Harry Brelsford's

SMALL BUSINESS SERVER 2000
Best Practices

Sheryn HARA PUBLISHING

Seattle, Washington

Published by
Hara Publishing Group
P.O. Box 19732
Seattle, Washington 98109
(425) 775-7868

ISBN: 1-883697-68-9
Library of Congress Number: 2001096682

Printed in USA
10 9 8 7 6 5 4 3 2

Editor: Vicki McCown
Design & Production: Lisa Delaney

Contents

Section 1: Starting with SBS

Section 2: SBS Management

Section 3: Using SBS to Communicate

Section 4: Extending SBS

Section 5: Appendixes

About the Author

Involved with SBS since June 3rd, 1997, at 9:00am, Pacific Standard Time (true story!), approximately half a year before its commercial release, Harry Brelsford is a longtime SBSer. His SBS accomplishments include:

- Serving a wide and diverse group of clients including Wallace Properties, EIS Group, the Peace Corps, and CainSweet.

- Acting as CEO for NetHealthmon.com, a start-up venture providing daily monitoring of SBS networks on a fee basis.

- Authoring books and articles on SBS, including the *Microsoft Press Small Business Server Resource Kit.*

- Serving as editor and publisher of a free monthly SBS newsletter, *Small Business Best Practices.*

- Serving the Microsoft SBS development team as a vendor, participating in SBS setup videos, and acting as the subject matter expert for Course 2301a and the advanced SBS 2000 computer-based training (CBT) module.

- Frequently delivering speeches on SBS at numerous venues, including Puerto Rico Direct Access event (Spring, 2001), the Gateway/Intel/ Microsoft Solutions Tour at ITEC (Fall 2001), *MCP Magazine* TechMentor, and SuperConference (accounting group, Chicago 2001).

When he's not being an SBSer, Harry works from his home office where he maintains his numerous certifications (MCSE, MCT, CNE-retired, CLSE, CNP). Harry holds two degrees (BSBA and MBA) and has written a total of nine books on technology topics. With his free time, Harry writes regular columns for *Microsoft Certified Professional Magazine* and *IT Contractor.* But, most of all, he enjoys his ski weekends at Snoqualmie
Pass, Washington, with his wife, Kristen, and two sons, Geoffrey and Harry Jr., engaging in Nordic (touring and racing) and Alpine skiing. The family, along with Springer Spaniels, Brisker and Jaeger, resides on Bainbridge Island, Washington. Harry can be reached at harryb@nethealthmon.com.

Dedication

To Kristen, Geoffrey, Harry, Brisker, and Jaeger. And all the SBSers out there!

Acknowledgments

Where oh where to start!

I certainly would not be where I'm at today in the SBS community without the grace and goodness of the Microsoft Small Business Server development team. I recently counted my Outlook contacts for this group and had over 50 names (too many to list!). You know who you are and I thank each of you.

The wonderful group at Hara Publishing helped immensely, including Sheryn Hara, Vicki McCown, and Lisa Delaney.

And I shan't forget those business people who prop me up daily. This includes my business manager, Lisa Wilhelm, and backup buddies, James Rose and Ty Christiansen.

And all the rest (that's et al. for y'all lawyers out there).

Foreword

Harry has done what I consider to be a remarkable job in portraying the heart and soul of what, in my opinion, a successful technology consultant needs to do. First, get competent with the tools of the trade, in this case Microsoft Small Business Server. Second, figure out what those tools can do in a practical, straight-forward, problem-solving manner with the client first and foremost in mind.

After all, there is incredible power in Small Business Server that just a few years ago was available only to well-budgeted IT departments of large companies. We at Microsoft have worked hard to make that technology more accessible and easy to use for the smallest businesses today and, frankly, we're pretty proud of what we've accomplished. But at the end of the day, regardless of how much technology you have at your disposal, it still takes a seasoned professional to both figure out exactly what that small business client really needs and then use your technical skill set to provide it. A lot of the time the first part is actually the hardest, which is why Microsoft will always depend on the broad network of value-added providers and resellers to bring the technology to life.

Harry's book will undoubtedly save you hours if not days out of your busy, billable schedules. Read it for the technology hints. Read it for the common-sense business ideas in front of that technology. And then implement what your customers uniquely need and what only you can uniquely provide.

Bob Clough
Vice President
Small Business Sales & Marketing
Microsoft Corporation

Preface

Welcome aboard the SBS 2000 boat, mate! This book is a comprehensive guide to Microsoft Small Business Server 2000 from a real-world, third-party perspective. Embedded herein you'll find the following highlights:

Methodology

Much care has been taken to develop a sample company storyline that is presented in each chapter. Over the course of the book, and I suspect after several weeks of reading and practice, you'll successfully set up the SBS 2000 network for Springer Spaniels Limited (SSL), a 10+ employee fictional firm located on Bainbridge Island, Washington. Fact of the matter is that, if you carefully follow each procedure, you'll be a bona fide SBSer within a month. All examples have been tested and include the implementation of third-party SBS solutions, such as virus detection and data backup. For example, after planning and setting up the SBS 2000 server for SSL, you'll download and install trial versions of Trend Micro's OfficeScan 5 for Microsoft Small Business Server 2000 (virus protection) and Veritas Backup Exec 8.x for Small Business Server 2000 (backup). You will implement necessary service packs and fixes (e.g., IIS CODE RED fix). So hang with me and this book, and you'll enjoy a completely satisfying SBS experience!

Real World

Part of the fun in writing a third-party book is that I can weave in real-world scenarios, such as client war stories. Equally important, this book is written on the released version of SBS 2000 plus six months hands-on, in-the-field, ass-kicking, real-world experience. It's the type of computer book I've always wanted to write! Heck – even several real-world SBSers have contributed guest columns in a few chapters to fortify things.

Microsoft SBS Team Insights

To balance my real world SBS-isms, I've asked for and received guest columns from several members of the Microsoft SBS development and marketing teams. In their own words, these kind souls speak about SBS in ways you won't find in other SBS books.

Best Practices

Central to this book are my BEST PRACTICES. These odd SBS facts are sometimes stranger than fiction. I attempt to divulge these hard-learned lessons and little-known nuggets from SBS 2000 between the covers of this book. As a rule, each chapter has at least several BEST PRACTICES.

Notes

Late in the writing process, I instructed the wonderful page layout artist to insert a section entitled "Notes" here and there on the pages of this book. That decision was made after looking at how readers have used my previous technology books. These books have become tattered, dog-eared daily references with handwritten notes squeezed in the margins, sandwiched between lines, and stuck on the end of sentences. I've now institutionalized that positive behavior by adding "Notes" sections on several pages per chapter. Go ahead and doodle away. Treat this book as your journal on your SBS 2000 journey.

Usual Stuff

Oh yes! This is a book with a start, middle, and finish. It features SBS 2000 planning, setup, deployment, administration, and troubleshooting issues. Each SBS 2000 component is explored in-depth including:

- Windows 2000 Server

- Exchange 2000 Server

- ISA Server 2000

- SQL Server 2000

- SBS Consoles and Wizards

- Client Computer Setup

- Shared Fax and Shared Modem

- IIS and Index Server

- Internet Connectivity

- Outlook 2000 and Internet Explorer

- And more…

Texas Accent

All authors like to think their books are unique, just as all homeowners feel their real estate is unique. While that's not true, one thing that helps make this book different than other technology tomes is my Texas accent. I knew those days at summer camp in the Kerrville, Texas, hill country would some day, some way yield royalties (literally!). Seriously, my shtick is to present technology matters in a kind, nurturing, sincere way that is friendly and affirming. Go ahead, thumb through a few pages now and see if my twisted Texas tongue doesn't tickle you!

Organization

On a more serious note, a lot of thought went into the design of this book. I first looked at how I and other SBSers work in this business. I then looked at how my paying clients use SBS 2000. This resulted in dividing the information into four sequential sections.

Section 1: Starting with SBS

This is the planning and setup section. It all starts here. Time to rock and roar!

Section 2: SBS Management

After you've set up an SBS network, you need to manage it. This section explores the two SBS Consoles, recurring administration tasks (daily, weekly, monthly, and annual), plus a super in-depth look at remote management via Terminal Services. By the end of this section, you'll be able to recite rhyme and verse as to what the SBS Baker's Dozen is.

Section 3: Using SBS to Communicate

SBS 2000 is, in many ways, here to help organizations communicate better. This section shows you how to connect securely to the Internet and configure Exchange-based e-mail (including Instant Messaging and Conferencing). You will learn how to take full advantage of Outlook 2000. You will configure the SBS 2000 sample network for remote connectivity and faxing.

Section 4: Extending SBS

So, you want more out of SBS 2000. You've got more! This section takes you to the next level with SBS 2000. It is here that you'll learn about SQL Server 2000, server health monitoring with Server Status Reports and Health Monitor, configure IIS (including the installation of FTP), and create an intranet Web page for the sample company. You even end with a "next steps" kinda chapter where you'll look at solutions that your SBS 2000 network infrastructure will support, including Microsoft Digital Dashboard, bCentral, and Great Plains "Blue" which is the new small business accounting solution.

Appendix Matter

Not only are you pointed toward some great SBS 2000 resources in Appendix A, but in Appendix B, the SBS 2000 upgrade issue is discussed. Because this book is based on SSL, the sample company that installs SBS 2000 fresh on a brand new machine, the upgrade discussion was better handled in Appendix B. Appendix C talks about the materials you need to add SSL staff members to the SBS 2000 network.

High Standards

This book should more than meet your needs and surpass your expectations. I expect it to be held to the highest standards; there should be no free pass here in SBS-land. I offer these measurements for judging how successful this book is:

- Save an hour, pay for the book. I believe that if this book has saved you one or more hours of SBS tail-chasing, it's paid for itself. At this basic level, the time and money you invested in this book should yield high dividends.

- Entertain yourself. Life's too short not to have fun with SBS 2000. Kindly accept my good humor in the spirit that it was written. You might find yourself laughing while reading a computer book, an oxymoron if I've ever heard one!

- Say "I didn't know that." Granted, there are many things you will already know in this book. However, I'm hopeful that just once (okay, maybe twice or more), you'll utter "I didn't know that" while reading this SBS 2000 book.

- Learn the next steps! This book picks up where other SBS resources end. That is, after surveying existing SBS resources and listening to feedback from other SBSers, I've handcrafted a book that flies higher, faster, and further than other SBS resources available to you.

Reader Feedback

As a writer, I welcome and relish reader feedback. This book is clearly better than some of my earlier books because of reader feedback over the years. For example, this book was delayed a few weeks so another quality control pass could be made against the final Adobe Acrobat PDF blue lines just before printing. I think this attention to quality will reveal itself to you.

But I digress. I need your feedback and, more important, the world needs your feedback. Could you be so kind as to post your feedback, hopefully positive, as reader reviews at the following online book reseller sites (I check occasionally, so I'll certainly hear you loud and clear).

- Amazon: www.amazon.com

- Barnes and Noble: www.bn.com

- FatBrain: www.fatbrain.com

So—turn the page! It's now time to start SBSing.

Cheers…harrybbbbb

Harry Brelsford
Bainbridge Island, Washington
harryb@nethealthmon.com
October 2001

PS—As an SBSer consultant and author, I live by referrals. If you like what you've read in this book, please tell all your friends, family, and of course, fellow SBSers! Thanks!

PPS—Be sure to subscribe to my monthly SBS newsletter "Small Business Best Practices" by sending e-mail to subscribe@nethealthmon.com.

Section 1

Starting with Small Business Server

Chapter 1
Welcome to Small Business Server

Howdy and welcome to Microsoft Small Business Server 2000, better known as *SBS*. SBS is nothing short of a major paradigm shift in Microsoft's view of network computing. This evolution, the SBS revolution, addresses a long-neglected area of client/server or personal computer-based computing: the small-business market. SBS clearly represents Microsoft's commitment to the small-business market, which as you will see later in the chapter, represents the largest computing market when measured by sheer number of businesses. Finally, with a single Microsoft networking product, it is possible to "right-size" a small-business networking solution, and all on one reasonably priced and powerful personal computer known as a *server*.

Before SBS, trying to implement Microsoft's default business networking solution—which I'll call *Big BackOffice* in this book—at a small-business site was a frustrating exercise in budget creep, much like placing too big of an engine in a small car!

> BEST PRACTICE: Microsoft is in the process of retiring the "BackOffice" name and replacing it with the term "Microsoft Servers". The retirement of BackOffice term will be completed by late October 2001, but to honor the BackOffice legacy, I'll continue to use this term in this book when appropriate.

And apparently enough of you agree that SBS fills a niche that needed filling: serving the business computing needs of the small business. You have made SBS one of the hottest-selling Microsoft offerings of the late 1990s. Perhaps you've discovered that a properly setup SBS network can improve the way you run your business, help lower your computing costs, and perhaps most important, make it easier for you, the technology consultant or SBS administrator, and your users to use and enjoy computers.

Defining SBS

Exactly what is SBS? Actually, there is more than one answer to that question. I like to think of defining SBS as akin to being a tax attorney: everyone's situation is different and tax codes can be interpreted differently by different people.

SBS provides cheap, reliable, and easy-to-manage business networking solutions. The business crowd wants to work with business applications, send and receive e-mail, print, and make sure the data is backed up. SBS scores high marks in these respects. And what a huge crowd this is. Of all the SBS installations that I've completed, this is by far the largest segment of SBSers.

For others, SBS is a cost-effective way of bundling Big BackOffice applications and the Windows 2000 Server operating system. Here, the emphasis in on bang-for-buck, and SBS is viewed as just a different stock keeping unit (SKU).

Presenting a larger than life image is the goal of some SBS clients who use SBS to look more impressive and bigger than their business size warrants. With a high-speed Internet connection and SBS, these businesses look and act as if they are much larger entities. More than once, customers who've conducted business with these small businesses, thinking they're engaging in transactions with a larger firm, are surprised to learn it's really been just three buddies, a pizza, and an SBS network all along. And get out your digital camera, for when these customers visit such an SBS site, you should photograph the look on their faces when they discover that the firm that appeared to be a big-time organization is just an incredibly efficient small business.

Many view SBS as Baby BackOffice and like to fully exploit SBS components, such as Microsoft Exchange 2000 Server and SQL Server 2000. This group, the SBS feature creatures, are interested in Table 1-1, which is divided, as much as possible, into the server-side (the powerful personal computer that typically resides in a closet) and the client-side (user workstations) components. Almost to a fault, this group is sometimes more interested in SBS than running the business, a dangerous and ominous warning sign to beware, as any college business professor will tell you.

Each component is discussed further in later chapters in this book, so don't worry if you don't understand, much less master, each one right now. Such comfort levels and expertise will be developed over the next several hundred pages together and in your career as an SBSer. For example, each server component is defined in great detail in its own chapter. Take Microsoft Exchange 2000 Server. You'll learn much more about this e-mail solution in Chapter 11.

Table 1-1 SBS Components at a Glance

Component	*Description*	*Server or Client Component*
Windows 2000 Server with Service Pack 1	Microsoft's 32-bit network operating system. An operating system controls the basic functions of a computer, including security, storage, printing, user management, remote communications, and so on. Supports Active Directory, Terminal Services in remote administration mode (discussed below), Group Policy for homogeneous Windows 2000 networks, disk quotas, advanced security such as encrypted file system (EFS). Windows 2000 Server is discussed across many chapters in this book.	Server
Microsoft Exchange 2000 Server	E-mail application that is used for communication and collaboration. Supports instant messaging and multimedia extensions. This is discussed in Chapter 11.	Server
Microsoft SQL Server 2000	Powerful database application. This is discussed in Chapter 15.	Server
Internet Security and Acceleration (ISA) Server 2000	Internet security and firewall gateway application with the capability to store or cache frequently accessed Web pages. This is discussed in Chapter 10.	Server
Microsoft Internet Information Server 5.0	Internet/Intranet Server development and management application. This is discussed in Chapter 17.	Server
Shared Fax Service	Fax pooling and management application. This is discussed in Chapter 14.	Server

Shared Modem Service	Modem pooling and management application. This is discussed in Chapter 13.	Server
Indexing Service	Search engine functionality. This is discussed in Chapter 17.	Server
Microsoft Front Page 2000	This application creates Web pages and can be used for desktop publishing. A single-license version can be installed on the server machine. FrontPage 2000 is discussed in detail in Chapter 18.	Server
Additional Goodies	VALUEADD and SUPPORT folders contain tools and sample software that are useful.	Server
SBS Management Consoles	GUI-based management consoles that use powerful yet friendly administrative wizards. There are two consoles in SBS: the administrator console for technology consultants and the simple console—"Small Business Server Personal Console—for use by power users, office managers and so on. The SBS consoles provide a central location to accomplish tasks. The consoles are discussed across the book and specifically in Chapter 5.	Server
Microsoft Management Console 1.2 (MMC)	This provides the framework for creating management consoles to perform task management. The SBS consoles are based on the MMC. This is discussed in Chapter 5.	Server
Server-based Wizards	Includes the Add User Wizard, Setup Computer Wizard, Internet Connection Wizard, device and peripheral management. Also includes numerous Windows 2000 Wizards. Wizards are discussed across the book.	Server
Health Monitor 1.2	Provides real-time network monitoring of critical performance variables. Has the ability to generate alerts. This is discussed in Chapter 16.	Server

Server Status Reports	This tool can be configured to send reports on system operations and third-party applications via e-mail or fax. This is discussed in Chapter 16.	Server
Server Status View	Provides a view of critical event, performance counters, and services. This is discussed in Chapter 16.	Server
Microsoft Connector for POP3 Mailboxes	Created with great pride by the SBS development team to allow small businesses to use existing POP3 e-mail services with Exchange 2000 Server. POP3 accounts are mapped to internal e-mail accounts. This is discussed in Chapter 11.	Server
Windows Terminal Services	Terminal Services is a multi-session solution in Windows 2000 that facilitates remote management of the SBS server by the technology consultant. Similar to remote control applications such as PCAnywhere. This is discussed in Chapter 8.	Server
To-Do List	Step-by-Step To-Do list. This is discussed across the book with special attention given to it in Chapters 3, 4, and 5.	Server
Online Guide	Robust online help for SBS administrators.	Server
Internet Explorer 5.x (IE)	Internet browser for navigating both the Internet and intranets. Installed on both the SBS server machine and SBS client's machine. This is discussed in Chapter 9.	Client/ Server
Default Page Internet	Connects IE to the Microsoft Network (www.msn.com) by default.	Client/ Server
Networking Setup Client Disk	A disk that is formatted and created on the SBS server machine. At the client workstation, the setup phase configures the client (TCP/IP protocol, NetBIOS name, user name assigned to machine, and so on). Affectionately known as the "magic disk." This is discussed in Chapter 4.	Client/ Server

Microsoft Outlook 2000	Client-based e-mail, client scheduling, and contact management application. Includes Service Release 1. This is discussed in Chapter 12.	Client
SBS Fax Sharing Client	Faxing functionality and capabilities. This is discussed in Chapter 14.	Client
SBS Modem Sharing Client	Modem pooling functions (port redirector). This is discussed in Chapters 4 and 13.	Client
SBS Firewall Client	Client-side ISA Server functions (WinSock redirector). This is discussed in Chapter 4.	Client
SBS Workstation Client	Basic SBS workstation client applications (assist in modifying client configuration). This is discussed in Chapter 4.	Client

Meanwhile, continuing with my broad definition of SBS, there is another group of SBSers that view SBS as a state of mind, or at least a different view of Windows 2000 computing. These are the people who get it; they know that SBS is different from regular Windows 2000 Server and Big BackOffice. Their view can best be summarized by Figure 1-1, the SBS Administrator Console snap-in based on the standard Microsoft Management Console (MMC).

Figure 1-1

The SBS Administrator Console is the classic view of Small Business Server 2000 and, at-a-glance, shows why SBS is different from other Microsoft product offerings.

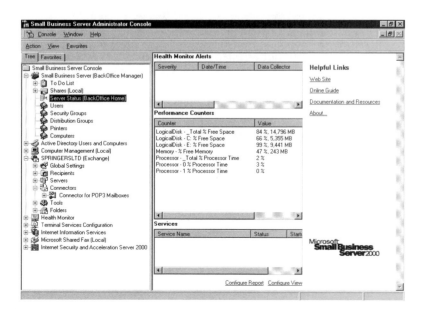

The SBS consoles (there are two: personal and administrator) are a feature that makes SBS a very different product from Windows 2000 Server. And when you get it with SBS, you'll understand why it is so different. That theme, *getting it*, is one that I'll often repeat as I draw out the difference between SBS, Windows 2000 Server, and Big BackOffice.

> BEST PRACTICE: Ironically, with the release of Small Business Server 2000, SBS and Big BackOffice now have more in common than ever before. The development teams were merged at Microsoft for the release, resulting in consoles that are very similar in appearance and functionality. I call it flattery at its finest. The Big BackOffice group finally saw the light and engaged in some pick-of-the-litter behavior on SBS. This is seen by the console's incorporation into Big BackOffice (in its BackOffice Server 2000 release).
>
> In fact, the more germane and interesting comparison is really between SBS and Windows 2000 Server.

Another view on defining SBS is looking at it from a business perspective: that is, how does SBS support the mission of the businesses to be efficient and successful? The SBS wheel in Figure 1-2 addresses this point of view.

Figure 1-2
The SBS wheel allows you to analyze SBS from using an analytical framework for gaining perspective on core SBS applications.

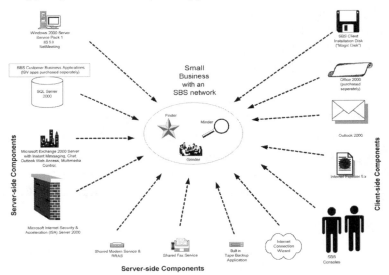

The left side of the wheel predominately speaks toward server-side components such as Windows 2000 Server, SQL Server 2000, and the like. The lower portion of the wheel speaks to the management function via the SBS Consoles. The right side of the wheel speaks to the client-side applications, such as Microsoft Outlook 2000.

Finder, Minder, Grinder

With respect to how SBS supports business operations, let me take a moment to speak about the three major functions of a small business: finder, minder, and grinder.

Finder

A finder is a rainmaker: the person who markets and gets the business. In many firms, it is the owner, CEO, or president; in others, it is a salesperson. Whoever has this important responsibility can directly benefit from SBS in many ways. I'll discuss two of those. First, there is the new area of electronic commerce. Electronic commerce includes everything from basic e-mail to elaborate Web pages that provide direct updates to your accounting system. At a minimum, a salesman in the early 21st century can benefit from using Internet e-mail. This feature is supported by SBS with the Microsoft Exchange 2000 Server.

A finder can also benefit from SBS applications such as Microsoft Outlook. Outlook provides contact management and scheduling capabilities in addition to serving as an e-mail client. Outlook is discussed in Chapter 12. You will learn basic Outlook functionality with an emphasis on e-mail use and how to create a company-wide contact list that is low maintenance yet allows everyone to have an updated list of contacts, such as important clients and vendors. You will even learn how to run Outlook over the Internet, via the Exchange Web Client (formerly known as Outlook Web Access), so you can check your SBS-based e-mail from a late model Web browser from any Internet connected PC in the world!

And then there is the CEO of the landscaping company in Issaquah, Washington, who wanted to use SBS to increase his company's sales. His idea was to fax a "spring cleaning" notice to his past landscaping clients. SBS does this very well with its desktop faxing and fax server support. Broadcast faxing is a breeze, and as an added bonus, this CEO found that he could fax directly to the names listed in the company-wide Outlook contact list. I'll talk more about faxing in Chapter 14.

Minder

There's one law of business that I've never seen successfully broken: For every finder, there is at least one minder. *Minders* serve as office managers, administrators, COOs, and all-around nags. Bless 'em, because we need them. SBS was designed with minders in mind (please don't *mind* the pun!). Typically, when I've deployed SBS from a minder's perspective, it has been to implement a piece of industry-specific business software. One of my examples is Xtek, a Redmond, Washington-based service firm that calibrates medical instruments. Norm serves as president and finder and Mike is the minder. You will see in Figure 1-2 that I listed business applications on the server side. One such application is BenchTop, a very powerful service management software application implemented on the SBS system at Xtek. BenchTop, which uses SBS's SQL Server for its engine, is very much a minder tool. This application brings control to the workflow and allows Mike to compile performance metrics specific to his industry. Mike unknowingly benefits from SBS because SQL Server is included as part of the SBS bundle. All Mike knows is that BenchTop makes his job easier and he is more productive.

> BEST PRACTICE: A moment of legal stuff that the lawyers would like to see put in. Benchtop is a business application being used by a firm in Redmond, Washington, on an SBS network. It is used for reference and example purposes only and is meant to be a representative business application on a representative SBS network. This is a narrow vertical market application, developed by an ISV, for the instrument calibration industry. I could have just as easily used a narrow vertical market application from the legal, real estate, or medical communities for my examples. You get the point. SBS doesn't live in a vacuum, but typically small businesses run some narrow vertical market application on top of SBS.

Another example of a minder tool in SBS is, in my opinion, Microsoft ISA Server. This is basically a firewall that not only protects the SBS network from the evil comings and goings of the Internet, but also allows the minder in all of us to control and monitor access to the Internet. You would be surprised how many firms place equal emphasis on controlling employee Internet usage as they do on their firewall to prevent intrusion. I guess you could call it *minding* the store.

And because minders are typically the ones who get stuck running SBS networks, the basic SBS Console (for power users), known as Small Business Server
Personal Console, is a fast friend. This is shown in Figure 1-3. Instead of having
to learn a variety of Windows 2000 Server tools that are "under the hood" in the
Administrative Tools program group (that is, not part of the SBS Personal
Console), SBS minders administer their networks with the push-button simplicity
of the basic Small Business Server Personal Console. More on the SBS consoles
in Chapter 5: Small Business Server Management Consoles.

Figure 1-3
The most basic SBS console is the Small Business Server Personal Console.

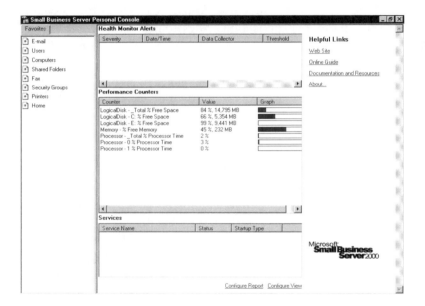

Grinder

Grinders are the worker bees. These are the people who are typically task-
oriented and look at the SBS infrastructure as a support system that makes them
more productive. Grinders benefit from SBS in two distinct ways.

First, applications such as BenchTop (mentioned above) that run on top of SBS's
SQL Server allow the repair staff to enter important job and task information.

This helps track the flow of goods in the system and effectively lowers cost by allowing better control. Another business application that uses SQL Server is Great Plains Dynamics, a robust accounting application. I've had tremendous success installing this on SBS machines and I can attest that the worker bees—typically accounting clerks and bookkeepers—have been able to complete their work in an efficient and reliable manner. Most important, in both cases with BenchTop and Great Plains, the grinders trust that SBS allows them to better do their work. Such has not always been the case with worker bees, known for coining such pithy phrases as "The #@%$!&* computer network is not working again" in the early days of computer networking.

Second, basic communication applications such as Outlook e-mail, contacts, and scheduling have allowed grinders to improve the quality of their work. Many times SBS is being introduced into environments that have no prior network or e-mail service. SBS often fundamentally changes how people do their work and, in its own way, reengineers workflow. The improvement in communications is but one example. Throughout this book many more business workflow improvements are presented.

SBS Philosophy 101

It is difficult to overlook the sheer numbers of small businesses that could benefit from a tailor-made BackOffice-type networking solution. Such was the idea behind SBS, a viewpoint that seems, on the surface, to fly right in the face of Microsoft's overt push into the enterprise with Windows 2000 Server. But the numbers speak for themselves. Although you can easily say that there are only 1,000 companies in the Fortune 1000 list, conversely you might be surprised to know that there are over 22 million small businesses in the United States, according to the U.S. Small Business Administration. It's a stretch, but can't you see the marketing wheels at Microsoft turning and dreaming of an SBS installation at every small business? You betcha.

Understanding that small businesses are fundamentally different from larger enterprises, SBS sells itself when positioned as a tool to help small business run better, with less effort, and, ultimately, more easily. You could say that SBS is nothing more than a return to the original LAN paradigm that both Apple Computer and Novell rode in the 1980s. This LAN paradigm, with a few modifications to accommodate SBS, is anchored by these key tenets:

- **Sharing:** The major justification for implementing SBS in the small business is the ability to share information. Sharing information, such as cost accounting data at the construction company, allows staff to work together with less redundancy (multiple entries are eliminated). Owners get better information about their operations. Staff works together as a team.

- **Security:** Like the enterprise, small businesses demand that reasonable levels of security be provided to protect sensitive information from competition and from loss or casualty. SBS provides regular Windows 2000 Server-based security (and there's a lot of security features there, let me tell ya) plus the security afforded by Microsoft ISA Server.

- **Cost Effectiveness:** Relatively speaking, SBS is cheap. The 25-user configuration of SBS, a popular option, can be purchased on the street for around $2,500. Add a very nice $5,000 server machine and very nice $1,500 workstations plus a few other necessities (approximately $1,000 for hubs, modems, cable, and so on) and you're up and running. Note you can get buy with servers in the $3,000 price range and workstations around $1,000 each. I've seen it done plenty of times!

BEST PRACTICE: When amortized, for accounting purposes, over the typical five-year holding period seen in many small businesses (versus the more aggressive three-year holding period typically seen at the enterprise-level), SBS is really cost-effective. After the basic installation, allowance for training (say, a onetime $500 per user outlay) and technology consulting fees, an SBS network typically costs less than $1,000 per user per year. If you've ever worked at the enterprise level, you'd be viewed as kooky if you told someone you had lowered your annual IT costs per user to less than $1,000 (more likely it would be over $5,000 per user per year).

- **Efficiency:** After an initial period of negative productivity while installing SBS and when everyone is learning the SBS network and its powers, company-wide productivity quickly increases to a level exceeding pre-SBS days. One example of this is the use of broadcast e-mails and faxes instead of making lots of telephone calls.

- **Better Work, New Work:** This includes fewer mistakes because of better communications, such as e-mail with staff, vendors, and customers; better scheduling with Outlook's calendar; and so on; and new work, such as winning new contracts because your work is of higher quality (proposals with accurate financial information derived from staff, and so on). In fact, as an SBS site starts using more and more SBS features, I've seen these small businesses dramatically increase their business. Meanwhile, back at the ranch, oops, I mean the previously mentioned landscaping company client, SBS's faxing capabilities are used to fax "Spring planting announcements" to its clients resulting in increased sales. Small businesses, enlightened by the powers of SBS, have also been known to enter into new business areas, feeling confident that they have the network infrastructure to back up promises. Need more convincing? A small construction company I worked with, confident that SBS-based e-mail and remote communications solutions wouldn't fail them, took on work in other cities.

- **Bottom Line:** How does SBS sum up? Properly implemented, SBS can help small businesses to enjoy higher quality work and get more work finished with the same resources:

  Land - Office space is used more efficiently as older office machines, file cabinets, and the like are eliminated.
  Labor - Existing staff works more efficiently, allowing owners to squeeze out more productivity. But fear not that SBS will result in staff downsizing. I've worked with a variety of SBS sites and have never seen a layoff or firing related to SBS. In fact, the opposite tends to occur. Small businesses get excited very quickly with SBS when they understand it and see it working. In short order, additional (and unplanned) work requests roll in. For example, several of my small-business clients that barely knew what the Internet was prior to the SBS installa-

tion call back and ask for WWW home page development assistance. I typically refer an intern from the local college to these clients, allowing them to save on Web page development costs and giving a starving college kid the chance to earn some money. And guess what! More often than not the college intern becomes a full-time employee, actually increasing headcount at the client site as a result of the SBS implementation.

Capital - Not to understate the initial capital investment in getting an SBS network up and running, but, after that outlay is made, the general consensus is that SBS delivers a positive return on investment (ROI) by increasing the firm's productivity and mitigating additional large capital outlays for the foreseeable future. One example of this is the reduced wear and tear on photocopiers. A client of mine who has aggressively exploited SBS features now stores documents electronically and faxes directly to vendors. By doing so, this customer found it could forego the purchase of a new, expensive photocopier.

So what does Microsoft think? Well, Microsoft extends this SBS paradigm specifically by adding these design goals:

- **Ease of Use/Simplicity:** The idea was to make everything easy, easy, easy. And when compared to the old command-line interface of NetWare 3.x (which a surprisingly high number of small businesses are still running, having foregone the opportunity to upgrade to NetWare 4.x, 5.x), you could say that SBS is easier to manage and use. For example, Dawn, who works at an athletic club I've assisted, took many years (appropriately so) to master NetWare. When Dawn was confronted with the decision to upgrade to the newly released NetWare 5.0, I loaned her a training machine that had SBS installed. One week later, Dawn was confident and had even confirmed that her narrow market vertical applications would run on SBS. Not surprisingly, Dawn and her firm became another SBS success story.

But *easy* is in the eye of the beholder. Whereas Dawn was coming from a more complex networking environment, allowing her to enjoy the ease of SBS when compared to NetWare, SBS has sometimes fallen short for small businesses that have never been networked. These firms, accustomed to working manually with file cabinets, fax machines, and basic word processing, are often disappointed with SBS initially when they (a) can't believe installing a network is so difficult and (b) don't understand why servers don't work perfectly all the time (for example, applications stop responding). So take Microsoft's SBS ease of use argument with a grain of salt.

However, if it is usability that you are measuring, clearly SBS wins when compared to other NOSs such as NetWare. With its Windows 9x-type interface, SBS encourages even those users unaccustomed to managing a network server to feel comfortable using the Start button, menus, mouse, and so on. Score one for SBS for high usability.

- **Making Decisions for the Customer:** In the context of having an automated setup and implementation process ("just add water"), SBS (in Microsoft's view) reduces the research, engineering, and guesswork that goes into making the networking decision. Microsoft correctly asserts that users do not have to decide whether the SBS machine should be a domain controller (it is because it controls the operations of the network) and whether to install Active Directory. Active Directory is the directory services database used to store user and computer account information.

- **Designed for Success:** This point speaks to the SBS consoles that I've previously discussed. The idea is that SBS administrators should enjoy a "simple, stupid" networking management experience and not really have to plan what they intend to do. Adding a user is a click away via the Users button in the basic Small Business Server Personal Console (see Figure 1-3). Simple.

BEST PRACTICE: Here again, I must interject a few clarifying comments regarding the pro-Microsoft comments. For new users and NetWare administrators coming over to SBS (such as Dawn), I've found the SBS consoles are great and really aid the SBS learning process. So on that count, Microsoft is correct with its ease of use, automatic decision making, and successful design assertions. But for good old Windows 2000 Server gurus with headstrong ways of doing things, the SBS consoles are sometimes more of an enemy. These Windows 2000 Server gurus begrudgingly use the SBS consoles (interestingly, the native tools are exposed in the Administrator Console, removing the need to drop down and use the Administrative Tools folder). I'll say it now and most assuredly say it again: Do everything from the SBS consoles (and its wizards).

Deciding Whether SBS is for You

Early in your decision-making process to either install a new network or upgrade the existing network at your business, you need to decide whether SBS is for you. SBS has several practical limitations that you should be aware of.

> BEST PRACTICE: In consulting, we call this frank assessment "expectation management." You should manage your expectations up front about what SBS can and can't do (especially the "can't do" part). That way, later on, you won't suffer severe disappointments.

User and Client Machine Limit

Only 50 users can be logged on at one time with SBS. And on a legal licensing note, only 50 client machines may be attached to the Small Business Server network. (Please read the license agreement in your SBS packaging for more details.) Microsoft imposed this 50-client machine limit as the break point between SBS and Big BackOffice. Typically, businesses that are growing rapidly and have over 40 users today need to consider Big BackOffice instead of SBS as the correct networking solution. The upgrade path to Big BackOffice retains your existing settings so that you don't have to do a complete reinstall of your network (however–with the demise of Big BackOffice in the next generation, the upgrade path to Big BackOffice will be irrelevant). Also note that more than 50 users can be entered on SBS as users, but only 50 may be logged on at any time. This preceding discussion assumes that you have the 50-user version of SBS installed. And under no circumstances may you have more than 50 machines attached to your SBS network.

There is another side to the concurrent-user-limit discussion. Suppose that you have a five-user license for SBS. That would mean the sixth user is locked out and is unable to work on the SBS network. In order for the sixth user to log on, you would need to purchase a five-license Client Access License (CAL) disk and install these additional licenses.

SQL Server 2000 Database Limits Removed

On a positive note, SQL Server 2000 no longer has imposed storage limits in SBS 2000. This wasn't the case with SBS 4.5 where the individual database (table and log file) size was limited to 10GB in SBS Server. The only practical limitation that I can now think of relating to SQL Server 2000 in SBS is that the application runs on the same machine as the other SBS applications. My point is that, if you're really serious about high transaction database activity such as electronic commerce, you can't install the SQL Server 2000 application in Small Business Server 2000 on another Windows 2000 Server machine. However, in this situation, you could purchase another copy of SQL Server 2000 (with the appropriate number of client access licenses) and install it on another Windows 2000 Server machine. Not a bad idea if you're fulfilling tons of customer orders each day over the Web, eh?

Exchange Optimization

To fit Microsoft Exchange Server on the same server as Windows 2000 Server and the other SBS components, its footprint was made smaller. Thus, SBS's Microsoft Exchange Server is optimized for a smaller environment than its big brother. One example of this trimming is that, by default, Exchange Server uses less RAM memory in SBS than its big league brother at the enterprise level. If you've ever worked with Microsoft Exchange Server, you know that it's a RAM hog, so the idea that a snippet of RAM memory has been removed from Exchange Server in SBS is significant. It's one of the reasons that Exchange Server in SBS runs a tad slower than when implemented in enterprises running Big BackOffice.

Don't let my sharing of limitations lull you into believing that SBS is somehow crippled. Such is not the case. SBS is a fully functional Microsoft networking solution. Period.

System Partition Limits Relaxed, FAT, and NTFS Issues

SBS 2000 no longer has the partition limits of its predecessors. In fact, a minimum of 4GB is recommended for SBS 2000. Note you can use multiple partitions for installing SBS 2000. For example, on one partition, you should consider installing the operating system and many of the SBS components. On another partition, you can install components such as SQL Server, Exchange Server, ISA Server, and user folders. This capability of redirecting the location at which applications are installed was first introduced in SBS 4.5 and it's still with us today. But, all praise aside, be advised of the 4GB minimum storage requirements and the relaxing of partition limits.

On a closely related note, you are no longer required to install SBS on an NTFS partition. Yes, you read correctly, SBS will install on a FAT partition. The only issue here is that ISA must be installed on an NTFS partition; so, theoretically, you could install all of SBS sans ISA on a FAT partition and then install ISA on an NTFS partition. To be brutally honest, this seems really crazy. Read the next tip.

> BEST PRACTICE: I highly recommend you only work with NTFS partitions in SBS 2000. Lose the FAT!

Single Domain, No Workgroups

SBS is limited to a single domain and must be the root of the Active Domain forest. (A domain is an administrative unit in a Windows 2000 Server environment.) This limitation is a hindrance if your organization is part of a larger enterprise that has other Windows 2000 Servers and typically uses Active Directory's implicit two-way "trust relationships" to interact with other domains. Don't forget this SBS rule: SBS trusts no one!

> BEST PRACTICE: A quick Active Directory primer for you: First, contrary to the rumors circulating in late 1999 and early 2000, domains are still with us in Windows 2000. In fact, there are two domains: the traditional NT-like NetBIOS domain name typically associated with the internal network domain and the Internet domain (ye olde dot-com) type. A forest is a collection of trees and a tree is a collection of domains. Whew!

Workgroups are not allowed in the SBS networking model because SBS must act as something called a *domain controller* (*DC*). A DC is the central security authority for the network. It is responsible for logging you on, auditing usage if so configured, and whatnot. Workgroups do not use such a robust security model, and interestingly, many small businesses that are upgrading to SBS have been using peer-to-peer networks built on the workgroup model. This change from workgroups to domains is often startling to the small business and requires extra care and planning. Why? For one reason, domains by their nature are a much more centralized management approach; workgroups are decentralized. So people who were comfortable with the workgroup sharing model are often put off by the heavy-handed centralized management domain view. Be careful here, especially if your working with peace-loving hippies from the 1960s!

Cost/Benefit Analysis

Another SBS consideration is cost. The standalone version of Windows 2000 Server is dramatically less expensive (by over 50%) than a comparably licensed version of SBS. I've lost SBS consulting opportunities in the past because customers decided that all they really needed the network for was to store common accounting files and print. One such case was a small construction company. E-mail, Internet connectivity, faxing, and other SBS features weren't part of the picture for this firm. Enough said. Out with SBS and in with regular Windows 2000 Server. I guess the $800 or so saved by this construction company by not purchasing SBS was used to make a monthly lease payment on the owner's $130,000 Mercedes sedan. It's a matter of priorities. For them, SBS wasn't a priority. And in fact, this construction company and other like-minded entities may well elect to use Windows XP's peer-to-peer networking feature in the future.

Not honoring these limitations might cause you to make a bad decision concerning your firm's computer network. The key point is to make sure that SBS is the right fit for your organization.

Business Reasons for SBS

Ultimately, it's a dollars-and-cents decision. How does SBS contribute to the bottom line? Does SBS have a favorable ROI?

It has been my experience in working with SBS and small businesses that the business software application typically drives the SBS decision (although there are exceptions that I'll mention in a moment). Although certainly not as lucrative as owning tons of Microsoft stock options, if only I received $10 for every time I've taken a call from someone on a Novell NetWare network saying their (pick from the following) accounting, design, CAD, CAM, retail, legal, medical, or time/billing software vendor will no longer support its NetWare version! These independent software vendors (ISV) typically migrate their applications to Windows 2000 Server, leaving their older NetWare installations orphaned. That translates into the small business taking a look at Windows 2000 Server to meet its ongoing computing needs. And if I can get a small business with fewer than 50 concurrent users to consider Windows 2000 Server, I can most likely right-size them right into SBS. So call it an SBS law: Business applications are clearly driving most of the migrations to SBS!

Other business reasons for migrating to SBS include cost-effectiveness. Microsoft has mastered the art of bundling software applications and selling these bundles at a price point far below the combined costs of purchasing these software applications on an individual basis. You saw this over the past several years with Microsoft Office. SBS is no exception. For approximately $1,500 (less if you are upgrading, which is discussed in the second part of Chapter 2, "Small Business Server Design and Planning"), you can have a five-user network with SBS's suite of applications.

I once sold SBS and my consulting services to a land development firm that was considering a new network for its four users. This firm had decided that its old NetWare 3.x server was ready for replacement. Initially, armed with a warehouse catalog showing the upgrade price for Windows 2000 Server at $400, this firm wanted regular Windows 2000 Server and only that, nothing else. But after we sat down and further discussed its needs, the firm decided that purchasing a third-party modem pooling and faxing solution to supplement regular Windows 2000 Server would exceed the SBS upgrading cost for five users. Needless to say, at the end of this meeting, SBS had sold itself with its built-in modem pooling and fax server capabilities.

Now for that "exception" in selecting SBS that I promised. First on this list is politics. Here I look no further than the Seattle athletic club, where many members are employees or vendors of Microsoft. Rumor has it that the big Bill (Bill Gates) himself is a member. Here, the management team concluded that having a NetWare network was a political negative that it didn't want to advertise. Exit NetWare and enter SBS. Whatever works!

Finally, more and more SBS purchases are being swayed by the increasing catalog of SBS-specific applications that are entering the market. First and foremost in this category are SBS-compliant and enhanced ISV-based tools and applications. Software vendors such as Seagate and Trend Micro have released SBS suites of their respective products (Backup Exec backup program and Office Scan 5.0 for Small Business Server 2000 virus protection, respectively). Note that I discuss these two applications in Chapter 6.

Guest Column

So, it's time to relax for a moment. My guest speaker for this chapter is Brian Jeans, an SBS product manager with Microsoft. His topic is especially meaningful as it helps bridge the morning basics session with the more advanced afternoon session. In particular, his message is directed toward Microsoft Certified Professionals who might like to provide SBS consulting services. Take it away, Brian!

Building a Business with Small Business Server

by Brian Jeans
Product Manager
Microsoft Corporation

Technology consultants and value-added resellers serving small- and medium-sized customers know that there's big demand for technology solutions in the small-business sector. To help small businesses meet their increasing business and technology demands, and to help technology consultants and VARs expand their business opportunities, Microsoft has developed Small Business Server.

As a small-business technology consultant and/or VAR, you likely are challenged by the need to implement, manage, and support the networking technology of a number of different businesses. One of the design goals of Small Business Server was to support a consultant's business practice. The flexible setup allows you to gradually deploy components over time so you don't overwhelm your customers with too many features at once. New monitoring tools have been added so you can set up alerts to notify you of potential issues such as low disk space or high CPU utilization. And finally, Small Business Server 2000 introduces native support for Terminal Services so you can resolve common server issues from a remote location – no more driving to your customer site to fix a minor issue.

The features designed for consultants and VARs offer a business model where you can charge for monthly server monitoring services or the ability to deploy additional services at a later time as the demands of the business increase. Further, Small Business Server should improve the efficiency of your business and enable you to service and support more customers without sacrificing your precious free time.

Best of all, Small Business Server is the right product for your small-business customers with less than 50 PCs. The product suite includes Windows 2000 Server, Exchange 2000 Server, SQL Server 2000, Internet Security and Acceleration Server (ISA), and Shared Fax and Modem Services all for a price of Windows 2000 Server plus less than what you would pay for just one of the additional applications. These server components offer features such as:

- *File, print, document indexing, and remote access services (Windows 2000)*

- *Internet Web server (Internet Information Server)*

- *Shared, secure Internet connectivity (Firewall) and Web site cache (ISA)*

- *E-mail, instant messaging, shared scheduling, shared customer lists, group discussions, and shared project tasks (Exchange and Outlook)*

- *Shared database (SQL Server)*

- *Faxing through networked PCs without employees getting up from their desks, while saving money on additional phone lines (Shared Fax Service)*

- *And more...*

Want to learn more? The latest information on Small Business Server, including details on one-day CTEC training courses, is available on-line at http://www.microsoft.com/smallbusinessserver. Also, be sure to check out our Direct Access Web site, specially designed for Microsoft resellers, at http://www.microsoft.com/directaccess.

Microsoft SBS Design Goals

There is no argument that Microsoft's primary SBS design goals were to serve the small-business market. That said, something that I've learned and heard from others is that serving the small-business customer is dramatically different from serving the enterprise. Because of this observation, I'd like to spend a few pages presenting these differences and defining the small-business market. Such discussions are bound to make you more successful in your SBS implementations. If you are a small-business person seeking to set up and use SBS, discover whether you don't see a little of yourself in these forthcoming section (although I make many comments that pertain specifically to SBS consultants).

Defining the SBS Market: The Small-Business Model

Now that I've installed several dozen SBS networks, I can wax poetically as an SBS elder statesman about the small-business firm. Small businesses are very different from the enterprise in three areas:

- Attitude
- Affluence
- Expertise

Attitude

Small businesses rightly are more focused on delivering goods and services than being concerned about the technology being implemented. In fact, many small-business people have a hostile attitude toward computers, viewing them as a drain on time and financial resources. Remember, these are the firms that complain long and loud when you purchase an unplanned network adapter card for $80!

Such antagonistic attitudes can be overt, such as criticizing your effort, or hidden, like not sending staff (including the owner) to basic computer training. Don't forget that the real measure of success of the SBS network one year hence will be a function of training. Are the users using the SBS network? Have they taken advantage of many of the SBS features such as robust Internet connectivity, faxing, and the SQL Server database application? If not, the significant investment of time and money in implementing the SBS network will be viewed unfavorably.

And even when you find and help a technology-friendly small business, you can't help but see that the owner and manager really should leave the SBS networking to you, the SBS consultant. Their energies are best allocated toward running their business, not running an SBS network.

I have one client, the aforementioned Norm, who is the owner of a small medical instrument repair facility. Norm is from the technical field, having worked for years in numerous technical roles in the firm he started. Several years ago, Norm hired a renowned management consultant who mentored Norm into being a president and CEO. One of the critical success factors in Norm's transformation from butcher, baker, and candlestick maker to president and CEO was his shift from doing the work to managing the work. It's arguably as difficult a shift as any small-business founder will ever have to make, and Norm is no exception. The point is this: When I arrived as Norm's SBS consultant, I inherited a large case of boundary definition and expectation management. Norm wanted to participate in the SBS administration, troubleshooting, and whatnot. But better senses prevailed, and Norm reluctantly did the things that presidents and CEOs do: go out and get the business.

Many times the negative attitude that is demonstrated by small businesses towards technology, such as SBS, is based on fear. We all get defensive when confronted with the unknown, and small-business people fear that SBS might make them look stupid. As an SBS consultant, you need to wear their moccasins for a moment.

> BEST PRACTICE: I have found that a fear-based negative attitude toward SBS by the small-business person is really a cry for more information. In the absence of sufficient information about SBS, small-business people make up their own information. And, as you will see in the next section, SBS occasionally suffers a product definition problem, so you hardly need anyone in your life manufacturing incorrect information about what SBS does and does not do.

> What's my recommendation? Over communicate with the small-business person about SBS. Once they're educated, expectations are kept in line, and you can chalk up another SBS victory. In fact, I've taken to communicating to my clients in writing, either via e-mail, fax, or mailed

letter every time I perform SBS-related work at their site. What's cool about this method is that, months later when both you and the SBS customer have forgotten something technically related, you can easily go back to your files and look up the facts (and, here again, prevent SBS misinformation).

So, assuming you either have clients who are wonderfully optimistic and need little communication about what SBS is or isn't, or you've sufficiently communicated to your clients needing more information about SBS, you're ready to move on. One transitional step is to make sure you've got your small-business hat on and are serving as a buddy and mentor to the client.

> BEST PRACTICE: Be sure to keep your own attitude in check. I can directly trace my SBS failures more times than not to having brought an enterprise "know-it-all" arrogance to the small-business person. In many cases, the small-business person has a perceived negative notion about arrogant computer people. Don't validate that perception. Remember that you're typically serving as both a technical consultant and a business consultant. At the small-business level, you wear multiple hats. It's hard to do, and few MCSE-types really do it well. But a few random acts of kindness go a long way with the SBS clientele (even though your enterprise experience frowns on such openness).

> What's my solution to this alleged attitude problem from the SBS consultant side? I now have more communicators on my consulting staff than I did in the past. Yes, there is still a role for tech heads who are appreciated for their expertise, but I've enjoyed great success with the SBS product line by taking liberal arts majors, training them on SBS, and having them score wins with my SBS clients. So, leave that big league Microsoft Servers attitude outside the door when working with SBS!

Affluence

One of the earliest lessons learned with SBS was that the small business isn't the enterprise. And remember that the small business truly watches dollars closer than the enterprise ever will. Remember the example at the top of this section regarding $80 network adapter cards? The enterprise-level Windows 2000 Server site probably has a half-dozen network adapter cards stacked in the server room ready for use. An enterprise-level Windows 2000 administrator wouldn't think twice about getting another network adapter card from the pile. But that cavalier attitude pales against the dollar-conscious small business that disapproves so greatly of unnecessary SBS-related expenditures that I've witnessed:

- A small firm makes do with the built-in SBS tape backup application instead of purchasing a $500 third-party tape backup solution, which provides greater services, such as the ability to backup SQL Server 2000 databases and Microsoft Exchange 2000 at the "bricks-level," and increased piece of mind.

- A small firm struggles with an older network adapter card for hours instead of buying a new card for $60 or less.

- A small firm didn't hook up an HP laser printer directly to the network (via the built-in HP JetDirect card) because it didn't want to run to the store to purchase another strand of CAT 5 cable. (Instead, this high-priced printer was attached to the SBS server via a parallel cable, which of course had significantly lower performance than a direct network connection.)

Expertise

One of the great consulting opportunities today in the world of Windows 2000 Server is SBS. When performing SBS engagements, I've found that I'm a large fish in a small pond. That's opposite of the typical enterprise-level Windows 2000 Server engagement at the Boeings of the world where, even as a know-it-all, you're really nothing more than a cog in a huge networking machine. So I guess you could say that rank has its privileges. Working with small businesses and helping them implement SBS can be tremendously rewarding.

The expertise coin has another side, however. As the SBS guru, you will be relied on in more, often unexpected ways than you might be at the enterprise level. Here is what I mean: When working with Windows 2000 Server at the enterprise level, you likely benefit from having someone on staff who can walk through a series of steps to solve a problem (often while you're speaking via telephone from a different location). But at the small-business level with SBS, this may not be the case. Here you are interacting directly with paralegals, bookkeepers, cashiers, clerks, and owners—not necessarily in that order! Not only do these people often lack the technical aptitude to assist your SBS troubleshooting efforts, but they usually become intimidated and nervous when working with you, the SBS guru.

So, while there may be a bona fide expertise gap when you work with SBS sites, your commitment will be certainly no less than the commitment you make to regular Windows 2000 Server sites. Just ask a friend of mine, who, approaching the front of the waiting line in Washington's San Juan Islands ferry, was paged by a small-business site. Apparently, this SBS site was unable to connect to the Internet. Without in-house technical competency, the SBS site doomed my friend to drive back to the city and assist it. Bummer! Somewhere here there is a lesson for the Windows 2000 Server guru who wants to master SBS.

Defining the SBS Market: The Small-Business Model

To understand who the SBS customers are, it is necessary to understand the small-business community. As previously stated, there are over 22 million small businesses in the United States alone. According to the U.S. Small Business Administration (SBA), these businesses account for:

- 39% of the gross national product

- Creation of two out of every three new jobs

- Creation of more than half of the nation's technological innovation

Given that basic premise, a lot is known about the small business from a technology perspective. According to IDC/Link, a highly respected East Coast (U.S.) research firm, of the small businesses that fit the profile for SBS:

- 74.6% of these small businesses currently have one or more PC

- 29.9% of these small businesses have their PCs networked

- Over 40.9% of these small businesses will have their PCs networked by the year 2001, which represents a 37% increase from 1998. In fact, I find this figure to be low if my former employer's (a regional accounting firm) portfolio of 800 active small-business clients is any measure. The IDC study most likely understates this rate because small businesses are feeling extreme competitive pressures to modernize by being attached to the Internet for e-mail and having a WWW presence. When these numbers are revisited several years hence, I suspect you'll see that over 50% of the eligible small businesses became networked during this timeframe. I'd bet the house mortgage on it!

Not every small business, as defined by the above business data, will be an SBS customer, but you get the idea. The potential SBS market in the small-business economic sector is, shall we say, huge!

Who Are the SBS Customers?

So would you have guessed that I'd provide an MBA lecture along the SBS journey? Well, here it is. This section is about customer profiling. The sections below answer the question: "Just who are all those SBS customers anyways?!"

Size Alone Doesn't Matter

One of the great fallacies that I've learned with SBS customers is the idea that business size alone matters. Such is not the case. Small businesses with fewer than 50 users typically have more than that in terms of head count or *fulltime equivalents* (*FTEs*). For example, the landscaping company I've mentioned previously has 20 SBS users (well within SBS's 50-computer limit) but over 100 employees. Many of these employees work in the field and don't fall under the traditional definition of user. But nonetheless, when at the office, some of these employees like to check e-mail, write reports, update the Outlook calendar, and so forth.

So, as you look at a small business and its fitness for implementing SBS, always consider the actual number of *users* when sizing up the organization. An employee headcount, sure to be the larger number, could be very misleading. More important, understand that the substance of the SBS licensing agreement relates to the number of client PCs attached to the SBS network.

Business Planning

More often than not, in the early planning stages of an SBS implementation, you will find yourself providing as much business-planning advice as you do technical SBS implementation advice. SBS planning is discussed in Chapter 2. Case in point is the lumber supply firm I once worked with where the founder was in the process of transferring ownership of the business to his well-qualified son for care and feeding. Implementing the technology at times played second fiddle to resolving delicate succession-planning issues. Other examples abound, including the property management firm that understood the need to implement SBS in its old space prior to its office move so that users could grow accustomed to the network and then introduce advanced SBS functionality (such as an Internet connection) later.

And you might really help the firm complete its actual business plan. Often the SBS planning documents result in the firm asking:

- Who has what functional responsibilities?

- What clients and markets are being served?

- Can SBS help increase sales? (Yes, it can with a WWW page, broadcast faxing, and e-mails.)

Cultural and Organizational Reengineering

If you think the paradigm shift I'm promoting today from regular Windows 2000 to SBS is hard going, think about how your SBS customer must feel when introducing a network into the organization. Communications go from traditional vertical lines on the organizational chart to horizontal democratic flows. (More than one small-business owner has grumped to me privately that introducing e-mail via SBS has increased organization dissension.) For many small firms, introducing SBS radically alters the work flow, and sometimes, especially in family-owned and -operated businesses, such radical reengineering efforts can ruffle the feathers of those at the top!

Keeping Up with the Joneses

In all seriousness, small businesses are demanding enterprise-level network functions at a fraction of the price. Enterprise-level technology that has been jealously eyed by small businesses includes powerful network operating systems (such as the Windows 2000 Server operating system include with SBS 2000), robust e-mail (such as the Microsoft Exchange 2000 Server product included with SBS 2000), and an effective firewall (such as ISA Server 2000 included with SBS 2000). While I won't list every SBS 2000 feature here in the context of the small businesses desire for enterprise-level technology solutions, you get the point. Small businesses find themselves with an increasing need for enterprise-level business technology to

- Provide better customer service

- Level the playing field with larger organizations

- Take advantage of the Internet

SBS delivers all of this with its implementation of proven BackOffice applications on top of Windows 2000 Server.

> BEST PRACTICE: In fact, this price differential from not having to purchase additional third-party solutions (such as modem pooling), which I call riding the SBS yield curve, has allowed me to successfully market SBS to reluctant small businesses. After they are educated that buying regular Windows 2000 Server would require an additional cash outlay for modem pooling and fax server functionality (sometimes approaching or exceeding the total cost of SBS!), they quickly reconsider and often select SBS.

Competitive Advantage

This issue speaks to playing both a good offense and a good defense. Consider it the universal challenge for all businesses.

Offense

Several of my progressive and proactive SBS customers have specifically sought out and implemented SBS for the advantages it brings to their business. For example, one client, a mail order solicitation firm that sells property tax reduction services to households, needed a robust networking solution, such as Windows 2000 Server with a workhorse database engine such as SQL Server. At first thought, you might suggest Big BackOffice. Wrong answer. This firm has two employees, and those two employees specifically wanted the easy-to-use SBS Consoles so that they could manage the network after the initial SBS installation and see less of you-know-who (me, the hourly SBS consultant). This is a case of SBS allowing a small business the opportunity to expand its marketing reach dramatically. Countless other examples exist.

Defense

Not to generalize, but the old, family-run businesses to which I've introduced SBS tend to implement SBS for defensive reasons. This is a completely legitimate decision-making framework for selecting SBS. These firms' defensive SBS strategy is analogous to the fax machine wave that hit the business community starting in the late 1970s. At first, only larger companies had faxes. Soon, as costs dropped, nearly every business had a fax machine. In fact, if you didn't have a fax number on your business card after the mid-1980s, you received a puzzled look from your clients. Nothing in that era was more embarrassing than having your receptionist recite to a caller "We don't have a fax machine." Fast-forward a decade or so. Today it's e-mail and a Web page. Lacking both, you're clearly behind the times and not a very attractive firm to do business with.

These old-thinking firms are actually some of the best SBS candidates, if for no other reason than prices have dropped so low on hardware (historically speaking), that you can leapfrog these customers right into the latest and greatest technology! Case in point: By being pulled into the SBS era, these Neanderthal firms have avoided suffering through the NetWare 2.x era (ouch!), and so on. This defensive strategy, usually unintended by these old-line small-business proprietors, kills a few birds with one stone. They can proudly tout their own Internet-registered domain name at their next fraternal lodge meeting and brag about how much money they saved as a late adopter of personal computer and networking technology!

Technical Considerations

Finally, as part of the goal to define and segment the SBS customer population, consider the following candidate firms for SBS:

- The soon-to-be newly networked

- Peer-to-peer upgraders

- Novell NetWare Converters

- Linux Losers

Soon-to-Be Newly Networked

These are the last frontiers in networking left today. Networking consultants, acting as explorers, seek out this type of SBS customer with a vengeance. Why? Because we can put our stamp on their successful network, and it's likely this type of client hasn't yet had a negative networking experience (or negative experience with their network consultant). Great SBS customers if you can find them.

Peer-To-Peer Upgraders

As you may or may not know, peer-to-peer networks are workstations that have been cabled together into a quick-and-dirty network. This is a significant SBS customer group because two factors are driving the upgrade decision: pain and gain. Peer-to-peer networks traditionally suffer from poor performance (that's the pain part) and many small businesses can easily see the gain a true client/server network such as SBS can deliver (that's, of course, the gain part).

And here's a late breaking peer-to-peer event for you. Recognizing this "micro market segment" within the small-business community, Microsoft was enabled surprisingly strong peer-to-peer networking capabilities in Windows XP. Seriously! The idea here is that a "micro" small business starts with Windows XP peer-to-peer and then, when growth happens, upgrades to SBS! Smart segment stratification, if I dare say so myself.

Pain

Having started on a peer-to-peer network, these SBS customers want to upgrade because the performance and reliability of the peer-to-peer network no longer cuts it. Either print jobs take forever, or they recently lost data because the decentralized nature of a peer-to-peer environment doesn't lend itself to proper backup procedures.

Gain

Revenues are up, earnings are exceeding expectations, you're growing like wildfire. Let's get a new SBS network. Enough said.

Novell NetWare Converters

This is perhaps historically one of the touchiest and most-difficult SBS customer groups to work with for several reasons. I know, I know, you're saying that

NetWare is dead. Not so quick my Missouri cousin! Why is it so many small businesses are running good old NetWare 3 even to this day? Granted, NetWare isn't the dominant force it once was, but it's a huge source of billable hours for me: converting NetWare to SBS.

Anti-Microsoft Sentiments

The big red crowd (existing NetWare users) find themselves in an interesting bind in the late 20th century/early 21st century. Having made the correct decision in the 1980s and most of the 1990s, this group is now faced with the prospect of converting to the often-perceived evil empire's network operating system.

In reality, many NetWare customers have taken a politically correct if-you-can't-beat-'em-join-'em attitude; but there are still some lingering "better red than dead" sites out there. Just be respectful of this customer group.

But NetWare Did It This Way

This trap requires you to show the former NetWare, new SBS customer how old NetWare features are implemented in SBS. Often, the client isn't interested in the facts but simply wants to vent some anti-Microsoft anger. Go ahead and let them; it's healthy.

> BEST PRACTICE: When you get caught in one of these donnybrooks, consider the following to win over the reluctant Red Heads. Quickly show off Health Monitor. Then compare that to the MONITOR.NLM monitoring tool on their NetWare server. Because Health Monitor is much more robust than NetWare's Monitor, you will have made your point.

Our New Software Runs Only on Windows 2000

I've saved the real reason small businesses are converting from NetWare to SBS for last. With the dramatic increase in popularity in the Windows 2000 Server operating system and the relative decline in NetWare's popularity, developers have flocked to the Microsoft development camp. In fact, this trend clearly started back in the Windows NT Server days. Within six months of release, Microsoft reported that Windows 2000 (Server and Professional editions) had sold a combined 3 million copies. With momentum like that, it's not surprising that many independent software vendors (ISV) have not only ported their applications over to Windows 2000 Server, but they no longer support NetWare.

A case in point is a product that a past employer sold: Great Plains Dynamics. Some time ago before its merger with Microsoft, Great Plains stopped future development work on its older NetWare/Btrieve-based accounting applications and shifted those resources to the Windows 2000 Server and Windows NT Server/SQL Server product line. That shift has been responsible for over one-third of my firm's SBS installs as customers have been forced to convert from NetWare to SBS to keep up with Great Plains latest accounting applications. (For example, its accounting/e-commerce module only runs on a server having SQL Server, which of course SBS does!)

I guess you could say that the ISV community has been very good to me, as it has to many SBSers in the SBS consulting trade! How can I be less subtle? If it weren't for ISVs pushing applications to the Microsoft networking environments such as SBS 2000, I wouldn't have my ski condo, island house and late model Volvo. SBS has been very, very good to me.

Linux Losers

So shareware is not your bag, at least when it comes to running a bona fide business operation? And the Linux user experience is just a tad too much on the bit twiddler side, eh? No hard feelings. Welcome back to SBS. And by the way, at the Microsoft FUSION conference in Anaheim, California, in July 2001, the Microsoft SBS team went into great lengths to compare SBS to Linux. Turns out, according to a Microsoft study, the argument that Linux is free is misleading. When considering the total cost of operations in a computer network (labor, hardware, training and operating system), the operating system is only 3% of the total costs.

SBS Architecture

SBS is essentially a trimmed-to-fit version of Big BackOffice. SBS can be viewed as a complex circle, as shown in Figure 1-4.

Figure 1-4

SBS architecture presented from an easy-to-understand "wheel" perspective.

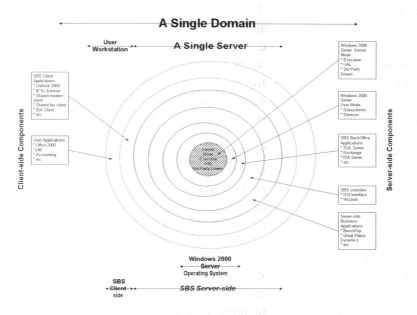

Let's discuss the SBS architecture model by starting with discussing a single domain (in a tree in an Active Directory forest, but more on that in a moment) and ending at the Windows 2000 Server operating system kernel. Note as you read the next few pages, that it's to your benefit to refer to Table 1-1, which not only lists the SBS components but makes a distinction between server-side and client-side components.

Root of Forest and a Single Domain

SBS must be the root of an Active Directory forest, which effectively prevents SBS from being another server (say a branch server) in an enterprise-level Active Directory domain infrastructure. In other words, practically speaking, you would say that SBS operates in a single-domain environment. As mentioned earlier, the SBS architectural model does not provide for multiple domains or explicit NT-like trust relationships. An Active Directory forest is a grouping of domains. A domain is an administrative or logical grouping of computers that participate in a common security model. This domain model manages the user accounts and security. Such security includes providing logon authentication for valid user accounts.

A Single Server

Only one computer on an SBS network can act as the root domain controller (DC). Out of the box, the SBS architectural model is to have one server, with the SBS machine acting as a root DC, per network. It is possible to have additional servers on the SBS network acting as domain controllers, non-domain controllers, or member servers.

Another DC on the SBS network houses a replica of the Active Directory database. Such a machine can verify a user's logon credentials; however, in my experience, it is extremely rare to have another DC on an SBS network. That's because additional DCs are typically placed on either a larger LAN or across slow WAN links on an enterprise-level network (two qualifications that typically aren't met with SBS).

Less rare on an SBS network is a member server. Member servers, known as *application servers*, typically run one or two specific business applications that can't run satisfactorily on the SBS root DC. Take the example of an animal service organization where I installed an SBS network. After installing the SBS server machine, I discovered that the fundraising software would run best on its own server. This software, known as Razors Edge, has its own SQL engine separate from SBS-included Microsoft SQL Server. Razors Edge's SQL engine proved itself to be quite a resource hog, necessitating the need for a standalone application server on this SBS network.

Because the BackOffice components included with SBS can't be installed on separate member servers (unlike Big BackOffice where several of the applications each have its own member server), it is critical that you purchase a machine with sufficient horsepower to optimally run SBS. I discuss hardware specifications in the second part of Chapter 2.

> BEST PRACTICE: Be advised that any additional servers on an SBS network may not be installed with the SBS product. Only one SBS server is allowed per network. The other servers must run regular Windows 2000 Server. Note that it is possible to have non-Windows 2000 Server application servers. I've worked on SBS networks where a NetWare server acted as a file/printer/application server on an SBS network (and did fine running a large Computer Associates business

accounting application). The wilderness advocacy organization kept the Sun UNIX-based servers as application servers so that the GIS specialists could continue using their high-end GIS/mapping software.

End-User Workstations

Assuming you have the full licensing allowed for SBS (50 computers), you know by now that up to 50 user workstations can be attached and concurrently logged on to the SBS network at any time. SBS natively provides full support for six operating systems: Windows XP, Windows 2000, Windows ME, Windows NT Workstation 4.0, Windows 98, and Windows 95. By *native support* I mean that the SBS client setup routine is fully supported, as well as client-side firewall (via ISA Server client-side support), fax, and modem.

SBS provides limited support for other clients including older versions (pre-4.0) of Windows NT Workstation, Windows For Workgroups, Windows 3.x, Macintosh, UNIX workstations, and LAN Manager Clients 2.2c. SBS does not offer support for OS/2 clients. Workstation support is discussed in the first part of Chapter 4.

User Applications

This area typically includes Office 2000 (or Office XP), a suite of applications including Microsoft Word for word processing, Microsoft Excel for spreadsheets, and Microsoft PowerPoint for presentations. Other user applications include narrow vertical-market software such as WESTMATE by Westlaw if you are an attorney, Timeslips if you're a professional who bills for your time, or QuickBooks if you are the bookkeeper in small company. You get the picture.

SBS Client Components

This includes many of the things listed as client components in Table 1.1. This includes not only common applications, such as Microsoft Outlook 2000 (discussed in Chapter 12), but also SBS components such as the modem-sharing redirector (discussed in Chapter 13). In order for you to have a fully compliant SBS network, the assumption is that the SBS client components have been installed on the user's workstations.

Be advised that after the initial setup of SBS, the majority of your time will be spent dealing with users, client workstations, end-user applications, and the like.

This isn't much different than any small network, but clearly Figure 1-4 isn't drawn to scale with respect to the time commitment you will ultimately make to end user workstations, user applications, and SBS client components.

Server-Based Business Applications

Next in the SBS architecture in Figure 1-4 is server-based business applications such as BenchTop and Great Plains Dynamics, two applications that use SBS's SQL Server as their engine. To reiterate, it is this layer of the SBS architectural model that is so important. Powerful business applications, typically server-based, will drive the purchase decision to implement an SBS-based solution. Every industry has its own narrow vertical-market application that the small business seeks to implement. It is critical to assess that the SBS architecture will faithfully support such an application.

SBS Consoles

The SBS consoles were discussed earlier today in Table 1-1. The SBS Administrator Console was shown in Figure 1-1. SBS consoles represent the server-based graphical user interface (GUI) from which the vast majority of your SBS management duties are performed. When an SBS console option is selected, an easy-to-use wizard is typically launched. This wizard often completes complex tasks without the user's knowledge. I discuss the SBS consoles in detail in Chapter 5, but here's a tidbit to whet your appetite: some human architectural considerations went into designing the SBS console, starting with an easy and advanced console to appeal to different types of users. Bottom line: SBS consoles can be customized, making the emphasis on usability. Many technology consultants and ISV are writing to the SBS Console, placing their own snap-ins on the SBS Console from which you can run and manage applications and processes. In the second part of Chapter 5, I'll discuss how to modify and customize the SBS consoles.

SBS BackOffice Applications

SBS includes several traditional BackOffice applications, such as Microsoft Exchange 2000 Server, SQL Server 2000, and several others that are listed in Table 1-1. As previously mentioned, some trimming, mainly licensing, has occurred when the SBS application suite is compared to its Big BackOffice brother. Each of these applications is discussed in this book, often in a chapter dedicated specifically to that topic.

Windows 2000 Server

As you might recall, Windows 2000 Server can be cleanly divided between user mode and kernel mode. Figure 1-4 reflects this division.

User Mode

This is where services and applications run in protected memory (Ring 3) environmental space. To make a long story short, that means an individual application or service can not explicitly crash the operating system. Each application enjoys its own protected memory space.

Kernel Mode

This contains the Windows 2000 Server executive, hardware abstraction layer (HAL), and third-party device drivers. More advanced discussion regarding User and Kernel mode can be found in Microsoft's TechNet subscription service. Further discussion here is beyond the scope of this book.

Bringing It All Together

So a lot of great information about Small Business Server 2000 has been presented to kick off your SBS experience. Granted, if you are new to SBS, you have much to digest and perhaps a good night's sleep is needed before jumping into Chapter 2 , where you meet the Springer Spaniels Limited methodology (the fictional company you will create an SBS network for the remainder of this book).

But allow me one last opportunity to shed light and impart knowledge on the SBS experience. This viewpoint, while oriented more towards technology consultants who implement SBS solutions, speaks towards an underlying foundational issue about why SBS is here (and why we're here using it). So here goes.

My clients (and perhaps yours too) are business people who first and foremost care about running their businesses profitably so that they can accumulate wealth in the long run. This is standard Economics 101 stuff from college. At the far upper left of Figure 1-5, the business person asks a simple enough question: "How can I run my business better?" This is a question that I encounter early and often with my SBS clients as I help them work through the decision to implement SBS. Such discussions usually lead to the business person understanding that they need better information. Take the example of an accounting report they haven't been able to receive before. Granted, this need for better information may not manifest itself as a better accounting report. It might well be another type of business report they haven't been able to compile prior to the introduction of a network such as SBS or, equally likely, a report that can be compiled faster (the information was always available but took to long to obtain). Now let me throw a quick twist at you. In order to get the superior accounting information in my example, the business must upgrade its accounting package (e.g., Great Plains Dynamics) to the latest version that runs best on Windows 2000 Server, the underlying operating system in SBS 2000.

Figure 1-5
The business purposes of an SBS network: running the business better!

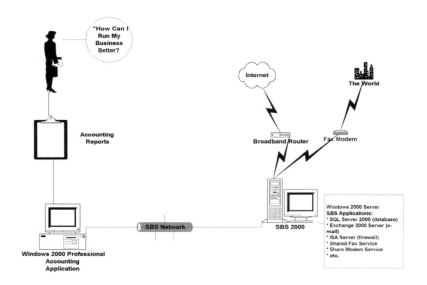

In the fictional example above, all the business knows or cares about is (and perhaps you have a real world situation in your life that you can relate to this) that the report is obtained by running the accounting client-application on his or her workstation. That's it. Anything between the workstation through the network wall jack in the wall to the machine running SBS and even out to the Internet are of little concern. This is where the SBSer technology consultant kicks in. We (you, me, and the other SBSers out there), know that the workstation has to be connected to the network via cabling, and cabling is typically connected to a hub in order to manage the network media. Also connected to the hub is the machine running SBS and the all-important accounting application (e.g., Great Plains Dynamics). This last point is something that will perk up the business person's attention again as you mention accounting application.

Well, in order for Great Plains Dynamics to run in my example, it needs SQL Server as its database engine, which is provided as part of SBS 2000. And yes, once asked, the business person agrees that they need internal and Internet e-mail capabilities such as those provided by Exchange 2000 Server in SBS 2000. And heck, if we're going to be connected to the Internet for e-mail, we better facilitate Web browsing (with Internet Explorer) and insure security with firewall protection (with ISA Server). Of yeah, and before I forget, the business person also see value in other SBS features such as the Shared Fax Service, the ability to work remotely via a secure VPN session (using ISA Server's VPN Wizard) and the ability to remote check e-mail (using Outlook Web Access). Lastly, the business person responds favorably when you mention that you can perform some of your network consulting work remotely using Terminal Services and better yet, keep an eye on the server machine with the built-in Server Status Reports. Whew! That's a long list of SBS success factors.

But understand what exactly has occurred here over the past few paragraphs. We've brought it all together from the point a business person expressed a desire to run their business better down to the nitty gritty details of SBS 2000. So as you can see, SBS really can help someone run their business better!

Competitive Analysis

No SBSer should blindly accept the virtues of SBS 2000 without doing their homework. By this I mean it's a healthy exercise to look at what competes with SBS 2000. By observing the competition, you can, of course, affirm the decision you've made to purchase and install SBS 2000. You'll eliminate any doubts you've had and answer any lingering questions. There are four primary competitors to SBS as near as I can tell:

- **Windows 2000 Server.** Good old, bare-bones Windows 2000 Server is a competitor for SBS 2000. This may be all you need, especially if you're using a POP3 mail account for your e-mail needs. God bless you is this is the case. Understand that you're missing out on so many other features of SBS by selecting this alternative.

- **Windows XP Peer-to-Peer.** This is the "micro" solution recommended for two-person offices (up to 10 people). Give the devil his due: Windows XP peer-to-peer is a competitor of SBS.

- **Novell Small Business Suite 5.1 (NSBS).** This is the closest bona fide competitor to SBS 2000 on the market. It darn near matches, feature for feature, the components in SBS 2000 (including consoles, wizards, and even remote management). It does at least two things differently than SBS 2000: makes it possible to add user licenses one at a time (SBS 2000 sells by the five pack); and has an integrated virus protection solution (SBS 2000 does not have a native virus protection solution but rather a close partner relationship with Trend Micro). However, NSBS doesn't have a robust database solution (SBS 2000 has SQL Server 2000), doesn't have modem pooling built-in and doesn't provide robust health monitoring. The pricing is comparable. NSBS is shown in Figure 1-6.

Figure 1-6
Novell's small-business offering can be found at www.novell.com.

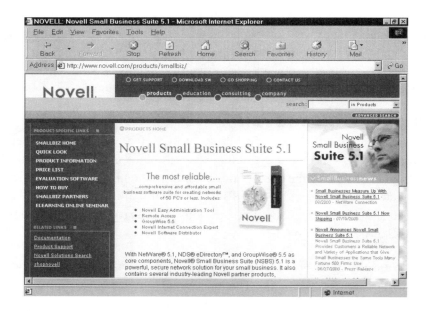

Oh, and did I mention that NSBS is based on the NetWare operating system, which while robust, is considered more difficult to work with and, more important, doesn't have the "mind share" or positive political support it once did in the business and technology communities (something to consider when looking at the investment you will make in a networking solution). The point I'm trying to make here is that business application developers, all things being equal, will typically develop their releases for a Windows 2000-based solution (SBS 2000) before a NetWare-based solution (NSBS).

- **IBM Small Business Suite for Linux.** Good old Big Blue (IBM) knows a good thing when it sees it: the small-business networking marketplace. So, it recently looked over its portfolio of technology assets and then borrowed, bundled, and stole to create its small-business networking solution seen in Figure 1-7.

Figure 1-7
IBM's Small Business Suite for Linux can be seen at www.ibm.com.

Certainly a couple of strengths about this offering are that IBM isn't likely to go out of business, the Linux operating system has grassroots support in the small-business community (Linux should not be underestimated as it causes lost nights of sleep for the SBS development team in Redmond, let me tell you!). Lastly,

IBM is the one company with the "goods" to build a bundle that is a legitimate competitive threat to SBS 2000. You heard it here first!

SBS 2000 Product Launch

A very special moment in SBS history occurred when SBS 2000 was launched in Atlantic City on February 21, 2001. It was at that moment that all the words in this book truly came to life. You could go forward, create the Springer Spaniels Limited sample network using this book and call yourself a true SBSer! I thought you might enjoy a few photos from that milestone event. In Figure 1-8, you are seeing the SBS signage at the hotel where the event was held. In Figure 1-9, you are witnessing the actual launch event. Figure 1-10 shows a break for the SBS launch cake. My SBS 2000 launch photo gallery concludes with a look at the SBS development team from Microsoft attentively answering questions from the audience in Figure 1-11.

Figure 1-8
Welcome to the SBS 2000 launch event!

Figure 1-9

The actual launch event was well-received by the attendees.

Figure 1-10

Let them eat SBS cake!

Figure 1-11
Microsoft's SBS development team getting feedback from the crowd.

So, what photos are missing? To protect everyone's professional reputations, I've decided not to show you the photos from the post-launch party on the evening of February 21, 2001, at the Hard Rock Café in Atlantic City. It was way too much fun for print!

The Future of SBS

There are two angles to this discussion. First is the SBS product itself. Microsoft, and more important, the marketplace, have given every indication that SBS is here to stay. SBS has crossed some significant financial thresholds inside Microsoft so that it positively contributes to the bottom line of the Mothership.

SBS 2000 will undoubtedly be followed by future SBS upgrades, each one providing more functionality and stability. In fact, Microsoft is already hard at work on "Bobkat" (that's Microsoft's code name for the next release), which will incorporate many components that didn't make it into the SBS 2000 release, including the talking computer named HAL (a nod to the classic movie *2001*).

Of course, I jest in order to provide a dose of humor at the end of a long chapter together. As an aside, the SBS development team was recently moved into the Windows operating system group. While I'm not sure what this means for SBS (will it be more operating system centric and less application focused?), you can't argue with it being underneath one of the cash cows and most successful business units at Microsoft (a positive sign).

The second dimension is what your future with SBS is. Ideally, if you have a growing business, SBS is merely a stepping stone to implementing Big BackOffice, and this path is certainly in alignment with Microsoft's view. If you can use SBS as an incubator to help you expand your business, Microsoft will be more than happy to upgrade you to Big BackOffice at a future date!

Summary

This chapter fulfilled several roles and met some very important goals. The first part introduced you to SBS with a brief introduction of each component and describes SBS's capability to deliver a single-server comprehensive networking solution that is relatively simple for the small business to implement and maintain. A key tenet to SBS—business application support—is emphasized. The guest column shared insights on the consulting opportunities for certified professionals that SBS brings. The back of the chapter defines the small-business market for SBS and provides an in-depth look at SBS's underlying architecture. The future of SBS is discussed in closing.

The chapter also provides you, in passing, with an overview of where this book is headed and how it is organized. Several topics are briefly described in Chapter 1 and cross-referenced to future chapters where the topic area or feature is covered in more depth.

You are now ready to proceed to Chapter 2. And before you know it, a short time will have passed, and you will be a competent SBS professional. Or as we say in the trade, SBSer!

Chapter 2
Small Business Server Design and Planning

Welcome to Chapter 2, where you will proceed with specific planning tasks, all of which increasingly work forward to the actual hands-on activity of implementing SBS. You are also introduced to Springer Spaniels Limited, the blessed sample company in this book.

Planning is considered an upstream function in a technology project. It tends to be less hands-on and more general than the actual setup and maintenance tasks that follow, these last two task areas being known as a downstream function. While it is easy to consider planning as an intuitive process that doesn't require much of a time commitment from the SBSer or business person, such an assumption is a fallacy. Indeed, planning is typically considered to be the best use of time in a technology implementation. In fact, you really can't escape planning. You can perform it upstream at the start of the technology implementation in an orderly and well-behaved way, or you can perform your planning the hard way when you find your self installing SBS multiple times at one business, realizing with each passing installation that you'd like to change the way you did things. Ouch!

Springer Spaniels Limited

First off, let's take a moment to meet Springer Spaniels Limited (SSL), the company for which you'll implement a complete and successful SBS-based networking solution throughout the remainder of the book. You will often hear me refer to the SSL methodology when I walk you through steps in a setup sequence. Understand that the context my references to the SSL methodology is this: While there are numerous ways that SBS can be implemented (for example, partition sizes can vary after the minimum requirements are met, company names and Internet domain names will most certainly vary, etc.), by following the SSL methodology, you will find the experience very educational, consistent, and even fun!

There are some very important reasons to work with an imaginary company the first pass through this book. It has been my experience with SBS (and life in general) that you know much more after you've done something once. It's another way of saying that hindsight is 20/20, a well-accepted old saw.

Such is the case with SBS. Typically, you set up SBS based on some assumptions that are made early in the planning process. Such assumptions might include the domain name you create, and so on. But fast-forward in the process, perhaps a few weeks. More than once an SBS administrator has commented to me that, now that she knows what SBS really is, she would have set it up differently. Those observations about getting it right are analogous to creating the chart of accounts when installing accounting software. You make some early decisions that you have to live with the rest of your life.

Now back to SSL. By using this company for the remainder of the book, you have the chance to learn SBS, warts and all, before installing it for real. These methods also allow you to avoid the scenario mentioned previously, wherein weeks after your "real" SBS install, you might lament that you would have done a few things differently if you had the chance to do it over again. With SSL, I'm providing you that chance at a very low cost.

By completing the activities in the remaining chapters, you will learn what works for you and what doesn't. When you go to install SBS for real, with live company data, you will have your feet on much more solid ground. That will result in a successful SBS install for you and your organization.

SSL, for these purposes, is a small company with 10 users and 30 employees. Please note that not every employee uses a computer (many clean kennels and so forth). The company breeds, raises, and shows prize-winning Springer Spaniels. SSL is headquartered on Bainbridge Island, Washington on a converted apple orchard. The SSL operations are seen in Figure 2-1. The two prize Springer Spaniels named Jaeger and Brisker are seen in Figure 2-2.

Figure 2-1
Springer Spaniels Limited operations on Bainbridge Island.

Figure 2-2
Lead dogs Jaeger and Brisker.

SSL has six departments in addition to the executive offices, as shown in Figure 2-3.

Figure 2-3
Springer Spaniels Limited (SSL) organizational chart.

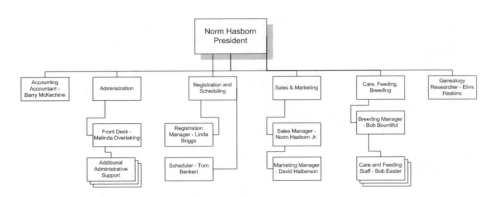

As you will see, SSL benefits from SBS in many ways, including its robust built-in Internet connectivity. How? Since canine breeders everywhere are worried about genetic variety in breeding (that is, they want to avoid inbreeding), the Internet is used to find suitable breeding partners. And I'm not talking about anonymous Internet chat rooms full of lonely Springer Spaniels looking for love in all the wrong places. Rather, SSL intends to search sophisticated and legitimate breeding databases around the world (if you are not aware, the Springer Spaniel breed is well-respected for its diversity in breeding, which is a kind way of saying the breed hasn't been ruined by inbreeding).

SSL also benefits from other easy-to-use SBS features, such as the two SBS consoles (Administrator, Personal) that were briefly introduced in Chapter 1 and are detailed in Chapter 5. As the chapters pass in this book, I will divulge more details of SSL as needed. Periodically, you will enter SSL information into SBS to complete exercises if you are following this book psalm and verse. It's the well-planned SSL methodology that is the foundation and backbone of this book.

Not surprisingly, I do want to tip my hat of acknowledgment to those of you who may not follow the exact steps of the SSL methodology, as you may be using this book as a quick primer to sharpen your SBS 2000 skills before building your own server (or the server of a client if you are a consultant). Right on! And for those of you who aren't dog lovers and find it hard to get excited about Springer Spaniels, I can appreciate that too. This book isn't a monument to dogs or the Springer Spaniel breed; rather the dogs and SSL serve as a convenient metaphor for telling a story and teaching you SBS 2000. So no e-mail from non-dog lovers please!

> BEST PRACTICE: Now is a great time to start your own *needs analysis* for your SBS project. A needs analysis typically involves looking at the ebbs and flows of business activity in your firm, often for the first time. Start by creating your own organizational chart similar to Figure 2-3. From that, you might discover that your company and SBS users are organized in ways that might not have been apparent. I have found that, early in the SBS planning process, many people use the SBS computer project as an opportunity to reorganize their businesses. In fact, an SBS consultant is often a management consultant as well.

SBS Project Management

You should never undertake an SBS project without sufficient planning. In fact, I typically spend a day or more with an SBS client doing nothing more than planning for the new SBS network. I can't emphasize enough how important planning is with an SBS implementation. These up-front hours are certainly some of the best you spend.

An SBS project can be divided into five phases. These phases, which will be described in detail, follow:

1. Planning Phase: The logical and physical design of the SBS network occurs here as well as some early expectation management to avoid future disappointments.
2. Server Installation Phase: The SBS server is installed.
3. Workstation Installation Phase: The workstations are installed and configured.
4. Follow-up Phase: Over the course of several weeks, new SBS features are introduced. This mirrors the layout of this book as later chapters present additional SBS features as well as general troubleshooting, user support, and network optimization.

5. Celebration Phase: Projects create stress, and an SBS installation is no different. Phase five is an opportunity to not only release some tension but also solicit feedback from SBS network stakeholders. This phase applies to both in-house SBS installations as well as those SBSers serving as consultants.

Planning Phase

For anyone considering SBS, the earliest planning exercises involve identifying and communicating why you want to implement SBS in your organization. That can be accomplished by answering the following questions. You will note that appropriate responses from SSL have been entered.

Early Planning Questions

I've got a secret for you about planning. To be honest, planning is very much about asking questions about the firm's existing and future situation with respect to technology and then actively listening to the responses given. It's harder than it looks. You might well find it easy to ask a lot of questions, but are the questions appropriate or effective? Do you have good listening skills and incorporate the client's feedback into your planning process?

Here are some sample planning questions to get things going:

Q   List the three reasons you plan to use SBS.

A   (1) Ultimately to install our accounting system, Great Plains Dynamics, using Microsoft SQL Server 2000 (which is included with SBS). (2) To have a secure and robust Internet connection for communications (e-mail) and Web-based research purposes. (3) To lower our information system costs by performing much of the ongoing administration ourselves via the friendly SBS Console.

Q   What is the time frame for implementing SBS?

A   We intend to set up, install, troubleshoot, and train everyone on the network over a 10-week period starting in two weeks when the new computer equipment arrives (and when you finish reading this book!).

Q   How have you arranged for training for the new SBS network?

A   The SBS consultant will train those responsible for network administration. The SBS administrators will show the users how to log on, print, and save information. These users will also attend three half-day training sessions on the following topics: Microsoft Windows 2000, Office XP, and Outlook.

Q   What roadblocks or problems can you identify today that might make the SBS project more difficult to complete?

A   First and foremost would be staff turnover. If our accountant leaves, not only would we have lost the individual we've identified as the SBS administrator, but we will have also lost our Great Plains Dynamics talent. To combat this potential problem, we plan to have the receptionist assist with the SBS setup and administration so she can act as a backup SBS administrator in an emergency. A second possible problem is the bank financing for our computer equipment purchase. We anticipate that the lending process will take only two weeks and the equipment will arrive roughly two weeks later. Being a critical path item, any delay in bank financing would delay the start of the SBS installation.

Existing Network Layout

Early on in the planning process, it is incumbent on SBS consultants and small-business owners alike to know exactly what they have when it comes to computer hardware and software. This baseline measurement allows you to determine what must be ordered, replaced, repaired, and so on. This information is typically gathered by inventorying the network and presenting your findings in a spread-sheet table or a network diagram. My preference has been to use a network diagram because its graphical views facilitate ease of understanding.

These network diagrams are typically drawn by hand, or with a network diagram-ming software application such as Microsoft's Visio, resulting in a schematic or drawing of your existing network. More information on Visio is available at www.microsoft.com. Visio can be purchased for under $500. Such a drawing might look similar to the drawing created for SSL in Figure 2-4.

Figure 2-4

Existing network for SSL.

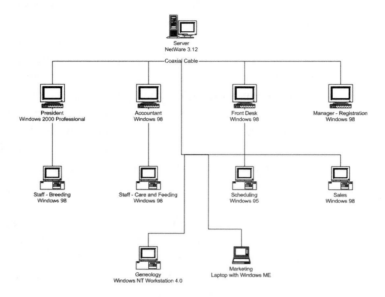

Check Existing Infrastructure

Assuming a network diagram has been created, you need to gather a little more information for SBS planning purposes. Take a tour of your existing physical site and make notes regarding the following items: cabling, hubs, and wall jacks. Table 2-1 shows the existing infrastructure information for SSL.

Table 2-1: Existing Infrastructure

Item	Condition/Notes
Cabling	Need to implement Category 5 10BASE-T, Ethernet-type cabling at site. Existing coaxial cabling will not work.
Hubs	Will purchase and install dual-speed hubs.
Wall jacks	Each office will have one wall jack plus extra wall jacks in hallway.

Cabling

In the case of SSL, you will note in Figure 2-4 that the existing cabling media is coaxial, which is considered inferior to the more modern Category 5, 10BASE-T, Ethernet-type cabling (or perhaps the new Cat 6 cable that was recently announced). Because SSL intends to replace the cabling, it is so noted on the proposed network layout (see Figure 2-6) later in the chapter.

Hubs

A hub is a central gathering point for network cabling. Many people today who are using the Category 5 cabling described previously are opting for high-speed hubs to replace older, slower hubs. Thus, when designing your SBS network, consider the faster (and more expensive) 100Mbps hubs over the 10Mbps hubs. With an eye on the future and getting the best long-term value from your SBS network, you will be glad that you did.

> BEST PRACTICE: Some older machines on a network, such as older laptops that use a parallel port-based network adapter, might not be able to run at 100Mbps (the new, higher network speed). If such is the case, you might need to purchase a dual-speed hub that supports both the older 10Mbps and the newer 100Mbps speeds. In fact, you will note in Table 2-1 that dual-speed hubs will be purchased and installed.

Wall Jacks

It is common when planning an SBS project to discover that you will need to increase the number of wall jacks at your site. This typically occurs for two reasons. The first is that additional networked workstations will be added as part of the SBS implementation. This is very common. More often than not, when a new network is installed, so are additional workstations. These additional workstations typically are purchased for new hires, suggesting company growth is a driving factor in implementing a new SBS network. Or, the additional workstations might be for existing employees—formerly reluctant players—now stepping up to the table to join the networked world.

Here is what I mean. At a property management firm I serve, the commissioned-based real estate agents must contribute financially to join the SBS network. That is, they have to buy a node on the network. Prior to introducing SBS, the old network was based on a NetWare server, something that didn't thrill many of the agents. Thus, several agents went without network connectivity in the past. Enter SBS, and these do-withouts became more excited about networking, especially with SBS's Internet connectivity. Thus, existing standalone computers were added to the network when the SBS network was up and running.

Another cause for ordering additional wall jacks is the pervasive use of network-connected printers. A popular setup is the Hewlett Packard (HP) laser printers connected directly to the network with a JetDirect card. These network printers are typically connected directly to the network using one of the wall jacks. Many firms use the SBS network project as an opportunity to upgrade their existing printers or add more printers, so it is very common when planning an SBS network to order additional network wall jacks.

> BEST PRACTICE: Attaching printers to the network in no way affects your user count with respect to SBS licensing. Some of you from the old NetWare days might recall that network devices, such as printers and Shiva LanRover modems, could and would consume one or more of your network logon licenses. Such is not the case with SBS. You can have as many network printers as you'd like. Your user limit in SBS is ultimately determined by counting how many machines are actually logged on to the SBS network at any one time.

Given that you probably need to order wall jacks for your SBS network, be sure to over-engineer the number of wall jacks ordered. I like to order up to 25 percent more wall jacks than I anticipate needing. These extra wall jacks are typically placed in the conference room where training occurs or temporary employees work. In my book, you can never have enough wall jacks. Plus it is cheaper to install them all at once rather than have the cabling specialist make return visits.

List of SBS Stakeholders

Another important SBS planning item is to create your list of SBS stakeholders. Stakeholders include yourself, any consultants, service providers, and so on who have a role on the SBS project. And because everyone today has multiple tele-phone numbers (work, work-private, work-fax, home, cellular, pager, and so on), I highly recommend that you add each stakeholder's telephone numbers and e-mail addresses to your SBS stakeholders list.

Table 2-2: SBS Stakeholders

Name	*Role*	*Contact Information*
Tom Jagger	SBS Consultant	SBS Staffing, Inc. 123 Main Street Redmond, WA 98000 W: 425-555-1212 Fax: 425-123-1234 Home: 206-222-2222 Cellular: 206-333-3333 Pager: 206-123-0987 Ski Condo: 503-200-1999 tomj@sbsrus.com
Jane Unionski	Cabling Specialist	Unionski Cabling Box 3333 Unionski, WA 98111 W: 222-333-4455 Cellular: 222-444-3344 Pager: 222-123-4567 union@cablespec.com
Bob Easter	Manager, SSL	Springer Spaniels Limited 3456 Beach Front Road Bainbridge Island, WA 98110 W: 206-123-1234 Fax: 206-123-1235 Home: 206-111-1234 bob@springersltd.com

Roni Vipauli	Lender, SBS	Small Business Savings
		123 Small Business Blvd.
		Small Town, WA 99882
		W: 425-111-8888
		Fax: 425-SBS-LEND
		roni@smallbusinesssavings.com
Ted Rockwell	Sales Associate	Overnight Warehouse
		PO Box 8855
		Acorn, WA 98234
		1-800-111-0000, ext. 334
		ted@sales.overnight.now.com

BEST PRACTICE: The users contained in Table 2-2 will be amongst the first names entered into Microsoft Outlook.

User List

Next in the general planning process under the SSL methodology would be creating a user list for your SBS network, those people you intend to allow to use the SBS network. It's not as easy as it sounds. First, you have to typically think through who needs SBS network access, as not all users do. Once it is decided who will be allowed on the network, you need to take extra care to spell each user's name correctly on the network and have an initial password to use. Each user's name at SSL (10 users) is shown below. These names will be entered into the SBS network in Chapter 4.

First:	Norm
Last:	Hasborn
User Name:	NormH
Password:	Purple3300
Job Title:	President
Office:	Executive
User Template:	Power User
Computer Name:	PRESIDENT

First: Barry
Last: McKechnie
User Name: BarryM
Password: 2Reedred
Job Title: Accountant
Office: Accounting
User Template: User
Computer Name: ACCT01

First: Melinda
Last: Overlaking
User Name: MelindaO
Password: Blue33
Job Title: Front Desk Reception
Office: Administration
User Template: User
Computer Name: FRONT01

First: Linda
Last: Briggs
User Name: LindaB
Password: Golden10
Job Title: Manager, Registration
Office: Registration and Scheduling
User Template: User
Computer Name: MANREG01

First: Bob
Last: Bountiful
User Name: BobB
Password: Bish4fish
Job Title: Breeding Manager
Office: Care, Feeding, Breeding
User Template: User
Computer Name: BREED01

First: Tom
Last: Benkert
User Name: TomB
Password: Whitesnow101
Job Title: Scheduler
Office: Registration and Scheduling
User Template: User
Computer Name: SCHEDULE01

First:	Norm
Last:	Hasborn Jr.
User Name:	NormJR
Password:	Yellowsnow55
Job Title:	Sales Manager
Office:	Sales and Marketing
User Template:	User
Computer Name:	SALES01

First:	David
Last:	Halberson
User Name:	DaveH
Password:	Grenadine2002
Job Title:	Marketing Manager
Office:	Marketing
User Template:	User
Computer Name:	MARKET01

First:	Elvis
Last:	Haskins
User Name:	Elvis
Password:	Platinium101
Job Title:	Researcher
Office:	Genealogy
User Template:	User
Computer Name:	GENE01

First:	Bob
Last:	Easter
User Name:	BobE
Password:	dogcatcher1
Job Title:	Dog Trainer
Office:	Care, Feeding, and Breeding
User Template:	Power User
Computer Name:	CAREFEED01

Security

Not surprisingly, small organizations have many of the same computer network security needs as larger enterprises. The owner of a small business typically has confidential information that should not be widely distributed.

Security is a recurring theme in this book as different SBS components are discussed, such as Microsoft SQL Server and ISA Server. But for your initial

SBS planning purposes, the first security issue to address is membership in the Administrators group. Administrators are the functional equivalent of Admins and Supervisors in NetWare or the super user account in a UNIX environment. Thus, it behooves you to select carefully who should have "full control" as an administrator over your SBS network. Typically, this membership group is limited to the organization's leader (owner, CEO, President), the day-to-day SBS administrator, and perhaps the SBS consultant you've retained.

Project Schedule

The next step is to create an SBS project schedule. Because of the nature of SBS projects—working with small organizations—it is not necessary to use Microsoft Project to create complex Gantt/Pert/CPM charts. These high-end project-scheduling applications are better left for putting pipelines across Alaska.

However, I do recommend that you create a simple calendar-based schedule for your SBS project. Microsoft Outlook has a calendar that works fine. The project schedule for SSL is shown in Figure 2-5.

Figure 2-5
SBS project schedule for SSL

BEST PRACTICE: For more complex scheduling, consider using other scheduling programs. These range from Calendar Creator (The Learning Company), which creates more detailed calendars than Microsoft Outlook, to Microsoft Project. Microsoft Project can be used for complex projects that track durations, resources, and predecessor/successor relationships.

Addressing Hardware, Software, and Services List and Budget Needs

You must now create the hardware, software, and services lists for your SBS network as the next planning step in the SSL methodology. The list shown Table 2-3 is the desired outcome. Regarding the hardware area, a new server and new hub are being purchased by SSL. With respect to software, SBS, sufficient user licenses, and additional software are being purchased by SSL. Several types of services will be required, including additional telephone lines for the new DSL Internet connection and new wiring, because a new star topology based on the Ethernet standard has been selected. A *star topology* occurs when each workstation and the server is connected to the hub in a "spoke and hub" configuration similar to a bicycle tire. You will also see that, by adding an additional column in Table 2-3 for costs, the list not only serves as your purchase specifications but also your budget. Note that I describe hardware, software, services, and budgets in much more detail later in the chapter.

Table 2-3: Hardware, Software, and Services List for SSL

Item	Description	Cost
Hardware	Gateway 7400 server, tape backup unit, hub, laser printer (network-ready), UPS backup battery, modems	$6,500
Software	SBS, Add'l Software (third-party tape backup, antivirus client/server suite, software). Note that NetMeeting will need to be downloaded and installed to facilitate remote user communications.	$3,500
Services	SBS Consultant, wiring with wall jacks, telephone line hookup, Internet service	$10,500

Proposed Network Layout

The next step is to create a drawing of the proposed network. The proposed network for SSL, shown in Figure 2-6, graphically depicts many of the items discussed previously in the section "Addressing Hardware, Software, and Services List and Budget Needs." Also shown is how the old NetWare server will be "recycled." Here, the old NetWare server will be reformatted as a Windows 98 workstation for use by staff for remote access via NetMeeting.

Figure 2-6

Proposed SBS network for SSL.

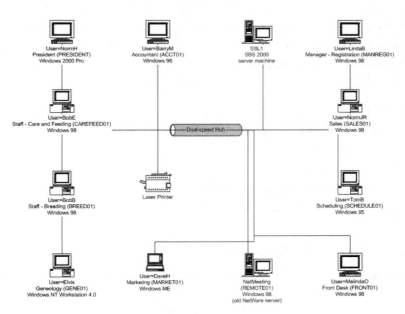

BEST PRACTICE: Granted, some of the more senior guru SBSers in the readership are asking why I don't simply have the remote users run a Terminal Services session on the machine running SBS. There are several reasons not to do this that I discuss in Chapters 8 and 13, but in a nutshell, Terminal Services sessions place a huge resource load on the server machine. And SBS is designed to run Terminal

Services in remote-administration mode, not application-sharing mode. Plus, as of this writing, Microsoft's position is that application-sharing mode will not be enthusiastically supported, meaning you more or less on your own if you try to jury-rig a remote-access solution via SBS's built-in Terminal Services (more on this in Chapter 8). Let's just say don't go there. But do go to the aforementioned two chapters for much more information.

Final Planning Activities

Three items remain as part of the SBS planning process: ordering, walkthrough, and documentation.

Ordering

A "critical path" item in your SBS project is the need to order your hardware, software, and services. Why? Under even the best of conditions, it can take 10 or more business days to receive your new server machine. Services such as scheduling your SBS consultant and ordering additional telephone lines can take even longer (especially when the telephone company is involved).

> BEST PRACTICE: If you use an SBS consultant, consider attending the calls placed when ordering. Typically I sit in a conference room with my SBS customer on "order day." The vendors are placed on the speakerphone, allowing for all parties to speak up and clarify anything. I've found that, by clarifying purchase specifications on order day, I save the client significantly more than my hourly consulting fees. Consider it another win for my SBS customer.

Walkthrough

Now that you are near the end of the planning phase, I highly recommend that you walk the floors of the site that will house the new SBS network again. By taking a fresh look at the site where the SBS network will be installed, you might notice a few things you initially missed. Items that have caught my eye on this final walkthrough include:

- Server placement: Where will the actual server reside? Is it near power outlets? Have you coordinated the extra telephone lines, some of which are used by SBS, to terminate at or near the SBS server machine?

- Workstation accessibility: Can you easily reach each workstation on the network? Is there enough room between the desks and walls to allow the cabling specialist to install wall jacks?

- Building access: Do your service providers have access codes and keys to perform after-hours work on the SBS project? Believe me, you can count on some unexpected late-evening visits from members of the SBS team!

Documentation and Loose Ends!

It is essential that you take a few moments to gather the letters, e-mails, bids, drawings, yellow sticky notes, and the like and organize these in an SBS project notebook. The SBS project documentation serves several purposes.

First, if you should leave the organization, you properly share your SBS knowledge with your SBS successors via the SBS project notebook. In effect, people who follow you don't have to start from the beginning. You, of course, would appreciate the same courtesy.

Second, because of the demands a small organization places on its staff, it's unlikely that you will remember the finer points of your SBS installation several months hence. Thus the value of an SBS project notebook.

Loose ends run the whole spectrum of SBS computing. You name it, and I've probably seen it. Some doozies in this category include:

- Sufficient quantity of telephone cable. Lesson learned: do you have enough telephone cabling to hook up the modems? And in this day and age, that might include DSL modems with its special cabling.

- Length of telephone cable: Lesson learned: are the telephone cables long enough?

- Environmental controls. Lesson learned: do you need a fan to help keep the server cool (because the work area is too warm)?

Another loose end to consider while planning your SBS network is training. One of the keys to success with an SBS network is to over-train your users! It's a theme worth repeating (and I do several times in this book!). Training can take several forms, all of which are discussed in Chapter 6.

BEST PRACTICE: Note the SBS project planning phase is typically 10 to 15 hours of consulting work. If you are undertaking your SBS project without a consultant, budget for one to two days of planning time.

Server Installation Phase

The big day arrives. Sitting in your workspace are large boxes on a pallet, representing the new server, monitor, and additional networking accessories (hub, modems, UPS, and so on.).

The server installation phase includes:

- Unpacking and physically building the server.

- Physically installing the network accessories such as the UPS, modems, and hub.

- Reseating the existing adapter cards that might have come loose during shipping.

- Installing SBS.

- Installing server-based applications, such as virus detection utilities, third-party tape backup applications, and so on.

- Performing several post-server installation tasks, such as creating the emergency repair disk (ERD), sharing folders, mapping drives, installing printers, and verifying security. This also includes completing SBS To Do List items (such as adding SBS licenses) and running SBS wizards from the SBS consoles.

- Configuring BackOffice applications. Typically Microsoft SQL Server must be configured for use. By itself, with no configuration out of the box, Microsoft SQL Server isn't especially useful. It is also common to configure Microsoft Exchange above and beyond its basic configuration to accommodate public folders, instant messaging, etc. This step may also include running wizards from the SBS consoles.

- Installing applications such as Great Plains Dynamics (accounting software).

It is important to have a server installation worksheet similar to Table 2-4.

Table 2-4 Server Installation Worksheet for SSL

Item	Description	Completed
Server Name	SSL1	
Domain Name	SPRINGERSLTD.COM	
Initial SBS Registration Name	Bob Easter	
Organization	Springer Spaniels Limited	
Installation Codes	Small Business Server, Outlook 2000 (use from Product ID stickers on Disc gem case)	
Area Code	206	
Dial Outside Number	blank	
Tone Dialing	Yes	
Address	3456 Beach Front Road	
City	Bainbridge Island	
State/Province	WA	
Zip	98110	
Country	United States of America	
Business Telephone	206-123-1234	
Business Fax	206-123-1235	
Initial Administrator Password	husky9999	
Hard disk	SBS operating system partition is 8GB. Data partition is approximately 9.5GB. Both partitions are formatted NTFS. Server has a three disk RAID-5 configuration. Each of the three disks is approximately 9 GB in size.	
Time Zone	Pacific	
User Accounts	Administrator (password= husky9999).	
Printers	Install new HP Color LaserJet 5M printer on network with HP5 share name.	
Registry	Modify Registry for opportunistic locking settings as per Great Plains Dynamics worksheet.	
Folders	Create additions folders on Data partition: **Accounting** (this is where Great Plains Dynamics will be installed along with the	

	storage area for the accounting data)	
	Old (this is where old data migrated from the NetWare server will reside until verified and either deleted or moved to Company Folders).	
	Applications (this is where third-party applications, such as virus utilities and so on, will be installed).	
	Backup (this folder will contain on-the-fly backups of company data between tape backups, such as internal SQL Server database backups)	
Shares	Create **ACCT** on the **Accounting** folder. Everyone allowed change rights. Full control rights to NormH, BarryM.	
Misc.	Windows 2000 operating system to be installed on C:. SBS components (Exchange, SQL Server, etc.) to be installed on C:. Will approve all licensing questions with "Yes". Will accept default SQL Server configurations (note additional items here). Note that remote access for users will be enhanced by NetMeeting running on a dedicated workstation.	

Regarding partitions, SBS requires that the partition containing the operating system (typically the C: drive) be formatted as NTFS to operate correctly. NTFS (NT file system) is the Windows NT Server partition scheme that allows advanced security and file management. The other partition selection is FAT (file allocation table), the type used primarily in the MS-DOS days of old. FAT partitions are less protected and considered less robust. The Microsoft Web site at www.microsoft.com provides extensive information on NTFS and FAT. Further discussion here would be beyond the scope of this book.

Workstation Installation Phase

The workstation installation phase is really the work that occurs in Chapter 4. That said, there are a few key steps in the workstation installation stage worth listing:

- Complete the SBS workstation installation sheet. This will be performed in Chapter 4.

- Physically unpack and construct workstations.

- Reseat the existing adapter cards that might have come loose during shipping.

- Complete installation of client operating system if necessary.

- Create the SBS client installation disk ("magic" disk) that will list each workstation. In SBS 2000, you only need one SBS client disk for the entire network setup instead of a diskette for each workstation. Very nice touch.

- Run the magic disk and configure the workstation for network and to receive its IP address dynamically from the SBS 2000 server (although you can use static IP addresses at the workstations as discussed in Chapter 4). If the workstations are Windows 2000 XP or Windows NT-based, the workstations will join the domain. If the workstations are Windows ME/98/95, the workgroup name will be made the same as the domain name and the logon condition setting will be set to log on to the domain. Next, the SBS client components are installed on each workstation.

- Perform basic SBS client component tests, answer limited-user questions, and so on.

- Enable and demonstrate network file sharing from client PCs.

- Enable and demonstrate network printing from client PCs.

- Enable and demonstrate basic *internal* e-mail via Outlook and Microsoft Exchange.

- Set a date to return to fully configure Outlook (shared calendar, shared contact list).

- Propose a date for network (logon, printing, saving) and Outlook training.

The middle steps involve testing the setup. Those are key steps in the success of attaching and using an SBS workstation. Too often I've observed homegrown SBS networks where the connectivity wasn't fully tested. In effect, the SBS network never did completely work. At one site the users joking called it an SBS notwork! Unfortunately, those SBS networks that forego workstation testing usually discover such things later rather than sooner.

And it shouldn't be lost on you that training is mentioned as the last step of the workstation installation phase. Again, training is important.

Follow-up Phase

As far as this book is concerned, the follow-up phase encompasses the balance of the SBS installation and administration experience. Why? For it is the follow up phase where additional SBS functions, such as faxing, and applications, and SQL Server, are introduced. There are important reasons for staging the introduction of many SBS features as separate, discrete tasks contained within a phase separate from server and workstation setup.

It has been my experience with organizations implementing SBS that the mere introduction of a computer network is enough to start with. The users need to become familiar with the basic Windows networking environment that is the foundation of SBS. In fact, for many users, being able to log on, save a file, and print are features enough to start out with.

Even network-experienced and computer-savvy organizations cannot absorb too many features too early. For example, e-mail is a great early candidate to introduce on the SBS network. But it has been my experience that even the best users aren't ready to tackle SQL Server and its strengths too early, so this speaks towards delaying the heavy stuff for awhile on your SBS networks.

Lastly, there is the Christmas-morning emotional response. Given a pile of wrapped toys, a child will eagerly attack, opening each and every gift until, several hours later, the child is overstimulated and sobbing in a corner. Such is the case with many SBS sites. Users want to do everything right now, on the first day the network is available, but by the end of the day, the same users are bewildered, frustrated, and, worst of all, have negative feelings toward the new SBS network. You, the SBS administrator, don't want and can't tolerate such an early defeat. Be smart. Stage the rollout of SBS features over time.

Celebration Phase

Yee-haw! Call it an opportunity to get a free lunch, but one of the most successful things I've accomplished as an SBS consultant is to have an end-of-project pizza lunch for all SBS users. Understand that there really is a method to this madness. Not only can I solicit user feedback that might not readily reveal itself during day-to-day SBS network use, but I can offer the opportunity to provide additional meaningful services that my SBS customer might not have initially considered. Four additional services have proven popular:

- Public folders - Many users, when they become addicted to e-mail, want additional help implementing public folders (shared resources) in Microsoft Exchange.

- Microsoft Outlook customization - When users start to use the contact list in Microsoft Outlook, the follow-up requests to create custom forms can be expected.

- SQL Server tables - The really hard-core SBS sites know that SQL Server can handle their most demanding database challenges, but few of these SBS sites actually know how to execute SQL queries and so on.

- Web page development – Last, but certainly not least, the discussion over the pizza lunch inevitably turns to Web pages and electronic commerce.

SBS Expectation Management and Perception

Avoiding disappointments is perhaps job one for an SBS administrator and certainly an SBS consultant. Recall that, in Chapter 1, I set the framework for understanding what SBS actually is. Disappointment can be avoided early, for example, by understanding that you will need to purchase a third-party virus scanning application because SBS is devoid of such a critical goodie.

Scope of Work

If you are using a consultant, a scope of work should be defined, largely based on much of the planning work accomplished previously. In my firm, the scope of work is typically delivered as a detailed proposal that describes how the work will be accomplished. Likewise, the engagement letter, which refers to the proposal for scope items, is a contract between my consulting firm and the client. An engagement letter typically covers items such as terms and conditions of payment, how disputes will be resolved, and so on.

BEST PRACTICE: Here is an additional thought for SBS consultants about the scope of work and engagement letters. Many SBS consultants ask how you get paid for your planning efforts if you haven't yet created a scope of work or gotten the client to sign the engagement letter.

Here you should contract with the client for 10 to 20 hours of your consulting time to assist with planning. Perhaps this consulting time could be evidenced with an engagement letter separate from the SBS project engagement letter you intend to present later. It has been my experience that if the customer is not interested in paying you for 10 to 20 hours of your planning time, that customer isn't very serious about having a successful SBS installation. Also, if the SBS customer is cautious about the planning phase, explain that the scope of work you create with 10 to 20 hours of planning time can be easily converted into a request for proposals (RFP) that could be distributed to other consulting firms and resellers.

The thought here is that you can get 10 to 20 hours into your SBS project with this customer, and either one (or both) of you decide that you don't care to work together anymore. This approach provides an out for all involved.

The scope of work would likely contain the following items:

- A detailed proposal

- A schedule

- A budget

- A project task list or checklist

Over communicate

Another theme to this book is that of over communicating before, during, and after your SBS project. It is very easy to do. You can do it in person via periodic SBS network meetings, pizza lunches, and the like. You might consider sending out an SBS project update e-mail, such as presented in Figure 2-7.

Figure 2-7

SBS e-newsletter.

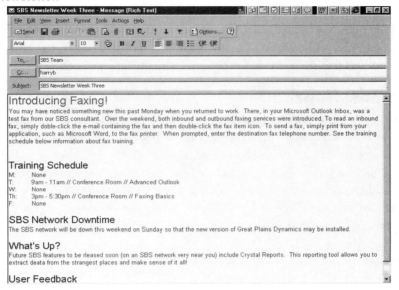

Selecting SBS Service Providers

Another planning issue is that of selecting the service providers for products and services for your SBS network. There are several types of SBS service providers:

- SBS consultants

- Hardware and software resellers

- Wiring and cabling contractors

- Telcos

- Internet service providers (ISP)

First, a comment regarding service providers. In general, the very best way to retain a service provider is via referral of a mutually respected third party, typically a friend at another organization that has used a service provider that he is pleased with. Acquiring or avoiding a service via this avenue is greatly recommended. In fact, as an SBS consultant, one of my key motivators to perform at the highest level is the prospect of getting referrals from my existing SBS client base!

Now here is a bit of advice they didn't teach you in the Microsoft Certified System Engineer (MCSE) program or the Harvard Business School for that matter. Avoid retaining a service provider based on an advertisement in the media, telephone book, and other outlandish promotional venues. Under these circumstances, it is very difficult to ascertain the quality of a service provider's work, communications style, and other critical factors.

SBS Consultants

Of course, one of the earliest and most important decisions you will make relates to whether you will engage the services of an SBS consultant. I wrote this book so that you could indeed implement an SBS network on your own with both study and practice (the two key tenets to this book). But many of you might want to extend the SBS best practices in this book by having an SBS consultant on your team for all or part of the SBS project. Furthermore, many of you are reading this book with the thought of becoming an SBS consultant.

Assume that you indeed plan to use an SBS consultant. You need to consider a few things up front. First, many Windows 2000/NT Server gurus have bestowed the title of SBS consultant on themselves because the shoe appears to fit. Such is not the case for reasons I presented in Chapter 1 that underscore how different SBS is from Big BackOffice and Windows 2000 Server. So what's my advice to you, the SBS customer? Avoid being the early training grounds for tomorrow's SBS guru (unless you're getting a significant discount on the billing rate being charged by the greenhorn SBS consultant, a point I surface in the next paragraph).

However, SBS gurus are in relatively short supply right now, so what should you do if all you have to select from are SBS newbies? At a minimum, negotiate a training rate that is significantly less (perhaps 50 percent) than the consultant's normal fees. That recognizes that your SBS installation will indeed be a learning exercise that at least you can afford. I also recommend that, armed with this book, you work side-by-side with the SBS consultant to make it right!

Those consultants who are SBS gurus tend to be nichers. Like a medical specialist, true SBS gurus basically live and breathe SBS all day long. You'll potentially pay extra for this level of expertise (perhaps a 50 percent premium over the bill rates of a general practitioner), but it's typically considered to be well worth it.

Hardware and Software Resellers

To be brutally honest, when purchasing for SBS networks, I've found the very best hardware and software buys on the Internet and via 800 numbers. A few vendors that I've used via this approach include the following.

Hardware

- Gateway. As seen in Figure 2-8 (www.gateway.com or 1-800-846-5211)

- Dell. (1-800-WWW-DELL)

- Compaq. (www.compaq.com)

Figure 2-8

Gateway has made a huge commitment to the SBS market.

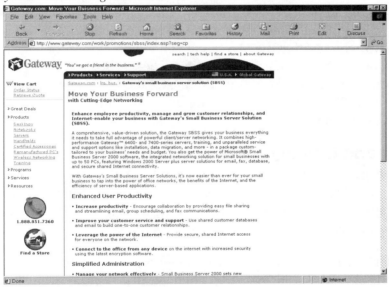

Software

- PCZone. (www.zones.com)

- CDW. (www.cdw.com)

BEST PRACTICE: If you are an SBS consultant, you may well want to resell software and hardware as another revenue source. While I personally don't do this, you should look at this possibility. For software sales, one firm has made it easy for the small-business consultant to become a software reseller and make a little pocket change at the same time. The firm, License Online, can be reached at 1-800-414-6596 or www.licenseonline.com. Good luck!

I've advised clients to be cautious about using resellers to perform the installation work because these organizations, often storefront retail establishments, typically lack SBS-specific expertise.

BEST PRACTICE: Hardware and software resellers can be a good source of free consulting as long as you keep in mind that you get what you pay for. For example, if you call Gateway to order your server (or better yet, visit a Gateway consultant at a Gateway Country store), the sales consultant can serve as a reality check regarding the number of processors, amount of RAM, and hard disk storage to order. That second opinion is of value and can be obtained for free. You will also note with interest that the SBS Online Guide, found via the SBS consoles, also addresses hardware scaling issues. To see this online information, look under the discussion area called "Getting Started" in Chapter 2: "Preparing to Install and Run Small Business Server" of the SBS Online Guide.

Wiring and Cabling Contractors

Here again, getting a reference is a great way to locate a competent wiring and cabling service provider. You might check with the property management firm that manages your office space. They most likely use one or two such firms when building out office space.

BEST PRACTICE: Be sure to have the wiring and cabling contractor test and certify his work (network cabling, wall jacks, and so on). Faulty network cabling can wreak havoc on an SBS network, and you should have some type of recourse against the contractor. A cabling and wiring certification provides the documentation you need to seek relief.

One of my SBS jobs, at a mortgage brokerage, suffered from faulty wiring. After trying to troubleshoot the software, server, other hardware, and so on, it was finally discovered the wiring was the culprit. So beware. Bad cabling happens.

Telcos

Here my options are limited for giving advice. You might not have the ability to select from multiple telephone companies (telcos) that can provide you with the additional lines needed for your Internet connection, faxing, and remote access. Increasingly though, many areas now have local telco competition, so choice is increasingly becoming available.

> BEST PRACTICE: Whenever working with a telco on any matter related to your SBS network, be sure to allow plenty of lead-time for the delivery of the services that you are requesting. Due to a booming demand for telephone lines, backlogs in filling service orders can be measured in weeks in many locations.

Internet Service Providers

Aside from using an ISP referral that you deem trustworthy, you have great flexibility in working with any old ISP you might stumble across. The Internet Connection Wizard (ICW) process is open to working with existing ISP accounts, large ISPs, small ISPs, even your dog's ISP (just a little Springer Spaniel humor there). The ICW is displayed and discussed in Chapters 5 and 9. But, seriously, in the planning phase of the SSL methodology, it behooves you to be a prudent purchaser of ISP services and shop around. Look at ISPs that best meet your technological needs and budget. For example, you might well find an ISP that is hurricane and earthquake proof (having backup batteries on-site that will run for weeks and other features) but such an ISP might be very expensive to do business with.

Guest Column

I asked my friend, John Martinez, to put the "B" back in SBS. That is, let's talk about "business." John has us take a few moments to ponder what being a small business is all about. This sets the table for a successful SBS installation: getting it right about being a small business. Take it away, John!

Owning your own business is the ultimate American dream—right after life, liberty, and the pursuit of happiness. It's that opportunity to bring to life an idea, plan or product and ultimately form and mold it and its many parts into a full-time, make-real-money job. But, boy, does it have its share of land mines, booby traps, and dead ends, especially when it comes to the business side of the operation. Some of us are great salesmen, others can dream up great ideas and some of us have the ability to invent cool, new products but that's not enough to be successful in today's business world. To succeed, you need a firm grasp of business principles, including accounting, human resources, marketing and sales, and have an understanding of the technology that holds it all together.

I'm the editor of a computer magazine, so I'm pretty up-to-date on hardware technology. But I'm struggling over where to go with our accounting software. Our current accounting firm is mired deeply into an old Novell Network version of Timberline software and is offering us some healthy discounts if we use the same system. They seem to be able to produce all the reports we'd ever need, but am I going to be left high and dry when Novell and Timberline eventually abandon support (and you know they will)? What happens if I want to change accounting firms? Will I have to go through this whole process all over again? Advice on the subject is cheap. Your bartender, the computer store sales person where you bought your first computer, and even your computer wiz nephew all have opinions. But who's right? Are any of them right?

Ultimately, I have to put aside valuable time I'd rather spend on other, more enjoyable projects and learn at least the rudiments of accounting technology. It's the only way I'm going to be able to know I've hired the right people to advise me on what software to use, and it will make me and my company better for it. It will make me look long and hard at a variety of practices within our organization. Will this software make hiring and people management easier? Will it improve our invoicing and data management? Does my current team have the technical ability to deal with these new tools in a positive and meaningful way? I also realize I need to make a real budget for my IT side of the business. I need to evaluate our current technology and look long and hard about paying good money for someone of talent to manage the whole process. It's kind of funny that we, as a computer magazine, know exactly what kind of components we're looking for in our production machines, but haven't a clue on what we need for computers and software on the money side of the business.

I look at a capital expenditure in an interesting way. I don't think of it as money. I think of it as ad space or editorial space because that's how I'll have to pay for the product. If we want to buy something, we need to go sell an ad. If we want to buy more than we can afford, we have to sell an ad and drop the corresponding amount of editorial space. If we buy too much, the magazine will be all ads and not a lot of people will want to read the magazine so I try to stick real close to the budget.

John Martinez, Editor
Computer Source Magazine
www.sourcemagazine.com

Advanced Planning Issues

This part of the chapter presents more details on software and hardware issues surrounding your SBS project. I offer a few comments with respect to SBS budgeting and the purchasing process. I will discuss software including the different SBS stock keeping unit (SKU) configurations.

Software

SBS ships in a variety of user-license, upgrade, and preinstallation configurations. There's even the free technology guarantee I'll mention in this section. I'll review each SBS purchase option here and provide only the estimated retail pricing. As you know, street prices are substantially lower. Also be advised that you should consult your software reseller for the very latest prices. No book could hope to stay current with pricing when even the monthly and weekly trade magazines are challenged to do so.

SBS 5-User Version - Full Product

SBS 2000 is sold off-the-shelf to the first-time buyer and the upgrade buyer in 5-user version. The estimated retail price for the 5-user version of SBS 2000 is $1,499. The estimated retail price for bumping your license count to the 25-user level of SBS 2000 is $2,500. To hit the 50-user level of SBS 2000, you're likely to be out of pocket to the tune of roughly $3,800. Nothing special here. The key point is that SBS 2000 is now sold as a 5-user edition, and then you simply add a 5 or 20 Client Add Pack. Details on all this good stuff can be found at http://www.mcirosoft.com/sbserver/howtobuy.

> BEST PRACTICE: Note that Microsoft can and often does change its "Stock Keeping Units" or SKUs in response to market demand. For example, if the market demands a 10-user full product version of SBS

2000, it is possible that this would be offered for sale as a retail product. Otherwise, as of today, you would create a 10-user network by purchasing the 5-user product and then purchase the 5-user Client Add Pack.

5-User and 20-User Client Access Licenses (CAL)

As alluded to above, and explained more here, additional SBS Client Access Licenses (CALs) are sold in 5- and 20-Client Add Packs. You cannot purchase individual SBS licenses for any lot other than 5 or 20. So, SSL would need to purchase a 5-user CAL in addition to its initial 5-user SBS version to reach a total of 10 users. But because SSL is actually migrating from an existing NetWare network, it qualifies for the upgrade pricing. A client add-pack containing 5 CALs has an estimated retail price of just under $300 (and a version upgrade price of approximately $159.00).

SBS Competitive Upgrade: 5 Users

Suppose, like SSL, you have a NetWare network that you are converting to SBS. You would qualify for upgrade pricing on the first 5 users on your SBS network. Additional CALs would have to be purchased at full price for any users over the initial 5. Currently, there is no 25-user or 50-user SBS competitive upgrade offering, although that is clearly subject to change as Microsoft reacts to customer feedback. The competitive SBS upgrade offering for 5 users has an estimated retail price of approximately $929.00. As you can see, it represents a significant discount of over $500 from purchasing the full-retail, 5-user version of SBS.

There are several ways to qualify for SBS competitive upgrade pricing. If you have an existing network that is running on the following operating systems, you will qualify for this competitive upgrade (as of this writing, subject to change):

- Novell: NetWare, IntranetWare, IntranetWare for Small Business

- Banyan Vines

- IBM: LAN Server, OS/2

- Microsoft LAN Manager

- DEC PATHWORKS

- Artisoft LANtastic

- SCO: Xenix, UNIX, OpenServer, or UnixWare

- Sun: Solaris 7 (Sparc or X86) or earlier, or SunOS

- Hewlett-Packard: HP-UX

- IBM: AIX

- Digital: Ultrix, OSF/1, or UNIX

- SGI: Irix

- Citrix WinFrame

- Tektronix WinDD

- NCD WinCenter

- Insignia Ntrigue

BEST PRACTICE: You are encouraged to check with Microsoft at www.microsoft.com/smallbusinessserver for updates to this competitive upgrade list.

SBS Version Upgrade

If you own SBS 4.5 you may upgrade to SBS 2000 for even less money than the competitive upgrade. The costs here would be $749.00 at the 5-user level. The mechanics of this are discussed at length in Appendix B: Upgrading to SBS 2000.

BEST PRACTICE: There is no practical difference in the regular or upgrade versions of SBS. Each contains the same features and functions. The version upgrade edition of SBS checks for an existing installation of a qualifying installation of SBS 4.5 but not a competitive upgrade (see my list immediately above). You might recall that this type of check is typically performed when upgrading desktop operating systems or common applications, such as word processing programs. The system check occurs two ways. You must either insert the SBS 4.x Disc #1 at mid-point of the Small Business Server Setup Wizard process when SBS 2000 is installed. Or you must already have SBS 4.x installed on the machine.

The competitive upgrade version of SBS 2000 does not perform a system check to verify you own or have in your possession the qualifying upgrade product, such as NetWare. It's the good old fashioned honor system here.

BEST PRACTICE: Be advised of the SBS 2000 setup experience I had at CFO2Go, a client that I serve. Here it was a late Saturday afternoon and SBS 2000 was essentially installed and running just fine. It was now time to add the CALs. Because CFO2Go had previously purchased and installed SBS 4.5, these smarty pants accountants realized they could save a few dollars by legitimately purchasing the SBS 2000 version upgrade, including the CALs (which are Microsoft part number E76-00131). I opened the oversized envelope containing the version upgrade CALs and find that only a paper license has been placed in the envelope, no CAL diskette. This is a major ouch because the worker bees are returning to the office on Monday morning and I'll only have a five user SBS 2000 network at that time. Why? Because without the ability to install CALs from diskette, the CAL counter in SBS 2000 will remain at five users. A quick call to Microsoft resulted in a CAL disk being drop shipped immediately to this client site and the accountants were only inconvenience for a day or two. But the real lesson learned was open all of your software packaging and confirm the media exists several days prior to starting an SBS installation!

OEM Preinstalled SBS

Another SBS purchasing option includes purchasing your server machine from an original equipment manufacturer (OEM) with SBS preinstalled. For example, if you purchase a server from Gateway, you might have SBS preinstalled (at the full retail price of the SBS software).

BEST PRACTICE: Having the hardware manufacturer install SBS is not the same as having SBS completely installed. A preinstall basically copies the necessary files over to the server's hard disk (which saves a good 30 to 60 minutes depending on the speed of your machine), but you must still answer several questions to complete the SBS installation. These questions relate to organization name, domain name, time zone, and so on.

Many of my SBS customers have considered the preinstall option with the thought that they wouldn't need to do anything to complete the SBS installation or hire an SBS consultant. Such is clearly not always the case.

I have evaluated this scenario several times, and it depends on your specific situation as to whether this option makes sense. The key point to consider when having hardware manufacturers install SBS is that they charge full retail price. Here is a story about why you might decline the SBS pre-installation option.

If you recall, several paragraphs ago we determined the difference between the 5-user version of SBS when comparing retail pricing to upgrade pricing was nearly $600. I had an SBS customer with 10 users, converting from an existing NetWare network, who hoped to see less of me, the SBS consultant, by having Gateway install SBS. In the purchase analysis for this client, two things became apparent. First, the nearly $600 difference between the preinstalled SBS version and the upgrade version this client qualified for made the Gateway preinstallation option unattractive. Second, I identified that the client would only save one of my billable hours by electing to have Gateway install SBS, so the $600 pricing differential that was identified didn't justify one hour savings of consultant's time (my SBS bill rates average $125 per hour). In this case, before I looked closer at the SBS purchase options for this client, there was a risk of being pennywise and pound foolish!

SBS 2000 and Office 2000/XP = Not!

SBS can not be purchased bundled with Office 2000 or XP Professional Suite. This is different from SBS 4.5 when such an SBS SKU configuration was made available (specifically for Office 2000). I suspect this SKU wasn't an overwhelming success to justify the marketing and packaging expense. Oh well, you can still purchase Office 2000 or XP Professional separately, and it works just fine on an SBS 2000 network. You might be interested in knowing that the Office 2000 (and XP) Professional Suite contains:

- Word 2000 (Word 2002 in Office XP)

- Excel 2000 (Excel 2002 in Office XP)

- Access 2000 (Access 2002 in Office XP)

- PowerPoint 2000 (PowerPoint 2002 in Office XP)

- Publisher 2000 (Publisher 2002 in Office XP)

- Microsoft Small Business Tools (financial analysis templates, and so on). Note that Office XP doesn't have these small-business tools as of this writing.

- Outlook 2002. One way to implement Outlook 2002 on your SBS network is to deploy Office XP (which contains Outlook 2002).

Many of these popular "front office" applications such as Word 2002 make your life much better and efficient as an SBSer. In fact, you'll find that your clients like 'em a lot too! Just show me someone that doesn't like Microsoft Office 2000 or XP.

SBS 2000 120-Day Version

If you attend the Microsoft Official Curriculum (MOC) Course #2301a: Implementing Microsoft Small Business Server 2000 (a one-day course), you will receive the full version of SBS 2000 (5-user) for your learning needs. But be advised this has a 120-day time bomb. The good news is that it can be upgraded (without reinstallation) to the full version of SBS 2000. Here you would purchase the "real" SBS 2000 at a future date (within the 120-day time frame) and then provide the authentic Product Key number from the back of the CD Disc "gem case." This is technically accomplished by re-running the Small Business Server Setup Wizard and "installing" SBS over itself. Fact of the matter is that the SBS setup really just asks for your Product ID and then removes the evaluation blocks. The Small Business Server Setup Wizard is launched from the **Small Business Server 2000** program under **Add/Remove Programs** in **Control Panel** (from **Start**, **Settings**).

This 120-day version of SBS is also available in the Microsoft Small Business Server 2000 Partner Guide that is liberally distributed at Direct Access events (see **http://www.microsoft.com/directaccess** for more information). The part number for this partner guide is 098-90807.

SBS Freshness

When ordering SBS over the Internet or through a national warehouse via a toll-free number, be sure to avoid the following problem that afflicted one of my clients in the early days of SBS. As planned, this client called a leading national warehouse on an 800 number to order SBS. A few days later, SBS arrived. When installed, the customer and I discovered that it was SBS version 4.0, not 4.0a. This occurred even though 4.0a had been shipping for several months. Further investigative work revealed that the reseller apparently was filling orders with old stock, not the latest SBS release. That realization was a major disappointment. Beware of resellers who aren't shipping you the freshest product. And although this story applies specifically to SBS 4.0/4.0a, you can bet that additional releases of SBS are forthcoming, making this issue germane.

Other Licensing Issues

It is no longer legally possible to upgrade individual SBS components to similar Big BackOffice applications. Such was the case in SBS 4.5 but it has been disallowed in SBS 2000. If you need Big BackOffice components you'll have to upgrade to the full implementation of Big BackOffice.

Also, SBS CALs are on a per server-basis, not a per seat basis. If you add another Windows 2000 Server to your SBS network (perhaps to work as an application server and run an accounting application), you will need to purchase Windows 2000 Server CALs (which are a different type of license from SBS CALs) for each user who intends to log on to the new Windows 2000 Server machine. And just to throw another twist at you, SBS CALs are not bona fide Terminal Services CALs. For your information, Terminal Services CALs are very expensive and a separate product from anything else that we have discussed here in this chapter. But I will talk about them in Chapter 8.

> BEST PRACTICE: And don't forget something discussed earlier in this book. The SBS license count applies to machines that are actually physically attached to the SBS network. So, a 50-user SBS network might actually support a company with 100 employees. However, in this scenario, only 50 machines could be both attached to and logged on to the SBS network simultaneously. I bet all this licensing legalese is starting to get old for you. Me too!

Other Software

It is not uncommon to purchase other software to run on the server machine running SBS. I have found that SBS customers typically purchase:

- Third-party tape backup applications, such as Veritas Backup Exec 8.6 for Small Business Server 2000

- Virus detection applications, such as Trend Micro's OfficeScan 5.0 for Small Business Server 2000

- Remote access applications, such as NetMeeting and PCAnywhere

- Accounting applications such as Great Plains

- Other business applications

Most of these application areas are discussed in future chapters. The key point is that SBS is rarely purchased and installed in a software vacuum. There is typically a support cast of other software applications running on the SBS machine to provide an organization with a complete computing solution.

Hardware

With respect to hardware, you name it, and it has probably been run on an SBS network. Why? Because smaller organizations often have lots of legacy equipment that they want to continue using on their SBS network. And small businesses aren't known for overspending.

Microsoft has a set of recommended hardware specifications for the server and client workstations on an SBS network. These specifications appear in the following sections. You should also consult Microsoft's SBS site occasionally (www.microsoft.com/smallbusinessserver) for any updates these hardware recommendations.

Microsoft's Server Requirements For SBS

Listed below are Microsoft's published server requirements for SBS 2000. It is interesting to note that during the development of SBS 2000, the minimum RAM memory requirement was lowered from 256MB of RAM to 128MB of RAM.

- Intel and compatible systems - Pentium II 300 MHz or higher processor (I personally recommend a dual processor machine for a performance level that will keep business people on an SBS network happy day in and day out.)

- 128MB of RAM (The more the better especially if you are running business applications.) See my discussion in the next section on what the RAM memory requirement really means in the real world.

- One 3.5-inch high-density disk drive

- 4GB of free hard disk space for the SBS-related installation. (You will really need this amount plus lots more for your data needs, including Exchange e-mail storage.)

- CD-ROM drive

- Super VGA or other video graphics adapter (800x600 x 256 colors)

- Ethernet network adapter card

- Fax/Modem card if you plan to use the Shared Fax Service or the Shared Modem Service. SBS 2000 has improved support for popular fax boards, such as Brooktrout.

- Microsoft mouse or compatible pointing device

- Optional: Uninterruptible Power Supply (UPS), tape backup, multiport board (for modem sharing). (The sky is the limit here as you can add hardware that I can't imagine as of this writing!)

Microsoft's Workstation Requirements for SBS

Listed below are Microsoft's published workstation requirements for SBS 2000. Again, just like the server requirements, these specific points are subject to change.

- Microsoft Windows XP, Microsoft Windows 2000 Professional, Microsoft Windows ME, Microsoft Windows 95, 98, or Microsoft Windows NT Workstation version 4.0

- PC with a Pentium 90 or higher processor

- 32MB of RAM

- One 3.5-inch high-density disk drive

- 300 MB of free hard-disk space, depending on the applications chosen to install.

- VGA, Super VGA, or other video graphics adapter

- Network adapter card

- Microsoft mouse or compatible pointing device

SBS Server Machine Role

The actual SBS server must be a domain controller (DC) at the root of the Active Directory forest. As a forest root DC, the SBS server machine maintains the original copy of the Active Directory database. This machine performs the basic logon authentication activities for the network. Note that an SBS server machine can only act as a forest root DC and there can be only one forest root DC per SBS network.

You might be interested to know that other "regular" (or non-SBS) Windows 2000 and NT Servers can be added to the SBS network. These machines can participate as domain controllers (DC) or member servers. In the case of a Windows NT Server, the machine would be a backup domain controller (BDC) as there is no generic DC designation in the Windows NT world. (Servers in the Windows NT world are either primary or backup domain controllers.) A member server is typically used for special functions such as running a specific application (for example, an Oracle database).

> BEST PRACTICE: To support legacy Windows NT services, SBS 2000 is installed in mixed mode.

Real-World Issues: Microsoft's Requirements

Allow me to speak for a moment to several real-world hardware matters, many with respect to Microsoft's recommended server and client configurations.

Realistic About RAM Memory and Hard Disks

Microsoft's recommended hardware configuration is sufficient except for one item: RAM. I've installed SBS 2000 on only one system with 128MB of RAM, and not surprisingly, it was a poor performer once real business applications were added to the same machine. Business applications and associated data and activity really take a toll on a server machine! I insist on a minimum of 256MB RAM for SBS server machines and I heartily recommend 512MB RAM. (Fortunately, several of my SBS clients have listened to me.) Oh, I almost forgot that using Terminal Services for remote administration is also a RAM hog. So, factor that into how much RAM you'll want to consider for the machine running Small Business Server 2000.

The hard disk storage requirements, after the first 4GB, are entirely up to you. Because SBS is typically used in business settings, it is common to see 20GB or more of hard disk space available for data.

Name Brands Versus Clones

At the server-level, I tend to recommend name-brand machines such as Gateway, Dell, or Compaq at, or slightly above, the $3,000 price point. Servers at that level provide over 512MB RAM, a small RAID array (around 20GB), or mirrored drives and dual processors (Intel chips in the P500 range). You can typically get a tape backup unit at this price level. As with any pricing estimate, understand that prices *might* have dropped dramatically since I wrote this.

These comments, of course, lead to the broader discussion of name-brand servers versus clones. Perhaps I have too many purple hearts from too many network wounds, but with any SBS customer that I take on as a client, I strongly push for using name brand equipment. The times that I haven't succeeded in that arrangement, I've gotten into trouble. Such trouble has taken many forms including unsatisfied warranty claims with the clone-maker.

One case was a tape backup unit on a clone server at a property management firm that the clone maker wouldn't replace. Across town, a client with the same tape backup issues (same type of backup unit, errors, and so on.), Dell had a technician out the same week providing a new backup device. What a difference the name brand warranty made in this case!

Another consideration relates to the tools provided by name brand server manufacturers. Gateway provides Server Companion, Compaq provides SmartStart and Insight Manager as part of its CD-ROM bundle. Likewise, Dell provides Server Assistant. Although these tools are oriented toward the one-time setup of the server and monitoring at the enterprise level, such tools are appreciated additions at SBS sites.

What's the final decision between name brand servers and clones? The choice is yours, but my vote is now with name brand servers (although I recognize many SBSers are also clone-makers, so no offense to my good bothers and sisters in the SBS family).

Real World Workstation Issues

Regarding workstations, rarely do I install SBS workstation components on anything less than a recent Pentium-class personal computer (say P500 or above) with at least 128MB of RAM. With workstation prices cheaper than ever, it is common to see such charged up or even more powerful workstations at the desktop. Now that's the kind of performance level that makes SBS look and feel good.

SBS Cheapskate Beware!

Don't poor boy that SBS hardware purchase. I've seen people scrimp several ways with SBS-related hardware, none of it acceptable. Here are three examples.

First, small businesspeople have attempted to recycle older monitors from retired workstations so that they didn't have to purchase a new monitor with the new server (a cost savings of perhaps $150). The problem is that older monitors can't provide the screen resolution you need to work with the SBS Console. In fact, improperly configured, the SBS Console might not show up on the screen or only part of it might appear on the screen, forcing you to scroll uncomfortably to reach distant SBS Console selection buttons.

Second, I've observed small businesses that wanted to use the SBS server machine as a workstation for one of its users. At a land development company, the president ran Microsoft Word, Outlook, and CompuServe right on the SBS server machine. The performance was unacceptable. Several months later, the president purchased a workstation, allowing the SBS server machine to do what it does best: act as a dedicated server. Needless to say, both the President and I were much happier from that point forward in our SBS relationship.

Finally, there is the case of the green machine. Here, a paving contractor decided to save a few bucks by using a workstation as an SBS server, result in some strange behavior. In this case, the BIOS-level energy saving function couldn't be turned off, so each night, when the server had several hours of inactivity, it went to sleep. Well, Windows NT Server, the underlying network operating system in SBS 4.5, didn't like that one bit, forcing the general manager at the paving company to reboot every morning. I finally solved this problem by creating artificial server activity every 15 minutes. To do this, I downloaded a program that executes the TCP/IP ping command on schedule. This tool, Ping Plotter, is available from www.winfiles.com as shareware. Richard Ness at Nessoft (www.nessoft.com) developed it. As seen in Figure 2-9, Ping Plotter can be set to generate ping activity on a fixed schedule. Such activity prevents green machine workstations, being used as SBS server machines, from sleeping.

Figure 2-9

Ping Plotter can be used to generate SBS system activity.

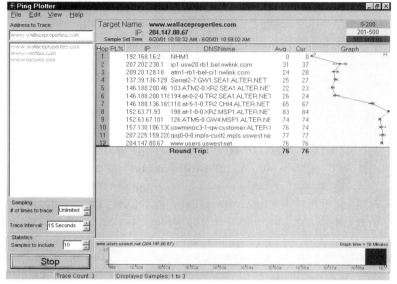

Better yet, buy an honest-to-goodness server to run SBS on and avoid many of the problems described above.

Hardware Necessities

It goes without saying that you should purchase the tape backup unit listed as "optional" in Microsoft's server requirements to back up your valuable data. Other necessities include an uninterruptible power supply (UPS) to protect your system and properly shut it down in a power outage. UPS devices from American Power Corporation (APC) ship with a free copy of PowerChute.

> BEST PRACTICE: Another item to consider is a Zip- or Jaz-type drive with removable cartridges. I've used these in one specific case with great success in an SBS scenario. That case is SQL Server. SQL Server allows you to run an on-the-fly database backup separate from the SBS-based tape backup you typically perform at night. This internal backup to SQL Server typically runs at midday, so you get a fresh SQL Server database backup between tape runs. I like to drop these internal SQL Server backups down on a Zip or Jaz drive or CD-ROM burner

so that the tape drive is not disturbed. It's something to consider if you are working with SQL Server on your SBS network. And, as an aside, if you ever hear a grinding sound with a Zip or Jaz drive, beware as trouble is looming on the drive.

Hardware Compatibility List

One of the final hardware issues to be discussed is also one of the most important. SBS 2000 is much less finicky about the hardware you select for use on the server machine compared to prior releases. Here is what I mean. If it (hardware) runs and is supported on Windows 2000, it'll work with SBS 2000! Hardware devices that have been tested for Windows 2000 are listed on the Hardware Compatibility List (HCL) at www.microsoft.com/hcl. This list should be honored under all circumstances. More important, if you don't select hardware from the Windows 2000 HCL, it is likely you won't receive official Microsoft support when you have problems.

Network Adapter Cards

I've narrowed my choices for the network adapter cards on the SBS HCL down to two brands (Intel and 3COM).

> BEST PRACTICE: I've had mixed results with the Intel EtherExpress PRO/100B PCI LAN Adapter. On many machines, it has been autodetected flawlessly. On other machines, it has shown up as the Intel 82557-based Ethernet Adapter, which is incorrect. Interestingly, this phantom Intel network adapter isn't even listed on the HCL.

The bottom line regarding SBS network adapters is that I've tried to stay with the major brands to avoid autodetection problems during setup of the SBS server machine. That darn MS loopback adapter is still with us in SBS 2000. The MS loopback adapter is installed when a network adapter card can not be found.

Selecting Business Class and High-Quality Modems

The Windows 2000 HCL lists several modems that are considered acceptable. This area of SBS computing has greatly improved, I can attest to this from a position of firsthand experience, but hear me now and pick high-quality business-class modems for your best success. And SBS 2000 now has bona fide support for fax boards including the industry leader Brooktrout! Finally, Microsoft and I wholeheartedly agree that you should avoid the new-fangled USB and PCI modems for a hundred and one reasons, the least of which is that they don't work very well.

SBS Budgeting

And as the corner is turned on Chapter 2 with its focus on planning, don't forget to keep an eye on the farm, that is the SBS budget. I've seen many a good SBS project fail not for technical reasons but because business basics, such as creating and adhering to a budget, were ignored.

> BEST PRACTICE: When budgeting for your network, be sure to consider the following budget tip: If you're eyeing a more powerful server than you planned on purchasing and are concerned about its cost, perhaps the more-powerful one isn't as expensive as it first appears. For example, let's say a server with more processors, RAM, and storage would cost you an additional $1,500. Now, assuming you recover your costs or depreciate the server over three years, that incremental amount ($1,500) adds up to an extra $500 per year, or roughly $1.50 per day. So ask yourself this: For an extra $1.50 per day, shouldn't I purchase the server I really want? In all likelihood, you will probably enjoy more than $1.50 per day in increased network performance, as measured by your staff's ability to get more work accomplished. Think about it!

Summary

I've now completed two chapters of SBS definition, needs analysis, and planning, and you know what? That is exactly the level of depth I delve into when working with SBS customers when performing the same tasks. Hang on to your hat—it is SBS setup time.

Chapter 3
Small Business Server Installation

Time To Install

The time has come to actually install SBS! The argument could be made that installing SBS is nothing more than swapping four setup floppy disks with four SBS CDs and performing a few reboots along the way. However, such an over-simplification of the SBS installation task is incorrect. You have already invested significant time defining what SBS is, performing a needs analysis, and planning.

> BEST PRACTICE: As you might have guessed from the last chapter, you will implement SBS 2000 based on the SSL methodology. That is how this chapter is constructed, after many hours of editorial design. By way of a disclaimer, let me say that your specific SBS implementation may vary slightly based on machine types, components installed, and so on. Furthermore, after I walk you through the step-by-step installation process under the broad jurisdiction of the SSL methodology, I then present some advanced setup topics in the second part of the chapter. If you are an advanced SBSer who is interested in these advanced topics, you may look at those now before you start the setup process or, preferably, follow the setup process under the SSL methodology, and then read the advanced setup topics, taking into account the advanced knowledge that will be imparted for your future real-world SBS setups.

I assume that you are using a new server machine for SBS. If you are using an old server machine that will be redeployed as an SBS server, many of these steps, such as unpacking the server, do not apply. Ditto for same server machine SBS upgrade scenarios. In the case of SSL, the firm has purchased the following hardware and software shown in Table 3-1. The following table is used to verify that everything ordered was indeed received.

Table 3-1 SSL Hardware and Software

Item	Description
Server	Gateway 7400 Server, dual Pentium microprocessors, 512MB RAM, 27GB HD-RAID (approximately 17 GB usable), 17" VGA Monitor, SCSI-based internal tape backup device, internal CD drive
Modem	US Robotics 56K External (Internal, PCI and USB modems are not recommended by Microsoft)
Network Adapter Card	Intel Pro 10/100 PCI Ethernet
Printer	HP Color LaserJet 5M with HP JetDirect Card
Other Hardware	External JAZ drive, APC UPS with PowerChute.
Software	Microsoft Small Business Server (SBS) version 2000 5-user version, 5-user SBS client access license (CAL) bump pack, Veritas Backup Exec v. 8.6 Small Business Server Suite (tape backup program), Trend OfficeScan 5.0 for Small Business Server 2000.
Miscellaneous	Modem cable, extra CAT5 patch cables, telephone cable, power strip/power tree

All of this required hardware adheres to the Windows 2000 hardware compatibility list (HCL) discussed in Chapter 2. You can find updates to the Windows 2000 HCL at www.microsoft.com/hcl. If you are an SBS consultant who regularly installs SBS for different clients, you are encouraged to monitor this site regularly and look for changes to either the HCL or System Requirements. If you are a business person or otherwise a non-SBS consultant installing SBS as a one-time discrete event, which it typically is for a single system at a single location, just initially verifying the hardware you intend to use for the SBS installation at www.microsoft.com/hcl is sufficient.

Note that you should acquire the most current Windows 2000 drivers you will need for the SBS installation if necessary. One example of this is to make sure your have on hand any needed SCSI or RAID drivers which will be needed if your SCSI or RAID controller isn't supported natively by the underlying Windows 2000 Server operating system. At the first step in the character-based setup phase (later in the chapter), you will be provided the opportunity to select the F6 key and provide these SCSI or RAID controller drivers (a very important step if it applies to you). Another example is to download the latest Iomega JAZ drive device drivers from www.iomega.com.

If you have a RAID-based system, such as what I'm listing above in Table 3-1 as part of my SSL methodology, you would need to perform the computer manufacturer's steps to prepare the hard disks in the RAID array for use by the operating system. In the case of my server, this is accomplished by selecting CTRL-M when instructed by the computer during the character-based POST setup phase of the computer boot cycle. This process will vary by manufacturer and computer model, so kindly use your very best judgment and consult the documentation that accompanied your computer.

Also note that while an SCSI-based tape backup device is the preferred hardware option, non-SCSI tape backup devices are supported via the ATAPI device driver in Windows 2000 Server. But be advised that non-SCSI tape devices run much slower than SCSI tape devices. Ouch!

Preinstallation Tasks

You need to perform several tasks before the actual setup process commences. Failing to perform these tasks will certainly result in failure.

Unpack and Connect

Assuming that your infrastructure, such as cabling, is in place and the server you have ordered has arrived, it's time to unpack the server and its components from the shipping boxes. If you haven't built a computer before from boxes, it's quite simple. Many name brand servers have color-coded guides so that you know which port the keyboard and mouse attach to. If you are still unsure of yourself, don't hesitate to hire a computer consultant to help you attach and build the computer. In fact, consider hiring a competent high school or college student who is both computer literate and seeking a few extra dollars. Again, putting together the computer from boxes is quite simple.

After physically building the server, make sure the following items are properly attached to the server box:

- A monitor or screen (be sure to attach the monitor to a power source). In the case of SSL, this is a 17-inch monitor.

- A keyboard

- A mouse

- A power cable

- External modems (if applicable; your modem might be an internal version, which, by the way, isn't recommended)

- An external tape backup device (if applicable and remember SCSI-based tape backup devices deliver higher performance)

- Other external devices that connect directly to the server (printers, Zip- or Jaz-type drives, scanners, and so on; and, if applicable, don't forget to gather the needed drivers before starting setup)

- A network cable (attach the network cable to both the network adapter card port and the wall jack; this connects your server to the network)

- UPS (you can connect the power cables to the UPS, but do not connect the serial cable from the UPS to the serial port on the server yet; see my note on this matter, later in this chapter)

BEST PRACTICE: If you have a UPS, do not attach it to the server at this time. UPS devices are attached to the SBS machine via COM ports (the same type of port used by modems). However, SBS tests each COM port as part of the installation of modems. Granted, modems are now an optional installation component during the setup of SBS (the Shared Fax Service and Shared Modem Service will install without a modem attached). What I'm getting at is this: If you elect to install a modem as part of the SBS setup, an attached UPS can cause the SBS machine to become confused during this installation period. Bottom line: After SBS is installed, you will hook up the UPS.

If you are interested in developing expertise as a hardware technician to supplement your SBS consulting practice or skills as an SBS administrator, you might also consider studying for and taking the A+ certification exam. The A+ certification is oriented towards computer maintenance from a technician point of view. It is a well-regarded designation created and managed by the Computer Technology Industry Association. For more information on the A+ certification, see www.comptia.com.

> BEST PRACTICE: Assuming the power is off and unplugged from the computer and external devices, and you are wearing a grounding strip on your wrist to discharge any built-up static electricity (before you touch an electronic component), take a moment to open the SBS machine and reseat all of the adapter cards. It has been my experience that a new server from "you know who" shipped across the country from Austin, Texas, can arrive with loosened cards, cables, and even memory chips! Such befallen cards have wreaked havoc with some of my early SBS installs when the internal network adapter card couldn't be detected during setup because it had become partially dislodged from its slot. Another experience I have had when working with new computers is that the ribbon cable located inside the machine (used to connect internal devices to cards or the motherboard) can come loose. If you need to reattach a ribbon cable, remember this rule of thumb: regarding which way the cable attaches is the side of the ribbon cable with the red line pointing to the power supply.

After you've completed the check on the system, plug in the power to the computer and the devices in order to proceed with the setup. And don't forget to verify (sorry to be a pest by mentioning this again and again) that you have sufficient power protection in the way of surge protection power strips and uninterruptible power supplies.

Check the Network

Has the cabling been properly attached to the hub? Perhaps this was a task that you assigned to the cabling specialist who installed the cabling at your site. If it hasn't been done, do that now.

To verify the fitness of your network, you must perform the "green light" test. After everything has been plugged in properly to the network, including the network hub, do the following:

1. Turn on the network hub.
2. Briefly turn on the server computer.
3. Observe whether a port light on the hub turns on. (This typically illuminates as the color green).
4. Observe whether the network adapter card connection light on the back of the server illuminates. (Again, typically green).
5. If you see green lights at both the hub and network adapter connection, you're green lighting!

Perform Server Quick Tests

So you've put the computer together and connected it to the network. Now is the time to turn on the computer for a few moments to see whether the BIOS information is correctly displayed on the screen during the power on startup phase. (This is called POST and is a term used in the technology community). This quick-and-dirty test is important for several reasons. It will check:

*   Video card - If you see no information displayed on the computer monitor, it is possible that the video card has failed. Such was the case during an SBS class I once taught. Not only was the computer unusable for the SBS class, but valuable time was wasted trying to determine exactly what the problem was. At first and second blush, it wasn't entirely clear that the video card had failed, as this type of problem can disguise itself.

*   Component attachment - Did you know that if a ribbon cable between the computer motherboard and floppy drive is incorrectly attached, the computer might fail to start, leaving you with only the sound of a failed start up: three quick beeps? This is but one example of how incorrectly configured internal components in your server can prevent you from having success with your computer. These are exactly the type of issues that you want to catch immediately, before you try to install SBS.

*   Hidden partition server tools - First, of all, let's just get this out in the open. SBS 2000 works fine with hidden system partitions (you may recall SBS 4.5 had a distinct problem with this, requiring you to delete the hidden system partition). Now for the next point. Starting up the computer also allows us to determine whether the computer manufacturer's server tools were correctly installed on a hidden partition

on the hard disk. When manufacturers ship their servers to you, they might or might not install their server tools (Gateway's Server Companion, Compaq's SmartStart, Dell's Server Assistant, and so on). Typically, the paperwork received with the server remains unclear on this point. The best way to test that is to look for language at the top of the screen during machine startup. In the case of Compaq, such language instructs you to hit the F10 key to launch SmartStart.

BEST PRACTICE: If the manufacturer's server tool hasn't been installed to a hidden partition on the server, it is essential that you do this now. Failure to do this now would mean that you would forever be prevented from installing these wonderful and helpful tools designed to configure and manage your server (although you could run these tools directly from CD). That's because after the operating system and SBS are installed, you cannot go back and install the manufacturer's server tools on a hidden partition.

To install the manufacturer's server tools on your system, be sure to follow the setup instructions for the specific tool. In the case of Compaq's SmartStart, it is very simple. Because a Compaq server is designed, by default, to boot from the CD drive, you simply place the SmartStart CD in the CD drive and restart the computer. On startup, and with no further fuss, you are presented with the SmartStart installation screen. Several minutes and one reboot later, SmartStart is installed on your system. Again, tools such as SmartStart provide the capability to configure your server properly, create driver disks, monitor your server's health, and so on.

- BIOS operation - There is simply no better test to make sure the computer's all-important BIOS is functional than to turn on the machine and observe that the BIOS information (copyright, date, storage device configuration, and so on) is displayed on the screen. Common BIOS names are American Megatrends and Phoenix.

BEST PRACTICE: It is very common for BIOS manufacturers to release upgrades shortly after the original BIOS has been shipped to market. These upgrades typically consist of bug fixes and the like. So consider downloading the BIOS upgrade and prepare to install or flash the BIOS upgrade. But be extremely careful about applying a BIOS upgrade to your server. If you've applied the incorrect BIOS version to your server, the server can be rendered inoperable or become unreliable. See the BIOS discussion on upgrades, installation, and flashing at your BIOS manufacturer's home page. And if you are at all uncomfortable with this, consider hiring a qualified technician or consultant to research and implement a BIOS upgrade for your server.

- Operating system status - By performing the quick power-up test, you can determine whether any operating system has been installed on the computer. It is common for clone-makers to both format and SYS (apply basic MS-DOS files) the primary drive (C: drive) of the server. If no operating system has been installed, you will see a character-based error message that indicates the operating system is missing. If you purchased a name-brand server and elected to have SBS preinstalled (OEM style!) as discussed in Chapter 2, you will notice the SBS setup process launches after the initial POST phase terminates.

- Windows 2000 Readiness Analyzer Tool - Yet another test exists that should be performed on your system. This test is the running of the Windows 2000 Readiness Analyzer Tool. As much as possible, this tool determines whether your computer is compatible with Windows 2000 Server. You will recall from Chapter 1 that Windows 2000 Server is the underlying network operating system for SBS. Thus, it is essential that you ascertain whether the system is Windows 2000 Server-compatible.

BEST PRACTICE: Although an important and necessary step, running the Windows 2000 Readiness Analyzer Tool isn't the final word on compatibility. It is meant to serve only as a guide or early warning system. I've installed systems that, at first appearance, weren't 100 percent Windows 2000 Server-compliant. This tool is an aid for you but not the final word.

You'll find the Windows 2000 Readiness Tool at http://www.microsoft.com/windows2000/server/howtobuy/upgrading/compat/default.asp (which is shown in Figure 3-1).

Figure 3-1

Windows 2000 Readiness Analyzer Tool home page.

And no discussion about tools is complete without pulling out a couple of oldies. When it comes to getting an old-fashioned view of your system, one tool, MSD, is very easy to acquire and use. Simply copy it from one of your machines running true MS-DOS 5.0 or greater and place it on a MS-DOS system-formatted floppy disk. Boot from the floppy disk and type *MSD* at the command prompt for the floppy drive (typically A:). MSD calls it as it sees it, reporting IRQ settings and the like. I've also used CheckIt, a relatively low-cost computer assessment application from Touchstone Software. For more information, visit www.checkit.com.

Backup Data

With SSL, you will recall that you are installing SBS on a brand-new Gateway server. The company's data initially remains on the old NetWare server until later, when it will be transferred over the wire or across the network to the new SBS server. That said, the data backup precautions are nothing out of the ordinary: Last night's backup should be verified.

Assuming you are like many small businesses and hope to reuse your existing server for SBS, you are confronted with major data backup issues. That is, how do you transfer data, via a single machine, from your previous operating system (say NetWare) to SBS.

> BEST PRACTICE: Please carefully read the following scenario and appreciate that is an advanced topic for guru SBSers. First and foremost, I do assume that the foreign environment you are migrating data from has a tape-back device attached to the server, the tape backup device works and you know how to make and verify a tape backup on the foreign system. My example uses Novell NetWare as its foreign system from which the data will be migrated to the new SBS system.

Assume that you are converting from a small Novell NetWare network to SBS. Also assume that, to save money, you plan to reformat the hard drive on your existing NetWare server and install SBS. Thus, your first challenge is to make darn sure that you've completely protected the businesses data located on the existing NetWare server prior to reformatting its hard disk. If not, let's just say that there aren't enough hours in the day to re-create the data you've lost!

The challenge here is that the tape created on a NetWare server using an NLM-based tape backup application isn't readable by the SBS's native tape backup application. In fact, relying on such a strategy results in an error message regarding a foreign tape when you try to access the tape under Backup in SBS.

So what can you do? I've performed the following work around to transfer this data from NetWare to SBS server-based environments. What makes this work around so SBS-specific is that you can play this trick in a smaller environment, the kind of environment that SBS caters to. Obviously, this trick wouldn't be possible in larger enterprise environments that the full versions of Windows 2000 Server and Advanced Server (heck, throw in Datacenter too!) cater to.

First, copy the NetWare-based data to a second server or even one or two client workstations. As you know, today's workstations have huge hard drives that are often larger than those found on older servers in smaller companies. In my case, I pursued both strategies. I literally copied the firm's data from its existing NetWare server (2.5GB of data on a NetWare partition) to a loaner NetWare 4.11 server that I brought from home. I also copied the same data to a subdirectory of a robust workstation. After I completed my SBS installation, I (of course) copied the data back to the newly created SBS server from the client workstation. Using the data copy stored on the workstation, I saved a lot of time by not dropping under the hood on SBS and performing a somewhat nasty Win2K-ism of install-ing Gateway Services For NetWare (GSNW) to retrieve the data from my loaner NetWare 4.11 server.

> BEST PRACTICE: I've done the same thing with an SBS installation converting from a Linux server to a new SBS server. In this case, I wasn't interested in wasting the time to perfect the ICE.TEN terminal emulation connection between the Linux box and the SBS server. Thus, I copied the data from the Linux box to a workstation and back to the new SBS server.

Read Release Notes

Take my advice and print the README.DOC and the READ1ST.TXT files, which together constitute the release notes and are found on SBS 2000 CD Disc 1 in the root directory (for example, E:README.DOC where E: is the CD disc). Not only are some of the preinstallation topics discussed, but many of your questions regarding SBS and its limitations will be answered.

SBS Site Review

Humor me and quickly walk around the site where the SBS 2000 Server-based network will be installed and make sure that there is no existing DHCP Server. Suffering from fatigue, I didn't do this at one of my first SBS 2000 installations, and sure enough, it came home to bite me bad. It turns out, as this story goes, the client site (a law firm) was a sublease from a former Dot-Com enterprise gone Dot-Bomb. The law firm, upon moving in, used much of the technology equip-ment, including the DSL router, from the former tenant. It turned out the DSL router, which no one had the password to, was acting as a DHCP server and issuing internal 10.x.x.x network IP addresses to workstations. When installing the SBS 2000 Server, I found this condition violated one of the cardinal laws in SBS land: SBS must be the one and only DHCP server on the network.

So the outcome of all this was that the SBS 2000 Server didn't complete its setup. I manually had to add the DHCP Server service and configure the default scope and add the Windows Internet Naming Service (WINS). The lesson learned was that more planning would have prevented this foolish error. My embarrassment is clearly your gain.

SBS Installation Overview

Allow me to take a moment to outline the SBS installation process for you. Understanding this setup blueprint is important because, if your setup fails somewhere along the line, you can quickly assess at what stage your setup failed. That failure assessment is extremely beneficial in troubleshooting any setup problems you might be having. Your understanding of the setup process will also help you communicate with your SBS consultant (a.k.a. SBSer Guru) or Microsoft support.

> BEST PRACTICE: These setup steps assume that you have purchased SBS as a standalone software package. These are not the same steps undertaken by the preinstalled (or OEM) version of SBS. The SBS OEM preinstallation approach is discussed later.

The SBS installation process can be divided into six discrete steps (shown in Figure 3-2).

Figure 3-2

SBS installation overview.

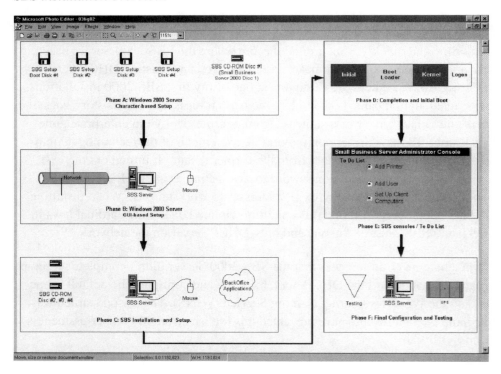

Windows 2000 Server Character-Based Setup (Phase A)

This phase consists of inserting the four SBS setup floppy disks and the first SBS CD (Microsoft Small Business Server 2000 Disc 1) when requested.

> BEST PRACTICE: SBS 2000 setup now boots directly from Disc 1 if you have a machine that has a bootable CD drive. This is a real timesaver and this wasn't possible with SBS 4.5. Most of the Phase A steps are the same except you don't have to swap those darn little floppies! Kindly adjust your expectations about the specific setup steps related to switching floppies as you read forward. Thanks in advance! And thank you to Microsoft for allowing us to avoid, in many cases, having to swap those darn floppies.
>
> By the way, I've heard from other SBSers that their clients use machines that support a bootable CD device and there is little reason to know or care about the need to set up floppy disks. Well, clearly these SBSers have more modern clients than I do; I'm still working with a few small businesses that have older server machines without that new-fangled CD boot capability. Regardless of whether the equipment you will use is modern or not, Microsoft supports these different setup media implementation approaches.
>
> And hey, before I forget, Microsoft even has a version of SBS on DVD. Because DVD discs hold so much more information, there is only one DVD disc for SBS. The use of DVD discs truly takes a modern server computer. Speaking only for myself, few of my clients have DVD-capable servers.

You must answer questions regarding the standard hardware and software components that were detected (Standard PC, Microsoft Serial Mouse, and so on). Create and format a hard disk partition that's 4GB or more in size. Extensive file copying occurs at this stage from each of the floppies and CD Disc 1. The computer reboots once.

> BEST PRACTICE: Also note that Windows 2000 Server, acting as the underlying operating system in SBS, no longer requires an emergency repair disk or a unique boot disk created for recovery efforts.

Recovery is now supported via the recovery console accessed by selecting the F8 key early in the boot phase of Windows 2000 Server (a text message at the bottom of the screen will advise you to hit F8).

This phase is represented by SBS setup tasks 1 through 12 several pages below in the bona fide, step-by-step SBS setup section of this chapter.

Windows 2000 Server GUI-Based Setup (Phase B)

After the second reboot, you are presented with a Windows-like graphical user interface (GUI) to complete the installation of Windows 2000 Server. Provide a user name for registration purposes and an organization name. Either accept the automatically created computer name or provide your own computer name.

Observe the networking components being installed and tell Windows 2000 Server to start the networking services. Select the correct time zone for the SBS computer. The correct computer monitor settings are tested and, after additional Windows 2000 Server files are copied over, the SBS computer reboots.

This phase is represented by SBS setup tasks 13 through 22 several pages below in the bona fide, step-by-step SBS setup section of this chapter.

SBS Installation and Setup (Phase C)

The computer automatically restarts, selects the Small Business Server boot option, and perform a logon. The Microsoft Small Business Server Setup Welcome dialog box appears, and you answer many, if not all, of these setup questions regarding the following topics (not necessarily in this order):

- Software licensing
- SBS CD Product Key entry
- Outlook 2000 CD Product Key entry
- Proof of ownership for upgrades
- Active Directory domain name
- NetBIOS domain name
- Installed hardware, including network adapters
- Company information

- Administrator's password

- Telephone settings

- ISA Server caching and LAT table

* SQL Server 2000 questions

- SBS installation paths for applications and data

After you provide this information, Active Directory and its required services, such as DNS, are installed and configured. Additional Windows 2000 Server services, such as DHCP and Terminal Services, are installed. Service Pack #1 for Windows 2000 is installed. Finally, all of the true SBS components (management consoles) and applications (Internet Explorer, SQL Server, Exchange Server, and the like) are installed. During this phase, you insert SBS CDs #2, #3, and #4. At the end of this phase, you need to click Finish in a dialog box indicating the SBS setup process has completed. The SBS computer asks you to approve a reboot.

This phase is represented by SBS setup tasks 23 through 45 several pages below in the bona fide, step-by-step SBS setup section of this chapter.

> BEST PRACTICE: Regarding the SBS installation process, actual installation time varies greatly. It can take anywhere from 90 minutes to over four hours depending on the speed of your CD drive, hard disk, and CPU microprocessor and the installation selections that you made. The amount of RAM also affects setup times. Believe me, I've seen both the fastest time and the slowest time listed here—and everything in between!

SBS Completion and Initial Boot (Phase D)

Assuming you have installed to a clean server machine (meaning not previously used or, if previously used, a machine whose hard disks have been reformatted), this phase represents the first logon to the underlying Windows 2000 Server operating system. Log on with the administrator user account and password.

> BEST PRACTICE: Carefully note that the context of my discussion herein assumes you are starting with a clean machine (as I alluded to in the paragraph above). Upgrading to SBS 2000 from an existing installation of SBS (say SBS 4.5) requires a slightly different process and is covered in great detail in Appendix B: Upgrading to SBS 2000.

As an aside, the reason I've placed the upgrade discussion in Appendix B is that the beloved SSL storyline centers around the use of a new server machine with no prior operating system installed. Understandably, your specific situation may vary (such as the upgrade discussion in Appendix B.)

SBS To Do List (Phase E)

When you first log on to the SBS computer after completing the installation, you are presented with a To Do List of tasks to complete:

1. **Welcome.** A general welcome notice is presented for you to read.
2. **Add Client Licenses.** This is a very important step where you add the additional client access licenses (CALs) to the system.
3. **Define Client Applications.** This allows you to specify software applications that can be installed on the client computer. Note that the applications must have a silent installation (not requiring input from the user during setup) and cannot be a Microsoft Software Installer (*.msi) file. Only setup.exe files are supported and I discuss this more in Chapter 5.
4. **Add User.** Here you would add a new user to the SBS network.
5. **Add Printer.** This is where you would add a new printer to the SBS computer and make it available to the network.
6. **Configure Internet Information Services.** This selection launches the **IIS Configuration Tool**. You will input your server's IP address and click **OK** to commence a process that will secure the IIS application in SBS 2000.
7. **Enable Network Interfaces.** This provides instructions to enable the second network adapter card (if present) in the machine running SBS so that the broadband or router-based (using the second network adapter card) Internet connection can be configured via the Internet Connection Wizard.
8. **Internet Connection Wizard.** Here you would configure both software and hardware components SBS for a new or existing Internet connection.
9. **Configure Remote Access.** This is where you configure dial-in and VPN (over the Internet) remote network access.
10. **Configure Modems.** This selection provides a help screen for information on how to configure the modems for use by the Shared Fax Server.
11. **Configure Access for Terminal Services.** This allows you to configure who can access Terminal Services remote administration.

12. **Configure Exchange Management.** This option is mildly confusing. SBS installs and configures Microsoft Exchange 2000 Server during the SBS setup phase (Phase C). This option allows you to assign users to an Exchange administrative management role to manage e-mail accounts (e.g., adding accounts) and distribution lists.
13. **Configure Server Status Report.** This option provides help on how to configure what information is sent in the Server Status Report, what format (there is an XML selection) and how the reports are sent.
14. **Getting Started.** This is an excellent online tour of SBS 2000.

Microsoft created the To Do List with the idea that you would complete each step in order (according to members of the SBS development team who shared this public information with me directly in late 2000), but experience has shown that this order isn't necessarily practical or desirable. Understand that nothing prevents you from either following the To Do List step-by-step or using an ad-hoc To Do List approach. As with the execution of any task on a computer, always think before acting and use your best judgment.

In the case of SSL, you will use an ad-hoc To Do List approach. Before lunch, as part of the initial SBS setup process, you will add additional user licenses and add a printer. You will also perform a task outside of the scope of the To Do List when you create the emergency repair disk (ERD). In Chapter 4, you will return to the To Do List and add new users and set up new computers. You will also create an updated ERD to reflect the new system configuration. In Chapter 9, you will return to the To Do List and configure your connection to the Internet.

> BEST PRACTICE: You can return to the To Do List at any time, not just the first time that you log on to the SBS computer. This is accomplished by clicking the To Do List selection in the console pane on the SBS Administrator Console.

> Also allow me a brief moment to mention something about the SBS Administrator Console and the SBS Personal Console. Both of these tools are technically snap-ins, using the Microsoft Management Console (MMC). Be advised that the user interface (UI) for both consoles spells out "Small Business Server" completely, although I've taken to abbreviating the term Small Business Server as "SBS" when discussing the console.

Final Configuration and Testing (Phase F)

This phase resolves loose ends, including attaching and making operational the uninterruptible power supply (UPS) that I discussed in Chapter 2. You also check the event logs to ensure that the SBS installation went well (from a Windows 2000 Server event logs via the Computer Management snap-in found in the SBS Administrators Console). You also perform some basic SBS system tests so that you know you're ready to proceed to Chapter 4, with confidence. Also during this phase, a tape backup of the system would likely be made to save your setup and configuration, and you might install third-party applications, such as a virus protection application at this phase.

Ready, Set, Go

Make sure you're familiar and armed with the numerous SBS setup sheets from Chapter 2. If this is your first pass through the book, these sheets, which reflect setup information for SSL, have been completed for you. If this is your second pass through the book, and you're installing SBS for real, gather the setup sheets from my Web site at www.nethealthmon.com. Much of the information on the setup sheets will be called for in the next section.

You are now ready to install SBS.

> BEST PRACTICE: Let's take a deep breath at this point to reflect and meditate for a moment on exactly what is going on here. The planning and installation presented to date, and the forthcoming setup steps, are based on the viewpoint of SSL. Why? Because this book has been written with the idea in mind that, if you invest some of your limited time and you follow each step in this book, you will be a bona fide SBSer with a functional network for SSL. That is the underlying paradigm to how I wrote this book, and as you might imagine, I jealously guard my SSL methodology for quality assurances purposes.

> Now, granted, your situation may be dramatically different if you install more than one SBS network (particularly if you are an SBS consultant). For example, one client site may use an EIDE-based older computer system as the server machine. Another site may use a SCSI-based computer as the server machine. And yet another site may use a RAID array hard disk storage system. Variations in SBS implementations will exist, depending on your unique situation. Another area of

variation is data migration. You may or may not have data to migrate from another machine, another partition of the existing machine that you are installing SBS on. Talk about an area where things can vary on a case-by-case basis, it's data (some data is comma separated value, some is text, some uses XML, etc.)

So what's the bottom line? Stick with me and follow this methodology exactly and you'll have a functional SBS network for SSL after completing this book. But in the very next breathe, I'm not as tough of old Angus bull as I first appear. If you are reading this book for pleasure and do not care to follow SSL rhyme and verse, God be with you and it's likely you'll still derive great value from these pages. But back to the SSL methodology. As an example, I have a printer installed on the SBS network later in the chapter but you might not have a printer in the real world of SBS implementations. While it's unlikely you don't have a printer, SBS can be implemented without incident without a printer. Heck, you can even install the Shared Fax Service and the Shared Modem Service without a modem attached!

Vary from this specific methodology and you're on your own. (Sorry!) And again, I do try to accommodate different scenarios as much as possible (such as the upgrade discussion in Appendix B). Thanks!

The first step assumes that you have the four boot floppy disks needed by SBS's setup process and you intend to install with the four floppy disks. Note that the SSL methodology assumes an SBS installation based upon the use of four floppy disks. Kindly recall that earlier in the chapter I discussed the ability to book directly to SBS Disc 1 to commence the SBS setup process. (You can consult the Planning and Installation Guide that shipped in the SBS product box for more information on an install started from SBS CD Disc 1.)

If you don't have the four setup floppy disks in hand, here are the steps for creating said disks. To create boot disks on an existing machine (running Microsoft Windows 2000, ME, NT or 9x):

1. Insert Disc 1 into the CD drive.
2. On the **Start** menu, point to **Run**. The **Run** dialog box appears.
3. In the **Open** field of the **Run** dialog box, type **e:\bootdisk\makebt32.exe**

(assuming your CD drive is E: but, if not, kindly change the drive letter indicator to the letter of your CD drive. Click **OK**.

4. Follow the on-screen instructions to create the four setup floppy disks. For example, the onscreen instructions will ask you to insert diskette one through four.

SBS Setup

Ladies and gentleman, it's time to rock and roll, SBS 2000 style!

1. Insert the Windows 2000 Setup Boot Disk in floppy drive A: and turn on your computer.

BEST PRACTICE: Immediately after the character-based setup commences at this step, you will note language at the bottom of the screen that asks you to "Press F6 if you need third-party SCSI or RAID driver."

There are several issues concerning this message. First, if you are using an unsupported SCSI or RAID disk controller, you would indeed press F6 at this point and provide the manufacturer's driver on a floppy disk. This is straightforward enough. However, I've installed SBS 2000 on Gateway, Compaq, and Dell systems which had SCSI and RAID controllers without having to hit F6. How can this be, you ask? Very easily. The SCSI or RAID controllers were supported by the underlying Windows 2000 Server operating system with its native drivers (many of which were supplied by leading hardware manufacturers and burned on SBS CD Disc 1.

Also note that I assume you have configured the hard disk to be used by the RAID subsystem as I discussed earlier in the chapter. (This is where you add the hard disks to the array using the steps provided by the computer manufacturer during the POST startup in the computer boot phase.)

2. When you see the following screen, insert Windows 2000 Setup Disk #2 and press **Enter**.

    Please insert the disk labeled

    Windows 2000 Server

    Setup Disk #2

into Drive A:

*Press ENTER when ready.

3. When you see the following screen, insert Windows 2000 Server Setup Disk #3 and press **Enter**.

    Please insert the disk labeled

    Windows 2000 Server

    Setup Disk #3

    into Drive A:

    *Please ENTER when Ready

4. When you see the following screen, insert Windows 2000 Server Setup Disk #4 and press **Enter**.

    Please insert the disk labeled

    Windows 2000 Server

    Setup Disk #4

    into Drive A:

    *Please ENTER when Ready

BEST PRACTICE: Note that steps #1 through #4 would not be explicitly performed if you started the SBS setup process by booting directly to the SBS CD Disc #1. Rather, the first step would be to put the SBS CD Disc #1 in the computer and turn on the machine. Your next steps, under a bootable CD scenario using SBS CD Disc #1, would be step #5.

5. A Windows 2000 Server Setup screen appears after several minutes that communicates the following text. After reading, press **Enter** to continue with the setup of the server for SSL.

    Welcome to Setup.

    This portion of the Setup program prepares

    Microsoft Windows 2000 to run on your computer.

    * To set up Windows 2000 now, press ENTER.

    * To repair a Windows 2000 installation, press R.

    * To quit Setup without installing Windows 2000, press F3

6. When you see the following screen, insert the SBS CD Disc 1 (this contains Windows 2000 Server). Press **Enter**.

> Please insert the CD labeled
>
> Windows 2000 Server CD-ROM
>
> into your CD-ROM drive.
>
> *Press ENTER when ready.

BEST PRACTICE: You would of course not see step #6 if you had booted from the CD Disc #1 for your SBS setup. Another way the screen in step #6 will not appear is if you had put in the SBS CD Disc #1 in the CD drive prior to this setup (maybe you put it in a step or two prior).

In the case of SSL and its setup methodology, you would see this screen because the setup routine started with the four setup floppy diskettes.

7. The **Windows 2000 Licensing Agreement** screen appears. After reading this license agreement, press **F8** to agree to the license and continue.

BEST PRACTICE: At this point, if you are installing on a machine that has a previous edition of Windows 2000 Server installed on it, you would receive a message that you could quit the installation (by pressing F3,) repair the Windows 2000 installation (by pressing R), or hit the escape key (ESC) to not perform a repair and proceed.

In the case of SSL, you would not be confronted with this screen as I assume you are starting with a new server machine that had not previously had Windows 2000 installed on it.

8. Assuming you have a new hard disk, you see the following hard disk partitioning screen. The actual space value (MB) varies depending on how large your hard disk is. In this case with SSL, the hard disk is a 27GB RAID array (with 7.5GB usable).

> The following list shows existing partitions and
>
> unpartitioned space on this computer.
>
> Use UP and DOWN ARROW keys to select an item in the list.
>
> * To install Windows 2000 on the selected item, press ENTER.
>
> *To create a partition in the unpartitioned space, press C.

*To delete the selected partition, press D.

```
| 17493 MB Disk 0 at Id 0 on bus 0 on atapi          |
|  Unpartitioned space              17493 MB        |
```

9. You need to create a partition for Windows 2000 Server and SBS to install on. Select **C** on your keyboard to create this partition. In the case of SSL, enter **8000** for approximately 8GB (just under 8GB, technically speaking, but don't worry about it) on the following screen.

> You have asked Setup to create a new partition on
>
> 17493 MB Disk 0 at Id 0 on bus 0 on atapi.
>
> *To create the new partition, enter a size below and press ENTER.
>
> *To go back to the previous screen without creating the partition, press ESC.
>
> The minimum size for the new partition is 8 megabytes (MB).
>
> The maximum size for the new partition is 17493 megabytes (MB).
>
> Create partition of size (in MB): 8001

Press **Enter** to return to the screen similar to that shown above in step #8 above.

10. On the screen below, select the new C: drive partition and press **Enter** to install Windows 2000 Server and (in several steps) SBS on the newly created 8GB (approximately) system partition.

> The following list shows existing partitions and
>
> unpartitioned space on this computer.
>
> Use UP and DOWN ARROW keys to select an item in the list.
>
> * To install Windows 2000 on the selected item, press ENTER.
>
> * To create a partition in the unpartitioned space, press C.
>
> * To delete the selected partition, press D.

```
| 17493 MB Disk 0 at Id 0 on bus 0 on atapi          |
|  C:  New (Unformatted)            8001 MB      |
|  Unpartitioned space              9492 MB      |
```

11. The following screen asks you to format the C: drive (or system partition). It is essential that you select the NTFS formatting option because SBS installs only on an NTFS partition. Press **Enter** after selecting NTFS.

> The partition you have chosen is not unformatted.
>
> Setup will now format the partition.
>
> Use the UP and DOWN ARROW keys to move the highlight
>
> to the file system you want and then press ENTER.
>
> If you want to select a different partition for Windows 2000, press ESC.
>
> Format the partition using the NTFS file system.
>
> Format the partition using the FAT file system.

BEST PRACTICE: Because you are following the beloved SSL methodology, you will indeed have seen the screen in step #11 above. However, if you were installing SBS in a scenario where you installed to an existing formated hard disk partition, you would not see the screen in step #11 because it would not be necessary to format the partition.

Setup now formats the hard disk partition you have just created. This formatting process takes several minutes. Feel free to get a cup of coffee to pass the time.

After the formatting is complete, the computer's hard disks will be inspected for hard disk errors.

After the initial partition formatting has been completed, numerous Windows 2000 Server-related files (.inf, .exe, .dll, .wav, .sys, .fon, .hlp) are copied over to the newly NTFS formatted partition. A screen will briefly appear communicating the newly copied files are being initialized.

12. You must now remove SBS Setup Disk #4 from your floppy drive A: even though nothing requests that you do so. After several minutes of file copying from SBS CD Disc 1, the computer automatically reboots itself (with only a brief, timed notice that it is doing so). If SBS setup Disk #4 is still in drive A:, the machine will not boot properly.

Remove SBS setup Disk #4 now from floppy drive A:.

BEST PRACTICE: You should remove the CD Disc #1 when the read activity to that disk ceases (near the end of step #12) if your computer automatically boots to the CD as part of its boot sequence. However, many computers require you to "hit any key" to boot to the CD, so the SBS Disc 1 could actually stay in the CD drive if your computer uses such a method to launch a boot routine from the CD drive and you do not touch any key. SBS Disc 1 will be used again shortly.

13. An autologon occurs and the GUI-based Windows 2000 Server phase commences. The **Windows 2000 Server Setup Wizard** appears and automatically starts installing devices. A screen is briefly displayed (for a few seconds), followed by an **Installing Devices** screen (which is displayed for a few minutes). Neither of these screens requires input from the user.

BEST PRACTICE: The Windows 2000 Server setup routine using SBS Disc 1 is slightly different than a Windows 2000 Server setup routine using a Windows 2000 Server Disc. Why? Because the setup information file (.sif) on SBS Disc 1 is different from that found on good old-fashioned Windows 2000 Server Disc. With SBS, the two screens described immediately above in step 13 (Welcome, Installing Devices) are instructed to run and proceed automatically without user input. Also, the SBS .sif file suppresses the Licensing (Per Seat or Per Server) and the Workgroup or Domains screens. Both of these decisions are made automatically by the SBS setup routine (based on .sif file input).

14. You are presented with the **Regional Settings** screen where you make select the system locale and keyboard layout. After accepting or changing the defaults (via the **Customize** button), click **Next**.

15. You are next presented with the **Personalize Your Software** screen. This allows you to enter the name and organization. Recall from Chapter 2, Table 2-4, that the information you need to enter is readily available. That information is

> Name: Bob Easter
>
> Organization: Springer Spaniels Limited

After entering this information, click **Next**.

16. The **Your Product Key** screen appears. Enter the product key found on the Small Business Server 2000 CD Disc case (it is a 25-alpha/numeric code). Click **Next**.

17. The **Computer Name and Administrator Password** screen appear. Provide the computer name (**SSL1**) for SSL in the Computer name field and the Administrator password (**husky9999**) in both the **Administrator Password** and **Confirm Password** fields and click **Next**.

BEST PRACTICE: You will note that a computer name has been automatically suggested in the Computer name field (e.g., SPRINGERSPA-B3KU6G but your suggested name may vary). There are several issues surrounding the suggested computer name.

First, the suggested computer name is typically long and difficult to remember. There are still applications that require you to manually type the server computer name during a setup screen or to map a drive via a uniform naming convention path (UNC). One of these applications, Outlook Team Folders, has a screen where you specify a folder by UNC naming convention and you must manually type in the machine name (you can't browse to the machine). In this case, a shorter machine name is desirable for spelling purposes. Note that Outlook Team Folders are discussed in Chapters 12 and 19.

Second, the SSL methodology used throughout this book demands you name the machine SSL1 in order to successfully complete the examples herein this text.

Third, while you should put care and thought into naming the computer at this point, you actually have one more chance to change the machine name in the SBS setup routine. This last chance to change the computer name occurs later in what I defined as Phase C: SBS Installation and Setup. There is a screen in the SBS setup routine at that time that allows you to modify the computer NetBIOS name (but after that naming screen, the only way to change your computer name is to reinstall SBS from the start!).

18. Select what components you want to install on the **Windows 2000 Components** screen and click **Next**.

BEST PRACTICE: I recommend you accept the default Windows 2000 component selections and click **Next**. At a later time, when your SBS network is up and running without any problems, you can add Windows 2000 components. If you add Windows 2000 components now and the system is badly behaved, it will be more difficult to determine whether it is SBS or the additional components that are causing the bad behavior!

19. Assuming you are adhering to the SSL story line and have a modem attached (as specified earlier in the chapter), the **Modem Dialing Information** screen appears. Complete the **What country/region are you in now?** drop down box (for SSL, select **United States of America**), the **What area code (or city code) are you in now?** field (for SSL, enter **206**), and the **If you dial a number to get an outside line, what is it?** field (for SSL, leave blank). Select between **Tone dialing or Pulse** dialing under **The phone system at this location uses:** and click **Next**. I am, of course, assuming you can find out all of the answers to the questions above relatively easily for your own real world use (for example, many businesses dial "9" to reach an outside line and use tone dialing). If you don't have a modem attached, the **Modem Dialing Information** screen will not appear and you will go immediately to the next step for date and time settings.

20. Select your date, time, and time zone when presented with the **Date and Time Settings** screen. For SSL, select **(GMT-08:00) Pacific Time (US & Canada), then Tijuana** in the **Time Zone** drop-down field. You can enter whatever day and time you desire (and this can be changed via Control Panel when the server machine is up and running after setup) in the **Date & Time** drop-down fields. Click **Next**. Note that for SBS sites in the United States, it makes sense to select the **Automatically adjust clock for daylight saving changes** checkbox to automatically adjust your server time in the spring (ahead) and fall (back).

21. Additional computer files to install the Windows 2000 networking components (the **Networking Settings** screen will be displayed requiring no input from you at this point, but that will change in just a moment) are copied and installed. You will then select either **Typical settings** or **Custom settings** on the **Networking Settings** screen. For SSL, select **Typical settings** and click **Next**. Additional Windows 2000 files are copied and installed (this may take upwards of 10 minutes).

BEST PRACTICE: Much like my comments previously about the default Windows 2000 component selections, I recommend you select **Typical settings** and click **Next**. At a later time, when your SBS network is up and running without any problems, you can add other networking components, such as the NWLink IPX/SPX protocol (for supporting NetWare servers if your situation warrants). If you add lots of networking components now and the system misbehaves, it will be the dickens to troubleshoot, let me tell ya!

22. **The Performing Final Tasks** screen appears to install Start menu items, register components, save settings, and remove any temporary files used. No input is required of you on the screen. Click **Finish** when the **Completing the Windows 2000 Setup Wizard** appears. The SBS computer reboots and Windows 2000 Server starts.

23. You are instructed to press **Ctrl-Alt-Delete** at the **Welcome to Windows** dialog box. **The Log On to Windows** dialog box appears. After you log on as **Administrator** (remember the password is **husky9999**), you are greeted by the initial SBS setup screen that is titled **Microsoft Small Business Server 2000 Setup**, which is shown in Figure 3-3.

Notes:

Figure 3-3
Initial SBS setup screen.

BEST PRACTICE: Depending on the hardware you have installed on your system, such as a USB device, plug-and-play device, or PCI-based device, you might receive a notice in the form of an informational dialog box titled **System Settings Change**. The message will read "**Windows 2000 has finished installing new devices. You must restart your computer before the new settings will take effect. Do you want to restart your computer now?**" You should reply **No** to this message because the initial SBS Setup screen (shown in Figure 3-3) is programmed to run once and, if you reboot, it won't run a second time.

However, if you inadvertently click **Yes** on the **System Settings Change** dialog box, all is not lost. Upon the next reboot, simply reinsert your SBS CD Disc 1 and the autorun routine on the CD Disc media will execute, launching the **Microsoft Small Business Server 2000 Setup** screen. Pretty cool, huh!

BEST PRACTICE: Now is the time to drop under the hood and run the **Computer Management** snap-in (found in the **Administrative Tools** program group from the **Programs** group from the **Start** menu) to create, format, and assign drive letters to your additional, unused hard disk space. By doing that now, when you're presented with the screens that allow you to redirect where specific applications are installed and data is stored, you will have additional hard disk space ready and able and willing to go to work.

In the **Computer Management** snap-in, expand **Storage** and expand **Disk Management**. In the details pane, **right-click** on the **Unallocated** space (in the case of SSL, this would be approximately 9.5GB).

Select **Create Partition** and click **Next** when the **Create Partition Wizard** launches and the **Welcome to the Create Partition Wizard** screen appears. In the case of SSL, select **Primary partition** on the **Select Partition Type** screen and click **Next**. Note that primary and extended partition types are defined on the Select Partition Type screen, so I won't repeat that definition here. In the **Amount of disk space to use** field on the **Specify Partition Size** screen, type the size you want the partition to be. In the case of SSL, the disk space would be approximately 9.5GB, entered as **9492 MB**. Click **Next**.

The **Assign Drive Letter or Path** screen appears. Select **Assign a drive letter** and select a drive letter. The first free drive letter will appear by default. Under the SSL methodology, this is assumed to be drive letter **E:** but it is entirely likely the first available drive letter may be the letter F (depending on how man CD Disc devices you have attached). This is entirely normal and depends on your unique situation. If for some reason you can not select the drive letter E and you are following the SSL methodology, it is OK to depart from the script and select a drive letter other than the letter E. (This specific selection will not materially alter the SSL experience!) Click **Next**.

On the **Format Partition** screen, select **Format this partition with the following settings:** and select **NTFS** for **File system to use:**, **Default** for **Allocation unit size:**, type **Data** for **Volume label:**, and check **Perform a Quick Format**. Click **Next**.

On the **Completing the Create Partition Wizard** screen, click **Finish**. You have now successfully created the data partition under the SSL methodology.

As you might have guessed, this is an undocumented trick with respect to the core SBS setup approach!

Note that you could have created the second partition back on the
partition screen in the Windows 2000 Server character-based setup
phase (approximately Steps 9, 10, 11), but I elected not to use that
approach as part of my SSL methodology.

24. Click Set Up Small Business Server. You will receive a notice to please
    wait while setup initializes and some low-level files are copied. The
    Welcome to the Microsoft Small Business Server 2000 Setup Wizard
    screen, seen in Figure 3-4, appears. Click Next. There may be a slight
    pause (ten seconds) before the licensing screen appears and the Welcome
    to the Microsoft Small Business Server 2000 Setup Wizard screen
    remains visible. This is a normal pause and there is no need to click Next
    twice (even though I've done it myself thinking something was wrong).

Figure 3-4
Welcome screen on the SBS 2000 Setup Wizard.

BEST PRACTICE: At this point, you might well receive a warning or a blocking message indicating your machine doesn't satisfy some SBS setup requirement. First and foremost, understand that either warning or blocking messages appear depending on machine settings, so one SBS setup on a specific machine might vary from another SBS setup on another machine (the point being you might receive a warning or blocking message on one machine and not the other).

As a general rule, a warning message does not stop the SBS setup routine and can be cured immediately. An example of a warning message is the 600X800 or higher display resolution warning message that basically communicates your display resolution is too low. When your machine is configured, it is entirely likely that the initial display resolution was 640X480. This has happened on many machines that I have installed SBS 2000 on. A warning message appears at this point indicating the display resolution is too low. To fix this, I simply **right-clicked** on the **display desktop**, selected **Properties**, clicked the **Settings** tab, and moved the slide bar towards **More** under **Screen area**. Moving the slide bar to the right toward More allows you to select a display resolution of 800X600 or higher. This satisfies the warning message's intent to have you make a change that would benefit the SBS setup process.

A blocking message is typically more severe and will require more extensive remedial action on your behalf. For example, you may have insufficient hard disk space or not enough RAM memory. These are the types of conditions that can generate a blocking message and the SBS setup can not continue. In the case of insufficient hard disk space, you would either free sufficient hard disk space or add another hard disk and then restart the SBS setup process from Step 23 and forward. In the case of insufficient RAM memory, you would purchase, beg, borrow, or steal suitable and sufficient RAM memory, install it inside the machine and restart the SBS setup process from Step 23 and forward.

Note there are numerous warning and blocking messages that will be identified on the display if you receive this message (e.g., network adapter card problems, etc.). I will not list other such messages here.

And, of course, if you did not receive a warning or blocking message, you will proceed with the setup.

25. You are presented with the **License Agreement** screen. If you select the **I Agree** button, the setup routine continues. If you select the **I Disagree** button, the SBS setup routine terminates.
    As part of the SSL methodology, read the software license agreement, select **I Agree**, and click **Next**.

BEST PRACTICE: If you are upgrading from a previous version of SBS, you will be presented with a screen asking you to insert Disc 1 from the older SBS version to verify your ownership. No pulling a fast one on Microsoft here when it comes to version upgrades.

Also note that if you are doing a competitive upgrade, no such screen will be presented.

26. The **Product Identification** screen now appears. You are shown the Name (Bob Easter), **Organization** (Springer Spaniels Limited), and **Computer Name** (SSL1) fields. This is your last chance to change the Name, Organization, and Computer Name fields without performing a reinstall of SBS from the very beginning!

BEST PRACTICE: So where does the Name, Organization, and Computer Name information come from? Is SBS a mind reader or what? Not exactly. The Name and Organization information was derived from Step 15 above, Computer Name from Step 17.

You also need to enter the 25-digit CD product key that is found on the yellow sticker on the back of your SBS CD case. But you're not done yet! You will enter the 25-digit CD product key for Microsoft Outlook as well. Your screen should look similar to Figure 3-5. Click **Next**. Note that for legal reasons and the fact I'd get my fanny spanked by Microsoft, Figure 3-5 does not display the full product keys. You will need to provide your own unique 25-digit CD product key as I won't provide it for you in a screenshot in a book.

Figure 3-5

Complete the Product Identification screen. Be sure to enter the 25-digit CD product keys carefully!

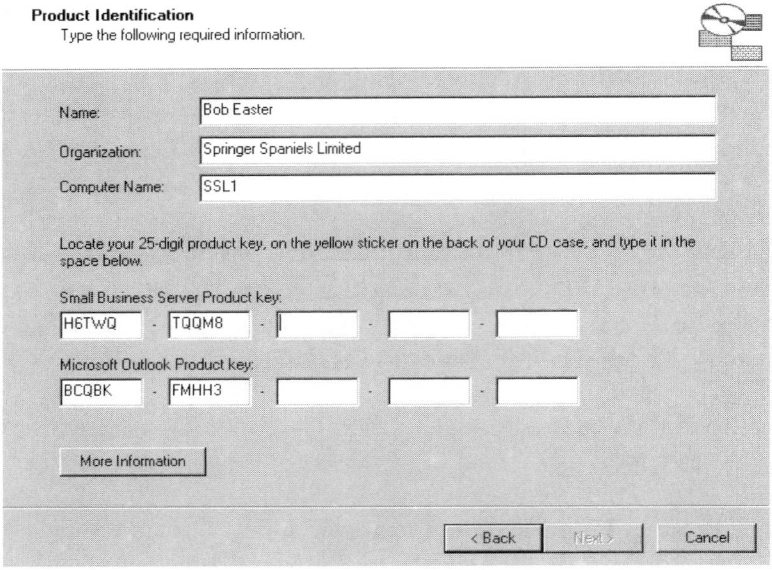

BEST PRACTICE: You should be aware of the More Information button at the lower part of each SBS 2000 Setup Wizard screen. Click **More Information** and you are presented a worksheet and a help topic for the screen being displayed. This is a big improvement over SBS 4.5 when only a few screens had the More Information button. More importantly, the More Information buttons help you install SBS 2000 correctly if you are unsure about a setting.

27. Provide the Administrator account password in the **Password** field (under **Automatically log on**) on the **Automatic Logon Information** screen. In the case of SSL, it is "**husky9999**". Click **Next**.

BEST PRACTICE: SBS checks the password instantly and notifies you if it was entered incorrectly. This is a nice touch because you have a chance to correct your error without disrupting the setup process. Better to find this out now than later when you try to autologon!

28. Complete the **Company Information** screen. Be sure to complete each field similar to that seen for SSL in Figure 3-6. You'll recall the SSL server setup information was presented in Table 2-4 of Chapter 2. Click **Next**.

Figure 3-6

Complete the Company Information screen.

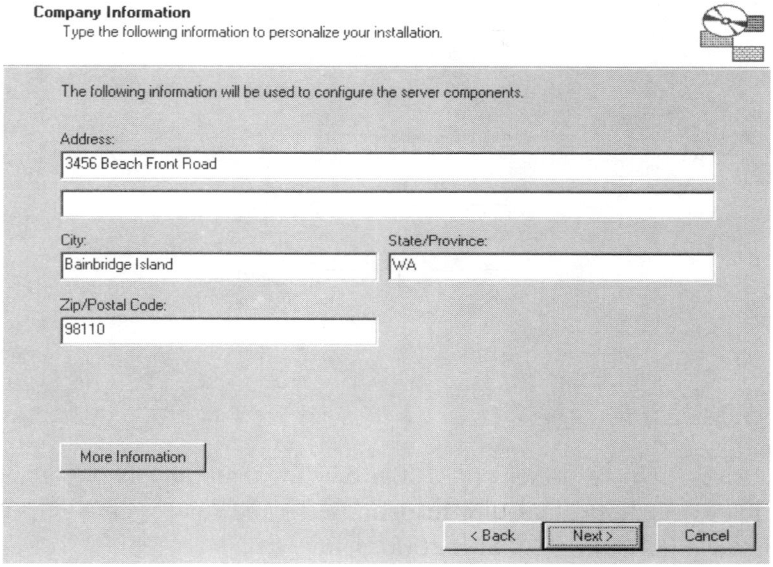

BEST PRACTICE: Complete as many fields as possible on all SBS setup dialog boxes when you set up your own SBS machine. Much of this information, known as metainformation, is used in other places within SBS for the life of the system.

29. Complete the **Telephone Information** screen) based on information from Table 2-4). For SSL, this is shown in Figure 3-7. Click **Next**.

Notes:

Figure 3-7

Complete the Telephone Information screen.

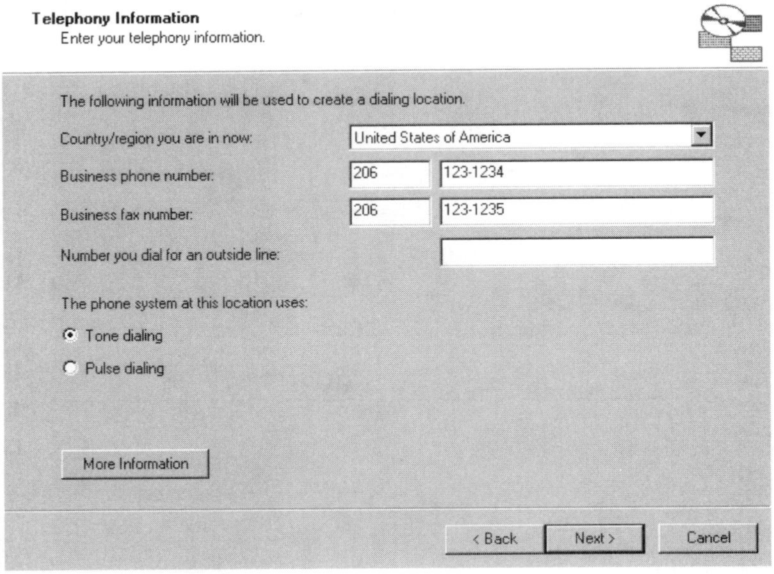

30. Select the network adapter that will be the internal network adapter on the **Local Network Card Information** screen and click **Next**. This is shown in Figure 3-8

Notes:

Figure 3-8

You select the network adapter card that will be associated with the local area network, not the external Internet connection. The network adapter card for the Internet will be configured later.

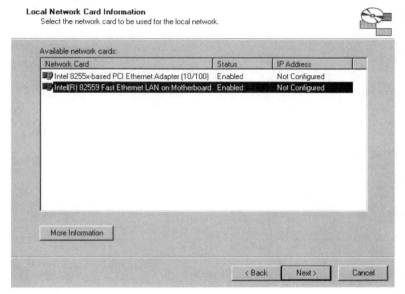

31. Complete the **Server Network Card Configuration** screen. You may enter the **IP address, Subnet Mask**, and **Default Gateway** values of your choice for the internal network. This is a major improvement over SBS 4.5, where you were assigned the private network address of 10.0.0.2 by default. You may accept the Class C private network address of 192.168.16.2 which is suggested (but not required) by default, as seen on Figure 3-9. Click **Next**. Note for SSL, the default IP address value (192.168.16.2) is accepted.

Notes:

Figure 3-9

You may enter the IP address of your choice on the Server Network Card Con-figuration screen or simply select the default private network address (the correct choice for SSL).

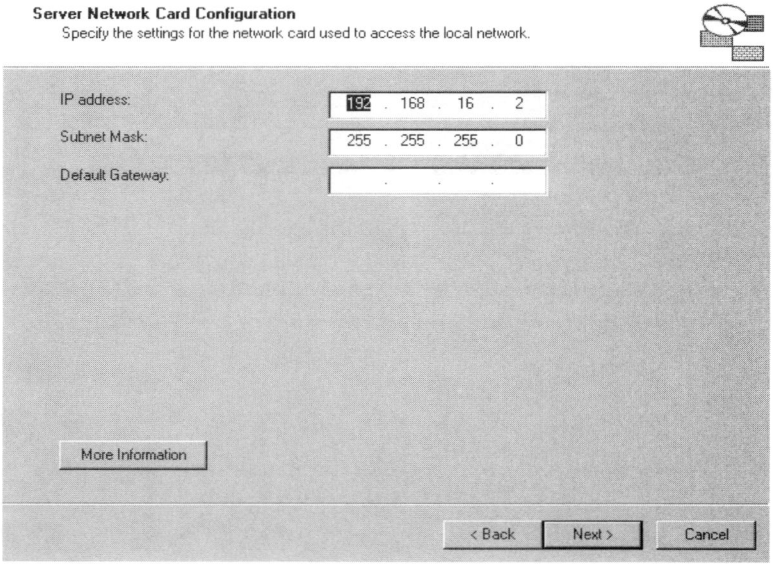

32. Provide your full DNS domain name information, as well as the down-stream NT-like domain name (NetBIOS domain name), on the **New Domain Information** screen. By default, the NetBIOS name field is completed with the first term you supplied in the Full DNS name for new domain name field. Your screen for SSL should look similar to Figure 3-10 where you have entered **springersltd.com** in the **Full DNS name for new domain:** field and the **Domain NetBIOS Name:** field was auto-matically populated with **SPRINGERSLTD**. Click **Next**.

Notes:

Figure 3-10

Complete the New Domain Information screen.

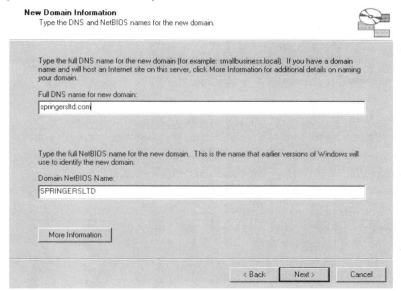

BEST PRACTICE: All that planning you did in Chapter 1 and 2 will pay off here. The domain name information you provide on the New Domain Information screen is used when Active Directory is installed and configured in a few moments.

Also note that it is not truly necessary to have a registered Internet domain name to install SBS. You can put in an "internal" DNS domain name that works for you and your organization. In the official SBS training course—2301a Implementing Small Business Server 2000—the DNS domain name used in the classroom is nwtraders.msft, and all of the examples worked fine. And you can literally enter "smallbusiness.local" as suggested in the text of the New Domain Information screen if you don't have anything or any other name to use.

You may click the **More Information** button on the **New Domain Information** screen if you'd like to be soundly taken to school on DNS and domain names. Seriously, the More Information button provides help on completing the field related to domain names.

Note that you can not change your domain name after this screen unless you reinstall SBS.

33. The **Directory Services Restore Mode Administrator Password** screen appears as seen in Figure 3-11. You will need to provide the administrator's password in both the Password: and the Confirm password: fields. For SSL, the password is "**husky9999**"—without the quote marks of course.

Figure 3-11

Active Directory needs to know the administrator password to run in Directory Services Restore Mode. This mode is only used to restore the Active Directory to a domain controller. Click More Information to learn more.

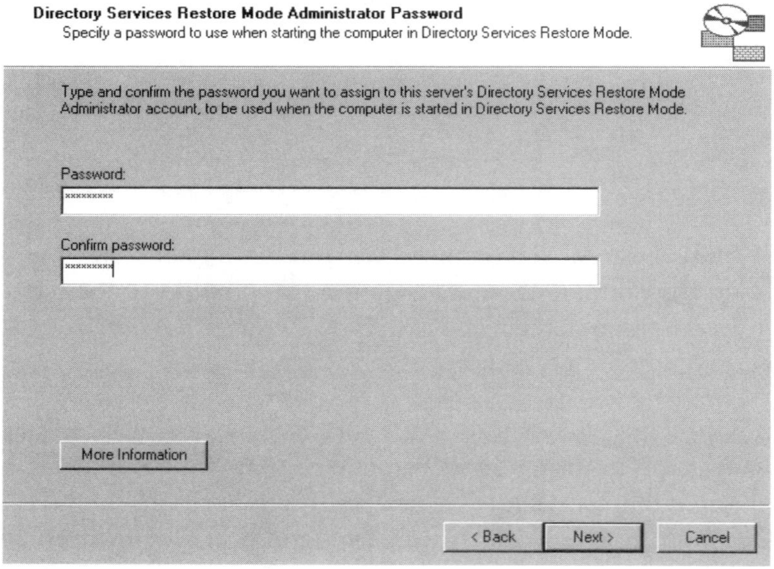

34. The **Scenario Baseline** screen appears and communicates that the several components will be installed at the Windows 2000 Server-level, as seen in Figure 3-12. This includes installing Active Directory, promoting the server machine to a Domain Controller at the root of an Active Directory forest, and installing necessary Windows 2000 Server components and configurations needed (including DNS, DHCP, and WINS) prior to the installation of SBS applications. Terminal Services is installed in remote administration mode. Click **Next**.

Figure 3-12

The Scenario Baseline screen communicates what Windows 2000 Server components will be installed and configured so that the SBS applications will successfully install.

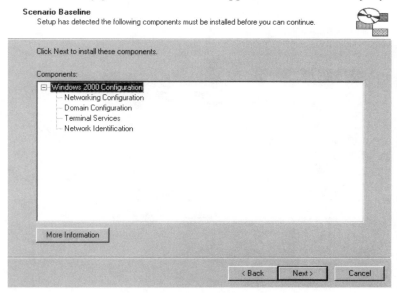

The Component Progress screen, seen in Figure 3-13, will inform you of the progress of the scenario baseline configuration.

Notes:

Figure 3-13

The scenario baseline activity will take several minutes, possibly just over 10 minutes depending on machine speed. The Component Progress screen is a way to track the configuration activity.

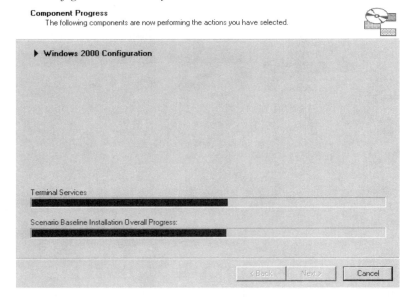

Windows 2000 will reboot automatically after Active Directory and related components are installed and the scenario baseline is complete. An automatic logon occurs and the SBS Setup Wizard starts again, allowing the Windows 2000-related components to continue installation and configuration. Hang in there! You are getting closer to the actual SBS components!

35. The **Component Selection** screen appears (Figure 3-14). This is where you will select the SBS components to install and the location for the installation. In the case of SSL, you will install all SBS components (including SQL Server 2000) to drive C:. Note that to select a component, you click the "down arrow" **Action** button to the left of the application name and select **Install**.

BEST PRACTICE: SQL Server 2000 is not installed by default. Too bad! More people would use it and appreciate it if this were a default installation in SBS 2000. Yes, you've guessed it. I'm a big fan of SQL Server 2000.

To install SQL Server 2000, which you must do as part of the SSL methodology, you will need to expand the parent object (SQL Server 2000 in the Component Name column) and select Install all of the children components (including Server Components, Management Tools, Books Online, Analysis Services and English Query). If you select only the SQL Server 2000 parent object for installation, some barebones SQL Server 2000 components are installed but not the true database application nor its components. This is clearly a misleading aspect of the SBS 2000 Setup routine.

Also, for the SSL methodology, please expand the Microsoft Exchange 2000 parent object and select **Microsoft Exchange Instant Messaging Service** for installation. I discuss Instant Messaging in Chapter 11.

After double-checking that you've selected the SQL Server and Microsoft Exchange Instant Messaging Server components (as dictated by the SSL methodology), click **Next**.

Figure 3-14
The Component Selection screen allows you to select which SBS applications you will or will not install.

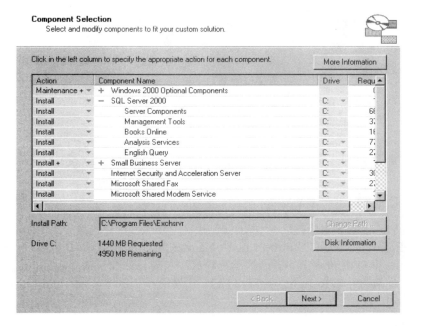

BEST PRACTICE: Revisit Table 1-1 in Chapter 1 if you need to refresh your memory about what each SBS component is and does. For example, Microsoft Exchange 2000 Server is the e-mail communications program in SBS.

36. On the **SQL Server 2000 Collation Settings** screen, accept the default **SQL Collations** (used for compatibility with previous version of SQL Server) selection of **Dictionary order, case-insensitive, for use with 1252 Character Set**. This is shown in Figure 3-15 and is acceptable under the SSL methodology. Click **Next**.

Figure 3-15
The default Dictionary order, case-insensitive selection is acceptable for most applications that use SQL Server. However, you should check with your ISV for any SQL Server settings it may require.

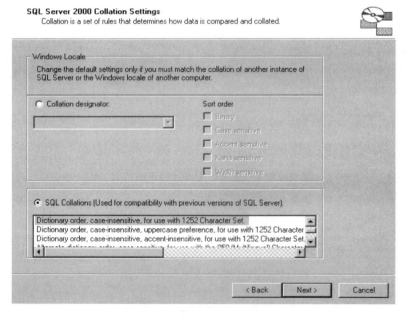

37. When the SQL Server 2000 Network Libraries screen appears (see Figure 3-16), accept the default Named Pipes and TCP/IP Sockets (note the default port number of 1433) selections for the SSL methodology. However, in the real world, an ISV that uses SQL Server might instruct

you to modify these settings. A common setting to select is Multi-Protocol to allow a SQL Server-based form of encryption. Click Next.

Figure 3-16
You will select Network Libraries for SQL Server to use. Note additional support for NWLink (for NetWare compatibility), AppleTalk, and Banyan VINES (which are not used by SSL).

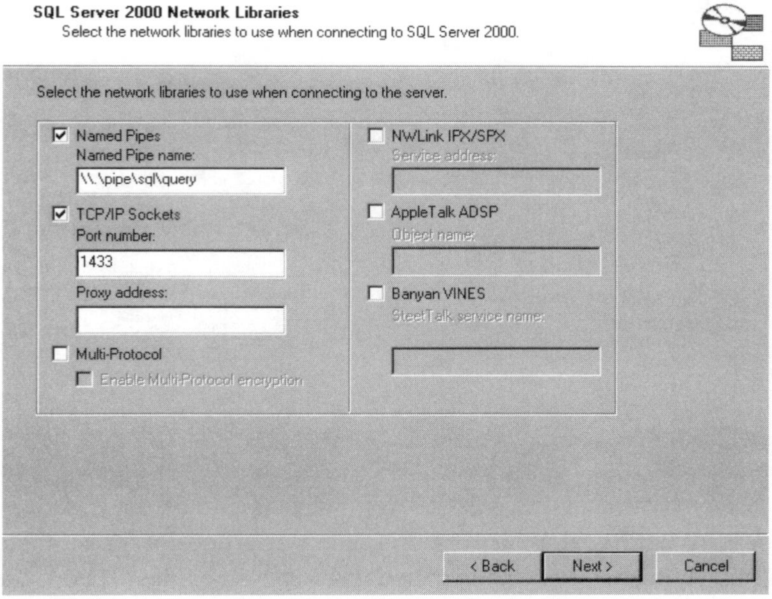

38. For SSL, accept the default ISA Server cache of 100MB on drive C: on the **ISA Server Cache Drives** screen and click **Next**. This is the screen that allows you to select whether ISA Server caching is enabled and which drive will hold the cache files. Note that only an NTFS drive can be used for ISA caching. ISA Server is discussed in Chapter 10. This is shown in Figure 3-17.

Notes:

Figure 3-17
The caching capabilities of ISA Server improve Web access for the SBS network.
The cache file size location is set on the ISA Server Cache Drives screen.

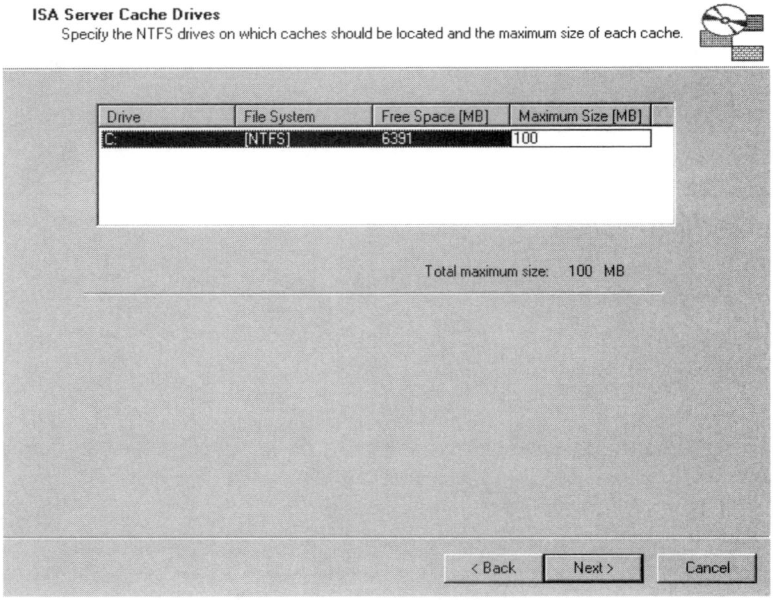

ISA Server Cache Drives
Specify the NTFS drives on which caches should be located and the maximum size of each cache.

Drive	File System	Free Space [MB]	Maximum Size [MB]
C:	[NTFS]	6391	100

Total maximum size: 100   MB

< Back   Next >   Cancel

39. Select your local (internal) network adapter card on the **ISA Server Construct Local Address Table** screen so a Local Address Table (LAT) can automatically be constructed. LAT is used by the network address translation (NAT) function in ISA Server. You would also select the **Add the private ranges 10.x.x.x, 192.168.x.x, and 172.16.x.x to 172.31.x.x. to the table** checkbox. Click **Next**. Note for SSL, your screen should look similar to Figure 3-18.

Notes:

Figure 3-18

You will advise ISA Server how to build the LAT table with the ISA Server Construct Local Address Table screen.

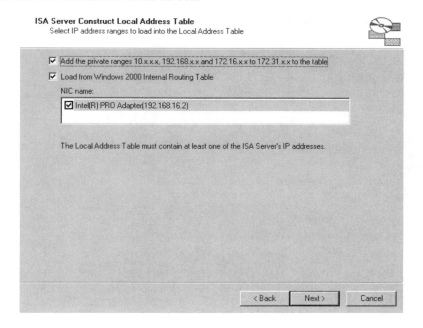

40. The **ISA Server Local Address Table Configuration** screen allows you to confirm the entries that were automatically made and further, to make manually LAT table entries if you so desire. Additional manual entries are not necessary for SSL. Your screen should look similar to Figure 3-19. Click **Next**.

Notes:

Figure 3-19

The ISA Server Local Address Table Configuration screen allows you to confirm the LAT that was automatically constructed.

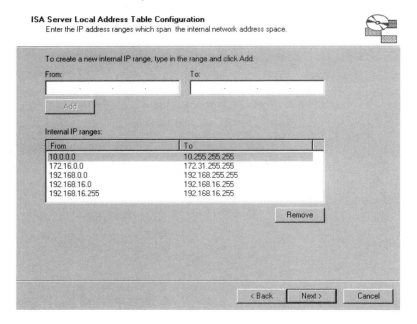

41. The **Data Folder** screen allows you to specify where data folders related to SBS and its components will be placed. For SSL, accept drive **C:** as seen in Figure 3-20 and click **Next**.

Notes:

Figure 3-20

SBS-related data folders may be redirected to other drives.

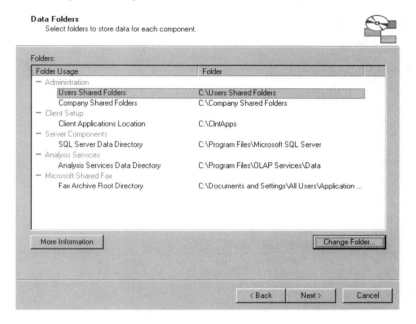

42. The **Service Accounts** screen appears for assigning a service account to SQL Server (Figure 3-21). For SSL, do the following. First, click the Assign Accounts button, then type **Administrator** in the Account name field and **husky9999** in the Password field of the **Microsoft Small Business Server 2000 Setup Wizard** dialog box that appears. Click **OK**. You are returned to the **Service Accounts** screen where you will need to click **Next**.

Notes:

Figure 3-21
You will need to specify the service account to be used by SQL Server 2000.

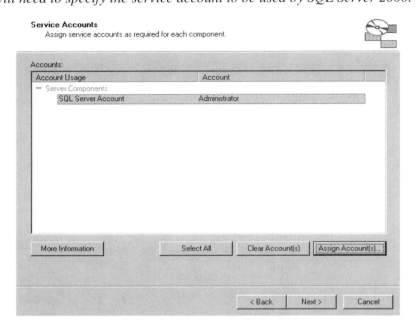

43. On the **Installation Summary** screen, seen in Figure 3-22, review your installation choices for correctness and click **Next**.

Notes:

Figure 3-22

The Installation Summary screen allows you to confirm and change, if necessary, your SBS components selected for installation.

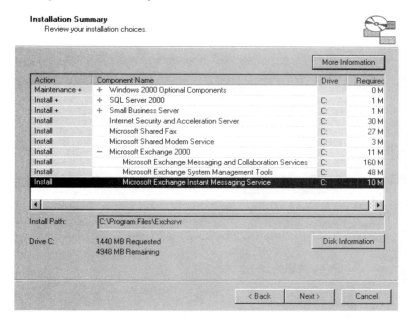

44. When asked to extend your Active Directory schema in the **Microsoft Small Business Server 2000 Setup Wizard** dialog box, click **OK**. The Components Progress screen, shown in Figure 3-23, lists the order of SBS components being installed plus the current installation status. You will need to swap SBS CD Discs as requested by the program. Depending on the speed of your machine, this part of the installation process takes between 30 minutes and over two hours! I'd like to say you could go to lunch, but not yet. You have to attend the installation to swap Small Business Server 2000 CD Discs when requested. Remember there are four Discs used as part of the SBS 2000 installation process. The cool thing is swapping Discs is relatively low bandwidth, so you can always use this time to use another computer to answer e-mails, etc.

Notes:

Figure 3-23

The Components Progress screen affords you the chance to monitor the status of your SBS installation. The overall progress indicator is a wonderful way to estimate how much time remains.

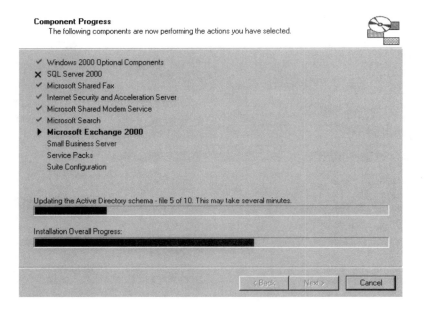

BEST PRACTICE: Did you notice the Shared Fax Service and Shared Modem Service were selected by default and are installed whether or not you have a modem attached? Its true in SBS 2000 and a major improvement compared to past SBS releases where a modem detection issues could kill the whole party.

Also note that Figure 3-23 shows a failed component during setup. Can you guess which one? It's SQL Server 2000 with the "X" next to it. When this occurs, you typically need to rerun the SBS 2000 setup process again to solve the problem. In this case, after SBS 2000 was installed, I simply ran **Small Business Server 2000** from **Add/Remove Programs** in **Control Panel** (**Start**, **Settings**, **Control Panel**) and selected the SQL Server components again for installation. Worked like a charm.

If for some reason you've had a faulty installation with failed components, the Components Messages screen will be displayed describing the failure, as seen in Figure 3-24. After reading this screen, click Next to continue.

Figure 3-24
SBS components that failed to install are displayed on the Components Messages screen.

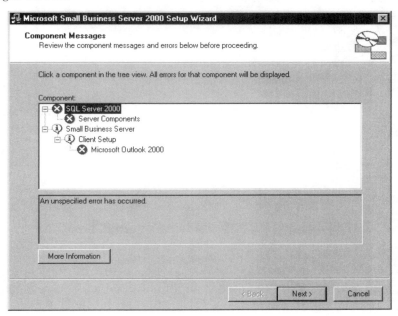

45. Click **Finish** on the Completing the Microsoft Small Business Server 2000 Wizard screen, shown in Figure 3-25. This screen will report that the setup was successful or that it was not successful because one or more components reported an error. Answer **Yes** when asked to reboot.

Notes:

Figure 3-25

The completion screen is the end of the Wizard-based SBS installation process, allowing you to use SBS after one final reboot.

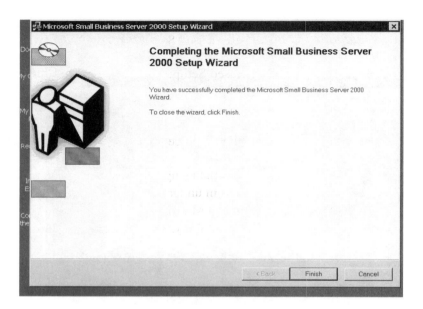

BEST PRACTICE: If your SBS installation was unsuccessful, you must stop and troubleshoot the failed components. Typically a reinstallation of the failed components as I described in the BEST PRACTICE above will cure the problem. However, I've had to call Microsoft's Product Support Services (PSS) in the past to solve the really tough ones!

So otherwise, assuming all went well, let me be the first to say congratulations! You have now completed the base installation of your SBS Server. Now, more configuration items await you.

BEST PRACTICE: After the computer restarts, SBS performs some background housekeeping duties. You see a dialog box that communicates that data access is being configured. Don't be alarmed. These are one-time configuration events.

SBS is completely installed. When the logon dialog box is displayed, provide your username (**administrator**) and password (**husky9999**).

Time Flies (Not!)

The basic SBS setup process from Phase A to the end of Phase D should take anywhere from 90 to 240 minutes, depending on the speed of your computer. I've noticed installation time breaks down as follows:

Phase A - Windows 2000 Server Character-Based Setup: 15 percent

Phase B - Windows 2000 Server GUI-Based Setup: 20 percent

Phase C - SBS Installation and Setup: 60 percent

Phase D: SBS Completion and Initial Boot: 5 percent

Dual-processor computers are much faster than single processor computers and can complete this SBS installation process in under 90 minutes. I've heard rumors that one SBS 2000 server machine at Microsoft was installed in just over 60 minutes with four processors, SCSI technology, and a 40-speed CD drive. That's flying!

Guest Column
The Successful SBS Setup Experience!

by Erin Bourke-Dunphy, Microsoft Corporation

A successful installation and configuration of SBS 2000 sets the stage for a successful experience with the SBS product. The SBS setup wizard provides an integrated setup experience tailored to the small-business scenario that is both predictable and repeatable – two very important factors to the technology consultant! It is by talking to the technology consultant about their previous experience with SBS setup and listening to their problems and ideas that we have been able to deliver on this.

While SBS 2000 is similar to previous releases of SBS in that it installs and configures all of the server applications shipped in SBS through a single wizard, we have made several changes to the architecture of setup in the 2000 release. The most important of these changes lies around how the operating system is installed and configured. In SBS 4.0 and 4.5, we installed the operating system using an unattended file. While this allowed us to ensure that the operating system was configured appropriately for the small-business environment as well as a successful server application installation, we received two pieces of feed-back from the technology consultants. First, the technology consultants were familiar with the operating system installation, and they expressed a desire for more control over this portion of the installation. Ultimately, they wanted to know what setup was doing under the covers. Second, when installing newer hardware, the technology consultants ran into problems with undetected hardware. As the newer drivers for the hardware were not on the installation media, and the unattended file did not provide the ability to "Have Disk" in new drivers, the technology consultants were often required to stop setup between the operating system install and the SBS server application installation to fix hardware issues.

Based upon this feedback, SBS 2000 setup was re-architected into three installation phases: Windows 2000 Server installation, Windows 2000 Server configuration, and then SBS server applications installation. In the Windows 2000 Server installation we have dropped the use of the unattend file to install the operating system, and placed the technology consultants on the same playing field as native Windows 2000 Server installation. The technology consultant can see how the operating system is being installed and has control over the installation. We do make a few modifications to simplify the installation: slipstreaming Windows 2000 Server SP1 into the base installation, and not displaying screens, such as the licensing and domain membership screen as these are not applicable to the small-business scenario.

In the Windows 2000 Server configuration phase, we pull all of the work previously accomplished by the unattended file into setup and allow the technology consultant to both see and customize this. In this phase we configure the networking (now using a default address of 192.168.16.2 which can be changed), install and configure the Active Directory, and install Terminal Services in remote administration mode. While the technology consultant has more flexibility in SBS 2000, setup still ensures that the operating system is configured to allow for a successful SBS server application installation. The last phase is the server application installation, which is similar to previous releases.

While this is the major change in SBS 2000, several additional improvements have been made based on feedback from the technology consultant, such as: no longer requiring a modem for installation, defaulting the setup to a typical small business needs that is still customizable, and supporting maintenance mode setup for a graduated deployment.

The above improvements ease the installation process and help the technology consultant perform a successful SBS installation time after time.

Erin Bourke-Dunphy graduated from Electrical Engineering at the University of Waterloo, in Canada and now works as a Lead Program Manager on the Small Business Server team at Microsoft.

Final SBS Setup Configurations and Advanced Setup Issues

Welcome back from lunch. This afternoon you complete the final steps necessary to initially implement SBS on the server machine. I then share with you a variety of advanced setup issues. These include adding the client licenses, adding a new printer, and basic server testing, including a ping test.

The To Do List Lives!

After successfully logging on for the first time, the SBS To Do List shown in Figure 3-26 automatically appears.

Figure 3-26
To Do List is your starting point for the SBS experience.

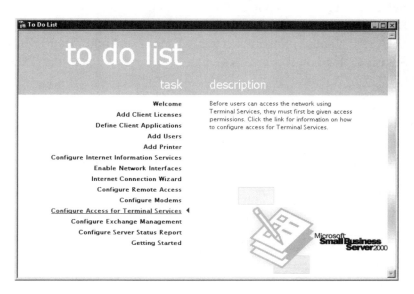

As mentioned earlier in this chapter, right now you will complete only a couple tasks on behalf of SSL. Why? Because it has been my experience that you should take baby steps with a new network and just get the darn thing up and running before you start introducing more advanced configurations. The tasks you will complete now include reviewing the SBS To Do List, adding the client licenses, and a connecting to the printer. Other tasks, such as adding new users, setting up computers, and Internet connectivity configurations, are completed on later.

BEST PRACTICE: I defined each To Do List item earlier in the chapter when I discussed major SBS setup phases (just before the step-by-step keystrokes commenced). This is in the SBS Installation Overview section.

Add Client Licenses

Selecting this option, **Add Client Licenses**, from the To Do List displays, a Help screen that instructs on how to add client access licenses (CALs).

The process for adding user licenses is very simple.

1. Put the license disk in floppy drive A.
2. Select **Server Status (BackOffice Home)** in the console pane of the **Small Business Server Administrator Console**.
3. Select the **About...** link in the Details pane. The **About Small Business Server** dialog box appears, as seen in Figure 3-27.

Notes:

Figure 3-27
Add Licenses link on the About Small Business Server dialog box.

4. Click **Add Licenses**.
5. Click the **Click Here to Start Setup** which will start the Microsoft Small Business Server Client Add Pack.
6. Follow the on-screen instructions where you will agree to the license and provide a Client Add Pack password. On a happy note, you do not need to reboot your SBS server machine as part of this process (you had to do this in the old SBS 4.5 days).

BEST PRACTICE: You need to perform the above activity for as many license disks as you have. Note the order in which you insert the license disks. The last license disk records the cumulative number of licenses you have installed. If you ever rebuilt SBS on your server machine, you'll only need to insert the last license disk to add client licenses. A very nice touch, I'll tell ya!

You might have to call Microsoft Product Support (PSS) if you've already used your license disk once before. The license disk makes an entry that it has been used previously by recording the network adapter card address (MAC address) on the disk. If you call PSS, they will give you a new code to unlock the license disk for another use. You might not encounter this problem at all, but just be advised.

To verify the CALs, look at the good old **About Small Business Server** dialog box (displayed by clicking **About...** on the **Server Status (BackOffice Home)** page in **Small Business Server Administrator Console**) and observe the number of licenses listed.

Add a New Printer

Adding a printer is very simple (like many tasks in SBS). Not only does SBS install a printer just like you may have done in Windows 2000, but it publishes the printer to Active Directory as an object. Once the printer becomes an Active Directory object, it is easily found by searching the Active Directory database. Granted, my last comment is more enterprise-centric, as finding a printer in a large company with thousands of printers may be a real challenge!

BEST PRACTICE: In fact, in SBS 2000, it's entirely likely that Windows 2000 has auto-detected your attached printer and installed the appropriate drivers for it. Windows 2000 has great device detection.

For SSL, assume that an HP Color LaserJet 5M is attached directly to the SBS computer via the LPT1 port (although in the section immediately following I discuss the use of a network-based printer using the HP JetDirect adapter):

1. From **To Do List**, select **Add Printer**. The **Add Printer Wizard** launches.
2. Click **Next** when the **Welcome to the Add Printer Wizard** screen appears in the **Add Printer Wizard**.
3. The **Local or Network Printer** screen appears. Select **Local printer** and click **Automatically detect and install my Plug and Play printer**. Click **Next**. Note that this is the suggested approach via the SSL methodology. I can appreciate that you might not have an interest in clicking the automatic detection of Plug and Play printers (perhaps your printer isn't Plug and Play).

Note if the printer was not automatically detected, you will be presented with a **New Printer Detection** screen that informs you Windows was unable to detect any Plug and Play printers. You will click **Next** to manually install the printer. You will then select the printer port (e.g., LPT1 under **Use the following port:** on the **Select the Printer Port** screen and click **Next**. The **Add Printer Wizard** screen appears, allowing you to select the printer manufacturer (e.g., **HP**) under **Manufacturers:** and the printer (**HP Color LaserJet 5M**) under **Printers**. Click **Next**.

4. Assuming the printer was detected and installed (at least in the case of an HP Color LaserJet 5M printer), provide a printer name in the **Printer name:** field on the **Name Your Printer** screen (you will note with interest that the suggested printer name is the same name as the printer, in this case with the SSL methodology, that is **HP Color LaserJet 5M**). Answer **Yes** or **No** to the **Do you want your Windows-based programs to use this printer as the default printer?** In the case of the SSL methodology, select **Yes**. Click **Next**.

BEST PRACTICE: You may need to provide a printer driver for your specific printer, but that tends to be the exception not the rule in SBS 2000 (a large number of printer drivers are stored on the hard disk of the machine running SBS).

5. On the **Printer Sharing** screen, select **Share as:** and type **HP5** in the field to the immediate right of this selection. Click **Next**.
6. On the **Location and Comment** screen, complete the **Location:** and **Comment:** fields if you want (these are optional). Click **Next**.
7. On the **Print Test Page** screen, you are asked if you want to print a test page. Answer **Yes** under **Do you want to print a test page?** and click **Next**.
8. Click **Finish** on the **Completing the Add Printer Wizard** screen.
9. You will receive a dialog box asking if the test page printed correctly. Click **OK** if the test page printed properly (click **Troubleshoot** if it didn't). I'm assuming you indeed followed the steps correctly and received a printout of the test page. You can perform the basic steps above for other brands of printers, such as Xerox, Lexmark, or any of the hundreds of printers supported by SBS 2000. I only selected the HP Color LaserJet 5M because it is the printer that I have available to me personally.

BEST PRACTICE: Let's assume for a moment that you don't have any printer available to you and you'd like to complete the steps above as much as is feasible. There is a work around for this that yours truly wrote into the Microsoft 2301a Implementing Microsoft Small Business Server 2000 one-day course. Here you can select **Generic** as the printer manufacturer and **Generic / Text Only** as the printer in Step 3 above. You can then delete the test page from the printer queue by opening the printer from **Start**, **Settings**, **Printers**, and highlighting the print job and pressing your **Delete** key.

You have now installed a printer in Small Business Server 2000. Next, I discuss an advanced SBS printer configuration using the an HP JetDirect card.

HP JetDirect Printers

Perhaps the most popular printer option on an SBS network is that of the network-installed printer. This is where the printer is cabled directly into the network. It plugs into a network wall jack just like a networked workstation. One of the most popular options for attaching network printers has been the HP JetDirect card.

To install an HP JetDirect networked printer on your SBS network, you must first install the JetAdmin application. You will need either the JetAdmin CD Disc that came with your HP printer or Jet Direct card or you will need to download the JetAdmin program from HP's Web site (*www.hp.com*). By installing the JetAdmin program, you install the HP JetDirect port need by Windows 2000 to interact with the JetDirect card. Bottom line? If you using an HP printer with a JetDirect card on your SBS network, you need the port discussed in this section to make a connection and make good things happen.

So, given that for the HP JetDirect port support to appear, you must first install the HP JetAdmin tool and follow these steps using the JetAdmin Disc provided by HP (alternately, you can download the JetAdmin application from the Web at www.hp.com).

1. Insert the HP JetAdmin Disc1 in your CD drive.
2. Launch the **jetsetup.exe** program from the **\Jetadmin\i386** directory on Disc 1. Note that, depending on the HP Jet Admin Disc version you have, it is possible the location of the jetsetup.exe file is different. Modify as necessary.

3. Click **Next** at the **HP JetAdmin Welcome** screen.
4. Select the JetAdmin components to install on the **Install Components** screen and click **Next**. The default is to install all JetAdmin components.
5. Accept or change the **HP JetAdmin Utilities** program folder name. Click **Next**.
6. Click **Next** at the **Start Copying Files** dialog box. The files will copy and JetAdmin will be installed. This process takes less than two minutes.
7. Answer **Yes** or **No** when asked to view the JetAdmin README file.
8. Click **Finish** in the **Setup Complete** dialog box.
9. Click **Yes** in the **Restart Windows** dialog box. You must restart Windows (SBS) for the HP JetDirect port to appear.

After rebooting, if you check the Printer Ports dialog box (**Start, Settings, Printers,** and select the **Properties** for a printer), you will see the HP JetDirect Port listed. You can now install a printer connected to the network via an HP JetDirect card.

Create an Emergency Repair Disk

This is one of the most important steps in the SBS setup routine, but there is no link to the task from either SBS Console. The Emergency Repair Disk (ERD) contains very important system information (user accounts, system settings, and configurations) that can recover your system in an emergency. You should update ERD periodically after significant changes have been made to your SBS network.

For the purposes of SSL, you create an ERD right now and again at the end of Chapter 4:

1. From the **Start** menu, select **Programs**, then **Accessories**, then **System Tools**.
2. Launch **Backup**.
3. Select **Emergency Repair Disk**.
4. Insert a blank 3.5-inch floppy disk into drive A: and select the **check box** that also backs up the Registry to the Repair folder on the SBS server machine (a nice touch).
5. Click **OK** as requested in the **Emergency Repair Diskette** dialog box.
6. Click **OK** and remove the floppy disk when you have been notified the emergency repair diskette was "saved" successfully.
7. Close **Backup**.

Final Configuration and Testing

You're almost finished, and the end of the day is near. You will add the UPS, check the event logs, and run an application before proceeding to the final section on advanced setup issues.

UPS

Attach the APC UPS device that was purchased for SSL. (Don't worry if you don't have this item at your site, but I highly recommend you purchase a UPS for your SBS network.) After the UPS is physically attached, via a serial cable from the back of the UPS to a COM port on the SBS machine, you then install PowerChute, a power management software application that ships with APC UPS devices.

When your site loses power, the UPS (via PowerChute) starts a gradual and safe shutdown of your SBS computer. This type of shutdown is critical for protecting important company data, such as accounting information, e-mail, and so on.

Event Log

I also enjoy checking the system and application event logs under Event Viewer to see how clean my SBS setup and installation was. This is where the rubber meets the road. You will also want to check the application event log to see how the SBS BackOffice applications are functioning.

To view the event logs:

1. Select the **Start** button at the lower left of your SBS monitor. Select **Small Business Server Administrator Console**.
2. Expand **Computer Management (Local)** in console pane.
3. Expand **System Tools**.
4. Expand **Event Viewer**. Select **System**. Your screen, displaying **System Log** information, should look similar to Figure 3-28.

Notes:

Figure 3-28

System log in Event Viewer.

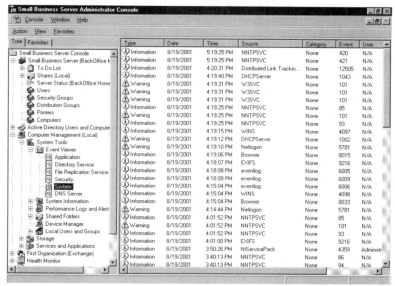

5. Click the Application log and the application log is displayed similar to that shown in Figure 3-29.

Figure 3-29

Application log in Event Viewer.

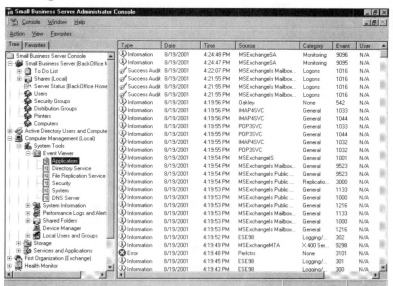

If you can't fully understand these logs, don't worry at this time. In general, you're only really worried about the red Stop signs. An experienced SBS consultant can interpret these logs for you.

> BEST PRACTICE: You will also be interested to know that in the system log, when an entry is made for Event Log (Event 6005), that represents a reboot or a restart of the SBS server machine. You can see this at the middle of Figure 3-28. Oftentimes an SBSer wants to know when the machine rebooted.

SBS Tests

You can now perform some basic tests to see whether your SBS server machine is functioning properly. You'll perform two such tests, but there are many. First, you'll test the networking capability of SBS with the simple ping test. You'll finish with an SBS application test.

Ping Test

The ping command allows you to quickly test the TCP/IP protocol (a communication) on your SBS network. When you *ping*, you establish that a low-level connection exists between two computers on a network. It is a very useful test for basic connectivity.

1. Click the **Start, Programs, Accessories, Command Prompt**.

> BEST PRACTICE: You may also launch a command prompt box by clicking **Start**, **Run** and typing **cmd.exe** in the **Open:** field in the **Run** dialog box.

2. At the command prompt (**c:>**), type **ping 192.168.16.2** (this command pings or "calls" the network adapter card with the 192.168.16.2 address located in your SBS server machine). If you used a different IP address for your network adapter card, be sure to substitute that IP address for this step.
3. You should see the successful reply activity shown in Figure 3-30. If you do not receive such results, you need to engage in basic network troubleshooting methodology for which there are many references on the Web, visit Microsoft TechNet (www.microsoft.com/technet), or rely on your

own troubleshooting knowledge and other SBSers. Basically you will want to double-check the physical network connection (see the green light test earlier in this chapter) and work from there.

Figure 3-30

A successful ping test.

Application Test

Now you want to know whether one of the SBS applications runs correctly. In this case, you are going to run the Exchange 2000 Server System Manager:

1. Click the **Start** button.
2. Select **Programs, Microsoft Exchange, System Manager**.
3. The **System Manager** application launches as seen in Figure 3-31.

Notes:

Figure 3-31

Exchange System Manager.

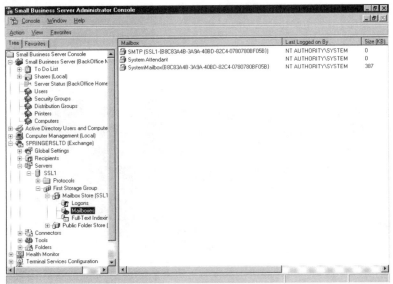

Advanced SBS Setup Issues

After you've installed SBS several of times, you'll likely recognize many of the following advanced SBS setup issues. It's also likely you'll see a thing or two not mentioned here. If so, be sure to share your wisdom with some of the SBS newsgroups and mailing lists listed in Appendix A, "SBS Resources." Let's face it. SBS is an evolving culture (oh, and an evolving product too), so you'll some day, some way, have something to share with the SBS community.

OEM Setup Scenario

As mentioned in Chapter 2, there are different SBS purchase and installation scenarios. One of these options was the preinstallation or OEM installation option. There, a hardware manufacturer partially installs SBS on your computer, saving you some installation time (less than one hour). For the record, the OEM installation option essentially takes the process through "Phase A: Windows 2000 Server Character-Based Setup" and starts with "Phase B: Windows 2000 Server GUI-Based Setup."

One Source for Source Media

Two topics, not part of the detailed SSL methodology, are nonetheless of interest to the SBSer. First, you can copy all four SBS 2000 CD Discs to a partition on your server (e.g., Drive D) and perform the installation from this location. Why would you do this? Because this prevents you from having to swap the Discs during the later steps of the SBS setup process. And just how did I learn this, you ask? Let's just say necessity is the mother of invention. While assisting Microsoft in the design of its Microsoft Official Curriculum (MOC) 2301a Implementing Small Business Server 2000 course, the test engineers and I concluded that we wanted the SBS 2000 source installation files to be located on a second partition. Why? Because this prevented delays in the class when students forgot to swap Discs (e.g., students take a coffee break and the machine simply waits for the next Disc). Also, hard disk input/output (I/O) is significantly faster than CD Disc I/O, resulting in a faster, in-class SBS 2000 installation experience. (This is important when you're trying to teach SBS 2000 in a one-day course, let me tell you!)

Second, if your server is a late-model cream puff, to borrow terms from the automotive industry, you might be able to use the DVD media that ships with SBS 2000. This single DVD Disc contains all of the SBS source installation media at a single source. Unfortunately, most of my small-business clients don't drive such cream puffs, but you get the point here: A late model server machine may well have a DVD device installed, saving setup time.

Terminal Services in Application Sharing Mode

Against the advice of me and Microsoft, you can technically place the Terminal Services component in application sharing mode on an SBS 2000 server machine. In Chapter 8, I go into great detail as to why this isn't preferable and you should adhere to the default remote administration mode for Terminal Services. And you can bet your boots that I didn't make this part of the SSL methodology, this rogue application sharing mode approach for Terminal Services!

> BEST PRACTICE: You are advised to consult the following KBase article: **Q282009** on Microsoft TechNet at www.microsoft.com/technet for all the reasons why you shouldn't place Terminal Services in application sharing mode.

But truth be told, if you want to place the Terminal Services component in Application Sharing mode, perform the following. You would minimize the SBS Setup Wizard after Step #34 above (just after the Scenario Baseline completes) and complete these steps:

1. Assuming you are logged on to the SBS 2000 server machine, click **Start, Settings, Control Panel**.
2. Launch the **Add/Remove Programs** applet.
3. Click **Add/Remove Windows Components**. In five seconds (approximately), the **Windows Components Wizard** will appear.
4. Click **Next**.
5. The **Terminal Services Setup** screen appears. Note the default selection is Remote administration mode. Here you would select **Application server mode** and click **Next**.
6. After the **Configuring Components** screen is completed (which will keep you informed of the installation progress), click **Finish** when the **Completing the Windows Components Wizard** appears.

The significance of switching Terminal Services to Application Sharing Mode at this exact point is simply this: None of the BackOffice applications have been installed yet. Prior to having the BackOffice applications contained in SBS 2000 installed, you need to make the election as to whether the server machine should run in Remote Administration Mode or Application Sharing Mode (I and others voting for the former). If you, at a future date, switch the SBS server machine from Remote Administration Mode to Application Sharing Mode, several applications, including Exchange 2000 Server, won't function properly! Why? Because in plain Texas talk, you've been messing around at the Executive level again (a low level in the operating system).

In Chapter 8, not only do I discuss this matter more, but you will also find my recommendation for setting up Terminal Services on another Windows 2000 Server machine that is a non-DC.

The Exchange Server 2000 Pre-Prep Maneuver

Another hidden hook in the SBS 2000 setup process is to save time in the later steps by "pre-preparing" Active Directory for Exchange 2000 Server. You may recall that one of the longest phases in the later part of the SBS 2000 setup process was the amount of time Exchange 2000 Server took to modify the Active Directory schema. This time can be minimized (but not completely eliminated) by running a command after the Scenario Baseline completes (just after Step #34). Here are the steps to run this command that modifies the Active Directory schema for Exchange Server 2000 before the SBS Setup Wizard proceeds to install the BackOffice applications.

1. Place SBS Setup Disc #3 in the CD drive on the SBS server machine.
2. Assuming you are logged on as the Administrator, click **Start, Run, Browse**.
3. Navigate to the following location: **\exchsrvr60\setup\i386\setup.exe**. Click **Open** to close the **Browse** dialog box.
4. In the **Open** field of the **Run** dialog box, append the command with / **Forest Prep**, so the total command would appear as **\exchsrvr60\setup\i386\setup.exe /Forest Prep**.
5. Click **OK** and the command will execute. The Active Directory schema will be prepared for Exchange 2000 Server.

So the big question is, why would you do this? Simply stated, you would do this if you wanted to save time during the last part of the SBS setup process. I've done this so that when I demonstrate the SBS setup process to clients and students, we don't have to spend up to (or more than) 30 minutes watching Exchange 2000 Server prepare the Active Directory Schema. Let me tell you, when you are in front of a crowd, those minutes seem like hours!

Unsupported Devices

Every SBS installation has a right way and a wrong way to do it. There is the easy way and the hard way. There is the "follow the rules way" and the "break the rules" way. Surprisingly, you're likely to try, suffer, cheer, celebrate, and curse all approaches during your tenure as an SBS guru. So far, I've demonstrated only the SSL methodology for installing SBS (which I believe to be a "best practices" methodology for installing SBS). Now, and I'm addressing the most advanced guru SBSers amongst us, let's break the rules and understand why you would do so.

Without question, one of the greatest SBS installation challenges today is that of managing your library of current drivers from third-party vendors. By that I mean, when you install and maintain SBS, you have the latest drivers from the vendors of the components attached to your system. This is extremely important because operating systems are built and released at a certain point in time. Although the periodic release of service packs allows the operating system to refresh its library of drivers, in no way can an operating system hope to ship with the latest and most current drivers from all of the third-party vendors. It's a common and daunting challenge that confronts system engineers everywhere.

What's the bottom line? If you have unusual or new drivers, you need to specify **F6** when installing SBS in the early character-based setup screen (immediately after the character-based setup process commences, which would be while disk 1 is still in the floppy drive if you selected to set up SBS with the four disks instead of booting directly from the CD Disc) when you are asked to specify additional controller and adapter cards. And when you communicate that you want to specify drivers, you often have to specify the drivers for existing controller and adapter cards, because the setup's auto-detection has not been stopped. That is, once you press **F6**, you'll likely have to specify all controller and adapter cards, not just the unsupported one you were trying to add.

> BEST PRACTICE: So of course there must be a Texas tale to accompany this section, and here it is. There I was on a sweaty summer Saturday afternoon installing SBS 2000 at an accounting firm called "CFO2Go" in Bothell, Washington. For some strange reason, the SBS installation kept "hanging" or stopping during the Scenario Baseline stage, right when the networking components were being installed. It was all very strange and I tried the setup a couple of times. No luck. I even tried installing the DNS, DHCP and WINS services manually thinking something was hung up there. Heck, I even tried manually installing Terminal Services in Remote Administration Mode. Lo-and-behold, it turns out the SCSI card was an older Adaptec brand card that had been mis-identified by the underling Windows 2000 Server operating system during setup. Once I download the correct and supported Adaptec driver for Windows 2000, it worked just fine and I was able to sail right past the Scenario Baseline setup stage in SBS 2000.

Upgrading to SBS

Earlier in this chapter I pointed out one instance in the setup process where you will need to provide proof of ownership if you are upgrading from SBS 4.5 to SBS 2000. This and other upgrade issues are discussed in Appendix B: Upgrading to SBS 2000.

> BEST PRACTICE: In Appendix B, I sneak in some discussion on how to upgrade to SBS 2000 from Windows 2000. Why? Because many small businesses purchased and installed Windows 2000 Server when it was released in February of 2000. You'll note that SBS 2000 wasn't released until 12 months later, creating a one-year timing mismatch between the operating system release and the SBS 2000. Needless to say, many of these small businesses now want to "upgrade" to SBS 2000 without losing all of their installed applications, data, and so on.

But you should also know at this point you cannot downgrade (Which is sorta like upgrading). If you have Big BackOffice 2000, there is no path for you to downgrade to SBS 2000 and retain your Registry settings, Active Directory database settings, etc. Can't you just imagine it? A dot-com grows from five to 500 employees overnight and upgrades from SBS 2000 to Big BackOffice 2000. So far this makes sense. But if the same dot-com laid off almost all of its staff in an attempt to become profitable, there is not a path for it to downgrade back to SBS 2000. This dot-com would be stuck with Big BackOffice 2000, which isn't the worst problem facing it in my little case study.

To go from Big BackOffice 2000 back to SBS 2000 on a single server machine, you would need to reformat the server machine and install SBS 2000 from scratch.

SBS supports upgrades from existing Windows 2000 Server machines and it is the scenario baseline activity in step 34 earlier in the chapter that facilitates this process.

> BEST PRACTICE: I can't resist telling you now and repeating myself later: I only perform "freshies" with SBS 2000. That is, I'm not performing in-place upgrades from SBS 4.5 to SBS 2000. Rather, I make data backups, FDISK the SBS 4.5 machine, and install SBS 2000 "fresh." Like downhill skiing on a new powder day, I prefer "freshies."

Troubleshooting Setup Errors

In your career as an SBS professional, you will possibly have occasion to troubleshoot setup errors. These errors come out of left field, but the Readme document contained on Small Business Server 2000 Setup Disc 1 discusses a surprisingly large number of setup errors and the suggested resolution steps. Hats off to the SBS development team for shipping this timely resource in time!

You may also want to consult the SBS resources listed in Appendix A: SBS Resources to stay current with SBS 2000 setup issues. Heck, don't hesitate to throw in your own two cents in the discussion group and news list (listserv) mentioned.

And consider simply re-running the SBS setup again as I discussed earlier with Figure 3-24.

Summary

As you reach the end of the SBS server machine setup and installation discussion, remember to go forward keeping a healthy perspective. Often I witness SBS professionals spending hours troubleshooting some setup- or installation-related problem. In many cases, that is not a good use of time. Remember that it often takes less than three hours to do a complete SBS server machine reinstall. Believe me, I've done plenty of fresh SBS installs and come out hours ahead. Just a thought!

Chapter 4
Client Computer Setup

Congratulations to you, good friends! You're well on your way to a completed, functional, and optimally performing SBS 2000 network. But one major set of tasks remains: setting up the workstations. This task area shouldn't be marginalized. Whereas you possibly performed the SBS 2000 server machine setup out of sight (and hearing range) from your end users, you don't have that same luxury with the workstation setup phase you are about to undertake. Your role will be very public, and so will the users' feedback. So, slow down, pardner, and take the extra time needed to get it right.

> BEST PRACTICE: Let me take a moment to reiterate a key point to our time together in the SBS tome. As you work through this and other chapters, understand that the book is based on the SSL methodology (the sample SBS client based on Bainbridge Island, Washington).
>
> The idea is that you spend the time upfront with this book creating a successful SBS network for a sample company following every keystroke in every chapter. It is paramount you try to follow through with each example and task. At the end of the book, you're a bona fide SBSer as far as I'm concerned. I also understand that your real world SBS experience will be slightly different from mine with my beloved dogs. You'll work on different equipment under different conditions. In fact, Microsoft reports that the majority of SBS sales are international, so you're likely setting up SBS in a different country than I or my Springer Spaniels live in. (And, by golly, perhaps your country favors different breeds of dogs – cool!)
>
> More important, where possible I try to compare and contrast different SBS features and functions, but sometimes I'll bypass some esoteric alternative path to accomplish a task in the spirit of maintaining

the purity of my SSL methodology. All I can say is that some excellent advanced resources that explore every conceivable SBS feature and function, starting with the online help system, exist for your academic researching pleasure. Thanks in advanced for your understanding. Long live SSL!

Workstation Installation Plan

The following half-dozen tasks are necessary to be completed prior to performing the SBS hands-on workstation configuration tasks, such as adding users and setting up the workstations. These tasks include the following:

1. Setting up a staging area

2. Building the new workstations

3. Completing the installation of the workstation operating system

4. Testing the workstation's network connectivity

5. Procuring floppy disks to use as the client setup disk

6. Completing the workstation installation worksheet

First

Be sure to find a place to set up the workstations if you purchase new workstations for your SBS network. This workstation staging area is typically a conference room. If you are converting from an existing network, or the users already have their workstations in place, you probably won't need a workstation setup area.

> BEST PRACTICE: If you indeed use a workstation staging area, it is very helpful to have a network hub (connected to the SBS network) in the center of your work area. That way, as you build each workstation, you can complete the workstation setup tasks in a good ol' blue-collar assembly line-like fashion. It's very efficient.

Second

If you have new workstations, physically build the workstation by unpacking all the components from the shipping boxes (monitor, computer, and keyboard). Be sure to reseat each adapter card inside the new workstation in case it came loose during shipping. After connecting all the workstation components, turn on the power and verify that the workstation is functional. I recommend that you check the workstation BIOS settings similar to how the server BIOS was observed in Chapter 3. (You typically press the Delete key during the power-on phase to see the BIOS settings.)

> BEST PRACTICE: Be sure to confirm that the workstations you speci-
> fied and ordered while you read Chapter 2 are the same as the work-
> stations now in your possession. And does each workstation have a
> network adapter card as specified and ordered?

Whether the workstation is new or not, take a moment to confirm that your workstation meets the minimum system requirements specified by Microsoft for participating on an SBS network (see Chapter 2 for discussion on this). In particular, make sure that you have enough hard disk space to accommodate the SBS client applications you intend to install in a few moments. The most popular SBS workstation setup error I've witnessed is a shortage of hard disk space on the client workstation. Unfortunately, you aren't always advised of such space shortage problems until well into the SBS client workstation setup process. The workstation space requirements in SBS have grown to over 300 MB if you install each client component.

Third

New workstations typically have no operating system completely installed. Depending on the workstation manufacturer, the workstation might have a partial installation of Windows XP, ME, or 98. Such is the case when you purchase from name-brand manufacturers such as Gateway, Dell, Compaq, and the like. With true clone workstations (sometimes called "white boxes"), such as the PC that your Uncle Chas built, it might or might not have any operating system (here it varies on a case-by-case basis). Regardless, it is essential that each workstation have a functional operating system such as Windows XP, ME, or 98. Now is the time to make sure that each of your workstations indeed has an operating system installed. In fact, the SBS client applications and networking functionality cannot be fully installed on a workstation until a supported workstation operating system is installed. Recall from Chapter 2 that SSL has a mixture of five popular operating systems: Windows 2000, Windows ME, Windows 98, Windows 95, and Windows NT Workstation 4.0.

BEST PRACTICE: SBS fully supports the following six workstation operating systems:

•Windows XP

•Windows 2000 Professional

•Windows ME

•Windows 98

•Windows 95

•Windows NT Workstation 4.0 with Service Pack #3

Full support includes use of the modem sharing client, fax client, and Firewall client (related to the ISA Server 2000 firewall protection).

SBS has limited (and I mean limited) support for other popular workstation operating systems:

•Microsoft Windows for Workgroups

•Windows NT Workstation version 3.x

•Windows 3.*x*

•MS-DOS

•Linux clients

•UNIX clients

•Macintosh

Operating systems that are not supported by SBS in any way, shape, or form include OS/2, CP/M, Apple DOS, and Apple ProDOS. If you have such a workstation, do yourself a favor and strongly consider purchasing an Intel-based workstation running one of the supported operating systems so that you can participate on the SBS network.

Fourth

Perform a workstation-level green light test: Plug a network cable (that is, CAT5 10BASE-T cable) into the workstation's Ethernet network adapter card jack.

Make sure the other end of the network cable is connected to an active hub connection (for example, the hub in your workstation staging area). Much like the testing you performed on the server in Chapter 3, make sure that both the hub and workstation network adapter card jack have a green or active light.

If you use existing workstations on an existing network, you can also perform this test with little effort. Simply turn on the existing workstation and see whether the network adapter card jack is green or active. Then trot over to the network hub and confirm the same.

Fifth

Be sure to procure at least a single floppy disk to create a networking setup diskette (a.k.a. magic disk). New in SBS 2000 is that you can use one magic disk for the entire network. That is, one diskette will accommodate all workstations you intend to add to the SBS network. The magic disk is discussed more in a moment.

Sixth

Be sure to revisit the SBS network user and machine information created in Chapter 2 (see the "User List" section following Table 2-2) and complete the Workstation Installation Worksheet for each user. The Workstation Installation Worksheet has been completed for Norm Hasborn, SSL president (see Table 4-1). The entries for the remaining employees are provided in Appendix C: "SSL Information."

> BEST PRACTICE: Remember that it is far better with SBS to populate each field, even with N/A (Not Applicable or Not Available). That way, you know at a later date that you didn't overlook any user and computer setup configuration field. Also, SBS uses user and computer setup configuration information in other areas of the SBS network, making it important to complete each and every user and computer setup configuration field.

Table 4-1 SBS Workstation Setup Sheet

Setup Field	Input/Value/ Description	Where Used
User's Full Name (First, Last)	*Norm Hasborn*	Add User Wizard
Logon Name	*NormH*	Add User Wizard
Phone	*206-123-1234*	Add User Wizard
Office	*Main*	Add User Wizard
Password	*Purple3300*	Add User Wizard
E-mail alias	*NormH (default)*	Add User Wizard
Exchange Server	*SSL1 (default)*	Add User Wizard
Exchange store	*Mailbox Store (SSL1) (default)*	Add User Wizard
Description for User	*Founder and President*	Add User Wizard
Allowed to change password (Y/N)?	*No*	Add User Wizard
SBS User Template	*Power User*	Add User Wizard
Workstation NetBIOS	*PRESIDENT*	Set Up Computer Wizard
SBS Programs to Install:	*Complete:* *Internet Explorer (IE),* *Microsoft Shared* *Modem Service Client,* *Microsoft Shared Fax* *Client,* *Firewall Client,* *Outlook 2000 SR1*	Set Up Computer Wizard
Operating System:	*Windows 2000 Professional*	Set Up Computer Wizard
Verify available workstation hard disk space based on SBS Programs to install listed immediately above (for example, 300 MB required)	*Yes*	Misc.
Turn off programs at workstation such as anti-virus programs.	*Yes/No?*	Misc.

Setup Field	Input/Value/ Description	Where Used
SBS server-based Shared Folders this user will access.	*NORMH, USERS, COMPANY, ACCOUNTING, OLD, APPLICATIONS*	Misc.
Printers	*HP5MCOLOR*	Misc.
Network Protocols	*TCP/IP*	Misc.
IP Address (Static or Dynamic)	*Dynamic*	Misc.
Mapped Drives	*S: \NORMH* *T: \USERS* *U: \COMPANY* *V: \ACCOUNTING* *W: \OLD* *X: \APPLICATIONS*	Misc.
Workstation Shares (shares on workstation)	*N/A*	Misc.
Additional Applications to install (for example, Great Plains Dynamics accounting):	*Great Plains Dynamics client FRX Report Writer*	Misc.
Special configuration issues	*Triple-check security. This is the president's PC.*	Misc.
Comments	*Complete this one last after all other workstations.*	Misc.
Tested Logon (Y/N)	*No*	Misc.
Repairs/Reconfiguration Needed		Misc.

BEST PRACTICE: Remember that the workstation name is typically based on job title or function. Thus, the workstation names associated with the users at SSL are closely related to the user's job title. This naming convention is helpful when you have staff turnover but the jobs remain the same.

Another useful practice, although not used with SSL, is to name machines after something neutral, such as fruits. A former client, Larry P, did this because he observed that while people change jobs, machines don't. Or sometimes you have people leave and the job is restructured with a new title. You get the point. Hey, if I'm going to have a machine named after a fruit, I want the machine named KUMQUAT01!

BEST PRACTICE: Access to the Internet is allowed by default.

BEST PRACTICE: You generally want to avoid giving any user account administrator privileges. Even the SBS project manager for SSL, Bob Easter, will only have power user rights assigned to his user name. When any administrative functions need to be performed on the SBS network, the best practice is to log on as the Administrator to perform that action. And don't forget to log off and log on again as a user after performing your required administrative-level duties.

SBS Workstation Setup Process

The SBS workstation setup approach is a four-step process, and compared to the SBS server machine installation, it is relatively simple. Another interesting point is that, whereas you perform the SBS server machine setup only once, you perform the SBS workstation setup several times, once for each workstation. I've found that such repetition breeds familiarity; your comfort level increases with this process.

Of the four steps, the first two (running the Add User Wizard and running the Set Up Computer Wizard) are performed on the SBS server machine via the To Do List (part of the SBS Administrator Console). The last two steps are performed on the SBS workstation. Run the Setup program on the magic disk and install the client applications. This process is shown in Figure 4-1.

A quick SBS 2000-specific comment for you: If you have worked with SBS in the past, say SBS 4.5, you will be very pleased to see that SBS 2000 has greatly simplified the add user and computer processes. This was accomplished in part by using user account templates, discussed in a moment.

Figure 4-1
SBS Workstation setup process.

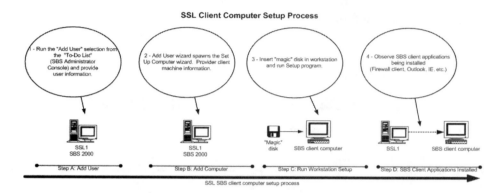

BEST PRACTICE: As promised in Chapter 3, you now revisit the To Do List in the next several steps. Recall that in Chapter 3, you completed a few of the To Do List items and promised to complete the Add New User and Set Up Computer Wizard items in Chapter 4. That time has now arrived!

Server-Side Setup Stuff

To get going, you would first add user NormH (refer to Table 4-1) to the SPRINGERSLTD SBS network. This task of adding a user has two stages. First, you add unique user information, such as Norm's name. Second, either via one of the default user templates or step by step, you add the common information, such as allowing Internet access (which is allowed by default). So, as you can see, the first part of the Add User Wizard is custom information; the second part is common information.

1. Make sure you are logged on to the SBS server machine as an administrator. In the case of SSL, the correct username is **Administrator**, and the correct password is **husky9999** (note the lowercase form).
2. Launch the **Small Business Server Administrator Console** by clicking the **Start** button on the lower left corner of your display monitor.

3. Launch the **To Do List** found in the left pane beneath **Small Business Server (BackOffice Manager)**.
4. Select **Add Users**. The Add User Wizard launches. Click **Next** after reading the basic welcome information on the **Welcome to the Add User Wizard** screen.
5. Complete the **User Account Information** screen, as shown in Figure 4-2, based on the information for NormH contained in Table 4-1. Click **Next**.

Figure 4-2
User Account Information.

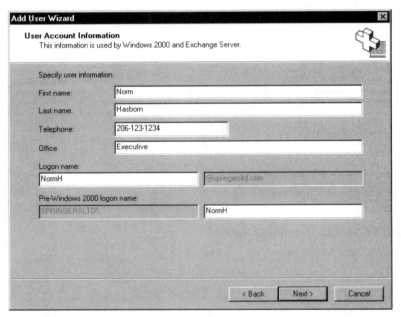

6. On the **Password Generation** screen, select **I will specify the user's password** (see Figure 4-3). Type the password for NormH (taken from Table 4-1, this password is **Purple3300**). NormH is not allowed to change his password, so select **Cannot change password**. Click **Next**.

Notes:

Figure 4-3

Create a Password for NormH.

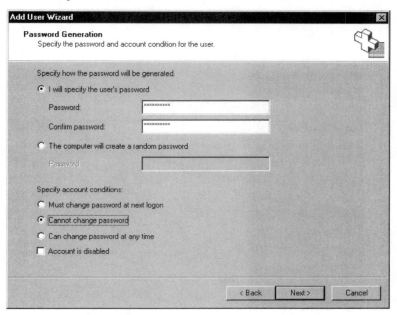

7. On the **Mailbox Information** screen, accept the default information shown in Figure 4-4. Click **Next**.

Notes:

Figure 4-4

Mailbox Information for NormH.

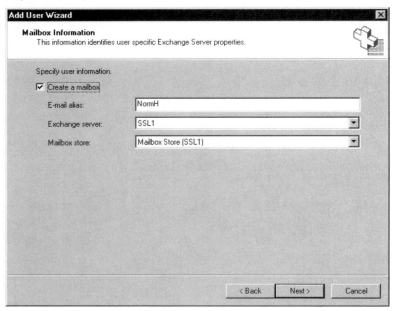

8. On the **User Properties** screen, select **Small Business Power User**, as seen in Figure 4-5. Click **Next**.

Notes:

Figure 4-5

Selecting the Small Business Power User template for NormH.

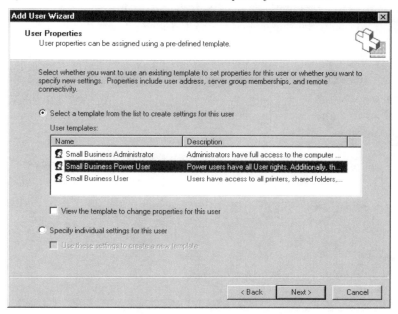

There are three user templates to select from in SBS. This allows you to select an account that has been configured with common information (such as allowing access to the printer and fax device) and avoid completing numerous screens. There are three user templates in SBS:

- **Small-Business Administrator.** These are gods. Administrators have full access to the computer and domain. Enough said.

- **Small-Business Power User.** These are junior gods. Not only do power users have all regular user rights, such as accessing the Internet, but they can manage users, groups, printers, shared fax devices, and so on.

- **Small-Business User.** These are just normal people showing up on time each day and doing their jobs. Seriously, users have access to all printers, shared folders, and fax devices. By default, they also have Internet access. To be honest, most of the accounts you add to SBS will be users.

You may look at the specific properties for each of these user templates to answer any questions you have. Such questions are often focused on exactly about what settings are being invoked by selecting one template as compared to another template. Simply select **View the template to change properties for this user** checkbox on the **User Properties** screen. You should do this while adding at least one of your users, so you better understand the background process that is occurring.

Interestingly, you can create your own user templates for use in SBS. This would make sense where you want to model a particular group of users around an application or function. For example, you might want to give users in the book-keeping department access to the shared folder containing the accounting data. You get the point.

9. Select whether to set up the computer now or later on the **Run the Set Up Computer Wizard** page. In the case of NormH and SSL, you would pick the **Set up computer now** radio button (see Figure 4-6) and click **Next**.

Figure 4-6
Elect to set up the computer now foNormH.

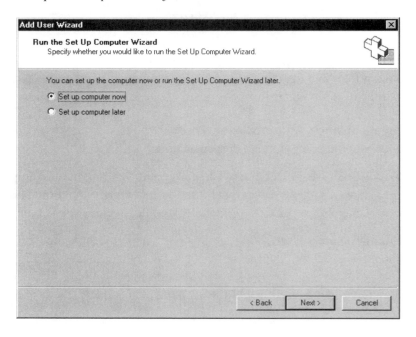

BEST PRACTICE: The Set Up Computer Wizard, affectionately known as the SCW, is chained to the Add User process you are currently completing. If, in the future, you want to add only a computer (but not a user), you need to run the SCW from the **Set Up Client Computer** button on the **Tips - Setting Up Client Computers** page on the SBS Administrator Console (assuming you are logged on as the Administrator, click **Start**, **Small Business Server Administrator Console**, **Favorites** tab, **Small Business Server Tips**, **Set Up Client Computers** link, and click the **Set Up Client Computer** button).

10. Provide a computer name on the **Computer Name** screen. In the case of NormH, the computer name is **PRESIDENT**, as seen in Figure 4-7. Click **Next**.

Figure 4-7

Machine Name Information for NormH.

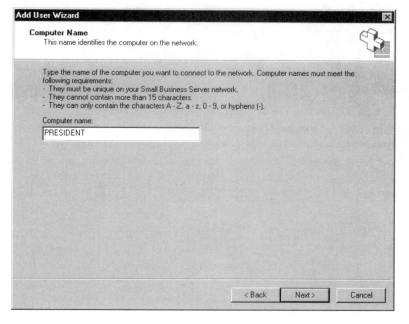

11. Select the SBS client-side applications to install on the **Applications** screen (Figure 4-8). In the case of NormH, select all applications by clicking **Install the selected applications** and you'll find that the checkbox next to each application has been checked under **Applications**. Click **Next**.

Figure 4-8

Installed Application List selection.

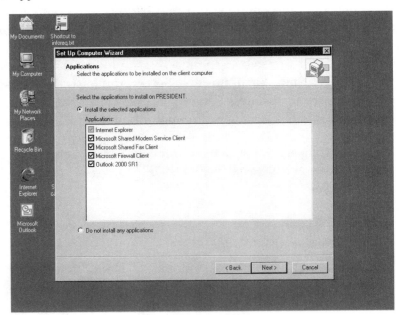

12. Elect whether to create a network setup disk or not on the **Networking Setup Disk** screen as seen in Figure 4-9. In the case of NormH, select the **Create a networking setup disk** and place a diskette in Drive A. Click **Next**. The networking setup files are copied to the diskette.

Notes:

Figure 4-9

Creating a Networking Setup Diskette for NormH.

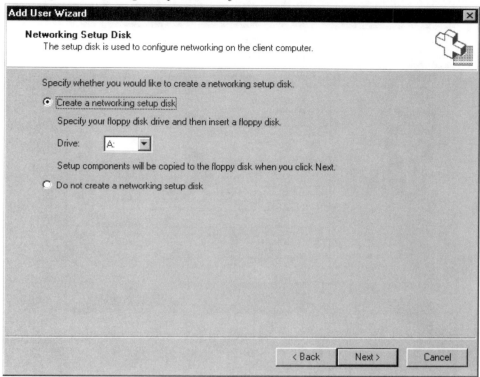

BEST PRACTICE: Another timesaver is to elect not to create a networking setup disk until you create the last user in your organization during your SBS setup project. By doing this, you avoid the couple of minutes of disk input/output (I/O) needed to write the user and computer setup information to the magic disk. When you create the last user, and you elect to create the magic disk, all of the prior user and client computer information is written to the magic disk at that time. A true timesaver.

13. Click **Finish** as seen on the **Completing Add User Wizard** screen (Figure 4-10) to complete the creation of the NormH account and the PRESIDENT client computer.

Figure 4-10

User NormH and PRESIDENT client computer successfully created.

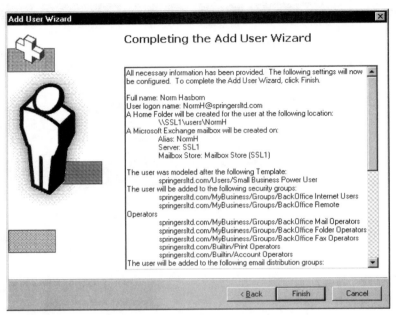

BEST PRACTICE: When the **Completing the Add User Wizard** screen appears, consider this tip for building your SBS network notebook: Copy the summary text by dragging your mouse (mouse button depressed to highlight) across the information presented in the text box (user name, group membership, etc.). Once this text is highlighted, perform **Ctrl-C**. Launch **WordPad** (**Start, Programs, Accessories, WordPad**). In WordPad, select **Edit, Paste** to paste this user information into the document. Save the document as "**SBS Network Notebook.doc**" in the My Documents Folder (**File, Save**, type file name, click **Save**). Do this for each user you add and you will nearly automatically create your much appreciated network notebook!

You can also perform this cut-and-paste trick to WordPad anytime you see a Completing screen in SBS 2000 (such as the Internet Connection Wizard). By performing this action, you'll generate an amazingly detailed network notebook with ease!

That's it! You've witnessed the setup of the first user and client computer on the SSL network. Trust me that you'll do this plenty more times in your career as an SBSer.

> BEST PRACTICE: After your network is up and running, this add-client computer step is often handled differently to account for new hires in your organization. Basically, you'll run the **Add User Wizard** to add a new user, then manually add the user to the local machine's Administrators group (for Windows 2000 Professional) and configure Outlook 2000 for the user, assuming the new hire will occupy a seat that's still warm from the last employee. I discuss this scenario later in the chapter.
>
> You might be interested to know you can customize the Set Up Computer Wizard to install programs outside of SBS. This is discussed in Chapter 5.

You have now completed the server side of the SBS client computer setup process. Now on to the client computer itself.

Client Computer-side Setup Stuff

You will now go to the workstation that you want to add to the SBS network and turn it on. After successfully booting into the workstation operating system (for example, Windows 2000 Professional), you start the SBS workstation setup tasks. The setup program installs and configures the workstation-side network components (networking protocol, networking client, domain name, and machine name), sets up the specified user (NormH), and reboots the client computer. You then log on to the client computer, and the desktop shortcuts to the shared network folders are created. You then go back to work for the boss.

> BEST PRACTICE: The following setup of the PRESIDENT machine for NormH reflects a Windows 2000 Professional machine. Other Windows operating systems setup using the SBS magic disk will have setup screens with a slightly different appearance. This is normal.

1. Insert the SBS workstation setup disk (magic disk) into the floppy drive of your computer. Run the **Setup** command from the disk. This is typically a:\setup.exe and can be executed from the **Run** dialog box of Windows 2000 Professional, Windows ME, Windows 9x, or Windows

NT Workstation 4.0. The **Run** command is accessed via the **Start** button from your desktop. In the **Open:** field, type **a:\setup**.

2. The **Microsoft Client Network Setup Wizard** launches and the **Welcome to the Small Business Server Client Network Setup Wizard** screen appears (see Figure 4-11). Click **Next**.

Figure 4-11
Welcome screen for Microsoft Client Network Setup Wizard.

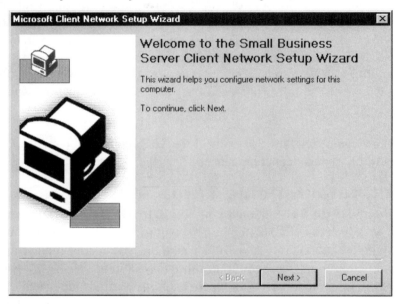

3. Select the computer name **PRESIDENT** on the **Computer Name** screen, shown in Figure 4-12. Click **Next**.

Notes:

Figure 4-12

Selecting a machine.

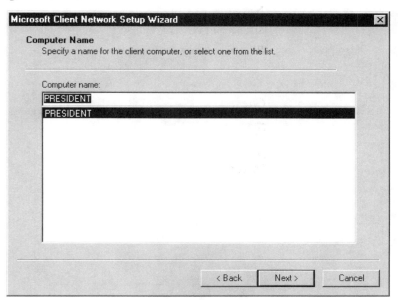

BEST PRACTICE: One of the most dramatic changes between SBS 2000 and SBS 4.5 relates to the magic disk used to setup workstations. The Computer Name screen allows you to select which computer you are setting up. This translates into something I've previously mentioned in passing—that is, you only need one magic disk to setup an entire SBS network of client computers. Wow!

4. On the **Assign Users** screen, select the user or users you want to associate with this client computer. **NormH** is selected by default under **Assigned users:** as shown in Figure 4-13. Click **Next**.

Notes:

Figure 4-13

Assign a single user or multiple users to the client computer.

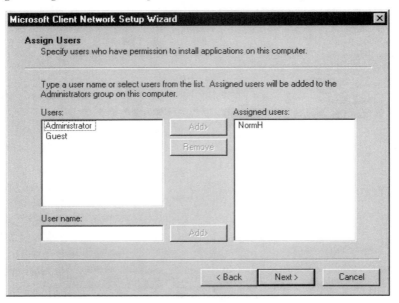

BEST PRACTICE: Let me repeat something I presented much too quickly in the last step. The magic disk also allows you, as part of its setup process, to assign multiple users to a client computer. This process really takes the assigned users and groups and makes them a member of the local Administrators group on Windows 2000 Professional client machines (but it does not configure Outlook 2000 profiles for each of these users, something I discuss later in the chapter). This is a badly needed real world improvement over SBS 4.5 (when you had to perform a workstation setup each time you wanted to add an additional user to a client computer). This is a major timesaver, let me tell you.

5. Provide the administrator account name and password on the **Network Authentication** screen, as seen in Figure 4-14. In the case of SSL, the account name **administrator** is entered in **Name:** and the password is **husky9999** entered in **Password:** (assuming you've completed the tasks in this book). Note the account name is not case sensitive and the password is case sensitive. Click **Next**.

Figure 4-14

The administrator logon credentials are necessary for the client computer to join the SBS domain during the client computer setup.

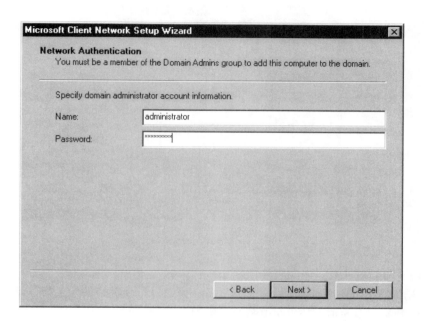

6. Click **Finish** on the **Complete the Small Business Server Client Networking Setup Wizard** screen. You will receive a message in the **Windows 2000 Networking Wizard** dialog box (see Figure 4-15). After reading the message, click **Begin**. The **Windows Client Setup Status** dialog box will inform you of the Windows 2000 networking setup status (installing, configuring, finishing).

Notes:

Figure 4-15

After reading the client computer setup message regarding user, machine, and domain name, click Begin to proceed.

BEST PRACTICE: The client setup program assumes that you have your Windows 2000, Windows ME, Windows 9x, or Windows NT Workstation 4.0 source files (a.k.a. CAB files) on your workstation's hard disk. The client setup program needs access to these source files in order to install the networking components. If these source files are not located on your workstation's hard disk, you are prompted for the location of these files (typically, you insert the CD-ROM for your workstation operating system). If necessary, direct the client setup program to your source files and continue.

7. After the networking is setup, the **System Settings Change** dialog box appears asking if you want to restart your computer. Click **Yes**.

BEST PRACTICE: Be sure you remove the SBS magic disk from the floppy drive of the workstation you're working on before you reboot. If you fail to do this, the workstation will report a missing command file or operating system, because the floppy disk, when left inadvertently in Drive A:, isn't bootable.

Finally, you get something of a well-deserved rest after lots of SBS network setup activities. Here, the applications you specified above to be installed on the client computer are automatically installed. So kick back and enjoy. At the end of the SBS client application installation process, which starts with the steps below, you need to reboot your workstation (if Windows 9x or NT) and log on to the SBS network as the user you are setting up. A Windows 2000 Professional workstation will not require a reboot (but it's not a bad idea to reboot anyway to get a clean start).

1. Press **CTRL-ALT-DEL** and when prompted via the **Log On to Windows** dialog box, log on as **NormH** in **User name:** with the password **Purple3300** in **Password:**. Make sure you are logging on to the **SPRINGERSLTD** domain and not performing a local logon to the **PRESIDENT** machine.

   BEST PRACTICE: If prompted to **Retain Your Individual Settings** in the Future via a **Windows Networking** dialog box, select **Yes**. This is the type of message you will receiving on a Win9x client computer.

   Again, relating to Windows 9x, if prompted, confirm your password (for example, Purple3300) in the **Set Windows Password** dialog box. This sets the local password file to be the same as the network password file in Windows 9x. Don't forget that passwords are case-sensitive.

2. Click **Start Now** when the **Small Business Server Client Application Installer** dialog box appears (see Figure 4-16). This will start the installation of the SBS client computer applications.

Figure 4-16
Clicking Start Now commences the SBS client computer application installation process.

The **Small Business Server Client Application Installer** dialog box will change to provide setup status information as seen in Figure 4-17. The applications are installed in the following order:

- Microsoft Shared Modem Service Client

- Microsoft Shared Fax Client

- Firewall Client

- Outlook 2000 with Internet Explorer 5

Figure 4-17
You may track the progress of the SBS client computer application setup process by observing the status information displayed in the Application Launcher dialog box.

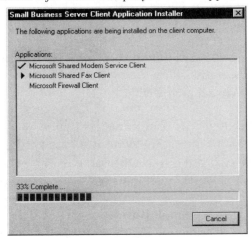

3. Click **OK** when the **Small Business Server Client Application Installer** dialog box reports that you have successfully installed the applications on the client computer.

BEST PRACTICE: As mentioned at the start of this section, a Windows 2000 Professional client computer will not require a reboot. However, a Windows 9x or NT client computer will ask you to reboot and log on again.

You will now want to prove to yourself that the SBS client applications have correctly installed. To do so, follow these steps:

1. If necessary, log on as **NormH**.
2. Select **Start**, **Settings**, **Control Panel**.
3. In Control Panel, double-click the **Internet Options** applet.
4. Select the **Connections** tab on the **Internet Properties** dialog box.
5. Click the **LAN Settings** button. The **Local Area Network (LAN) Settings** dialog box appears and should display SSL1 in the Address field, as seen in Figure 4-18. This confirms that Internet Explorer and the ISA Server (proxy settings) have been correctly installed.

Figure 4-18

Confirming the SBS client machine setup is easily done by looking at client application settings, such as Internet Explorer.

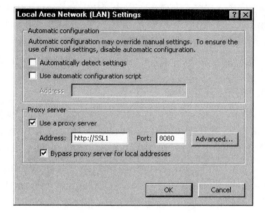

6. Click **OK** to close the **Local Area Network (LAN) Settings** dialog box.
7. Click **OK** to close the **Internet Properties** dialog box.

Congratulations! You have now set up the SBS server, a user, and a workstation. You now have a functional SBS network. It is a milestone to be proud of!

BEST PRACTICE: Now is the time to enter all of the cast of characters under the employ of SSL. These user names are found in Appendix C of this book. By entering this information, you can more closely track to SSL examples in forthcoming chapters.

ERD Update

Take a moment to update the Emergency Repair Disk (ERD). Because you've added a lot of information to the SBS network (users, machines, and so on), it is important to capture these updated settings on the ERD (just in case bad things happen!).

To update the ERD, select the **Emergency Repair Disk** option in **Backup (Start, Programs, Accessories, System Tools, Backup)**. This is similar to the same ERD steps you performed in Chapter 3.

Advanced Workstation Setup Topics

I now take a distinct shift in the flow of the chapter. The first part of the chapter was somewhat linear, wherein you added a user to the SSL SBS network in step-by-step fashion. Now, an array of advanced topics is presented. I start by spending several pages sharing different workstation setup scenarios with you, based on my experience with SBS out in the real world, not my test laboratory.

SBS vs. Windows 2000

The SBS workstation setup phase has been especially perplexing to seasoned Windows 2000 Server gurus who typically view workstation setups as a quick secondary click on My Network Places in Windows 2000 Professional, the installation of the TCP/IP protocol and Microsoft networking client, and a reboot. In fact, I'll never forget overhearing a Windows 2000 Server wizard telling a gullible small-business client that the magic disk would screw up everything. Boy, was he wrong!

The magic disk process is very different from setting up a workstation on a regular Windows 2000 Server network. Over the past several pages, that much has become clear to you, I'm sure, but let me take one more stab at making the distinction. The three closest processes in regular Windows 2000 Server that even come close to the wonderful magic disk are the Windows 2000-based Intellimirror solution set, the use of a pair of setup diskettes to configure a client computer for connection to a Terminal Services server machine, and using Group Policy to install software applications.

Intellimirror

Intellimirror is a set of Windows 2000 installation-related technologies typically used on large Windows 2000 networks. In plain English, using the Intellimirror approaches is similar to using disk duplication products, such as Ghost, to quickly install the Windows 2000 Professional operation system in a consistent manner on a large number of client machines. Admittedly, I've oversimplified the process, because this discussion is really beyond the scope of my time with you in SBS land. However, if you are interested in this topic, I can offer the following Intellimirror setup solution topics you should read more about at Microsoft's Windows 2000 Web site (www.microsoft.com/windows2000):

- **Setup Manager in the Windows 2000 Resource Kit.** This tool, the Windows 2000 Setup Manager Wizard, allows you to create an answer file (unattended.txt) for automating the setup of Windows 2000 Professional on client computers.

- **Disk Duplication.** Running the System Preparation Tool (sysprep.exe) allows you to implement a disk duplication setup solution. You first configure the "model" client computer just the way you want it. After using the System Preparation tool, in conjunction with a third-party disk duplication application, such as Ghost (see, you don't completely get away from ghosting!), you create an image of this "model" client computer by deploying the image to identical machines for final setup and configuration. The key word here was "identical," let me tell you. Basically, the System Preparation Tool is striping out the unique Security Identifier (SID) and allowing the SID to be uniquely set at each machine. (Other process are occurring as well that you can read about on your own time.)

- **Remote Installations.** Another efficient way to deploy Windows 2000 Professional on a fleet of machines is to use the Remote Installation Server (RIS) in Windows 2000. Two thoughts to send you forward with about RIS (assuming you are interested in performing your own research to master this enterprise-level tool) are: RIS must be installed on the Windows 2000 Server machine via the Add/Remove Software applet in Control Panel, and the client machine must support RIS. Good luck, my SBSer friend.

- **Other Intellimirror capabilities.** To completely round out the Intellimirror discussion, understand that additional capabilities exist, including user data management via replication (folder redirection, offline folders, and synchronization), that support mirroring of user data for the network. Conversely, you may also allow the user machine to hold local copies of network data. The software installation and maintenance capabilities also include the use of the Windows Installer, made popular by Office 2000 and now used by a number of applications. But I've broken my promise to you not to go into too much detail on Intellimirror, so I'll now stop. Please visit Microsoft's Windows 2000 Web site (I provided the URL earlier) for much more information.

Terminal Services Client Computer Setup Diskettes

In order to implement the Terminal Services client on a client computer, you will use two setup diskettes. These are created using the Terminal Services Client Creator program found in the Administrative Tools program group (Start menu, Programs). I discuss this process in great detail in Chapter 8. Note you can also run the Terminal Services client setup process from the \TSCLENT share on the SBS 2000 server machine (this approach assumes the client already has a reasonably fast network connection to the SBS server, which isn't always the case).

Software Installation with Group Policy

Assuming you have both Windows 2000 Professional clients on your SBS network and modern applications that provide an *.msi setup file, you can deploy applications using the Group Policy software installation capabilities. This capability is widely known as Assign and Publish and it allows the administrator to install software applications on the client computer. You assign applications that you want installed on the machine as a mandatory installation. You publish applications when the installation on the client computer is optional and you want the user to know about its availability. The key difference between the SBS magic disk, SBS's ability to assign software to a client computer, and the use of Group Policy-based software installation are these points.

- The SBS magic disk is typically a one-time discrete event that occurs when the client computer is set up initially to work on an SBS network.

- Using the SBS Setup Computer Wizard to install client computer software application post-setup is limited to installing software on one individual machine at a time. You can't create control conditions where the software is installed based on an individual logon name or group membership (either user or machine objects to group membership). The SBS Setup Computer Wizard is exactly as it appears: you install client applications on a selected client computer. At the next logon performed at the client machine, the software is installed as you would expect. To be honest, this is typically sufficient for the day-to-day operations of an SBS network but might be too limited at the enterprise level.

- Group Policy-based software installations are infinitely configurable based on user name, machine name, group membership, Organization Unit (OU) membership, domain membership, and heck, even Active Directory site membership. This is big-league stuff here, beyond the scope of most SBS networks but necessary to know if you're trying to pass your MCSE exams.

BEST PRACTICE: It is important to note and appreciate that none of these alternatives are mutually exclusive and necessarily unavailable to SBS. You can pick and choose from the above three choices to effectively select the level of client computer setup you want to use on a regular Windows 2000 network. You may also use any or all of the above traditional Windows 2000 tools to supplement your SBS network client computer setup and management process, assuming you've met the prerequisites, such as having a Windows 2000 Professional client computer.

And, as a parting shot at other automated setup methods, don't forget a well-received friend at the enterprise level: Microsoft System Management Server (SMS) 2.0. SMS 2.0 allows administrators to manage Windows-based desktops and servers in the enterprise with software distribution, inventory management and control, remote diagnostics, and remote troubleshooting (including remote control). SMS is included with BackOffice 2000, but not SBS 2000. You can get more information on SMS at www.microsoft.com/smsmgmt.

Part of the magic in the SBS magic disk is best displayed by pulling back the curtain and looking at the Netparam.ini file. This file resides on the SBS magic disk. Below is the Netparam.ini file for NormH.

; This file is revised by the Setup Computer Wizard and written to the
; startup floppy disk. It is subsequently used by the SAM Integrated Client
; Setup process.

```
;

[NetParams]

Domain=SPRINGERSLTD

;

Server=SSL

;

; The computer name is generated by the Setup Computer Wizard.

;

ComputerName=PRESIDENT

;

User=NormH

;

; The computers are found by enumerating the computers in the domain.

;

Computers=PRESIDENT\

;

; The users are found by enumerating the users in the domain.

;

Users=NormH\Administrator\Guest\TsInternetUser\IUSR_SSL1\IWAM_SSL1\krbtgt\EUSER_EXSTOREEVENT\Small
Business User\Small Business Power\Small Business Admin\CB6C4506-EEBC-4302-B\

;

; Admins is determined by the end user during setup on the client computer.

;

Admins=NormH\
```

BEST PRACTICE: When discussing the beloved Netparam.ini file, I can't resist the opportunity to describe how you would re-create the magic disk if it were ever lost or destroyed (such as being eaten by a Springer Spaniel). You could, of course, add another user to the SBS network (perhaps a fake user) and create the magic disk so all prior user and machine information is laid down on the diskette. Fair enough.

But there is another way. If you copy the contents of the following folder to a floppy disk, you've nearly re-created the magic disk:

%systemroot%\Program Files\Microsoft BackOffice\ClientSetup\Floppy

However, the Netparam.ini contained at this location does not contain the most current user and machine information for your network. This is the original Netparam.ini file that was installed when you set up your SBS 2000 server machine. What you need to do is find the most current Netparam.ini file to place on your new magic disk. This exists in the Response folder for the most recently created user (where a machine was also created and the magic disk had been created). In other words, go to the **Response** folder for the last user that you created on the SBS network. The path to poke around at is:

%systemroot%\Program Files\Microsoft
BackOffice\ClientSetup\Clients\Response

At this location, you will find folders named after the client computers. Look for the folder the with most recent date, open it, and confirm that the Netparam.ini contains the collective user and machine setup information. Copy this Netparam.ini file to your new magic disk.

Whew! That's a lot of work to create a magic disk, eh? The very last step, finding the most current Netparam.ini file, can be shortened by using the **Find** command from the **Start** menu to search on **Netparam.ini**. When all of the Netparam.ini files are listed, simply copy the most recent version to your new magic disk. You read it here first!

Windows For Workgroups

Believe it or not, I have a customer with a couple of old, dusty 486-based machines that are still running Windows for Workgroups. Being the fussy, self-made millionaire from the old school (make that World War II generation), he won't listen to me about upgrading to a modern desktop operating system. I guess that's why he's the millionaire and I'm not (he doesn't spend any money, as proved by using a really old operating system). But back to the storyline. In the old days of SBS 4.x, Microsoft claimed that SBS supported Windows for Workgroups (WFW). Microsoft has since deemphasized that claim in the SBS 2000 era, recognizing that WFW client machines are now few and far between and the fact that the SBS client support never really worked very well. One catch to using WFW on an SBS 2000 network: You must use the 16-bit versions of the following applications with SBS when working with workstations running WFW:

- Microsoft Internet Explorer (IE)

- Microsoft Exchange client

- Microsoft Schedule +

Officially, there is no support for Microsoft Outlook, Firewall Client, the shared modem client, or the shared fax client program (none of these are available in 16-bit versions).

There is really no problem configuring this legacy desktop environment to log on to an SBS network, but understand that the WFW setup process on an SBS network is manual, not automatic. First, you must use with the 32-bit TCP/IP protocol that is not native to WFW (but can be downloaded from Microsoft's downloads site at www.microsoft.com/downloads); or you can use an alternative networking protocol on both the SBS server machine, such as NWLink IPX/SPX or NetBEUI. Second, you must configure the network settings, such as SBS domain name (for example, SPRINGERSLTD). Third, after you reboot and log on to the SBS network, you must configure your drive mappings and printer resources. You then manually install the client applications, including IE, Microsoft Exchange client, Microsoft Schedule +, and proxy client software.

So far, so good, if it all works. The bad news is that, for all the discussion concerning WFW support on SBS networks, I've had very little luck with WFW. There are several culprits regarding WFW on an SBS network, starting with a misbehaving TCP/IP protocol trying to get a dynamic IP address. Bottom line? In nearly 100 percent of the cases, I have upgraded WFW workstations to at least Windows 95 in order to make them functional workstations on an SBS network. So, I leave you with the advice from the field: WFW and SBS don't mix. Sorry.

> BEST PRACTICE: But let's not end the WFW discussion on such a negative note. Be advised that Terminal Services supports 16-bit operating systems such as WFW. By installing the Terminal Services client on a WFW and connecting to the SBS server machine (that runs Terminal Services), you will have a bona fide Windows 2000 Professional environment right before your very eyes on the WFW machine. Note that Microsoft has designed Terminal Services in SBS 2000 to be accessed for remote administration purposes (and I agree). So, in this case, you would use the WFW machine to remotely manage the SBS server.

If you want to extend the life of legacy desktops such as WFW using this Terminal Services trick, and have these machines use the Terminal Services sessions to run bona fide business applications, you want to add a pretty darn powerful Windows 2000 member server to your SBS network running Terminal Services in application mode. I discuss this much more in Chapter 8.

Other Workstation Operating Systems

Why would you ever be concerned about supporting UNIX-related, Macintosh, or NetWare clients on an SBS network? Because, in the real world, you will have to, as have I. Needless to say, there have been a few lessons learned along the way. I'll tell one war story from the UNIX, Macintosh, and NetWare camps.

UNIX Scenarios

Many industries have historically rallied around solutions that were UNIX-based for a huge number of reasons. An example is the fundraising field in the nonprofit sector, which is exactly where I gained my experience. Here, the disease research organization needed to maintain access to its existing UNIX server in order to continue using its Raiser's Edge fundraising software. I easily accomplished this by installing the ICE.TEN terminal emulation package, which allowed me to establish a character-based session from the SBS clients to the UNIX server. ICE.TEN runs on the client workstations with no involvement from the SBS server. The one observation was that I had to carefully select the same the IP addressing scheme taken from the existing UNIX network in order for SBS and the client machines to see the UNIX server. Once that setup task was accomplished and the SBS was up and running, the UNIX and SBS networks coexisted very well together.

The above example involved Intel-based PCs (with Windows 9x) to access the UNIX server. But what if you are running a UNIX workstation trying to access an SBS server machine? Here, the situation is no different from regular Windows 2000 Server. You need to implement a network file system (NFS) client/server solution such as NetManage's Chameleon or WRQ's Reflection applications. This scenario limits you to basic logon, file, and printer services. You in no way, shape, or form participate as an SBS client.

One final comment on UNIX and SBS: You should be aware of two Windows 2000-level UNIX support mechanisms. First, there is the Print Services for UNIX in Windows 2000 that enables UNIX clients to print to any printer available on the Windows 2000 network (which in our world is the same as the SBS 2000 network). This is installed via the Windows Components Wizard launched from the Add/Remove Programs applet in Control Panel. Second, Microsoft has released Services for UNIX 2.0, which can be purchased for approximately $150 to enhance the Windows 2000/UNIX interoperability (such as the ability to share resources). Services for UNIX capabilities include:

- Client for NFS. Allows Windows 2000 clients to mount exported file systems directly from UNIX NFS servers as if they were regular Windows shares.

- Server for NFS. Shares directories from Windows 2000-based servers as if they were native UNIX exports.

- Gateway for NFS. Shares UNIX NFS exports as Windows-based shared directories, allowing any Windows client access without installing NFS client software.

- Server for PCNFS. Enables Windows 2000 to act as a PCNFS daemon (PCNFSD) server, providing seamless user authentication services when connecting to NFS servers.

- Over 60 UNIX Utilities. Enables you to run familiar UNIX commands such as cat, grep, ls, ps, rshsvc, and vi natively from Windows 2000.

- Korn Shell. Provides a full-featured implementation that enables you to run UNIX shell scripts from Windows 2000.

See Microsoft Services for UNIX 2.0 Web site at www.microsoft.com/windows2000/sfu for more information. You might also consult Chapter 11: "Services for UNIX" in the *Internetworking Guide in the Windows 2000 Resource Kit*.

Macintosh Clients

This was certainly one of my more interesting SBS gigs. Here, the investment analysis firm was upgrading from its older Macintosh network to a brand-new SBS network. For reasons known only to the managing partners of the client firm, I was asked to allow a few Macintoshes to exist past the network conversion date. That meant these Macintosh workstations needed to access the SBS server for a limited period of time for e-mail, file sharing, printing, and logon/logoff purposes. No problem. Hey, years ago I once set up a Macintosh/Windows NT Server network for the world's largest Macintosh temporary agency.

In fact, it wasn't a problem. Here is how you support Macintosh clients on an SBS network:

There are three sides to this puzzle: the SBS server machine, the Macintosh workstation, and the applications.

On the server side, you need to confirm that you indeed installed SBS on an NTFS partition. (That should be an automatic affirmative, because NTFS is the default file system for SBS server machine.)

You then need to install both the File Services for Macintosh and Print Services for Macintosh via Windows Components Wizard launched from the Add/Remove Programs applet in Control Panel. File Services for Macintosh automatically installs the AppleTalk Protocol, which allows file and printer sharing (this last point assumes the Print Services for Macintosh have been installed as well).

On the Macintosh client side, you will need to install the Microsoft user authentication module (UAM). This process is well-documented in the Windows NT Server 2000 Resource Kit in Chapter 13: "Services for Macintosh" of the Internetworking Guide in the Windows 2000 Resource Kit. It is essential that you use Macintosh OS version 7.5 or higher to take advantage of the UAM's robust logon security. On the application side, you might be interested to know that Microsoft has a full-featured Outlook client available for Macintosh workstations (see www.microsoft.com/office/outlook).

SBS 2000 and NetWare Clients

Many small businesses migrate from NetWare networks to SBS, even SSL! That fact is well-established. But many times, things don't go quite as scheduled, and, for a period of time, both the SBS network and NetWare network are up and running. I have seen this primarily in the context of accounting system conversions. Whereas the SBS network might be functional as planned, often the accounting system isn't ready for conversion. So, you have a situation where users are logging on to the NetWare network to run the accounting application (for example, Great

Plains Dynamics) and logging on to the SBS network for e-mail, Internet access, printing, and so on.

Based on this need, how well do SBS and NetWare networks coexist? I've found that the two environments get along remarkably well. But there are several steps on both the SBS server and the SBS client workstation that must be performed to work with a NetWare network. If you want the SBS server to communicate with the NetWare server, you need to install the Nwlink IPX/SPX protocol and the Gateway Servers for NetWare (GSNW) services on the SBS server machine. (This process is well-documented in Chapter 12: "Interoperability with NetWare" in the Internetworking Guide in the Windows 2000 Resource Kit.)

If you want the client workstation to log on to both the SBS network and the NetWare network, you need to do the following: For the SBS network, no further changes are necessary, assuming you performed the steps earlier in the chapter and are logging on to the SBS network without any incidents. For the NetWare network, you need to install the IPX/SPX-compatible Protocol and the Client Service for NetWare on your Windows 2000 or the Client for NetWare Networks on your Windows 9x machine. Upon rebooting your workstation, log on to both the SBS network and the NetWare network.

> BEST PRACTICE: Make your username and password the same on both the SBS and NetWare networks for simplicity. Also, on a Windows 9x machine, I highly recommend that the Primary Network Logon be the Client for Microsoft Networks so that the SBS network is the first network to provide your logon authentication and drive mappings.

The Barrister's Skinny Machine

Small businesses are always up for saving a buck or two. Such cost-saving behavior takes many forms, include the barrister's skinny machine. This Seattle lawyer is an expert in the legal field of labor law. He has little interest in mastering computers, and that lack of interest was manifested in his workstation configuration. This barrister hadn't upgraded for many years, resulting in his continued use of an older Compaq 486 workstation running Windows for Workgroups with 12MB RAM and 10MB of free hard disk space (on a 125MB hard disk to begin with). When I arrived on the scene to implement SBS at the law firm, I knew the barrister's machine would present some interesting challenges.

By hook and by crook, I was able to upgrade the barrister's machine to Windows 95, which, as you recall from the section "Windows for Workgroups," removed several SBS-related workstation issues. This was accomplished by removing old versions of Lotus 123, WordPerfect, and an unusually large amount of .tmp (temporary) files. But I still didn't have close to the minimum amount of disk space required for the full SBS client applications.

Here I had to go under the hood on the SBS workstation setup process. First, I created a skinny magic disk for the barrister's workstation with no SBS applications installed. The magic disk was used to simply change the machine and domain name. Next, I installed IE and Microsoft Outlook manually from these application's respective stand-alone CD-ROMS. When installing these applications, I selected the custom installation options and not only deselected unnecessary IE and Outlook features (such as holiday clip art), but I also installed these applications to the barrister's user directory on the network. This, of course, dramatically reduced the application footprint on the workstation's hard disk, but not as much as you might think. Microsoft Outlook isn't without a footprint when a network installation of this application is installed. No matter what you do, Outlook insists on installing some components on the workstation's local hard disk. And because I manually installed IE and Outlook, I had to manually configure these applications to work with the SBS network. For IE, I had to modify the connection properties to use SBS's ISA server. For Outlook, I had to create a profile that attached to the barrister's Exchange-based mailbox.

When all was said and done, the barrister literally had 2MB of free space on his local hard disk, but he didn't care. Heck, he was participating on the SBS network, barrister-style!

Alternative Workstation Installations

There are two ways to implement the necessary SBS components without using the client installation or magic disk. The first involves a scenario using Windows 2000 Professional machine. The second approach is much more manual, whereby you explicitly run the setup for each SBS program.

Magic Diskless #1: Windows 2000 Professional Machine

As promised, here is how you can add a Windows 2000 Workstation to an SBS network without the magic disk (a.k.a. magic diskless):

1. Make sure you are logged on to the SBS server machine as an **Administrator** or equivalent.
2. Launch the **Small Business Server Administrator Console** from **Start**.
3. Expand the **Active Directory Users and Computers** link in the console pane.
4. Expand the **Springersltd.com** domain object (the domain object will reflect the name of your network).
5. Right-click on the **Computers** folder and select **New**, **Computer** from the secondary menu.
6. Complete the **New Object – Computer** dialog box similar to Figure 4-19 with the machine name **CONTRACTOR1**. Click **OK**.

Figure 4-19
Adding a computer in Active Directory Users and Computers.

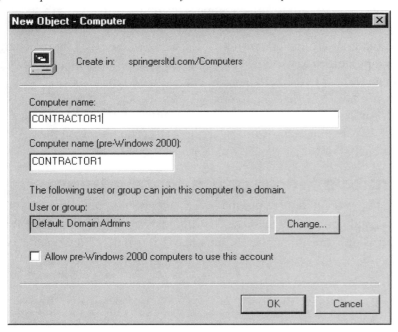

7. Select **Computers** beneath **Small Business Server (BackOffice Manager)**.
8. Highlight the computer you just created (**CONTRACTOR1**) in the details pane under **Name**.
9. Click on the **Add Software to Computer** link in the details pane.
10. Click **Next** when you see the **Welcome to the Set Up Computer Wizard**.
11. Select the SBS client applications you want to install on the **Applications** screen listed beneath **Applications:**. Click **Next**.
12. Click **Finish** on the **Completing the Set Up Computer Wizard** screen.
13. Now, go to the workstation that you named in step 4 and log on to the SBS network. Make sure that you've configured the Windows 2000 Workstation, via the Network Identification tab on the System Properties dialog box (accessed via the System applet in Control Panel), to use the same computer name you indicated it would (in this example, Contractor01).
14. Upon successful logon authentication, observe that the SBS client programs you selected in step 9 are installed. After the SBS client programs have been installed, you do not need to reboot the Windows 2000 Professional (although it's never a bad idea to do so after installing applications). You will want to add the SBS users who intend to use this machine to the local Administrators group.

I have seen this approach used on SBS networks that had Windows 2000 Professional clients and the SBS consultant (me!) wanted to save valuable time by not trotting around and running a:\setup.exe from the single SBS magic disk at each workstation. This way, at the next logon of the client machine, the SBS client application installation process commences.

Shifting Gears Manually

I've used another nontraditional workstation setup approach that is also magic diskless: I manually install the SBS client applications. I've used this approach several times when, for reasons I've never been able to explain, the darn magic disk simply didn't work on a client machine. This is typically caused by a hardware failure on the client machine, specifically the floppy drive. I usually discover the broken floppy drive on a Sunday evening at 11:00 p.m. with the client's worker bee staff arriving in about nine hours.

To perform this, I assume that you're on a Windows 2000 or 9x workstation with basic logon connectivity with the SBS network and you can browse via My

Network Places (Windows 2000 Professional) or Network Neighborhood (Windows 9x) to see the SBS server machine (for example, SSL1). That is, you've correctly installed and configured the TCP/IP protocol and have logged on to the SBS network.

1. On the client workstation, browse via My Network Places (Windows 2000 Professional) or Network Neighborhood (Windows 9x) to the SBS Server machine (SSL1).
2. To install the SBS client applications, run the appropriate setup file as shown in Table 4-2. This is typically accomplished by double-clicking on the setup file for each applications and performing the necessary setup steps, such as answering setup wizard-based questions, clicking **Next** and the clicking **Finish**. You get the picture.

Note that I assume you are installing these applications to a Windows 2000 Professional client machine. If you are installing to a Windows 9x and NT4 client, the path will be different on the Shared Modem client application (you would select the appropriate subfolder for Windows 9x or NT4 inside the Modem Sharing Client folder).

Table 4-2: SBS Client Application Setup Files

SBS Client Application	Setup File (share name\directory\setup file)
Microsoft Shared Fax client	\ClientApps5\Fax Client\Setup.exe
Microsoft Internet Explorer	\ClientApps5\IE5\Ie5setup.exe
Microsoft Shared Modem client	\ClientApps5\Modem Sharing Client\Win2K\NetSetupWin2K.exe
Microsoft Outlook client	\ClientApps5\Outlook2000SR1\Setup.exe
Microsoft Firewall client	\Modem Sharing Client\Firewall Client\Setup.exe

BEST PRACTICE: Notice I didn't provide the SBS server machine NetBIOS computer name component (\\SSL1) in the second column of the above table. My assumption is that you know how to construct a UNC path and would automatically add the SBS server machine NetBIOS computer name before the path listed in column two. I discuss UNC paths in Chapter 6.

BEST PRACTICE: If you manually install the SBS client applications using the method presented above, you need to manually configure the applications to participate on the SBS network. That is because the applications don't benefit from some of the SBS macro code that automatically performs such configurations for you. One example of this would be the connection type used by IE. You will need to configure IE to use the SBS-based ISA Server (typically the NetBIOS name of the SBS server machine, for example, SSL1).

Client Support for SQL Server 2000

While SQL Server 2000 has client components, such as SQL Server management applications that can be run at the client machine, these components are officially ignored by the SBS client machine setup process. I guess Microsoft figures the hard-core SQL Server crowd won't mind manually installing such components. Also, when interacting with SQL Server 2000 in a small-business environment, you're far more likely to install some SQL Server 2000-related client-side application on behalf of a third-party software application, such as an accounting program. Enough said.

Any User, Any Time!

One of my clients has a policy that any user may use any machine at any time. This policy has been put in place so that organization productivity isn't impeded by a failed workstation at someone's desk. This policy has several ramifications. First, I've noticed that each user keeps a workstation that is clean as a whistle. No unacceptable Internet-based photos here, given that anyone may use anyone else's machine on short notice. Second, the users no longer have an excuse for why they can't work. Third, organization productivity has indeed risen, I guess based on the first two reasons, but all amounting to this: The workstations are a business tool viewed much like a photocopier or fax machine.

To implement this any user/any time system, there are two approaches: Group Policy and adding users to existing machines.

Group Policy Again!

Assuming you are on an all-Windows 2000 network, Group Policy may be just what you're looking for. That is, on your SBS 2000 network, if the client computers are Windows 2000 Professional-based, Group Policy allows you to effectively create roaming user profiles that follow the user. That is, the user can log on at one Windows 2000 Professional machine and have certain applications installed for immediate use. The same user can log on at another Windows 2000 Professional machine and the cycle repeats itself.

Group Policy is very effective for creating a user profile that follows the user amongst Windows 2000 Professional machines, as long as the setting you are trying to modify are Windows 2000-related or you are trying to generically install applications (without a lot of application customization). Basically, Group Policy is incredibly effective at the infrastructure-level. You can read more about Group Policy in Chapter 22: "Group Policy" in Part 4: "Desktop Configuration Management of the Distributed Systems Guide" of the Windows 2000 Resource Kit. Heck, all of the aforementioned Part 4: if the Resource Kit is worthwhile reading. You might also cast an eye to Chapter 8: "Customizing the Desktop of the Windows 2000 Professional Desktop."

Adding Users to Existing Machines

So let's say you run an SBS network where every user does not run a Windows 2000 Professional client machine, eliminating Group Policy as an effective tool. This fact requires you to implement the any user at any time policy using a variety of Microsoft tools that address the following user information management areas.

> BEST PRACTICE: When working with Windows 2000 Professional client machines, remember that you'll want to add each user who intends to use the client machine to the local Administrators group.

Basic SBS Client Applications

The core SBS applications, subject to the Outlook 2000 and Internet Explorer 5 discussion below, are ready, able, and willing to serve any user that logs on to a configured SBS client machine. For example, the ISA client, shared modem client, and shared fax client don't implicitly discriminate by the logged on user. That is, the ISA client will continue to redirect Internet-bound traffic for a Telnet session, regardless of who is logged on, subject to this one major point. At the SBS server machine level, you can set permissions for which users have Internet access, ability to use the fax device to send faxes, and ability to use the shared modem pool (these are server-level security settings). In other words, while the locally installed Shared Fax Service client may start on the local client machine when a user-driven outbound faxing function commences, it might be all for naught if said user is not allowed to use the fax device(s) on the SBS network. Note I'm implicitly referring here to global security settings that would impact a user regardless of the client machine logged on to. I continue to touch on the SBS client applications on future days of this text. For example, in Chapter 14: "Faxing," the faxing model will be discussed in greater detail.

Mapped Drives

When a user logs on to any machine, the expectation is that he or she would see the mapped drives they are accustomed to seeing. Fair enough. Using Windows Scripting Host (WSH), you may create robust logon scripts for use on the SBS network. I discuss the concept and application of mapped drives in much greater detail in Chapter 6.

Outlook 2000

The any user/any time policy for sharing client machines requires you to create Outlook 2000 profiles for each user that might use a given machine. Needless to say, with 10 machines and 10 users, you're ultimately creating over 100 profiles (10X10) in this implementation model. In Chapter 12, I discuss how to accomplish this task.

Another data management topic that falls into the any user/any time discussion is the use of public folder in an Outlook/Exchange e-mail scenario. Using public folders allows the user to, for example, use a common shared calendar and contact list, regardless of the machine logged on. Again, this topic is discussed in Chapter 12.

Internet Explorer 5

SBS users participating in the any user/any time client machine deployment model will scream long and loud when, after logging on at a client machine (other than their own), does not see the Web page bookmarks they are accustomed to using. Prepare them for this reality.

Office 2000

Ah, last but certainly not least in the any user/any time model is the Office 2000 suite, a popular front office solution for nearly all SBS users on this planet. This is a larger discussion area than you might imagine, ranging from allowed applications the user may run, the user's expectation to find custom Office templates when logging on to any machine, using common Office templates in the entire organization, and so on. This big area of discussion, including Office 2000 administrative installation to a network share point, Office 2000 transforms, and the Office 2000 Custom Installation Wizard are discussed Chapter 19.

> BEST PRACTICE: The any user/any time approaches discussed above allow each user to enjoy secure and confidential e-mail and file storage on the SBS network. That is because the e-mail is managed via a Microsoft Exchange mailbox that uses robust, Active Directory-based network logon security. The stored files on the network also use this same network logon security along with share-level and NTFS permissions. Thus, the CEO of a small company can have another employee use her machine without lingering concerns that her private e-mails will be exposed. (That's as long as she hasn't exported selected e-mails to an unencrypted personal folder (*.pst file) on the workstation's hard drive. Such a *.pst file could, theoretically, be imported into the mailbox of another user for viewing.)

Active Directory Organizational Units

A hidden jewel in SBS 2000 that isn't emphasized by Microsoft is the Active Directory organizational unit (OU) area. In this round of SBS, Microsoft is emphasizing the use of security and distribution groups, based in part on feedback from SBSers during the SBS 4.x era. The SBS consoles now allow you to create and configure security and distribution groups, to which SBSers recite a resounding "Cool!"

However, the SBS consoles really don't allow you to create and configure OUs in any meaningful SBS kinda way. To create and configure OUs in SBS, you need to select the Active Directory Users and Computers item in the SBS Administrators Console, but, alas, this is the same Active Directory Users and Computers MMC you see in the Administrative Tools program group from the Start menu.

Specific keystrokes aside, it appears Microsoft is, for whatever reason, deemphasizing the use of OUs. One legitimate reason might be that OUs are really geared to the enterprise level to assist in the grouping of users, computers, printers, and other objects. OUs are containers that typically reflect the name of a department ("Marketing") or the location of the branch office ("Downtown"). Technically speaking, OUs are popular in Windows 2000 in migrations from legacy Windows NT 4 networks where resource domains are now collapsed into OUs. In fact, you can kinda think of an OU as a resource domain, holding users, computers, printers, and so on.

> BEST PRACTICE: An object, such as a user, can only belong to one OU at a time, which is the same fundamental rule that applied to domains in Windows NT 4.

I like to use OUs to organize, as in the above discussion, resources by organizational department. This isn't a super big deal in SBS except for one major point. Group Policy in an all-Windows 2000 scenario is typically applied at the OU level. So, the Marketing OU might have a different Group Policy Object (GPO, the official term for Group Policy settings) applied to it than the Management OU. In other words, OUs are really a business tool, as far as I'm concerned.

SBS 2000 creates a default OU titled MyBusiness, which is used to store such objects as the default SBS security groups (e.g., BackOffice Internet Users) via three additional OUs (Distribution Groups, Folders, Groups). MyBusiness is displayed in Figure 4-20. However, amazing as it sounds, the SBS users and client machines you create are not placed in MyBusiness. Rather, SBS users are created in the default Windows 2000 Users container and client machines are created in the default Computers container. Kinda bewildering, to say the least, as this approach effectively marginalizes the role that the MyBusiness OU could assume if it were honored more.

Figure 4-20

The default SBS OU, MyBusiness, displayed in Active Directory Users and Computers.

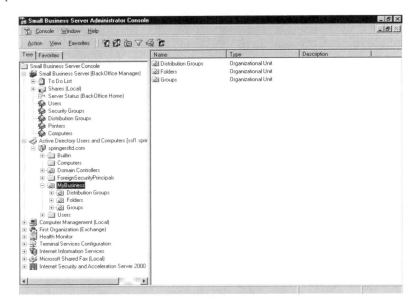

But, again, fear not! Here are the explicit keystrokes to create your own OU (which I'll call "Marketing") in the Active Directory.

1. Assuming you are logged on to the SBS server machine as an **Administrator**, launch the **Small Business Server Administrative Console** from **Start**.

2. Expand **Active Directory Users and Computers** in the console pane.

3. Right-click on the domain object in the left pane (e.g., **Springersltd.com**).

4. Select **New**, **Organizational Unit**. The **New Object – Organizational Unit** dialog box appears.

5. Provide a name for the new OU, such as **Marketing,** in **Name:** and click **OK**. The new OU should appear in the list of OUs for the domain, as seen in Figure 4-21.

Figure 4-21

Creating your own OUs in the Active Directory in SBS offers additional management possibilities.

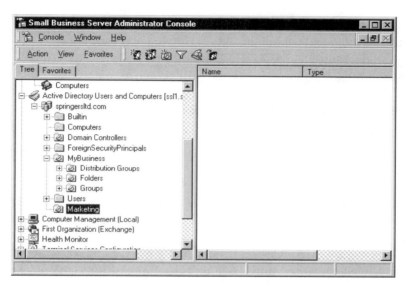

To move an object such as a user to a different OU, say the Marketing OU, you simply right-click on the object and select **Move** from the secondary menu. The **Move** dialog box that appears will allow you to select the OU you want to move the object to. It's as simple as it sounds.

> BEST PRACTICE: The Move command for moving objects between OUs in Active Directory does not allow you to move objects between domains. Thus, this is not a move utility to facilitate an SBS implementation from an existing multiple domain Windows 2000 network or a multiple domain Windows NT 4 network. And this move command certainly won't allow you to migrate users from Novell NDS-based networks to SBS. Nope! Don't even try.

A final note on OUs: You can nest an OU inside of an OU. This is helpful when you might be working on special projects with contractors and temporary employees. For example, in the Marketing OU, you might create an OU titled "Jones Project." You would then toss all the temps you've added to the SBS network into here so you could apply a special GPO.

If you'd like to learn more about OUs, select the **Help** menu option from the **Start** menu to launch the traditional Windows 2000 help system and follow these keystrokes:

1. Expand the **Active Directory** book.
2. Expand the **Concepts** book inside the **Active Directory** book.
3. Expand the **Planning for Active Directory** book.
4. Select the **Planning organizational unit structure** link.

Troubleshooting SBS Workstation Setups

A few rules of the road help you drive when troubleshooting workstation problems. These range from official Microsoft support proclamations to streetwise knowledge.

In general, the SBS workstation setup routine is a finicky process. You should not only adhere to the formal magic disk setup process, but you should also use common sense. Consider the following:

*   Be careful about overwriting existing, newer applications with older, SBS client applications. For example, with SBS it may be a mistake to install an older version of IE or Microsoft Outlook, via the magic disk, over newer versions you might have on your hard disk. The version numbers change every few months, so it is likely the programs versions shipped with SBS 2000 have aged. My advice, given that frequent upgrades and fixes are a fact of life? Try your SBS client installation routine on one machine that is representative of the fleet of client machines at your SBS location. If it works without incident, you are armed with great information to make the decision to install the SBS client applications on all client machines. Also, consult with another SBSer or two (perhaps other SBS consultants) about their experience in upgrading over existing client applications, such as IE and Outlook 2000. The rules of the road are constantly changing here!

*   Be careful when using light versions of popular applications. For example, Outlook Express, a lightweight e-mail client with IE, never did work under SBS 4.0 or 4.0a. Believe me, I tried to make it work on workstations with too little local hard disk space.

- Workstation operating system versions. Throughout the history of SBS, my experience has been that the SBS releases (4.0, 4.0a, 4.5, 2000) can't keep up with the more frequent workstation operating system releases and upgrades. Your challenge as an SBS administrator, consultant, and user will be to keep your SBS version in synch with your workstation operating system. For example, if you use SBS 4.0 or 4.0a with Windows 98, you will, of course, notice that all the SBS Console references to workstation operating systems didn't include Windows 98. Look for this same type of dilemma when Windows XP is released and you want to use it with SBS 2000.

The point is this. With workstation operation systems growing and changing literally all the time, your SBS network possibly won't natively support the latest workstation operating system. You must use vision and common sense to make the marriage of your SBS network and your workstation happen. Here is what I recommend. First, monitor the SBS-related newsgroup and support articles at www.microsoft.com. Second, consider subscribing to Microsoft TechNet, a monthly CD-ROM library subscription server (approximately $300 annually and can be purchased from your favorite reseller). Third, interact with other SBS sites via local computer user groups. And fourth, take full advantage of third-party SBS support resources, such as Grey Lancaster's e-mail listserv discussed in Appendix A: "SBS Resources."

- Can't read the magic disk. Perhaps your workstation can't read the formatting method used by SBS (called distribution media format). Simply copy the setup.exe, netparam.txt and other files from the SBS magic disk to another already-formatted disk. Then continue with the SBS workstation setup as usual. Errors occur when attempting to run the magic disk at the workstation. Here I recommend you start over. Delete the user and computer from the SBS network (via the SBS Console) and then re-create the user and computer again. Hiccups happen, but less often in SBS 2000 than previous versions.

- Read the README.DOC file on Disc #1 of the SBS 2000 media. This readme document contains the latest Microsoft-known bugs relating to SBS setup, clients, applications, and so on. Be sure to print it out and read it. You might recall I recommended this step prior to building the SBS server machine, but it's worth repeating.

- Others. Over the course of the remaining days, you will learn, on a feature-by-feature and application-by-application basis, how SBS client applications might or might not function as expected. For example, in Chapter 13, I'll show you how to troubleshoot modem pooling from both the server and workstation sides.

SBS Upgrade Scenarios

Assuming you are upgrading from an older version of SBS to SBS 2000, you will need to rerun the magic disk at the workstations to upgrade the SBS client machine applications. I discuss this more in Appendix B: "Upgrading to SBS 2000."

Uninstalling SBS Clients

This is a great area of improvement in SBS 2000 compared to SBS 4.x. To uninstall SBS client applications, simply use the Add/Remove Programs applet in Control Panel. This is a process typical to many applications and I discuss this area in more detail in Chapter 6.

Summary

Whew! You've made it through four demanding chapters and your reward is a functional and operational SBS network. I started today by offering you congratulations and I end on the same note. In the next chapter, you will master My Small Business Server Console and the Small Business Server Administrator Console.

Section 2

SBS Management

Chapter 5
Small Business Server Management Consoles

Spank me silly for placing this chapter here just after you've set up the SBS network, but I have methods to my madness. It's my belief that, with the SBS network up and running at a basic level, you need to take a deep breath and learn a thing or two about some of the SBS management tools. I actually deliver this information over the next four chapters, starting here with the SBS consoles. Later in the book you will delve deeply into the individual server-side applications, like Exchange 2000 Server, but just hold your horses for a couple hundred pages please. This chapter, based not surprisingly on the SSL methodology that weaves across this book, fills knowledge gaps about the consoles you might have at this point. You've already seen the consoles as part of your SBS setup, but this chapter takes the time to explore the consoles thoroughly.

So, right here and right now you'll tour and learn about the SBS consoles. Yes, you read correctly in that SBS consoles are now plural! A major change from SBS 4.5 was the creation of a Personal Console in addition to the main (known as Administrator Console) console. And as you'll see at the end of the chapter, you can even create custom consoles.

Many screens on the SBS consoles are task-oriented; others are display- or report-oriented. You need both to properly manage your SBS network. And this insight applies whether you're an SBS newbie or SBS guru.

> BEST PRACTICE: My advice for learning the SBS Console is to both read this chapter and play with the SBS consoles along the way. Because the recommended path with this book is first to set up an imaginary company—SSL—you really can't do any business harm to your system. The benefit of playing with the SBS consoles now is that, after you've completed this book and then installed SBS for your real com-

pany or clients, you will have learned the SBS console inside and out. Not a bad idea when you think about it. Tinker with the consoles now and effectively pay your dues with the SSL organization. Later on, when it's for real, you'll minimize mistakes and downtime with your real company.

But there is, of course, another parallel question: Why play with the SBS consoles at all? In my experience, few SBS administrators actually take a few hours out of their busy days to click each object in the SBS consoles. These few hours make a world of difference when it comes to improving how you use your SBS network at your small business.

In the first part of the chapter, I'll focus on the SBS Personal Console. In the middle of the chapter, we'll hear from Dean Paron, a product manager on the SBS development team at Microsoft who had a big say in how the SBS consoles were created. In the back part of the chapter, the focus shifts to the SBS Administrator Console and its capabilities. So gussy up to a cup of espresso to charge your engines, as I suggest in the next section.

First Things First – Take Five and Celebrate!

To set the proper tone about what I have in mind for this chapter, please do the following. Take a five-minute break to stretch, fill and drink that coffee cup, and celebrate the fact you've implemented a bona fide SBS 2000 network, having completed the first four chapters of this book. That's no small accomplishment, so massive congratulations are in order. In fact, if you're wondering what the "real" SSL SBS 2000 server machine looks like in its server room, take a gander at Figure 5-1.

Figure 5-1

The SSL SBS 2000 network powered by its Gateway 7400 Server (lower center).

BEST PRACTICE: Want to win your next round of SBS trivia? In Figure 5-1, the monitor is displaying the "bobrand" background on the desktop (this is the default desktop background in SBS 2000). In English, this stands for BackOffice brand and is a photo looking up at the Tacoma Narrows Bridge in the Puget Sound area. This Pacific Northwest landmark is approximately 50 miles southwest of Microsoft's Redmond campus where the SBS development team works.

SBS Surf's Up Dude!

Before we begin looking at virtually every click of the SBS consoles, take a moment while you're finishing that cup of coffee this morning to launch both the **Small Business Server Administrator Console** and the **Small Business Server Personal Console** from **Start**. Such creative play breeds familiarity and increases your comfort as we proceed. And by creating a console-centric technology culture in your organization, I hope to indoctrinate you into the belief and mantra of "do everything from the console." You can repeat that phrase several times now in a Tibetan monk-like chant! So, surf the SBS consoles for a spell.

> BEST PRACTICE: The old guard in the SBS community will appreciate the following tidbit of information. Back in the days when knights were bold and Microsoft blue cards owned all the gold, under SBS version 4.0 or 4.0A it was essential that you set your screen area to 800X600 pixels under **Display** (accessed via **Start**, **Settings**, **Control Panel**) and 256 colors, so that the SBS Console was properly displayed. Failure to do so resulted in only part of the SBS Console being displayed, which was unpleasant. This also required a silly game of physically moving the SBS console around the screen in order to see it. Now neither the color scheme nor screen area matters with SBS 2000 or its predecessor SBS 4.5. That is, the full SBS consoles will be displayed even at 640X480 (ouch!). Note at the lower resolutions, the SBS consoles get jumbled, but they still work in their self-contained screen area.

If you're a Microsoft Certification candidate, you might recall that one of the challenges on the exams was that there were several ways to answer the questions (meaning several ways to perform the same action). For example, in Windows 9x, there are seven ways to Egypt to run an application. The SBS consoles have some similarities in this case. You will quickly see that the SBS consoles have a habit of task repetition. That is, as you gain experience with the SBS consoles, you'll discover there are multiple ways to accomplish or perform the same task. When such repetition occurs, I will try to alert you to that point and cross-reference the repetition.

Getting Started – Personal Console

So we begin the formal lesson delivery by clicking **Start, Small Business Server Personal Console.** The resulting console is shown in Figure 5-2.

Figure 5-2

Meet the SBS Personal Console.

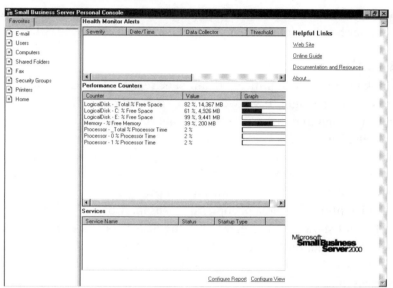

So what are your initial reactions? I have a couple thoughts centered on the design goals and artistic merit. In the design goals category, I heartily endorse the SBS development team's decision to create a second console oriented towards the power user at the SBS site (and not necessarily for use by the SBS consultant). So, two thumbs up in design goals. For artistic merit, here's my take, even though I'm not a qualified User Interface art critic. The little "stars" on a page image next to each link are disconcerting to me. This looks far too much like the icon I see in Internet Explorer when a *.jpg screen image doesn't display on a Web page. Seriously, my expectation is that I'd see a cute button here, but I'm left with the impression that such artwork hasn't rendered itself correctly in the SBS Personal Console. Oh well, moving on, as they say.

Home Page

When first started, the SBS Personal Console is launched to its "home page" view (this is seen in Figure 5-2). The left side has the links you can click (and we'll look at each and every one of them). The right portion of the screen, known as the details pane, actually is displaying what's called the Server Status View. Basically, the Server Status View provides a quick-and-dirty view of important server health information. To be honest, the Server Status view is an advanced topic that is better handled later, when you and I wear our advanced SBSer hats.

Helpful Links

Don't overlook the fact that significant detail pane real estate is dedicated to the Helpful Links on the far right. If we were Kremlin-watching or tea leaf-reading, we'd take this as a sign that these links are as important (even more important) than anything else on the SBS Personal Console. Such is really not the case, and you'll see that, if you turn your SBS server machine screen area up to some ungodly value like 1280x1024, the Helpful Links portion of the details pane shrinks relative to the Server Status View portion of the details pane. So, at lower resolution, the Helpful Links area occupies a "disproportionate" amount of real estate. Note I won't show you a screenshot of the SBS Personal Console at a high screen area value, as that type of screenshot doesn't reproduce well in a book (but you can try this experiment from **Start**, **Settings**, **Control Panel**, **Display**, **Settings**, **Screen area**).

In the next breath, let me trumpet the value of the Helpful Links to the SBS newbie and power user. The specific Helpful Links are:

- **Web Site.** This selection spawns an Internet Explorer 5.x Web browser window, taking you to the hard-coded SBS Web site of www.mcirosoft.com/sbserver. I have it on good word that this is a permanent link (hence the term hard-coded) and won't be changed or suffer a sudden death. The Web site is shown in Figure 5-3.

Notes:

Figure 5-3

The Microsoft SBS Web site.

- **Online Guide.** The crack SBS documentation team at Microsoft really poured their hearts and souls into this link (as well as the next one). The goal here was to let you, with just a click, jump easily into the new and improved online guide. This is shown in Figure 5-4.

Figure 5-4

Online Guide (aka Online help) for SBS 2000. Try the nifty Introductory Tours and Troubleshooting Microsoft Small Business Server 2000 selections in the left pane.

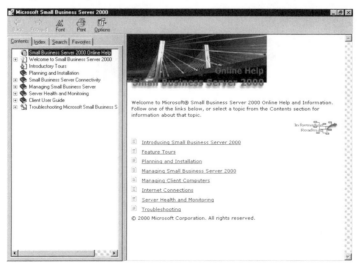

- **Documentation and Resources.** Talk about a paradigm shift in assisting users. The title of this link does an injustice to the cool tool that is a mere click away: the **Information Roadmap**. Shown in Figure 5-5, this is Microsoft's attempt to try new approaches to jazzing up user help. At a minimum, it's awfully nice eye candy for delivering user support content. Join me in clicking each button (Figure 5-6 is the result of clicking the **Migration** button). Man, I want some of whatever that SBS documentation team has been smoking!

Figure 5-5
The cool tool in online help: Information Roadmap.

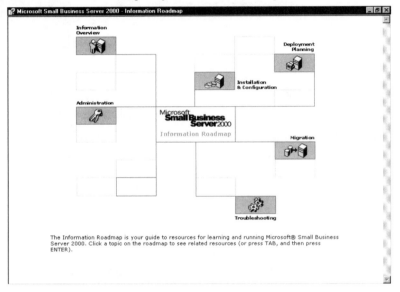

Notes:

Figure 5-6

The Migration links.

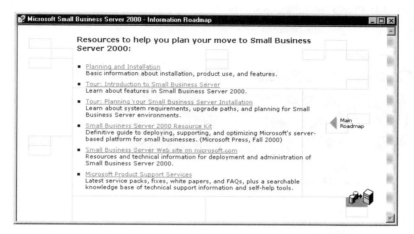

BEST PRACTICE: Truth be told, it's the online help guide of a software product like SBS 2000 that often has more up-to-date information than printed books and resource kits. This is another reason you want to take the Helpful Links seriously: You are getting better information in many cases than with the printed word. That's because the printed word is often frozen 60- to 90-days out from the release date of a software product (even this book suffers this time lag, as it takes 60 to 90 days for the book to hit the shelves after I've written the last word). Contrast that with online documentation that, theoretically, can be modified up to the release-to-manufacturing (RTM) date of a software product. RTM is generally considered to be six weeks before release.

Of course, don't overlook the first link that takes you to the SBS Web site at Microsoft. This is where you can obtain the very latest information pertaining to SBS.

- **About.** Ahhh, the good old **About** dialog box. This is actually very valuable in SBS 2000 as it's one of two places you can tell how many Client Access Licenses (CALs) you've actually installed. In Figure 5-7, you can see that number is five in the case of Springer Spaniels Limited. The **Add Licenses** link is a place to add more CALs. I discuss the art of adding licenses later in this chapter.

Figure 5-7
There's more to the About dialog box than a copyright notice.

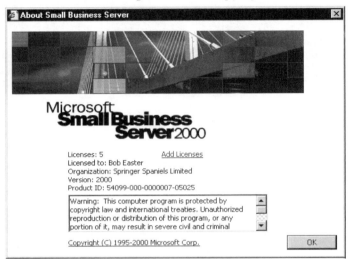

BEST PRACTICE: These same helpful links exist on the SBS Administrator Console, but I thought the discussion was more germane to the first part of the chapter focusing on the Personal Console. That's because these helpful links are likely to be of more interest to the SBS newbie or power user than the SBS guru. Don't you agree?

So it's now time to click on and explore each of the links on the **Favorites** tab on the SBS Personal Console. That process starts in the next section.

Notes:

E-mail

Let's face it. Whether you're a newbie, power user, or guru, few things are more important on an SBS network than e-mail. With that acknowledgement, it's not lost on the SBS community that the E-mail link is first in the SBS Personal Console. The E-mail link spawns the E-mail taskpad in the details pane, as seen in Figure 5-8.

Figure 5-8
The E-mail taskpad for your configuration pleasure.

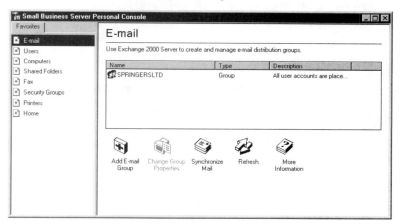

There are several tasks you can perform, including:

- **Add E-mail Group.** This is your chance to add a distribution group to Active Directory. In other words, you can create an e-mail group, such as "Accounting." You place users in the group and then, viola! You only have to send one e-mail to the e-mail group to reach everyone. Nifty!

- **Change Group Properties.** This button is shaded, meaning it's not accessible from the E-mail taskpad on the SBS Personal Console.

- **Synchronize Mail.** When clicked, a silent action is performed in the background that does the old GET/PUT of e-mail at the Internet Service Provider (ISP). This is the same as clicking the Send/Receive button on your Outlook toolbar in Outlook 2000.

- **Refresh.** This command simply refreshes the distribution group list shown in the center of the taskpad.

- • **More Information.** This button launches a separate window for the Managing E-mail section of the online help system.

Users

As seen in Figure 5-9, this is where you can allegedly manage end users on the SBS network. But, in reality, all you can do is add users via the **Add User** button. The other important buttons (**Reset Password**, **Change User Properties**, **Add User to Groups**) are grayed out and unavailable for security reasons. Huh? Take the ability to reset passwords. A malcontent power user could easily reset the passwords for other employees, read their e-mail, and so on. Thus, that type of option is grayed out.

Figure 5-9

The Users taskpad.

As defined above, the **Refresh** button simply refreshes the list of users that are displayed. The **More Information** button takes you to the Manage Users section of the online help system.

Computers

So finally the power user is loose in the Palouse! The Computers taskpad has no grayed out buttons, as seen in Figure 5-10.

Figure 5-10

A power user has all options with Computers.

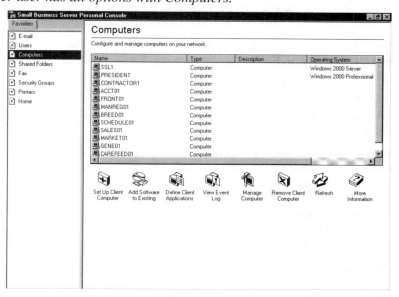

- **Set Up Client Computer.** This is a very interesting button. You might remember from Chapter 4 that the Add User process spawns the Set Up Computer Wizard (SCW). But the challenge facing SBSers was where to go if you wanted to run just the SCW? This button is your answer.

- **Add Software to Existing Computer.** This is where you can add a native SBS client-side application such as Outlook 2000 to a workstation. And any third-party applications you've correctly defined via the next link (Define Client Applications) will appear here as well. What really occurs is the SCW runs and displays the Applications screen.

BEST PRACTICE: By default, no computer is selected in the detail pane. If you click **Add Software to Existing Computer**, nothing will happen at this point. However, if you highlight a computer in the detail pane and then click **Add Software to Existing Computer**, the SCW will launch.

- **Define Client Applications.** This is the same as the Define Client Application link on the To Do List (from the SBS Administrator Console). This is where you can define third-party client applications that are to be installed to the client workstation using the SCW. I discuss some of the Define Client Applications issues of this approach, including limitations such as not being able to use Microsoft installer files (*.MSI), in Chapter 6 in the discussion on installing and removing applications.

- **View Event Log.** When you highlight a listed computer in the display, and click the **View Event Log** button, the Event View snap-in will launch for that computer. However, this assumes the computer is Windows 2000-based in order for this to work (for example, this won't work with Win9x/ME). The basic assumption here is that you would select the SBS 2000 server machine and simply view the event logs (which include Application, Security, System, Directory, DNS, File Replication). If no computer is selected from the list, the View Event Log will perform no action when clicked.

- **Manage Computer.** This button will launch the Manage Computer snap-in for Windows 2000-based computers. And you guessed it. You first select the Windows 2000 computer in the list that is displayed and then click the **Manage Computer** button.

- **Remove Client Computer.** Just as the button name suggests, you would highlight a computer and click the **Remove Client** button to remove it from the SBS network. But, upon closer examination, what's really occurring here? First, a Windows 2000 Professional or Windows NT Workstation 4.0-based computer is truly removed as a member of the domain. If your computer is Windows ME/9x-based, the listing on the computer screen is updated to delete that computer name. But since these machines have no Security ID (SID) at the domain level, no SID removal process occurs. If this doesn't make much sense to you, don't worry about it. If at some future date you want to remove a machine that you had originally added to the SBS network, then simply use the **Remove Client Computer** button as described at the top of the paragraph.

The **Refresh** and **More Information** buttons act in a manner similar to the other taskpads (refresh the display, launch the online help system).

Shared Folders

The fourth link down on the left pane of the Small Business Server Personal Console is Shared Folders. There are only two things you can do here: observe existing folders and add a shared folder. Observing the listing of shared folders is more interesting than might seem at first glance. If you expand the Shared Path column on the Computer screen, as I've done in Figure 5-11, you can actually see the path to the folder that is shared. This answers a huge question I often have (and I'm sure you join me) about exactly where a shared folder is pointing.

Figure 5-11

This (the Shared Folders screen) is the best way to see what exact folder is being shared both by share name and hard disk location.

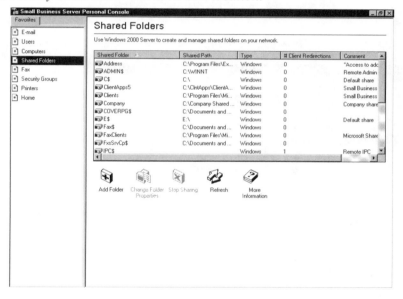

You will note that you can't find this type of information navigating via My Network Places. (Even if you right-click and select **Properties** for a shared folder, it doesn't display its hard disk location). You could use Windows Explorer at the server machine to do some serious hunt-and-peck keystroking to ultimately find out what folders are shared (as seen by the shared hand symbol in Windows Explorer) using which share names.

The **Add Folder** button launches the **Add Shared Folder Wizard**. Note the **Change Folder Properties** and **Stop Sharing** buttons are grayed out. The **Refresh** and **More Information** buttons have previously been defined on other screens and act the same here.

> BEST PRACTICE: I discuss issues related to the sharing of folders, including share-level and NTFS permissions, in Chapter 6.

Fax

The Fax screen, shown in Figure 5-12, allows the power user (who I assume is granted your blessings to use the Small Business Server Personal Console) to interact with the Microsoft Shared Fax Service in SBS 2000.

Figure 5-12
This is where fax activity is managed in the Small Business Server Personal Console.

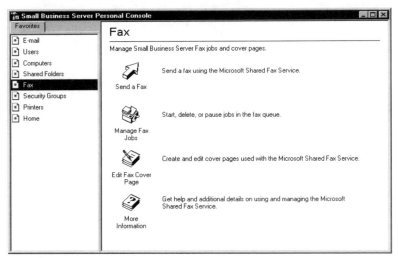

- The **Send a Fax** button launches the **Send Fax Wizard**. This is, of course, where you could immediately send a fax on-the-fly without being inside an application, such as Microsoft Word.

- **Manage Fax Jobs** launches the **Microsoft Shared Fax Service Console** that is great for managing fax traffic (including the all-important task of quickly viewing which faxes your organization has sent or received).

- The **Edit Fax Cover Page** button allows you to, not surprisingly, view and edit existing fax cover pages (including the default four fax cover pages included in SBS 2000: **confident.cov**, **fyi.cov**, **generic.cov**, **urgent.cov**). When the **Fax Cover Page Editor** launches, you can also create new fax cover pages.

- The **More Information** button launches the context-sensitive online help system for faxing.

BEST PRACTICE: I discuss faxing in much greater detail in Chapter 14.

Security Groups

Here's another example of the SBS development team at Microsoft listening to feedback from you and me. An oft-requested feature was the ability to manage security groups from the SBS Consoles (both Administrative and Personal). Here it is as seen in Figure 5-13.

Figure 5-13
Meet a welcome addition to the SBS Console family: Security Groups.

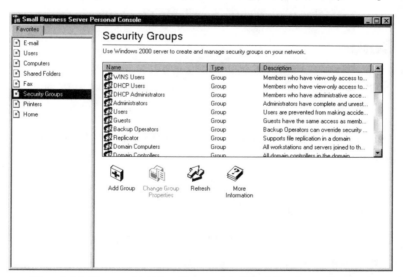

- The **Add Group** button allows you to add and configure a security group (via the **Add Security Group Wizard**).

- The **Change Group Properties** button is unavailable and the **Refresh** and **More Information** buttons have previously been defined.

Printers

To be honest, the Printers screen just puts a pretty face on the Printers folder that is also found in Control Panel. Not that there is anything wrong with that, but I do want to manage your expectations. If you're used to working with the Printers Folder, then you really don't need the Printers screen on the SBS Personal Console. But, that said, the Printers screen has the following buttons:

- **Add Printer.** This launches the Add Printer Wizard and allows you to add and configure a new printer.

- **Change Printer.** When you select a printer and click this button, a property sheet for the selected printer appears.

- **Manage Print Job.** First, select a printer and then click the button to display the printer queue window that shows active print jobs.

- **Refresh** and **More Information.** Ahem – these have previously been defined.

Home

This displays the Small Business Server Personal Console home page which has the Server Status View. This was discussed earlier in the chapter

Guest Column

On the Microsoft SBS Development team, there are few more qualified to discuss the SBS Consoles than Dean Paron. It's an honor and a pleasure to present Dean's words of wisdom:

When designing the administration model for SBS 2000, we held a few goals paramount in importance:

  *Present the VAP with a set of flexible administration tools that were 100 percent compatible with Windows 2000 practices.

  *Identify the typical users of the Small Business Server environment and enable the quick creation of those types of accounts.

To achieve these means, the SBS 2000 administration model differs in a few key ways from the SBS 4.5 model. Most important, and probably most noticeable, access to network resources (such as printers and file shares) is now controlled via group memberships, instead of the per-user basis that was previously em-

ployed in SBS 4.5. This scheme not only follows Windows 2000 best practices, but it also grants the administrator much more flexibility than was previously present. This flexibility may seem daunting at first, but SBS 2000 setup creates all the security groups and organizational units required to enable the small-business users to immediately access resources. For example, at setup time, a group called "BackOffice Internet Users" is created. Members of that group can (not surprisingly) access the Internet.

At first blush, the experienced SBS administrator might think that these groups are simply substitutes for the per-user configuration that was previously supported, i.e., instead of clicking on a checkbox to give a user Internet access, now I need to add him to a group. However, with SBS 2000 we've actually shortened administration task time by introducing the idea of user templates. Think of these templates as shortcuts to creating user accounts: By modeling a new user after an existing template, an administrator can quickly transfer key administration data to new users, including group memberships.

No discussion of templates would be complete without diverting into the thought process that went into creating them. When we studied how our VAPs created user accounts, the data they entered typically fell into two distinct categories: 1) the information about the user that was specific to that account – items of this sort include the account name, password, home folder, and mailbox; and, 2) the information about the user that was typically similar to other classes of users in the organization – items of this sort include group and distribution list memberships, remote access settings, and address information. After reviewing the data, we thought it made sense to design our Add User Wizard so that all the information similar to classes of users could just be inherited and skipped at creation. Thus, the idea of templates was born, and to make the SBS 2000 administration model even easier to use out-of-the-box, we created several templates that are available for use immediately after install of the server.

Small Business User: *This template account corresponds to the typical knowledge worker that encompasses 95 percent of the users of the network. Users modeled after this template can, by default, read from all the file shares, print to the printers, send faxes, and access the Internet. These users are prohibited from performing any administrative tasks and even from logging into the server itself.*

Small Business Power User: *Users modeled after this template contain all the same access permissions that Users own, but they also have administrative access over some key tasks. For example, these users can clear Fax and Printer queues and create other user and group accounts. Furthermore, when these users log on to the server via terminal services, they are immediately entered into a task-based administration console that only exposes those tasks for which they have permission. When that console is closed, their remote session to the desktop is also closed. In the small-business marketplace there would typically be one or two of these users present at a small business – probably the most techno-savvy user at the business and someone a VAP would entrust to perform easy administrative tasks in her absence.*

Small Business Administrator: *This template account typically maps to that individual who performs the SBS install and has extensive computer knowledge. Users modeled after this template have complete unrestricted access to the computer and domain.*

So, now, when an administrator creates a new user, he simply adds the name, password, mailbox, and selects a preexisting user template to finish the creation of a brand new account. That new account contains distribution and security group memberships, remote access settings, and address information with which the administrator didn't need to bother entering. The account just works.

Once this model has been introduced, it's only natural to wonder how extensible it is, namely:

Q: Can I still create users without using templates?

A: Yes. If desired, an administrator can choose to create a new user from scratch and individually decide any settings and group memberships. In fact, an administrator can pick an existing template, review the settings, and tweak individual properties that might be different for that specific user.

Q: Can the templates and groups be modified using the Windows 2000 administration tools?

A: Yes. The Add User Wizard will inherit properties of any template user on the system, and any group on the system, regardless of the tools with which it was created. The Add User Wizard is effectively generic to these items, a big improvement from the SBS 4.5 timeframe, which some of you might remember.

Q: Can I easily make my own templates?

A: Yes. If an administrator wants to create a new template account that will map to the settings of several users, say the "Hygienist" template at a dental office, or the "Secretary" template at a law office, he can simply check a box when the user is being created and the new user will be added to the list of available template users. In fact, the beauty of the template accounts is that they are simply user accounts _ no more, no less. What registers these accounts as templates within the Add User Wizard are their memberships in the "BackOffice Template Users" Group. To add more templates to your system, simply add members to that group. To modify the properties of a template, simply open the property sheet of the account. It's that simple.

So, in recap, the SBS 2000 administration model is significantly more powerful and flexible than previous versions of the product – the core model is based around security groups, and the Windows and SBS tools can modify all the data interchangeably. To give the administrator an easier way to reuse and default large portions of user administration, the idea of templates was introduced. A set of working templates ships with the product, but an administrator can tailor the tools to meet his own needs.

Dean Paron has been a Program Manager at Microsoft since 1997 and currently works on the Small Business Server and BackOffice development team. An accomplished conference speaker, he has recently presented at Comdex, TechEd, MTB, and Networld InterOp. He currently resides in Bellevue, Washington, but wants to live on Queen Anne Hill in Seattle someday.

More Console Stuff

Welcome back from that masterful speech by Dean Paron. In particular, I like the point Dean raised about allowing access to the native tools (see Dean's early comments about 100 percent compatibility with Windows 2000 practices).

My translation on this relates to a situation I've observed countless times: the enterprise weekend warrior. Perhaps you've observed this in SBS land. A well-meaning MCSE who works at the enterprise level during the week volunteers to help his brother's small business implement SBS. In the SBS 4.x days, this was a common occurrence, with the MCSE mocking the SBS console as a "sissy tool" that isn't used at the enterprise level. Perhaps you know the rest of the story. The well-meaning MCSE did great harm by not using the SBS console (and its bevy of integration processes and SBS wizards) and then proceeding to drop under-the-hood to use native Windows NT tools.

So, in SBS 2000, this same enterprise-level MCSE can now help his brother and, much to this weekend warrior's pleasure, see that the SBS Administrator Console allows direct access to the native Windows 2000 tools. Now, of course, we die-hard SBSers are grieving that the SBS Consoles have been less SBS-like and more native Windows 2000-like (and thus removing some of the mystique of SBS in my eyes). But it's a small price to pay to simplify the SBS experience for one and all (including the MCSE weekend warriors!).

Let's jump into the good stuff: the Small Business Server Administrator Console, which is accessed directly from the Start button.

Architecture

I'll start at the grassroots level. You will notice the SBS Administrator Console conforms to the classic snap-in view of an MMC. In the left-pane are two tabs: Tree and Favorites.

Tree Tab

When the Tree tab is selected, several SBS tools and many native Windows 2000 Server tools are displayed. This is shown in Figure 5-14.

Figure 5-14

Viewing the Tree tab that displays several SBS-specific tools and many Windows 2000 Server tools.

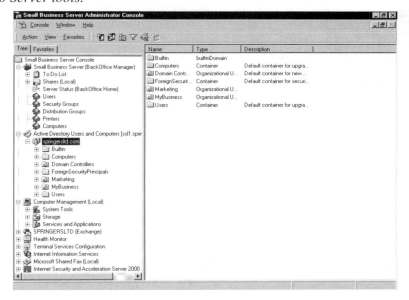

Favorites Tab

The Favorites tab displays two links: Small Business Server Tips and Management Shortcuts. These will be explored shortly, but I would share with you now that the selections accessed via the Favorites tab display taskpads that are similar in appearance to the SBS Personal Console.

Now I'll proceed to describe the individual components of both the Tree and Favorites tabs. Note that in the case of the Tree tab, many of the individual components will receive introduction here but are more fully explored in the chapter that directly applies to the native tool. For example, when I discuss First Organization (Exchange), I'll quickly point you to Chapter 11 where Exchange is discussed in great detail. Got it?

Small Business Server BackOffice Manager

So when you launch the Small **Business Server Administrator Console** from the shortcut on the **Start** menu, you'll see the **Server Status View** by default, as seen in Figure 5-15. That's because the Server Status (BackOffice Home) object is selected in the tree. I'll discuss the other sub-objects in a moment.

Figure 5-15

The cool Server Status View page in the SBS Administrator Console.

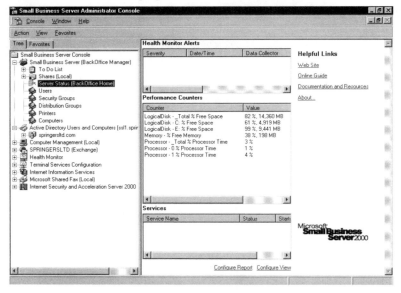

I liken the Server Status View as an executive information system (EIS) for SBSers wherein only critical SBS variables are presented and the nonessential malarkey is filtered out. An EIS is a business tool that shows important business information to executives. I discuss the Server Status View in much greater detail in Chapter 16, but for now, consider it your at-a-glance buddy for monitoring your SBS server machine. You will note with interest that the major monitoring areas of disk, memory, and processor are presented in the Performance Counters section.

Perhaps you've been like me and have, after a few glances, started to take the Server Status View for granted. A recent SBS client experience helped me appreciate the value of the Server Status View more than I realized. At this particular client site, I replaced a consultant who was, shall we say, exited from his engagement. Turns out he recommended stand-alone implementations of Windows 2000 Server and Exchange 2000 Server as the technology solution for this firm. As you know, this client could have had SBS for essentially the same price. But, more to the point, the network administrator was trying to monitor the server machine using a combination of Task Manager and Performance Monitor when the information she really wanted and needed is presented in the SBS Server Status View. Problem was, she didn't have SBS installed, based on the former consultant's recommendation. Bummer.

Also note that the Small Business Server (BackOffice Manager) parent object contains more children objects than just the Server Status View shown when Server Status (BackOffice Home) is selected. There is the infamous To Do List, which is truly your SBS deployment methodology, shown in Figure 5-16.

Figure 5-16

The genius of SBS is its in-a-box system methodology led by the To Do List.

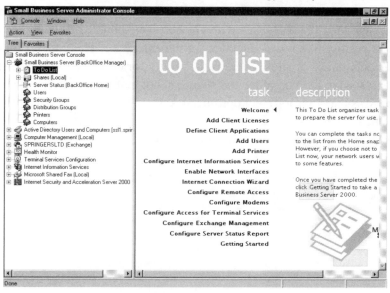

The Shares (Local) link is the same one found under Computer Management (Local) which I describe fully in a few pages. Next up are the query nodes, the green objects for Users, Security Groups, Distribution Groups, Printers, and Computers. These query nodes, also seen in Figure 5-16 above, give you direct access to the list of users, groups, printers, and computers. I often click a query node when I just want to see a list of users and not get caught up in any wizardry.

> BEST PRACTICE: On a more advanced note, if you right-click a query node and select **Edit Query**, the Find Custom Search dialog box appears and displays how the query was built and how it interrogates the Active Directory database. The SBS gurus in the readership of this book will find this fascinating! If you right-click and query node and select **Properties**, you will not only see how the query was constructed, but the Content Menu and Columns tab allow you to recast the appearance of how the query results look in the right display pane of the SBS Administrator Console. Advanced but fun stuff, let me tell ya!

Active Directory Users and Computers

Talk about good timing. While writing this chapter, I had lunch with one of the product managers from the Active Directory team at Microsoft who has since moved over to the SBS team. His insights into SBS and Active Directory were especially interesting to me. I offered and he confirmed that SBS doesn't really use Active Directory like it was intended for the enterprise. There aren't multiple forests, trees, domains, or sites. There is the ability for effective use of organizational units (OUs) to help organize the business, but that's about it. We both agreed that SBS had appropriately optimized Active Directory for the small business. One of these optimizations is the inclusion of the Active Directory Users and Computers snap-in, as seen in Figure 5-17.

Notes:

Figure 5-17

Meet the Active Directory Users and Computers snap-in in the SBS Administrator Console.

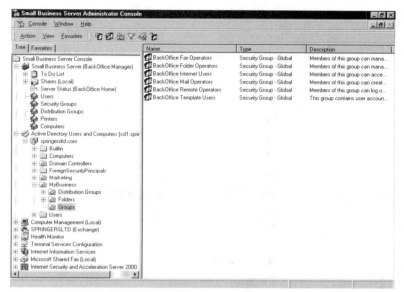

BEST PRACTICE: One way in which SBS uses Active Directory functionality that you might not have known concerns replication. If you add another Windows 2000 domain controller to SBS network, the Active Directory databases will be replicated between DCs. This is discussed more in Chapter 19.

So in all likelihood, you'll use the Active Directory Users and Computers snap-in to:

- Add and manage users

- Add and manage groups (security, distribution)

- Add and manage OUs

- Apply Group Policy Objects (GPOs)

- Add miscellaneous items. You might add an Exchange-based Global Address Contact, publish a printer to the Active Directory, and publish a shared folder to the Active Directory.

Computer Management (Local)

And just when you thought that some of the more useful native tools were ignored in the SBS Administrator Console, along comes the Computer Management (Local) object. This is where many of the individual tools found in the Administrative Tools program group are hidden. To be brutally frank, it took a lot of SBS use for me to discover that the Computer Management (Local) snap-in is one of the most valuable objects in the SBS Administrator Console. Computer Management (Local) is shown in Figure 5-18 and is proof-in-the-pudding that you can do nearly EVERYTHING from the SBS consoles just as the SBS development team intended.

Figure 5-18
A true buffet of SBS tools, meet Computer Management (Local).

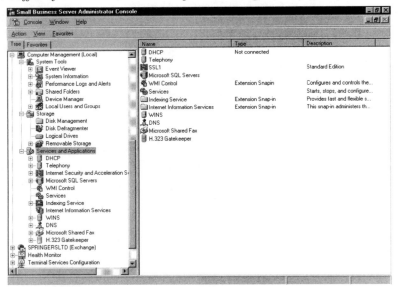

There are three sub-objects in Computer Management (Local) that I will now explore.

System Tools

Microsoft has grouped several tools together here under the belief that these relate to management of the operating system. I think they've done a good job in creating this logical grouping of the following tools:

BEST PRACTICE: Kindly note that I further explore the meaning and purpose for these tools in much greater detail in Chapters 6 and 7. Here my intention is to provide simple definitions.

Event Viewer

Here's a frequently accessed snap-in for all SBSers, the Event Viewer. This is where you can view the following logs.

- Application. This reports start-up and on-going information on Windows 2000, services and applications. Very useful and a common place to troubleshoot application problems.

- Directory Service. Not surprisingly, this reports Active Directory information. Because SBS interacts with Active Directory in a superficial manner compared to large enterprises, this log isn't that meaningful. It'll basically tell you that Active Directory has started. Big woop, eh?

- File Replication Service. This is not a useful log in the SBS world and will tell you that the File Replication Service has started and is no longer preventing your server machine from acting as a domain controller.

- Security. Assuming you want to audit logons and the like (such as file access activity), the Security log is very important to you. Otherwise it's blank by default.

- System. Now we're talking important. This is where critical operating system information is reported, including start-up conditions and failures. It's safe to say the System log will be heavily used during your tenure as an SBSer.

- DNS Server. This log reports the startup and current state of the DNS server component in SBS. DNS is the default name resolution mechanism in SBS, so looking at this log is important if names aren't resolved when clients browse the network.

BEST PRACTICE: Most of the time, the DNS log will report Event #2, which indicates that DNS has started. Interestingly, in the System Log, you might occasionally receive notification that the DNS server attempted to start and failed when you reboot your SBS server. Don't be alarmed. The DNS server service will continue its attempts to restart and ultimately succeed after predecessor operating system-level services finally start.

BEST PRACTICE: Because the Event logs were moved to the Event Viewer snap-in in SBS 2000, you can now sort on each of the columns (Type, Date, Time, Source, Category, Event, User, and Computer). This is much more efficient than trying to configure the fan-dangled Event log filter that you used in SBS 4.5 and is still found under the View menu.

System Information

This snap-in reports information that can not easily be found anywhere else, such as hardware IRQ settings. There are six major categories, each with additional subcategories of information:

- System Summary
- Hardware Resources
- Components
- Software Environment
- Internet Explorer 5
- Applications

Performance Logs and Alerts

This is good old Performance Monitor, a tool that dates back to the earliest days on Windows NT, the predecessor to Windows 2000. I discuss Performance Monitor, which is also known as System Monitor, in Chapters 7 and 16.

Shared Folders

This is one of the few places that you can see what physical disk location is mapped to what share name, as seen in Figure 5-19. And by clicking on Sessions, you can actually see what users are currently logged on the network. More on both of these topics of shared folders and users logged on in Chapter 6.

Figure 5-19
Observe how share names relate to physical disk storage folders.

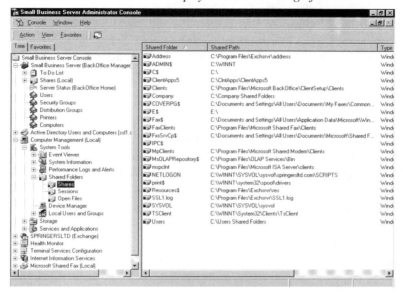

Device Manager

One of the most welcome additions to SBS 2000 is Device Manager. This tool was clearly lacking in the SBS 4.5 environment, when managing hardware devices in real-time was something of a CompTIA A+ certification. Seriously, hardware device management is much improved and it occurs right here.

Local Users and Groups

Huh? Aren't we on an SBS network with a domain and not a workgroup? You bet we are and that's why Local Users and Groups has a red "X" across it. Because you are not using a workgroup, this option is unavailable.

Storage

The Storage object has several selections that allow you to manage your hard disks and removable media. There are a couple of reasons you might click here:

- **Healthy Disks.** Clicking on the Disk Management icon provides the old Disk Administrator view in SBS 4.5, but with a twist. Not only is storage space and disk format displayed, but you are alerted as to whether disks are healthy or not, and are online or offline. This is very handy when troubleshooting storage problems.

- **Mirroring.** It is Disk Management again where you create dynamic volumes by **right-clicking** on the **Disk** indicator (e.g., Disk 0) and selecting **Upgrade to Dynamic Disk**. The **Upgrade to Dynamic Disk** dialog box appears and allows you to select which disks should be upgraded from Basic to Dynamic disks. Make your selection and click **OK**.

BEST PRACTICE: To implement mirroring, your disks must be dynamic, something that many SBSers overlook in the rough-and-tumble life of the real world!

- **Media Pools.** When using the native Windows 2000 backup utility in SBS 2000, if you want to use the scheduler, with one method you'll need to create a "media pool" of tapes. This is accomplished under Removable Storage by **right-clicking** the **Media Pools** object and selecting **Create Media Pool**. I discuss this further in Chapter 6.

Services and Applications

By all means, take an extra few minutes to click on each of the components beneath Services and Applications. I've listed these components in the order of importance to the SBSer. That is, this is the following order that I've found myself using these objects, the most popular being first.

- **Services.** So many times in your life as an SBSer you'll need to stop and restart services. This occurs here.

- **Routing and Remote Access.** Believe me on this one. You're on the telephone with an SBS network user who can't create a VPN connection. This is where you monitor remote logons.

- **DNS.** So, did the new workstation dynamically register itself in the DNS tables? Here's where you will find out.

- **DHCP.** Suppose you need to see why a workstation isn't getting its IP address from the DHCP server service on an SBS network. Start your investigation here.

- **WINS.** For legacy name resolution matters where DNS isn't part of the picture, click on the WINS object to see what machines have registered their NetBIOS names correctly.

- **All the rest.** The other tools have minor roles in the life of an SBSer (or are important and are accessed elsewhere in the SBS Administrator Console) and are listed here only for reference purposes: Telephony, Internet Security and Acceleration Server, WMI Control, Indexing Service, Internet Information Services, Microsoft Shared Fax, H.323 Gatekeeper.

First Organization (Exchange)

This is where one of the most mission-critical functions—e-mail—is managed in SBS 2000. In fact, this is so important, I've dedicated all of Chapter 11 to the use and management of Exchange 2000 Server. When you click this object, as seen in Figure 5-20, you are looking at System Manager. Enough said for now.

Figure 5-20

E-mail is managed from First Organization (Exchange), which is also known as System Manager.

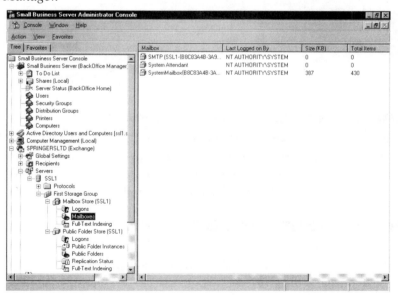

Health Monitor

This is a tool that is unique to SBS and BackOffice 2000 that allows you to dynamically monitor your server in real-time. I consider it much more effective than Performance Monitor mentioned above. Health Monitor, shown in Figure 5-21, is discussed at-length in Chapter 16.

Figure 5-21
Health Monitor is a way cool tool.

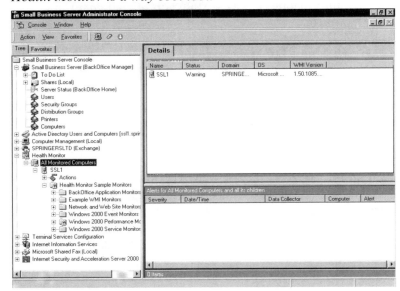

Terminal Services Configuration

This is the Terminal Services Configuration snap-in and allows you to configure the finer points of Terminal Services on the SBS server machine. Remember that Terminal Services is set up in Remote Administration Mode by default when you install SBS 2000. I discuss Terminal Services in depth in Chapter 8.

Internet Information Services

Again, the subject of its own chapter, Internet Information Services (IIS) is managed from this snap-in in the SBS Administrator Console. This is also where you add and configure the FTP service. See Chapter 17 for more details.

Microsoft Shared Fax (Local)

I'm really excited about the revamped faxing capability in SBS 2000 and devote Chapter 14 to this topic. Faxing is managed from this snap-in in SBS 2000 and is shown in Figure 5-22.

Figure 5-22

All fax management occurs from the Microsoft Shared Fax (Local) snap-in.

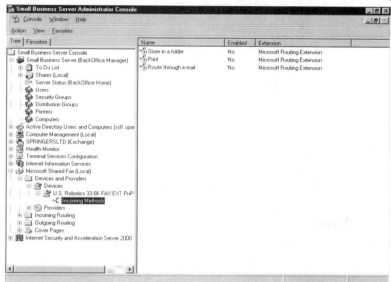

Internet Security and Acceleration Server 2000

Certainly one of the more important snap-ins in the SBS Administrator Console, you can perform hundreds of adjustments, tweaks, and fine tunings to your firewall and caching capabilities right here. And you guessed it – an entire chapter is dedicated to ISA Server: See Chapter 10. The Internet Security and Acceleration Server 2000 snap-in is shown in Figure 5-23.

Notes:

Figure 5-23
The SBS firewall and caching solution known as ISA Server.

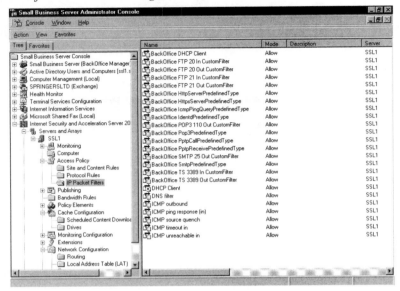

Favorites Tab

The Favorites tab is truly a blast from the past for us old SBSers. It has buttons galore, divided between the two objects: Small Business Server Tips and Management Shortcuts. I'll explore both in this section.

Notes:

Small Business Server Tips

As seen in Figure 5-24, Small Business Server Tips displays several links listed below.

Figure 5-24:

Small Business Server Tips under the Favorites tab.

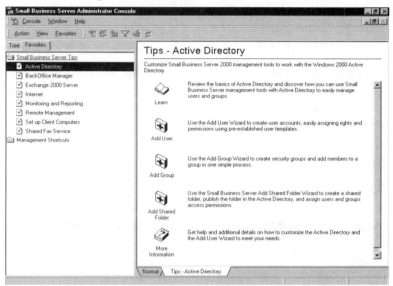

- **Active Directory.** This allows you to add users and groups and to publish shared folders to the Active Directory. It is one of the few places you can launch the Add User Wizard without having to go through the To Do List.

- **BackOffice Manager.** I recommend SBS gurus spend a few moments with the **Customize** and **Create a Query** buttons here. Customize allows you to modify which query nodes are displayed under the Small Business Server (BackOffice Manager) when the Tree view is selected in the SBS Administrator Console. Create a Query launches the Add Query Node Wizard to create your own query nodes to use in the SBS Administrator Console and elsewhere. This is very powerful and fun guru stuff when you're sitting around bored with absolutely nothing to do, my good friends!

- **Exchange 2000 Server.** Numerous help buttons on this page allow you to learn more about Exchange 2000 Server. You can also add an e-mail distribution group here. Nothing too exciting, to be honest with you.

- **Internet.** This tip page allows you to run the Internet Connection Wizard from a location other than the To Do List and also change the password you use to log on to your ISP for e-mail services.

- **Monitoring and Reporting.** You can configure the server status reports and view from this tips page.

- **Remote Management.** Just a couple of help system links here for remote management matters.

- **Set up Client Computers.** This is one of the few places that you can run the Setup Computer Wizard (SCW) without having to first run the Add Computer Wizard from the To Do List! This is very cool because sometimes you just want to run the SCW for an existing user that has a new computer. That task is accomplished here. The Tips – Setting Up Client Computers page is shown in Figure 5-25.

Figure 5-25

This page is a one-stop shop for managing client computers on an SBS network.

BEST PRACTICE: This is also one of the few places you can remove a client computer from an SBS network. Click on the **Remove Client Computer** link to accomplish this task.

- **Shared Fax Service.** What can I say other than this is where you can manage the faxing function on an SBS network.

Management Shortcuts

Whew! As we approach the end of our long journey exploring the SBS Consoles, we have the management shortcuts remaining. These are basically shortcuts to things you've already seen before, such as the query nodes for users, groups, printers, and computers. The point to management shortcuts is that they providone-click links to "raw" objects. No fancy buttons here, buddy boy! The following management shortcuts are available and basically self-explanatory. (Or, you can go to your SBS server and click on the darn things to learn more about them!)

- Users

- Security Groups

- Distribution Groups

- Printers

- Computers

- Fax Devices

- Web Sites

- To Do List

- Shared Folders

- Home

Console Customization

One thing that the SBS gurus latched upon when SBS 2000 was released in February 2001 was the ability to more easily modify the console. In prior releases of SBS, modifying the console took the smarts of a computer science major in college and the backbone of a Texas ranger. This is no longer the case.

Truth be told, I've been somewhat perplexed by the SBS guru's excitement for customizing consoles. I'm perfectly satisfied, except in one or two cases, with the two consoles offered by default in SBS 2000. The exceptions are when you install SQL Server 2000 and need to manually add the SQL Server Enterprise Manager, want to view the RRAS snap-in, and when you install third-party applications and want the application manger(s) for these products to appear in the SBS consoles. But more on that in a moment.

Back to the issue at hand: the need for a custom console at all. I've had it explained this way to me by one of the leading SBSers, Curtis Hicks, at the Center for Computing Resources in the Detroit, Michigan, area. He explained that at many of his SBS clients, which number over 200 sites, he likes to deploy standardized management consoles that meet their specific needs. Curtis has a valid point. With such a large SBS client base, he can certainly benefit from standardization at each site when it comes to custom SBS consoles. However, for those of us with small client portfolios (including yours truly), you might scrutinize the need for custom consoles.

In this section, I explore a couple of different types of customization, including creating a new MMC, modifying the existing SBS Administrator Console, and creating your Administrator type console.

A Naked MMC

First off, you can create a Microsoft Management Console (MMC) for just about darn near anything in the Windows world. Click **Start**, **Run**, and type **MMC** in the **Open** field. You'll be presented with a bare-naked MMC that you can add your own snap-ins to by selecting **Add/Remove Snap-in** from the **Console** menu. Your console can be shared with other users. This is the most basic form of working with MMC-based consoles.

Modifying the Administrator Console

A little history is in order first and foremost. There are really two copies of both consoles on an SBS server machine. This is a little known fact in SBS land. The copies are located at:

```
Copy #1:  %system drive%\Documents and Settings\All
Users\Application Data\Microsoft\BackOffice\Management
```

```
Copy #2:  %system drive%\Program Files\Microsoft
BackOffice\Management
```

The first copy listed above is the copy that maps directly to the SBS console shortcuts from the Start menu and can be edited directly. By that I mean these files don't have a read-only restriction on the MMC-based file. Contrast that with the second console location under Program Files. This is the "master copy" of the SBS consoles that is flagged as read-only and not intended to be modified. Rather, these SBS console copies, located underneath Program Files, are intended to be backup copies if the working copy is somehow damaged.

> BEST PRACTICE: Even though I've shown you the two locations of the SBS consoles above, there is actually a better way to modify either the Administrator Console or the Personal Console. This is accomplished by clicking **Start** to display the Start menu and then right-clicking either **SBS Console** (e.g., **Administrator Console**). Then select **Author** from the secondary menu and you are placed in author mode in the SBS console located at the location of "Copy #1" listed above. This is far easier than drilling six layers deep to get to the edit copy of the SBS consoles.

Modifying The Existing Administrator Console

So, let's follow an example of why I'd want to modify the SBS Administrator Console. In this case, I'd like to add the SQL Server Enterprise Mananger. This example assumes that you've installed SQL Server 2000 to the SBS server machine, which is something you SHOULD have completed in Chapter 3, believe me. You might be interested in knowing that none of the SQL Server components are added to the SBS consoles when you in fact install SQL Server.

Follow these steps right now as part of the SSL methodology:

1. Log on to the SBS server machine, which in this book is **SSL1**, as **Administrator** with the password **husky9999**.
2. Click **Start**.
3. Right-click **Small Business Server Administrator Console** and select **Author** from the secondary menu that appears. This is shown in Figure 5-26.

Notes:

Figure 5-26
*The easiest way to modify the SBS Administrator Console is the Author second-
ary menu selection.*

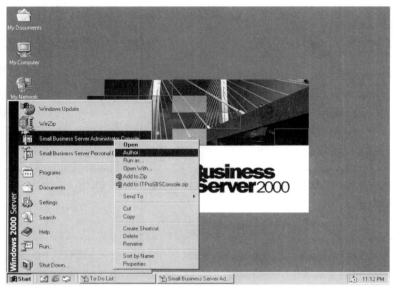

4. Select **Add/Remove Snap-in** from the **Console** menu.
5. Click **Add** when the **Add/Remove Snap-in** dialog box appears.
6. Select **Microsoft SQL Enterprise Manager** from the list of snap-ins
    displayed in the **Add Stand-alone Snap-in** dialog box.
7. Click **Add** to add the **Microsoft SQL Enterprise Manager** snap-in.
8. Click **Close** to close **Add Standalone Snap-in**.
9. Click **OK** to close the **Add/Remove Snap-in** dialog box.
10. Observe in Figure 5-27 that the Small Business Server Administrator Console
    displays the Microsoft SQL Enterprise Manage. Mission accomplished!

Notes:

Figure 5-27

Merci-merci! It's a modified SBS Administrator Console showing the Microsoft SQL Enterprise Manager (displayed as Microsoft SQL Servers).

Creating a New Administrator Console

It may well be that you want a new SBS administrator-type console that is in fact separate from the SBS Administrator Console provided by Microsoft. This actually makes sense in that you might want to create an administrator-like console that doesn't impact the existing SBS Administrator Consoles.

Here's what I recommend. Refer to the procedure above, and between steps #2 and #3, simply select **Save As** from the **Console** menu and provide a new MMC name (such as **SSLAdmin**). You've now effectively created a new MMC with the existing SBS Administrator Console snap-ins. Think about it, and I bet you'll agree this makes a lot of sense!

Notes:

Oh – MyConsole

There is another console in title only called MyConsole. This is really a Web-enabled interface to commence a Terminal Services session with Internet Explorer. MyConsole is displayed in Figure 5-28 and is discussed in much greater detail in Chapter 8.

Figure 5-28

MyConsole is not really an SBS console but a way to utilize Terminal Services with a Web browser.

Relationship to Windows 2000 Server and Big BackOffice 2000

So, how do the SBS consoles relate to Windows 2000 Server and Big BackOffice —if at all? Well, let me take those matters one at a time. With Windows 2000 Server, you can dig, hunt and peck, and find much of the functionality presented in the SBS consoles. For example, the Administrative Tools program group contains much of the native tools I've displayed to you via the SBS Administrator Console. However, some things like the Add User Wizard are truly unique to SBS and can't be re-created in the nekkid version of Windows 2000 Server in a million years! What's important for you, the SBSer, to understand is that you should ALWAYS use the SBS consoles!

The relationship between SBS and Big BackOffice in the console area is very interesting. It is here that the joint-development, team nature of these respective products is really apparent. The Administrator consoles are basically the same, with only a few minute differences such as different To Do Lists. Big BackOffice doesn't have the Personal Console for power users; SBS has more push-button functionality. But, if you placed both SBS 2000 and Big BackOffice 2000 servers side-by-side, you'd quickly see their similarities!

Summary

You have now been exposed to the heart and soul of SBS: the SBS Consoles. This foundation, combined with the server and client setup experience gained from Chapters 3 and 4, now allows you to master the daily baker's-dozen tasks of an SBSer in Chapter 6. So, I've talked long enough about the two SBS consoles and must now take a break and go take my power walk. See you next chapter.

Chapter 6
SBS Administration: Daily and Weekly

This important chapter takes a very real-world view of SBS. You will find an assortment of tasks and duties you are likely to perform on a daily or weekly basis. Granted, the frequency that you perform the "baker's dozen" of tasks will depend on your unique situation. You may even have your own tasks to add to this list, such as performing some reindexing job on a business accounting application.

It has been my observation that how and when daily and weekly SBS tasks are performed depends on the following factors. It might be that your skill level as an SBS administrator or consultant affects the tasks you perform. A newbie might perform minimal tasks and a guru might perform more tasks. The activity on your SBS network can determine which tasks you feel comfortable performing and when. Don't overlook how the computer knowledge of your users can determine what maintenance tasks are performed (especially the end-user support tasks). And believe it or not, the quality of your network from wiring to server brand, can affect your task list too!

At this point, I assume that you've correctly set up a robust SBS network based on the SSL methodology used in this book (yes, it's the sample company Springer Spaniels Limited again). This SBS implementation should be stable, functional, and allow you to continue forward with this and the remaining chapters. If such isn't the case, don't be afraid to rewind and redo your SSL network (I'm not going anywhere and I'll wait for you).

The SBS Baker's Dozen

It's now time to impart the top thirteen things (aka baker's dozen) that confront us SBSers during the day-to-day activities of running our SBS networks. Without much further ado, let's get to it and look over the baker's dozen list, which I've attempted to list in order of importance. Table 6-1 shows where we are headed and how we'll get there!

Table 6-1 The SBS Baker's Dozen

Task	Frequency
1 - Virus Detection and Protection	Daily
2 - Tape Backup	Daily
3 - Sharing Files and Folders	Weekly
4 - Mapping Drives	Weekly
5 - Managing Users, Groups, Computers	Daily/Weekly
6 - UPS Power Levels	Daily
7 - Logon/Logoff Status	Daily
8 - End-User Support	Daily
9 - Check System Health	Daily
10 - Go Online	Daily
11 - Installing/Removing Applications	Weekly
12 - Reporting	Daily
13 - Working Smarter Each Day	Daily

BEST PRACTICE: Granted, this list is representative of the life in a day and week of a typically SBSer. Your situation may vary.

1 - Virus Detection and Protection

There is literally no day in the life of an SBSer on which a virus isn't released. Many viruses are harmless and never make the news. But there are those whoppers that surprise us all, such as ILOVEYOU, CODE RED I and II, and NIMDA.

This list of both mellow and harsh viruses will most assuredly continue to grow; thus the elevation of the virus protection and detection function to the top of my SBS 2000 baker's dozen list of daily tasks.

Out of the box, SBS 2000 doesn't have virus protection. Therefore, you must take the bull by the horns, run it through the china shop, and find a virus protection solution to your liking. There are several virus protection solutions on the market, but the one that aligns with SBS 2000 is Trend Micro's OfficeScan 5 for Microsoft Small Business Server 2000. This is the virus protection product that you will download (30-day version) and install as part of the SSL methodology. Time's a wasting – let's get started.

1. Log on to **SSL1** as **Administrator** with the password **husky9999**.
2. Double-click **Internet Explorer** from the SSL1 desktop. Surf over to the following uniform resource locator (URL) by typing **www.antivirus.com/ download** in the **Address** field.
3. Under the **Network Desktop** listing, click the **OfficeScan SBS 2000** link. Complete the **Download Now** fields (**Number of Seats**, **Time to Buy**) and **Contact Information** fields (**First Name**, **Last Name**, **Telephone**, **State/Province**, **Country**, **E-mail Address**, **Company Name** and **Title**). Note in all fairness to the Trend Micro folks, kindly complete the fields just listed with your real name and contact information (hey – this helps Trend Micro with its business!). Select the check boxes for more information and a sales call under **Trend Offers** if you so desire and click the **Download Now** button.
4. When the **Network & Desktop** listing appears, click the link under **Server** for the product (as of this writing, this link is **osbs51_100201.zip**). When the **File Download** dialog box appears, accept the **Save this file to disk** and click **OK**. In the **Save As** dialog box that appears, save the file to **My Documents** (navigate to this folder and click **Save**).
5. Once the download is completed (which can take a spell, as this is a 60 MB file), click **Close** on the **Download complete** dialog box. Close **Internet Explorer** from **File, Close**.
6. Double-click the **My Documents** shortcut on the **SSL1** desktop.
7. Double-click the OfficeScan 5 for Microsoft Small Business Server 2000 30-day trial file that you have downloaded (as of this writing, that file is **ossbs51_100201.zip**).

BEST PRACTICE: My bad! I might have just done you wrong if the *.zip file above didn't launch. If you don't have WinZip installed on your SBS server machine, which at this point would be unlikely if you've followed the SSL methodology, I need to ask a favor of you. Please jump down in the chapter to Task 11: Installing/Removing Applications and complete the steps to download WinZip and install it. Then jump back here and repeat Step 7. It'll work at this time.

8. When **WinZip** launches, click **I Agree** on the **Thank You For Trying WinZip!** page. Click **Extract** and save the file to **\My Documents\Trend** (you will need to type this path and the Trend folder will be created).

9. From the **My Documents** folder, open the **Trend** folder and double-click **Setup.exe**.

10. Click **Next** at the **Welcome** screen.

11. Click **Yes** at the **Software License Agreement** screen.

12. Review the **Information** dialog box (about disk space and so on) and click **OK**.

13. Accept the default installation location of **C:\Program Files\Trend** on the **Choose Destination Location** screen and click **Next**.

14. Accept the default information (**Bob Easter**, **Springer Spaniels Limited**) on the **User Information** page (Figure 6-1). Note you will leave the **Serial:** field blank in order to invoke the 30-day trial period. Click **Next**.

Notes:

Figure 6-1

Creating the 30-day trial period with Trend Micro OfficeScan 5 for Microsoft Small Business Server 2000.

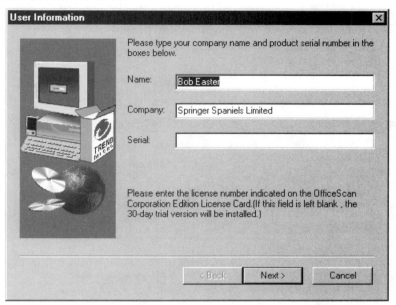

BEST PRACTICE: One of the totally cool things about the Trend Micro OfficeScan 5 for Microsoft Small Business Server 2000 30-day version is that, once your purchase the real, licensed version, you don't have to reinstall said program again. In other words, you like the product so much you purchase it. At that point, all you have to do is enter the serial number as per instructions from Trend. Very easy and a nice user-friendly touch!

15. Click **OK** when informed of the trial period expiration in 30 days on the **30-day trial version** dialog box. The program installation will begin.

16. On the **Domain Name and Port Configuration** screen, accept the default settings shown in Figure 6-2. The fully qualified domain name of **ssl.springers.com** is acceptable in the **Domain name:** field. The **Port number** of **80** is acceptable, believe it or not! That's because this setting isn't being used for external HTTP-based communications where the port is now 8080 in SBS 2000. Rather, this port setting is used for internal

communications between the server and client computers, plus the interaction between the HTML-based OfficeScan Management Console (HTML) which you'll observe later in the Trend OfficeScan Corporate Edition-SSL1 program group. For these forms of communication, the proxy features of ISA Server 2000 are bypassed (see Chapter 10 for this discussion). Click **Next**.

Figure 6-2
This screen facilitates server and client computers communications.

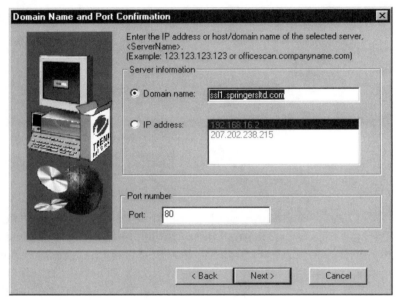

BEST PRACTICE: If you mistakenly place 8080 in the Port: field, the OfficeScan Management Console (HTML) will not function when you attempt to configure and administer the OfficeScan product. Read on.

What is really occurring with the information from Figure 6-2 is that the **ofcscan.ini** file is being populated. In the **[INI_SERVER_SECTION]**, the **Master_DomainName** field is set to **ssl1.springersltd.com**. The **Master_DomainPort** is set to **80**. I learned this when I once set the Port: field in Figure 6-2 to 8080 thinking I was being SBS 2000 smart, but later I had to find a way to fix my mistake. Ergo—the Master_DomainPort setting must be 80.

Oh, by the way, if you are trying to be a smarty pants, such as myself referenced immediately above, you'll need to make one other correction to return the internal HTTP-based communications back to port 80. Navigate to and right-click on the following file and select **Properties:**

```
c:\WINNT\Trend OfficeScan Corporate Edition-SSL1.url
```

The property sheet for this file will appear. In the URL field, at midpoint in the HTTP:// command, replace the **8080** port reference with just **80**. Click **OK** to close. You have now taken the manual steps necessary for OfficeScan 5 to function correctly with respect to internal communications in SBS 2000.

17. Click **Yes** after reading the **Confirm OfficeScan Server ID information** dialog box.
18. On the **Management Console Password Setting** screen, enter **husky9999** in the **Password:** and **Confirm password:** fields. Click **Next**.
19. Review the message on the **OfficeScan Client Alert Message** screen and click **Next**.
20. Accept the default client path settings on the **OfficeScan Client Installation Path** screen and click **Next**.
21. Accept the default program group setting (**Trend OfficeScan Corporate Edition-SSL1**) on the **Select Program Folder** screen and click **Next**.
22. Read and complete the **Installing E-mail Virus Protection** screen (**Domain** is **springersltd.com**, Login is **Administrator**, Password is **husky9999**). Your screen should look similar to Figure 6-3. Click **Next**.

Notes:

Figure 6-3

It's important to get this screen correct as there is no password confirmation field.

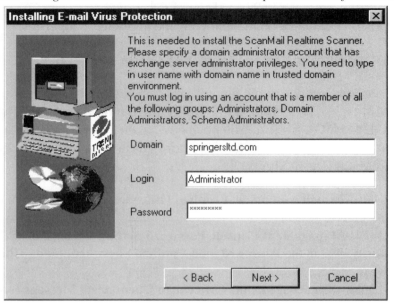

23. Click **OK** when the **Changing Installation Folder Privileges** screen appears.
24. Click **Next** when the **Trend OfficeScan Directory Sharing** screen appears.
25. Click **Finish** when the **OfficeScan Server Setup Completed** screen appears.

Now, refill the coffee and stretch the legs. You've nearly completed the OfficeScan 5 setup, but you'll need to answer a few questions that follow regarding the setup of ScanMail for Microsoft Exchange 2000.

26. Click **Next** when the **Welcome to ScanMail for Exchange 2000 Installation Program** screen appears. The setup process will automatically commence. Note if the installation appears to stall by displaying the Trend ScanMail for Exchange – Real-time Scan Monitor screen, it hasn't! Simply minimize this screen.
27. When the **Trend ScanMail for Exchange Installation** screen appears, communicating that you are done, simply click **Next**, as seen in Figure 6-4.

Figure 6-4

A cheerful Done! message awaits you as well as a Successful field.

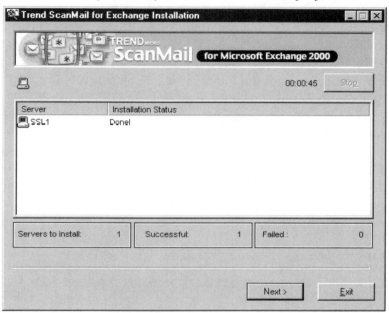

28. Click **Finish** followed by **OK** (on the Setup dialog box). Reboot SSL1 from **Start**, **Shutdown**, **Restart** in order for the Exchange Information Store to stop and start again.

You're done with server-side installation of OfficeScan 5. Now you need to configure the OfficeScan product and have it update its scan engine and virus definition files. Follow these steps.

1. Log on to **SSL1** as **Administrator** with the password **husky9999**.
2. Click **Start**, **Programs**, **Trend OfficeScan Corporate Edition-SSL1**, **OfficeScan Management Console(HTML)**.
3. Type **husky9999** in the **Log On** field and hit **Enter**.
4. Click the **Update & Upgrade** button when the **Trend OfficeScan Corporate Edition** page appears.
5. Click the **Internet Proxy** button.
6. On the **Internet Proxy** screen, type **localhost** in the **HTTP Proxy** field under Proxy Setup. Type **8080** under **Proxy Port**. Select the **Connect to**

the Internet through a proxy server check box. Your screen should look similar to Figure 6-5. Click **Apply**.

BEST PRACTICE: Note that the need to use the term **localhost** in the **HTTP Proxy** field is poorly documented. Fail to enter this information correctly and you'll not receive automatic virus engine and virus definition file updates from the Internet, which, let's face it, is just as bad as not having any virus detector at all.

A quick rant about OfficeScan. Not only does Trend use its standard "corporate" user interface for an SBS product, it doesn't proffer port 8080 in the Proxy Port field (in Figure 6-5). My complaint is that this product, while honoring much of what SBS is all about, doesn't completely get there. It'd be nice to see an SBS OfficeScan release that is truly 100 percent SBS. Hint-hint to Trend.

Figure 6-5
Be careful to complete this firewall information correctly.

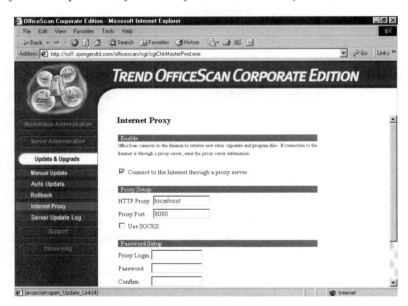

7. Click on the **Auto Update** button. Accept the default settings but select **Hourly**. Click **Apply**. This will force the virus protection program to

look hourly at Trend to download the latest virus scan engine and virus definition file.

8. Click on the **Manual Update** button. Under **From Internet**, click **Update**.

9. Click **Update Now** when the **Update From Trend Screen** appears. This will force the first update of the virus scan engine and virus definition file, as seen in Figure 6-6.

Figure 6-6

Downloading and installing the latest OfficeScan updates from Trend to give you a current virus protection baseline.

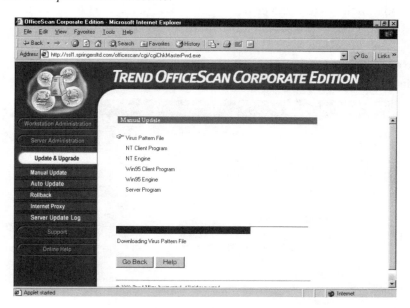

10. After the download is complete, close management console from **File**, **Close**.

You will now configure and update the ScanMail for Exchange component. Note this process is indeed separate from the OfficeScan configuration tasks you just performed. Follow these steps.

1. Log on to **SSL1** as **Administrator** with the password **husky9999**.

2. Click **Start**, **Programs**, **Trend ScanMail for Exchange**, **ScanMail Management Console**.

3. Type **husky9999** in the **Password** field on the **Server Logon** dialog box. Click **Logon**.

4. Click **Close** on the **Get the full version** dialog box to start your 30-day trial period. The ScanMail management console will now appear.

5. Click the **Active Update** bar on the lower-left.

6. Click the **Scheduled Update** button on the left.

7. Select the **Enable scheduled update** check box. Accept the default hourly update frequency.

8. Click the **Proxy Settings** button and select the **Enable proxy server** check box. In the **Proxy server** field, type **SSL1**. In the **Port number** field, type **8080**. Your screen should look similar to Figure 6-7. Click **OK**.

Figure 6-7

Completing the Proxy Settings dialog box.

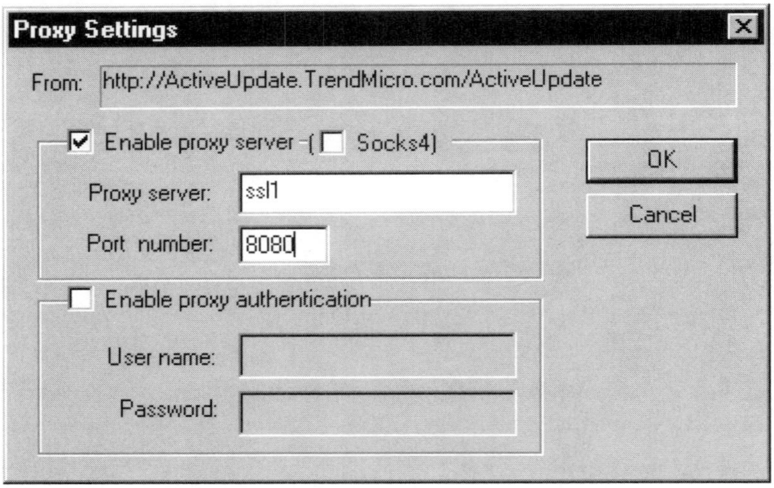

Notes:

9. Click the **Apply** button and your screen should look similar to Figure 6-8.

Figure 6-8
You've now configured the e-mail virus protection mechanism to stay current.

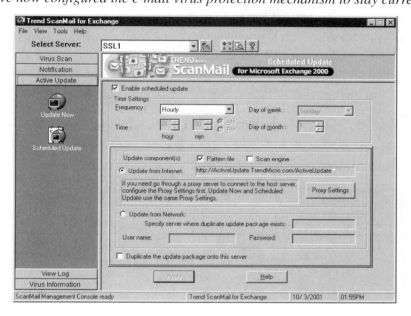

10. Click the **Update Now** button on the left to immediately force an update and bring ScanMail current! When the center screen changes, click the **Update Now** button at the bottom. Granted, this procedure sounds like the old "Department of Redundancy Department" thang. The **Active Update** window will keep you posted on the download progress.
11. After the update is complete, close the **ScanMail Management Console** from **File**, **Exit ScanMail**, **Yes**.

Take a short bow, as you've made the SBS server-side pretty darn virus-proof at this point. You'll now implement the solution to update all client computers. The OfficeScan 5 suite for SBS 2000 is both server- and client-side protection, one of its greatest strengths, let me tell ya! Moving on, the first step will be to update the SBS_Login_Script as per the OfficeScan 5 ReadMe file (**Start**, **Programs**, **Trend OfficeScan SBS**, **ReadMe**). Follow these steps:

1. Log on to **SSL1** as **Administrator** with the password **husky9999**.
2. Click **Start, Search, For Files or Folders**.
3. Type **SBS_L*.*** in the **Search for files or folders** field. This will search for the SBS logon script.
4. Right-click on **SBS_LOGIN_SCRIPT.bat** located at **c:\WINNT\SYSVOL\sysvol\springersltd.com\scripts** and select **Edit**. The file will appear in a NotePad session.
5. At the bottom of the file, type: **\\ssl1\ofcscan\autopcc**. Your screen should look similar to Figure 6-9.

Figure 6-9
You have now added the line of script code that will automatically update the client computers with Trend-based virus protection.

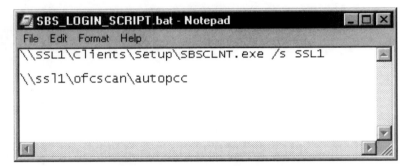

6. Click **File, Exit** and **Yes** when asked if you want to save your changes.
7. Close the **Search Results** window from **File, Close**.
8. Now, go over to the **PRESIDENT** client computer, turn it on, and log on as **NormH** with the password **Purple3300**. When the SBS logon script runs, the Trend OfficeScan 5 client computer components will automatically be installed.
9. Double-click on the **OfficeScan** icon on the lower right **Start task bar** (near the clock) on the **PRESIDENT** desktop. The **OfficeScan Monitor** should appear and look similar to Figure 6-10. Click **OK** to close the **OfficeScan Monitor**.

BEST PRACTICE: The OfficeScan setup script will actually run each time the user logs on to their client computer. The issue at hand is this: If OfficeScan sees that the client computer program is installed and the virus definition file is current, nothing else will occur. If needed, the virus definition file will be updated on the client computer. This "push" approach is very nice for keeping all client computers protected from virus outbreaks.

As a general practice, OfficeScan will delete other virus detection programs that it finds on the client computer. This is normal and entirely acceptable.

Figure 6-10

Proof positive that the client computer is protected by OfficeScan in real time!

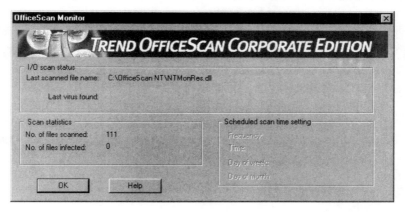

BEST PRACTICE: I've had end users fuss that their client computers appear to run slower after OfficeScan is installed. This is probably true, because OfficeScan looks closely at and scans each file opened and closed on the local machine. So a small speed hit is to be expected.

However, I've seen one or two client computers in my day where the speed hit was excessive relating to OfficeScan. I cured that performance problem by disabling the OfficeScanNT Listener service (Start, Settings, Control Panel, Administrative Tools, Services). The effect of disabling this is that the client computer won't receive virus definition file updates during the day while a user is logged on. Rather, the virus definition file updates will only be made upon user logon. You may find this to be an acceptable outcome and balance between performance and protection!

So, you've now completely implemented an up-to-date end-to-end virus protection solution specifically tailored to SBS 2000! Congrats. There is one last advance exercise I'd like you to perform. This involves blocking common file types that are known for transporting virus payloads (*.vbs, *.com, *.wav)

1. Log on to **SSL1** as **Administrator** with the password **husky9999**.
2. Click **Start**, **Programs**, **Trend ScanMail for Exchange**, **ScanMail Management Console**.
3. Type **husky9999** in the **Password** field on the **Server Logon** dialog box. Click **Logon**.
4. Click **Close** on the **Get the full version** dialog box to start your 30-day trial period. The ScanMail management console will now appear.
5. On the default screen **Virus Scan, Options**, select the **Enable attachment blocking** check box and click **OK** when the warning message appears (**smmc** dialog box).
6. Click the **Setting** button.
7. Click the **Attachments with specified extensions** radio button and type **vbs;com;wav** in the field. This will block a common method of virus transportation. Your screen should look similar to Figure 6-11. Click **OK**.

Figure 6-11
Attachment blocking is now in place.

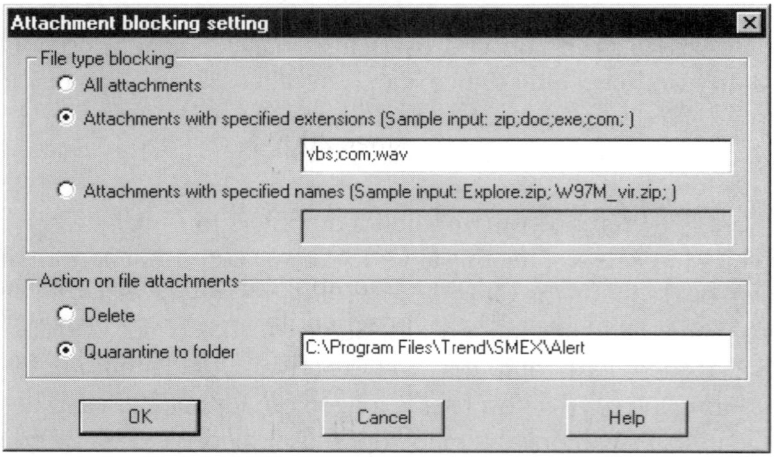

BEST PRACTICE: You may well want to add more attachment extension types in the above step. For example, you might want to add *.exe, *.bat, *.zip. However, for the SSL methodology in this book, we'll keep it simple in Step 7 above, okay?

8. Close the **ScanMail Management Console** from **File**, **Exit ScanMail**, **Yes**, **Continue**.

Now you're really secure with the addition of attachment blocking. Even though Trend only suggests attachment blocking during a virus outbreak, I use it all the time for certain file types, such as those listed above. It's the world we SBSers now live in.

BEST PRACTICE: In Chapter 7 you will undertake three more virus protection-related steps as part of your monthly duties. First, you will apply MS Security Bulletin (MS01-044) from August 2001 that is the CODE RED and NIMDA fix for IIS. This process occurs in the Service Packs, Patches, Upgrades, and Fixes section of that chapter. Second, in the same chapter section, you'll apply Windows 2000 Server Service Pack 2 followed by Exchange 2000 Server Service Pack 1. This allows you to, as of this writing, be ship-shape on your SBS network.

Third, you'll download and install Trend Micro's ScanMail 5.1 which is a fix to the OfficeScan 5 for Microsoft Small Business Server 2000 product that you've just installed. Long story short, Trend Micro and other virus protection independent software vendors (ISVs) got the short side of the match stick when Exchange 2000 Server was first released. The application programming interface (API) needed by virus protection IVSs wasn't perfected with the initial release of Exchange 2000 Server, or so the story goes. Basically the first generation of Exchange 2000 Server-specific virus protection applications could scan the e-mail storage group on a manual or scheduled basis (that is, complete a scan at a discrete point in time, not real-time scanning). So the inability to conduct real-time scanning was a major impetus for Exchange 2000 Server Service Pack 1 and the API fix. Lo and behold, it worked, except in the case of Trend Micro's virus protection application where you had to download and install a minor upgrade to one of the suite components (ScanMail 5.1). And you'll do exactly that in Chapter 7.

A couple of concluding thoughts on Trend's OfficeScan 5 for Microsoft Small Business Server 2000 virus protection application.

- A huge tip of the Texas cowboy hat for having an SBS specific release out there!

- It's a crying shame the product didn't go one step further and install buttons and links for its use on the SBS Consoles.

- Ahem – the branding could have been updated to remove words like "enterprise" on screens and programs items. The correct branding would reflect the SBS name.

- I'm a fan of Trend with its end-to-end client/server protection model plus the easy updating capability. It works very well!

2 - Tape Backup

Now, second things second. The SBS server machine is virus-free, so it's time to back up your important data in SBS. You have basically two options. The first option is to use the native backup utility (**Backup**), accessed not from any SBS Console but rather the **System Tools** program group (**Start**, **Programs**, **Accessories**). The second option is to use a more sophisticated third-party backup program, such as Seagate's Backup Exec 8.x Suite for Small Business Server application to perform your data backups. In this book, I'll honor the native backup application with a few kind comments and keystrokes upfront, but the focus of this section is to have you download the Seagate Backup Exec 8.x SBS product, install it, and use it.

> BEST PRACTICE: For every backup, you need to think about how you are going to restore. However, I for one don't perform daily restores from tape, so in Chapter 7 I have a section on how to restore from tape once per month. Hang on.

SBS's Native Backup Application

This backup and restore program is relatively easy to use.

The native Windows 2000 backup utility can be used to back up your data, e-mail, and system state information. Here's how to make a manual backup using the native Windows 2000 backup utility in SBS 2000.

BEST PRACTICE: Button, button, where is the button? In SBS 4.x, the SBS Console provided a button that instructed you in great detail on how to make backups. No such link or button exists on either the Administrator Console or the Personal Console in SBS 2000. This is the first SBS release to contain no such backup guidance.

1. Log on to **SSL1** as **Administrator** with the password **husky9999**.
2. Click **Start, Programs, Accessories, System Tools, Backup**. The Backup program launches.
3. Click the **Backup** tab.
4. Select your hard disk drives under **My Computer** (for example, C: for the main hard disk). DO NOT select Drive M: Exchange, as Microsoft Exchange 2000 Server is backed up in a different way.
5. Select **System State**. This will back up the all-important Registry and other system files (Click **Help, Help Topics** to learn more about System State)
6. Expand **Microsoft Exchange Server**. Expand the **server object** named after your server. Select **Microsoft Information Store**. This will back up the e-mail system at a high-level, not the individual mailbox level.
7. Select your backup tape system under **Backup Destination**. It is acceptable for the Backup media or file name to report "**New Media**".
8. Click **Start Backup**.
9. Review the information in the **Backup Job Destination** dialog box for correctness, and click **Start Backup**.
10. If you receive an error message that says "**There is no unused media available with the selected type, but unassigned media named "Untitled 00001" is available. Do you want to use the unassigned media for this backup?**" you should click **Yes**.

The tape backup will now proceed and you will ultimately receive a completion notice.

BEST PRACTICE: So, you're an SBS guru and you've attempted to schedule an unattended backup using the native Windows 2000 backup utility only to have the job fail in the middle of the night. The KBase article titled "How to Schedule Unattended Backups Using a Stand-Alone Tape Library" (Q239892) goes into great detail on how to fix this problem. But consider this easy step hidden at the end of this article: Simply add the **/um** switch to the backup job command.

Assuming you have already created a scheduled tape backup job using the native Windows 2000 backup utility; add the **/um** switch this way:

1. Log on to **SSL1** as **Administrator** with the password **husky9999**.
2. Click **Start**, **Settings**, **Control Panel**, **Scheduled Tasks**.
3. Right-click the **backup job** (e.g., FULL DAILY BACKUP), and select **Properties** from the secondary menu.
4. On the **Task** tab, scroll to the far right in the **Run** field and add the following switch: **/um**.
5. Click **OK**.

This will now allow the tape backup to proceed regardless of which tape is physically located in the tape drive. It's called the unmanaged method, but it's by far the most simple to manage, if that makes sense.

Note that the tape scheduling capability, much improved in SBS 2000, allows many SBSers to seriously consider using the native backup application. Hey—more power to you, but as the next BEST PRACTICE suggests, this native backup application has limitations.

BEST PRACTICE: The native backup application in SBS does a very poor job of backing up SQL Server-based databases (.dat files). You need to use the Daily Maintenance Wizard in SQL Server to create a successful backup of your SQL Server databases (see Chapter 15). Databases backed up in SQL Server (which reside as a closed file on your server's hard disk) can then be successfully backed up by the native backup application. Better yet, consider the Backup Exec program in the next section to back up SQL Server data successfully (as well as back up e-mail at the "bricks-level").

Backup Exec for Windows NT and Windows 2000 Small Business Server Edition

Now for the primary focus of the backup discussion in the context of the SSL methodology: using a third-party backup application. In this section, you will download and install Veritas's Backup Exec for Windows NT and Windows 2000 Small Business Server Edition. You will then perform a backup of a sample folder, the Exchange 2000 Information store and the System State to a location on the hard disk. Note that I assume you don't have a tape backup device attached to your server machine (even though SSL1 does) so that you can complete the backup exercise to hard disk successfully. To be honest, the incremental steps to back up to tape instead of hard disk are minor and easily performed. In Chapter 7 you will perform a restore.

So, let's download the Backup Exec for Windows NT and Windows 2000 Small Business Server Edition trial software version.

1. Log on to **SSL1** as **Administrator** with the password **husky9999**.
2. Double-click **Internet Explorer** from the SSL1 desktop. Surf over to the following uniform resource locator (URL) by typing **www.veritas.com/products** in the **Address** field.
3. Click the **Product Listing** link on the left side.
4. Click the **VERITAS Backup Exec for Windows NT and Windows 2000 Small Business Server Edition** link in the center of the screen.
5. Beneath **Downloads**, click **Trial Software**.
6. Complete the required **name, address, job,** and **demographic information** on the Web page titled **Get your copy of VERITAS Backup Exec for Windows NT and Windows 2000 Small Business Server Edition**. Click **Submit**.

BEST PRACTICE: Please do me a favor and provide your real name, address, job, and demographic information here instead of Bob Easter from SSL. Veritas is kind enough to provide its backup software on a trial basis, so you should be kind enough to provide real contact information. Thanks!

7. On the **Trial Version** page that appears, select the **http** link, which as of this writing is a 92 MB file titled: **bnt86i03_237889.exe**.

8. In the **File Download** dialog box, select **Save this program to disk** and click **OK**. In the **Save As** dialog box that appears, accept **My Documents** and click **Save**. The file will be saved to a name, such as **bnt86i03_237889.exe**. Note this 92 MB file will take some time, eh? Over my DSL connection, it took approximately 21 minutes.

BEST PRACTICE: Note that as part of your visit to Veritas, you can elect to have the backup software sent to you via snail mail instead of downloading it. Whatever your pleasure.

9. After the download has finished, click **Close** on the **File Download** dialog box and close **Internet Explorer** from **File**, **Close**.

You have successfully downloaded the Backup Exec for Windows NT and Windows 2000 Small Business Server Edition trial software at this point. In the next procedure, you'll install it on SSL1.

1. Log on to **SSL1** as **Administrator** with the password **husky9999**.
2. Double-click **My Documents** from the SSL1 desktop.
3. Double-click the **Backup Exec for Windows NT and Windows 2000 Small Business Server Edition trial software file** (e.g., **bnt86i03_237889.exe**).
4. The **Veritas Self-Extractor** launches. In the **Extract to:** field, accept the initial location of My Documents, but append the command line on the far right to extract the files to a sub-folder under My Documents titled Veritas. The entire extraction path should read **c:\Documents and Settings\Administrator\My Documents\Veritas**. Click **Extract**. Your screen should look similar to Figure 6-12.

Notes:

Figure 6-12

Unpacking the Backup Exec files you just downloaded.

5. Click **OK** when the **Finished** dialog box appears.
6. With the **My Documents** window still displayed, open the **Veritas** folder, followed by the next folders, **WINNT, INSTALL, ENG**.
7. Double-click **SETUP.EXE**.
8. Click **Next** at the **Welcome** screen.
9. Click **Yes** on the **Software Licenses Agreement** screen.
10. Click **Next** after reading the **PLEASE READ** page.
11. Click the **button** immediately to the right of **Install Backup Exec software or options on this computer**.
12. On the **VERITAS Backup Exec Serial Numbers** page, click **Next**. This will start the 60-day evaluation period.
13. Click **OK** on the **Backup Exec Evaluation Information** dialog box.
14. On the **Backup Exec Install Options** page, accept the default selections

and click **Tape Device Drivers**, **Online Documentation**, **Agent for Microsoft SQL Server** and **Agent for Microsoft Exchange Server**. Your screen should look similar to Figure 6-13. Click **Next**.

Figure 6-13
Selecting the Backup Exec suite components that you will need.

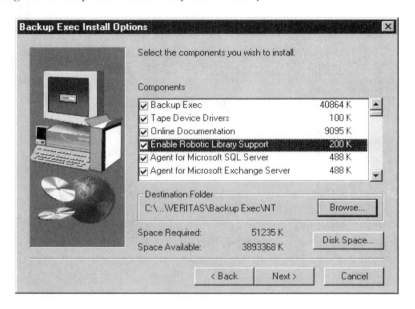

15. Accept the default **Claim that device...** setting on the **Device and Media Manager** screen and click **Next**.
16. Click **Next** on the **Start Copying Files** screen.
17. On the **Service Account** dialog box, type **husky9999** in the **Password** field and click **OK**.
18. Click **OK** on the **Previous Backup Exec Installation** screen.
19. Click **Next** on the **Welcome to the VERITAS Windows NT/2000 Device Driver Installation** screen.
20. Accept the **Use VERITAS tape drivers for all tape devices** selection on the **Choosing tape drives** screen and click **Next**.
21. Click **Next** on the **Scanning Hardware** screen.
22. Click **Next** on the **Installing VERITAS drivers** screen.
23. Click **Finish** on the **Completing the VERITAS Windows NT/2000 Device Driver Installation** screen.

24. Select **Common Program Group** on the **Select type of Program Group** screen and click **Next**.
25. Click **No** on the **Question** dialog box about installing agents on remote systems.
26. Click **Finish** on the **Setup Complete** dialog box.

Close any open windows such as My Documents or Internet Explorer. You've now successfully installed Backup Exec for Windows NT and Windows 2000 Small Business Server Edition. Cool! Take a break and get ready to use it for real.

Welcome back from your break. Let's back up a sample folder, the SBS System State, and the Exchange 2000 Server-based e-mail system, eh? But first, complete this procedure:

1. Log on to **SSL1** as **Administrator** with the password **husky9999**.
2. Click **Start**, **Programs**, **VERITAS Backup Exec**.
3. When the **Welcome to the Online Registration Wizard** page appears, select the **Register later** check box and click **Next**.
4. Click **Next** when the **First Time Startup Wizard** displays the **Welcome to the First Time Startup Wizard**.
5. Click the **Select Overwrite Protection Level** button on the **Media Overwrite Introduction** page.
6. Select **None** and uncheck the **Prompt before overwriting allocated or imported media** checkbox. Click **Next**.
7. Accept the **Overwrite scratch media...** selection on the **Preferred Overwrite Media Type** screen and click **Next**.
8. Click **Next** at the **Virus Protection** page. Note that if you weren't using Trend's OfficeScan SBS 2000 suite, you might want to have your virus protection occur here!
9. Click **Finish** on the **Backup Exec Windows Explorer Interface** page.
10. Click **Next** at the **Welcome to the Device Configuration Wizard** page.
11. Verify that Backup Exec has detected your tape drive correctly and click **Next** on the **Detected Hardware** screen.
12. On the **Detected Backup-to-Disk Folder** screen, click the **Add Backup-to-Disk Folder** button.
13. Click **OK** after reading the **Backup-to-Disk Warning**.
14. Accept the default settings on the **Add New Backup-to-Disk Folder** shown in Figure 6-14. Click **OK**.

Figure 6-14

Creating the backup folder you need for the SSL approach.

15. Click **Next** when returned to the **Detected Backup-to-Disk Folder** screen.
16. Click **Next** on the **Drive Configuration** screen.
17. Click **Finish** on the **Completing the Device Configuration Wizard** screen.

Okay, my SBSers, you'll now, at long last, make a data backup!

1. Log on to **SSL1** as **Administrator** with the password **husky9999**.
2. Click **Start**, **Programs**, **VERITAS Backup Exec**.
3. Select **Create a Backup Job** on the **Backup Exec Assistant** screen that appears.
4. Click **Next** on the **Welcome to the Backup Wizard** screen.
5. You will now make your backup selections. You will first select the My Documents folder for the Administrator by selecting **Local Selections**, **Documents and Settings**, **Administrator**, **My Documents**. Next, select **Microsoft Exchange Information Store** and **System State**. Your screen should look similar to Figure 6-15. Click **Next**.

Notes:

Figure 6-15

Making your backup selections as part of the SSL methodology.

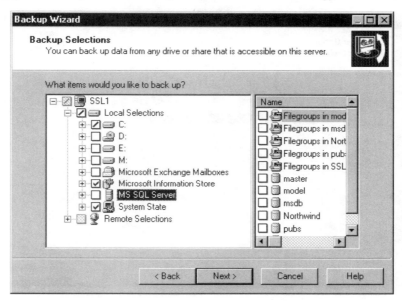

6. On the **Backup Names** screen, name the backup job **SSL-Practice** and name the backup set as **SSL-Set1**. Click **Next**.

7. On the **Backup Devices and Media** screen, select **Backup Folder 1:1** under **Which device would you like to use to back up your data?** and click **Next**.

8. Select **Overwrite media** on the **Backup Overwrite Media Method** screen and click **Next**.

9. Accept the default **FULL-Back Up Files – Reset Archive Bit** setting and **Yes, verify after backup** selection on the **Backup Options** screen and click **Next**.

10. Accept the **FULL-Database & Logs (flush committed logs)** selection on the **Exchange Options** screen as seen in Figure 6-16 and click **Next**.

Notes:

Figure 6-16

Get it right – flush those Exchange 2000 Server logs.

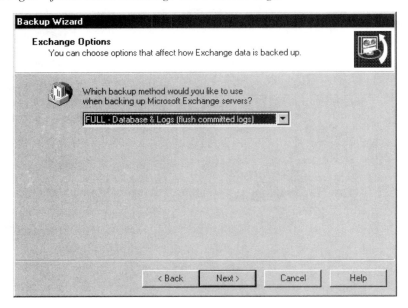

BEST PRACTICE: This is a very important screen to get right (Figure 6-16) in SBS 2000. It's essential that you flush the Exchange 2000 Server logs when you make a backup. Otherwise, each and every day, a new 5.12 MB log is written to the Exchange MDBDATA folder (see Figure 6-17). Over 30, 60 or 90 days, this can grow to a huge amount of disk consumption. Worse, SBS newbies who don't make proper Exchange 2000 Server backups wonder why the heck they're quickly running out of disk space (hint: it's the Exchange logs that are accumulating).

Notes:

Figure 6-17

Three Exchange 2000 Server logs have been created. After the backup is performed, there will only be one (the older logs will be automatically deleted). Check back for yourself.

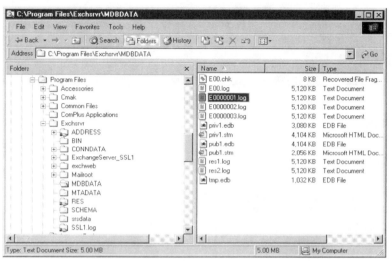

11. Select **Yes, run the job now** on the **Completing the Backup Wizard** page. Select **Finish**.

Take a break while the job runs. When you return, in the **Backup Exec** program, click on the **Activity** tab and confirm the job has successfully completed, similar to Figure 6-18. Afterwards, Click on the **Reports** tab to view the reports relating to the backup. You can also right-click and select **Properties** on the **SSL1-Practice** job on the **Job Definitions** and create an ongoing backup schedule to run the job each night. Finally, back on the **Activity** tab, if you double-click the job **SSL-Practice** and select **Job Log**, you can get the most detailed backup report view.

Notes:

Figure 6-18

Congratulations! The backup job you have created was successfully completed.

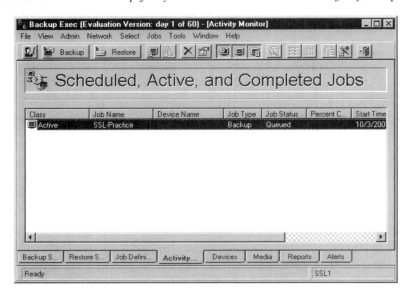

So what's the wrap on Backup Exec for Windows NT and Windows 2000 Small Business Server Edition? A few thoughts.

- Kudos for having an SBS 2000 specific release.

- Thumbs wavering downward for essentially providing the "big" Backup Exec for Windows NT and Windows 2000 without truly customizing the screens and logos for SBS.

- It's too bad that the darn product doesn't install itself on the SBS Console as a button or link. That'd be a nice SBS touch.

- This product won't fail you when it comes to your hard-core backup and restoration needs, or so it has been my experience.

Notes:

Suggested Backup Routine

Now you need a backup schedule that ensures you get the backups you need to protect your information. Start with a group of nine tapes. Place a blue dot on the outside of each tape (you'll see why in a moment). Four tapes are used for normal backups between Monday and Thursday. Four tapes are used for normal backups each Friday (Friday1, Friday2, Friday3, Friday4). The last tape is used for normal backups performed at month's end. Label each tape for its respective role (Monday and so on). So far, so good.

Now, at the end of the month, remove the end-of-month tape that contains a verified normal backup from the group and store off-site. (Of course, you might want to have other tapes, such as the Friday tapes, rotated off-site as well.)

Purchase a new tape, place a red dot on it and label it Monday. Take the existing Monday tape (blue dot) and label it for the end-of-month-two normal backup. Repeat this scenario the next month, removing a used blue-dot tape from the mix.

So what's the bottom line? Threefold:

1. Each month you purchase a fresh tape that has a recent "born on" date from the manufacturer.
2. Each month you retire a tape from the original "blue dot" group so that after nine months, all of the tapes have red dots and are fresh.
3. By taking a daily or Friday tape and promoting it to the monthly role, ideally no daily or Friday tape suffers excessive usage before being replaced.

BEST PRACTICE: Don't forget that excessive media usage is a common cause of restoration failure, so keep those tapes fresh!

Notes:

3 - Sharing Files and Folders

Historically, a huge reason for having a computer network was sharing information in an easy and secure manner. Hardly an hour, make that a day, goes by where users won't ask you to assist them in gaining access (legitimately so) to information they need to do their jobs. You can satisfy this request by sharing files and folders.

Sharing files and folders is very easy and can be accomplished completely from the SBS Administrator Console. Follow these steps to create a shared folder and publish it to Active Directory. Afterwards, NTFS folder and file-level permissions will be discussed.

1. Log on to **SSL1** as **Administrator** with the password **husky9999**.
2. Click **Start, Small Business Server Administrator Console**.
3. Click **Favorites, Active Directory, Add Shared Folder**. The Add Shared Folder Wizard will launch.
4. Click **Next** at the **Welcome to the Add Shared Folder Wizard** screen.
5. On the **Folder Identity** screen, click **Browse**. The **Browse For Folder** screen will appear and you will need to click **Local Disk (C:)**.
6. Click the **New Folder** button. A folder will appear at the root of C: that you should name **Transfer**. Click **OK**. You will be returned to the Folder Identity screen.
7. In the **Shared folder name** field, type **SSL-Transfer**.
8. In the **Comments** field, type **This is a temp folder to transfer files quickly**. Observe the **Publish the shared folder in the Active Directory** check box is selected. Your screen should look similar to Figure 6-19. Click **Next**.

Notes:

Figure 6-19

The Folder Identity screen tells the whole story.

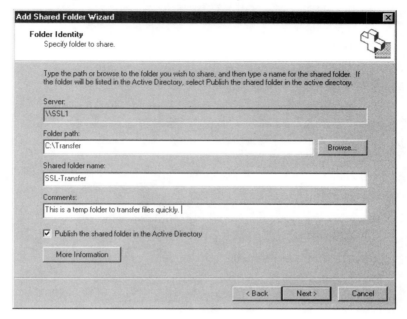

9. Carefully read the **Permissions** screen. Notice that access is granted by default to Administrators, Domain Users, and BackOffice Folder Operators. Go ahead and add **Norm Hasborn** with the **Full** permission. Your screen should look similar to Figure 6-20. Click **Next**.

10. Click **Finish** on the **Completing the Add Shared Folder Wizard** page.

Notes:

Figure 6-20
Norm Hasborn with the Full permission can be seen on the Permissions screen.

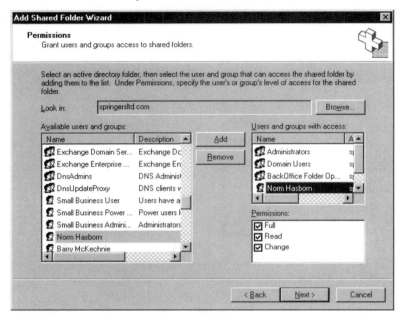

To manage file permissions, it is necessary to go under the hood and use a traditional Windows 2000 Server tool, Windows Explorer. It is also essential that you've formatted your partition as an NTFS partition. If, for some reason, you are working with a FAT partition, you will not be able to manage permissions at the file level. Managing user access at the file level is typically a larger concern in enterprise-level organizations (several hundred users and larger). But, small business owners have unique security needs, such as allowing access to their user folder but invoking strict security on their TurboTax data file (true story!).

To set file permissions, you simply use **Windows Explorer** to navigate to the file you want to set permissions on. Then right-click on the file, select **Permissions**, **Security**. Next, add or remove the user and security groups that you seek to allow or deny permission to. Still on the security tab, select the permissions you want (e.g., **Read & Execute**). Click **OK** to close the property sheet. It's really that easy!

Let's visit folder and file security at a great level of depth. The share permissions that you set in the SBS Administrator Console are but one level of security known as share-level security. For most small businesses, share-level security is sufficient. Share-level security can be applied to both FAT and NTFS-formatted partitions. Typically, share-level security acts as a mask that sets the tone for other types of security. Note that share-level permissions can not be applied to files, only folders. But be advised that more robust security implementations surround the use of NTFS-based security. NTFS security can be applied to folders and files that might or might not be shared. Let's take a moment to distinguish between share-level and NTFS security.

This mask, the share-level permissions, acts as a filter that allows certain types or classes of permissions to flow or not flow through. For example, suppose you had a shared folder named FOOBAR (see Figure 6-21). Note that the FOOBAR folder contains two additional folders and also some files.

Figure 6-21
Look closely – share-level and folder- and file-level security.

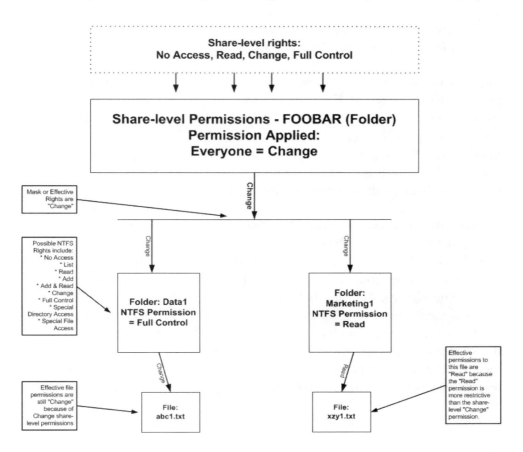

So, assume for a moment that you applied the Change permission to the FOOBAR folder for everyone. This permission means that the users on your staff could only change the files stored in FOOBAR. Change includes the following characteristics:

- View file and folder names
- Change folders (for example, rename)
- View data in files and folders
- Add files and folders to the shared directory
- Modify or change data in files
- Delete files and folders

The primary difference between Change and Full Control is ownership. The Change permission allows neither a change in the underlying folder ownership nor the capability to change permission on the folder. Only someone with Full Control can actually change permissions on the folder.

> BEST PRACTICE: When discussing SBS security, the terms *folders* and *subdirectories* are interchangeable.

Thus, the change permission at the share-level sets the mask from which all lower permissions are evaluated. For most SBS sites, this highest layer of security, share-level security, is sufficient. Now, going to the next level of complexity, assume you apply NTFS-level security settings to the folders and files contained in FOOBAR. You might do this because you have unusual security requirements. An example of this is the restaurant I once worked with that was especially concerned about the dissemination of its proprietary recipes.

If such is the case, return to Figure 6-21 and observe that the Change mask flows down from the top part of the figure where the share-level security was implemented. Then, NTFS-level security is applied to the folders Data1 (NTFS permission = Full Control) and Marketing1 (Read). So what's the bottom line in the example on Figure 6-21? The abc1.txt file would have the Change right applied to it because the more restrictive Change share-level permission is acting as the mask that sets the tone for all other security rights. The file xyz1.txt would have the Read permission set on it because the Read permission, applied via NTFS at the folder-level, would pass through the Change mask created at the upper share-level. Whew! I'll stop now as I'm beginning to go beyond the scope of this book.

Let's tackle one more area – hidden shared folders. There are numerous hidden shared folders in SBS that you may not have even known about. For example, take a look at Figure 6-22. The folder share names that end in $ will not appear when you browse the SSL1 server via My Network Places. However, you can still map a drive to these hidden shared folders from a client computer (assuming you have sufficient user permission to access said hidden share).

> BEST PRACTICE: NetWare users should recognize this hidden trick in SBS as the Hidden permission in good old NetWare.

Figure 6-22
Observe the hidden shares where the share name ends in "$". Also, note that you can manage both share-level and NTFS permissions from the SBS Administrator Console with this view.

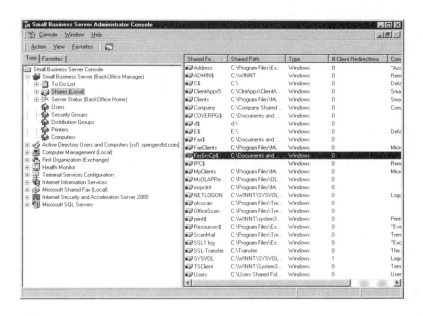

Consider the following challenge that I will now issue to you. A page or two ago you created the Transfer folder and shared it (remember?). Now I want this folder to have a hidden share name. I'll give one hint before setting you free: Find the folder with **Windows Explorer**, right-click on the folder, select **Properties** and **Sharing**. Good luck in completing this task.

BEST PRACTICE: Might I dare say that share-level and NTFS permissions are too generous by default. The default sharing permission in SBS 2000 is Everyone = Full Control. The default NTFS permission on a folder and file, all things being equal, is Everyone = Full Control. These are extremely generous and dangerous default security levels. Enough said.

4 - Mapping Drives

In order to create, modify, and otherwise use data on a server, you must first have access to folders on the server. There are three ways to gain this access to folders located on a server that involve creating a path or mapping a drive to the server.

Graphical Method

The first method is the easiest and the most preferred method. This method, also known as point-and-shoot, consists of browsing via the My Network Places applet, finding the shared folder of interest, and mapping a drive with an alpha letter.

1. Log on as **NormH** at **PRESIDENT** with the password **Purple3300**.
2. Double-click **My Network Places** and navigate to the **COMPANY** shared folder on **SSL1**.
3. Right-click **COMPANY** and select the **Map Network Drive** command.
4. Select a drive letter to identify this mapped drive to this shared folder. For example, you might select **Drive F:** as being mapped to **COMPANY**.
5. Select the **Reconnect at Logon** check box if you want this drive to be remapped each and every time you log on to the SBS network. This is what you would typically select.
6. Click **OK**. You have now mapped a network drive via the graphical method.

The Dialog Box Method

This method requires that you know the folder's share name in advance of mapping it. Assuming that you do, right-click **My Network Places**, select **Map Network Drive** and type the UNC path (discussed in the section below in step 3 and beyond) in the **Folder** field.

The Command Line Method

You can also map drives from the traditional command line (a.k.a. command prompt). If you follow these steps, use the <u>NET USE</u> command to map drives to SSL1.

1. Log on as **NormH** at **PRESIDENT** with the password **Purple3300**.
2. Click **Start**, **Programs**, **Accessories**, **Command Prompt**.
3. At the command prompt, type the following command if you want to map drive F: to \\SSL1\COMPANY on your SBS network: **NET USE F: \\SSL1\COMPANY**.
4. Type **EXIT** to close the command prompt window and return to your desktop operating system.

BEST PRACTICE: The <u>NET USE</u> command must be executed each session to map your network drives. The <u>NET USE</u> command does not offer the option of Reconnect at Logon like the graphical or dialog box methods.

Advanced Drive Mapping

In this section, I will discuss the Uniform Naming Convention (UNC) definition of drive mappings, how to map drives via user logon scripts, and mapping drives to other client computers.

UNC

SBS 2000 uses the UNC approach to make network drives from the workstation to the server. The UNC can be broken down into two parts, as shown in Figure 6-23.

Notes:

Figure 6-23

Breaking down the UNC step-by-step.

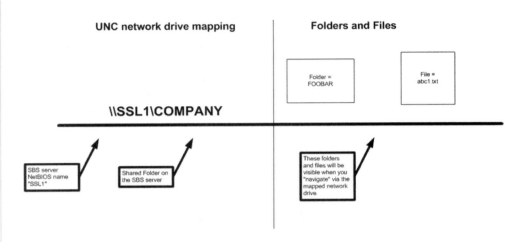

The left side of Figure 6-23 shows the traditional UNC drive mapping command. This command comprises the SBS server machine's NetBIOS name (SSL1) and the share name (COMPANY). The right side of Figure 6-23 displays the folders and files you would see when you explore or navigate the mapped drive.

> BEST PRACTICE: You cannot map a drive to an unshared resource, such as an unshared folder.

Mapping Via a Login Script

In order to implement drive mappings that are centrally administered and enforced, consider the NET USE drive mapping statements in the **SBS_LOGIN_SCRIPT.bat** located at **c:\WINNT\SYSVOL\sysvol\springersltd.com\scripts**. This login script file was discussed and shown earlier in Figure 6-9 of this chapter. Here is an example of a NET USE statement you might add to the SBS login script to map drive F: to the Company share:

```
NET USE F: \\SSL1\COMPANY
```

Mapping Drives to Other Client Computers

Did you know that you can map a network drive to a shared resource on another SBS user's client computer? It is very simple to do. Running the SBS magic disk on the client computer automatically turns on file and printer sharing, making the client computer eligible to share a folder for others to use. Assuming this has been accomplished, you would simply map a drive to the shared folder on the client computer, using the UNC drive mapping approach (any of the three methods discussed above will work). For example, if the workstation was named ACCT01 and the shared folder was MONEY, the UNC command would be \\ACCT01\MONEY.

Guest Speaker

Here's a light-hearted tale of woe and winning from a fellow SBSer, Richard Prangnell. He shares his experiences from over the years, so while some references are to SBS 4.5, his wit and points are well taken.

Would you like to hear my SBS installation tale? I think it's a good one for the consultant's notebook. For my sins, I'm Webmaster for the Academy of Internet Commerce Limited (www.academyinternet.com). We are business-to-business specialists providing a range of services from training to marketing in the area of e-commerce.

Our focus is more entrepreneurial than technical. In fact, I am the only "techie" on a payroll of some 20 employees, so I get to do the LAN administration as well as my primary website-related work. When I joined the company last December, we had, in theory, an SBS server running our LAN – except that one of my colleagues must have done a boot-up using the Emergency Recovery Disk at some stage, because all I could find on it was a minimal set of NT functionality.

The SBS disks had disappeared, too, but after a charm offensive and on the strength of the original invoice from Dell for "2300 Poweredge Server + SBS 4.5," I managed to get a replacement set of media from Microsoft for just the cost of postage and packaging (Thanks, Bill!). I went to all this trouble because the CEO was convinced we weren't making the most of the SBS system. He was quite right; it was being used solely for file and print serving.

One quiet evening I backed up the public folder on the server onto my workstation hard disc, did a low-level format on the server, and reinstalled SBS 4.5 with all the Office 2000 trimmings. It was then, when I saw the SBS console for the first time, that I realized just what a serious piece of kit I was landed with. I decided it would be prudent to go on using the SBS server just for filing and printing until I could get a clued-up MCP onto the site for a days' worth of post-installation integration.

An MCP was duly hired and, following an initial consultation, it was decided that we would go for a slightly nonstandard implementation of SBS in order to gain some performance advantages; i.e., the SBS DHCP service would be turned off. Instead, DHCP would continue to be handled by our D-Link DI-300 ISDN Router. The reasoning was simply that, as every one of our 20 employees required efficient, ongoing access to the Internet on a daily basis, it made sense to off-load the Internet tasks from the server completely onto an existing piece of kit that had already proved itself. The bonus would be faster throughput of other server tasks.

The MCP also advised us that if we wanted to gain the maximum functionality from Exchange Server (and we did), we would need to get our ISP to provide us with SMTP rather than POP3 for our outbound mail. So far, so good. A date was agreed for the rollout of expanded server functionality and I got our ISP to commit to an exact time for throwing the switch from POP3 to SMTP.

The big day dawned and our MCP arrived as promised. The server was soon reconfigured but things didn't go quite according to plan. We discovered that mail was not getting past our router. It turns out that the DI-300 router doesn't support network address translation (NAT) in DHCP mode. Apparently, we should have gotten the DI-300M. It was a bad time to find this out.

The quickest work-around that we could come up with was to forget about the new SMTP feed to our existing ISDN-only ISP and immediately set up a fresh SMTP account with a dial-up ISP. We would then use one of the modems that had been earmarked for faxing for handling all our e-mail traffic instead. Not such a daft idea as it sounds, because it means a lighter load on the router and therefore faster Internet page download times (at least, that's what I told the CEO!).

A little bit of tweaking inside Exchange, a request to the original ISP to set up an appropriate MX line to point to the new destination for e-mails, and we had a working system. The panic over, the MCP and I spent the rest of the day setting up the workstations and doing initial training on Outlook. The euphoria did not last, however. Over the next few days, it became apparent that something of a nightmare scenario was emerging. A high proportion of e-mails were being bounced. Try as I might, I could not find anything in common or unusual about the bounced e-mails, so I was at a loss to explain the phenomenon. It was as if we were being bedeviled by that bane of all techies, an intermittent fault.

It turned out to be a most fascinating problem. As a professional SBS guru, you've no doubt already guessed the cause. It took me a considerable amount of brainstorming before I began to realize it was something to do with the fact that our set-up gave rise to no less than four possible server states with regard to e-mail: 1. modem off-line and router off-line: e-mail queued; 2. modem off-line and router on-line: e-mail sent via router (bounced!); 3. modem on-line and router off-line: e-mail sent via modem (success!); 4. modem on-line and router on-line: e-mail sent via router (bounced!). When you consider that the timing of transitions between any of the above states were quasi-random (dependent on size and quantity of e-mails and patterns of Internet usage), the conditions were perfect for apparent mayhem!

The cure was simply to delete all reference to the router gateway in the appropriate network adapter applet on the server. The one drawback is that the server cannot now be used for browsing the Internet, but that is not a significant problem - it is not used as a workstation. In fact, in terms of RAS, barring Internet access via the server is a very useful ploy. It is good for overall site security and avoids the potential problem of modem-hogging by remote users who would like to browse the Internet all evening via RAS and the LAN gateway, instead of just uploading or downloading files.

So, it seems we have stumbled upon an interesting alternative to the traditional SBS model that is performance-tuned for intensive Internet-browsing applications. What's more, it came about more by accident than design. Just make sure that the server knows nothing about the Internet gateway! At least in the SBS 4.5 era.

All the best, Richard Prangnell

5 - Managing Users, Groups, and Computers

On any given day, you likely need to either add or delete a user or computer from your SBS network. Hey, people come and go from organizations all the time.

You might recall from prior chapters, including Chapters 3, 4, and 5, that users and computers are added, deleted, and managed from the SBS Consoles. In fact, the step-by-step process for adding users is shown during Chapter 4. So, I'm not going to repeat the step-by-step here for you (you can simply revisit those other chapters). However, I'll speak to a management issue: disabling user accounts. Typically, when an employee is terminated, you first disable the account prior to deleting the account. That way, just in case the employee legitimately returns, you can reactivate the account for proper use. In fact, I typically disable an account for up to two weeks before deleting it. It's just another best practice in network management.

To disable the account, right-click a user account and select **Disable Account** from the secondary menu (user accounts are found in the **Users** folder under **Active Directory Users and Computers** in the **Small Business Server Administrator Console** from **Start**). To reactivate the account, simply uncheck the **Disable Account** menu option for the user account.

6 - UPS Power Levels

As part of your SBS network management stewardship, it is critical that you periodically monitor the power feed to the server machine. Recall from Chapter 2 that I planned for and purchased a backup battery known as an uninterruptible power supply (UPS).

One popular brand of UPS is the Smart UPS series from American Power Corporation (APC). Typically, a UPS shipped by APC includes a UPS monitoring application called PowerChute. PowerChute is far superior to the UPS application included with SBS (found in Control Panel). In fact, some people out in SBS land will bomb my e-mail box if I don't call a spade a spade: The UPS application in the Control Panel is the absolute worst. Don't ever use it.

PowerChute installs like any other application, but you must do this after you have completely installed SBS 2000. That's because PowerChute requires that you attach a serial cable from the back of the UPS battery to one of the COM ports of your SBS server machines.

> BEST PRACTICE: Be prepared to purchase a multifunction I/O card to provide you with an additional physical COM port on your SBS server machine. I've had the great pleasure of looking behind the SBS server machine, ready to cable the UPS, only to discover that I have no free COM port available. Later, after installing a new multifunction I/O card on my server, I have the ability to attach the serial cable from the UPS to my SBS server machine.

To view the power level that your UPS is monitoring, simply launch the PowerChute application (assuming you're using PowerChute and it has been correctly installed). You can observe power level information on the main power level screen.

7 - Logon/Logoff Status

In SBS 4.5 it was easy to tell who was logged on at any time. That was done by selecting the Manage User Connections option from the Manage Users screen (accessed via the SBS Console). Being able to determine who is logged on to your SBS 2000 network is a little bit tricky. Here, you will look at **Sessions** beneath **Shared Folders** in **System Tools** under **Computer Management (Local)** in the **Small Business Server Administrator Console** (from **Start**). This is shown in Figure 6-24.

Figure 6-24

Observing who is logged on currently.

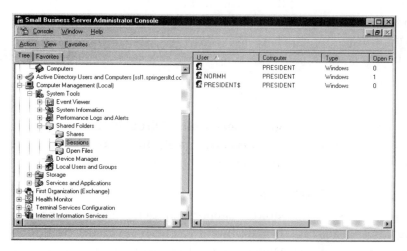

Knowing who is logged on is important in that it quickly enables you to answer a user who asks "Am I logged on?" Why might a user ask such a question? Most likely, this question would be asked when a user is unable to accomplish something such as being able to access a file or print a document. Thus, the need arises to know whether the user is logged on to the SBS network.

Likewise, it is very easy for users not to log on to your network, even though their intentions are good. I call it the CEO factor. On occasion, a CEO or other prominent businessperson, accidentally escapes past the SBS network logon dialog box from his Windows 9.x workstation (often while distracted on telephone call). Soon thereafter, said CEO believes the SBS network is broken because he can't get his e-mail, print, or surf the Web. And it is I, the SBS consultant, who receives his call.

There is a quick way to verify the logon status of a Windows 2000 Professional client computer. You can easily check the SBS user's login status by pressing **Ctrl+Alt+Delete** to display the **Windows Security** dialog box. The top part of the Windows Security dialog box contains a **Logon Information** section. It is here that the user's logon name, the domain name, and the logon date and time are displayed. Once they're displayed, you can click **Cancel** to close the **Windows Security** dialog box and return to your desktop.

There are two more ways to determine login status. These are the net session command and the netwatch.exe file contained in the Windows 2000 Server Resource Kit. At **SSL1**, at the **Command Prompt** (from **Start**, **Programs**, **Accessories**, **Command Prompt**) simply **type net session**. The netwatch.exe file would be copied from the Windows 2000 Server Resource Kit and run on SSL1 to observe logged on users.

> BEST PRACTICE: Consider imposing login restrictions from the user account property sheet under **Users**, **Active Directory Users and Computers** in the **Small Business Server Administrator Console** (from **Start**). This will bring order to chaos.

8 - End-User Support

Something you do every single day is support end users. End-user support is a truly a multifaceted area; issues can come at you from any angle. Here are some of the most common end-user support issues I've encountered on SBS networks, but, of course, the sky is the limit.

Printing

"I can't print" is a frequent cry for help from the SBS user base. From the Printers folder (**Start**, **Settings**, **Printers**) you can correct most, if not all, of the printing management issues you are likely to encounter. This includes verifying that the server received the print job for processing (queuing) and canceling a print job.

But exceptions exist. For example, if you use a printer that is directly connected to the network, you likely use a printer management software application such as HP's JetAdmin software to manage the printer.

> BEST PRACTICE: By the way, you can turn off the annoying printer feature of writing out an event to the System event log for every successful print job. Click **Start**, **Settings**, **Printers**, **File**, **Server Properties**, **Advanced** tab and deselect the **Log spooler information events** check box. Click **OK**.

Applications

"How do I do that?" is an applications refrain that SBS users sing. Even though you might not have application-specific expertise, SBS users associate you, the SBS guru, with anything and everything related to the SBS network. Perhaps that's why I've found myself supporting Westlaw's WESTMATE legal application at the law firm in the morning and the MasterBuilder construction accounting software at the homebuilding company in the afternoon. Such is a day in the life of an SBS guru. More important, being an SBS guru requires that you think quickly on your feet and have the ability to learn new user applications very quickly. Hey, it's not like I'm certified in WESTMATE or MasterBuilder!

E-Mail

Want to find yourself providing user support, as if you didn't have other things to do? Just do something to interrupt the e-mail service on an SBS network. A few words to the wise regarding e-mail service: If the user hasn't successfully logged on to the SBS network, it is entirely likely that the user's e-mail won't function. First, verify whether the user is logged on to the SBS network (see the "Logon/ Logoff Status" section above). If the user is not logged on, simply have him log on. It is likely that e-mail service will be restored. Second, see if you can you distinguish whether local e-mail on your internal SBS network is working and whether the Internet e-mail service is working. Often the internal e-mail system is working while the Internet e-mail isn't. It's an important distinction that you will want to make. Third, find out if only one user is experiencing e-mail problems or there are other users displaying similar problems. Here, the individual user might have somehow corrupted his Microsoft Outlook profile, resulting in an interruption in the specific individual's e-mail service.

Special Requests

"Can you just do…" is typically the opening phrase of a special request from an SBS user. Such requests are really an affirmation that the SBS users want to do more with the SBS network. I think that's a good thing: SBS network acceptance! However, it is a time management challenge for SBS administrators and gurus alike everywhere to respond to such requests (perhaps you have other duties pulling at your limited time availability as well).

End-User Training

One easy way to mitigate support requirements is to better train your SBS end users. The training might take the form of guide-by-the-side, where you mentor SBS end users one-on-one by assisting individual users who have a need to know something SBS-related. The other training method to consider is sage-on-the-stage. Here, you, or a trainer you retain, provide traditional classroom-style training for SBS end users on SBS network usage or applications, such as Microsoft Outlook and Microsoft Office 2000.

Advanced Support Issues

If you can't beat 'em, join 'em. This SBS strategy concerns using end users to support end users on your SBS network. Having end users as support resources takes two forms. First, you might be able to enlist one or two of your power users into mentoring the weaker SBS users. Second, you should strongly consider using local college interns for part-time SBS end-user support. Either approach can save you from the endless parade of SBS end-user support issues (and spend your time introducing enhanced SBS features, such as new Web pages).

9 - Check System Health

You can do a couple of things each day to quickly check the health of your SBS server machine: run Task Manager and check Event Viewer.

Task Manager

Task Manager is my SBS buddy. It reports a wide range of current information about your SBS 2000 server. To launch Task Manager, simply right-click the task bar at the bottom of your screen on your SBS server machine. From the secondary menu, select **Task Manager**. Task Manager launches and offers you three tabbed sheets to select from: Applications, Processes, and Performance.

Applications

Here, open applications are displayed. You can end the applications via the End Task button. More important, the Applications tab enables you to determine whether an application has crashed or stopped running. If an application has crashed, Not Responding is displayed in the Status column. At that time, you need to use the End Task button to crash the application.

Processes

This technical tab displays processes currently running on the SBS server. To be brutally honest, it's likely you would view this screen if you were answering questions posed to you over the telephone by a Microsoft technical support engineer. Enough said.

Performance

The Performance tab is my absolute favorite! Here, at a glance, I can tell what the CPU utilization (processor activity) is on my machine (see Figure 6-25). Typically, the CPU Usage value is in the single digits. But if that value remains above 80 percent for an extended period of time (say, several days), I'm on notice that I have performance issues on my SBS network and perhaps I should purchase a more powerful processor (or additional processors) for my SBS server machine.

Figure 6-25

The Performance tab of Task Manager.

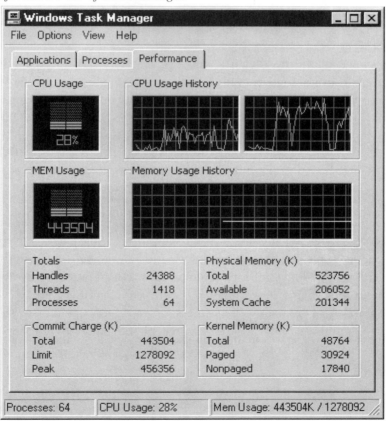

The other cool thing on the Performance screen is the memory usage information. The Memory Usage History histogram enables me not only to determine what amount of my SBS server machine's RAM memory is being consumed, but if I observe an upward sloping trend line, I know I might have leaky applications (an application that is robbing memory). I discuss the performance area in much greater detail in Chapter 16.

> BEST PRACTICE: In fact, I try to mentally note the Mem Usage value located at the lower-right of the Performance screen every several days. This value might appear similar to Mem Usage 87824K/130928K. If you reboot, the numerator (the top number) is smaller because the SBS server machine's memory has been flushed and reset. Over time, moderate growth in the numerator value is acceptable. However, if I have a major problem with an application robbing memory, the numerator can grow rapidly to a very large number. In fact, I've seen badly behaved applications eat up all the memory to the point that the SBS server machine runs out of memory, causing it to stop functioning!

Event Viewer

The Event Viewer application enables you to peek at the health of your system. You can observe several logs, but only the system and application logs hold real meaning for most of us. The security logs require that you implement auditing, a feature that is typically beyond the scope of the average SBS site.

> BEST PRACTICE: Please revisit my discussion in Chapter 5 when I explore the SBS Administrator Console for greater details on all of the logs in Event Viewer. I won't repeat that discussion here.

A few general comments regarding Event Viewer are in order. First, blue is a great color. When viewing any of the Event Viewer logs, blue-dotted information entries are good. Typically, blue-dotted information entries reflect the starting of a service. The yellow-dotted information messages reflect, just as a yellow traffic signal does, caution. Further investigation is necessary, but often yellow-dotted information messages are relatively harmless. The red Stop sign messages can be bad, reflecting a service that failed to start. But, when it comes to red Stop sign messages, Event Viewer is often a "wolf crier," in my opinion.

System

The system log in Event Viewer shows operating system-related information. Here is where important network information is communicated to you, such as the network card failing.

> BEST PRACTICE: The system log is where you can also tell when the SBS server machine was last restarted or rebooted. This is accomplished by looking for the most recent entry titled EventLog (it has a blue information dot associated with it). This is the moment the computer restarted, as far as SBS is concerned, and can be seen in Figure 6-26.

Figure 6-26
Taking a look at System in Event Viewer.

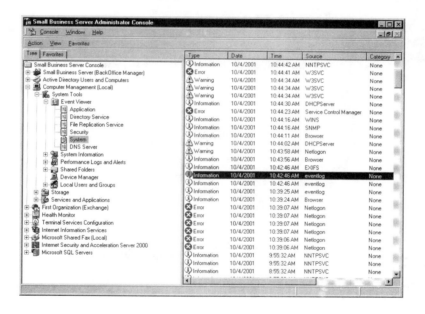

Application

The application log reports important information on various applications, including tape backup applications, the Microsoft Exchange e-mail application, and the Microsoft SQL Server database application (as well as many other applications that write to the application log).

10 - Go Online

Make a habit each day of sitting at the SBS server (or creating a Terminal Services session to the SBS server machine) and running Internet Explorer. This does two things. First, you can quickly verify the fitness of your Internet connection. Second, you can look at a couple of Web sites that might have some useful information for you. One Web site, www.sbsfaq.com, is discussed in Appendix A. Another one that I really like is www.dslreports.com if you have a broadband connection. This allows you to see where DSL service outages are occurring presently as well as run a broadband speed test. DSL Reports is shown in Figure 6-27.

Figure 6-27
One heck of a cool online tool is DSL Reports.

Notes:

11 - Installing/Removing Applications

You can count on installing and removing applications on any given day or week. While most programs are installed and removed via the **Add/Remove Software** applet in **Control Panel** (**Start**, **Settings**), I'll use this discussion to download and install WinZip, a shareware program you'll need on SSL1 as part of the SSL methodology.

1. Log on to **SSL1** as **Administrator** with the password **husky9999**.
2. Launch **Internet Explorer** from the SSL desktop and type **www.shareware.com** in the **Address** field.
3. In the **Search** field, type **WinZip**.
4. Under **CNET Downloads**, click **WinZip (32-bit)**.
5. Click **Download Now**.
6. Select a download site under **All download sites:** (e.g., ftp.simtel.net).
7. In the **Save As** dialog box, click **Save** to save the WinZip file to **My Documents**. The file should have a name similar to **winzip80.exe**. Click **Close** after the download is complete.
8. Close **Internet Explorer** from **File**, **Close**.
9. Double-click **My Documents** from the SSL1 desktop and double-click on the **WinZip** file.
10. Click **Setup** on the **WinZip 8.0 Setup** dialog box.
11. Accept the default installation path (**c:\Program Files\WinZip**) by clicking **OK** at the **WinZip Setup** dialog box.
12. Click **Next** on the **Thank you for installing WinZip!** screen.
13. Click **Yes** on the **License Agreement and Warrant Disclaimer** screen.
14. Click **Next** on the **WinZip Quick Start** screen.
15. Select **Start with WinZip Classic** and click **Next**.
16. Select **Express setup (recommended)** and click **Next**.
17. Click **Finish**.

That's it! You've now installed an application and one that's central to the SSL methodology, my friend! Note that WinZip will automatically create a shortcut on the Start menu for you and appear whenever you look at a secondary menu in Windows Explorer.

12 - Reporting

Oh, did I forget to mention along the way that you should create an SBS network notebook to record information about your network, such as the setup sheets you observed in Chapter 2? If I did forget (or you forgot to do it), please take a moment now to find a three-ring notebook and label it "SBS Network." Then consider printing out the numerous settings you've saved as part of the SSL step-by-step methodology and placing these printouts in the notebook.

Now that you've finished that, let's look at a few reports you might like to look at each day and periodically place in your SBS Network notebook. Based on my experience, the reports SBS administrators most like to see are Internet usage. This area is covered in detail in Chapter 10, but for giggles, the path is to launch the Small Business Server Administrator Console from **Start**, expand **Internet Security and Acceleration Server 2000**, expand **Servers and Arrays**, expand **SSL1**, expand **Monitoring and expand Reports**. You would then select from five reports: **Summary, Web Usage, Application Usage, Traffic** and **Utilization, Security**. A sample report is shown in Figure 6-28.

Figure 6-28
Looking at an Internet report.

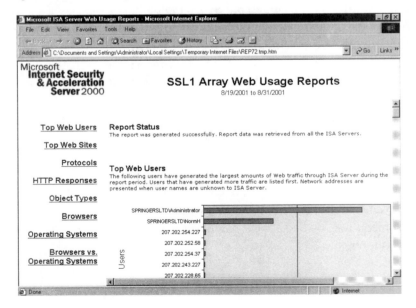

13 - Working Smarter Each Day

I'd like to close by encouraging you to consider the following SBS paradigm: working smarter each day. The best way to get value from your SBS network is to – as they say at IBM – think!

The Web

One easy way to work better each day is to browse the Web for SBS topics. A list of SBS-friendly Web sites is included in Appendix A, "SBS Resources." I would also encourage you to use a popular engine, such as Google (www.google.com), and search on the word "SBS".

Microsoft TechNet

Consider subscribing to Microsoft's monthly CD-ROM subscription service known as *Microsoft TechNet*. For approximately $300 per year, you will receive a set of CD-ROMs that provide invaluable SBS support information.

> BEST PRACTICE: To search in Microsoft TechNet, click the binocular-looking icon on the toolbar and type the term SBS. The results of such a search are shown in Figure 6-29.

Figure 6-29

SBS search on Microsoft TechNet.

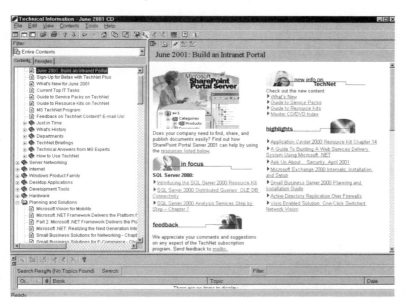

Research

Keep an eagle eye out for SBS articles in technical trade journals, such as *InfoWorld*. I am also seeing in increase in SBS-related articles in business magazines, such as *INC.* and *Success*. I've always felt an hour of research saves many hours of learning the hard way (the trial-and-error method). Oh, and don't forget in Appendix A I provide details on how to subscribe to my free monthly SBS newsletter.

Summary

This chapter presents the 13 most important and frequent tasks you are likely to perform to keep both your SBS network and SBS users up and running, but feel free to add to this list as your own unique experience dictates. The point is that, in just a large handful of pages, I've tried to present many common tasks you'll encounter as an SBSer. These were ordered, to the extent possible, by priority. Granted, virus protection and backups are probably both number one, but for this edition of the book, virus protection won. Onward to Chapter 7 and the view of monthly and annual SBS tasks!

Chapter 7
SBS Administration: Monthly and Annual

This chapter extends the daily and weekly view from Chapter 6 to include SBS network monthly and annual tasks. Although these tasks are not as extensive as the daily and weekly tasks you undoubtedly perform on your SBS network, monthly and annual SBS-related tasks are no less important. In fact, overlooking some of the monthly tasks such as defragmentation can result in declining performance, frustrated users, and, ultimately, a doomed SBS server before it's time to put it out to pasture.

> BEST PRACTICE: As always, this chapter will present the topics contained herein in the context of SSL, the sample company in this book.

For the first part of the chapter, I'll discuss the monthly tasks you should perform on your SBS network. These tasks are outlined in Table 7-1. In the second part of the chapter, I'll discuss important annual tasks that you must perform.

Table 7-1 SBS Monthly Dozen Tasks

Task	Description
1	The Monthly Reboot
2	Disk Defragmentation
3	Service Packs, Upgrades, Hot Fixes
4	Hard Disk Space Management
5	Virus Protection Again!
6	SBS Toolkit Updates
7	Adding Hardware
8	Test Restore
9	Research
10	Performance Monitor Logging
11	Updating SBS Network Notebook
12	Update the ERD

1 - The Monthly Reboot

Much like the popular graduation song where the singer advises students to always use sunscreen, in a similar vein I offer up the following advice to SBSers: Always reboot your SBS server once per month. Seriously, for several reasons, I like to reboot the SBS machines under my stewardship once per month. First, all computers suffer from RAM leaks as services, processes, and applications are opened and closed. These memory leaks occur because whatever used the memory doesn't completely return it to the computer when finished. Second, computers just get plain fussy from time to time and need a reboot to effectively get up on the right side of bed.

Granted, for most services, processes, and applications, the memory leak is very small (sometimes none at all). But, as they say in my neighborhood, Bainbridge Island has always had one bad kid. Such is life with your SBS network. You can count on one bad service, process, or application to be a RAM robber at some point. These are typically poorly developed applications that the software vendor fixes at a future date.

BEST PRACTICE: Bear with me as I dust off a golden oldie. Memory leaks are discussed extensively in two older Microsoft Certified System Engineer courses: Windows NT Core Technologies and Windows NT Server Enterprise Technologies. In fact, in the Core Technologies course, you will complete a lab with bad applications that consume excessive resources including RAM. Granted, it's unlikely that you'd go out and explicitly take these courses in the Windows 2000 era. However, if you're an MCSE from the older days (or know such a person), revisit the courseware books that accompanied these courses to bone up on this topic. In the Windows 2000 era, both the Windows 2000 Professional and Windows 2000 Server Resource Kits contain discussion on memory and performance.

Before rebooting, be sure to observe the following memory value via Task Manager and record it in the Monthly SBS worksheet discussed later. This memory value is the Mem Usage value in the lower right corner of Task Manager's Performance tab sheet. It is shown in Figure 7-1 as 612156K/1277976.

Figure 7-1

Mem Usage before reboot.

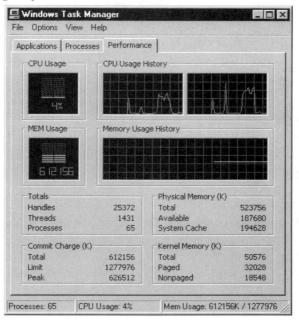

After performing a reboot on your SBS machine, once again observe the Mem Usage value in Task Manager. The numerator portion of the Mem Usage value should be lower (perhaps significantly lower). That is because the reboot flushed the RAM (your SBS machine now has more RAM to work with).

And the second reason I like to reboot an SBS machine each month? I need to know that any SBS machine I'm working with is basically healthy, at least to the extent that I'm not afraid to reboot it. Believe me, in other networking environments, such as the early days of LAN Manager or NetWare, I managed machines I was afraid to reboot! Today, with better machines and better operating systems, such as SBS, that fear of rebooting doesn't cut it. Thus, the monthly reboot shows me the machine is in good working order.

Rebooting your SBS machine is, of course, very simple. Follow these steps:

1. Log on to **SSL1** as **Administrator** with the password **husky9999**.
2. Select **Shutdown** from the **Start** menu at the desktop.
3. When the **Shut Down Windows** dialog box appears, select **Restart** under **What do you want the computer to do?**
4. Click **OK**. The SBS server machine will reboot.

Or, if you prefer, simultaneously hold down **Ctrl+Alt+Delete**, and the **Windows Security** dialog box appears. Select **Shutdown..** and when the **Shut Down Windows** dialog box appears, select **Restart** under **What do you want the computer to do?**

> BEST PRACTICE: The reboot time in SBS 2000 is much faster than SBS 4.5 and certainly much, much faster than SBS 4.0/4.0a, if you haven't already noticed. This has occurred because of optimization improvements, especially with Microsoft Exchange 2000 Server.

So, post-reboot, observe the new memory settings in Figure 7-2. Some memory has been returned to the SBS server machine for use, in part because the reboot "flushed" memory and gave it a fresh start, for lack of a better explanation. The MEM value reads 578468K/1277976.

Figure 7-2

Mem Usage after reboot.

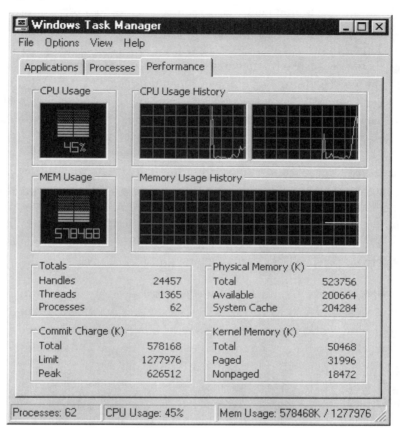

I have a final thought on rebooting. Make sure you've notified your SBS users that a reboot will occur so that they can log off properly and not leave any important files open (such as Great Plains accounting files). Better yet, consider coming in after hours to reboot the server when no one is around. And as you'll learn in Chapter 8, you can even use the Terminal Services remote management approach to reboot the server at night when you're sitting on an island thirty miles away.

Notes:

2 - Disk Defragmentation

Believe it or not, the hard disks in your SBS machine, as well as your SBS user's machines, are subject to fragmentation. Fragmentation occurs when information is written, in a fragmented way, to different locations. Here is what I mean. Suppose you had a large Microsoft Excel spreadsheet file titled CASHFLOW.XLS. It is possible this file could be written to numerous spots or locations on your hard disk to get it to fit when performing a file save. On the surface, this notion that one file is really stored across different locations on your hard disk isn't terribly bothersome, but when this happens with many files, including important operating system files, both you and I should be much more concerned.

Why concerned? Because these files, being stored in a somewhat discontiguous manner, have become fragmented. Such fragmentation results in poor performance on your machine because the hard disk must perform additional read/write I/O activity to either retrieve or save the file. You see this phenomenon when you observe an incessantly grinding hard disk on your SBS machine during normal network activity (such as SBS users opening files to work on).

> BEST PRACTICE: Contrary to popular belief, the NTFS formatting scheme used on SBS machines is indeed subject to fragmentation. Rumors have abounded during the life of Windows NT Server and haven't been completely quashed under Windows 2000 (the underlying operating system in SBS), that NTFS partitions didn't suffer from fragmentation. That is wrong, as you'll see shortly in Figure 7-3.

So, if we agree that fragmentation is bad, how might you address this problem? Simply stated, on a monthly basis (more frequently on heavily used SBS systems), you should defragment the hard disk on your SBS machine. SBS 2000 now supports two types of disk defragmentation! This is a change from SBS 4.5, which supported only the first method (the CHKDSK command) out of the box and required you to purchase a third-party disk defragmentation program.

The Beloved CHKDSK command

Call it an oldie but a goodie, the command line utility CHKDSK (known as check disk) is provided from the command-line in SBS 2000. CHKDSK tests the integrity of your SBS machine's hard disks and marks bad spots as off-limits for future storage. If you've ever shut off an SBS machine before you were notified it was kosher to do so, CHKDSK will run automatically at the next reboot. To see the different options for CHKDSK, simply type **CHKDSK /?** at the command prompt. For example, if you run CHKDSK with the /F switch, problems with the file system that are detected will be fixed (/F = fix). CHKDSK runs in five stages:

1. File verification
2. Index verification
3. Security descriptor verification
4. Journal verification
5. Reporting (reports total disk space, files, indexes, bad sectors, space in use by the system, size of log file, and free space on disk. There is additional information on allocation units reported).

SBS's Native Disk Defragmenter

I still haven't answered the underlying question about defragmenting a hard disk. To defragment a hard disk, you need to use the new Disk Defragmenter included in SBS 2000 (click **Start**, **Programs**, **Accessories**, **System Tools** and **Disk Defragmenter**). Basically, Disk Defragmenter, when using the steps below, identifies how badly fragmented your hard disk is and then proceeds to defragment the hard disks. The defragmentation process recombines files, resulting in free space that is contiguous or whole, not chopped up. Bottom line? When the hard disks on your SBS machine are defragmented, you will notice better SBS machine performance, and thus higher network performance. Meanwhile, back at SSL, please complete the following steps:

1. Log on to **SSL1** as **Administrator** with the password **husky9999**.
2. Make sure you have a good tape backup of everything (data, System State, applications, and so on) on the hard disks of your SBS machine. You want this in case something goes terribly wrong during the defragmentation process. Tape backups were discussed earlier in Chapter 6.
3. Click **Start**, **Small Business Server Administrator Console** and expand **Computer Management (Local)**. Expand **Storage** and click **Disk Defragmenter**. The Disk Defragmenter tool appears in the right-pane and looks similar to Figure 7-3.

Figure 7-3

The default view of Disk Defragmenter in the Small Business Server Administrator Console displays the hard disks on the system.

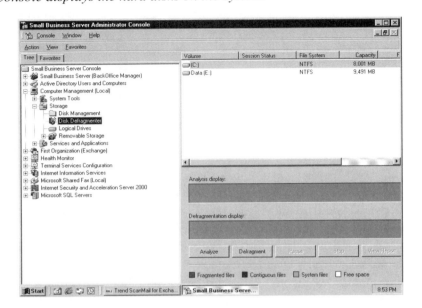

4. Select the hard drive that you want to analyze and defragment (say Drive C:). Click the **Analyze** button. The Disk Defragmenter program will run for a few minutes and report back to you (in the screen), the condition of the disk, as seen in Figure 7-4.

Notes:

Figure 7-4

Drive C: has been analyzed and visually reports moderate disk fragmentation.
And, yes, this figure is truely different from Figure 7-3.

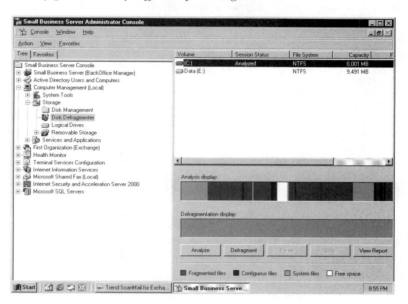

5. The **Analysis Complete** dialog box appears after the analysis is complete,
    allowing you to view the report, shown in Figure 7-5, by clicking the **View
    Report** button. You can start the defragmentation process by clicking the
    Defragment button or clicking **Close** to close the **Analysis Complete**
    dialog box. Go ahead and click the **View Report** button, and after observ-
    ing the information in the **Analysis Report** screen, click **Close**.

Notes:

Figure 7-5
Meaningful disk information is displayed on the Analysis Report screen.

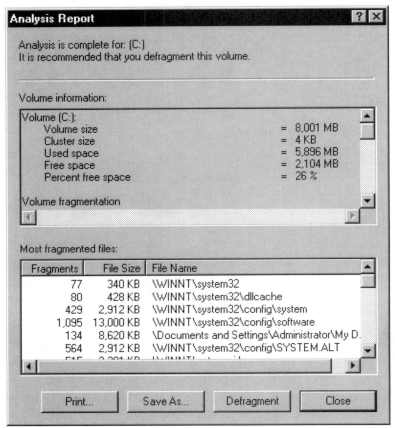

BEST PRACTICE: You can print (Print) or save the disk report information (Save As) shown in the Analysis Report screen and add it to your
SBS network notebook. The network notebook is discussed later in the
chapter as monthly duty 11.

6. Click the **Defragment** button on the **Disk Defragmenter** screen to start
    the disk defragmentation process.
7. Click **Close** when the **Defragmentation Complete** screen appears. If
    you look at the display bars in the center of Disk Defragmenter, you will
    note that these have been updated to show fewer areas of fragmented files.

8. Close the Disk Defragmenter program by clicking the close button (**X**) in the upper right part of the window.

BEST PRACTICE: The same steps for running Disk Defragmenter should be used on your Windows 2000 Professional workstations on your SBS network. The same tool is used.

Also note that Disk Defragmenter must be started manually, as there is no schedule or timer to run this tool in the off-hours (nights and weekends for most companies). If your want to automate the disk defragmentation process (and have one less thing to worry about), consider purchasing a third-party disk defragmentation program such as Executive Software Diskkeeper (full version, as the lite version is included in SBS 2000).

Defragmenting Windows 9x clients

Like the SBS machine, the user's Windows98 workstations aren't immune to fragmentation. And, on a monthly basis, you should strongly consider defragmenting their hard disks as well.

BEST PRACTICE: If you've been especially negligent and haven't performed disk defragmentation in ages, it might take more than one pass for the disk defragmentation utility to optimize your hard disk space. That's reasonable. Use your judgment, but if the shoe fits, run the defragmentation utility twice.

1. Log on to a Windows 98 computer.
2. Click **Start**, **Programs**, **Accessories**, **System Tools**, **Disk Defragmenter**.
3. When Disk Defragmenter is running, identify the drive you want to defragment (for example, drive C). Click **OK** to start the disk defragmentation process..
4. Observe the disk defragmentation activity in the Disk Defragmenter dialog box (see Figure 7-6). Click **Close** when the process is complete.

Notes:

Figure 7-6
Windows 98's Disk Defragmenter.

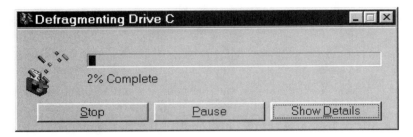

3 - Service Packs, Patches, Upgrades, Hot Fixes

Whatever name you use, be it service packs, patches, upgrades, or hot fixes, software
manufacturers such as Microsoft periodically release enhancements to either fix
problems or add features. These enhancements, known generically as the aforementioned service packs, et al., can be released for the operating system (which is
Windows 2000 Server in SBS 2000) or the applications (such as Microsoft Exchange
Server on the server-side or Microsoft Office on the client computer-side).

One of the largest ongoing SBS administration challenges is keeping track of the
service packs, et. al. that are released for your SBS computer system. If you are an
SBS consultant, this is just another day at the office. Customers running SBS look to
you to know this information and use it to watch out for the clients' best interests.

If you are an SBS administrator working for a small business, the challenge is
knowing what service packs, et. al. have been released for your SBS network and
applications. For starters, allow me to walk you through two service packs and one
virus/worm-related fix you need to add at a minimum to your SBS server machine.
You will then implement the fix to the SBS 2000 license logging service. From the
top, the order of the specific tasks you MUST complete for SSL are:

1. Deploy Windows 2000 Server Service Pack 2
2. Implement Microsoft Exchange 2000 Server Service Pack 1
3. Install Microsoft's IIS/Code Red/Nimda Fix (Security Bulletin 44)
4. Apply the SBS 2000 License Logging Service (LLS) fix

BEST PRACTICE: These need to be added in order, as far as I'm concerned, because Security Bulletin 44 correctly overwrites the older

ISAPI IIS-related file implemented from the Exchange 2000 Server Service Pack #1.

In Chapter 11, you'll apply the Exchange 2000 Server Conferencing Server Service Pack, but not here. This is because you will first download and install the Exchange 2000 Conferencing Server solution.

Note that I recognize these fixes are only as current as the date I penned these words. The world changes rapidly with respect to technology, and SBS 2000 is no exception. It's likely when you're reading these words several months hence, the service pack-level will have incremented and perhaps other important fixes will have been released. Bear with me, but understand this example works perfectly within the context of the SSL methodology.

Also, you should consider subscribing to my monthly SBS newlsetter as discussed in Appendix A.

First, complete the following procedure to create the necessary folders to store the files you'll download and apply as part of this section on service packs, et. al.

1. Log on to **SSL1** as **Administrator** with the password **husky9999**.
2. Double-click the **My Documents** shortcut on the SSL1 desktop.
3. Right-click on the right-pane (details pane) and select **New**, **Folder**. Repeat this task as necessary to create the following folders:
   •**Windows 2000 Server SP2**
   •**Exchange 2000 Server SP1**
   •**MS-Security44**
   •**SBS2000 LLS Fix**
4. Double-click the **Exchange 2000 Server SP1** folder and in the right-pane, right-click and select **New**, **Folder**. Name the new folder **Exchange 2000 Conferencing Server SP1**.
5. Close **My Documents** from **File, Close**.

You will know proceed to download each of the service packs and fixes and place these in their respective folder.

1. Log on to **SSL1** as **Administrator** with the password **husky9999**.
2. Double-click the **Internet Explorer** shortcut on the SSL1 desktop.

3. Surf to the Microsoft Windows 2000 site by typing **www.microsoft.com/ windows2000/server** in the **Address** field and pressing **Enter**.

BEST PRACTICE: Note the addresses (URLs) listed in this section may change over time. Please adjust the addresses for the Microsoft Web site as necessary.

4. On the **Windows 2000 Server** page, select **Downloads, Service Packs**.
5. On the **Service Packs** page, select **Windows 2000 Service Pack 2**.
6. On the **Windows 2000 Service Pack 2** page, select **Get SP2 Now**.
7. Under **Get Windows 2000 SP2 Now**, select **Download Windows 2000 SP2**.
8. Accept the default settings (English) and click **Go**.
9. On the **Windows 2000 Service Pack 2 U.S. English** page, click **SP2 Network Installation**.

BEST PRACTICE: Note the file you will download is 101 MB in size, so there will be plenty of time to go out for coffee, even with a broadband connection. I have you download the entire service pack, so it'll be easy to apply again when you make systemic changes to your SBS 2000 server machine. I've also found the express installation option to be unreliable.

10. On the **File Download** dialog box, select **Save this program to disk**. Click **OK**.
11. On the **Save As** dialog box, select the **Windows 2000 Server SP2** folder under **My Documents** and press **Save**. The download will commence.
12. Select the **Close this dialog box when the download completed** check box on the **File Download** dialog box. Now go get a cup of coffee.
13. Okay, welcome back from the Windows 2000 Server SP2 download. You've got a lot of work remaining. In the **Internet Explorer,** click on the **Address** field and type **www.microsoft.com/exchange/downloads/ 2000/** and press **Enter**.
14. On the **Downloads for Exchange** page, select **Download or Order Exchange 2000 Service Pack 1**.
15. On the **Exchange 2000 Server Service Pack 1** page, select **Go** under **Exchange 2000 Server**. Accept the default language (English).

BEST PRACTICE: Note that the second service pack listed is for Exchange 2000 Conferencing Server. You will download this next.

16. On the **Exchange 2000 Server and Exchange 2000 Enterprise Server Service Pack 1 English** page, click on the files listed below and select **Save this program to disk** on the **File Downloads** dialog box. Click **OK** and save to the **Exchange 2000 Server SP1** folder under **My Documents**. You will repeat this exact step for each of the files listed below. (Sorry, but this is time-consuming and detailed-oriented work to download all 13 files – too bad it's not one huge file to download, eh?)

    1. E2KSP1_setup1.exe
    2. E2KSP1_setup2.exe
    3. E2KSP1_setup3.exe
    4. E2KSP1_setup4.exe
    5. E2KSP1_setup5.exe
    6. E2KSP1_support1.exe
    7. E2KSP1_support2.exe
    8. E2KSP1_support3.exe
    9. E2KSP1_calcon.exe
    10. E2KSP1_instmsg.exe
    11. E2KSP1_migrate.exe
    12. E2KSP1_adc.exe
    13. ReleaseNotes.htm

17. In **Internet Explorer**, click **Back** to return to the **Exchange 2000 Server Service Pack 1** page.

18. On the **Exchange 2000 Server Service Pack 1** page, select **Go** under **Exchange 2000 Conferencing Server**. Accept the default language (English).

19. On the **Exchange 2000 Conferencing Server Service Pack 1 English** page, click **E2KSP1_Conf.exe**.

20. On the **File Downloads** dialog box, select **Save this program to disk** and click **OK**. Save the file to the **Exchange 2000 Conferencing Server SP1** folder under **Exchange 2000 Server SP1** under **My Documents**. Click **Save** to close the **Save As** dialog box and start the approximately 11 MB file download. Note the saved file name will be **e2ksp1_conferencing.exe**. Select the **Close this dialog box when the download completed** check box on the **File Download** dialog box.

BEST PRACTICE: I've noticed something very strange about the download process from the File Downloads dialog box. If, for some reason, you're distracted for several minutes (say to answer a telephone call) while at midpoint in this process, right before you click Save from the Save As dialog box, the download will fail. Only the shortcut to the file but not the file will be downloaded. The shortcut download only takes a few seconds with a broadband connection, not the several minutes you would expect for the entire file.

The cure for this malady is to simply repeat the file download operation again, and not answer the telephone if it rings!

21. You will now download Microsoft Security Bulletin 44. In the **Address** field of **Internet Explorer**, type **www.microsoft.com/security/downloads**.
22. In the left pane, expand **Security, Bulletins** and select **Microsoft Security Bulletin (MS01-044)**.
23. Under **Patch availability**, click the link beneath **Microsoft IIS 5.0**.
24. On the **Security Update, August 17, 2001** page, click **Go** under **Download**. Accept English as the default language.
25. On the **Security Update, August 17, 2001 U.S. English** page, click **Security_Update** under **Download**.
26. On the **File Downloads** dialog box, select **Save this program to disk** and click **OK**. Save the file to the **MS-Security44** folder under **My Documents**. Click **Save** to close the **Save As** dialog box and start the approximately 2.1 MB file download. Note that the saved file name will be **q301625_w2k_sp3_x86_en.exe**. Select the **Close this dialog box when the download completed** check box on the **File Download** dialog box. Now take a quick break!
27. You have one download task left. In **Internet Explorer**, type **www.microsoft.com/sbserver/downloads** in the **Address** field.
28. Click the link for the **License Logging Service fix** (as of press time, this link hadn't been posted yet, so bear with me).
29. Click **Go** beneath **Download**.
30. Under **Download**, click the link for the **License Logging Service fix** (*.exe).
31. On the **File Downloads** dialog box, click select **Save this program to**

disk and click **OK**. Save the file to the **SBS2000 LLS Fix** folder under **My Documents**. Click **Save** to close the **Save As** dialog box and start the approximately 200 KB file download. Select the **Close this dialog box when the download completed** check box on the **File Download** dialog box. This relatively small file should only take a moment to download.

You have successfully downloaded the baseline of service packs, et al., that are necessary to make the SSL SBS 2000 network shipshape. You will now apply each and every one of these fixes. Let's get going and remember to complete these procedures in the order presented. You will first install Service Pack 2 for Windows 2000 Server.

1. Log on to **SSL1** as **Administrator** with the password **husky9999**.
2. Click **Start, Run**. In the **Run** dialog box, click **Browse,** navigate to **My Documents, Windows 2000 Server SP2** folder, and click **W2KSP2.exe**. Click **Open**.
3. Click **OK** in the **Run** dialog box. The **Extracting Files** dialog box will appear and report file extraction activity.
4. Click **OK** when the **Service Pack Setup Error** dialog box informs you that a reboot is needed.
5. Click **Start, Shut Down**, select **Restart** on the **Shut Down Windows** dialog box, and click **OK**.
6. Log on to **SSL1** as **Administrator** with the password **husky9999**.
7. This command and the next will look familiar, but you need to complete them! Click **Start, Run**. In the **Run** dialog box, click **Browse,** navigate to **My Documents, Windows 2000 Server SP2** folder, and click **W2KSP2.exe**. Click **Open**.
8. Click **OK** in the **Run** dialog box. The **Extracting Files** dialog box will appear and report file extraction activity.
9. On the **Windows 2000 Service Pack Setup** dialog box, click the **Accept the License Agreement (must accept before installing the Service Pack)** check box and click **Install**. At this point, progress bars will display the service pack setup activity, so you can quickly stretch your arms!
10. When the process is completed, click **Restart** on the **Windows 2000 Service Pack Setup** dialog box. You now complete the installation of Windows 2000 Server Service Pack 2.

BEST PRACTICE: Time to go get a refill of that cup of coffee here. For some reason, right after you apply this service pack, the reboot time is longer than normal. See you back here in several minutes!

Next, you'll complete the following procedure to install the Exchange 2000 Server service pack.

1. Log on to **SSL1** as **Administrator** with the password **husky9999**.
2. Double-click the **My Documents** on the SSL1 desktop.
3. Double-click the **Exchange 2000 Server SP1** folder.
4. You will now double-click on the following files in the order listed below. Each time you do this, the **Win2K Self-Extractor** dialog box will appear. In the **Unzip to Folder** field, make sure the follow path is entered: **C:\Documents and Settings\Administrator\My Documents\Exchange 2000 Server SP1**. Click **Unzip**. Click **OK** when notified that the files have been successfully extracted. Repeat this exact step as necessary to unzip each of the files (granted, this takes a fair amount of time to accomplish).
   - `E2KSP1_setup1.exe`
   - `E2KSP1_setup2.exe`
   - `E2KSP1_setup3.exe`
   - `E2KSP1_setup4.exe`
   - `E2KSP1_setup5.exe`
   - `E2KSP1_support1.exe`
   - `E2KSP1_support2.exe`
   - `E2KSP1_support3.exe`
   - `E2KSP1_calcon.exe`
   - `E2KSP1_instmsg.exe`
   - `E2KSP1_migrate.exe`
   - `E2KSP1_adc.exe`
5. With the **My Documents** window still open, navigate to **Exchange 2000 Server SP1\setup\I386** and double-click on **update.exe**.
6. Click **Next** when the **Welcome to the Microsoft Exchange 2000 Service Pack Installation Wizard** appears.
7. Click **Next** on the **Component Selection** screen, as seen in Figure 7-7.

Figure 7-7

The default selections on the Component Select screen are correct.

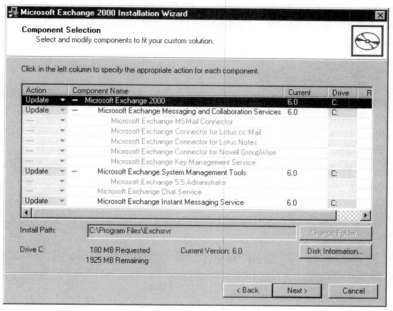

BEST PRACTICE: You might note with interest that the amount of disk space requested at the bottom left of Figure 7-7 is over 180 MB! To me that says the entire Exchange 2000 Server application is darn near being replaced.

8. Click **Next** on the **Component Summary** screen.
9. The **Component Progress** screen will communicate the service pack installation progress. This service pack takes several minutes to install if you'd like to take a short break.
10. If you receive an error message that a file can't be overwritten because it's in use, via the **Microsoft Exchange 2000 Installation Wizard** dialog box, click **Continue** so the service pack installation can continue. When you reboot, the service pack installation will replace the file referenced here. Note this is a normal error message to appear on the screen.
11. Click **Finish** on the **Completing the Microsoft Exchange 2000 Wizard** page.
12. Click **Yes** when asked to restart on the **Microsoft Exchange 2000 Installation Wizard** dialog box.

When SSL1 restarts, some background tasks will complete the Microsoft Exchange Server 2000 Service Pack installation. Your work on this procedure is complete and you'll now proceed to install Microsoft Security Bulletin 44, which is the comprehensive IIS fix for CODE RED and Nimda.

1. Log on to **SSL1** as **Administrator** with the password **husky9999**.
2. Click **File, Run** and **Browse**.
3. In the **Browse** dialog box, navigate to **My Documents** and the **MS-Security44** folder. Highlight the **q301625_w2k-sp3_x86_en.exe** file and click **Open**.
4. Click **OK** in the **Run** dialog box. The files will be extracted.
5. In the **Windows 2000 HotFix Setup** dialog box, click **Continue** when notified that several services will be stopped and started. Some file copying activity occurs.
6. On the **HotFix Setup** dialog box, click **Continue** to reboot SSL1.

You have now successfully applied Microsoft Security Bulletin 44. Next, you'll apply the License Logging Service fix specific to SBS 2000.

> BEST PRACTICE: Note these steps are based on the beta release of the License Logging Service fix. When you perform this procedure, check the README file that accompanies the License Logging Service fix in order to verify the exact steps you should perform.

1. Assuming you are still logged on to SSL1, you will now reboot and start in Safe Mode. Click **Start, Shutdown, Restart**.
2. When SSL restarts, press the **F8** key when prompted for advanced startup options and select **Safe Mode** from the **Windows 2000 Advanced Options Menu**. Press **Enter**.
3. Log on to **SSL1** as **Administrator** with the password **husky9999**. Click **OK** when the **Desktop** dialog box notifies that you are running in safe mode.
4. Click **Start, Programs, Accessories, Windows Explorer**. Navigate to **C:\WINNT\System32** directory.
5. Select and right-click on the file **llssrv.exe** in the **System32** directory. Select **Rename** and name the file **llssrv.old**. Click **Yes** on the **Rename** dialog box.

6. Navigate to **My Documents**, **SBS2000 LLS Fix**, right-click **llssrv.exe**, and select **Copy**.

7. Navigate to **C:\WINNT\System32** directory, right-click in the detail pane (right-side), and select **Paste**. This will copy-and-paste the new llssrv.exe to the System32 directory.

8. Navigate to the **dllcache** directory under **System32** (full path is **C:\WINNT\System32\dllcache**).

9. Rename the **llssrv.exe** in the **dllcache** directory to **llssrv.old** (right-click, **Rename**).

10. Right-click in the detail pane of the **dllcache** directory and select **Paste**. This will effectively copy-and-paste the new llssrv.exe to the dllcache directory.

11. Close **Windows Explorer** from **File**, **Close**.

12. Reboot SSL1 from **Start**, **Shutdown**, **Restart**.

You've now created the procedures necessary to bring SSL1 into line with the latest service packs and fixes. Other examples in this chapter and the remainder of the book will now work without incident!

So, now that you've got your baseline of service packs, you could peruse www.microsoft.com each month. At Microsoft's Web site, click the **Support** button to learn more about service packs, et al. You should typically view information for each operating system you have (Windows 2000 Server, Windows 2000 Professional, Windows XP, Windows ME, Windows 9x) and each application. Remember that applications include the BackOffice applications, such as Microsoft Exchange and Microsoft SQL Server, plus user applications, such as Microsoft Word. For non-Microsoft applications, such as accounting software applications, visit the specific software manufacturer's site

> BEST PRACTICE: Even for the best of us, keeping up with new service packs, et al., is difficult. So, while giving yourself a break, don't be negligent. Each month, make it part of your SBS administration duties to seek out service pack, et al., information (or at least seek out someone who knows this information).

I have a few final thoughts regarding service packs, et al. First, assess whether you really need to apply it. Does your computer system actually benefit from the service pack, et al.? If not, think twice about installing it. Second, understand the political dimension to this area. For example, some IT managers won't install an operating system or application until the first service pack has been released. The conventional wisdom is that when an operating system or application is initially released, it's fit for testing. When the first service pack is released for the operating system or application in question, it's fit for duty. And when the second service pack is ready, even the most conservative SBS customer can't plug the dike of SBS momentum any longer.

Third, one of the SBS challenges you will ultimately face is knowing which version of the service packs, et al., you have installed on your machine. Don't laugh! It's easy to forget sometime whether hot fix 2000.1a was already applied. To assist you with this dilemma, consider **Service Pack Manager 2000** from Gravity Storm Software (**home.san.rr.com/gravitystorm**). This is an application that allows you to see which service packs, et. al. have been applied to a system running on Windows 2000. Information on Service Pack Manager 2000 is shown in Figure 7-8. There are other similar applications that can be found on the Winfiles shareware site (**www.winfiles.com**) by searching on words such as "**hotfix**". One such other tool is HotFix Control.

Figure 7-8
Service Pack Manager 2000.

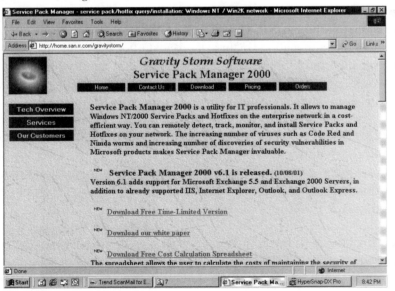

Fourth, understand that service packs, et al., are typically acquired one of two ways. You can either download the files from your software manufacturer's Web site or order the files on a CD-ROM (again, from your software manufacturer). My advice? If you have a high-speed connection to the Internet, simply download the files you need. However, if you have a modem-based connection, be sure to order the files on CD-ROM. Modem downloads of any significant size not only take forever, but the download process is often unreliable (the modem drops the connection at midpoint or creates corrupted files).

> BEST PRACTICE: Please consider clicking **Windows Update** program item from the **Start** menu periodically. This is a way to stay current with Windows 2000 Server-specific fixes. However, this approach will not specifically address SBS 2000 fixes. But, heck, it's a good start toward better managing your system, eh?

And last, countless stories in the short history of network computing relate to inappropriately applied service packs. Here is admittedly an oldie but a doozy! Just ask your networking guru buddy about Service Pack 2, circa Windows NT Server 4.0 several years ago. It was the infamous service pack that, in many cases, broke more than it fixed. Perhaps you have your own story about a service pack, et al., that was more problematic than you anticipated. The point is this: Don't always be the first on your block to apply the latest service pack, et al. You probably want to wait a few weeks while the larger computing community acts as your personal fleet of regression testers. In other words, let them pay too much and pass the savings on to you.

4 - Hard Disk Space Management

Each month, you should monitor the amount of hard disk storage space you have remaining on SBS machine. Tracking this information monthly assures that you won't be caught by surprise as applications take more and more space for data. One such example is an accounting application. Month in and month out, accounting transactions and the like cause the accounting software database to grow. Often, before you know it, you're out of hard disk space on the SBS machine, and that can clearly be problematic.

Notes:

There are a few good reasons for not letting the hard disk space on your SBS server machine become in short supply:

- **The 20 Percent Rule.** Long known by veteran network administrators, it is essential that you maintain at least 20 percent free space on your SBS machine hard disks. This free space allows file swapping and accounts for bad sectors on the hard disks. In my experience and that of others, falling below 20 percent free space can cause operating system instability. See Chapter 16, where I discuss using Health Monitor to notify you of low disk space conditions on your SBS server.

- **Printing.** You might not have known that a print job, sent by an SBS user, first prints to the printer queue on the SBS machine's hard disks. In effect, you first print to the hard disks before the printer (whether you like it or not). The good news is that this approach allows print jobs to queue up and await actual printing. The bad news is that running out of hard disk space on your SBS machine means the network printing capabilities are kaput!

- **New Applications.** Monthly monitoring of your hard disk space allows you to plan for the installation of new applications on your SBS machine. Hardly a month goes by when one of your SBS users won't suggest some new application they have read about. You need to anticipate such requests when observing how much free disk space you have on your SBS machine. Don't underestimate the space you need; rare is the day that you truly have too much hard disk space. Of course, with the low prices of storage space today, adding another drive isn't really a problem for many small businesses.

BEST PRACTICE: See Chapter 16 where I discuss hard disk space management with Server Status View, Server Status Report and Health Monitor. Below I discuss hands-on approaches to hard disk space management.

Checking Free Space

Checking the amount of free hard disk space on your SBS machine is very simple. Instead of the CHKDSK command from DOS days of old, I prefer the SBS Administrator Console method followed by the GUI method. The SBS

Administrator Console method has become much easier in SBS 2000 compared to SBS 4.5/4.0a/4.0.

1. Log on to **SSL1** as **Administrator** with the password **husky9999**.
2. Click **Start, Small Business Server Administrator Console**.
3. Expand **Computer Management (Local)** and **Storage**.
4. Click **Disk Management**. In the right-pane, disk information is reported as seen in Figure 7-9. The **Status** column reports the disks are healthy. The **Free Space** column reports the amount of free space. The **% Free** column reports the percentage of free disk space.

Figure 7-9
Basic at-a-glance, very useful hard disk information is reported under Disk Management.

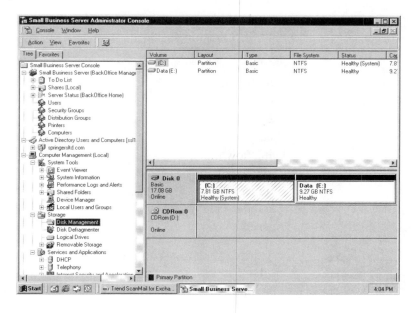

Now I'll present the old-fashioned GUI method. Simply launch My Computer from the SBS machine desktop and look at a hard drive's properties. The GUI method steps are

1. Log on to **SSL1** as **Administrator** with the password **husky9999**.

2. Double-click the **My Computer** icon on the SSL1 desktop.
3. **Right-click** the hard disk **Local Disk (C:)**.
4. Select **Properties** from the secondary menu.
5. Select the **General** tab sheet in the **Properties** dialog box. The results should be a screen similar to Figure 7-10.
6. Click OK when you have recorded the amount of free space to close the Properties dialog box.

Figure 7-10
Determining hard disk free space using the tried and true old fashioned GUI method.

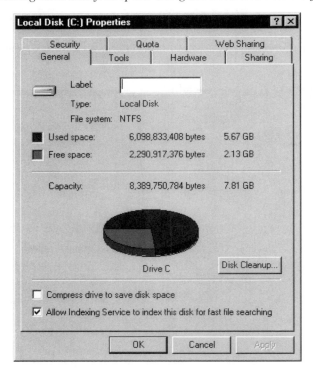

BEST PRACTICE: The old-fashioned GUI method that makes use of My Computer is a fool-proof method for checking free disk space on Windows 2000 Professional, Windows ME, and Windows 9x workstations. However, under SBS 2000, you could use the **Small Business Server Administrator Console** to accomplish this as well. Expand **Computer Management (Local)**, expand **Disk Management,** right-click a drive (say **C:**), and select **Properties**. Click the **General** tab.

Increasing Free Space

There are three approaches for increasing the amount of hard disk space on your SBS machine, should you find one month that you've fallen below the 20 percent free space threshold: the cheap way, the trade-off way, and the moderate cost way.

Cheap Way

The cheap way is to use the WinZip compression application long favored by network professionals to send large files as e-mail attachments. WinZip can also be used to compress data files stored on your SBS machine that you are not frequently accessing. An example of this might be files specific to a project that has been completed. As you recall, WinZip was downloaded and installed in Chapter 6. Typically *.zip files are only 10 percent the size of the original data that was compressed, but that number can vary depending on the type of file being compressed. Text files tend to compress better or more efficiently than files containing photos. That's saving disk space, my friend. Later, when you need to access a file contained in a WinZip archive, simply double-click the .zip file containing the files you seek. WinZip automatically launches and allows you the opportunity to expand the files of interest.

Trade-off Method

For the trade-off method of gaining more space, simply use the compression capabilities provided by Windows 2000 Server. This approach is very simple to implement. If you revisit Figure 7-10, where you learned to determine the amount of free space on your hard disk, you will notice a check box in the lower-left corner of the General tab that allows you to Compress C:\ (or whatever drive letter you are looking at). Simply select the option by clicking on the **Compress drive to save disk space** check box. You're finished, but at a steep price. Because you will be compressing folders and files you'll be actively using, the computer will have to decompress these files on-the-fly for you to use them. This decompression/compression activity negatively affects overall SBS server machine performance.

You can compress selected folders instead of entire drives, as I implied earlier today. To compress a folder:

1. Log on to **SSL1** as **Administrator** with the password **husky9999**.

2. Click **Start, Programs, Accessories, Windows Explorer**.
3. Navigate and right-click the folder you want to compress to display the secondary menu and select **Properties**.
4. Select the **General** tab.
5. Click the **Advanced** button. The **Advanced Attributes** dialog box appears.
6. Select the **Compress contents to save disk space** check box in the **Compress or Encrypt attributes** section.
7. Click **OK** to close the **Advanced Attributes** dialog box.
8. Click **OK** to close the folder's **Properties** dialog box.
9. The **Confirm Attribute Changes** dialog box appears. Select **Apply changes to this folder only** and click **OK**. The compressed folder appears in a blue color when observed in Windows Explorer.

BEST PRACTICE: Compression provided by Windows 2000 Server, as discussed in this section, is available only on NTFS partitions. FAT partitions don't enjoy such powerful capabilities.

Moderate Cost

The expensive method of increasing your hard disk space is simple: Add more hard disk space. This can take the form of another hard disk or an external array or collection of hard disks. The sky (and your budget) is the limit! But I serve up these dramatics half in jest. Hard disks are far cheaper today than just a year or two ago, so although some cost is associated with adding a hard disk to your SBS server machine, the cost is much lower than you might imagine if you haven't looked at hard disk prices lately.

SBS Disk Cleanup

Another cool tool for hard disk space management is to use Disk Cleanup, a native Windows 2000 tool accessible under the System Tools folder in SBS 2000. This tool looks for ways to free up space on your hard disk. To use Disk Cleanup:

1. Log on to **SSL1** as **Administrator** with the password **husky9999**.
2. Click **Start, Programs, Accessories, System Tools, Disk Cleanup.**
3. When the **Select Drive** dialog box appears, select the drive that you want to clean up under **Drives:** and click **OK**. Under the SSL methodology, select **drive (C:)**.

4. The **Disk Cleanup** dialog box appears, giving you a progress report. It will report that it is calculating how much space you will be able to save on the drive you selected.

5. The **Disk Cleanup for (C:)** dialog box will appear. On the **Disk Cleanup** tab, select the check box options under the **Files to delete:** list that you want to delete in order to free space. If you click the **More Options** tab, you can perform advanced action, such as removing unused Windows components (for example, Games) and removing applications that you no longer use. Accept the default selections on the **Disk Cleanup** tab and click **OK**.

6. Answer **Yes** when the small **Disk Cleanup for (C:)** dialog box appears asking **Are you sure you want to delete files?**

7. The **Disk Cleanup** dialog box will appear and report the progress of the cleanup operation. This box will automatically disappear when the cleanup operation has concluded. This is the end of the process.

Error Checking

You can perform a scan disk function to surface test and fix your hard disk media on the machine running SBS. This is accomplished by running an error-checking capability with the following steps:

1. Log on to **SSL1** as **Administrator** with the password **husky9999**.

2. Click **Start, Small Business Server Administrator Console.**

3. Expand **Computer Management (Local)**.

4. Expand **Storage**.

5. Select **Disk Management**.

6. **Right-click** one of the **disk drives** listed under **Volume** in the right pane. In the case of the SSL methodology, select **drive (C:)**. Select **Properties** from the secondary menu.

7. Select the **Tools** tab.

8. Click the **Check Now** button under **Error-checking**.

9. The **Check Disk** dialog box appears. Under **Check disk options**, select **Automatically fix file system errors** and **Scan for and attempt recovery of bad sectors**.

10. The **Checking Disk C:** dialog box will appear, notifying you that the disk check function can not commence until the next reboot, as the operating system could not obtain exclusive access to the drive. Click **Yes**

to schedule this task at the next restart. And as you might have guessed, this disk check capability will run without user intervention as part of the character-based boot process.

Disk Quota

A most desired hard disk space management capability, previously provided by third-party utilities, is the Disk Quota functionality in the underlying Windows 2000 Server operating system in SBS. This allows you to restrict the amount of hard disk space a user can consume. I think it can be considered like applying the old "an ounce of prevention is worth a pound of cure" paradigm to hard disk space management. To invoke the Disk Quota capability:

1. Log on to **SSL1** as **Administrator** with the password **husky9999**.
2. Click **Start, Small Business Server Administrator Console.**
3. Expand **Computer Management (Local).**
4. Expand **Storage.**
5. Select **Disk Management**.
6. **Right-click** one of the **disk drives** listed under **Volume** in the right pane. In the case of the SSL methodology, select drive **(C:)**. Select **Properties** from the secondary menu.
7. Select the **Quota** tab.
8. Click the **Enable quota management** check box. Several options on the Quota tab will now become visible. Under the SSL methodology, select the following: **Deny Disk space to users exceeding quota limit, Limit disk space to 100MB**, and **Set warning level to 75MB**. Also select **Log event when a user exceeds their quota limit** and **Log event when a user exceeds their warning level**. Your screen should look similar to Figure 7-11. Note that these are the default settings for the hard disk.

Notes:

Figure 7-11

Configuring the disk quota capability for SSL.

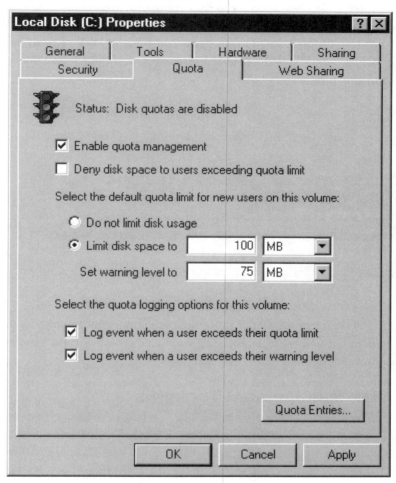

9. Click **Quota Entries**. The Quota Entries for Local Disk (C:) appears. This is where you can set individual quota limits that override some of the default settings you created in the last step (Step 8).
10. Click **Quota, New Quota Entry**. The **Select Users** dialog box appears. The default container (or location) is **springersu.com**.
11. In the screen area that lists the names (under **Name**), scroll down and select **Norm Hasborn** and click **Add**. Click **OK**.

12. The **Add New Quota Entry** screen for NormH will appear. Select **Limit disk space to 250MB** and **Set warning level to 225MB**. Click **OK**. The reason for allowing NormH to have more disk space is that he is the company president, and those with the gold make the rules, eh?
13. You are returned to the **Quota Entries for Local Disk (C:)** window, which should look similar to Figure 7-12. Close the window by selecting **Quota**, **Close**.

Figure 7-12
Individual disk quota configurations are displayed in the Quota Entries for Local Disk (C:) window, allowing you to observe at a glance what user has which settings.

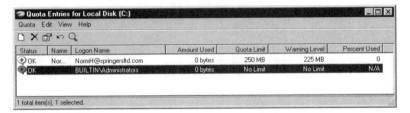

14. Click **OK** to close the **Local Disk (C:) Properties** dialog box.
15. Click **OK** when the **Disk Quota** dialog box appears asking you to confirm your action and advising you that the disk will be "rescanned," an operation that will take several minutes.

Final Disk Management Thoughts

Allow me to give you a quick peek at the future when I discuss performance monitoring topics in great detail in Chapter 16, where I will show you the Server Status View, Server Status Report, and Health Monitor in the context of managing hard disk space. You will also recall that I discussed these three cool tools in the context of daily and weekly duties in Chapter 6. I guess I'm repeating myself, but I can't get enough of this stuff. Plus these tools transcend fixed boundaries, such as daily or monthly tasks.

But, specifically discussing monthly tasks, you should consider using the following three cool tools in this way. On the first day of the month, observe the hard disk settings related to space. Do this again on the last day of the month. By comparing the start- and end-of-month figures, you can monitor disk consumption on a monthly basis. It's actually very interesting to do this as, over time, you'll see a trend line develop that can help you plan for your hard disk requirements. The three cool tools are:

- **Server Status View.** The Server Status view is the default display on your screen when you select **Server Status (BackOffice Home)** in the **Small Business Server Administrator Console**.

- **Server Status Report.** The Server Status Report is an automatically e-mailed or faxed report that can provide a wealth of information on the machine running SBS. It is configured by clicking the **Configure Report** link on the **Server Status (BackOffice Home)** screen. By default, the e-mail that is sent as the Server Status Report communicates significant hard disk-related information.

- **Health Monitor.** Ah, good old Health Monitor, an application that receives attention later in Chapter 16. You can configure this to alert you when some important performance monitor is out of whack.

A final question for you about storage management. What other ways can you think of to recover hard disk space? Approaches that I've seen include moving the Windows 2000 Server paging file to another hard disk on systems with multiple hard disks, or selecting some of the disk cleanup actions discussed earlier in this section, including removing unused applications, or clearing out the \temp folder of unused and unneeded temporary files (*.tmp) files. Care to add to this list? For example, you might know of a way that a line of business application, such as an accounting application, can recover disk space by compressing its internal database or re-indexing. These strategies will vary on a case-by-case basis.

5 - Virus Protection Again!

Your monthly duties demand that you not fall asleep at the wheel. In the virus detection area, are there any fixes you should apply beyond the periodic virus protection signature files? In the SSL methodology, such is the case with Trend Micro's OfficeScan 5 for Small Business Server 2000. You might recall from Chapter 6 that I mentioned that Exchange 2000 Server Service Pack 1 fixed an application programming interface (API) issue that would allow modern virus detection applications, such as OfficeScan, to scan e-mail in real time. Well, it turns out that you need to also update a specific OfficeScan component. You'll do this buy downloading and installing ScanMail 5.1 (the ScanMail version contained in OfficeScan is 5.0 by default as of this writing). Follow this procedure and OfficeScan 5.0 for SBS 2000 will stop e-mail viruses dead-cold in real time.

BEST PRACTICE: There was initially some confusion in the SBS community as to "what" was to be downloaded from Trend's Web site. Some believed a download called OfficeScan 5.1 for Small Business Server 2000 was needed. There is no such OfficeScan version available as of this writing (however, see my last BEST PRACTICE in this section). Rather, it is just version 5.1 of the ScanMail component.

1. Log on to **SSL1** as **Administrator** with the password **husky9999**.
2. Double-click **Internet Explorer** from the desktop and type **www.antivirus.com/download** in the **Address** field. Press **Enter**.
3. Click on the **OfficeScan SBS 2000** link on the right side of the Web page.
4. You will then be presented with the **OfficeScan SBS 2000 – Download 30-day trial software** page. Note that if you're using SSL1 to connect, the Trend Micro Web site remembers your name (otherwise you'll need to complete a customer signup form that will appear next). Complete the **Number of Seats** and **Time to Buy** fields and click **Download Now**.

BEST PRACTICE: If you actually own OfficeScan 5 for Small Business Server 2000, complete the **Already a customer?** field with the first part of your ScanMail 5.0 serial number and proceed to download and install this update. Note that the ScanMail serial number is found by observing the serial number field in the **About Trend ScanMail for Exchange** dialog box (from **Start**, **Programs**, **Trend ScanMail for Exchange**, **ScanMail Management Console** [you will need to provide the password **husky9999** to log on], **Help**, **About**). It is VERY IMPORTANT that you correctly write down this complete serial number for use when you install ScanMail 5.1, so that it doesn't install in 30-day evaluation mode.

5. On the **Network & Desktop** screen, click the **patches** link under **Patches Available**.

6. On the **Updates/Patches** screen, click the **ossbs2000_smex_patch.zip** link.
7. On the **File Download** dialog box, select **Save this file to disk** and click **OK**.
8. Save this file to **My Documents** and click **Save** in the **Save As** dialog box. This 12.1 MB file will now download.
9. Click **Close** when the **Download complete** dialog box appears.
10. Close **Internet Explorer** from **File, Close**.
11. Open **My Documents** from the SSL1 desktop.
12. Open the **Veritas** folder (that you created in Chapter 6). Right-click and select **New, Folder**. Name the folder **ScanMail5-1**.
13. Click **Back** to return to **My Documents**.
14. Double-click **ossbs2000_smex_patch.zip**. Click **I Agree** at the **WinZip** dialog box.
15. Click the **Extract** button and navigate in the **Extract** dialog box to the **ScanMail5-1** folder you created in Step 12 above.
16. Click **Extract**.
17. Close **WinZip** from **File, Exit**.
18. Navigate to the **ScanMail5-1** folder and double-click **setup.exe**.
19. Click **Next** at the **Welcome** screen.
20. Click **Yes** on the **Software License Agreement** screen.
21. Complete the **Domain (Springersltd)**, **Login (Administrator)**, and **Password (husky9999)** fields on the **Installing E-mail Virus Protection** screen and click **Next**.
22. Close the **My Documents** window, currently pointing to ScanMail5-1, when the installation progress screen disappears.

You've now updated the ScanMail component of OfficeScan 5 for Microsoft Small Business Server 2000. It's likely in future months that you'll undertake similar upgrades.

BEST PRACTICE: Here's some late breaking news. Just as this book is going to press, Trend Micro has announced that OfficeScan 5.1 for SBS 2000 is coming soon.

6 - SBS Toolkit Updates

If you're an SBS network administrator or consultant, you'll need to carry a toolkit, which can consist of physical tools to open a computer and add components as well as CD-ROMs containing valuable software.

The hardware toolkit is easy enough to obtain. For this, go to an online merchant, such as PC Zone (www.zones.com), and order a computer hardware toolkit, ranging in price from $25 to $200. Often, the lower-priced toolkits will meet your needs just fine. You will want to have some of the basics, including:

- T-10 and T-15 6-point drivers

- IC inserters

- 1/4" and 3/18" nut drivers

- 3-pronged parts retriever

- Reversible and 4 5/8" tweezers

- Screwdrivers: 5-1/4", 6", and 7-1/4" flathead

- Screwdrivers: 0, 1, and 2 Phillips head

- Wire cutter/stripper

- 5" needle-nose pliers

- Adjustable wrench

BEST PRACTICE: You should be able to purchase such a kit for under $50, with an imitation-leather case thrown in.

The software-side of your toolkit can take longer to build. In fact, I suggest you set a goal of adding one meaningful program each month to make your life more pleasant (and more effective) as an SBS administrator. Start with a subscription to Microsoft's TechNet monthly CD-ROM service. You might also try shareware Web sites and stores to find little-known and low-cost utilities.

Guest Column

Fellow SBSer and writer, Jonathan Hassel, provides these insights for you.

So, you've got that SBS server sitting in that corner there. It's a fairly powerful machine, loaded with some complex software. It's supposed to do a lot of neat stuff for the business—e-mail, Internet access, central file storage. But, like a pet, it won't live without constant care and feeding. It looks like you're the "designated one."

So, what comes with the territory? Well, people are depending on the server to coordinate the new automation that is now part of their everyday computing experience. And while Microsoft has designed SBS 2000 to be as self-sufficient as possible, sometimes things need to be tweaked, settings need to be changed, dust needs to be blown off, and so on.

The first step in SBS maintenance is being aware of what's happening on the server side of the network. SBS includes the neat Server Status Report feature that you can configure to e-mail copies of logs, monitors, and general resource information to a designated administrator. I have set my SBS 2000 server to e-mail me this report every morning at 4:30 a.m. It tells me things like:

- *how much of the time the processor isn't being used*

- *how much free memory the server has*

- *how much free disk space the drives on the server have*

- *how much data the Ethernet interfaces have transferred*

The tool can also send copies of the ISA Server logs and the current contents of the event logs on the server. This is a very useful tool—it's easy to remember to log onto the server and check the logs, and having them automatically e-mailed to you every night is a great way to ward off problems before they become chronic or dangerous.

The next step is to protect your network. There are several lines of defense you can put up for your network. First, if you don't have an anti-virus (AV) product for the server, get one. Virus creators are wreaking havoc on business networks everywhere, and all the businesses I know can't afford the downtime a virus infestation would cause. Products to look for include those that protect SMTP servers, Exchange, and the file server hard disks. If you already have AV soft-ware, update the virus signatures or definitions. Most of the time this is a fairly simple automated Internet download, but it has to be triggered manually in a lot of software. Better still, put a recurring appointment in your personal informa-tion manager (PIM) software that reminds you to do this.

Second, get an uninterruptible power supply (UPS) for your server. Trust me, I know this from personal experience: I had discarded a ton of advice from fellow SBS administrators, authors, and colleagues about the value of a UPS. The power where I was living at the time was fairly reliable and I hadn't much need for an expensive UPS. Then I moved, and my building's power was flaky. I was hard at work on a chapter for my book, was about to save, and the power went out. It cost me sixteen hours to recreate the data I had lost. That convinced me so much that I now run all of my client machines (I have six of them) on UPSs. Maybe you don't need to buy UPSs like they're going out of style, but I heartily, sincerely, and passionately implore you to protect your business's data with a UPS. It could be the best $400-$500 you ever spent.

Finally, satisfy the CYB (cover your butt) principle by making regular backups to another device. There are some great software titles out there, like Veritas BackupExec and BEI's UltraBac, that automate this procedure to a large extent. I recommend a weekly full backup, which should be run on the weekend, and nightly incremental backups (incremental backups of only those backup files that changed since the last backup). The other part of backing up is performing test restores. After all, what good is a backup if the backup is full of useless garbage? Weekly, using your backup program, select a small text, document, or spreadsheet file and restore it to a temporary location on your hard disk. If it comes out OK, you shouldn't have any errors in your backup. You might even install a CD-RW drive in the server and make periodic copies of the Users Shared Folders and Company Shared Folders directories. New DVD-RAM technology will make this even easier.

All in all, the Microsoft designers have made SBS 2000 as hands-free as possible. Some gentle course correction, however, is always in order. Good luck!

Thanks Jonathon. Be sure to read more of Jonathon's words in his frequent contributions to *Windows 2000 Magazine* or at www.hasselltech.net/hassell/ journal/thisweek.html.

7 - Adding Hardware

Let's face it. Hardly a month passes that you won't add hardware somewhere on your SBS network. These additions can occur at the SBS machine itself (say a CD-ROM tower) or at an SBS user's workstation (say a PocketPC docking station). It's simply part of your job as an SBS administrator.

At the SBS machine, you might add a CD-ROM tower so that your SBS users can access libraries of information in an instant. This is a common addition I make at small law firms, as their collections of CD-ROM-based libraries grow. By deploying a CD-ROM tower, all these CD-ROMs are available in real-time for all the users.

To add hardware, right-click on **My Computer** from the SSL1 desktop and select **Properties, Hardware**. Your screen should look similar to Figure 7-13. Click the **Hardware Wizard** button to add hardware to the SBS 2000 server machine.

Notes:

Figure 7-13
The Hardware Wizard is a welcome way to add hardware in SBS 2000.

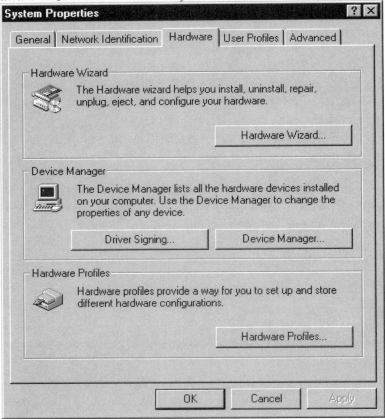

One of the great improvements in SBS 2000 is the Device Manager tool provided by the underlying Windows 2000 operating system. This is where you can manage hardware that has already been installed. For example, Device Manager would allow you to update a hardware driver for a device.

8 - Test Restore

Time for another task to perform. Each month you should perform a test restore just to make sure the backup you made in Chapter 6 was valid, as Jonathan commented in his guest column above. Follow these steps to complete that procedure.

1 . Log on to **SSL1** as **Administrator** with the password **husky9999**.

2. Click **Start**, **Programs**, **VERITAS Backup Exec**.
3. Select **Create a Restore Job** on the **Backup Exec Assistant** screen.
4. Click **Next** on the **Welcome to the Restore Wizard** screen.
5. Expand **C:**, then select the backup job you created in Chapter 6. Expand **Documents and Settings**, **Administrator**, **My Documents** and **My Pictures**. Click **sample.jpg** in the right-pane. Your screen should look similar to Figure 7-14. Click **Next**.

Figure 7-14
Select a sample file to restore.

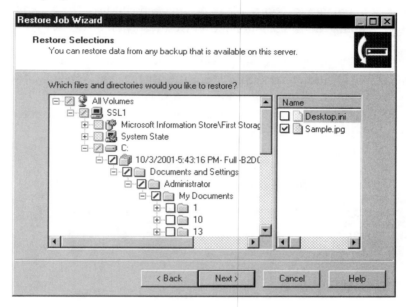

6. Accept the default name on the **Restore Job Name** screen and click **Next**.
7. Accept the default device on the **Data Source Selection** screen and click **Next**.
8. Select **Overwrite the file on disk** on the **Existing File Options** screen and click **Next**.
9. Accept the **Yes, run the job now selection** on the **You have completed the Restore Wizard** screen and click **Finish**. The restore job will commence.
10. Close **Backup Exec** from **File**, **Exit**.

Now you will open the restored file to see for yourself that it truly is valid and "works." Simply double-click **My Documents** from the **SSL1** desktop and open the **My Pictures** folder. Double-click **sample.jpg** and see for your very own eyes that it's a picture of a runner in the sprinter start position. Cool! Mission accomplished.

9 - Research

An hour of research will save countless hours of misdirected effort when managing your SBS network. That said, take at least an hour each month to surf the Internet for SBS issues. Likewise, peruse popular computer magazines and other periodicals for computer network, SBS-specific, and end-user issues. And don't forget to pick up this book each month to review a section or two.

I can suggest a few Internet sites to consider in the context of SBS network administration. Other interesting SBS Web sites are listed in Appendix A. Take a look at **www.eventid.net**, as seen in Figure 7-15. This is a Web site that cross-references all Windows 2000 Event ID numbers you're likely to encounter in the event logs seen in Event Viewer.

Figure 7-15
Finally, a Web site to help you translate Event IDs in Windows 2000.

I highly recommend that you visit BugNet at **www.bugnet.com**. Here you can assess whether any recently found software bugs pertain to either your SBS network or any applications being used by your SBS users.

> BEST PRACTICE: The full BugNet service requires a subscription fee, but the free stuff isn't bad either!

Because SBS-related Web sites come and go, you should, once a month or so, visit a search engine such as Google (**www.google.com**) and type in the key words **Small Business Server**. You'll be rewarded with a buffet of SBS Web sites from around the world. Go ahead and eat it up!

10 - Performance Monitor Logging

This monthly task isn't the most exciting, and to exploit it fully, you'll likely need to retain a Microsoft Certified System Engineer (MCSE) to interpret the results. But the results can be invaluable when tracking the performance of your SBS network over time. Basically, you will use Performance Monitor to create a trend line of core computer system data. And as that trend line either improves or displays degrading performance, you'll have the ammunition you need to justify the purchase of a new server or better hub.

The Performance Monitor tool is located via **Performance** the **Administrative Tools** program group (which you can access via **Programs** from the **Start** button on the SBS machine's desktop). Performance Monitor is an MBA-type's dream come true! This tool allows the capture and reporting, in a graphical format, of SBS computer system information.

Each month, using Performance Monitor, I recommend that you capture or log the following SBS computer system items (known as objects) in Table 712. These items represent common measurements that MCSEs need to look at over time to fully assess the health of your SBS network. Better yet, something I've always felt was going on with Performance Monitor logging was recently confirmed when I attended an SBS focus group on Microsoft's Redmond campus. There, participants shared that, although Performance Monitor logging is a foundation for solving really complex problems, it's more likely to be used for showing long-term performance declines. This use of logging to display trends is typically used to get budget approval for bigger and better toys, like a new server.

BEST PRACTICE: I've included descriptions of the objects so that you can better understand what is being measured. However, full discussion of this complex area is beyond the scope of this book. Refer to the *Windows 2000 Professional and Server Resource Kits* (respectively) from Microsoft Press for more information on Performance Monitor.

Note that I suggest you log the following information for a 24-hour period each month.

Table 7-2 Performance Monitor Objects to Log

Object	Description
Cache	Primary memory area that holds such items as recently used documents and file pages, data. With caching file pages, access time is dramatically improved.
Logical Disk	Logical views of disk space, including disk partitions.
Memory	This allows you to analyze performance matters relating to real memory. Includes both primary (RAM) and virtual (paging file) memory.
Objects	Relates to system software objects. Objects have properties and are subject to access control restrictions imposed by SBS security.
Physical Disk	Secondary storage, such as hard disks. Physical Disk measurements can be unreliable when you have a RAID array (a discussion that's beyond the scope of this book).
Process	A software object that is an active or running program.
Processor	Provides measures relating to the central processing unit (CPU).
Redirector	Assesses network connections between your computer and other computers.
Server Work Queues	Used to measure processor backlogs on your SBS machine.

System	Measures the activity on system hardware and software.
Thread	The basic unit of execution. Every running process will contain one or more threads.

11 - Updating SBS Network Notebook

Last but not least, you need to update your SBS network notebook to reflect your monthly findings. Such an update, although not especially meaningful when viewed at one month, is incredibly valuable when viewed over, say, several months. It is here that you can see what changes to your system have been made and what the effect of those changes was. What you should do is record many of the topics presented in both Chapters 6 and 7 in this notebook. For example, the starting and ending hard disk free space on a monthly basis would be a valid entry.

12 - Update the ERD

Something that is so darn easy to forget is the periodic update of the emergency repair disk (ERD). The ERD contains critical system information. This ERD update is very simple to do, following these steps:

1. Log on to **SSL1** as **Administrator** with the password **husky9999**.
2. Click **Start**, **Programs**, **Accessories**, **System Tools**, **Backup**.
3. Click the untitled button next to **Emergency Repair Disk** on the **Welcome** tab.
4. When instructed by the **Emergency Repair Diskette** dialog box, insert a blank, formatted floppy disk in drive A. Select the **Also backup the registry to the repair directory** check box. Click **OK**.
5. Click **OK** when notified by the **Emergency Repair Diskette** that the update was successful.
6. Close **Backup** from **Job**, **Exit**.

Now remove and label the ERD floppy disk with today's date and save it in a fire-proof safe! Don't forget to do this each and every month. Good show, mate, and we now leave the monthly tasks to consider some annual tasks for the SBSer.

Annual Tasks

I want to present a half-dozen annual tasks related to SBS for you to perform:

1. Getting Help from Consultants and Interns
2. Security Review
3. Hardware and Software Upgrades
4. Training
5. SBS Budget
6. SBS Retreat

Allow me the opportunity to set the discussion framework for the half-dozen topics listed immediately above. As your planning horizon expands from daily to weekly to monthly to annually, the tasks you perform necessarily become broader and more general. If you're a businessperson, it's similar to why a mission statement reflects general rather than specific tactics in the world of strategic planning. My remaining conversation in this chapter necessarily echoes that perspective. Whereas the first part of Chapter 6, with its daily tasks, was very detail-oriented, the end of this chapter is much broader in scope. Put on the SBS strategic planning hat and enjoy the discussion.

1 - Getting Help from Consultants and Interns

In my experience with SBS 2000, the average SBS customer is stuck between a rock and a hard place when it comes to getting competent yet cost-effective SBS 2000 support and consultation. Here is what I mean. Larger firms can afford to have MCSE-types on staff to administer, engineer, maintain, and otherwise optimize their networks. SBS sites can't afford the $60K per year computer gurus (hell – many small business owners *themselves* don't make $60K per year). Yet the needs of the SBS site aren't that different from the large sites: allowing people to do their jobs better with the aide of a computer network.

So, most SBS 2000 sites need to maintain some form of consulting relationship with an outside guru. Armed with a book such as this one, the on-site SBS administrator (usually a staff person at the business) can usually perform most of the duties to run the SBS network. That way, you can selectively use SBS 2000 consultants with bill rates well into the $100/hour range (depending on region) to complete the toughest SBS 2000 assignments. (SBSers around the country report bill rates ranging from $50 an hour in smaller towns to over $200 an hour in the largest cities. The $100/hour rate is the median, as best I can tell.)

One trick I've shared with one of the SBS 2000 sites that I work with is the use of low-cost college interns. Each quarter, a bright and eager intern arrives at this SBS site to provide a presence in the ongoing administration and oversight of the SBS network. By being there, the intern can respond immediately to user requests like "How do I do this?" (the kind of question asked several times per day). Clearly, we rather expensive (and more experienced) SBS consultants can't be sitting around every day to field those questions, but interns potentially can be. And, as the British say, BEHAVE when it comes to working closely with young interns of the opposite gender!

2 - Security Review

Each year it behooves you to review the security you have placed on folders on your SBS 2000 network. Perhaps something slipped by last year and, now identified, the security needs to be tightened and made more restrictive. More likely, you might want to make someone on your staff a member of the Administrators group. Why? Because, over the course of a year, you're likely to see one or two staff members take a keen interest in the operations of your SBS 2000 network. If this person can be trusted, add them to the Power Users group template and have the curiosity turn into competent SBS administration.

3 - Hardware and Software Upgrades

Each year, you will likely need to replace one or two workstations due to failure or obsolescence. In fact, many small businesses replace between 20 percent and 33percent of their fleet of workstations each year so that they stay current. And as mentioned earlier in this chapter in the monthly discussion, you'll always be adding hardware to your server and workstation during the year. Count on it.

> BEST PRACTICE: Although I haven't seen it at my SBS 2000 sites, word has reached me that some sites lease hardware for financial reasons and to match the life of the asset (hardware) with the actual use. The point is, in certain situations, leasing allows you to acquire hardware for little money down and get rid of it before it becomes obsolete.

With respect to software upgrades, you can safely plan on major upgrades to SBS and your applications every 18 months or so. It's the nature of the computer business. Not only do you need to factor in the costs for both your hardware and software upgrades, but you also need to account for the time it will take to implement these upgrades. And time not only includes the time to install software, but also the lost time, as the staff learns to use the new upgrades. Yes, you guessed it. It's the software learning curve now playing at your SBS site!

4 - Training

Consider offering an annual reimbursement to your SBS users to get computer training each year. For the small business, perhaps $500 per year per staff member is sufficient. Larger companies often offer greater training dollars, but their needs tend to be greater. If you're worried that you might be training your competition, that is, your trained staffers will join another firm to make more money, consider having a training dollar repayment plan in place. Such an arrangement is, of course, evidenced by an agreement.

Most importantly, because you're dealing with knowledge workers here when it comes to using the SBS network, anything you can do, such as computer training, to increase the user's knowledge will yield dividends in excess of your outlays.

5 - SBS Budget

Ah, the annual technology budget. This is actually a simple topic to address. In large companies, I've seen annual technology budgets of $3,000 to $5,000 per user per year! Smaller companies can get by with smaller technology budgets, thank goodness. At a minimum, I can't envision you budgeting less than $1,000 per user per year when you account for recovering the costs of your SBS user's workstations and spreading out the costs of your server machine and SBS software. More likely, you're probably spending at least $1,500 per user per year if you're sufficiently training your staff, upgrading your software, and so on. Although that number seems large, remember that it's only $5 per day per person to give them the tools they need to do a better job for you.

Let me share a few budget specifics with you that I've encountered in the SBS world:

- **Tape backup machines.** Due to the mechanical nature of these devices, I've observed that tape backup devices can fail after only one year. A new tape backup device can cost in excess of $700, but I've had little trouble receiving purchase approval from an SBS site after they understand that hours of data are at stake!

- **Training pays off.** Unfortunately, small-business owners often cut training from budgets. Perhaps it's because many small-business owners fit the mold of the "millionaire next door" and never complete college, thus they have an underlying anger toward education. More likely, the small-business owner has been burned by newly trained employees who leave for higher-paying jobs. First, you need to convince the reluctant budget gods at your SBS site that training returns more value in increased productivity than it extracts from the corporate coffers. Okay, so that didn't work. More practically speaking, small-business owners might be more receptive to an arrangement wherein employees receiving training will reimburse the company if they depart within 24 months, as I discussed in the training section above.

- **MBA stuff.** Don't overlook the comments I made earlier about justifying your technology outlays via reports, such as the type you can create from the data you obtain from your Performance Monitor logs.

6 - SBS Retreat

Did someone suggest an *SBS retreat*? Once per year or so, treat your SBS stakeholders to some type of planning retreat not only to review the year that just passed, but more important, to plan for the year ahead. You'd be surprised that a simple planning retreat might enable you to think of ways to better use SBS in your organization. For example, consider the following:

- Small business electronic commerce via SBS

- Lowering your SBS costs by performing more SBS management yourself (armed with this book, of course)

- The SBS faxing capabilities as a tool to increase your sales

- The future of SBS (thinking about SBS dot-NET)

Who knows, you might even come out of your annual planning retreat with an SBS Mission Statement! Try this one on for size: "Saving the world with SBS."

Summary

This chapter provides you with the fundamentals needed to administer your SBS network on a monthly and annual basis. Combined with Chapter 6, you now have the knowledge to manage your SBS network from daily, weekly, monthly, and annual perspectives. In particular, you worked with third-party SBS 2000 products, such as those offered by Trend Micro and Veritas. You made your systems as shipshape as possible by applying several critical updates in the form of service packs, patches, hot fixes and upgrades. In short, you've started to make great strides in the management of your SBS 2000 network. In the next chapter, you'll learn how to manage your SBS 2000 network remotely with Terminal Services.

Chapter 8
Remote Management with Terminal Services

The final chapter in this section on SBS administration features Terminal Services. Terminal Services is technically a lot of things, but to the SBSer, it's a chance to perform much of the day-to-day drudgery from the privacy of home (or in my case, the good old home office!). In short, Terminal Services allows you to create a session showing the actual SBS server desktop from a remote location or another client computer on the network. One way you might use this feature is rebooting the server from home at 10:00 PM at night when all of the users have logged off of the SBS network. Another might be managing your SBS server machine, which is locked securely in a supply closet, from the comfort of an oversized Aeron chair in the president's office (true story!).

80/20 VAP Power

The systematic deployment of Terminal Services on SBS 2000 is nothing short of a major paradigm shift in how value added providers (VAPs), also known as consultants, work with SBS. The good news is that no longer do you need to drive an hour in traffic across the urban landscape (or heck, an hour of boring straight roads across the Texas rural landscape) to add a user to an SBS network. Rather, you simply log on from a remote location via a Terminal Services session and add that darn-tootin' user. To be honest, this task only takes a few minutes with Terminal Services instead of the hour it took before. Such efficiencies and suggested Luddism acts are discussed in a moment.

Defining 80/20

So what's really going on here is the MBA phenomena known as the 80/20 rule. Simply stated, that means 80 percent of all tasks take 20 percent of the time to perform and vice-versa. Nowhere in the world of SBS is that more true than Terminal Services. It is now possible to perform 80 percent and perhaps even more of your tasks from the Terminal Services session. This session, running on the SBS server machine at work (or a client site if you're a technology consultant), is displayed on the remote computer. So as long as the task is virtual in nature—where you don't have to physically replace something—it's all possible with Terminal Services.

> BEST PRACTICE: Early in your Terminal Services education it's important to understand that this management capability applies to the SBS server machine. Terminal Services is not used to manage client computers. You will typically use a desktop remote control application, such as NetMeeting or PCAnywhere, to manage a client computer. NetMeeting is discussed later in the chapter.

You can have multiple Windows 2000 Server-based machines running Terminal Services and manage each of those machines via Terminal Services sessions. This is discussed later in this chapter.

There is still that 20 percent of the work that requires a physical presence, such as replacing a failed tape drive. Another part of the workload is end-user support, which typically requires a combination of telephone and onsite support. Depending on how much end-user support is needed at the SBS site, you might perform much of your server-machine-related work remotely, with tons of end-user support provided onsite. But with respect to management of the SBS server machine, it's critical to appreciate the nature of your work has changed and the 80/20 rule is alive and well.

SBS Luddites Unite!

So, a few comments directed to those SBSers who make a living as billable-hour consultants. First, understand that Luddites, according to www.dictionary.com, are "(1) Any of a group of British workers who between 1811 and 1816 rioted and destroyed laborsaving textile machinery in the belief that such machinery would diminish employment or (2) one who opposes technical or technological change." It's this second definition that might relate to the introduction of Terminal Services in SBS 2000. I've found that I can perform many tasks in 25 percent of the time that it previously took in SBS 4.5. The problem is that, as a billable-hour consultant, I'm finding my existing client base greatly appreciates the same level of service from me and the dramatically smaller invoices. However, my accountants have noticed that on a per-client basis, my billings are down with SBS 2000, in part due to the management efficiencies gained by Terminal Services (the product is also much more stable leading to a lower demand for technology consultants).

So what's an SBSer to do in this era of Terminal Services? On the Luddite side of the equation, you could unleash a Terminal Services killer, such as a destructive worm, but that's unethical and would quickly be fixed by a patch from Microsoft. It's also a negative behavior not seen in the SBS community. More likely, you'll put on your MBA hat and modify your business model to adapt to this new world. In Economics 101 we'd call this a shift in the supply curve due to a change in technology. As for me, I'm looking at two new approaches for conducting business: grow my portfolio of clients or charge a flat fee rather than by the hour. If you're an SBSer who is also a technology consultant, you'll need to confront this basic business issue or else risk being BBQ-ed.

Defining Terminal Services

In this chapter so far, hints and allegations have been issued as to what Terminal Services is and is not. Let's take a second to define it technically.

What You See Is What You Get

To borrow from the late comedian, Flip Wilson, who portrayed a sassy woman named Geraldine on the Flip Wilson Show in the mid-1970s, "what you see is what you get." The SBS twist on this comedic line is that a remote Terminal Services session looks and feels just as if you were sitting in front of the SBS server machine itself. This is demonstrated in Figure 8-1 where Bob Easter from Springer Spaniels Limited (SSL) is working from home one night using his wife's laptop computer.

Figure 8-1

A diagram of a laptop at home can manage the SBS server machine desktop using Terminal Services.

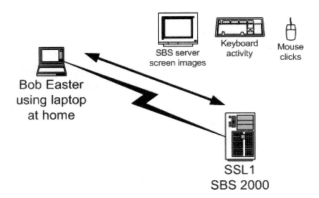

Bob is able to manage the SBS server by observing the desktop (the screen image), typing commands on the keyboard that are passed back to the SBS server, and making mouse clicks to select options as necessary. In Figure 8-2, you can see how SSL1 actually looks on Bob's borrowed laptop computer.

Figure 8-2

A peek at Bob's laptop shows you the same view is diagram in the earlier figure. Note that Bob is logged on as Administrator in the Terminal Services session.

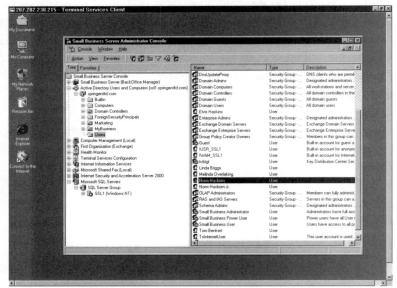

BEST PRACTICE: Notice in this mini-example that I didn't tell you how Bob Easter was accessing the SBS 2000 server machine back at the SSL office? This was by design to get you thinking for a spell. Truth be told, Bob might have accessed SSL1, the SBS server machine at SSL, any number of ways. He might have dialed in via a routing and remote access service session (RRAS). You might recall in the old days we called this RASing. Bob might have initiated the Terminal Services session directly from the Terminal Services Client (I discuss the Terminal Services Client in a moment) over the Internet simply by typing in the wild-side IP address of SSL1. As configured on SSL1 with SBS 2000, this would have worked (and was the actual approach used). Another approach might have been to first establish a virtual private networking (VPN) connection and then launch the Terminal Services Client and have it initiate a Terminal Services session on SSL1.

One Terminal Services access method I've not suggested that could have worked right here, right now for Bob Easter was the Web-based MyConsole, which I'll hide from you until later in the chapter.

RAM Hog

No, I'm not speaking of the latest Harley Davidson model at the Sturgis summer motorcycle rally. Rather, I'm putting on your radar screen the fact that the virtual machine created by a Terminal Services session uses massive server-side resources. This includes RAM memory and processor time. Those people who are serious about Terminal Services at the enterprise level often have multiple servers performing this function, and each server has quad processors and a couple of gigabytes of RAM memory. When I discuss Remote Administration and Application Sharing Mode below, I'll speak to specific performance matters.

Historically Speaking

Terminal Services has a dark and mysterious past. It originated as a third-party product called WinFrame from Citrx (which had an expensive variation called MetaFrame, a product still around today). It was possible for this remote computing solution to exist because Microsoft licensed some of its kernel code to Citrix. Citrix ran with the kernel code to develop the ICA communications protocol that was the basis for WinFrame. This became known as thin-client computing. In the heat of the Netscape battle, where thin-client computing was hot and Microsoft was facing "not," Microsoft released the Windows NT-era product called Windows NT Server – Terminal Server edition. It did not license the Windows NT 4 interface to Citrix, so the WinFrame was stuck with the Windows 3.51 interface. In a matter of months, Citrix lay bleeding on the beach in its home state of Florida. Fast forward and Citrix is a minor player in the thin-client marketplace today, providing MetaFrame as an add-on to Terminal Services. MetaFrame provides additional features on which Terminal Services doesn't do a good job, such as supporting NetWare networks and multimedia. It is possible that more sophisticated SBS sites might have a need to implement MetaFrame (visit www.citrix.com), but I'll warn you, this add-on is one expensive dude!

That historical tour behind us, I want to highlight the five functions of Terminal Services, three of which are typically deemphasized in SBS 2000.

Remote Control

What has really been presented so far in this chapter is the remote control feature. An administrator can remotely control a Windows 2000 Server-based machine, such as SBS 2000, and complete administrative tasks. Enough said for now.

Application Management

A huge selling point for Terminal Services is the ability to place it in Application Sharing Mode on a Windows 2000 Server machine (not the SBS 2000 server machine thank you, a fine point I discuss in a moment). This mode allows numerous client computers to connect, initiate a Terminal Services session, and run an application (such as a business database). One benefit to the IT staff is that legacy client computers can now run powerful applications with the heavy lifting really being accomplished on the server. The client computer only receives the screen image. The IT staff greatly appreciates having to only update the applications on the Windows 2000 Server machine running Terminal Services, not run around to touch hundreds of client computers.

Thin Clients

Don't overlook the possibility of thin clients in small- and medium-sized businesses, subject to my discussion later about multiple servers running Terminal Services on an SBS network. Thin clients are those cheap, mainframe-era, dumb terminals that, revamped for the 21st century, are now in color and only have a keyboard and mouse attached. This is a popular option for retail, where a powerful desktop computer isn't needed or desired at the sales counter. Thin-client pricing typically starts at $300.

Ultimate Profiles

Before the advent of more powerful native operating system tools, such as Group Policy, the uses of Terminal Services allowed IT managers to lock down client computers – big time. You could make it so an end user couldn't do anything except perform a very narrow task. You'll actually see a variation of this when I show you how SBS users created with the Power User template have extremely limited mobility with this lockdown capability in Terminal Services (this is discussed a tad later in the chapter).

> BEST PRACTICE: Perhaps you've seen the fallacy of my argument immediately above about Group Policy. Remember that Group Policy requires the client machine be a Windows 2000 Professional or XP-based desktop operating system. Such is not always the case in a small business. So, a Terminal Services-based session is the way to apply more configurations and control to a legacy client computer.
>
> Technically speaking, Terminal Services is the solution to applying Group Policy to a legacy client computer. That's because the Terminal Services session running on the client computer can have Group Policy applied to it. Cool huh!?!?

So, wrapping up the ultimate profile discussion, in the old days, IT administrators really enjoyed the way that a Terminal Services session profile could easily be recreated if the user somehow trashed the computer environment. Instead of having to go deal with a screwed up C: drive, the IT administrator could perform a simple fix at the server. This is part of the centralized administration paradigm with Terminal Services.

Spying and Support

Another traditional benefit of Terminal Services is spying and support. When a user is running a Terminal Services session, you can view the user session. This can be configured to alert the user to snooping and require the user's permission to view their session, or let you view in stealth mode where the user is unaware of your activities. This capability is provided in the spirit of providing end-user support, but I'm sure it's abused on a regular basis.

It's a Service Stupid

One thing that separates Terminal Services from remote control applications is that it runs as an operating system-level service, not an application. And, speaking straight for a moment, Terminal Services is really more than just a service. In reality, when Terminal Services is installed at the scenario baseline stage during the SBS 2000 setup, the Windows 2000 kernel is switched out to be multisession, much like UNIX operating systems are. In SBS 2000, Terminal Services is placed in Remote Administration Mode at that time, something I discuss in the next section.

What the multisession kernel means to you is that one machine can run several computing sessions at once. This is accomplished by creating virtual machines for each Terminal Services session. This is one of Terminal Services greatest strengths compared to remote control applications, such as NetMeeting or PCAnywhere. Truth be told to you, with a program like NetMeeting or PCAnywhere, you need a dedicated client computer to support each and every remote session. The contrast between the two approaches is shown here in Figure 8-3.

Notes:

Figure 8-3

Terminal Services is a true service with a multisession kernel. Remote control applications having a 1:1 ratio between user session and session machine providing remote control support.

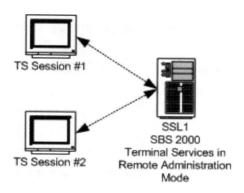

Terminal Services

TS Session #1

TS Session #2

SSL1
SBS 2000
Terminal Services in
Remote Administration
Mode

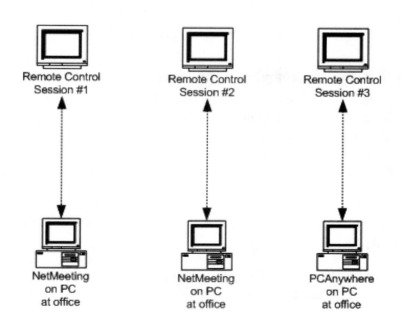

Remote Control
Session #1

Remote Control
Session #2

Remote Control
Session #3

NetMeeting
on PC
at office

NetMeeting
on PC
at office

PCAnywhere
on PC
at office

Remote Control Applications

Further proof positive that Terminal Services is a service and not an application in SBS 2000 can be found in Figure 8-4. This figure displays the services listed in the SBS Administrator Console.

Figure 8-4
The description for the Terminal Services service, partially displayed in the Description column, is quite informative.

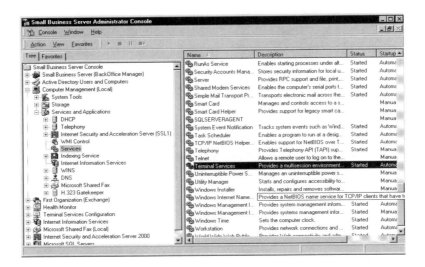

Remote Administration Mode

When SBS is installed, as detailed back in Chapter 3, Terminal Services is configured in Remote Administration Mode at the Scenario Baseline step. This is part of the optimized and best practices setup of SBS 2000. You don't need to do a thing as Terminal Services is set up and configured for you on the server-side. On the client-side, you'll need to implement the Terminal Services Client, which is discussed later in this chapter.

To see for yourself that Terminal Services is in Remote Administration Mode, follow these steps.

1. Log on to **SSL1** as **Administrator** with the password **husky9999**.
2. Click **Start**, **Small Business Server Administrator Console**.

3. Expand **Terminal Services Configuration**.
4. Click on **Server Settings**. Observe that the **Terminal server mode** setting has the **Remote Administration** attribute.

Remote Administration Mode allows up to two users with sufficient authority to log on and establish a Terminal Services session. Those users who are members of the administrators group or were created with the power user setup template will by default have access to Terminal Services on the SBS 2000 server machine. The key regulatory point with Remote Administration Mode is that no additional client access licenses are needed.

From a technical perspective, Terminal Services in Remote Administration Mode behaves differently than its other mode (Application Sharing Mode, which is discussed in a moment). With Remote Administration Mode, the Terminal Services session is what I'd call "background." That is, operating system functions, programs, and services have foreground priority over Terminal Services sessions. Also, receiving foreground would be the BackOffice applications installed as part of SBS (e.g., Exchange 2000 Server). Relegated to background processing priority is the lowly Terminal Services session that an administrator might run from home to work on the SBS server machine. It's a good thing because this background priority means that the "real" users on the network inside the four walls at work won't suffer when the administrator is working on the system from afar.

Application Sharing Mode

It is Application Sharing Mode that many technical types think of when they are really discussing Terminal Services. At the enterprise-level, this is where tons of users log on to a Windows 2000 Server running Terminal Services in Application Sharing Mode and run applications. When Terminal Services is in Application Sharing Mode, the Terminal Services sessions receive foreground processor priority (exactly opposite of the situation discussed above in Remote Administration Mode). That means the Terminal Services session users enjoy zippy performance and the underlying operating system (including services, processes, and even server-side applications) will act in a subordinate role.

The election to implement Terminal Services in either Remote Administration Mode or Application Sharing Mode is made from Add/Remove Programs in Control Panel on a regular Windows 2000 Server machine. However, in SBS, this election would theoretically be made just after the Scenario Baseline step runs.

As mentioned earlier in the chapter, Terminal Services is installed in Remote Administration Mode during the Scenario Baseline setup stage. If you were crazy enough to do so, right after the Scenario Baseline completes you would place Terminal Services in Application Sharing Mode from Add/Remove Programs. This is a critical step for making such a move, because the server machine must be placed in Application Sharing Mode prior to any BackOffice applications being installed. If down the road you decided to place your SBS server machine in Application Sharing Mode, BackOffice applications, such as Exchange 2000 Server, will fail horribly because these applications have operating system kernel sensitivity and they don't like being messed with!

> BEST PRACTICE: You should NEVER place your SBS server machine in Application Sharing Mode! There are so many reasons why. First, supporting this is the same as allowing your remote users to log on locally at the domain controller (DC) to perform their work. This is a bad idea and is not recommended because all internal users take a performance hit since the remote Terminal Services sessions will receive foreground priority. An excellent KBase article (Q282009), found at http://support.microsoft.com/support/kb/articles/q282/0/09.asp, lists all of the reasons you should not run SBS 2000 in Terminal Services in Application Sharing Mode.
>
> So, while it's technically possible to place an SBS 2000 server machine in Terminal Services – Application Sharing Mode, both Microsoft and I do not recommend it. If you do, you do so at your own risk and you may or may not receive sincere and kind support from the SBS Product Support Service team when you call with unspeakable maladies.
>
> Later in the chapter I suggest an appropriate strategy for supporting a Windows 2000 Server as a non-DC running Terminal Services in Application Sharing Mode. I'll also tackle a few dreaded Terminal Services licensing topics. Ouch!

Further Application Sharing Mode discussion of Terminal Services is a tad beyond the scope of my SSL methodology, so I'll defer some of the finer points on this matter to the advanced topics section at the end of this chapter. In Figure 8-5, I attempt to depict the finer points between Remote Administration Mode and Application Sharing Mode.

Figure 8-5

Visualizing the difference between Remote Administration Mode (default SBS 2000 server condition) and a Windows 2000 Server machine running in Application Sharing Mode.

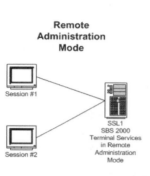

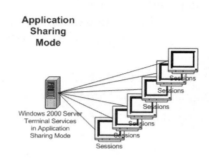

* Background priority
* No CALs needed
* Two user session limit
* Default SBS configuration

* Foreground priority
* CALs needed (extra $$)
* Lots of user sessions possible
* NOT recommended on SBS 2000 server machine

Using Terminal Services

Now that I've set the table for a Terminal Services BBQ, let's eat! I've told you once. And I've told you twice. And I'll tell you again. Terminal Services is configured in Remote Administration Mode during the Scenario Baseline phase of the SBS 2000 setup routine. You'll remember this as Step 34 and Figure 3-12 in Chapter 3. So, there really aren't any magical keystrokes for performing the server-side configuration of Terminal Services. Rather, we pick up with installing the Terminal Services Client on NormH's client computer (PRESIDENT). Let's get it on!

1. Log on to **PRESIDENT** as **NormH** with the password **Purple3300**.
2. Double-click **My Network Places**.
3. Double-click **Entire Network**.
4. Click the **entire network** link on the lower left-side of the screen.
5. Double-click **Microsoft Windows Network**.
6. Double-click the **SPRINGERSLTD** domain object.

7. Double-click **SSL1** server object.

8. Double-click the **TSClient** shared folder. This is where the Terminal Services client is located. Note this method assumes the client computer on which you are installing the Terminal Services Client has a network connection (either local or remote) in order to access the TSClient shared folder. In the BEST PRACTICE listed in a moment, I describe how to create the installation diskettes for those cases where an existing network connection isn't feasible (which happens, surprisingly, a large part of the time).

9. Double-click the **Net** folder.

10. Double-click the **Win32** folder.

11. Double-click **Setup.exe**.

BEST PRACTICE: Do not double-click acmesetup.exe. This is a standard Microsoft setup routine that is actually called from setup.exe.

12. Click **Continue** after reading the **Welcome to the Terminal Services Client installation program** information on the **Terminal Services Client Setup** dialog box.

13. In the **Name and Organization** dialog box, type **Norm Hasborn** in the **Name** field and **Springer Spaniels Limited (SSL)** in the **Organization** field. This is shown in Figure 8-6. Click **OK**.

Figure 8-6
Entering the Terminal Services user name and organization.

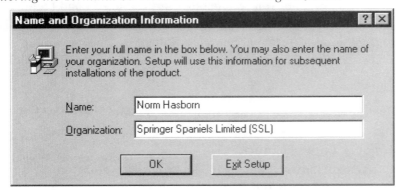

14. Click **OK** when the **Confirm Name and Organization Information** dialog box appears.

15. Click **I Agree** at the **License Agreement** dialog box.

16. Click the **large button** to start the setup process on the **Terminal Services Client Setup** dialog box. Said button is in the upper left-hand corner (see Figure 8-7) and looks like two screens on top of one another. (There is really no name for this button, something that drove the SBS documentation team nuts at Microsoft!)

Figure 8-7

Click the large unnamed button to start setup.

17. Click **Yes** at the **Terminal Services Client Setup** dialog box when asked if you want the same settings for all users on this client computer.

18. Click **OK** when notified by the **Terminal Services Client Setup** dialog box that the setup was successfully completed.

BEST PRACTICE: Often times you are not connected to the SBS network where you can run the above steps to install the Terminal Services Client. In these cases you will create the Terminal Services Client installation diskettes. There are two ways to accomplish this.

The first method is from the Start menu. At the SBS server machine (e.g., SSL1), click **Start, Programs, Administrative Tools, Terminal Services Client Creator**. Follow the on-screen instructions to insert each diskette. Other than the diskette-related steps, the steps are similar to Steps 12 to 18 immediately above.

The second method is even easier. If you complete Steps 1 to 8 immediately above and then double-click the **Win32** folder, double-click the folder titled **Disks** and you will see two additional folders titled **Disk1** and **Disk2**. Simply copy the contents of Disk1 to the first diskette and – you guessed it, pardner – the contents of Disk2 to the second diskette. You've now created your Terminal Services Client setup diskettes. This is very handy to have when you're traveling across the state in a car and pull into a Kinko's to rent an Internet-connected computer that doesn't have the Terminal Services Client software installed. Let's just say I've been there and done that (and I've committed to memory where the Kinko's in Bozeman, Montana, is located!)

So now it's time to have NormH launch a Terminal Services session. Perform the following keystrokes at NormH's client computer (PRESIDENT).

1. Log on to **PRESIDENT** as **NormH** with the password **Purple3300**.
2. Click **Start**, **Programs**, **Terminal Services Client**, **Terminal Services Client**.
3. The **Terminal Services Client** dialog box appears. Select **SSL1** under Available servers. Note the Servers field is populated with the server machine name automatically, as seen in Figure 8-8. Select **Cache bitmaps to disk** to improve performance. You will also adjust the **Screen area** to **800x600**. Click **Connect**.

$$\boxed{\text{Notes:}}$$

Figure 8-8

Completing the Terminal Services Client dialog box.

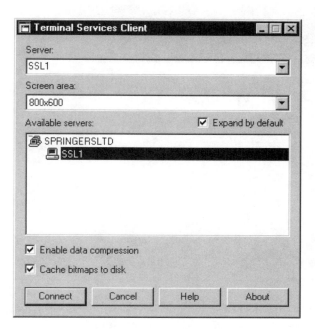

BEST PRACTICE: Note that you can access the SBS server by server name, internal IP address, or even external IP address. In fact, as configured by SBS automatically, and if you select **Terminal Server** on the **Configure Packet Filtering** screen of the **Internet Connection Wizard** (this is shown in Figure 10-2 of Chapter 10, for example), you can directly access the SBS server machine over the Internet via its **external IP address** in the **Server** field of the **Terminal Services Client** dialog box. This is a trick to play when you install the Terminal Services Client on a rented computer at Kinko's in Bozeman, Montana. (It's an inside joke, but see my prior BEST PRACTICE above).

4.　As seen in Figure 8-9, the Terminal Services session window appears in the center of the desktop on NormH's client computer. At this time, a logon is needed via the **Log On to Windows** dialog box. Complete the **User name** field with **Administrator**. Complete the **Password** field with **husky9999**. Click **OK**.

Figure 8-9

Log on as Administrator to launch the Terminal Services session.

5. In the Terminal Services session window, click **Start, Small Business Server Administrator Console**. The result should look similar to Figure 8-10. You can now manage SSL1, the SBS server machine at SSL, just as if you were sitting in front of the actual machine!

Notes:

Figure 8-10

A fully functional Terminal Services session.

6. To terminate the Terminal Services, in the session window, click **Start**, **Shut Down** and then select **Log off administrator** under **What do you want the computer to do?** in the **Shut Down Windows** dialog box. Click **OK** and the Terminal Services session will be terminated.

BEST PRACTICE: In the **Shut Down Windows** dialog box, it's very important that you understand what each option under **What do you want the computer to do?** does:

- **Log off administrator.** This will log off the administrator and terminate the session.
- **Shut down.** This will shut down the SBS server machine.
- **Restart.** This will reboot the SBS server machine.
- **Disconnect.** This will disconnect but not terminate the Terminal Sevices session. This is a critical point that I discuss in the Advanced Topics section below, but basically when you log on again, the prior existing Terminal Services session you had is alive and kicking (and consuming server-side resources to boot!).

In most cases, you'll either select **Log off administrator** or **Disconnect.**

Advanced Topics

It's now time for a whole bevy of advanced topics for you. This section includes understanding how the different SBS user setup templates affect who can run a Terminal Services session, the use of the Web-based MyConsole, a couple of server-side tricks, configuring session settings, and a second look at Application Sharing Mode.

Power Users and Normal People

For the record, only users created with the Power User setup template (discussed in Chapter 4) or those with administrator-level permissions can run a Terminal Services session on SBS 2000. If someone attempts to initiate a Terminal Services session who is just, shall we say, a normal person, the error message in Figure 8-11 results, making it perfectly clear that the person does not have the right to log on and start a Terminal Services session.

Figure 8-11
Busted! A normal user attempts to start a Terminal Services session in SBS 2000 and is denied.

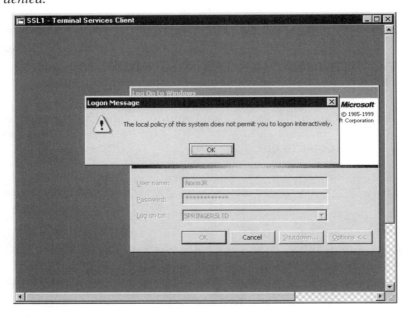

Likewise, when a user created with the Power User setup template starts a Terminal Services session, it's not like they will get free run of the SBS server machine. Far from it. The users created by the Power Users setup template can only run the SBS Personal Console, which severely restricts their ability to roam around the SBS server machine. Think for a moment about the limiting features of the SBS Personal Console from Chapter 5 and how these users are limited in their system scope. So, just how are these users restricted to the SBS Personal Console? Look no further than the **Environment** tab on the property sheet for a user (see Figure 8-12). You will recall that you can access a user's property sheet by double-clicking a user name (e.g., **Bob Easter**) in the **Users** folder under **Active Directory Users and Computers** in the **SBS Administrator Console**.

Figure 8-12

*Observe the power user is locked into the SBS Personal Console with the entries in the **Program file name:** and **Start in:** fields.*

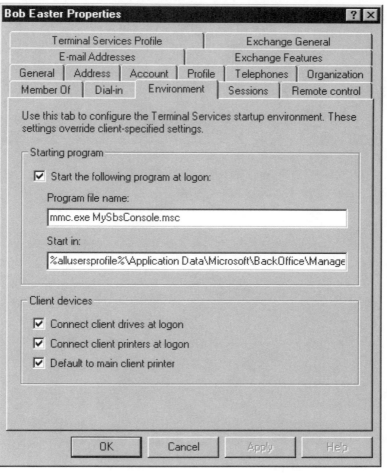

Now what if you wanted a normal person, not created with the Power User template in SBS 2000, to have access and the ability to log on and initiate a Terminal Services session? How would you accomplish that? You would follow these steps (using the SSL methodology, you'll perform these steps for Tom Benkert).

1. Log on to **SSL1** as **Administrator** with the password **husky9999**.
2. Click **Start, Small Business Server Administrator Console**.
3. Expand **Active Directory Users and Computers**.
4. Expand **Springersltd.com**, the Active Directory domain object.
5. Click on the **Users** folder.
6. Double-click on **Tom Benkert**. The **Tom Benkert Properties** dialog box will appear.
7. Click on the **Terminal Services Profile** tab. Select **Allow logon to terminal server** as shown in Figure 8-13.

Notes:

Figure 8-13

The Terminal Services Profile tab allows you to set Terminal Services usage conditions.

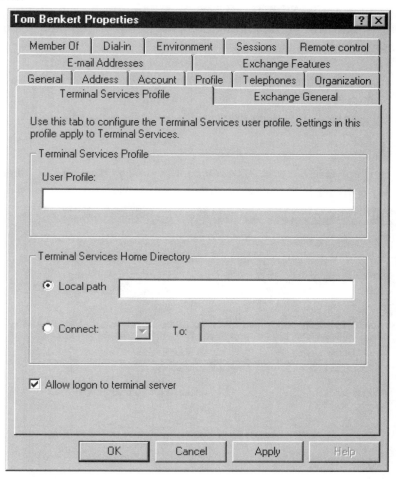

8. Click on the **Member of** tab.
9. Click **Add**. The **Select Groups** dialog box appears.
10. Select **BackOffice Remote Operators** and click **Add**.

BEST PRACTICE: If you want to learn more about the role of the **BackOffice Remote Operators** group, look at the description for this group in the **Groups** organizational unit (OU) under the **MyBusiness** OU under **Active Directory Users and Computers**. The description explains how this group allows members to log on remotely to run a Terminal Services session.

11. Click **OK**. Observe that Tom Benkert is now a member of the BackOffice Remote Operators group. This is shown in Figure 8-14.

12. Click **OK** to close **Tom Benkert** Properties.

Figure 8-14

Tom Benkert is a member of the BackOffice Remote Operators group and can log on locally for the purposes of Terminal Services.

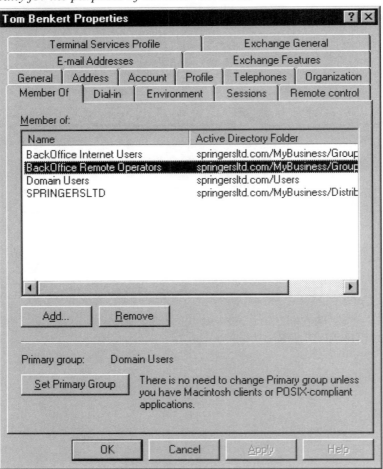

Note that the steps you've just performed immediately above are automatically performed for you when you create a user with the Power Users setup template with the Add User Wizard. This was discussed in Chapter 4.

Now, test the adjustment that you made for Tom Benkert on the PRESIDENT machine by launching a Terminal Services session from the Terminal Services Client. Log on as Tom Benkert. Notice that you have control of the SSL1 server machine desktop.

> BEST PRACTICE: So I ask you. Why wasn't Tom Benkert locked into the SBS Personal Console like other nonadministrators (i.e., power users) who have the right to log on to Terminal Services? Give up? Because you didn't make the entries shown in Figure 8-12. Thus, the SBS Personal Console wouldn't launch automatically.

There are two other tabs on the property sheet that relate to Terminal Services. First is the **Sessions** tab, shown in Figure 8-15. It is here that you can implement individual settings relating to disconnected sessions and how reconnections are handled.

Notes:

Figure 8-15

Creating individual session settings for Terminal Services.

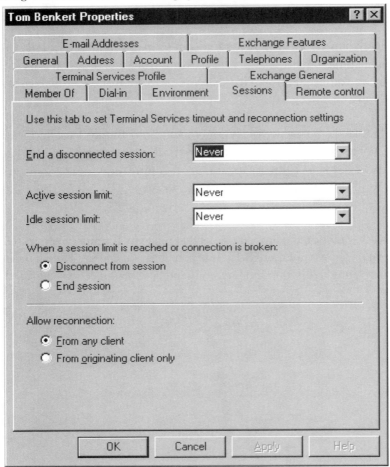

The other Terminal Services-related tab is **Remote Control**. Shown in Figure 8-16, this is where you can invoke settings on how this user's Terminal Services session may be observed.

Figure 8-16

There are the "spy settings" for a user session in Terminal Services.

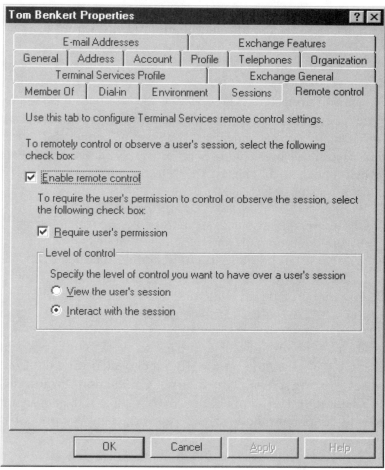

BEST PRACTICE: Note that you can't actually spy on a user while sitting at the SBS 2000 Server machine. Nope! Microsoft had that in mind when it implemented Terminal Services. In fact, there is an error message in a Terminal Services Manager dialog box that reads as follows:

"Certain features, such as Remote Control and Connection, work only when you run this tool from a Terminal Services client session. When this tool is run from the console session, these features are disabled."

Rather, as the administrator from a client computer, you initiate a Terminal Services session. In the Terminal Services session window, you click **Start**, **Programs**, **Administrative Tools**, **Terminal Services Manager**, right-click on a user, and select **Remote Control** from the secondary menu.

MyConsole

An exciting variation of using Terminal Services is the MyConsole Web-based Terminal Services console tool. This is installed and configured by default when SBS 2000 is installed. At a client computer that was set up with the SBS magic disk, you launch MyConsole by selecting **Small Business Server Administration** under **Favorites** in Internet Explorer. This selection maps to http://ssl1/myconsole in the SSL methodology.

> BEST PRACTICE: You can also access MyConsole over the Internet by typing a fully qualified domain name (FQDN) that has an "A" record registered with your ISP pointing to the IP address of your wild-side network adapter card. This FQDN would be followed by "/myconsole". Alternatively, you can type the wild-side IP address in the following manner: **http://207.202.238.215/myconsole**.

Note that for this Internet access approach to work, you'll need to make darn sure you select the **Terminal Server** check box on the **Configure Packet Filtering** screen of the **Internet Connection Wizard** (discussed in Chapter 9). The Terminal Server checkbox allows users on the Internet to connect to the local SBS network using Windows Terminal Services.

Notes:

So, without further ado, meet MyConsole in Figure 8-17.

Figure 8-17

Meet MyConsole in its default state awaiting a logon.

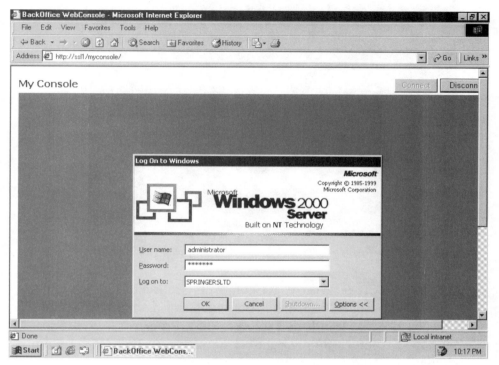

When you enter the Terminal Services session, notice how the SSL1 desktop appears under the SSL methodology (Figure 8-18). But perhaps you agree with me that something doesn't look exactly right. It shouldn't be lost on you that you must scroll down to see the remainder of the SSL1 desktop. This can be fixed by making the adjustment in the following BEST PRACTICE.

Notes:

Figure 8-18
The SSL1 desktop as viewed from MyConsole.

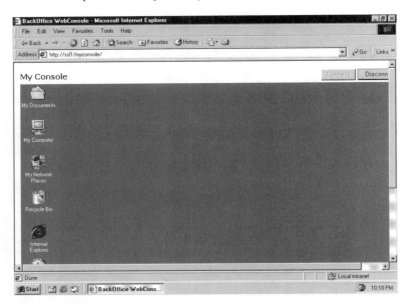

BEST PRACTICE: So, you're not completely satisfied with the basic look of MyConsole? This can be adjusted. Using a common file management tool like **Windows Explorer** (**Start, Programs, Accessories, Windows Explorer**), simply right-click and select **Open With** on the following ASP file on the **SSL1** server machine:

c:\Inetpub\WebAdmin\WebConsole.asp

When asked to select an editor in the list on the **Open With** dialog box, select **Notepad**. Click **OK**. Scroll down to the bottom of the file and change the **WIDTH** value to **640** and change **HEIGHT** to **480**. Your screen will look similar to Figure 8-19. Select **File, Exit** to quit **Notepad**. Click **Yes** when asked **Do you want to save the changes?** in the **Notepad** dialog box that appears.

Notes:

Figure 8-19

Modifying WebConsole.asp will modify the display area of MyConsole.

```
WebConsole.asp - Notepad
File  Edit  Format  Help
</td>

<td id=td2 valign=middle align=right>
      <input type=Submit name=Connect value=<%=L_Connect_Button%> onC
      <input type=Submit name=Disconnect value=<%=L_Disconnect_Button%
</td>
</tr>

<tr>
<td id=td3 colspan=2>
      <OBJECT language="vbscript" ID="MsTsWCl"
      CLASSID="CLSID:1fb464c8-09bb-4017-a2f5-eb742f04392f"
      CODEBASE="mstscax.cab#version=5,0,2221,1"
      WIDTH=<%="640"%>
      HEIGHT=<%="480"%>>
      </OBJECT>
</td>
</tr>

<tr>
<td id=td4 colspan=2 class=directions align=center>
      <%=L_Directions_Text%>
</td>
</tr>

</table>
```

Now at a client computer such as PRESIDENT, launch MyConsole again, log on
as a user, and observe the screen area is a better fit on the screen. This is shown in
Figure 8-20.

Figure 8-20

*Changing the width and height settings allows you to make MyConsole a better
fit on your screen.*

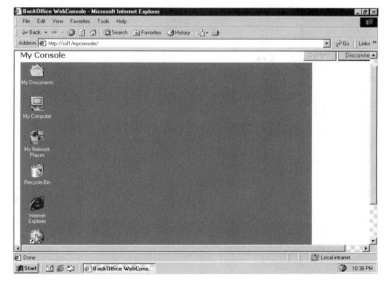

Server-side Settings

There are a few server-side configurations you can make with Terminal Services in SBS 2000. And there's even a trick you can play where you run multiple local Terminal Services sessions on the server machine.

RDP Protocol Settings

If you delve deeply into the depths of Terminal Services, you will find a property sheet for the RDP protocol that offers several interesting configuration possibilities. I'll explore the tab sheets on the RDP-Tcp Properties property sheet. To display this property sheet, follow these steps.

1. Log on to **SSL1** as **Administrator** with the password **husky9999**.
2. Click **Start, Small Business Server Administrator Console**.
3. Expand **Terminal Services Configuration**.
4. Click on **Connections**.
5. Right-click on **RDP-Tcp** and select **Properties** from the secondary menu. Observe the RDP-Tcp Properties property sheet in Figure 8-21.

Notes:

Figure 8-21

The General tab displays version and encryption information. Note that the
Encryption level: *is set to* ***Medium*** *by default, proving Terminal Services ses-*
sions are secure.

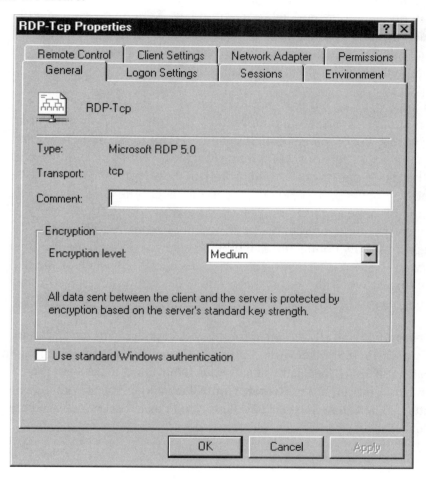

The **Logon Settings** tab allows you to set global logon conditions to override
individual user settings. For example, you could have everyone log on as a guest.
The **Sessions** tab would allow you to set how disconnects and reconnections are
handled (again, overriding user settings).

BEST PRACTICE: This talk about configuration disconnects is more important than you think. One of the great strengths in Terminal Services is its ability to maintain disconnected sessions. Suppose you were remotely connected to the SBS server and were adding a user. Now pretend your modem connection fails. When you reconnect to your Terminal Services session later on, you are taken back to the exact same user setup screen you were working on at the point of modem failure. You don't lose your work.

Let me give you another example of this. At a CPA firm I worked for as a consultant some years ago, Terminal Services ran in Application Sharing Mode. Tax preparers dutifully worked from home at night via Terminal Services sessions, completing lengthy tax forms. If someone else in the tax preparer's household picked up the telephone and killed the modem connection to the office, you might assume all work was lost on the 75-page tax form, right? Nope! Because the disconnection feature can be configured to maintain Terminal Services sessions, the tax preparer simply connected to the office again and found the Terminal Services session still running and at the exact same spot he or she was working at when the connection failed. This approach saved many hours of work!

The **Environment** tab allows you to force a certain program to run at startup. This is wonderful in retail environments where Terminal Services is running in Application Sharing Mode and you only want a thin client to act as a cash register. Not surprisingly, the **Remote Control** tab allows you to configure global spy settings. The **Client Settings** tab allows you to map local printers and drives on a global basis.

Notes:

One tab sheet that I really want to highlight for you is **Network Adapter**, seen in Figure 8-22.

Figure 8-22

The RDP protocol bindings are set on the Network Adapter tab.

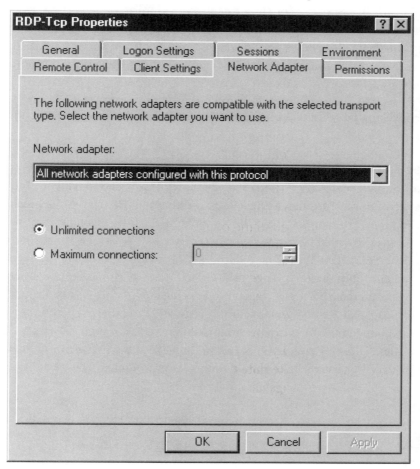

BEST PRACTICE: On the **Network Adapter** tab sheet, under the **Network adapter:** dropdown menu, you can bind the RDP protocol to the internal network adapter card. This is easily accomplished by selecting the **internal network adapter card** from the list and clicking **OK**.

So what does this do for you? This has the effect if making the Terminal Services capability inaccessible from the Internet, even if you enabled the Terminal Services-related ISA Server firewall port you set when you selected the **Terminal Server** check box on the **Configure Packet Filtering** screen of the **Internet Connection Wizard** (this is discussed in Chapter 9). Some SBSers feel this is a good thing – to bind the RDP protocol to the internal network adapter card. As such, this forces you to establish a VPN connection (discussed in Chapter 13) prior to launching a Terminal Services session. You be the judge here on what your needs are.

The **Permissions** tab allows you to set RDP protocol management permissions. Yawn!

Server-side Sessions

One cool trick you can play to amaze your fellow SBSers and make your life easier is the multiple Terminal Services sessions on the SBS server machine trick. First, install the Terminal Services Client on the SBS server machine itself using the same steps presented earlier in the chapter (navigate to the **TSclient** shared folder, select **Net**, select **Win32** and launch **setup.exe,** and complete the Terminal Services Client setup screens). Then proceed to launch multiple Terminal Services sessions on the SBS server machine (a maximum of two sessions can be launched because of Remote Administration Mode). Note that earlier in the chapter I explained how to start a Terminal Services session with the Terminal Services Client (**Start**, **Programs**, **Terminal Services Client**, **Terminal Services Client**). Your SBS server screen should look similar to Figure 8-23.

Notes:

Figure 8-23

Multiple Terminal Services sessions on the SBS server machine are useful for logging on as different users and troubleshooting problems. You can also use this approach for testing server-side business applications before rollout to the end users.

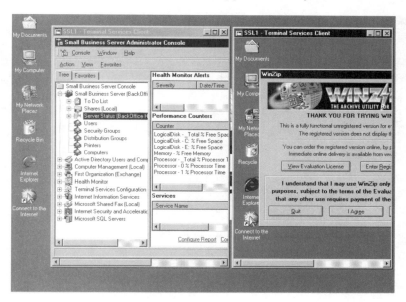

Other Remote Management Approaches

While Terminal Services is the preferred approach to managing your SBS server machine, there are at least two other tools that'll do the trick. Granted, these tools were more popular in the legacy SBS era prior to the introduction of Terminal Services, but I mention both here in the spirit of delivering to you a well-rounded remote administration chapter. These tools are NetMeeting and Virtual Network Computing.

NetMeeting

If the truth be divulged to you, I love NetMeeting. It's a tireless workhorse that I've used for years for remote administration, video conferencing, and collaboration (e.g., chatting). It was the remote administration tool of choice in SBS 4.x. You'll have a chance to use it legitimately in this book as the client application for Exchange Conferencing Server in Chapter 11 and as remote desktop management tool in Chapter 13. In Figure 8-24, I show NetMeeting.

Figure 8-24

Good ol' NetMeeting – one of the last truly valuable freebies!

Virtual Network Computing

A client turned me on to Virtual Network Computing (VNC), a lightweight application for remote administration. This client, a government agency, selected VNC because it provides the required remote administration functionality, has low bandwidth requirements, and can be run as a service. And, perhaps most reassuring of all, VNC was developed by ATT, so you know it has some smarts to it! VNC's home page at www.uk.research.att.com/vnc/ is shown in Figure 8-25.

Figure 8-25

Consider VNC as a possible remote administration solution, especially if you manage platforms other than SBS 2000.

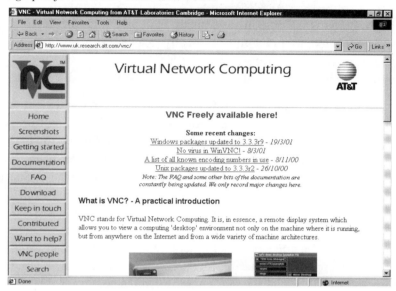

Application Sharing Mode

So, I've saved the best for last: How to run Terminal Services in Application Sharing Mode. Foremost in this discussion is that, as mentioned earlier in the chapter, you should never run Terminal Services in Application Sharing Mode on the SBS 2000 server machine. Accepting that belief, you and I can now move on to a bona fide Terminal Services solution that'll keep the stakeholders happy.

Additional Terminal Services Server on SBS Network

Central to my Application Sharing Mode solution set is the notion that you'll install a second server running Windows 2000 Server on your SBS network. Might I suggest this Windows 2000 Server be a non-domain controller (non-DC) or what we commonly refer to as a member server. There are two reasons for making this machine a non-DC:

- **Performance.** Any server running Terminal Services in Application Sharing Mode is a very busy machine. This machine doesn't need bothersome tasks such as acting as a DC. And don't forget such a machine likely needs multiple processors and more RAM memory than you might imagine! Additional gigabytes of RAM aren't unheard of.

- **Security.** Perhaps you join me as something of an old fuddie duddie, but I simply don't like users logging on locally to a DC, which is the case when Terminal Services runs on a DC. It's all member servers for me when implementing Terminal Services in Application Sharing Mode.

The point is this: Everyone digs Terminal Services and wants to use it right way, including remote users who want to work from home. You'll feel a lot of pressure to allow them to log on locally to the Terminal Services capability on the SBS server machine. You must resist and insist on a second, powerful server machine where Windows 2000 Server is running Terminal Services in Application Sharing Mode. Got it?

Licensing

The last section primed you conceptually for deploying a second server running Terminal Services in Application Sharing Mode. So far so good. Now it's time for the harsh realities of Terminal Services licensing in the context of Application Sharing Mode. It gets ugly early, as they say on a slow Saturday night at a country and western bar in Texas.

First, there is the basic fact that, after you install Terminal Services in Application Sharing Mode on a Windows 2000 Server, you have only 90 days to acquire your special Terminal Services Client Access Licenses (CALs) for non-Windows 2000 Professional clients.

BEST PRACTICE: Windows 2000 Professional clients are "exempt" from needing a Terminal Services CAL. Why? Because Windows 2000 Professional is "granted" a Terminal Services CAL as part of its basic licensing. Given that Terminal Services CALs can run as high as $130 each, you might take a look at just upgrading your legacy desktops to Windows 2000 Professional. Think about it. You can upgrade a legacy desktop OS to Windows 2000 Professional for approximate $200 and not have to deal with this whole big mess. That delta difference of approximately $70 is sure worth it. I recommend to all of my SBS clients in a Terminal Services Application Sharing Mode scenario that they just take client computers up to Windows 2000 Professional and get on with their lives.

These Terminal Services CALs are not part of the generous client license granted with the SBS CALs. And like SBS CALs, Terminal Services CALs are enforced, so we're not talking some paper-based honor system here.

> BEST PRACTICE: Be sure to catch my point about the 90-day grace period earlier. Such a time frame passes quickly and you're likely to forget about the whole darn matter until an end user reports that they can't log on to Terminal Services one day. You'll find yourself counting backwards, just like you do when a baby is born a tad soon to a newly married couple, only to discover that indeed 90 days has passed. Worse, you're likely to need a few days to order the paper-based Terminal Services CALs from a distributor as this particular stock-keeping unit ain't stocked on the shelves of your local computer reseller. You put at risk having a user hit the 90-day mark and then be unable to log on to Terminal Services for a few days while you acquire the CALs. Ouch!

> So, the best practice here is to order your Terminal Services CALs early and often, as they say in Chicago on voting day. And speaking of actually purchasing these CALs, if you're working with your reseller, consider providing the Microsoft manufacturer part number to the reseller for the five CAL – stock-keeping-unit (SKU) of: C79-0001. This may allow the reseller to find the Terminal Services CAL product, which can be a challenge in itself. Believe me.

Second, when you place Terminal Services in Application Sharing Mode, you'll need to install the Terminal Services License Manager component. The Terminal Services License Manager is installed from **Start**, **Settings**, **Control Panel**, **Add/Remove Programs**, **Add/Remove Windows Components**, then selecting **Terminal Services Licensing**. Click **Next** and **Finish** to close the **Windows Components Wizard**.

This is a critical component that starts the 90-day CAL grace period and it's where you add and manage the CALs.

BEST PRACTICE: The Terminal Services Licensing Manager component must be installed on a DC. However, I just told you that I want the second Windows 2000 Server machine running Terminal Services in Application Sharing Mode to be a non-DC. Have I committed one of the seven sins of computer book writing here and walked myself into a box canyon? Nope! You'll simply install the Terminal Services License Manager on the SBS 2000 server machine to manage the Terminal Services licensing for the entire network.

That last statement begs two more interesting points.

First, you'll recall that Terminal Services on the SBS 2000 server machine has no licensing issues because it is running in Remote Administration Mode.

Second, there was a real problem for the first six months in the life of SBS 2000. That's because the License Logging Service in SBS had a bug in it wherein it didn't correctly release license tokens for users that had logged off. Microsoft PSS told SBSers to simply turn off the License Logging Service in the Services applet. But if you did that, the Terminal Services License Manger wouldn't run. This raised the specter that you'd need a third server, running as a Windows 2000 Server DC, to properly run the Terminal Services License Manger. Ouch Again! Fortunately, Microsoft resolved this in the fall of 2001 by releasing a fix for the errant License Logging Service in SBS 2000. All is well and the SBS 2000 server machine can again run the Terminal Service Licensing Manager for you under the scenario presented in this section on Application Sharing Mode.

Note that the Licensing Logging Service fix is discussed in Chapter 7.

So, just what are the steps to implementing Terminal Services licensing in a Application Sharing Mode scenario? Well, it's been said you should always be careful what you ask for as you might just get it. Here you go!

Assuming you missed the mark and used up your 90-day Terminal Services CAL grace period, you'll appreciate the following storyline:

You've fought off the remote end users who, quite frankly, were out for your head while the Terminal Services CALs were being shipped! The big shipment finally arrives and you open it to find a standard license agreement and a page titled "Microsoft License Code" with a 25-alpha/numeric license code. Cool you say! Time to add the CALs using the following steps:

1. Log on to the SBS 2000 server machine (e.g., SSL1) as **Administrator** with the password **husky9999**. Remember that the SBS 2000 server machine will be the required DC to support Terminal Services licensing.
2. Launch the **Terminal Services License Manager** from **Start, Programs, Administrative Tools, Terminal Services Licensing**. **Terminal Services Licensing** appears as seen in Figure 8-26.

Figure 8-26

The Terminal Services Licensing snap-in.

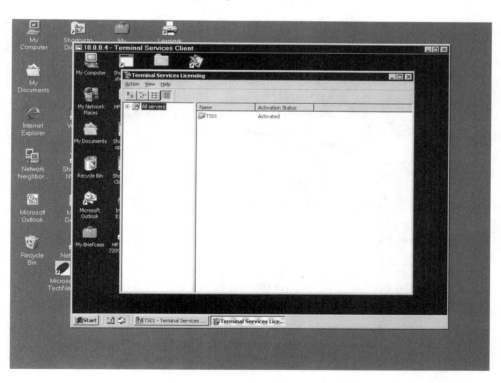

3. Highlight the **Terminal Services machine** in the right pane with a single-click.

4. Click **Action**, **Install Licenses**. The Licensing Wizard launches.

5. After reading the **Welcome to the Licensing Wizard** page, click **Next**.

6. If necessary, select the **licensing program** you use (in my scenario, it is "**Other**") and click **Next**. This screen will not appear if you've previously selected a licensing program.

7. The **Obtain client license key pack** page is displayed. You are now at a critical juncture. You would expect at this point to enter the 25-character license code in the **Type the client license key pack ID in the boxes below** field. However, upon closer examination, you note the field accommodates 35-characters, not the 25-character license code you have in your possession. Perhaps you've noted that the license server ID, also displayed on the **Obtain client license key pack** page, is 35-characters (see Figure 8-27). If you're like me, you enter that number in the blank fields. But it doesn't work. Stand by for the next step.

Figure 8-27
The Obtain client license key pack page in the Licensing Wizard.

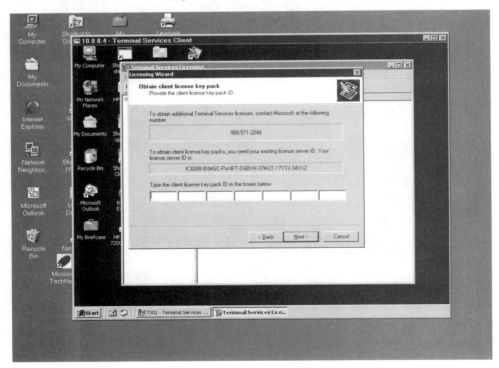

8. You must now perform a poorly documented step (heck, I think it's undocumented). Call the telephone number listed on the **Obtain client license key pack** page (888-571-2048) and provide the person on the other end both the 35-character licensing server ID and the 25-digit licensing code. They will feed both numbers into a computer and it will hash out (or generate) a unique 35-character code that you enter in the **client license key pack ID in the boxes below** field on the **Obtain client license key pack** page. Click **Next**.

9. Click **Finish**. Your remote users can now log on and return to work via their beloved Terminal Services sessions.

BEST PRACTICE: So what were the lessons learned about Terminal Services licensing?

- Don't wait until the end of the 90-day Terminal Services licensing grace period to purchase and install your Terminal Services CALs (or else you'll suffer some downtime with your end users!).

- Consider using all Windows 2000 Professional clients to access Terminal Services. These clients, as stated in passing earlier in the column, don't need Terminal Services CALs. In fact, the license record-keeping for Windows 2000 Professional clients is handled via the Existing Windows 2000 License entry shown in Figure 8-28 (below) in the right pane. Note that if you pursue the Windows 2000 Professional client strategy, you will still need to call Microsoft at the telephone number shown in Figure 8-27 above and have them help you activate your Terminal Services licensing server.

- Have a deep appreciation that this licensing is enforced. (Aside from Microsoft Small Business Server 2000, this is one of the few products from Microsoft that actually enforces licensing.)

- Note that an upgrade from Windows NT Server 4.0 – Terminal Server edition to Windows 2000 Server running Terminal Services doesn't upgrade the Terminal Services CALs (which you will still need to purchase). Early in this consulting experience, I thought the CAL issue would be resolved by virtue of my upgrade (and, of course, I was caught by surprise!).

Figure 8-28

Observe the two types of licenses in the right pane: Windows 2000 and Terminal Services CALs.

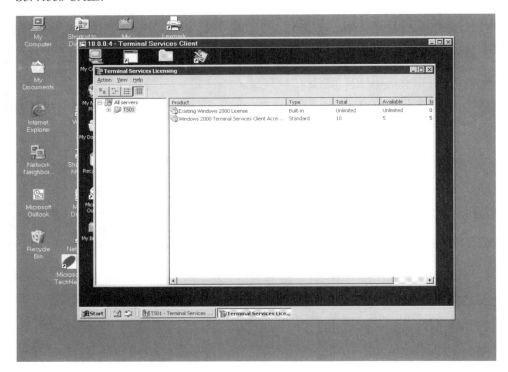

BEST PRACTICE: Note that you can complete this license activation process over the Internet or via fax, but these alternative registration methods assumed you obtained your Windows 2000 Server media via a volume purchasing program, which typically does not apply to my SBS clients.

Not to leave you hanging, but see the Resources section at the end of the chapter for places to go and find out more about Terminal Services and its most interesting licensing scenario.

Notes:

Installing Office 2000

Time to wrap this chapter on Terminal Services all up. But not before I honor the end user and the need to truly use Terminal Services, when allowed, in Application Sharing Mode to accomplish real work (such as using Office 2000). As you know all too well as a bona fide SBSer, end users just want to get their work done. For most, it's nothing more and nothing less, just a fair day of work for a fair wage. Central to this is the Microsoft Office bundle as a common productivity solution.

Granted, today many people are starting to deploy Office XP (as of this writing), but I want to interject a few comments for those using Office 2000. Installing Office 2000 on a Windows 2000 Server running Terminal Services in Application Sharing Mode is a total bearcat that scratches and eats young'uns! In Microsoft English (not the Queen's English, mind you), you'll use a sophisticated transform with a preconfigured Microsoft installer file (*.msi) specifically for Terminal Services setup scenarios.

I've successfully completed installing Office 2000 in what appears to be a corkscrew of a project in under 60 minutes. To accomplish this, I had to slow down and read the section of the Office 2000 Resource Kit, found online at www.microsoft.com/office/ork/2000/default.htm. In Figure 8-29, I show the specific Web page, found via the **Installing Office in a Windows Terminal Services Environment** link in **the Installing Office 2000 in Your Organization** in the **Office 2000 Resource Kit**.

Notes:

Figure 8-29

Read this entire section on installing Office 2000 in a Terminal Services environment at least twice before you make any attempts.

BEST PRACTICE: If this is the only time that you are inclined to listen to me in this entire tome, great! If you follow my advice here, you've gotten full value for the price that you paid for this book and then some.

Notes:

Resources

Not enough books have been written, quite frankly, on the Terminal Services area. But there are a lot of good articles on Terminal Services that give you your next steps.

- See the *MCP Magazine* article "Progress at the Speed of Thin" (www.mcpmag.com/members/00jul/fea2main.asp) that thoroughly defines Terminal Services.

- One of the most technical theses on Terminal Services that I've every seen is "My 10 Favorite Tips for Increasing Windows 2000 Terminal Server Performance" by Ron Oglesby at www.certcities.com/editorial/tips/story.asp?EditorialsID=5 (note that CertCities is related to *MCP Magazine*).

- For general information about Terminal Services, visit Microsoft's Web site at www.microsoft.com/windows2000/technologies/terminal/default.asp as seen in Figure 8-30.

Figure 8-30
Ground zero for anything and everything Terminal Services is Microsoft's own Web page dedicated to the technology.

- Regarding Terminal Services licensing, sink your teeth into the following Microsoft Web page, at http://www.microsoft.com/windows2000/guide/server/pricing/terminal.asp

- And last, visit *IDG InfoWorld* columnist Brian Livingston's Web site at www.brianlivingston.com as seen in Figure 8-31 for a series of columns in early to mid-2001 on the Terminal Services licensing story. Brian applied his unique viewpoint plus his Mensa intellect to solving this regulatory Rubic cube of legalese.

Figure 8-31

Visit Brian Livingston's collection of Terminal Services articles at his Web site www.brianlivingston.com.

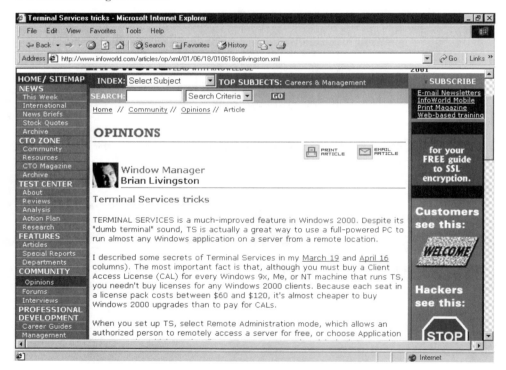

Summary

Whew! That was one heck of a chapter on Terminal Services for you. Truly, before it turns into a book in itself, I'm going to spear this bull with a sword and end it. In this chapter, the primary focus was on Terminal Services in Remote Administration Mode under SBS 2000. But once you start talking about Terminal Services, there are inevitably other considerations that must be addressed. For example, there are server-side configurations to consider and tricks to play, such as running a couple of Terminal Services sessions on the SBS 2000 server machine itself. But all roads and discussions concerning Terminal Services ultimately lead to Application Sharing Mode and supporting herds of end users that just want to work remotely. I spent the second part of the chapter doing exactly that. And with that, I conclude this section of the book dedicated to SBS management issues. The next chapter starts a new section focusing on communications.

Section 3

Using SBS to Communicate

Chapter 9
SBS Internet Connectivity

Call it a case of being an oldie but goodie that was copied as a form of flattery. Introduced in the original SBS version in 1997, the capability to connect your SBS network with ease to the Internet has been greatly improved with each release. It has also been built into Big BackOffice 2000, proving that a little brother can teach a big brother a thing or two along the way.

Not only can you connect via the traditional modem, but also via digital connections ranging from ISDN, DSL, and even WAN-like connections. The WAN connection types vary but include frame relay communications. Figure 9-1 shows the basic Internet connection for Springer Spaniels Limited. Here, the SPRINGERSLTD.COM network is connected to an ISP that is hosting the springersltd.com domain name. The Internet connection allows each user of the SPRINGERSLTD.COM network to send and receive e-mail, browse the Internet, and engage in other fun activities such as Instant Messaging.

> BEST PRACTICE: Kindly be sensitive to the fact that, with each passing month, more and more Internet gizmos are introduced that both empower and distract users. It is widely believed that e-mail and Web browsing have empowered users to do their jobs better. However, the jury is still out on Instant Messaging, which is viewed by many as a toy. So, just be aware that this issue exists in the business community with respect to Internet connectivity.

Figure 9-1

SSL, SBS, and the Internet.

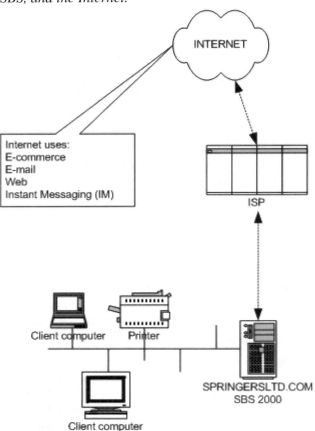

Internet Connection Phases

Here's a look at the Internet connection life cycle as I've observed it from the SBS peaks and valleys. Interestingly, even as some of the technologies have changed during the SBS product life, the basic Internet adoption behaviors have remained consistent. You should find this valuable in managing the expectations of your SBS stakeholders. The three SBS Internet connection life cycle phases are:

1. Ignorance or Early Adapter
2. Modem
3. High-speed Broadband

Ignorance or Early Adapter

During the earliest stages of an SBS network, the SBS community is typically divided between those who don't see the business benefit of an Internet connection (the low-enders of the world) and those who want to ride the Internet wave immediately using the Internet Connection Wizard from the To Do List. The latter group, early adapters, usually has a compelling reason to sign up with an ISP as soon as possible. One such example is the printing shop that needs File Transfer Protocol (FTP) capabilities to transfer large Linotronic files. Another example is the architectural firm that needed to transfer large AutoCAD drawings for the new Seattle Seahawks stadium. In my experience, the average SBS site is skewed toward the ignorance category rather than early adapter. However, that can quickly change once Internet enlightenment arrives at these businesses.

Modem

Most SBS sites start with a simple dial-up modem connection to the Internet. This is typically done just to get the ball rolling. And much like that, the ball quickly grows larger and larger until you've unleashed an Internet monster. But experienced computer consultants shouldn't ignore or laugh at this phase; they should embrace it! That's because, if you listen to your SBS clients, they most likely will communicate three things:

- **Small budgets.** They have a small budget for the Internet connection to start with (until it proves itself and larger monthly outlays are justified).

- **Past dial-up experience.** The boss might suggest that they can have a $20/month dial-up Internet connection via America Online (AOL) or Microsoft Network (MSN). Although it's unlikely you will find $20/month dial-up service for your ISP for a bona fide business, it is likely that a simple dial-up solution between your SBS network and your ISP will be significantly cheaper than the hotshot broadband solutions that are out there.

- **Fear factor.** The third message your SBS clients and users might be communicating is that they are somewhat fearful of the Internet with its potential power and abuses. By starting with a dial-up connection, the SBS client can, as I alluded to previously, get the ball rolling. Interestingly, these SBS clients tend to become my best Internet clients within 6 to 12 months. At that point, they are educated on Internet use and can now appreciate more speed and will gladly pay for it. The moral? Today's SBS modem-based Internet connection is tomorrow's high-speed digital connection. This moral works almost every time.

High-speed Broadband

So here's a pop quiz for all the SBSers out there. What three things are unavoidable for every SBSer? Answer: death, taxes, and a high-speed Internet connection. Sooner or later, the need for speed will infect your SBS site. The reasons are varied and the following are all true:

- A hotshot future employee won't join the company unless you implement a high-speed broadband Internet connection. I hear you laughing on this one but it's really happened. Just ask the law firm in the Pike Place Public Market in Seattle that was trying to hire an experienced legal secretary from a competing firm.

- A younger, more computer-savvy person takes over the company from Dad.

- The sales force needs a faster Internet connection for more immediate e-mail and Web browsing.

- The popularity of the SBS network and the Internet grow so that a modem connection is inadequate.

It's likely you can name your own reasons that high-speed connections have been implemented. And although many SBS sites might not opt for a high-speed Internet connection early on, like death and taxes, most SBS sites will have such a connection within 12 months. Trust me on this one.

Internet Connection Wizard

Many SBSer gurus associate the SBS magic with the Internet Connection Wizard (ICW). The ICW can be launched from two places in the SBS Administrator Console: the To Do List and the Tips – Connecting to the Internet page on the favorites. The ICW is the preferred way to connect your SBS network to the Internet.

BEST PRACTICE: Here is the ICW law for all SBSers to follow. Always try to connect to the Internet via the ICW before going under the hood and manually configuring SBS much like you would regular Windows 2000 Server. Also, here is an important piece of advice that I'll mention later in the chapter: Update your network notebook with SBS Internet connection information. Remember that, on the completion page of a wizard, you can select the summary text and copy and paste it into your network notebook.

The ICW supports three types of Internet connections: dial-up connections, router connections, and broadband connections.

Dial-up Connections

The simplest and most common form of ICW configured connection, a dial-up connection to the Internet, uses an analog or ISDN modem to call the ISP. This is seen in Figure 9-2 and is reflected as callout (A), and it really is as straightforward as it appears. A connection to the ISP is established at modem speed which is typically 28.8 Kbps or greater.

BEST PRACTICE: Modems that purport to have speeds of 56 Kbps typically connect at speeds slightly less, such as 38.5 Kbps, due to telephone line connection quality. ISDN modems operate at speeds greater than twice those of analog modems, depending on the ISDN configuration (one or two ISDN channels).

Notes:

Figure 9-2

SBS and a modem connection to the Internet via ICW, a Shared Modem Service approach and direct dial.

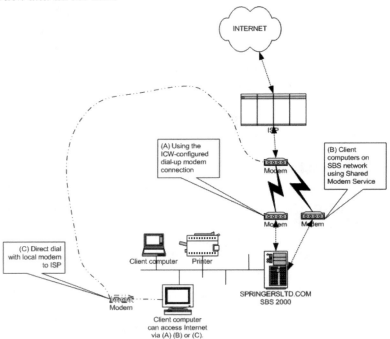

Perhaps you noticed something else that is interesting about Figure 9-2. Properly configured, a client computer can dial out to the Internet by calling an ISP directly using the Shared Modem Service in SBS 2000, as seen in callout (B). I discuss the Shared Modem Service more in Chapter 13. Good old-fashioned direct dial wherein a client computer has a local modem and simply dials the ISP directly is displayed in callout (C) of the figure.

As in many life matters, there are pros and cons with respect to modem connections to the Internet. The positives are the simplicity found with a single analog modem connected to an ISP. Throw in the ease of connection configuration, maintenance, and the relatively low cost to initiate and continue this type of connection. And heck, in many parts of the world, this is the only connection available, as is the case for one of my clients who has outposts in several third-world countries where a telephone line is still a luxury.

Cons tend to focus on transmission speed. Not only do many people view an analog modem connection as too slow when deployed on a stand-alone PC, the situation is exacerbated when a single analog modem is servicing an entire SBS network!

Router Connections

A *router* is a device that directs traffic from one network to another. In the case of SBS and the Internet, a properly deployed router sends SBS information to the Internet and vice versa. Routers are deployed in SBS environments in one of two ways: with a single network adapter card or two network adapter cards. For giggles, I also show a hybrid method to interact with routers on an SBS network.

Single Network Adapter Method

Typically a router configuration is such that the single network adapter exists in the SBS 2000 server machine. A network cable, plugged into the network adapter card, runs between the SBS server and the network hub. Likewise, a network cable connects the router from its Local Area Network (LAN) port to the network hub. That basically communicates that the LAN-side of the router is on the same subnet as the SBS network. The actual "routing" between the local network (known as the inside) and the Internet network (known as the wild side) occurs inside the router between the LAN port and the Internet port. This is shown in Figure 9-3.

Figure 9-3
Anatomy of a router: the inside and the wild side.

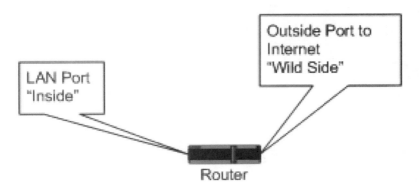

Double Network Adapter Method

Here, the SBS server machine has two network adapter cards. This approach, known in technical circles as the *multihomed approach*, results in one network adapter card having an internal IP address (192.168.16.x on SBS networks by default). The second network adapter card has a real Internet IP address and, via a crossover cable (a special network cable), connects directly to the router. The space between the two network adapter cards is what allows ISA Server to function as a firewall in addition to its local address table (this is explained in Chapter 10). The double network adapter card router method is shown in Figure 9-4.

Notes:

Figure 9-4
Double NIC method.

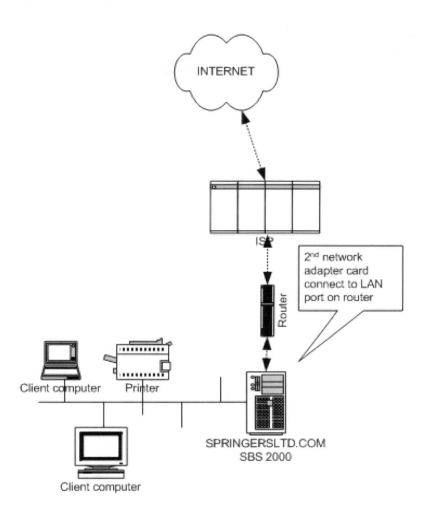

BEST PRACTICE: To be honest, the router approach is really designed to use a single network adapter card approach. On one of the ICW screens where you're configuring the router connection, there is a check box whereby you can tell SBS that you are using two network adapter cards. Said check box almost strikes me as something of an afterthought.

Hybrid Method

The hybrid method is more often than not the "confused" method. Here, the TCP/IP properties on the client workstation are somehow configured as follows: The gateway IP address entry on the client computer is the LAN port IP address on the router. The client computer has no firewall configuration (such as the manual proxy configuration in Internet Explorer). So when I've seen this pretzel logic method shown in Figure 9-5, it usually reflects the work of someone who didn't know what in the heck they were doing when the client computers were set up on the SBS network.

Figure 9-5
Hybrid method.

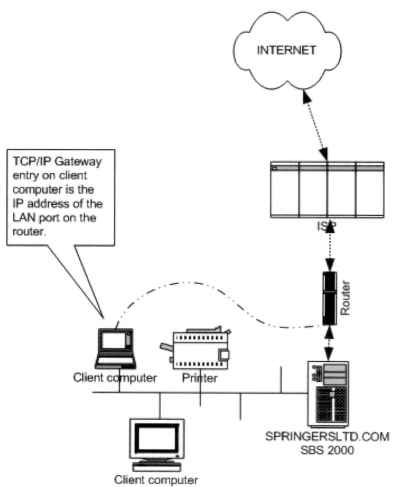

Pro and Con

So what are the pros and cons of using the router connection approach for your SBS network? The pros are obvious: higher speed and the ability to expand your Internet connection by changing the service you have with your telco (either more or less bandwidth). There are a couple of cons. A router-based Internet solution can be inherently more complex than simple analog modems or broadband connection. Routers must be programmed initially and reprogrammed if changes or problems occur. And when you're dealing with a router connection, you're typically dealing with a potentially more expensive telecommunications solution, such as frame-relay.

Broadband Connections

This is a newer type of Internet connection solution and depends largely on whether your geographic area offers such services. I can tell you that broadband is typically offered in urban areas instead of rural areas. Broadband services are more likely to be found in developed countries instead of developing countries.

Two broadband solutions that are available in some areas are (1) digital subscriber line (xDSL) and (2) dedicated digital line (DDL) cable modems. Note that there are different variations of DSL, so I'll generically refer to DSL as xDSL in this book to accommodate all variations. An xDSL solution requires that you are located within 15,000 linear feet of your telco's central office (CO). That's because the strength (or lack of it) requires the host be relatively close to the CO. QWest is an xDSL service provider and is shown in Figure 9-6.

Notes:

Figure 9-6

Most major telcos such as QWest provide DSL services

BEST PRACTICE: Call it a case of the avoiding the bankruptcy blues, but I never felt right steering my SBS clients towards cut-rate xDSL service providers. Rather, I've recommended the bulky, huge telcos. Boy was I reassured by the big bulky telco xDSL selection decisions I made when the popular media started reporting serious business interruption problems occurring when cheapo xDSL providers started going bankrupt (and I avoided this problem in my client base). You're likely aware of the fact the Covad and other xDSL providers have run into financial difficulty lately, causing service delays and problems for xDSL subscribers. My advice? Love them or hate them, the big bulky telcos will still be here tomorrow.

A cable modem solution requires that your cable service provider offer such a service. A popular cable modem service provider is AT&T's @HOME solution. Beware that @HOME and competing cable modem service providers have recently reported financial troubles. The @HOME Web page is displayed in Figure 9-7.

Figure 9-7

AT&T is the major investor in @HOME, suggesting this service may survive the broadband shakeout occurring in the life of SBS 2000.

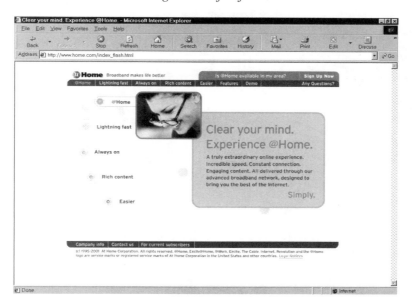

BEST PRACTICE: Although these services are truly wonderful and often very cost effective, I want to emphasize my point about service limitations. Whereas my house is located three long country blocks from a QWest CO (which I knew from the telltale, windowless telco building in my neighborhood), a construction company client of mine, on a popular street with many businesses, was measured as being too many miles from the nearest CO as the crow flies. That means they were disqualified from using an xDSL solution because they easily exceeded the 15,000 foot limit as measured by the telco.

Likewise, cable modem service providers have geographic areas that are not served, so you'll want to check closely as to the availability of this form of broadband service prior to making an assumption that it'll all work out in the end!

As seen in Figure 9-8, the broadband solution assumes the double network adapter card approach.

Figure 9-8

Broadband approach.

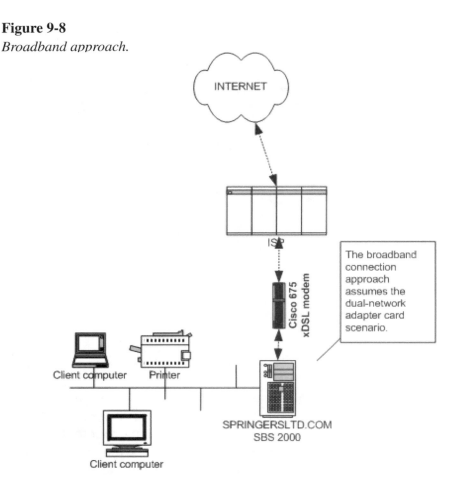

Interestingly, these broadband solutions often offer faster download speeds than upload speeds. Why? Because Internet users typically download far more traffic than they upload! This approach also allows the telco to multiplex existing capacity and provide service to more users than if the upload and download speeds were exactly the same. In Chapter 6 I show how to test your DSL network speed using www.dslreports.com.

The pros for using a broadband solution include having a high-speed Internet connection for a cost often dramatically lower than traditional router-based Internet connection solutions. The cons include the limited service availability: It is possible your location will not have either service available. Bummer!

Futuristic Approaches

A new arrival on the small business networking front is the use of satellite dishes for broadband, high-speed Internet connectivity. This stuff really works, man! For a reasonable price, say $100/month in the Western United States, you can enjoy 1MB transfer speeds (slightly higher than the average DSL service) plus a buffet of cable TV channels. One service provider, Starband (www.starband.com), is displayed in Figure 9-9.

Figure 9-9

Consider Starband and other satellite service providers when you decide you might need this form of broadband service.

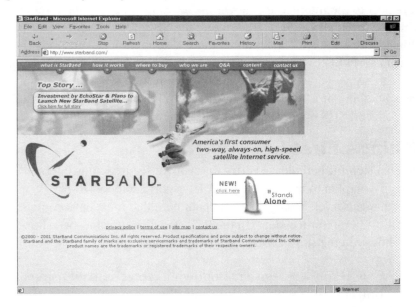

BEST PRACTICE: If you purchase Starband, learn from my friend VanWinkle, who lives in rural Oregon and implemented Starband. There are different ways to acquire Starband service. For example, Radio Shack wants you to purchase a computer at the same time you sign up for the Starband service. So good old VanWinkle settled on making his purchase from Starband itself, saving him lots of money and allowing him to sleep better at night.

So why would anyone fuss with this new-fangled, satellite-bouncing, UFO-infested Internet connection approach such as Starband? Well, your beloved SSL, the sample company in this book, almost had to consider it! Turns out small businesses located in rural areas, such as Bainbridge Island where SSL is located, are often shut out of conventional broadband services. Truthfully, on Bainbridge Island, this tends to be the waterfront homes that are too far from the QWest CO. Look for Starband and similar satellite broadband service providers to do very well in rural areas.

Meet Your Creator: The ICW

Now that you have spent the past few pages better understanding how SBS 2000 networks connect to the Internet, it is now time to connect SSL to the Internet. The ICW in SBS 2000 allows you to configure the SBS 2000 machine for the ISP of your choice, based on the connection method of your choice. This is a big difference from early SBS versions that had you select an ISP from a referral list. And speaking as someone who advised one of the referral ISPs on how to support SBS, it was something of a Texas-sized hurricane of madness! Those days are safely behind us and SBS openly supports your Internet connection needs.

First Things First

Before you go a step further, please verify that you've secured your Internet domain name if you plan to use Simple Mail Transport Protocol (SMTP) e-mail with your Exchange server. This is a critical path item that must be accomplished first and foremost before proceeding. In the SSL storyline, this has been done for you, but I'll show you the steps I used to accomplish this.

> BEST PRACTICE: You will register your own Internet domain name in the real world, but you won't register the domain name for SSL (I've already done that!).

Registering Your Internet Domain Name

As part of the SSL storyline, the Internet domain name SPRINGERSLTD.COM will be registered. I'll use Networksolutions.com to accomplish this. These are the steps to follow:

1. Launch a Web browser such as Internet Explorer and surf over to www.networksolutions.com.

2. At the Network Solutions home page, search for the domain name www.springersltd.com under **Search for a domain name – no obligation**. Click **Go**.

3. As seen in Figure 9-10, the domain name was still available for SSL to purchase on the **Select An Address** page. Click **Continue**.

Figure 9-10

The springersltd.com domain name is available. Note that several variations are suggested by Network Solutions.

4. On the **Choose Your Services** page, click **Select** to purchase your domain name of springersltd.com.

5. Review your order on the **Review Shopping Cart** screen and click **Continue**. This is shown in Figure 9-11.

Notes:

Figure 9-11

The shopping cart for springersltd.com appears to be in good order.

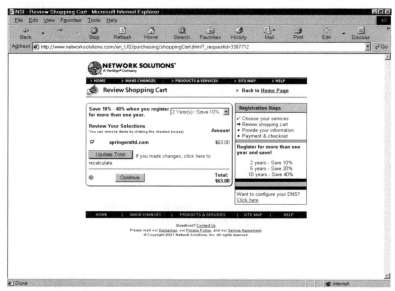

6. On the **Provide Your Information** page, select **Business** and click **Sign Up**.

7. Complete the **Account Holder Information** page similar to Figure 9-12. Click **Continue**.

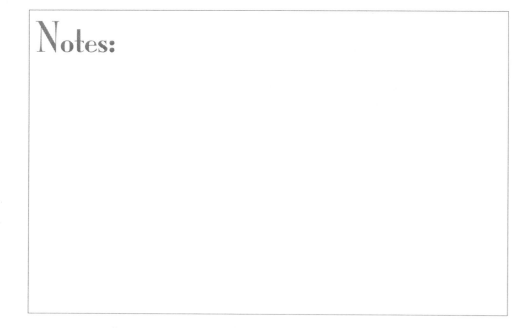

Notes:

Figure 9-12

Registering springersltd.com for Springer Spaniels Limited.

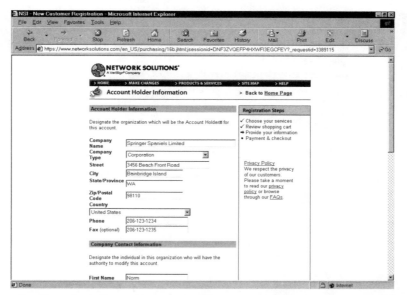

8. Confirm the information on the **Payment & Checkout** page and provide credit card payment information. Agree to the terms of the service agreement by selecting the **I have read the service agreement and agree to its terms** check box. Click **Submit**.

9. Print out the **Thank You** page which summarizes your domain name acquisition transaction. This is seen in Figure 9-13. Close your Web browser.

Notes:

Figure 9-13

Success! SSL now owns springersltd.com.

Later on, to verify the Internet domain name you've acquired has been processed and is truly yours, return to the Network Solutions Web site, click the WHOIS button in the upper-right corner, and enter your domain name in the **Domain** field. Your Internet domain registration information should appear.

Assigning Your Internet Domain Name to Your ISP

Now that you've acquired your Internet domain name, you have to assign it to your ISP. This is a process where your ISP becomes your technical contact, makes your DNS record entries, points your Mail Exchange (MX) record to your SBS server machine for SMTP-based e-mail, and serves as your primary and secondary DNS servers. This step varies on a case-by-case basis, as the ISP area is highly fragmented and not standardized. Consequently, you should contact your ISP directly for more information on how to assign your Internet domain name.

Running the ICW

The time has arrived. In the SSL storyline, you will configure your SBS 2000 server for SMTP e-mail using a broadband connection. Let's get started.

BEST PRACTICE: Ah, but not so fast, buckaroo. You will need to enable the second network adapter card if you plan to use a full-time broadband connection, which is the case with SSL. After Step 3 below, select Enable Network Interfaces on the To Do List. Carefully read the instructions under To check the network connection for proper IP address and network settings and To re-enable a network connection. Gather the IP address information for the second network adapter card from the full-time form below. For the purposes of SSL, you may ignore the instructions provided under To configure ISA Server.

1. Log on to **SSL1** as **Administrator** with the password **husky9999**.
2. Click **Start, Small Business Server Administrator Console**.
3. Select the **To Do List** under **Small Business Server (BackOffice Manager)**.
4. Click the **Internet Connection Wizard** link on the **To Do List**. The Internet Connection Wizard launches.
5. Click **Next** when the **Welcome to the Small Business Server Internet Connection Wizard** page appears.
6. Select **Full-time Broadband Connection** on the **Configure Hardware** page, as seen in Figure 9-14. Click **Next**.

Notes:

Figure 9-14

Select the Full-time Broadband Connection screen. Observe the three connection options that were explained earlier in the chapter.

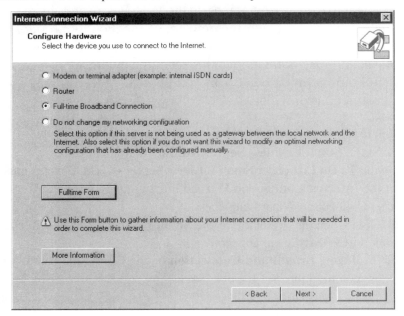

BEST PRACTICE: A tip of the Texas cowboy hat to the SBS development team at Microsoft when it comes to the forms button. If you look at Figure 9-14, you'll see the Fulltime Form on the middle of the page. Click and print this to fill in the blanks with the information you will need to complete the ICW correctly. Some fields will require you to call your ISP for information. Note that each connection method has its own form.

The information for the fulltime form is displayed below and completed in **BOLD** for SSL. :

Full-Time Broadband Connection

To identify your server, would you like to:

*   Obtain an IP address automatically from a DHCP server?

- Specify an IP address? USE THIS FOR SSL.

If you are specifying an IP address, complete the one you use for your second network adapter:

IP Address: _207._202._238._215
Subnet Mask: _255._255._255._0
Default Gateway: _207._202._238._1

Primary DNS server address (provided by your ISP): _209._20._130._35
Secondary DNS server address (optional): _209._20._130._33

What type of mail do you receive (choose one type)?

- Use Exchange (SMTP) Server **USE THIS FOR SSL.**

- POP3

- No e-mail

If you are using Exchange (SMTP) Server, what service do you use to deliver your mail?

- Forward all messages to host

Host Name or IP address of your ISP's mail (SMTP) server (example: exchange.microsoft.com or 170.10.10.10)

_____

- DNS **USE THIS FOR SSL.**

If you are using Exchange (SMTP) Server and automatically obtaining an IP address:

Host Name or IP address of your ISP's mail (SMTP) server (example: exchange.microsoft.com or 170.10.10.10)

_____

How do you signal your ISP to send mail to you?

- ETRN
- TURN with authentication
- No signal

How often should this signal be sent?

_____

Your domain name (example: microsoft.com):
__**springersltd.com**_

A couple of comments about the Fulltime Form and what it's really saying. First, SBS 2000 supports the dynamic assignment of the external IP address. This is seen in the top part of the Fulltime Form where you circle whether the external IP address is dynamic or static. For static IP address information, you complete the middle part of the form with the appropriate IP address information. Both SMTP and POP3 e-mail are natively supported. And you can specify whether your ISP needs a "signal," such as ETRN, to deliver its mail.

7. On the **Configure Network Adapters** page, select the network address card with the IP address of **192.168.16.2** as the local network card under **Select the network card you want to use for your local network card**. Select the other network adapter card as the external network card (or the wild side card) under **Select the network card you want to use for your external network**. This is shown in Figure 9-15. Click **Next**.

Notes:

Figure 9-15

Complete the Configure Network Adapters page similar to what you see here.

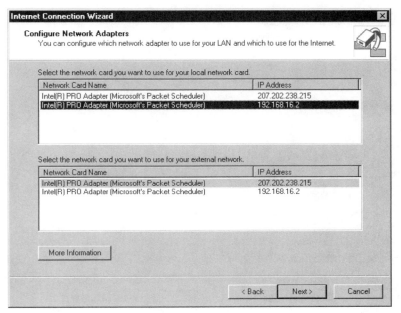

8. Confirm or change the settings for your second network adapter card on the **Specify your ISP connection information** page. This information, derived from the IP address information for the second network adapter card, is shown in Figure 9-16. Click **Next**.

BEST PRACTICE: Perhaps you've noticed that, in SBS 2000, a More Information button is present on each page of the ICW. This time the information is truly meaningful. Use it!

Notes:

Figure 9-16
Carefully verify the IP address for the second network adapter.

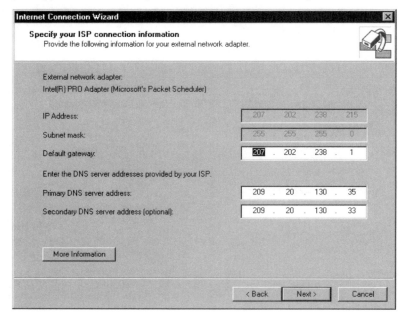

9. On the **Configure Internet Mail Settings** page, accept the default
    settings of **Use SMTP for Internet mail** and **Disable POP3 electronic
    messaging**. This is seen in Figure 9-17. Click **Next**. Note that Exchange
    2000 Server and its e-mail settings are discussed in Chapter 11.

Notes:

Figure 9-17

SSL will use SMTP-based e-mail.

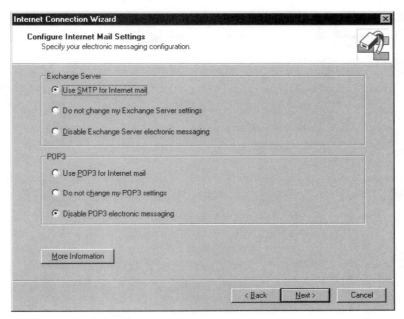

10. Accept the default Internet domain name of **springersltd.com** in the
    Your Internet domain name field on the **Configure Internet Domain
    Name** page. This is shown in Figure 9-18. Click **Next**.

Notes:

Figure 9-18

The Configure Internet Domain Name page is auto-populated with the domain name information you provided during the setup of SBS 2000.

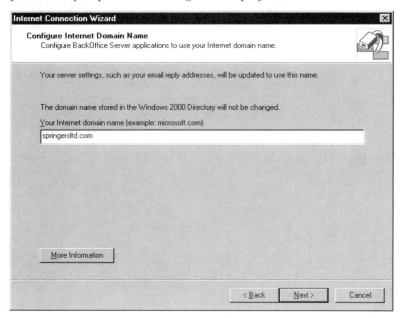

11. Accept the default **Use domain name system (DNS)** for mail delivery on the **Configure SMTP Server Address** page. Click **Next**.

12. Select each check box under **Enable ISA Server packet filtering** on the **Configure Packet Filtering** page, as seen in Figure 9-19. These selections are necessary to complete the exercises related to SSL in this book. Click **Next**.

Notes:

Figure 9-19

This is where you perform much of the firewall configuration in SBS 2000!

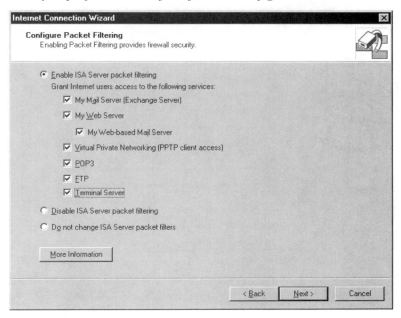

13. When the **Configure Packet Filtering** dialog box appears, read the message and click **OK**. Basically, this states your existing ISA Server configuration will be modified.

14. Carefully read the summary information on the **Completing the Small Business Server Internet Connection Wizard** screen (see Figure 9-20). Be sure to select this summary text and copy and paste it into your SBS network notebook. Click **Finish**.

Notes:

Figure 9-20

You've reached the tail-end of the ICW configuration process.

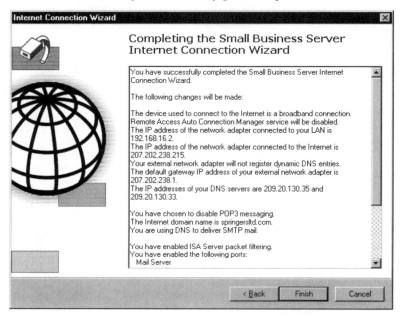

15. The **Internet Connection Configuration Status** dialog box (see Figure 9-21) will advise you on the progress of the configuration. Click **OK** when the process is complete, which may take several minutes, so go get a cup of coffee.

BEST PRACTICE: Old habits are hard to break. Whereas you technically do not need to reboot the SBS 2000 server machine after running the ICW, I always do. To me, there is nothing like a fresh baseline to increase my comfort level.

Notes:

Figure 9-21
Kick back and watch the ICW perform its configurations via the Internet Connection Configuration Status dialog box.

Using Internet Explorer

While not a big part of this chapter or the book, the Internet Explorer (IE) browser merits a quick mention. Granted there are short books out there if you really need to learn how to use a Web browser such as IE, but it's common knowledge in this day and age. So here is an opportunity to revisit your skills in using Microsoft's Web browser of choice in SBS 2000, IE version 5.01.

> BEST PRACTICE: The default configuration for IE in SBS, both at the server and client levels, is 56-bit encryption. You can see this by selecting **About Internet Explorer** from the Help menu in IE.

> There are many cases where this needs to be upgraded to 128-bit encryption. I look no further than a client company that does business in the area of worker compensation. This firm interacts with the State of Washington Department of Labor and Industries (L&I) on confidential worker injury claims. Recently, this form of interaction changed to a Web-based application, and I upgraded each of the client's computers to IE's 128-bit encryption to satisfy the security requirements of this L&I application. I even had to deploy a "smart card" in the USB port of each client computer as part of the security requirements. Whoa!

To upgrade your IE browser in SBS 2000 to 128-bit encryption, you'll need to click the **Update Information** link on the **About Internet Explorer** dialog box. You will be directed to a Microsoft Web site to download and apply the 128-bit encryption fix.

My advice is that you should upgrade IE at each client computer to 128-bit encryption for the highest level of security. Heck, just about everyone is making credit card purchases over the Internet these days.

IE is, of course, a Web browser. A *Web browser* is the tool you use to surf or navigate the Web. To surf the Web, you simply type a valid Web site address in the Address field located near the top of IE and press the Enter key. Such an address might look like www.microsoft.com or www.mcp.com. Or heck, you might enter Internet addresses that end in .net or .org. After a connection to the Internet is established (using one of the approaches discussed previously), the home page for the Web address you selected will be displayed. There are, as you probably know, millions of Web addresses on the Internet (and plenty of search engines such as www.google.com to help you find these addresses).

By default, IE launches the Microsoft Network (MSN) home page when you double-click the Internet Explorer icon on the desktop of an SBS user's computer. You might be interested to know that several SBS-related links are listed under Favorites.

- Small Business Server Users Guide. This is the online user manual, seen in Figure 9-22. It's actually very useful during this round, so please at least look at it once.

- Small Business Server Administration Console. This is the MyConsole Web-based Terminal Services capability discussed in Chapter 8.

- Microsoft Small Business Server Web site. This is ground-zero in the SBS movement, comrades! It points to www.microsoft.com/smallbusinessserver.

- My E-mail. This displays the Outlook Web Access (OWA) interface that is discussed in Chapter 12.

- Microsoft Small Business Internet Services. This points to Microsoft bCentral and in part creates a linkage between the bCentral and SBS communities.

Figure 9-22

The coveted SBS 2000 user guide. Goodbye printed manuals and hello online books!

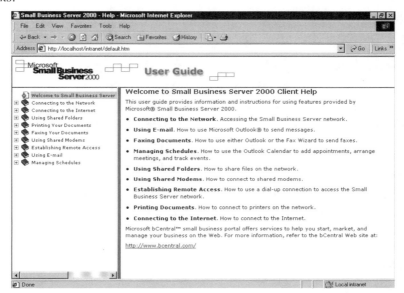

In Chapter 18 I'll show how IE can be used to publish documents to an intranet for collaboration. If you are interested in learning the finer points about IE 5.x, consult *Sams' Teach Yourself Internet Explorer 5 in 24 Hours* by Jill Freeze (ISBN 0-672-31328-6).

BEST PRACTICE: A couple of thoughts here.

Although I only introduced IE 5.01 here, don't underestimate the importance of IE 5.01 on an SBS network. With the world moving toward Web-based network computing, SBS users will likely use IE 5.01 often during the day and keep the browser open at all times.

Also, please consider upgrading IE to the latest version, which as of this writing is IE 5.5 (Service Pack 1). Often the upgrades include increased stability, more functionality, and, most important, security patches!

Note that I've not observed negative effects from having the SBS client setup program install IE 5.01 over a more recent IE version (e.g., 5.5).

This often occurs when you've purchased new client computers with the Microsoft operating system preinstalled and a more current IE version than ships with SBS. So what's my best practice here? Let the SBS networking setup disk setup the client computer with IE 5.01 and then come back and install the very latest edition of IE again.

Advanced Internet Configuration Issues

I'll now share a hodgepodge of tips and tricks related to SBS 2000's Internet connectivity. This includes how SBS 2000 configures IE in the background, how broadband networks with existing DHCP server do and do not affect SBS 2000, and how to support the roaming SBS user with respect to Internet Explorer.

IE Setup

About four layers deep in IE, you see that SBS 2000 has configured IE to use the ISA Server firewall service. Follow these steps to see for yourself.

1. Start **IE** from either the **Programs** group from the **Start** menu or the **Internet Explorer** desktop shortcut.

2. Select **Tools**, **Options**. The **Internet Options** property sheet will be displayed with the **General** tab.

BEST PRACTICE: In the Address field under Home page on the General tab, you can change the default home page that appears when you launch IE. Let's face it. For many of us, MSN doesn't cut it. Rather, you might consider a SBS-related page that is informative and, most important, updated frequently. This home page, www.sbsfaq.com, is Wayne Small's SBS frequently asked questions page. I discuss Wayne's page at length in Appendix A. By the way, once you've typed in the new address URL in the Address field, click Apply and continue with this set of steps.

3. Click the **Connections** tab.

4. Click the **LAN Settings** button. The **Local Area Network (LAN) Settings** dialog box appears.

5. Observe that the **Proxy server** section contains settings for **SSL1** (or

whatever your server name is along with port **8080**. This is shown in Figure 9-23. Perhaps you share in the irony that the firewall in SBS 2000 is called ISA Server 2000, yet IE's user interface refers to a proxy server. Sounds like someone on the IE development team violated the Microsoft style guidelines!

Figure 9-23
SBS 2000 automatically configures IE for its default firewall settings.

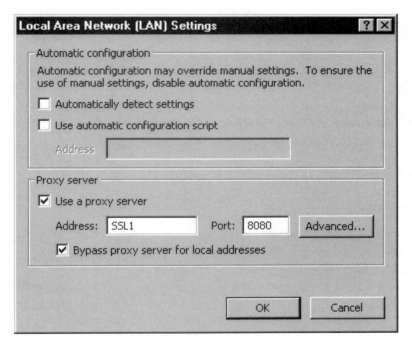

BEST PRACTICE: Notice that the **Automatically detect settings** check box under **Automatic configuration** isn't selected in Figure 9-23. That's too bad, because if it were selected and it worked in SBS 2000, that would solve the roaming user problem that I describe in a moment. I've tried IE on an SBS network where only the **Automatically detect settings** check box is selected and the **Use a proxy server** check box is deselected. The SBS 2000 server did not automatically configure IE in my test, but you never know—perhaps I was doing something wrong.

6. Click **Advanced**. The **Proxy Settings** dialog box appears. Note that all Internet server types except Socks are selected. This is a huge improvement over prior SBS releases where only the **HTTP** server type was automatically configured, and then SBS users who tried to access their secure (HTTPS) day trading stock brokerage accounts could not do so until they selected **Secure** on the **Proxy Settings** dialog box. Sometimes I truly do not miss the old days.

7. Close all dialog boxes by clicking **OK** successively and returning to IE's Web page view.

IE is configured via the install.ins file. This file is displayed below and certainly provides the meat on the IE configuration bone. You can see several IE configuration sections, including Favorites and the Proxy Settings. The **install.ins** file is located at **\%system drive%\Program Files\Microsoft BackOffice\Client Setup\Clients\Setup**.

```
[Branding]

CompanyName=Microsoft Corporation

Version=5,00,2014,0200

NoClear=1

Type=0

Wizard_Version=5.00.2014.200

Custom_Key=MICROSO

Win32DownloadSite=0

Window_Title_CN=

Window_Title=

Toolbar Bitmap=

FavoritesOnTop=0
```

```
User Agent=

Global=1

Platform=2

[URL]

Quick_Link_1_Name = %QL10%.url

Quick_Link_1    = http://www.microsoft.com/isapi/
redir.dll?prd=ie&pver=5.0&ar=CLinks

Quick_Link_2_Name = %QL20%.url

Quick_Link_2    = http://www.microsoft.com/isapi/
redir.dll?prd=ie&ar=hotmail

Quick_Link_3_Name = %QL30%.url

Quick_Link_3    = http://www.microsoft.com/isapi/
redir.dll?prd=ie&ar=windows

NoWelcome=0

[BatchMode]

URL="http://www.microsoft.com/windows/ie/ie5/download/
rtw/x86/en/download"

URL2="http://www.microsoft.com/windows/ie/ie5/down-
load/rtw/x86/ie5sites.dat"

[Strings]

QL10 = "Customize Links"

QL20 = "Free Hotmail"

QL30 = "Windows"

FAV1 = "MSN"
```

```
FAV2 = "Radio Station Guide"

FAV3 = "Web Events"

FAV4 = "Microsoft Small Business Server Website"

FAV5 = "Microsoft Small Business Internet Services"

FAV6 = "My E-mail"

FAV7 = "SBS User Guide"

FAV8 = "Small Business Server Administration"

[Media]

Build_Download=1

Build_CD=0

Build_LAN=0

Build_MultiFloppy=0

Build_Floppy=0

Build_BrandingOnly=0

[ActiveSetupSites]

SiteUrl0=http://www.microsoft.com/DOWNLOAD/win32

SiteName0=Download Site 0

SiteRegion0=North America

SiteUrl1=

SiteName1=

SiteRegion1=
```

```
SiteUrl2=

SiteName2=

SiteRegion2=

SiteUrl3=

SiteName3=

SiteRegion3=

SiteUrl4=

SiteName4=

SiteRegion4=

SiteUrl5=

SiteName5=

SiteRegion5=

SiteUrl6=

SiteName6=

SiteRegion6=

SiteUrl7=

SiteName7=

SiteRegion7=

SiteUrl8=

SiteName8=

SiteRegion8=
```

```
SiteUrl9=

SiteName9=

SiteRegion9=

[CabSigning]

pvkFile=

spcFile=

InfoURL=

Name=

[CabSigning]

pvkFile=

spcFile=

InfoURL=

Name=

[Internet_Mail]

Window_Title=

[Animation]

DoAnimation=0

[Small_Logo]

Path=

[Big_Logo]

Path=
```

```
[FavoritesEx]

Title1=%FAV1%.url

URL1=http://www.microsoft.com/isapi/
redir.dll?prd=ie&pver=5.0&ar=IStart

Title2=%FAV2%.url

URL2=http://www.microsoft.com/isapi/
redir.dll?prd=windows&sbp=mediaplayer&plcid
=&pver=6.1&os=&over

=&olcid=&clcid=&ar=Media&sba=RadioBar&o1=&o2=&o3=

Title3=%FAV3%.url

URL3=http://www.microsoft.com/isapi/
redir.dll?prd=windows&sbp=mediaplayer
&plcid=&pver=5.2&os=&over=&olcid=&clcid=
&ar=Media&sba=Showcase&o1=&o2=&o3=

Title4=%FAV4%.url

URL4=http://www.microsoft.com/smallbusinessserver/

Title5=%FAV5%.url

URL5=http://www.bcentral.com

Title6=%FAV6%.url

URL6=http://%sbsserver%/exchange

Title7=%FAV7%.url

URL7=http://%sbsserver%/intranet

Title8=%FAV8%.url

URL8=http://%sbsserver%/myconsole
```

```
[Channel Add]

No Channels

[DesktopObjects]

Channel Bar=0

Delete Old Channels=0

[Proxy]

HTTP_Proxy_Server=http://%sbsserver%:8080

FTP_Proxy_Server=http://%sbsserver%:8080

Gopher_Proxy_Server=http://%sbsserver%:8080

Secure-_Proxy_Server=http://%sbsserver%:8080

Socks_Proxy_Server=http://%sbsserver%:8080

Use_Same_Proxy=1

Proxy_Enable=1

Proxy_Override="<local>"
```

BEST PRACTICE: Did you see in the last few lines of the install.ins script how SBS is populating IE's proxy settings with the SBS server name? It's the %sbsserver% variable. I share that with you because this would be the "hook" other developers could use to configure their respective SBS-compliant products. For example, Trend Micro's OfficeScan 5 for SBS 2000, which I discuss in Chapter 6 does not in any manner auto-populate its proxy server settings (and it assumes Port 80 when SBS uses Port 8080). In the case of Trend, they could have used both the %sbsserver% variable and Port 8080 automatically so that you would automatically receive updated virus definition files without having to fuss with a manual proxy configuration. Another alternative would have been for Trend to simply copy the IE settings.

Dealing with Broadband Networks and DHCP

One network topology issue you're likely to encounter concerns broadband networks, an area in which I happen to have lots of personal experience. The issue here is rogue DHCP servers on a broadband network connection. I've seen a rogue server take two forms. First, it can be your DSL router/modem that is acting as a DHCP server (this can usually be turned off with a **SET DISABLE DHCP** command on the router). The other occurrence involves bona fide DHCP servers out on the Internet that are issuing dynamic addresses.

The presence of another DHCP server does and does not affect SBS 2000. During the SBS setup phase, discussed in Chapter 3, another DHCP server on the network will cause the SBS setup to massively fail at the Scenario Baseline stage. Basically the DHCP Server service in the underlying Windows 2000 Server operating system shuts down and the SBS installation fails. But, after SBS is set up, ISA Server has disabled the DHCP Client filter so that an external rogue DHCP server won't affect the SBS server and thus shut down the DHCP Server service in SBS 2000. Follow these steps to see for yourself.

1. Log on to **SSL1** as **Administrator** with the password **husky9999**.
2. Click **Start, Small Business Server Administrator Console**.
3. Expand the **Internet Security and Acceleration Server 2000** snap-in.
4. Expand **Servers and Arrays**.
5. Expand the **SSL1** server object.
6. Expand **Access Policy**.
7. Click on **IP Packed Filters**. Notice the IP Packet Filters displayed in the right detail pane, as seen in Figure 9-24.

Notes:

Figure 9-24

Although it is difficult to see in a book, the DHCP Client filter is actually disabled by a red "Stop Light" next to the entry.

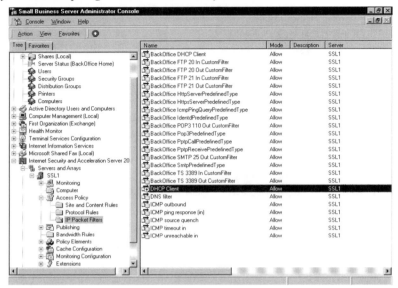

8. Double-click the **DHCP Client** entry. The **General** tab on the **DHCP Client Properties** dialog box is displayed. Note the **Enable this filter** check box is not selected, as seen in Figure 9-25. Click **OK**.

BEST PRACTICE: However, SBS implicitly supports an external DHCP server in that the external network adapter card can have a dynamically assigned IP address. To implement this scenario, you would configure the external NIC card to receive its IP address dynamically (right click **My Network Places** on SBS desktop and select **Properties**).

Notes:

Figure 9-25

Proof positive the DHCP Client filter is disabled by default in SBS 2000.

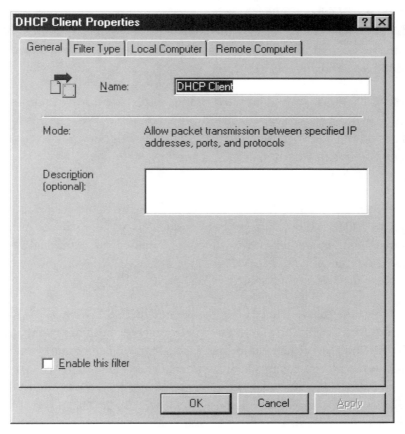

BEST PRACTICE: Note my discussion above relates to external rogue DHCP servers. A rogue server on the "inside" of your SBS network (which is the 192.168.16.x subnet by default) will still cause the DHCP Server service on the SBS 2000 server machine to shut down and create operational problems to say the least.

Changing an Internet Domain Name

Perhaps you already suspect why I'm doing with this. When it comes to changing an Internet domain name in SBS 2000, you can and you can't. First the "can" argument, followed by the "can't" argument.

Can

If the real question is whether you can change the Internet domain name in order to receive SMTP e-mail from a new domain name, the answer is yes, you can do this. Simply rerun the ICW and change the domain name in Step 10 in my ICW configuration steps earlier in the chapter (see Figure 9-18). This will update the Exchange 2000 Server recipient policies.

> BEST PRACTICE: You can even have multiple Internet domain names associated with your SBS server machine for SMTP e-mail purposes. This is accomplished by creating multiple recipient policies. I discuss recipient policies in Chapter 11.

Can't

If you're really asking whether the Active Directory domain name can easily be changed in SBS 2000, the answer is no. I present this discussion here because, more often than not, the internal Active Directory domain name is the same as your registered Internet domain name. This is the case with SSL and you made this entry in Chapter 3 during the setup of SBS.

In order to change the Active Directory domain name in SBS 2000, you basically have to reinstall SBS 2000. There is one trick where you can run **dcpromo** and demote the SBS 2000 server to a workgroup (and away from a domain). You then rerun the SBS setup process again and at the Scenario Baseline stage, you can define the new Active Directory domain name and proceed to reinstall all of the SBS applications. This is effectively a reinstallation of SBS 2000 and you'll lose your existing account and e-mail settings. But if you've changed your company name or merged with another company, let's face it, you may need to reinstall SBS 2000. Be sure to write that into your business plan!

> BEST PRACTICE: Any time you obtain or change an Internet domain name, be sure you're working hand in hand with your ISP. Your failure to do so will result, at a minimum, in a disruption of service.

Rogue and Roaming Users

At more SBS sites than I care to recall, there is always a couple of roaming and/ or rogue SBS users. First, let me talk about the rogue SBS users. These are the SBS users who insist on maintaining their existing ISP services (typically AOL,

MSN, or CompuServe). Often, these users have a local modem that they've used for years to call their ISP (and they're not interested in giving it up!). Because accommodating an SBS user's request is a virtue, I often permit these dual ISP service scenarios to exist. However, you must make one minor change at the SBS user's workstation to allow multiple ISP services to coexist.

This change is simple, but it must be managed by the end user because you, the SBS administrator, can't constantly be performing this action. First, you need to understand that, as part of the SBS client installation process, the Firewall Client applet is added to the SBS user's workstation Control Panel. It is automatically selected to redirect Internet-related activity, such as Web browsing, to the ISA Server running on the SBS server machine. A quick-link button for the Firewall Client is also added to the Start menu bar on the desktop on the right side next to the clock. This is normal and good.

But, when the SBS user wants to call AOL, MSN, or CompuServe, the user needs to disable the Firewall client. Simply click the **Firewall Client** link on the **Start Menu bar** and select **Disable** from the context menu that appears. You can also disable this capability via the **Firewall Client** applet in **Control Panel**. At that time, Internet traffic is not redirected to the **ISA Server** on the SBS server machine, and the SBS user can surf via AOL or her old ISP to her heart's content.

Likewise, when the AOL-type session is over, the same SBS user must reconfigure the Firewall Client by selecting the **Enable** from the **Firewall Client** context menu.

> BEST PRACTICE: Great news. Perhaps the only thing hated more than the tea tax in Boston over 225 years ago was the need to reboot the client computer after changing the proxy firewall setting in the SBS 4.5 era. It meant the rogue user had to reboot after to use AOL and then reboot again to use the SBS network. It was a major source of SBS user tension. In the SBS 2000 era, the end user doesn't have to reboot after changing the client-side firewall settings. Let the celebration start.

I end this chapter with a story about the prominent Northwest developer I featured extensively in the Outlook chapter (Chapter 12). This gentleman, a surprisingly savvy SBS user given his executive position, wanted to understand how he could easily use IE via the SBS network and ISA Server's firewall function on his laptop to connect to the Internet while at work. But he also used IE via a dial-up connection while on the road or at night when cuddling up with his Britanny Spaniel (yes, related to the Springer Spaniels so prominently featured in the SSL storyline of this book).

The problem he faced is a common one. In IE 5.x, you have to manually configure the proxy settings as seen above in Figure 9-23. Talk about a bummer. If you want to use IE via a dial-up modem connection while out of the office, you have to deselect the **Use a proxy server** check box on the **Local Area Network (LAN) Settings** dialog box. And it's vice-versa when you return to the office.

Troubleshooting Internet Connections

Talk about a book unto itself: troubleshooting Internet connections. In a few short sentences I can't educate you on this vast topic. Rather, after humoring you, please consult the SBS resources in Appendix A.

Take the Northwest shopping center owner who, prior to my arrival, had engaged the services of a low-cost ISP with some funky name I've long forgotten. The ISP pointed the MX record down to the external network adapter card on the server machine (which as inappropriately running nekkid Windows NT Server 4.0 with Exchange 5.0, by the way). I arrived on the scene and implemented SBS on a brand new server. Because the new server's external network adapter card used the exact same IP address, there was no apparent need to notify the ISP of the upgrade to SBS. WRONGO! After a couple billable hours of tail chasing, it turns out this ISP points the MX record to the external network adapter card by registering the MAC identification number of the network adapter card. Huh? In English, change the external network adapter card in any way shape for form, like a new server, and the new business doesn't receive its SMTP e-mail. Once discovered, this was fixed with a telephone call to the ISP, wherein I provided the MAC address for the external network adapter card for the new server running SBS. That was a strange event, to say the least.

Summary

What can I say at this point? There is perhaps no more important chapter in this book because I address a most important issue to SBSers: connecting your SBS network to the Internet. This chapter reviewed various SBS Internet connection scenarios. That was followed by a walkthrough of connecting SSL to the Internet with a full-time broadband connection. Then a whole bevy of advanced and random Internet connection topics, all related to SBS, were presented for your reading pleasure. In the next chapter, I make the leap to security issues surrounding use of the Internet in a small business.

Chapter 10
Using Internet Security and Acceleration Server

Just when you thought it was safe to go out in the SBS network neighborhood again, I throw the whole firewall security matter at you. This chapter explores the firewall issue in several ways. First, there is a basic definition section on firewalls. Not being a security niche specialist, I only provide introductory comments here. Note that at the end of the chapter I direct you to some detailed security resources. Next I focus on Internet Security and Acceleration (ISA) Server 2000 and explain how it was configured as part of the Internet Connection Wizard (ICW) in Chapter 9. After this, I present the well-hidden naughty and nice reports that allow you to monitor Internet usage. Next, a walkthrough of configuring ISA Server to accommodate the needs of Internet applications is provided, where you will open ports. This is followed by a discussion about how ISA Server acts as a gateway and a router. I also have an advanced discussion on using a hardware-based firewall instead of ISA Server and the importance of staying current with security patches.

And, have no fear, I'll be weaving the Springer Spaniels Limited (SSL) method-ology into this chapter just like all the others.

ISA Basics

It may be news to you that, if you did nothing more than install SBS 2000 and complete the ICW's Configure Packet Filter page by enabling ISA Server packet filtering, you would indeed have basic and effective firewall protection. Assum-ing you don't need the advanced security requirements for military contractors and financial institutions, this is sufficient protection from the Internet. Many an SBSer will never perform additional configuration work on ISA Server save for configuring the Virtual Private Network (VPN) capability in Chapter 13. So, since I've just summarized the whole firewall protection area as "just add water," this chapter is effectively done, right? Not so fast.

Defining the Need for ISA Server

Let's face it. You need to know a thing or three about firewall protection and ISA Server as an SBSer. Why? I've come up with a few reasons for reading this chapter and implementing ISA Server on your SBS network.

- **Curiosity**. It's just plain SBSer nature to wonder about the ebbs and flows of Internet goblins. There is a hunger amongst us to better understand security issues since SBS was designed to be connected to the Internet and, in many cases, connected full-time! Hey, from curious minds come better security decisions based on fact, not fiction and misunderstanding.

- **The Boss/Owner/Client**. Few of us operate truly independently, meaning we all have bosses at some level. So, if you're not that interested in Internet security, someone in your professional life, such as a boss or client, is. You better brief yourself on ISA Server basics so you can answer their questions.

- **Placating Your Attorney and CPA**. If you're interacting on the Internet for business purposes, your advisors – attorneys and CPAs (accountants), for example – will insist on effective and defensible security. That is, not only should the security protect confidential business information, such as client matters, but you need to be able to demonstrate to judge and jury that you tried your darnedest using acceptable solutions like ISA Server to protect your network from Internet hackers.

- **Minding the Store**. It's just a BEST PRACTICE in the truest sense. Who doesn't want to have protection for their business information? But that is an exterior view looking in. There is another view that has more of an insider's twist to it: the naughty and nice reports. Part of minding the store is monitoring how your internal users are behaving (or misbehaving if the shoe fits) in their use of the Internet. I explain the naughty and nice reports later in the chapter.

- **Nichers**. Perhaps you purchased and installed SBS 2000 to learn a little of this and a little of that of Microsoft's operating system and BackOffice offerings. Fair enough. Nothing like eating at a Texas-sized buffet to help you decide what your favorite dish is. I've seen it more than once: Someone dabbles with SBS because the price is right and then they take a keen interest in one of the components, such as ISA Server. Hail to the nichers of the SBS world.

Defining ISA Server Architecture

Hats off again to the SBS documentation team at Microsoft. If you right-click the **Internet Security and Acceleration Server 2000** snap-in in the **SBS Administrator Console** and select **Help**, followed by a click on the **Concepts** book, you'll more than learn everything you wanted to know about ISA Server. The online book explains in greater detail than I will here the following ISA Server firewall and caching capabilities:

1. **Application Filters.** One of the ISA Server control mechanisms is to use data-aware filters to manage application-specific traffic. Management includes accepting, modifying, redirecting, or rejecting specific-application traffic, subject to a filter. Look to third-party software developers to introduce ISA Server filters for their computer programs in the future.
2. **Authentication.** Several authentication modes are supported in ISA Server, including basic, client certificates, digest, and Integrated Windows authentication.
3. **Caching.** Several caching methods are supported, including distributed, hierarchical, scheduled, forward, and reverse. With caching, the ISA Server stores recent copies of the Web pages that have been visited by users on the SBS network so the future access attempts are first made against the caches at LAN speeds. The stored Web pages are updated occasionally (the frequency of which can be modified by the SBS administrator). You might remember that you created the 100 MB cache on an SBS setup screen in Chapter 3. And as you'll see later in the chapter, the naughty and nice reports display the percentage of Web hits that were returned from cache.

BEST PRACTICE: Because an SBS network is kinda a world unto itself with a single Active Directory domain and the SBS server being the root of the Active Directory forest, these small business limitations impact how you might exploit certain ISA Server features. One of these impacted features is ISA Server caching. In reality, you're only going to take advantage of scheduled caching (where cache updates can be scheduled) and forward caching (which provides internal users with access to the Internet but checks requests against cache first). The other caching features relate to arrays of ISA Servers at the enterprise level.

4. **Intrusion Detection.** ISA Server can alert you anytime day or night if a specific type of attack (several attack types are supported, including port scanning) occurs.

5. **Outgoing Access Policy.** You can configure which users and security groups have access to the Internet, during what hours, and even which sites are allowed or restricted from visits. That last capability is via the Site and Content Rules. By default, in SBS 2000, all users are allowed 7X24 Internet access from the SBS network, assuming you have a functional connection to the Internet.

BEST PRACTICE: Just a tad of expectation management here. Site and Content rules are not a net nanny to the rescue. You might beware that there are several services on the Internet that can be used to restrict Web surfers from inappropriate adult sites on the Internet. This is accomplished by subscribing to such a service, one of which is actually called Net Nanny at www.netnanny.com. All Web-bound traffic is compared to a huge database of adult Web sites and you are denied access to off-limit locations. The Net Nanny entity is constantly updating its database tables with new naughty Web sites as those sites seem to bloom like flowers during the spring in Texas hill country! Site and Content rules allow you to specify sites to which access is disallowed, so, to be honest, the list you could reasonably expect to provide would be relatively short compared to the naughty Web site database maintained by Net Nanny.

6. **VPN Wizard.** The one ISA Server security wizard you will use as part of the SSL methodology is the ISA Server VPN Wizard. This is where you configure ISA Server to allow users to establish a VPN connection and work on the SBS network from remote locations. The ISA Server VPN Wizard is discussed in detail and step-by-step with the SSL methodology in Chapter 13.

BEST PRACTICE: By the way, many SBS sites that deploy ISA Server still use a hardware-based firewall, which is discussed later in the chapter. So, the question posed to you is this: Why would you use ISA Server if you are using a hardware-based firewall? The answer is caching. Many sites enjoy the increased Web retrieval speed facilitated by caching frequently accessed Web content on the SBS 2000 server using ISA Server. This is especially apparent when using a dial-up connection with slow Internet access speed or remote sites that have expensive Internet connections (read third-world and developing-country locations) whereby the Web pages can be cached locally and updated once a day.

I've not personally worked with hardware-based firewalls that provide a sufficient Web caching solution, so chalk one score up to ISA Server over hardware-based solutions.

One thing you might have noticed is the changing face of ISA Server compared to Proxy Server 2.0 that was contained in SBS 4.5. You will recall that Proxy Server 2.0 was actually managed as a snap-in in the Internet Information Server (IIS) MMC. It was here that several services were listed, including Web Proxy Server services (this was the main service in Proxy Server 2.0 that regulated Web surfing). ISA Server has been dramatically re-architected from its predecessor in look, feel, and complexity. ISA Server is managed from the Internet Security and Acceleration Server 2000 snap-in in the SBS Administrator Console, as seen in Figure 10-1.

Figure 10-1
Meet the ISA Server snap-in where you will perform ISA Server-related configurations as necessary.

Services that relate specifically to ISA Server include the following:

- **Microsoft Firewall.** Provides firewall protection to Firewall and SecureNAT clients.

- **Microsoft H.323 Gatekeeper.** Supports communication with H.323 Gatekeeper-compliant applications.

- **Microsoft ISA Server Control.** Controls ISA Server services.

- **Microsoft Scheduled Cache Content Download.** Downloads cache content from Web servers based on specified scheduled jobs.

- **Microsoft Web Proxy.** Provides Web connectivity to Web Proxy clients. This service support amongst other things, the HTTP and HTTPS protocol standards.

- **World Wide Web Publishing Service.** Provides Web connectivity and administration through the Internet Information Service snap-in.

BEST PRACTICE: Not only was the ISA Server component one of the last applications to join the SBS Suite, added just weeks prior to SBS 2000's release-to-manufacturing date, it's a component more in common with its enterprise space than the small business space. How can I share that with you? If you look at the other SBS components, they've been, shall we say, SBSed. For example, Exchange 2000 Server has both the SmallBusiness SMTP connector and the Connector for POP3 Mailboxes. There are features unique to how Exchange 2000 Server is deployed in SBS. But in ISA Server, did you notice the user interface (UI) element called **Servers and Arrays** in Figure 10-1? That's enterprise talk when you say arrays because it highly unlikely you'd have an array of ISA Servers in SBS 2000. Personally, I'd like to just see that UI element say Servers.

Configuring ISA Server

As I've alluded to already, you will perform very little configuration work with ISA Server in SBS 2000. Much of the configuration tasks are performed in three locations:

- **Small Business Server Setup.** The SBS setup process has several ISA Server configuration screens. The first ISA Server-related setup screen you will encounter is the **ISA Server Cache Drives** screen shown in

Figure 3-17 of Chapter 3, where SBS proposed a 100 MB cache on the %system drive% (which is typically C: drive). Next, you complete the **ISA Server Construct Local Address Table** screen, where you tell ISA server how to build the Local Address Table (LAT). This typically includes browsing the network for known internal address ranges and using the subnet address range allocated to the internal network adapter card (192.168.16.2 – X). This is seen in Figure 3-18 of Chapter 3. Next, on the **ISA Server Local Address Table Configuration** screen (shown in Figure 3-19 of Chapter 3), you have the chance to accept the automatically populated LAT subnet address ranges and even add your own. It might be useful to add your own subnet address range if you're effectively running a second network in your business, such as the legacy UNIX system at my former not-for-profit SBS client that was ultimately unprofitable for me to serve.

- **ICW - Configure Packet Filter.** This screen was displayed in Chapter 9 in Figure 9-19 and it is where you declare what forms of packet traffic are acceptable between the Internet and your SBS network. This is shown again here as Figure 10-2.

Figure 10-2
The ICW is used to set the baseline firewall settings in SBS.

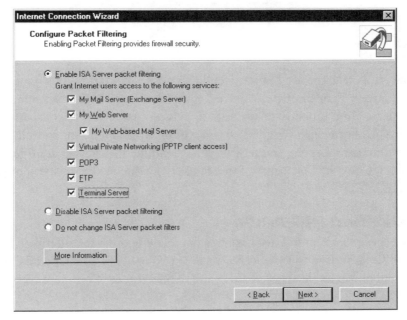

- **ISA VPN Wizard.** The ISA VPN Wizard is launched from the Configure a Local Virtual Private Network (VPN) link on the Configure Network Connection task pad shown in Figure 10-3. This is a wizard that is several screens in duration and is a central focus of Chapter 13.

Figure 10-3
The almighty ISA Server VPN Wizard is launched deep inside the ISA Server snap-in on the SBS Administrator Console.

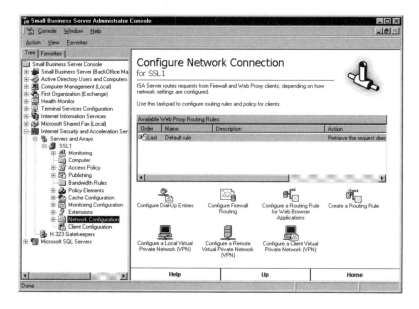

After that, it's off to the land of advanced ISA Server configurations. Later in this chapter, I have you open up ports needed by Exchange 2000 Conferencing Server in order to function properly on an SBS 2000 server machine. This is part of the SSL storyline, because in Chapter 11 you will install and configure Exchange 2000 Conferencing Server. You may well have unique ISA Server configuration needs that are beyond that scope of this book. Good luck and Godspeed to you my friend.

The Old Two NIC-A-Roo

No ISA Server architectural discussion is complete without the old two NIC-a-roo. Here I'm referring to ISA Server's use of two network adapter cards: one internal and one external. These cards were defined on the Configure Network

Adapters screen of the ICW (see Figure 9-15 in Chapter 9). Basically what you're doing here is using two network adapter cards to create a Great Barrier Reef (GBR) between the evils of the Internet and the goodness of your internal SBS network. This is shown in Figure 10-4. You will see that I'm using the terms "network adapter cards" and "NICs" interchangeably in this section.

Figure 10-4

Viewing the old two NIC-a-roo.

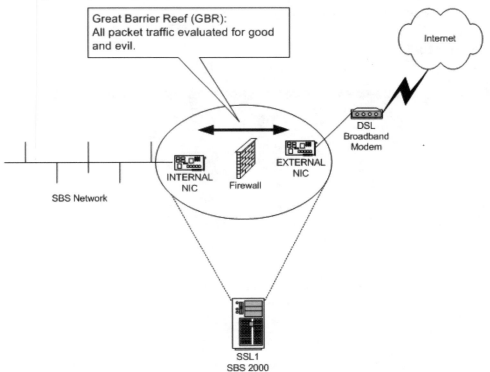

Note that you can do great harm by inadvertently circumventing the intent of the properly configured two NIC-a-roo. When I've seen this setting implemented in the past, it's typically by mistake. To be frank, it's a smarty pants MCSE who learned this cool technique in their enterprise-level MCSE training class and then applied it to an SBS server. IP forwarding between two network adapter cards has the effect of bypassing the GBR zone managed by ISA Server. To see if IP forwarding has been enabled on SBS 2000, you need to dig deep down for that gold nugget. Perform the following steps:

1. Log on to **SSL1** as the **Administrator** with the password **husky9999**.
2. Click **Start**, **Run** and type **regedit** in the **Open** field of the **Run** dialog box.
3. Expand the tree view to the following location:
   HKEY_LOCAL_MACHINE\SYSTEM\CurrentControlSet\ Services\Tcpip\Parameters.
4. Click **IPEnableRouter** and observe that the **REG_DWORD** value is **0x0000000 (0)** by default, which means IP routing has been disabled. This is seen in Figure 10-5 and confirms ISA Server is empowered to works its GBR magic for you.

Figure 10-5
The "zero" values in IPEnableRouter mean the routing capability is turned off.

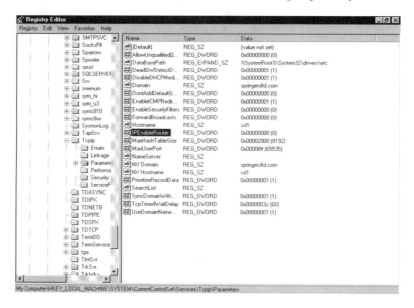

BEST PRACTICE: I'm honor-bound to say that you should not change **IPEnableRouter** value to **0x0000001 (1)** in the **Edit DWORD Value** dialog box that is disabled by double-clicking the existing entry. To do so would enable IP routing and render ISA Server's GBR useless.

How Users Are Impacted

So how are users impacted by ISA Server? In several ways. First, all users are granted Internet access by default in SBS 2000. This is different from SBS 4.5 where users were explicitly denied access to the Internet unless you specifically allowed for it in the Add User Wizard. Well times change, and in SBS 2000 you may have noticed in Chapter 4 that the Add User Wizard didn't have a screen that specifically allowed you to set Internet access permissions.

> BEST PRACTICE: I've just told you something of a Texas tall tale. There actually is a screen in the Add User Wizard that allows you to elect whether a particular user is granted Internet access. When running the **Add User Wizard**, if you select the **View the template to change properties for this user** check box on the **User Properties** screen, you will be exposed to all of the background settings being completed for you based on the user template you've selected. Click **Next** and the **Group Membership** screen appears in Figure 10-6, showing the default membership in the **BackOffice Internet Users Group**. This membership is applied to all users.

Figure 10-6

Observing how users are allowed Internet access by default on the Group Membership screen.

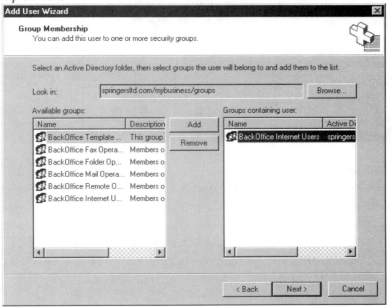

There is one other screen that relates to ISA Server settings that I'll share with you now. If you complete the ISA VPN Wizard when you read Chapter 13, the Allow access and Deny access on the Dial-in tab of the user's property sheet takes on an important meaning. As seen for Melinda Overlaking in Figure 10-7, she is denied the ability to establish a VPN connection to the SSL network. Granted, this point relates more to remote access and will be discussed in greater depth in Chapter 13.

Figure 10-7
By default, regular users are denied the right to establish a VPN connection on an SBS network. Power Users and Administrators are allowed access.

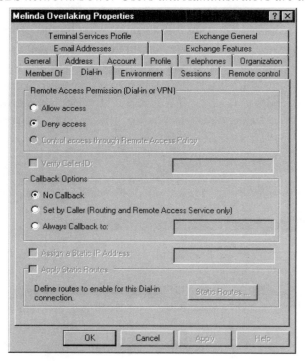

Naughty and Nice Reports

Some of my SBS clients are control freaks who want to snoopervise users on Internet usage. Some are motivated by deeply held religious beliefs that viewing pornographic sites is simply wrong and immoral. Others have financial motivations that employees should work, not play, during business hours at their place of employment. Interestingly, with some of these control freaks, they often don't care what you do with your own computer at home on your own time.

At first blush, I thought the wonderful naughty and nice reports had been eliminated from SBS 2000. These are reports that take the nearly unreadable raw
Internet activity data, shown below, and put on a happy face with a readable
pseudo Crystal Reports look and feel (in fact, older versions of SBS actually used
a run-time version of Crystal Reports to render the naughty and nice reports).
Here is the "raw" ISA Server logs (ouch!) as seen in Figure 10-8.

Figure 10-8

*The raw reports that hold the secrets as to who has been naughty or nice on the
Internet.*

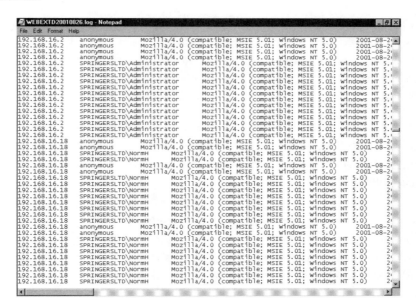

BEST PRACTICE: If you must, you can view the raw ISA Server logs
at:**%system drive%\Program Files\Microsoft ISA Server\ISA Logs**.
However, read on in this section for how to view this data in a friendly
report format.

Fist, you must create a report job. Perform these steps.

1. Log on to **SSL1** as **Administrator** with the password **husky9999**.
2. Click **Start, Small Business Server Administrator Console**.

3. Expand the **Internet Security and Acceleration Server 2000** snap-in.
4. Expand **Servers and Arrays**.
5. Expand the **SSL1** server object.
6. Expand **Monitoring Configuration**.
7. Right-click the **Report Jobs** folder and select **New**, **Report Job**.
8. The **Report Job Properties** dialog box appears. Type **SSL Naughty and Nice Reports** in the **Name** field.
9. Select the **Period** tab and select **Monthly**.
10. Select the **Schedule** tab and select **Immediately**.

BEST PRACTICE: It is on the Schedule tab that you could have the report run every day at a specific time. You could elect to only generate the report once per month. For the SSL methodology, you have selected the option to generate the reports immediately so that you can see your reports instantly.

11. Select the **Credentials** tab and complete the three fields that are displayed. In the **Username** field, type **Administrator**. In the **Domain** name field, type **SPRINGERSLTD**. In the password field, type **husky9999**.

BEST PRACTICE: In the **Domain** field of the **Credentials** page, you will type the internal NetBIOS domain name, not the external Internet domain name. This is very clear, but you can prove this by trying to type **SPRINGERLTD.COM** and observing that the field isn't wide enough to accommodate this entry.

12. Click **OK** to close the **Report Job Properties** dialog box.

Next, surf to the naughty and nice Web sites of your choice. A nice site to consider is one of my favorites, www.sbsfaq.com. Then complete these steps to look at the naughty and nice reports.

1. Log on to **SSL1** as **Administrator** with the password **husky9999**.
2. Click **Start**, **Small Business Server Administrator Console**.
3. Expand the **Internet Security and Acceleration Server 2000** snap-in.
4. Expand **Servers and Arrays**.

5. Expand the **SSL1** server object.
6. Expand **Monitoring**.
7. Expand **Reports**.

BEST PRACTICE: Even though the report job is displayed in the details pane when you click on Reports, you can't launch the naughty and nice reports from here. Move on to Step #8.

8. Expand **Summary** and double-click the **SSL Naughty and Nice Reports** entry. An IW Web browser is launched that displays the SSL1 Array Summary Reports.
9. Click on the **Top Users** link on the left. As seen in Figure 10-9, NormH is the top user.

Figure 10-9

NormH just edged out the Administrator as the top user in this example.

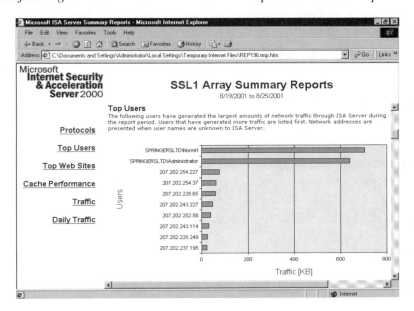

10. Click on the **Top Web Sites** link and observe Figure 10-10. It appears some Web surfing has been nice, such as entries number two (www.microsoft.com) and number seven (www.cbsnews.com). However,

some surfing has been naughty, as in entries number three (www.penthouse.com) and number ten (www.playboy.com).

Figure 10-10

Some SBS users have been naughty and some have been nice, if you look closely at the URLs of the Top Web Sites report.

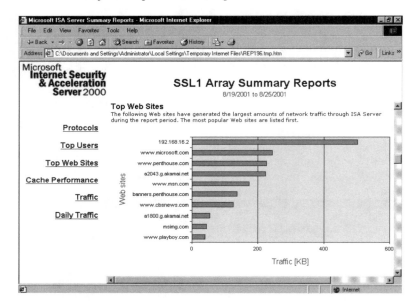

BEST PRACTICE: What the naughty and nice reports do not do is relate which user was naughty and which user was nice. That is, the Top Web Sites report shows total hits as an SBS network, not by individual. To find out which specific user has been naughty, you'd need to look directly at the ISA Server logs shown earlier in Figure 10-8.

Note that the reports won't be compiled until enough data has been collected. For example, a weekly report won't be created and displayed until a week has passed.

11. Selecting the **Cache Performance** link shows a pie chart of how many hits are drawn from cache. This is displayed in Figure 10-11.

Figure 10-11

In the case of SSL, the Cache Performance report indicates that most hits are returned from the Internet, not cache.

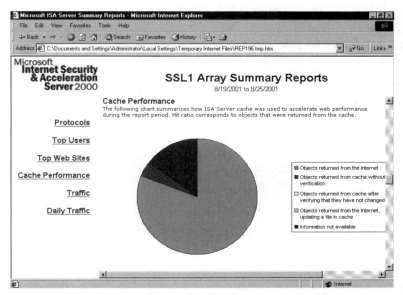

12. Click the **Traffic** link to display the **Traffic** report. This shows traffic over a range of dates.

13. Click **Daily Traffic** to observe traffic by time of day for a specific day. This is shown in figure 10-12.

Notes:

Figure 10-12

The Daily traffic report is very valuable to observe when most of the Web surfing activity is occurring. For example, too much Web surfing over lunch might indicate horseplay by the employees at the firm.

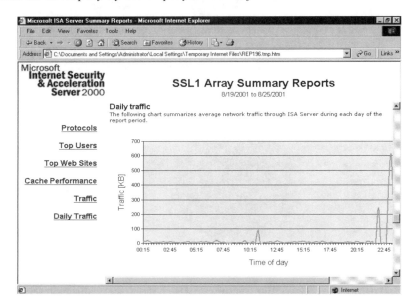

BEST PRACTICE: Matter of factly, I've used the **Daily traffic** report to exonerate the wrongly charged in organizations more often than to obtain convictions for naughty behavior. Here's what I mean (as in the reports are a double-edged sword just like DNA evidence in criminal proceedings). An employee is suspected of surfing the Web for pornography on a company workstation. Perhaps this was determined by a supervisor viewing the History folder in Internet Explorer. But upon closer inspection, it might be revealed that the employee had left a workstation logged on each night and there was unusually high traffic at 1 a.m. when the janitors perform their work. I've now introduced reasonable doubt in the equation and allowed the shaken employee to retain his job. Whew!

Configuring ISA Server

One configuration example that I want to talk you through is how to configure firewall ports so that Exchange 2000 Conferencing Server can run on an SBS server that uses ISA Server as its firewall. This information is based on the Microsoft KBase article from Product Support Services titled "**Q158623: How To Establish NetMeeting Connections Through A Firewall**" The firewall ports needed by NetMeeting are the same as the ports needed by Exchange Conferencing Server. You will open the firewall ports listed in Table 10-1:

Table 10-1: ISA Firewall Ports Opened For Exchange Conferencing Server.

Port	Purpose
389	TCP – Internet Locator Server
522	TCP – User Location Server
1503	TCP – T.120
1720	TCP – H.323 call setup
1731	TCP – Audio call control
Dynamic	H.323 call control and H.323 streaming (RDP over UDP). You will pass through secondary UDP connections on dynamically assigned ports 1024-65535.

You will complete the following as part of the SSL methodology.

1. Log on to **SSL1** as **Administrator** with the password **husky9999**.
2. Click **Start, Small Business Server Administrator Console**.
3. Expand the **Internet Security and Acceleration Server 2000** snap-in.
4. Expand **Servers and Arrays**.
5. Expand the **SSL1** server object.
6. Expand **Access Policy**.
7. Click **IP PacketFilter** and select **Taskpad** from the **View** menu. .
8. Click on the **Create a Packet Filter** link shown in Figure 10-13.

Figure 10-13

Clicking the Create a Packet Filter link is where you start the journey to open firewall ports.

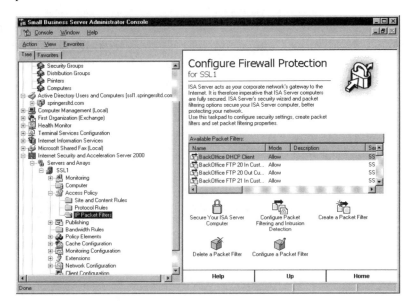

9. The **New IP Packet Filter Wizard** launches. Type **TCP – Internet Locator Server** in the **IP packet filter name** field. Note the filter name as taken from the Purpose column of Table 10-1. Click **Next.**

10. On the **Filter Mode** screen, select **Allow packet transmission** and click **Next**.

11. On the **Filter Type** screen, select **Custom** and click **Next**.

12. Complete the **Filter Settings** screen similar to Figure 10-14. Click **Next.**

Notes:

Figure 10-14

The mechanics of opening Port 389 for the TCP protocol.

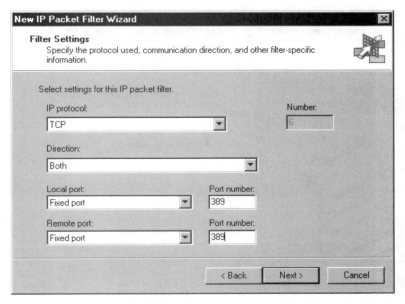

13. On the **Local Computer** screen, accept the **Default IP addresses for each external interface on the ISA Server computer** selection and click **Next**.
14. On the **Remote Computers** screen, select **All remote computers** and click **Next**.
15. Observe the summary information shown in Figure 10-15 on the **Completing the New IP Packet Filter Wizard** and click **Finish**. You've just shot a hole through the firewall by design.

Notes:

Figure 10-15

This summary information can be copied and pasted into your network notebook for future reference.

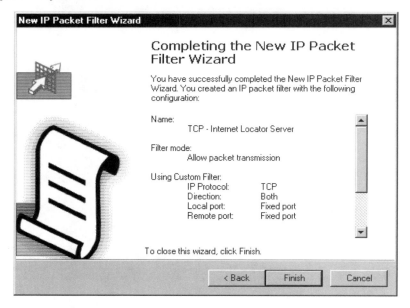

Now you need to repeat Steps 8 through 15 for each of the remaining ports in Table 10-1. This should be a fairly routine set of keystrokes for you to perform. For the last entry, Figure 10-16 shows the Filter Settings screen configuration for the dynamic UDP ports.

Notes:

Figure 10-16
Configuring the UDP ports. Remember that these are not open all of the time, but rather are opened dynamically as needed by Exchange Conferencing Server.

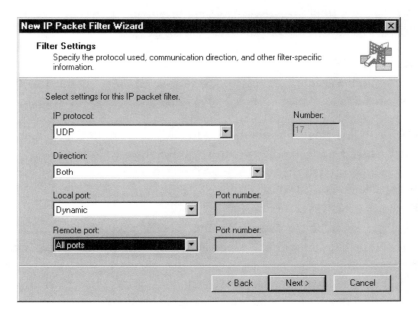

BEST PRACTICE: You should also see the KBase article "**Q278339 TCP/UDP Ports Used By Exchange 2000 Server**" for even more detailed information about all IS Server ports used by Exchange Conferencing Server.

Notes:

Advanced Internet Security Topics

In this section, I discuss a hodgepodge of advanced security topics that relate to using ISA Server on an SBS network. This includes caching settings, autodial configuration, the use of hardware-based firewalls, and the importance of applying security patches.

Hyperactive Caching

You can configure the caching aggressiveness in ISA Server by completing the following steps. First, you must turn on Active Caching.

1. Log on to **SSL1** as **Administrator** with the password **husky9999**.
2. Click **Start, Small Business Server Administrator Console**.
3. Expand the **Internet Security and Acceleration Server 2000** snap-in.
4. Expand **Servers and Arrays**.
5. Expand the **SSL1** server object.
6. Right-click **Cache Configuration** and select **Properties**.
7. The **Cache Configuration Properties** dialog box appears. Click on the **Active Caching** tab.
8. Select the **Enable active caching** check box. Observe that **Normally** is selected by default in Figure 10-17.

BEST PRACTICE: In SBS 2000, note that Active Caching is disabled by default. This is exactly the opposite of how previous editions of SBS handled this, where Active Caching was enabled. One of the big complaints in past SBS versions was that Active Caching generated too many dial-outs via modems (where modems were the Internet connection approach). In fact, at a construction company client of mine during the good old days of SBS 4.5, I well recall the day that I was called out to explore "phantom" modem dial-outs Turns out the Active Caching feature was updating cached Web pages with frequent dial-outs to the Internet.

Note: You would invoke hyperactive caching by selecting **Frequently** on the **Active Caching** tab on the **Cache Configuration Properties** page.

Figure 10-17

Turning on active caching is accomplished on the Active Caching tab.

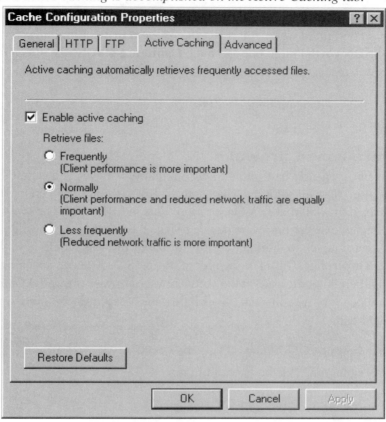

9. Click **OK**.

You've now invoked Active Caching on SBS 2000. And if you followed the BEST PRACTICE above, you've also invoked hyperactive caching.

> BEST PRACTICE: By invoking active caching, you will also modify the ratio in the caching pie chart of Figure 10-11. More Web hits will come from cache than was previously the case.

Dial on Demand

In the old days of SBS 4.x, you might recall that Proxy Server could be configured for dial-up activity. In ISA Server and SBS 2000, the dial-on-demand
capability is configured when you select the **Modem or terminal adapter
(example ISDN cards)** radio button on the **Configure Hardware** screen of the
ICW. This was discussed in Chapter 9. No additional configuration is necessary.

Note that a dial-on-demand failure will be reported as an ISA Server entry in the
Application event log.

Hardware-based firewalls

On any given day, nearly half of the SBS community believes you should have a
hardware-based firewall solution. That is, these SBSers don't fully endorse the
software-based firewall that ISA Server represents in SBS 2000. The reasons vary
from wanting an exterior hardware device to take the brunt of the abuse in a
denial of service attack to thinking a software-based firewall should never be run
on a domain controller (DC). For the record, the SBS 2000 server machine is a
DC. I'm not here to participate in the software vs. hardware firewall debate in
this chapter, but simply to present how a hardware-based firewall solution is
implemented with SBS 2000.

The solution that I intend to implement is Pivio from Crossport Systems in
Bellevue, Washington. This is shown in Figure 10-18.

Notes:

Figure 10-18

Pivio is a hardware-based firewall solution for small business networks such as SBS 2000.

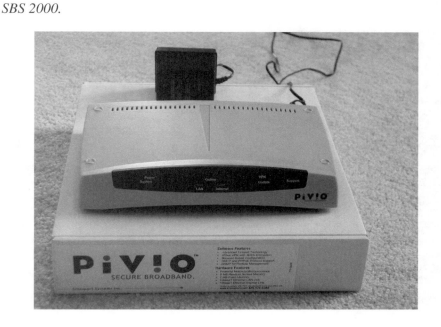

Hardware firewalls such as Pivio start at a couple of hundred dollars (US) and go up from there. Different hardware-based firewall solutions have different twists. In the case of Pivio, its purchase and use is tied to subscribing to a monthly security monitoring service. This is described at www.crossport.com, shown in Figure 10-19.

Notes:

Figure 10-19

For a modest monthly fee starting at under $100, Crossport Systems will monitor your hardware firewall.

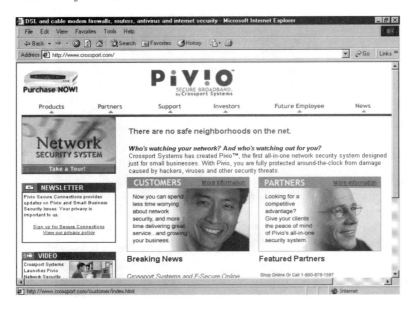

So, time to put the pedal to the metal. To configure SBS 2000 to use a hardware-based firewall, you'll basically complete three phases.:

Physical

You will physically attach the router to the network and plug it in. Note that the hardware-based firewall will be plugged into the hub on the SBS network from its LAN port because you'll use a single network adapter card (not the two NIC-a-roo described earlier in the chapter). That's because the hardware-based firewall, in this case, Pivio, have both a LAN and an Internet port. This is shown in Figure 10-20. In Figure 10-21, you can see how the Pivio hardware-based firewall fits into the SBS network. Pivio's Internet port is plugged into the back of the broadband router (in the case of SSL, this is a Cisco 675 router).

Figure 10-20

The left port is the LAN port and the right port is the Internet port (also known as the "wild side," WAN or external port).

Notes:

Figure 10-21

The LAN port is plugged into the hub on the SBS network. The Internet port is attached to the back of the broadband router.

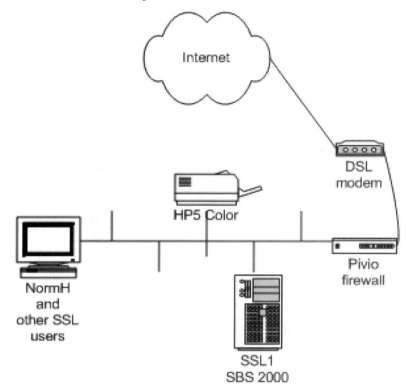

Router configuration

You will use a Telnet session or Web browser to attach to and configure the router. The configuration information is typically provided by your ISP and relates to how the LAN and Internet ports are configured with IP addresses. In the case of Pivio, insert the Disc that accompanies the hardware into the CD Disc drive on the SSL1 server. The **Welcome to Pivio** screen appears as seen in Figure 10-22.

Notes:

Figure 10-22
Welcome to Pivio.

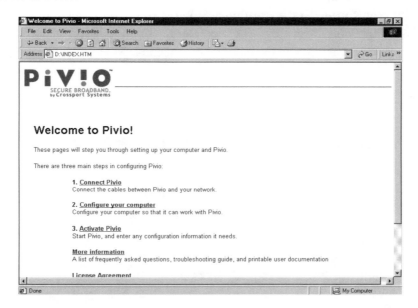

Screens will vary depending on the hardware firewall manufacturer, but basically you are provided configuration information as requested. In the case of SBS 2000, might I suggest the router be configured for the address 192.168.16.1 (one address below the default LAN IP address on the SBS server, such as SSL1). The subnet mask is 255.255.255.0.

Run ICW

You will now run the Internet Connection Wizard and complete the following steps.

1. Log on to **SSL1** as **Administrator** with the password **husky9999**.
2. Click **Start, Small Business Server Administrator Console**.
3. Click the **Favorites** drop-down menu, select **Small Business Server Tips** and select **Internet**.
4. The **Tips – Connecting to the Internet** page appears. Click **Manage Connections**.

5. The **Internet Connection Wizard** launches. Click **Next** at the **Welcome to the Small Business Server Internet Connection Wizard** screen.

6. Select **Router** on the **Configure Hardware** screen, as seen in Figure 10-23. And don't hesitate to click the **Router form** to help you correctly complete the ICW in the next few steps. Click **Next**.

Figure 10-23
Select the Router radio button.

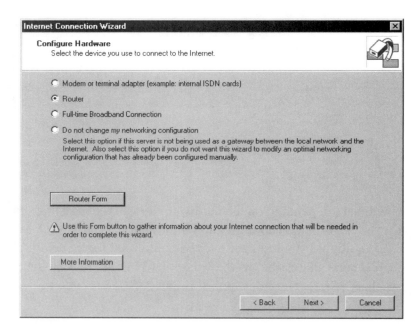

7. Complete the **Set Up Router Connection to ISP** screen similar to Figure 10-24. In this case, if you followed my thinking, the router's LAN port is 192.168.6.1 (a reserved IP address that is allowed in SBS 2000 for another device). Click **Next**.

Notes:

Figure 10-24
You enter the hardware-based firewall's local IP address. Note this is a single NIC scenario.

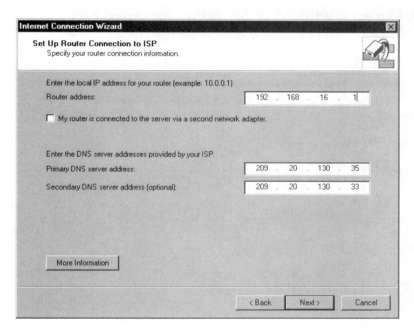

8. On the **Configure Network Adapter** screen, notice you only tell SBS 2000 which card is the local network card if you previously had two network cards installed and configured. The external network selection is grayed out. This is shown in Figure 10-25. Click **Next**.

Notes:

Figure 10-25

If your SBS server has two NIC cards, select which one is the inside card.

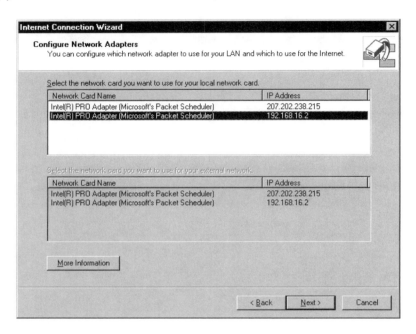

You will now complete the ICW in a manner similar to that described in Chapter 9. You would provide Exchange 2000 Server e-mail information, packet filtering information, domain name information, and so on. At the end, you will click **Finish** and the configuration for a hardware-based firewall solution will be implemented. You will click **OK** when the configuration tasks are complete.

BEST PRACTICE: If you've forgotten the remaining ICW configuration steps, start with Step 9 next to Figure 9-17 in Chapter 9 and continue to Step 15.

Security Patches

In all likelihood, there isn't a perfect firewall in existence. Witness how the CODE RED worm was able to penetrate into SBS 2000 servers and disable IIS in the late summer of 2001. Of course, Microsoft had released the CODE RED patch much earlier than the outbreak, and once network administrators FINALLY applied it life continued as normal. But you should be diligent and monitor the Microsoft Web site at www.microsoft.com/technet/security for announcements of fixes, patches, and service packs for ISA Server. Just as sure as it rains in Seattle in the winter, you'll find that ISA Server vulnerabilities are exposed from time to time. Hey – the good news is that at least you've got a company the size of Microsoft with its legions of blue-card coders to quickly kick out ISA Server patches, fixes, and service packs as necessary.

> BEST PRACTICE: Tattoo this one on your forehead. Don't ever fall into the trap as an SBSer whereby you communicate to a boss, owner, or client that ISA Server guarantees nothing bad will enter from the Internet. Business people like assurances and they might well try to trap you in a box canyon. They'll solicit comments that no Internet evil will occur because you've installed SBS with ISA Server. Such is not the case. Rather, you should take the SBSer position that ISA Server is an effective firewall that provides reasonable protection from the Internet. If more Internet security is needed, then the firm should not be connected to the Internet. Not being connected to the Internet is the highest form of Internet security known to the SBS community.

Resources

Internet security, the primary thrust of ISA Server, is an ever-changing and evolving area. You'll need to cast an eye toward developments in the security community. I have three ideas for you to consider.

> BEST PRACTICE: Scoot to the Microsoft SBS Web site and navigate to the following article titled: How to Maintain a Secure Small Business Server Installation. This is a MUST READ for all SBSers and can be found specifically at: http://support.microsoft.com/support/kb/articles/q303/3/23.asp?id=303323.

Roberta Bragg

World-renowned computer security author Roberta Bragg is a dear friend of the SBS community. She in fact runs her own small business and has consulted to other small businesses over the years. Roberta Bragg has several computer books on the market, including one book dedicated to ISA Server. Her monthly column, *Security Advisor*, shown in Figure 10-26 is well-received and thought-provoking.

Figure 10-26

A must-read is Roberta's column at Microsoft Certified Professional Magazine (www.mcpmag.com).

Security Newsletters and Web sites

There are numerous security newsletters circulating, and I don't proclaim to know all of them. But I've been receiving the *Security UPDATE* for years and like its timeliness. To subscribe, send a blank e-mail to **subscribe-Security_UPDATE@list.win2000mag.net**. A Web site recommended by this newsletter is www.windowsitsecurity.com as seen in Figure 10-27.

Figure 10-27

A security site supported by Windows 2000 Magazine is a top security resource for you to monitor.

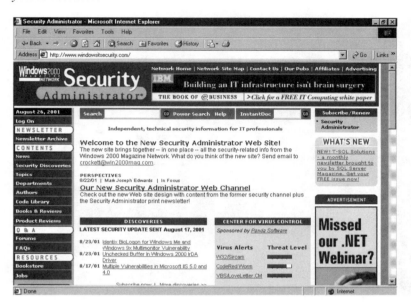

Take a Security Consultant to Lunch

Finally – take a security consultant to lunch and develop both a business and personal relationship with this most valuable person (MVP!). Having a security guru an e-mail or telephone call away does wonders for an SBSer. In the spirit of the SSL methodology, might I suggest the pub in Figure 10-28 on Bainbridge Island as the location for your lunch with your security buddy? Brisker, Jaeger, and all of the other Springer Spaniels at SSL would be proud of you!

Figure 10-28
You can take your security consultant to this pub near SSL on Bainbridge Island, Washington.

Summary

This is certainly one of the more important chapters in this book no matter how you slice it. Few topics cause more stress in the SBS world than Internet security. This chapter set out to accomplish several aggressive goals, including both introducing you to and having you configure ISA Server. General security topics were presented and you were even shown how to use a hardware-based firewall on an SBS 2000 network. Oh – and who could forget the time we devoted to dissecting the naughty and nice reports! On to Exchange 2000 Server in Chapter 11. See you there, pardner.

Chapter 11
Configuring Microsoft Exchange 2000 Server

Truth be told, out of the box Microsoft Exchange 2000 Server is a ready-to-roll application. Very little configuration is necessary to provide robust e-mail, scheduling, and groupware support for Outlook 2000. That darn thing just works from day one, period. Oh sure, you'll need to complete a few screens in the Internet Connection Wizard (ICW) if you want (and who doesn't?) Internet e-mail capabilities (SMTP or POP3). But otherwise, it's entirely possible that, as an SBSer, you'll have very little interaction at the nuts-and-bolts level of managing Exchange 2000 Server.

> BEST PRACTICE: Don't let my ease-of-use comments dissuade you from believing that you're not working with the real Exchange 2000 Server. You are! In fact, my enterprise-level Exchange guru buddy, who, by the way, has implemented an SBS network for his church in his spare time, provided the following unique perspective. His basic position is that the average SBSer knows more about Exchange than they give themselves credit for. As long as Exchange is providing its support for internal messaging and groupware along with Internet e-mail, you've likely got 80 percent of the Exchange 2000 Server functionality down. In most organizations, you'd function just fine. The missing 20 percent, something you could master, not necessarily in a fortnight but over the course of a year, relates to optimizing Exchange 2000 Server. And it is here you're on your own as you go to the next level. This would include Exchange sites and support for foreign e-mail systems.
>
> You might find it interesting to know that one service related to advanced Exchange 2000 Server functionality is disabled. That's the Microsoft Exchange Site Replication Service. By default, Exchange 2000 Server in SBS 2000 is optimized to only support one site. That is, inter-

site communications in Exchange 2000 Server under SBS are not supported. To enjoy this support, you'd need to upgrade your network to Big BackOffice or the full Microsoft Servers family.

So this chapter isn't about mastering Exchange 2000 Server. Like many components in SBS 2000, this one could truly be a big thick book in its own right. In fact, searching on the keywords "Microsoft Exchange 2000 Server" yielded 30 matches, and many of these books had four stars (or higher) ratings. No sir, this chapter is about extending Exchange 2000 Server with a couple of add-ons that many SBSers will find to be cool: Instant Messaging and Exchange Conferencing Server. Advance topics will be discussed at the end of the chapter. And, as always, the topics presented herein will be in the context of Springer Spaniels Limited (SSL), the sample company used in this book.

Instant Messaging

Believe it or not, Instant Messaging (IM) is gaining momentum in the SBS community. Sure, the old form of IM in small companies – standing and yelling "Hey you!" – worked fine for generations. But my client, Surface Engineering in Sunnyvale, California, taught me the importance of IM in a small business. This company is in the precision machining industry that kept its old NetWare server around in part so it could run the NoteWorks popup messaging service (this was kinda similar to the chat applet in Windows For Workgroups 3.11 a generation ago). Dick, the founder and president, claimed that NoteWorks historically met his needs in two ways. First, if he was already on a telephone call, he could receive a popup note that told him a telephone call was waiting on line two or someone was in the lobby to greet him. Second, the ability to communicate in real-time across his physical plant, which includes a large and noisy machining area where "Hey you!" doesn't cut it, was needed.

Needless to say, Dick and his Sunnyvale company were bright-eyed when they learned SBS 2000 contains IM support in Exchange 2000 Server. It's likely that you (or your clients if you're a consultant) will see great value in introducing IM on the SBS 2000 network at some point.

So, let's get started. You'll follow a handful of procedures in this section, so go ahead and refill the coffee first.

I assume you installed the IM component in Chapter 3 as part of the SBS server setup (see the discussion surrounding Figure 3-14). But, if for some reason you were errant and didn't follow the step-by-step SBS 2000 setup in Chapter 3, your first procedure will be to add the server-side Instant Messaging capability to Exchange 2000 Server. In all likelihood, most of you will NOT need to perform this first procedure.

1. Log on to **SSL1** as **Administrator** with the password **husky9999**.
2. Click **Start**, **Settings**, **Control Panel**, **Add/Remove Programs**.
3. Select **Microsoft Small Business Server 2000** and click **Change/Remove**.
4. Click **Next** at the **Welcome** page of the **Microsoft Small Business Server 2000 Setup Wizard**. Remember, there is a slight 5- to 10-second pause here before the next screen appears.
5. Click **Next** on the **Product Identification** screen.
6. On the **Automatic Logon Information** screen, type **husky9999** in the **Password** field and click **Next**.
7. Click **Next** on the **Company Information** screen.
8. Click **Next** on the **Telephony Information** screen.
9. Click **Next** on the **Domain Information** screen.
10. Finally, you reach the **Component Selection** screen. Expand **Microsoft Exchange 2000** and select **Microsoft Exchange Instant Messaging Service**. Click **Next**.
11. Click **Next** on the **Component Summary Screen**.
12. Insert **Disc 3** when requested and click **OK**.
13. Click **Finish** on the **Completing** screen.
14. Click **Yes** when notified that your system must be restarted.

BEST PRACTICE: Every time you run the SBS 2000 Setup Wizard and modify the SBS environment, the legacy service pack (Windows 2000 Server Service Pack 1) that shipped with SBS 2000 will typically run again (watch the setup screen closely to see if that occurs). If such is the case, that means you need to again run Windows 2000 Server Service Pack 2 and Microsoft Security Bulletin 44 (or its successors) again. Deploying additional service packs, hot fixes, upgrades, and patches was discussed in Chapter 7, so revisit that if needed

In this next procedure, you'll configure the server-side IM components.

1. Log on to **SSL1** as **Administrator** with the password **husky9999**.
2. Click **Start, Small Business Server Administrator Console**.
3. In the Tree pane, expand **SPRINGERSLTD (Exchange)**, **Servers**, **SSL1**, **Protocols**.
4. Right-click on the **Instant Messaging (RVP)** protocol and select **New**, **Instant Messaging Virtual Server** from the secondary menu.
5. Click **Next** on the **Welcome to the Virtual Server Wizard** screen of the **New Instant Messaging Virtual Server Wizard** screen.
6. In the **Display Name** field on the **Enter Display Name** screen, type **IM-SSL** and click **Next**. This is shown in Figure 11-1.

Figure 11-1
Naming the virtual server, which can have a different name than the NetBIOS name of the SBS 2000 server machine.

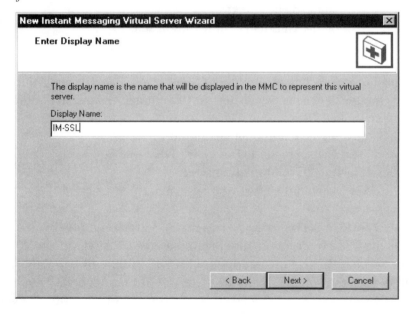

7. Accept the **Default Web Site** entry under **IIS Web Sites** on the **Choose IIS Web Site** screen and click **Next**. This is displayed in Figure 11-2.

BEST PRACTICE: This is one area that IIS interacts with other components. Break IIS in any way, form, or fashion and you can kiss IM functionality goodbye! I discuss IIS interaction with SBS 2000 in Chapter 17.

Figure 11-2
Just accept ye olde Default Web Site here.

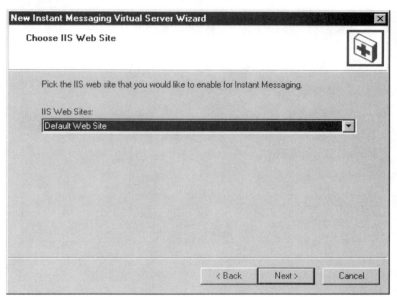

8. In the **DNS Domain Name** field on the **Domain Name** screen, accept **ssl1** as the **DNS Domain Name** and Port **80**. This is shown in Figure 11-3. Click **Next**.

Notes:

Figure 11-3

Please verify that your screen looks similar to this one with respect to DNS domain naming.

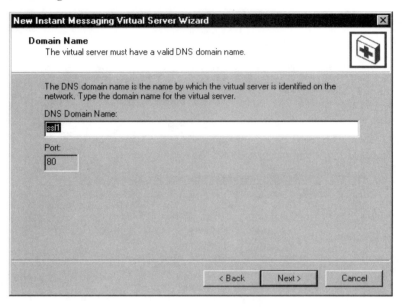

BEST PRACTICE: Call it a case of been there and done that, but DO NOT enter the NetBIOS domain name in Step 8 of springersltd.com. An IM domain is a strange, virtual beast. Just accept the **ssl1** suggested domain name and the remainder of the procedures will work. Otherwise they won't!

9.   Select the **Allow this server to host user accounts** check box on the **Instant Messaging Home Server** screen and click **Next**.

10. Click **Finish** on the **Completing the Virtual Server Wizard** screen.

Now, forward to the next server-side IM configuration procedure: invoking IM capabilities on a user-by-user basis.

1.   Log on to **SSL1** as **Administrator** with the password **husky9999**.

2.   Click **Start**, **Small Business Server Administrator Console**.

3.   In the Tree pane, expand **Active Directory Users and Computers (ssl1.springersltd.com)**, **springersltd.com**, **Users**.

4. Right-click **Norm Hasborn** and select **Exchange Tasks**.
5. Click **Next** at the **Welcome to the Exchange Task Wizard** page of the **Exchange Task Wizard**.
6. Select **Enable Instant Messaging** and click **Next**.
7. Click the **Browse** button in the **Enable Instant Messaging** dialog box.
8. Select **IM-SSL** on the **Select Instant Messaging Server** dialog box and click **OK**.
9. You are returned to the **Enable Instant Messaging** screen that should look similar to Figure 11-4. Click OK.

Figure 11-4
SSL-IM is selected and note the springersltd.com domain name for the IM domain.

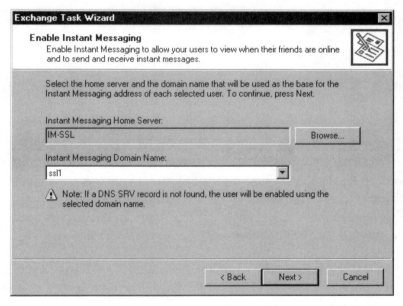

10. Click **Finish** on the **Completing the Exchange Task Wizard**, as seen in Figure 11-5.

Notes:

Figure 11-5

Success! You've configured Norm for IM. Don't forget to select the important information under Task summary and copy-and-paste it into your SBS network notebook.

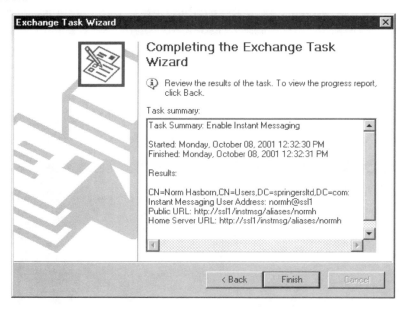

Now you will repeat Steps 4 – 9 for each SSL user to give each individual IM capabilities, at least on the server-side. Next up is the procedure for configuring the IM application on the client computer. There is a kinda funky twist here wherein you'll insert SBS 2000 Setup Disc 3 into the workstation.

> BEST PRACTICE: You'll be using the Exchange 2000 Server IM client, not the popular MSN IM client for IM-based communications on your SBS 2000 network. That's because the MSN IM client doesn't have the ability to point to an Exchange 2000 Server.
>
> However, the Exchange 2000 Server IM client has the ability to support MSN-based IM, so if you want both internal and external IM capabilities, the client you install next will do it! You would use external IM to communicate with clients, friends, and family in the real world. When you've installed the Exchange 2000 Server IM client, click **Tools**, **Options**, **Accounts** to invoke MSN functionality

1. Log on to **PRESIDENT** as **NormH** with the password **Purple3300**.
2. Insert **SBS 2000 Setup Disc 3** into the CD drive of the client computer.
3. Double-click **My Computer**, expand the CD drive icon (e.g., drive **D:**), expand **Exchsrvr60,** and double-click **LAUNCH.EXE**.
4. The **Exchange 2000 Server** splash screen appears. Click **IM Client Setup**. This is shown in Figure 11-6.

Figure 11-6
This is where the IM client you will need is installed from.

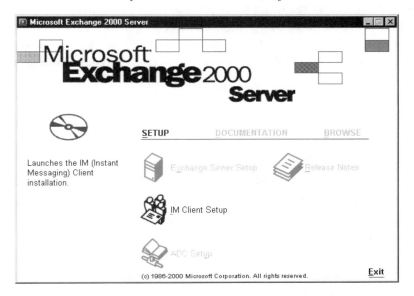

BEST PRACTICE: Although I won't do it here as part of the SSL methodology, in the real world, you'd likely want to download the latest Exchange 2000 Server IM client from the Web at **www.microsoft.com/ exchange/downloads/imclient.htm**. This would insure you're working with the latest and greatest IM client that has additional features (and fixes).

5. Expand the **USA** folder.
6. Double-click the **MMSSETUP.EXE** file to start the IM client setup.

BEST PRACTICE: I know a couple of you smarty-pants SBSers are already thinking ahead here. If you copy the MMSSETUP.EXE file to a network shared folder, such as COMPANY on the SBS server machine, you don't need to carry Disc 3 to each workstation to launch the file. Rather, you can launch said file from one central location on the SBS 2000 network.

And the very sharpest amongst you have probably figured out that the IM client could be installed to client computers as part of the SBS client application setup process. Pursue this solutions set from the **Add Software to Computer** button on the **Tip – Setting Up Client Computers** from **Set up Client Computers** under **Small Business Server Tips** on the **Favorites** tab of the **Small Business Server Administrator Console**.

Bravo!

7. On the **Messenger Service 2.2** screen, click **Yes** to agree to the end-user license.
8. Click **Next** when the **MSN Messenger Service Welcome** screen appears.
9. On the **Provide Microsoft Exchange Instant Messaging information** screen, keep the **Use this program to talk to my Microsoft Exchange contacts** check box selection. In the **E-mail address** field, type **normh@ssl1** and click **Next**. Note this is the IM domain name you defined in the last procedure (see Figure 11-3).
10. On the **Get a free Passport** screen, select the **Use Exchange Instant Messaging only. (Do not connect to the Internet.)** check box. Click **Next**.

BEST PRACTICE: There are strong feelings about Microsoft Passport, a service that allows you to enjoy a single sign-on experience at Web sites (for example). My advice? See the Window Manager columns on this topic by Brian Livingston at www.brianlivingston.com. Note that if you plan to download and install Exchange 2000 Conferencing Server in the second part of this chapter, you will need to register with Microsoft Passport.

11. On the **Congratulations! Setup is now complete** screen, click **Finish**.

12. Ah, but you not truly done yet. After the MSN Messenger Service automatically starts, click the **Click here to log on** link. Verify that the **E-mail** field reads **normh@ssl1** on the **Log On – MSN Messenger Service** dialog box and click **OK**.

Your screen should now look similar to Figure 11-7. You are truly "IM-ing" at this point, and as other SSL users are added, their names will appear on your list on Contact Currently Online. At that time, you could send a message to one or more users by clicking the Send button. Please enjoy IM, as many people in the SBS community currently are.

Figure 11-7
You've got old NormH IM-ing at this point. And who said you couldn't teach an old dawg new tricks? (Just a little Springer Spaniels humor here!)

Now it's on to Microsoft Exchange 2000 Conferencing Server.

Exchange 2000 Conferencing Server

So, now for something really neat: Exchange 2000 Conferencing Server. This is a world-class video conferencing system that even small businesses see the value of. Client computers, armed with NetMeeting (discussed in both Chapters 8 and 13) plus a small computer camera (e.g., Intel) can participate in real-time video conferencing with others. Granted, you'll want a broadband connection to make this work effectively, but such bandwidth is well within reach of small businesses today.

> BEST PRACTICE: Once this is deployed and in use, have the attendees turn off the sound. Save that precious bandwidth for video. To enjoy sound, place a conference call between the participants and let the telephone excel in what it does best: transmitting voice.

In this section, you'll first go read and follow a KBase article on how to prepare your SBS 2000 server machine for using Exchange 2000 Conferencing Server (a little bit of Active Directory modification stuff here). This is followed by the download of the 11.6 MB Exchange 2000 Conferencing Server application file from Microsoft (this is a 120-day trial version). Exchange 2000 Conferencing Server is then installed. Next you apply the Exchange 2000 Conferencing Server Service Pack 1 that you downloaded in Chapter 7. Finally, you configure Exchange 2000 Conferencing Server, including some adjustments to Outlook 2000, and host your very first video conference. It's a lot of work, so let's get going, eh?

> BEST PRACTICE: It's payoff time. The firewall port configuration procedures you completed in Chapter 10 with Table 10-1 will pay off in spades now. These are critical ports to open for the video conferencing capability. Good deal, eh?

Modifying Active Directory

Your first task is to point your Internet Explorer Web browser to www.microsoft.com/technet and search for KBase article Q280444 that is titled *XCCC: How to Configure Exchange 2000 Conferencing Server for Internet Attendees*. Read the summary section, located at the start of the article, about creating a fictitious site in Active Directory. This is the procedure to create that fictitious Active Directory site.

1. Log on to **SSL1** as **Administrator** with the password **husky9999**.
2. Click **Start**, **Programs**, **Administrative Tools**, **Active Directory Sites and Services**.
3. Right-click on **Sites** in the left-pane and select **New**, **Site**.
4. Type **Conferencing** in the **Name** field of the **New Object – Site** dialog box and click **OK**.
5. Click **OK** when the **Active Directory** dialog box appears.
6. Right-click **Subnets** and select **New**, **Subnet**.
7. In the **New Object – Subnet** dialog box, type **231.107.16.2** in the **Address** field. Type **255.255.255.255** in the **Mask** field. Under **Site Name**, select **Conferencing**. Your screen should look similar to Figure 11-8. Click **OK**.

Figure 11-8
This is where you make critical multicast site configurations.

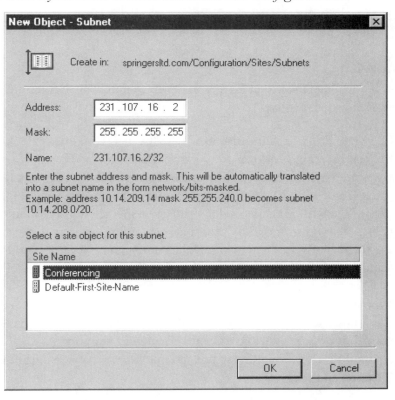

8. The **AD Sites and Services** snap-in should look similar to Figure 11-9. Close from **Console**, **Exit**.

Figure 11-9

Viewing AD Sites and Services and you've completed your configuration.

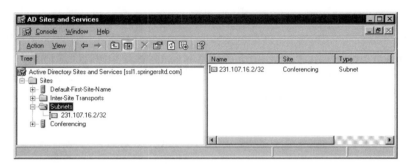

BEST PRACTICE: Please keep KBase article Q280444 handy as you'll need it later on.

Downloading

Next, you'll download the actual Exchange 2000 Conferencing Server file from Microsoft. Follow these steps.

1. Log on to **SSL1** as **Administrator** with the password **husky9999**.
2. Launch **Internet Explorer** from the SSL1 desktop and type **www.microsoft.com/exchange/evaluation/trial** in the **Address** field.
3. Click **Go** beneath **Exchange 2000 Conferencing Server** (accept English). You will be challenged to provide your Microsoft Passport credentials. After you successfully pass this step (either log on with your existing Microsoft Passport credentials or complete several steps to acquire such credentials), you will proceed to the next step. Oh, click **OK** and **Yes** to any notices that you are entering a secure site.
4. On the **Exchange 2000 Conferencing Server English Version** page, scroll down and click the **E2K_Conferencing.exe** link under the **Description** column under **Required Download Components**.
5. On the **File Download** dialog box, accept the **Save this program to disk** selection and click **OK**.
6. In the **Save As** dialog box, select the **Exchange 2000 Conferencing**

Server SP1 folder you created in Chapter 7 (it's beneath the **Exchange 2000 Server SP1** folder) and click **Save**. The file will download.

Installing

Whew, so close yet so much work to do before you have a bona fide video conference running. Hang in there and complete these steps.

1. Log on to **SSL1** as **Administrator** with the password **husky9999**.
2. Open the **My Documents** shortcut on the SSL1 desktop. Open the **Exchange 2000 Server SP1** folder. Open the **Exchange 2000 Conferencing Server SP1** folder. Create a folder titled **EC** with a right-click and select **New, Folder**.
3. Double-click the file **E2K_Conferencing.exe**.
4. In the **WinZip Self-Extractor** dialog box, extract the file to the **EC** folder you created in Step 2 above. Click **Unzip**.
5. Click **OK** when the files have been successfully extracted. Click **Close** to close **WinZip**.
6. Navigate to the **EC** folder from the **My Documents** window.
7. Open the following folders: **Conferencing, Setup, I386** and double-click **setup.exe**.
8. Click **Next** at the **Welcome** screen of the **Microsoft Exchange 2000 Conferencing Server – Installation Wizard**.
9. On the **Licensing Agreement** screen, click **I accept the terms of the license agreement** and click **Next**.
10. Accept the sample 25-digit product identification number on the **Product Identification** screen and click **Next**.
11. Select **Complete** on the **Setup Type** screen and click **Next**.
12. On the **Administrative Group** screen, accept **first administrative group** and click **Next**.
13. Click **Install** on the **Ready to Install the Program** screen. A progress bar screen will keep you informed of the setup progress.
14. Click **Finish** on the **Installation Wizard Completed** screen.
15. Close the **My Documents** window from **File, Close**.

Okay, now it's time to apply the Exchange 2000 Conferencing Server service pack in the next section to make your installation as current as possible.

Applying the Service Pack

1. Log on to **SSL1** as **Administrator** with the password **husky9999**.
2. Open the **My Documents** shortcut on the SSL1 desktop. Open the **Exchange 2000 Server SP1** folder. Open the **Exchange 2000 Conferencing Server SP1** folder.
3. Double-click the file titled **e2ksp1_conferencing.exe**.
4. In the **WinZip Self-Extractor** dialog box, extract the file to the current folder (**Exchange 2000 Conferencing Server SP1** folder). Click **Unzip**.
5. Click **OK** when the files have been successfully extracted. Click **Close** to close **WinZip**.
6. Open the following folders: **Conferencing**, **Setup**, **I386** and double-click **update.exe**.
7. When asked if you want to proceed with the service pack installation on the **Microsoft Exchange 2000 Conferencing Service Pack 1** screen, click **Yes**.
8. Click **OK** when the **Microsoft Exchange 2000 Conferencing Service Pack 1** dialog box notifies you that the service pack was successfully installed.
9. Close the **My Documents** window from **File**, **Close**.

Configuring

Now you will perform the baseline configuration procedures that must be completed before that elusive, first video conference can occur! This includes procedures to configure Exchange 2000 Conferencing Server itself and Outlook 2000 on the SSL1 server.

Exchange 2000 Conferencing Server

Complete the following procedure.

1. Log on to **SSL1** as **Administrator** with the password **husky9999**.
2. Click **Start**, **Programs**, **Microsoft Exchange**, **Conferencing Manager**.
3. Right-click **Exchange Conferencing** and select **Manage**.
4. Click **OK** when the **Default-First-Site-Name** selection is listed under **Select a conference management site** on the **Exchange Conferencing** dialog box as seen in Figure 11-10.

Figure 11-10

Don't change a thing here.

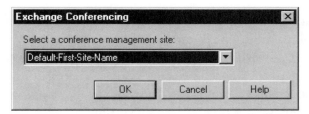

5. Click **Yes** when asked if you want to specify a Conference Calendar Mailbox.
6. Click **Create** on the **Conference Calendar Mailbox** dialog box.
7. Complete the **Create Conferencing Calendar** dialog box similar to Figure 11-11. In **Display name**, type **Room1**. In **Logon name** type **Room1**. In **Password** and **Confirm password**, type **husky9911**. Click **OK**.

Figure 11-11

This e-mail box will be a conferencing resource.

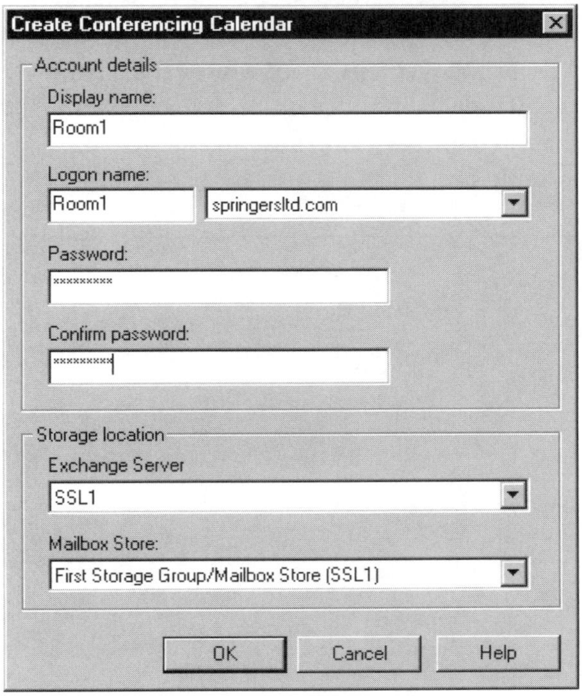

8. Click **Close** on the **Conference Calendar Mailbox** dialog box.

9. Right-click **Default-First-Site-Name Conferencing Site** and select **Properties**.

10. Click **Resources** and click **Add**. The **New Resource Mailbox** screen appears. In **Display name**, type **Room1-seats**. In **Logon name** type **Room1-seats**. In **Password** and **Confirm password**, type **husky9912**. Click **OK**.

11. Click **Add** on the **Resource Properties** dialog box.

12. Select **Data Conferencing Provider** and **Video Conferencing Provider** and click **OK**.

13. On the **Data** tab, accept **20 meeting participants** and click **OK**.

14. On the **Video** tab, select the **Enable H.323 Data Provider fallback** checkbox and click **OK**.

15. Click **OK** to close **Resource Properties**.

16. Click **OK** to close **Default-First-Site-Name Conferencing Site Properties**.

17. On the **Exchange Conferencing Manager** snap-in, expand **Default-First-Site-Name Conferencing Site** and click **Data Conferencing Provider**. Right-click the **SSL1** server object in the right-pane and select **Properties**.

18. On the **General** tab, select the **Accept client connections from the Internet** check box and type the fully qualified domain name (FQDN) of **ssl1.springersltd.com** in the **Use network name** field. Your screen should look similar to Figure 11-12.

Notes:

Figure 11-12

The FQDN is an important entry. Note that you might need to add a DNS re-source record at your ISP that points to this FQDN to allow Internet access.

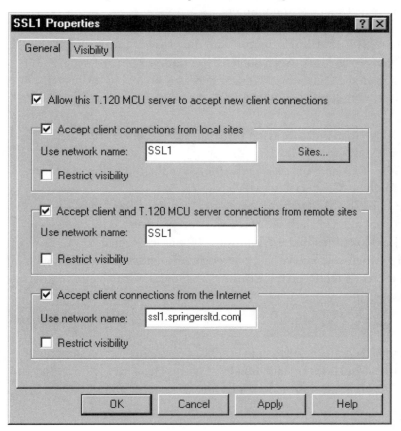

19. Click **OK**.
20. Close the **Exchange Conferencing Manager** snap-in from **Console**, **Exit**.
21. Restart the SSL1 server from **Start**, **Shutdown**, **Restart** so the DNS cache will flush and update.

Notes:

Outlook 2000

Time to make a simple adjustment to Outlook 2000 on the SSL1 server. This is a registry entry that allows you to schedule Exchange Conferencing Server conferences when you create Calendar appointments.

1. Log on to **SSL1** as **Administrator** with the password **husky9999**.
2. Click **Start**, **Programs**, **Accessories**, **Notepad**.
3. The Notepad application will launch. Type the following text exactly in two lines (the first line is the REGEDIT4 command):
   ```
   REGEDIT4
   [HKEY_CURRENT_USER\Software\Microsoft\Office\9.0\
   Outlook\ExchangeConferencing]
   ```
4. Select **File**, **Exit** and **Yes** to save the file. Save the file to the **My Documents** folder as **Conferencing.reg**.
5. Double-click the **My Documents** shortcut from the SSL1 desktop.
6. Double-click the **Conferencing.reg** file you just created to modify the Outlook 2000 entries in the Windows 2000 Server Registry.
7. Click **Yes** when you receive a warning on the **Registry Editor** dialog box.
8. Click **OK** when the **Registry Editor** dialog box informs you the Registry was successfully updated.

Using

In this section, you'll create an Exchange 2000 Conferencing Server appointment, e-mail it to Norm Hasborn, and then have Norm Hasborn log on and attend the conference. It's all good stuff and a lot of fun, so let's get going.

Create Appointment

1. Log on to **SSL1** as **Administrator** with the password **husky9999**.
2. Double-click **Microsoft Outlook** from the SSL1 desktop.
3. Click on the **Calendar** button under **Outlook Shortcuts**.
4. Click the **New Appointment** button.
5. A **New Appointment – Meeting** dialog box will appear. In **Subject**, type **SSL Conference**. Select the **This is an online meeting using** check box and select **Microsoft Exchange Conferencing Server**. Set the start and end times for your current date and time.
6. Click **Invite Attendees**. Click the **To:** field. Add **Room1-seats** to the **Resources** field. Add **Norm Hasborn** to **Required**. Your screen should look like Figure 11-13. Click **OK**.

Figure 11-13
It is essential that you identify the conference resource in the Resource field or else the conference will fail.

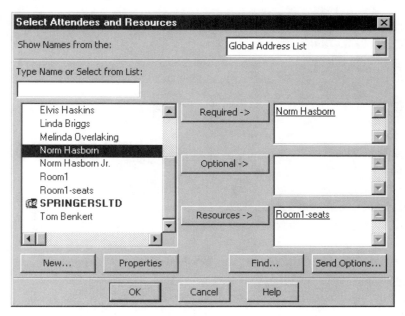

7. The **SSL Conference – Meeting** screen should appear and look similar to Figure 11-14. Click **Send**.

Notes:

Figure 11-14
You are SO close to enjoying a video conference at this point.

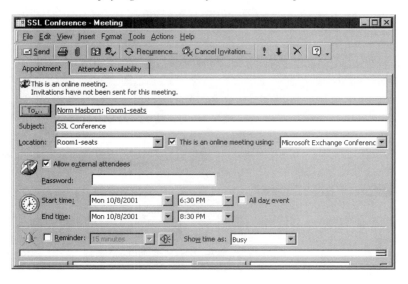

8.   Click **OK** when the **Resources Booked** dialog box appears.

To wrap up this discussion on creating the appointment, I display Figure 11-15 to show how the appointment will appear in the Outlook Calendar.

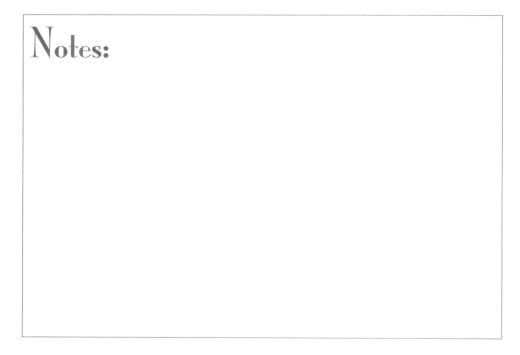

Notes:

Figure 11-15
Notice the Calendar entry has a long http path that you can copy and paste into a browser to join the conference.

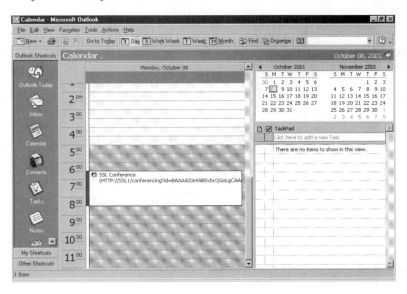

Log on to Conference

At this point, Norm Hasborn will attend the conference you just created. Complete this procedure.

1. Log on to **PRESIDENT** as **NormH** with the password **Purple3300**.
2. Double-click **Outlook 2000** from the **PRESIDENT** desktop.
3. Open the e-mail received for the conference and highlight and copy (**CTRL-C**) the **HTTP address** (aka Uniform Resource Locator – URL).
4. Double-click **Internet Explorer** on the **PRESIDENT** desktop.
5. Paste the address you copied in Step 3 into the **Address** field. Press **Enter**.
6. Lickity-split, you'll be participating in a video conference similar to that shown in Figure 11-16.

Notes:

Figure 11-16

Enjoying a video conference with Exchange 2000 Conferencing Server!

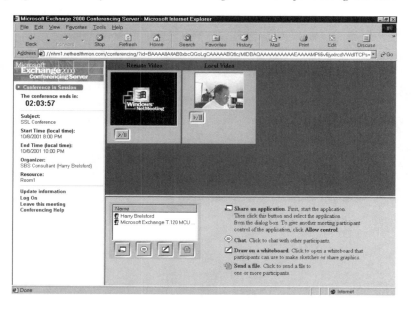

Resources

To be more than honest, there are few good Exchange 2000 Conferencing Resources on the market today. Much of my learning was trial and error, including a visit to the Exchange Conferencing Server lab at Microsoft in Redmond. But consider the following:

- **White Paper.** Surf to **www.microsoft.com/technet/prodtechnol/ exchange/featusability/ecsh323.asp** and read the white paper titled **Exchange 2000 Conferencing Server and H.323**.

- **Book.** I found one book titled **Microsoft Exchange 2000, Conferencing Server, and SharePoint Portal Server 2001** (SAMS, ISBN: 0672321793, $49.99), but be forewarned that I've not read it.

- **Online conference.** Surf to **www.microsoft.com/seminars** and expand **Exchange** in the left margin. Click and launch the online seminar titled **Exchange 2000 Conferencing Server Deployment and Configuration**.

You can look for more resources on this topic as its use increases, so hang in there!

Advanced Topics

Here are a few advanced topics for your consideration as you go and grow as an Exchange guru.

- **POP3 Connector.** Get to know the POP3 Connector found in the Internet Connection Wizard. This is a tool, created by the SBS development team, to effectively redirect incoming POP3 e-mail to an internal SMTP-based Microsoft Exchange 2000 Server e-mail accounts. This allows you to slowly migrate a small business from POP3 e-mail to SMTP e-mail over time.

- **Recipient Policies.** In the Small Business Server Administrator Console, under SSL1 (Exchange), Recipients, get to know Recipient Policies. The online help system will guide you, but basically you can have multiple registered Internet domain names with SMTP e-mail residing on one Exchange 2000 Server. This might be neat in situations wherein a small business running SBS 2000 is really an executive suites operation, with several sublease tenants that have their own unique Internet identities.

- **Forwarding e-mail.** I'm sure you'll run into this one as an SBSer. On a user's property sheet under **Active Directory Users and Computers**, select the **Exchange General** tab and click the **Deliver Options** button. It is here you can configure e-mail to be forwarded to a Blackberry handheld device or another e-mail system.

Notes:

Guest Column

No other computer manufacturer has dedicated so much effort into selling and supporting SBS than Gateway Computers. In speaking with Gateway employees, it became apparent that they've got the message straight about SBS. So who better to ask for a column on the importance of communication, e-mail-based and otherwise, than Gateway. Heather Finnemore stepped up to the table to share these words.

The Benefits of Using Technology to Communicate

The power of communications should not be underestimated by businesses today. And effective communications isn't a luxury reserved for big business. It's just as important, if not more so, for smaller companies too.

Communicating effectively can:

- *Enhance your professional image*

- *Provide customers with a sense of confidence in your services*

- *Make your small company seem larger*

- *Make your business more effective and efficient*

And while nothing beats talking to customers face-to-face, recent advances in technology make it easier and more affordable than ever for companies to leverage this powerful medium.

So exactly what do we mean by communications? As defined by Webster's, "communication is the exchange of ideas, messages or information." And at the heart of business communications is connectivity.

There are a number of technologies companies can use to communicate – Web sites, intranets, extranets, e-mail, networks, to name a few. And to be most effective, businesses should draw upon a variety of these, as each implementation serves a unique and important role in supporting the overall communications effort. Below we've listed a couple of the simplest and most effective ways a business can use technology to communicate more effectively.

Web sites *– whether you have a simple "home" page or a complex site with e-commerce capabilities, a Web site instantly gives your business visibility with a global audience. Many customers research and evaluate product and company information before they purchase, so having a Web presence is mandatory if you want your company's offerings to even be considered with today's buyers.*

Intranets and Extranets *– these are special sites accessible only to a specific and limited audience, such as employees (intranets) or special customers (extranets). These sites provide customized information, and can be automated based on the viewers' profile. For instance, an extranet can provide customers with the ability to track purchases, view historical service records, receive special promotions or read about new offerings specific to their business.*

E-mail *– keep in touch with your customers 24-hours-a-day, 7-days-a-week. Customers don't have to wait for the phone to be answered or get frustrated with being put on hold. Automated responses can provide instant responses and updates, giving customers the confidence their request was received and is being handled.*

Networks *– in their most basic sense, allow employees to share information and peripherals (such as printers and scanners) and have access to company data. For security reasons, dedicated servers and networks can be set-up to allow certain employees and customers access to limited information. Wireless networks provide employees with the ability to be "disconnected" from a wall while still having complete access to company data. Wireless networks are most beneficial for campus-style environments and jobs that require employees to move about during the day. In addition, wireless networks can be extremely cost-effective, as walls and floors don't need to be torn apart for the installation of network cabling.*

Whatever communications vehicles you choose for your company, it's important to start with a comprehensive strategy that supports your overall business objectives. It's not always necessary to start big, and it's important to evaluate the effectiveness of your communications as you go.

Heather Finnemore is the Gateway's Territory Director for the Northeast in the U.S.

Summary

On the one hand, your next step is clearly to purchase a big thick tome dedicated to Exchange 2000 Server. Whether you believe that or not, such a book is in your future as an SBSer and the mission-critical nature of e-mail messaging. This chapter painted one picture wherein Exchange 2000 Server is correctly viewed as ready to run right out of the box, with perhaps a few advanced native configurations you might consider. But the second picture that emerged in this chapter is that Exchange 2000 Server can be extended beyond its basic configuration. I proved that point with my step-by-step examples to deploy Instant Messaging and Exchange 2000 Conferencing Server. I rest my case and I'll see you in Chapter 12 where we'll study Outlook 2000.

Chapter 12
Outlook 2000 Implementation

Fact of the matter is, Outlook is important in nearly all SBS installations and quickly follows after the Internet connection is made in a secure way. Why? Users will want to take advantage of Outlook with its e-mail, scheduling, contact management, and general groupware functions. The first part of the chapter focuses on basic Outlook use; the second part of the chapter zeroes in on advanced Outlook use, including a couple of cool Outlook tools: publishing your Outlook calendar as a Web page and using Outlook Web Access.

> BEST PRACTICE: Note that I introduce advanced Outlook capabilities in Chapter 19, such as Outlook Team Folders and Digital Dashboard. I delay introducing these totally cool capabilities until then as I want you to gain more experience with your SSL network first. Also, this chapter necessarily presents a limited view of Outlook 2000, given the real estate this book must traverse. I highly recommend that you purchase another thick book dedicated to Outlook 2000. At last count, searching on Amazon, there were over 100 books on Outlook.

The Role of Outlook

Who said an SBS client can't teach me a thing or two along the SBS journey? On paper, during the SBS planning phase, it appeared as if the networked business accounting application would be the most popular feature of the SBS network. When planning for SBS, business applications are typically the primary reason for implementing the new SBS network. But leave it to users to decide for themselves what is the most popular SBS network application. And without question, literally from Day One of the SBS network's life, that application has been Outlook.

A true story serves to make the point. It was a late winter afternoon, and I was across the desk from a prominent Northwest businessman. I had just completed installing the SBS network at his small company, but something was wrong. I could sense he wasn't completely pleased with the new SBS network. So I launched into a long (and tiresome) dissertation about the high performance levels of his new server, 100MB-per-second dual-speed hub, DSL Internet connection, and so on. Still, he wore his disappointment outward and openly. Ah, I thought. He must be disenchanted with the new construction/property management accounting software running on the SBS server. (Whew—that was installed by the other consultant!). Wrongo! The CEO felt the full pain of his $10,000-plus outlay for his SBS network because his Outlook application ran too slowly. For him, having to count seconds when he switched between Outlook's e-mail and calendar modules represented a failed SBS implementation, and, as you know, the SBS client is always right!

Closer examination revealed that this individual maintained over 700 Outlook calendar entries and had a notoriously finicky machine. So we archived many of his historical calendar entries and moved much of his information into public folders (something I'll discuss with you later today). Bottom line: We solved his Outlook problem and changed his attitude, for the better, about his new SBS network.

This learning experience taught me an important lesson about Outlook. It's a mission-critical application on an SBS network and, in many cases, it's how you—the SBS consultant or administrator—are evaluated. So take Outlook's role very seriously on your SBS network. Your users do.

Outlook Overview

Let's you and I take a moment to learn what Outlook is. For many SBS users, Outlook is simply e-mail. It is where e-mail is composed, sent, received, and read. End of story, chapter, and book. Other SBS users not only take advantage of e-mail, but also enjoy Outlook's other functions, all of which are listed in Table 12-1.

Table 12-1: Outlook Defined

Outlook Feature	Description
Calendar	This is the appointment schedule where you can enter appointments for yourself and others.
Contacts	This is the contact manager for tracking names, addresses, telephone and fax numbers, e-mail addresses, and basic contact information.

Journal	This tool allows you to enter journal entries that are time-stamped for you, track the editing of popular data files by date, and create quick-and-dirty project schedules.
Mailbox	This contains the Inbox, Outbox, Sent Items, and other electronic mail folders you might create.
Notes	These are basically electronic yellow sticky notes that allow you to capture quick thoughts on a time-stamped note.
Tasks	This is a To Do List, where you can enter items that need to be accomplished. When accomplished, these items are typically marked as complete.

Much like SBS on the server-side, you could consider Outlook the SBS user's all-in-one solution (that is, "just add water"). Combined with a popular application suite such as Microsoft Office, Outlook rounds out the tools that the average SBS user needs. I've heard Outlook referred to as the Swiss Army Knife of business communications.

In my experience, these are the most popular Outlook functions, ranked in order: e-mail, calendar/scheduling, and contacts (see Figure 12-1). I'll review these three popular functions with you starting right now!

> BEST PRACTICE: If you're a betting SBSer, don't place your hard won moolah on the ponies, but rather bet that most of your calls from users will relate to e-mail. E-mail support has edged out other forms of support, such as printing problems. I previously discussed SBS network administration much more in Chapters 6 and 7.

Notes:

Figure 12-1
Microsoft Outlook - Opening Screen.

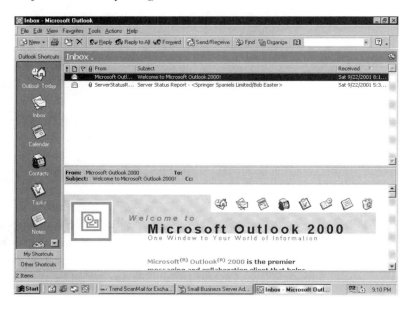

Basics of E-mail

For SBS users at any given moment, using Outlook is all about sending and receiving e-mail. I guarantee that this is something your users will want immediately when logged on to the SBS network. Electronic mail is, of course, a way to communicate with internal and external (via the Internet) parties. It is often used for communicating with business associates, friends, and family. It has gone from circus sideshow to main act in just a few years of local area network-based business computing.

Sending a Message

One of your first acts in Outlook is to send an e-mail message with an attachment. Funny how that is. No sooner is the SBS network is up and running than the first thing the new SBS users do is try to send e-mail to each other. It's safe to say that, during those first few hours of the SBS network's life, the brand new accounting system plays second fiddle to those who want to fiddle with the e-mail capabilities of Outlook.

In the following text, you'll send e-mail with an attachment to several employees of SSL as well as an Internet e-mail account.

1.　Log on to **SSL1** as the **Administrator** with the password **husky9999**.

BEST PRACTICE: You will need to install Outlook 2000 on the machine running SBS in order for the Administrator to have e-mail. This, of course, begs the question about why the Administrator would need e-mail on the machine running SBS. Shouldn't the machine running SBS not be used to run applications? The Administrator needs Outlook 2000 set up on the machine running SBS in order to send out administrative announcements, such as the one used in this task. And yes, in general, the machine running SBS shouldn't be used to run applications.

To install Outlook 2000 on the machine running SBS, double-click **My Network Places** from the desktop of the machine running SBS. Double-click **Entire Network**. Click the **entire contents** link. Double-click the **Microsoft Windows Network** link. Double-click the **SPRINGERSLTD.COM** domain. Double-click **SSL1** (the server machine that runs SBS). Double-click **ClientApps5**. Double-click **Outlook2000SR1**. Double-click **Setup.exe** and the Windows Installer will run. Accept **Bob Easter** as the registered customer in the **User Name** field on the **Please enter your customer information:** screen. The name Bob Easter was taken from the information you input when you installed SBS on in Chapter 3. Accept **Springer Spaniels Limited** in the **Organization** field and click **Next**. Click the **Install Now** button in the upper page of the **Setup is ready to install Microsoft Outlook 2000 SR-1** screen. Click **OK** when the **Microsoft Outlook 2000 Setup** dialog box reports that Microsoft Outlook 2000 SR-1 setup was completed successfully. Close any open windows, such as the **My Network Places** window that probably remained open in the background.

Double-click the **Microsoft Outlook** icon on the desktop of the machine running SBS. If necessary, reply to the Setup screen that the Outlook 2000 application will be used in a **Corporate or Workgroup setting** and click **Next**. Select **Microsoft Exchange Server** on the next screen to identify the services to be set up and click **Next**. Provide the server name as **SSL1** and the user name as **Administrator** and click

Next. Click **Finish**. Outlook 2000 will now launch into its default Inbox view with the generic **Welcome to Microsoft Outlook 2000** e-mail waiting in the Inbox.

2. If you haven't already done so in the BEST PRACTICE above, launch **Microsoft Outlook** application from the SSL1 desktop.
3. Select the **New Mail Message** button. An untitled message appears.
4. Select the **To:** button in the **Untitled - Message** window. This is found on the left side. The **Select Names** box appears, displaying the usernames for SSL. You will also note that the default e-mail distribution group **SSL1** is also displayed.

BEST PRACTICE: My preceding comments about the SSL employee names that will appear assume that you entered all the employees for SSL when you read Chapters 4 and 6. Enter those SSL employees now if you intend to follow the methodology of this book.

5. Double-click the following names: **Barry McKechnie**, **David Halberson**, and **Norm Hasborn**. The names appear on the right of the **Select Names** dialog box in the **Message Recipients** field. Click **OK**. You are returned to the **Untitled - Message** screen.
6. In the CC address field, type the following Internet address: **harryb@nethealthmon.com**.
7. In the Subject line, type **System Reboot and Downtime Announcement**.
8. In the body of the message, type the following:
    Good Greetings, Fellow Earthlings...
    The SBS network will be down most (if not all) of next weekend, starting late Friday night, for maintenance. Please plan to take the weekend off and enjoy. Don't forget the beloved Washington Huskies play Stanford that weekend!

BEST PRACTICE: You can enter partial names in the To: field, and the names are automatically resolved. For example, if the name you want to enter is Barry McKechnie, you could simply enter **Bar** in the To: field, and the remainder of the name, *Barry McKechnie*, would automatically appear. This is great stuff!

9. To insert a file, use the Insert menu (**Insert**, **File**). You are presented with the **Insert File** dialog box.

BEST PRACTICE: When you forward an e-mail in Outlook that contains an attachment, the attachment is also forwarded. Other e-mail programs do not behave this way and the attachment isn't forwarded.

10. Navigate and select **c:\WINNT\setuplog.txt** as the file to insert. Note that I assume you know how to find a file. Click **OK** in the **Insert File** dialog box to insert this file. Your e-mail message should look similar to Figure 12-2.

Figure 12-2

Completed e-mail message with an attachment.

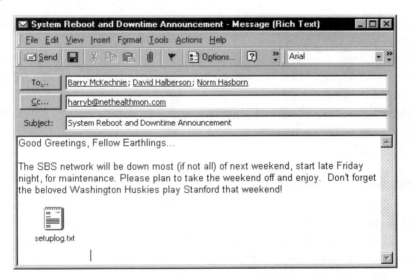

BEST PRACTICE: Be careful not to send extremely large files as attachments. The person who receives your e-mail with the attachment might not be able to open it (some e-mail servers restrict incoming attachment sizes). Worse yet, large attachments take forever to download when you have a modem connection to the Internet. Large file transfers are better handled via File Transfer Protocol (FTP), which is discussed in Chapter 17.

11. Click the **Send** button in the upper-left corner of the Message window.
12. Yee-haw and congratulations, pardner! You've sent your first e-mail message with an attachment in Outlook.

Reading a Message Sent to You

In order to read an e-mail message, go ahead and send an e-mail to yourself (meaning to Administrator - assuming you are still logged on as Administrator) using the steps just presented immediately above for sending an e-mail. Feel free to give the e-mail any subject line and text message.

To read the e-mail that you sent yourself (assuming you are currently logged on as Administrator), double-click the message.

> BEST PRACTICE: Y'all know that good e-mail etiquette suggests that you acknowledge, to the extent possible, the receipt of e-mail messages. This act of courtesy allows the sender to know that you received the message. This approach is what I call the sailboat racing method. In sailing, the crew always acknowledges the skipper's command so that everyone knows the command was heard and understood. I try to live by the same set of rules while on land using my e-mail system. Sometimes my replies are nothing more than "got it and will get back to you later with the information." Call it over-communicating but it's what e-mail is all about.

Saving Messages in Folders

You can save messages in folders similarly to the way that you save documents into folders on the SBS network. The difference between saving an e-mail in Outlook versus a file on the network is this: When you save an e-mail in Outlook, it is saved to an Outlook-based folder. When you save a file on the network, it is saved to a traditional file folder or subdirectory.

Thus, the folders you create in Outlook aren't folders in the traditional sense. These are not folders that you can see via Windows Explorer. Rather, Outlook folders are designed to help you organize your e-mail.

> BEST PRACTICE: If you're an SBS network administrator or consultant, I highly recommend that you teach your users to delete e-mail early and often. I can't tell you how many SBS users simply let old e-mail

languish in their Inbox folder. And if you subscribe to the opinion that information that is over 90 days old has expired, far too many of us carry around far too many e-mail messages. Having too many e-mail messages in your Outlook Inbox negatively affects Outlook's performance and your SBS experience.

And yes, this is a case of the pot calling the kettle black. My Outlook Inbox currently has 1,452 items, of which 224 are unread. Major Texas-sized ouch!

You'll create a folder to manage the Administrator's important e-mail. Follow these steps:
1. Log on to **SSL1** as the **Administrator** with the password **husky9999**.
2. Launch **Microsoft Outlook** from the **SSL1** desktop.
3. Select **View, Folder List** to display the center vertical pane of folders in Outlook 2000.
4. Select the **File, New**. The New command spawns another submenu. Select **Folder** from this submenu.
5. The **Create New Folder** dialog box is displayed. In the **Name** field, title the folder **Hot-Hot**. Allow the folder to contain **Mail Items** under **Folder contains:**. Make the Hot-Hot folder a subfolder of **Mailbox – Administrator** (click on this line in the **Select...** box).
6. Click **OK** in the **Create New Folder** dialog box to create the Hot-Hot folder. The Administrator intends to use this folder to store very important e-mail that needs attention.
7. If you are asked to **Add shortcut to the Outlook Bar**, please reply **No**. Shortcuts are displayed at the far left of the Outlook window in the Outlook Shortcuts pane. You may elect to answer **Yes** to creating Outlook shortcuts in the real world. Good for you.

Observe that the Hot-Hot folder now appears under Mailbox - Administrator in the center View Folders pane, as seen in Figure 12-3.

Figure 12-3
Hot-Hot Folder.

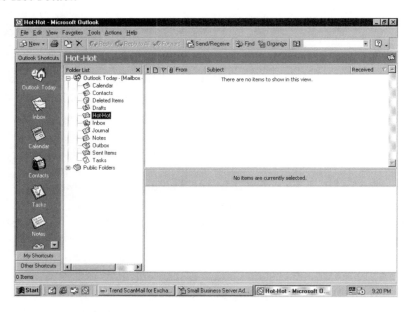

BEST PRACTICE: Be careful what e-mail you save in folders. If the e-mail message isn't work-related, such as those silly e-mail messages you receive from friends and family, perhaps you should delete (not save) the e-mail. I'd hate for you to save e-mail that might prove embarrassing to you later, as in litigation proceedings, such as a recent anti-trust case I know about.

E-mail Security

One of the biggest concerns expressed regarding e-mail has been that of security. The e-mail security issue has several angles, including secure transmission over the Internet, secure transmission over the SBS network within your four walls, and the all-important question answered by small-business CEOs and staff alike: "Can anyone else read my e-mail?"

The SBS network security issue is easily answered. Because the Microsoft Exchange site is housed on your SBS server, it benefits from being on a protected server (both physically secure and password protected). Furthermore, the Microsoft Exchange Information Store (where e-mail is stored on the server) isn't readable by mere mortals.

That leaves the all-important question: "Can anyone else read my e-mail?" The answer to this is that it depends. Your Outlook e-mail is inherently secure on an SBS network because of the use of Mailboxes. To access a Mailbox, you must successfully log on to the network. If you aren't logged on to the network, you can't access your Mailbox-based e-mail housed on the SBS server via Outlook. In this case, the answer is no, your e-mail is secure (as long as someone else doesn't log on to the network using your username and password).

If you are the type of user who leaves his or her workstation logged on to the network while away (say at lunch, evenings, weekends), your e-mail isn't as secure as you think it is. Under this scenario, the answer is then yes, other people can swagger on up to your workstation and read your e-mail. Think about it. If you keep your workstation logged on to the network and go to lunch, I can come along behind you, launch Outlook, and read your e-mail. Worse yet, I can send an e-mail on your behalf, giving everyone on the staff a 25 percent salary increase. I truly have the keys to the SBS kingdom, don't I?

> BEST PRACTICE: One SBSer I know uses screen saver passwords to attempt to restrict access to a workstation that is running. You can invoke a screen saver password via the **Screen Saver** tab in **Display** applet in **Control Panel** (from **Start**, **Settings**).

Calendar Basics

Meanwhile, back to my relationship with the prominent Northwest small-business CEO. Hands down, his main use of Microsoft Outlook was the Calendar. Not only did he keep at least historic appointments in his calendar for both legal and memory recall reasons, he kept several years of future appointments in his Outlook calendar as well. All told, he kept over 7,000 appointments spanning several years in Outlook. This gentleman was the most impressive user of Outlook, especially for an SBS site, that I've every witnessed. You name it, and he booked an appointment for it. This list of appointments included Rotary, Chamber of Commerce, political events, and even baseball games.

I share that story with you to underscore this fact: The calendar in Outlook isn't a toy. In fact, it's reliable and ready for your most demanding uses. It works well with external handheld personal digital assistant (PDA) devices to help you track your appointments, such as the Windows CE-based PDA from Phillips. I discuss handheld devices at the end of this section.

So, let's create an appointment for the Administrator on the SSL network.

1. Log on to **SSL1** as the **Administrator** with the password **husky9999**.
2. Launch **Microsoft Outlook** from the **SSL1** desktop.
3. Select the **Calendar** shortcut icon under **Outlook Shortcuts** (the far left column).
4. Select a date on the small monthly view on the right side of your Outlook Calendar. Select a date that is several days hence (e.g., **December 12, 2003**).
5. Click the **New Appointment** button (upper far left on toolbar). The **Untitled - Appointment** dialog box appears.
6. Enter **Upgrade to SBS 2004** in the **Subject** field.
7. Enter **Bainbridge Island** in the **Location** field.
8. Select a start time of **8:00 AM** and an end time of **5:00 PM,** using the time drop-down menus.
9. Allow the **Reminder** checkbox to remain selected. If you have Outlook open on your workstation, you will receive a reminder 15 minutes prior to the appointment. Allow the **Show Time As** field to remain as **Busy** (this would reflect a busy or occupied time if others looked at your schedule over the SBS network).
10. Underneath the Reminder checkbox is the appointment description area. Enter the following: **Make backups first**. The appointment dialog box should look similar to Figure 12-4.

Notes:

Figure 12-4

Completed appointment for a future SBS upgrade.

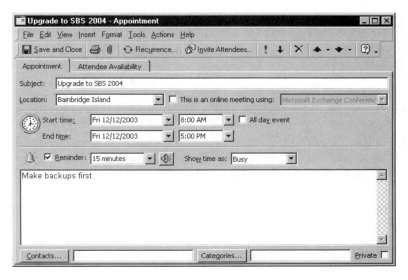

11. Click **Save and Close** in the upper-left corner of the appointment dialog box to book the appointment in Outlook. The appointment you just created will appear in the Outlook calendar.

BEST PRACTICE: Recurring appointments can be scheduled with ease in Outlook 2000. These are typically staff meetings that occur each week at the same time. To create a recurring appointment, simply click the **Recurrence** button when you are creating a new appointment.

Alternative Uses

There are many ways to use the Calendar in Outlook above and beyond simply maintaining your own personal schedule. Alternative ways that Calendar is used on real-world SBS networks include:

- Scheduling rooms - Some small firms with SBS use Calendar to schedule conference rooms.

- Group calendars - The Calendar function can be used to schedule group meetings, company ski days, the annual golf tournament, and so on.

- Check-in/Check-out – Front-desk receptionists in many companies on SBS networks use Calendar as an In/Out board to know of your whereabouts.

- Equipment scheduling - Scheduling the overhead projection unit or company car can be managed via Outlook's Calendar.

Contacts Basics

Of the three Outlook capabilities discussed today, this has been the least popular on SBS networks that I've worked with. I suspect this to be true for four reasons:

- It takes too much effort to enter data. Few small-business people truly have the time to sit and enter their contacts, business cards, loose scraps of paper, and so on into Outlook.

BEST PRACTICE: As an SBS consultant, I always enter my own name, address, and telephone number into my client's Outlook Contacts so that they see Contacts being used and, of course, I'm first on their list for a call when SBS-related work is available.

- Outlook's Contacts aren't as powerful as third-party applications Some of my SBS clients are indeed into contact management in a big way. These tend to be sales and marketing people. The problem I've encountered with "Contactmanics" is that they use more powerful, third-party stand-alone contact management applications, such as GoldMine. Indeed GoldMine has some capabilities that are absent in Outlook, such as a stronger database management function, but you would expect that with a stand-alone, specialized application. My position is simple. Although the Contacts feature in Outlook might not surpass the GoldMines of the world, the integration with the schedule, e-mail, and other capabilities of Outlook outweigh any feature-by-feature shortcomings.

- People still use business cards. The old school still likes paper business cards as their contact management system, God bless them. And don't forget there are many good business card scanners to convert business cards to Outlook contact records. You can see these at your favorite computer super store.

- Many SBS users simply don't know the power of Outlook and its Contacts capabilities. That's the underlying purpose of meeting today.

Training and education make a heck of a difference in how your users take advantage of Contacts. For example, some SBSers are enamored with the automatic dialing feature (AutoDialer) in Contacts (a feature that speed dials the telephone number displayed on your screen).

Add a Contact

It's time to add a contact for SSL. Again, I assume that you are currently logged on as **NormH** but just in case such is not true, I'll start the steps from the logon step at the workstation (**PRESIDENT**) used by NormH.

1. Log on at the **PRESIDENT** workstation as **NormH** with the password **Purple3300**.
2. Launch **Microsoft Outlook** from the **PRESIDENT** desktop.
3. Select the **Contacts** shortcut icon under **Outlook Shortcuts** (the far left column).
4. Click the **New Contact** button on the left side of the upper toolbar. A dialog box titled **Untitled - Contact** appears.
5. Enter the following information from Table 12-2. Note this name, Jane Unionski, is taken from the SBS Stakeholders list on Chapter 2 (see Table 2-2) and a Web page site has been added for Jane at this time for you to complete the contact record.

Table 12-2 - Sample Contact Information

Contact Field	Information to Enter
Full Name	**Jane Unionski**
Job title	**Cabling Specialist**
Company	**Unionski Cabling**
Address	**Box 3333 Unionski, ST 98111**
This is the mailing address	**Select this check box**
Phone - Business	**222-333-4455**
Phone - Mobile	**222-444-3344**

Phone - Pager	**222-123-4567**
E-mail	**union@cablespec.com**
Web page	**www.cablespec.com**
Description	**This is the cabling specialist for the SSL SBS network. Jane does very good work.**

The contact information you've entered should appear similar to Figure 12-5.

Figure 12-5
Jane Unionski contact information.

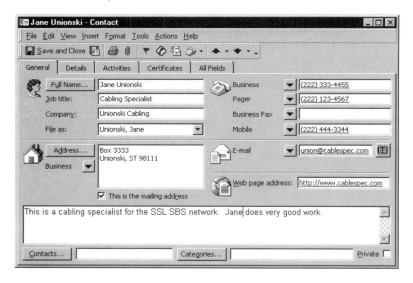

6.   After entering the information from Table 12-2, click the **Save and Close** button.

Observe your entry in the Contacts window. Congratulations. You've entered your first contact.

Additional Contact Considerations

Anyone using Contacts in Outlook, including yourself, will quickly expect the contact information to be preserved as metainformation. That is, you want to enter the information into the system once, maintaining it in a central location, such as Contacts, but using it in multiple ways, such as merge lists for Microsoft

Word. It is a very common expectation, one that is expressed at just about every SBS site I've worked at.

For example, the CEO of a landscaping company where I set up an SBS network expressed a desire to take the Contacts information and use it for marketing letters, faxes, and e-mail. No problem with Outlook Contacts.

Guest Column

For this chapter, I looked north to Canada for an interesting diddy on an Outlook conversion.

Outlook2000 Conversion

One of my local clients, a management consulting firm with 10 professionals and two support staff, agreed to my review of their site and plan to install a new SBS network with Windows2000 workstations to replace the mixture of hardware, software and procedures that had developed over the years.

Converting from individual POP3 boxes at the ISP and each person polling themselves was replaced with Exchange and the POP3 connector polling frequently over a DSL line. Although all users changed from Outlook Express of various versions to Outlook2000, we had no major surprises and most coped well.

To facilitate moving mail from personal file folders to Exchange, all older versions were first converted to Outlook Express 5.0 then to Outlook2000 – that combination worked well after several unsatisfactory attempts. As the staff use email as a long term filing system, it was a key benefit that individual mail files (as big as 200 megabytes) were now on the server for backup. All were encouraged not to have thousands of unsorted messages in their SINGLE inbox – coaching in setting up folders got the results.

Prior to the switch, the users had personal contact lists maintained in dBaseIII by support staff and printed several times a year as well as having their email addresses in Outlook Express. With some tricks, like converting the dBaseIII files to spreadsheets then importing them in Outlook2000, we got all the contacts for each professional into their Exchange folder. It did take brute force to review and combine the duplicate names from the two sources.

Scheduling+ data migrated very well as Outlook was able to import it without any hoops.

So finally we have all the data – contacts, email, and schedule for each professional in 1 place, fully backed up nightly.

But two additional features have made a big difference.

Palm IIIxe and IIIc units were given to each professional and now each can have the latest schedule and contact info available when out of the office. We have chosen not to implement the email to Palm as it is too difficult to use. The Palm is essentially a read only device for checking schedules and phone numbers – sure beats manually keeping daytimers up to date.

Secondly, we have implemented the Outlook Web Access as we now have a persistent connection to the Internet. When the professionals are in client offices or waiting in airport lounges – its just a few keystrokes to check their email and reply as well as having access to their latest appointments (made by their support staff).

The overall satisfaction level has risen substantially and the transition has not been difficult for any of the staff.

Joel Robinson (joel@askjoel.com) is a technology consultant in Toronto, Canada supporting sites in SBS and Linux and also develops custom solutions for non-profits.

Advanced Outlook

Now that we've gotten the basics relating to Outlook out of the way in the first part of the chapter, shall we move on to the more advanced discussion? Great. Let's get rocking and rolling.

Early on, SBS users embrace the use of e-mail as a core business tool. For that reason, many of the most common features of Outlook's e-mail capabilities were shown to you in the first part of the chapter. I will now show you several features relating to Internet e-mail and Outlook that you might not have been aware of, starting with Internet e-mail distribution lists. Why? Because SBS users quickly favor Internet-based e-mail, often more than any other Outlook feature. As you guessed, I don't stop with Internet e-mail distribution lists, but show you more cool tools, such as Outlook Web Access (OWA) and how to publish your Outlook calendar as a Web page.

Internet E-mail Distribution Lists

Assume that you still get together with the old ski team for Wednesday night cross-country skiing. E-mail is a powerful tool for quickly getting the word out to the gang. You can, of course, enter each individual e-mail name, but did you know that, much like internal e-mail names (SBS users on your internal network), you can also create e-mail groups with Internet e-mail addresses? You can! This capability of Internet e-mail groups is a little-known feature of Outlook.

To create an Internet e-mail group, complete the following steps (and yes, if necessary, log on as NormH again using the first step).

1. Log on at the **PRESIDENT** workstation as **NormH** with the password **Purple3300**.
2. Launch **Microsoft Outlook** from **PRESIDENT** desktop.
3. From the **Tools** menu, select **Services**.
4. Verify that **Personal Address Book** service is installed. If not, click the **Add** button to display the **Services** dialog box. Select **Personal Address Book** under **Available information services:** and click **OK**. The **Personal Address Book** dialog box appears. Accept the name **Personal Address Book** in the **Name:** field and accept the default file path in **Path:** and click **OK**. Click **OK** after reading the **Add Service To Profile** dialog box. Click **OK** to close the **Services** dialog box.

BEST PRACTICE: If you added the Personal Address Book service installation, then exit and restart Outlook to complete the Personal Address Book service installation.

5. From the **Tools** menu in Outlook, select the **Address Book** menu option. This option can also be selected with the **Ctrl+Shift+B** keystroke. Make sure the **Show Names From The:** drop-down menu displays **Personal Address Book**.
6. Enter several names and Internet e-mail addresses into the Personal Address Book (feel free to make up a few names for the purposes of this task). You can enter new names via **New Entry** from the **File** menu. When the **New Entry** dialog box is displayed, select **Personal Address** Book in the **In the** radio button field. Select **Internet Address** in the **Select the entry type** field and click **OK**. The **New Internet Address**

Properties dialog box appears. Complete the **Display name:** and the **E-mail address:** fields and click **OK**. Repeat these steps to add more names with Internet e-mail addresses to the Personal Address Book. Alternatively, you can have names in Contacts with Internet e-mail addresses as well. As you will see in a moment, e-mail distribution lists can be created with names listed in either a Personal Address Book or Contacts.

7. Next, to create an e-mail group containing these names and Internet e-mail addresses, select the **File** menu, and then select **New Entry**.

8. From the **New Entry** dialog box, select **New Distribution List**. Under **Put This Entry**, at the **In The** radio button field, select **Contacts**. Click **OK**.

9. The **Untitled - Distribution List** dialog box appears. Select the **Select Members** button. You can select **names** from your Personal Address Book (select the names you entered in Step 6 by selecting **Personal Address Book** from the **Show Names from the:** drop-down menu. You can also select other names from the Contacts, or the Global Address List depending on what selection you make in the **Show Names from the**: drop-down menu. I've selected three names from the Personal Address List and one name from the Global Address List.

10. Be sure to enter a group name in the **Name** field of the **New Personal Distribution List Properties**. Give the group the name **Skiing**. Click **Save and Close**.

11. Close the **Address Book** dialog box.

12. You are returned to Outlook. Select the **Contacts** shortcut icon under **Outlook Shortcuts** (the far left column).

13. Notice that the distribution group **Skiing** now appears in **Contacts**.

What's important here is that you now have an e-mail group that contains a variety of e-mail recipients (Internet e-mail address, Contacts, and local e-mail names). This is a wonderful feature in Outlook 2000.

Advanced Contacts Topics

As SBS users experiment more with Contacts, naturally their needs change for working within Contacts. Three such needs are discussed in this section, including e-mailing a Contact, writing a letter to a Contact, and performing queries against your Contact list.

One obvious need is to send e-mail to Contacts from the Contacts view. You accomplish this by following these steps:

1. Log on at the **PRESIDENT** workstation as **NormH** with the password **Purple3300**.
2. Launch **Microsoft Outlook** from **PRESIDENT** desktop.
3. Select the **Contacts** shortcut icon under **Outlook Shortcuts** (the far left column).
4. **Right-click** the Contact name that you would like to send an e-mail to (e.g., Jane Unionski). Select the **New Message To Contact** menu option from the secondary menu.
5. Compose the e-mail message as you normally would in Microsoft Outlook. The **To:** field is automatically filled in for you.
6. Send the e-mail by clicking the **Send** button.

Another advanced Contacts feature often requested is the capability to write a letter to a Contact easily, using the basic Contact information as the address for your letter.

> BEST PRACTICE: Note that I'm assuming you have installed Office 2000 (and, in particular, Microsoft Word 2000) on the machine you will use. I further realize that I've not walked you through the steps for installing Office 2000 on your machine (or my often referenced PRESI-DENT machine). If you have Office 2000, please consider installing it on the workstation you are using as part of your sample SSL SBS network. The setup instructions for Office 2000 are found in its accompanying documentation.

1. Log on at the **PRESIDENT** workstation as **NormH** with the password **Purple3300**.
2. Launch **Microsoft Outlook** from **PRESIDENT** desktop.
3. Select the **Contacts** shortcut icon under **Outlook Shortcuts** (the far left column).
4. Select the **Contact name** in the list of **Contacts** that you want to send a letter to. I suggest you select **Jane Unionski** (a name that you just entered).
5. From the **Actions** menu, select **New Letter to Contact** menu option.

(This option assumes that you have Microsoft Word 2000 installed on your workstation, a condition I discussed in the BEST PRACTICE before these steps started.)

6. A Microsoft Word 2000 session starts and the **Letter Wizard** launches.

7. Follow the on-screen instructions of the Letter Wizard. Start by selecting or deselecting any items of interest in **Step 1 of 4** in the Letter Wizard. Click **Next**.

8. Complete **Step 2 of 4** in the Letter Wizard. This is the **Recipient Info** tab. Typically at this stage you simply confirm that the address information is correct. You can also select the greeting (for example, Dear Jane) for the letter. Click **Next**.

9. Complete **Step 3 of 4** in the Letter Wizard. This is the **Other Elements** tab. Click **Next**.

10. Complete **Step 4 of 4** in the Letter Wizard. This is the **Sender Info** tab. Click **Finish**.

You would now complete the rest of your letter with your own information.

BEST PRACTICE: There is no easy way to perform a mail merge for a group of Outlook Contacts with Word. That's unfortunate, because other personal information managers, such as GoldMine, do a very good job of this. To do a mail merge between Outlook and Word, you would export the Contacts via the Import and Export menu option under the File menu. The problem with that is that the export is global for complete export. You can't selectively export all Contacts in, say, a range of zip codes. Bummer!

Queries on Contacts

Remember the landscaping company that I've mentioned throughout the book? I hope you remember the story in Chapter 1 where the landscaping company owner wanted to take advantage of SBS to increase his business. One of the ways in which he intended to do this was via Contacts in Outlook. This effective use largely centered around the ability to query Outlook and mail to selected groups, and so on.

There are two ways to apply queries against the Contact list in Outlook: Categories and Advanced Find.

You can display contacts by categories. Here, the idea is to define your Contacts by Category when creating them. To select a Category for a Contact, perform the following steps:

1. Log on at the **PRESIDENT** workstation as **NormH** with the password **Purple3300**.
2. Launch **Microsoft Outlook** from **PRESIDENT** desktop.
3. Select the **Contacts** shortcut icon under **Outlook Shortcuts** (the far left column).
4. Click the **New Contact** button on the Contacts toolbar (far left).
5. Complete the **Contact information** (**name, telephone numbers**, and **e-mail**). I suggest that you enter several contacts from the SBS Stakeholders list shown Chapter 2 (see Table 2.2). The steps for entering a contact were provided several pages ago under Add a Contact section.
6. Open a Select the **Categories:** button at the bottom of the **Contact** dialog box.
7. Observe the list of categories in the **Categories** dialog box.
8. Select the categories that you want associated with this contact. Select a similar category (for example, **Business**) for at least two of the Contacts. Click **OK**. Then you will **Save and close** the Contact. Repeat this step as necessary.
9. To view Contacts by the categories you have selected, choose the **Current View** menu option under the **View** menu. Select **By Category** as you view.

You can now manipulate Contacts by different groups of Categories. Expand the Business category (assuming you placed several Contacts in the Business category). Such manipulations might include sending an e-mail to each Category member inviting them over to the company back lot for a Friday afternoon BBQ.

Using Advanced Find

Using the advanced find capability in Microsoft Outlook is closer to performing a real database query. Here is how you use the advanced find capability. Note I assume you entered the stakeholders as Contract records as suggested in Step 5 above.

1. Log on at the **PRESIDENT** workstation as **NormH** with the password **Purple3300**.

2. Launch **Microsoft Outlook** from **PRESIDENT** desktop.
3. Select the **Contacts** shortcut icon under **Outlook Shortcuts** (the far left column).
4. Select **Find** from the **Tools** menu (you can also click the Find toolbar object)
5. Select the **Advanced Find** link in the upper right corner. The **Advanced Find** dialog box is displayed.
6. Select the **Advanced** tab. Enter field-specific search criteria in the **Define More Criteria** portion of the Advanced Find dialog box. In this example, I have selected **ZIP/Postal Code** by clicking the **Field** button and selecting from Address fields. I then entered the zip code **98234** in the **Value:** field. Click Add to List.
7. Click **Find Now**. This should display Ted Rockwell when I run the query.
8. Be sure to save your query for future use, so you don't have to rebuild it again. To save your query, select **Save Search** from the **File** menu of the Advanced Find dialog box.
9. Close the **Advanced Find** dialog box by selecting **File** menu, **Close**.

You now see a list of Contacts that meet your criteria. You might use these listed contacts for sending e-mail and so on.

Advanced Calendar Topics

The last discrete advanced area I want to cover is Calendar. Again, Calendar remains a wildly popular function in Outlook, and my SBS clients are using Calendar in ways that are somewhat unusual, but highly effective. These areas include group appointments, automatic meeting planning, scheduling resources, and Public Folders.

Making Group Appointments

No sooner do you get your own scheduling act together with Calendar than you will want to extend its capability to schedule group meetings with fellow SBS users. You can easily accomplish this by following these steps.

1. Log on at the **PRESIDENT** workstation as **NormH** with the password **Purple3300**.
2. Launch **Microsoft Outlook** from **PRESIDENT** desktop.
3. Select the **Calendar** shortcut icon under **Outlook Shortcuts** (the far left column).

4. Create a new appointment by selecting the **New Appointment** button on the Outlook toolbar.
5. Create a new appointment (for example, **SSL Annual Meeting**). Add an appointment location, time, and description.
6. Click the **Invitee Attendees** button on the Appointment toolbar. The appointment is modified to include the **To:** line.
7. In the **To:** field, add names of individuals you would like to invite to the meeting. You can use the names of internal SBS users (shown by clicking the To: button), or you can simply type an Internet username (for example, **NormH@springersltd.com**). Using the SSL methodology that is the basis for this book, select the group **SPRINGERSLTD**.
8. Click the **Send** button.

You have now invited users to a meeting.

> BEST PRACTICE: The key to using this approach is the ability to invite individuals via Internet-based e-mail. That's a practical way of scheduling meetings and doing business today.

Automatic Meeting Planning

There is an algorithm in Outlook that reminds me of that darned linear programming class I took in college. You might or might not know that *linear programming* is oriented toward finding an optimal solution given constraints. This Outlook-based tool is called the *AutoPick*, which evaluates the calendars for SBS users and selects a time that is mutually agreeable or open on all calendars. Then, potential attendees are scheduled for this meeting. Two caveats must be noted when using AutoPick: First, all SBS users must maintain up-to-date calendars. Second, this feature works only with SBS users on your network. That said, AutoPick is a great feature.

To use AutoPick, complete the following steps:

1. Log on at the **PRESIDENT** workstation as **NormH** with the password **Purple3300**.
2. Launch **Microsoft Outlook** from **PRESIDENT** desktop.
3. Select the **Calendar** shortcut icon under **Outlook Shortcuts** (the far left column).

4. Create an appointment in Calendar. Consider scheduling a retreat several months hence.
5. Select the **Attendee Availability** tab.
6. Add Attendees in the **All Attendees** column by clicking the **Invite Others** button (the **Select Attendees and Resources** dialog box will appear and you will add attendee names from the left column to the right fields of **Required** or **Optional**. Click **OK** to close the **Select Attendees and Resources** dialog box when you have selected the people you want to attend the event). Their calendar busy times should show up as filled lines. I suggest you select several employees of SSL.
7. Click the **AutoPick right-find arrows** (the double arrows pointing to the right next to the AutoPick button) and AutoPick automatically runs and reports to select a mutually agreeable time.

You have now automatically scheduled a meeting in Microsoft Outlook.

Public Folders

You can use Public Folders in numerous ways. I'll discuss three here: scheduling a conference room, creating company-wide calendars, and creating a company-wide contact list. The underlying idea, all specifics aside, is to manage critical company information at a single location (centralized management). That way, your SBS users know what is occurring when, how to contact individuals, and so on.

Scheduling Resources

Another popular use of Outlook is the scheduling of resources, such as the company car or conference room. You can easily accomplish this by creating a Calendar item in the Public Folders. Complete the following steps:

1. Log on at the **PRESIDENT** workstation as **NormH** with the password **Purple3300**.
2. Launch **Microsoft Outlook** from **PRESIDENT** desktop.
3. Select the **Calendar** shortcut icon under **Outlook Shortcuts** (the far left column).
4. Make sure the folder list is displayed in the center pane by clicking the **Folder List** button on your Microsoft Outlook toolbar.
5. Expand the **Public Folders** icon.
6. Expand the **All Public Folders** icon.

7. While **All Public Folders** is highlighted, display the secondary menu via a **right-click**.
8. Select **New Folder** from the secondary menu. The **Create New Folder** dialog box appears.
9. Name the folder something meaningful, such as **Conference Room B Calendar**.
10. Verify that the **All Public Folders** object is highlighted in the **Select where to place the folder:** screen area. Make sure the **Folder Contains** field reflects **Appointment Items** (if not, drop down the menu to show Appointment Items). Click **OK**.

BEST PRACTICE: If asked by the Assistant to Add shortcut to Outlook Bar, click **No**.

11. To modify the permissions for this calendar item, right-click the new Calendar icon under **All Public Folders**. In this example, you would right-click **Conference Room B Calendar**.
12. Select **Properties** from the secondary menu to display the Calendar Properties dialog box. The **Conference Room B Calendar Properties** dialog box appears.
13. Select the **Permissions** tab.
14. Select which SBS users may have permission to author the calendar (this means they can add appointments). In the SSL methodology, click the **Add** button. The **Add Users** dialog box appears. Select **Bob Easter** in the left column and click **Add**. Click **OK**. Bob Easter now appears under the **Name:** and **Role:** screen area. By default you will note that Bob Easter is an author who can create and read items. Click **OK**.

However, you will typically give reviewer rights for read only (for simply viewing the schedule). The author or higher right (such as editor right) would allow you (or any SBS user with this right) to schedule the resource. That means, given the editor right, an SBS user may schedule Conference Room B for a meeting. More important, even as a reviewer, an SBS user may see whether the resource is available. This approach prevents double-bookings of resources.

You have now created a shared calendar for scheduling a resource.

Company-wide Calendar

Back to the small law firm I assist. One huge need, met by Outlook, was the use of Outlook's Calendar for scheduling law firm-wide appointments, litigation, and employee schedules. I specifically satisfied this need by the following approach:

- A Calendar, titled Law Firm, was placed in a Public Folder. To do this, I followed the same steps you used to create a resource calendar.

- All SBS users were given the edit right to the calendar. To do this, I followed the steps related to granting Calendar permissions that I presented earlier today.

- Entries booked into the Calendar adhered to a code system. Each entry was preceded by the SBS user's initials to reflect who the appointment related to. For example, "HMB - In Court (Johnson Matter)" as a calendar entry would reflect that a lawyer with the initials *HMB* was booked in court for the Johnson matter.

Company-wide Contacts

Similar to having a company-wide Calendar, there is great merit in having a company-wide Contact book. Why? Because of all Outlook features, Contacts are probably the best suited to centralized management. Clients, stakeholders, associates, and prospects come and go. Not only that but last names, telephone numbers, and most of all, e-mail addresses, are tricky to type correctly.

By having company-wide Contacts, you can centralize both the presentation and administration of key contacts. Typically, one of the SBS users, such as an administrative assistant, performs the administration of the Contacts.

> BEST PRACTICE: Only one user should have the right to edit the company-wide Contacts for many of the reasons stated earlier, such as correct spellings. Identify who that person in your organization might be. In a moment, I'll show you how to set permissions on the company-wide Contacts to implement this approach.

The process of creating company-wide Contacts is similar to that for the Calendars that you just created. The steps are these:

1. Log on at the **PRESIDENT** workstation as **NormH** with the password **Purple3300**.
2. Launch **Microsoft Outlook** from **PRESIDENT** desktop.
3. Make sure the folder list is displayed in the center pane by clicking the **Folder List** button on your Outlook toolbar (or selecting **Folder List** from the **View** menu).
4. Expand the **Public Folders** icon.
5. Right-click the **All Public Folders** icon to display the secondary menu.
6. Select **New Folder** from the secondary menu.
7. Name the folder **SSL Company-wide Contacts**.
8. Select **Contact Items** in the Folder Contains field.
9. Make sure **All Public Folders** are highlighted in the **Select where to place the folder:** list.
10. Click **OK**.
11. Right-click the new **Contacts** item under All Public Folders in the Folder List to set permissions. Under the SSL methodology, you would right-click on **SSL Company-wide Contacts** and select **Properties** from the secondary menu.
12. Select the **Permissions** tab when the **SSL Company-wide Contacts Properties** dialog box is displayed.
13. Note that the default permission of Author is much too generous. Make the **Default permission** that of **Reviewer** by highlighting **Default** under **Name:** and selecting **Reviewer** under the **Roles:** drop-down menu. Give one user, Melissa Overlaking the rights of Editor by clicking the **Add** button (which displays the **Add Users** dialog box), selecting **Melissa Overlaking,** and clicking the **Add** button followed by **OK** to close the **Add Users** dialog box. With Melissa Overlaking highlighted, selected **Editor** under the **Roles:** drop-down menu. Melissa Overlaking will maintain the company-wide Contacts (everyone else will review the Contacts). Click **OK** to close the **SSL Company-wide Contacts Properties**.

Start entering and using the company-wide Contacts! This will be of great benefit to you in the real world. Having a current Contacts list that has correct spellings can offer your firm a significant competitive advantage. Why? Because as you enjoy this new century, the new phrase that pays is "You Are Your Database!" Thus, accurately maintained company metainformation, such as company-wide Contacts, can significantly enhance your competitiveness.

Security

And now, I'll provide a quick commentary on security. When SBS configures the workstation, the Outlook application is configured to use a mailbox for the user who is assigned to that workstation. That is good, because it means if another SBS user tries to work at your workstation, that person can't see your Outlook mailbox.

Basic Security Conflict

Assume your workstation is attached to an SBS network. If I log on to your workstation as myself (not you) and I launch Outlook, I receive an error message when I try to access your Outlook mailbox. This error message indicates your Outlook mailbox can't be opened. Why? Because I am not logged on as you. Your Outlook mailbox is protected by Windows 2000 Server-level security. This is a roundabout way of saying that, in this scenario, your private and confidential e-mail remains private to you, even if I am logged on.

However, if you somehow installed the Personal Folders capabilities under the Services dialog box (found under the Tools menu as discussed earlier), I'm possibly on my way to reading your e-mail. Why? Because if you use Personal Folders to manage your Outlook activity (e-mail, contacts, calendar, and so on), you do not benefit from the Windows 2000 Server security model described immediately above. In fact, if I merely walk up to your workstation, log on as myself or even bypass the SBS network logon dialog box by hitting the Esc key (on Windows 9x machines), I can easily read your e-mail simply by opening your Outlook application. So you better hope that if you operate under the personal folders scenario, you don't keep any incriminating or embarrassing e-mails in your Inbox.

> BEST PRACTICE: You should take seriously the weaknesses discussed earlier regarding Personal Folders. Few SBS users appreciate having their e-mail read without first providing permission to do so! You should also note that there is a way to password protect your Personal Folders, but few people actually take the time to do this. See the Outlook 2000 online help system for further details.

Any User, Any Time Revisited.

The solution to having multiple users on one workstation, each having the ability to read their own Outlook-based e-mail, is very simple. You will recall I discussed this capability in the context of users sharing workstations in the Group Policy discussion in Chapter 4. I mentioned it again in Chapter 5 when I discussed adding multiple users to a single machine. And for those of you who are reading especially closely, you remember that this topic of adding multiple users was briefly discussed in the BEST PRACTICE that followed Step 4 of setting up the client computer (and near Figure 4-13) in Chapter 4.

BEST PRACTICE: If the user you intend to log on with next was not added as a user to the specific workstation during the SBS workstation setup process in Chapter 4 (which adds the users as local administrators with the ability to install programs locally), you will need to do this manually at this point. You can not rerun the magic disk at the workstation again to cure this (where you would be presented with a screen to add more users to a workstation) as you'll get an erroneous error message saying the users have already been added locally, which they haven't).

Log on to the **SPRINGERSLTD** domain at the workstation as **Administrator**. In the case of the SSL methodology, you will use the password **husky9999**. Click **Start**, **Settings**, **Control Panel**. **Administrative Tools**, **Computer Management**. The Computer Management snap-in appears. Expand **System Tools** in the left pane and then expand **Local Users and Groups**. Expand **Groups** and open via a double-click on the **Administrators** group in the right pane. In the **Administrators Properties** dialog box, click **Add**. Select **springersltd.com** in the **Look in:** drop-down menu. The **Select Users or Groups** dialog box appears. Select the **users** you want to add as local Administrators to the machine and click **Add**. In the SSL methodology, in order to complete the forthcoming keystrokes, you will need to add **Linda Briggs**. Click **OK**. Click **OK** to close the **Administrator Properties** dialog box. Close the **Computer Management** snap-in. Log off as the **Administrator** by pressing the **Ctrl-Alt-Delete** keys and selecting **Log Off**. Click **Yes** when you see the **Log Off Windows** dialog box. You may now return to the step-by-step in this section.

And, of course, you could have saved this painful step if you had added the users who you thought might use this workstation in the future at the time you created the magic disk in Chapter 4. But, granted, few of us think that far ahead nor do we always have all of our future needs so explicitly defined when we create the network, eh? Oh, and I almost forgot—in all fairness, needs do change over time, so you might never have thought of addressing this matter in Chapter 4 when you created the magic disk!

So, follow these steps to configure the PRESIDENT machine for use by Linda Briggs.

1. Log on to the **PRESIDENT** workstation as user **LindaB** with the password **Golden10**.
2. Click **Start**, **Settings**, **Control Panel**, **Mail**. The **Microsoft Outlook Properties** dialog box appears.
3. Click **Show Profiles**.
4. Click **Add** on the **General** tab of the **Mail** dialog box. The **Microsoft Outlook Setup Wizard** appears.
5. Select **Microsoft Exchange Server** under **Use the following information services**. Click **Next**.
6. Type **Linda Briggs** in the **Profile Name** field. Click **Next**.
7. On the **Microsoft Exchange Server** page of the Microsoft Outlook Setup Wizard, type **SSL1** in the **Microsoft Exchange server:** field and confirm that **Linda Briggs** appears in the **Mailbox:** field (otherwise type **Linda Briggs** in that field). Click **Next**.
8. Answer **No** to **Do you travel with this computer?** Click **Next**.
9. Click **Finish** on the **Done** page.
10. Select the **Linda Briggs** profile under **When starting Microsoft Outlook, use this profile:**.
11. Click **Close** to close the **Mail** dialog box and close the **Control Panel** window (**File**, **Close**).

BEST PRACTICE: Assuming you have added the user that will use this machine to the local administrators group on the machine, you will need to perform Steps #1 to #10 again for each user that you want to have use this machine and see their Exchange-based e-mail in Outlook.

12. At this point you are still logged on as LindaB. Click **Start**, **Programs**, **Microsoft Outlook**. The **Windows Installer** dialog box will inform you the Outlook 2000 will complete its installation. You can now view the e-mail for Linda Briggs.

13. Do me a Texas-sized favor while you are still in Outlook and click **Tools**, **Options**, the **Mail Services** tab, and then the **Prompt for a profile to be used** button. Click **OK**. This will stop Outlook briefly when its launched and allow whomever to select their specific Outlook profile and proceed to read their e-mails. If you don't select this, the default profile tries to load regardless of the logged on user, and all users except the one whom the profile refers to will receive a nasty error message. This is the error message that says Outlook couldn't open the mailbox and would you like to open the default folders on your local hard disk instead. Thanks in advance.

BEST PRACTICE: So, what are the lessons learned here? Most important, I wanted you to see that users who intend to use a Windows 2000 Professional workstation need to be added to the local Administrators group in order to be fully functional (including the ability to install applications locally). Second, adding users to a workstation process performed by the magic disk in during the workstation setup phase doesn't automatically create Outlook profiles for each user, just the first user. Finally, you will have to manually create the user profiles for Outlook for each user that intends to use the Windows 2000 Professional workstation. Whew!

Third-Party Devices

Lastly, I address the use of popular third-party, handheld personal digital assistants (PDA) such as a Windows CE-based device (the Nino from Phillips is an example of this). These PDAs can integrate with Microsoft Outlook so that you have an up-to-date calendar, your contacts and tasks, and even your e-mail Inbox with you when you're out of the office.

The key to this integration is the synchronization process that must occur between the PDA and your Outlook mailbox. This process is shown in Figure 12-6.

Figure 12-6
Outlook/PIM Synchronization.

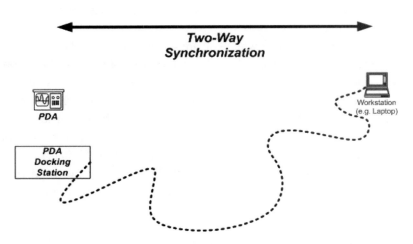

In the case of the Phillips Nino, you first install the Windows CE software that accompanied the PDA on your workstation (to do this, follow the setup instructions that accompany the Windows CE CD Disc). Then, you configure relationship between the PDA and the workstation. In the case of Nino, you define a PDA device in the Mobile Devices window (e.g., Harryb2) as seen in Figure 12-7.

Notes:

Figure 12-7

The Phillips Nino PDA is configured by naming the PDA device in the Mobile Devices window.

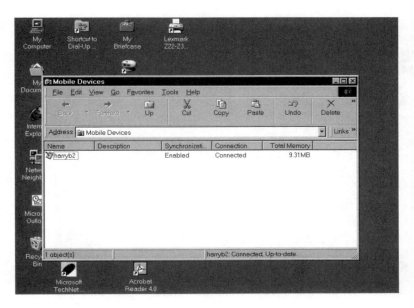

By selecting ActiveSynch Status from the Tools menu in the Mobile Devices window, you can observe what items are configured to synchronize and what their current status is. This is shown in Figure 12-8.

Notes:

Figure 12-8

This PDA is configured to only synchronize the Outlook Calendar (as Appointment) and the Outlook Contacts (as Contact).

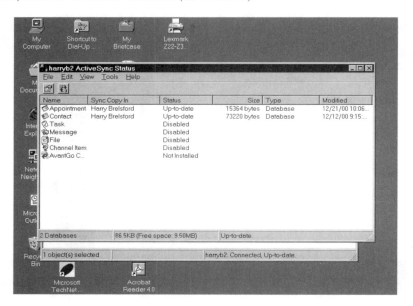

> BEST PRACTICE: The steps to configure a PDA with a workstation vary by manufacturer, so the steps presented above, while they relate specifically to the Nino, give you a general idea of what's involved. Consult the user documentation that accompanied your PDA for configuration specifics that relate explicitly to you.

Now, assuming you have configured your PDA to work with your workstation, you would simply dock it into its docking station. In the case of the Nino, it will then automatically launch Outlook and perform the synchronization of the items you've configured to synchronize. It works very well (and easily!). More important, it allows you to store critical data (contacts, calendar, e-mail) in two locations (the workstation and the PDA) with ease. It is this last point that is a basic tenant to disaster recovery in information technology. I thought you might enjoy that insightful tidbit of knowledge.

More Cool Capabilities!

It just keeps getting better with Outlook in an SBS environment, but I'm starting to approach the end of today, so I'll hurry. In this section, I show you two more cool capabilities in Outlook: publishing your schedule as a Web page and using Outlook Web Access. Later in the book, in Chapter 19, I'll introduce a couple of more cool tools including Outlook Team Folders and Digital Dashboard.

Creating a Calendar Web Page

A little know feature in Outlook that is pretty cool is the ability to publish your calendar as a Web page, viewable from any modern Web browser (such as the latest release of Internet Explorer or Netscape). To accomplish this, complete the following steps as part of my SSL methodology to publish Norm's calendar.

1. Log on at the **PRESIDENT** workstation as **NormH** to the SSL SBS network. Remember that his password is **Purple3300**.
2. Launch **Outlook 2000** either from the desktop or **Start**, **Programs**, **Microsoft Outlook**.
3. Select the **Calendar** shortcut icon under **Outlook Shortcuts** (the far left column).
4. Click **File**, **Save as Web Page**. You will receive a **Microsoft Outlook** dialog box informing you that you need to configure the Web Publishing Wizard in Internet Explorer.

BEST PRACTICE: The dialog box titled **Microsoft Outlook** provides the steps to configure Web Publishing via the Web Publishing Wizard (via Add/Remove Programs in Control Panel) but the steps are valid for Windows ME/9x. These steps are faulty for Windows 2000 because Internet Explorer doesn't appear in the list of installed applications in Add/Remove Programs in Control Panel. It's a god-awful oversight, if you ask me, and it's because Internet Explorer in Windows 2000 does not allow you to customize the installation or use of any advanced options in the Setup program. This behavior occurs because of the new Windows File Protection (WFP) feature in Windows 2000. For more information, be sure to read the Microsoft Knowledge Base article Q256340 found at www.microsoft.com/support. Believe me, any further discussion is way beyond the scope of this course! But hang on to your hats as I've got a work around for Windows 2000 Professional users in the next paragraph.

Okay, welcome to the next paragraph. Here's the work around. For Windows 2000 Professional users, go to Microsoft's Web site at **www.microsoft.com** and search (click the **Search** button in the tool bar) on the terms **Web Publishing Wizard** (type these in the **Search for:** field). You will see several results are returned, but select **Microsoft Web Publishing Wizard: More Information** at the following address: http:www.microsoft.com/Windows/SOFTWARE/webpost/wp2.htm (note that I didn't send you here initially as the Web address may change over time. Click the **Download Microsoft Web Publishing Wizard** link, followed by clicking the **microsft.com Download Center** link. Click **wpie415-x86.exe - 455Kb**. When the **File Download** screen appears, select **Save this program to disk** and click **OK**. Save to a location such as **C:\Temp** in the **Save As** dialog box and click **OK**. Click **Close** when the **Download Complete** dialog box appears. Click **Start**, **Run**, **Browse** and navigate to and select **wpie415-x86.exe**. Click **Open** and then click **OK** in the **Run** dialog box. Click **Yes** after reading the license agreement on the **IExpress Wizard** dialog box. The Web Publishing Wizard will automatically be installed. And you thought roping calves in the Texas hill country was hard.

BEST PRACTICE: Granted, I'm assuming that you are at PRESIDENT (a Windows 2000 Professional machine) and attempting to perform these actions across the SSL SBS network, using the Internet connection you established in Chapter 9. However, if for some reason you're not able to establish a bona fide Internet connection as you work through this book, you may very well need to simply read this section today to appreciate what is occurring and then perform the steps at a later date (or when you set up an SBS network for real).

5. If Outlook is still open, close and restart **Outlook**. Outlook is closed from **File**, **Exit** and restarted from the Outlook icon on your desktop.
6. Select the **Calendar** shortcut icon under **Outlook Shortcuts** (the far left column).
7. Click **File, Save as Web Page**.
8. The **Save as Web Page** dialog box will appear. Complete the **Start date:**, **End date:**, **Calendar Title,** and **File name:** (where you will save the file) fields. Note that the **Open saved web page in browser** option is selected, which will display the calendar in Internet Explorer. Click **Save**.
9. When the **Microsoft Outlook** dialog box-based notice appears saying that you need to install the publishing capabilities of Outlook, click **Yes**. The Windows Installer will run automatically.

10. The calendar will appear as a Web page in Internet Explorer.

BEST PRACTICE: You would use a program such as a File Transfer Protocol (FTP) application to copy the Web page representing Norm's calendar to the location where your Web site is hosted (typically some hard disk space provided by your ISP) if you wanted to truly make it viewable over the Internet. Alternatively, you could place the calendar Web page in a folder on the SBS server and share said folder as a Web folder via Internet Information Server (IIS), a topic I discuss in Chapter 17.

Also – I assume that you created an Internet connection in Chapter 9 to facilitate Internet-based activity, such as using the FTP application.

And that's it! Publishing a calendar to a Web page is useful for a small business that wants to communicate its free and busy times to external parties such as friends, family and the all important customers.

Using Outlook Web Access

Many people have come to appreciate the usefulness of Outlook Web Access (OWA), which allows you to check your e-mail on the SBS network from distant Internet locations. It is automatically configured as part of Microsoft Exchange 2000 Server in SBS 2000, a change from prior SBS versions where you had to manually configure the server-side OWA capabilities.

From any modern Web browser (e.g., Internet Explorer or Netscape), you can type in the external IP address of your sever as the Uniform Resource Locator (URL) in the Address field (say **131.107.6.200**) followed by **/exchange**. You will be challenged by a logon dialog box and, assuming you are properly authenticated on the network, OWA will run and you'll see your Inbox in your Web browser!

BEST PRACTICE: I assume that your SBS network has either a full-time broadband connection or router-based connection to the Internet, so the machine running SBS has full-time availability to receive incoming OWA requests. The Internet connection was created in Chapter 9.

You will now check Norm's e-mail via OWA with the following steps. Note these steps could be performed across the Internet, but are performed on the internal SBS network in this example for simplicity.

1. Log on at the **PRESIDENT** workstation as **NormH** to the SSL SBS network. Remember that his password is **Purple3300**.

2. Launch Internet Explorer from the desktop or **Start**, **Programs**, **Internet Explorer**.

3. In the **Address** field of Internet Explorer, type the external IP address of the machine running SBS followed by /exchange. Alternately, to complete this task, you can type the internal IP address so the command would appear as: **http://192.168.16.2/exchange**. (Again, I'll use the internal IP address in my screenshot as it is something you can replicate if you didn't create the Internet connection in Chapter 9). Tap your ever-faithful **Enter** key in order for Internet Explorer to read the address.

4. When the **Enter Network Password** dialog box appears, complete the following: User name (e.g., **NormH**), Password (**Purple3300**), and Domain (**SPRINGERSLTD**). Click **OK**. You will be authenticated on the SSL SBS network.

5. OWA will launch and you will see the Inbox for NormH, as seen in Figure 12-9. Notice that OWA has nearly the same full functionality as the regular Outlook 2000 client including Inbox, Calendar, and Contact.

Figure 12-9

The default view in OWA is the Inbox, as shown for NormH.

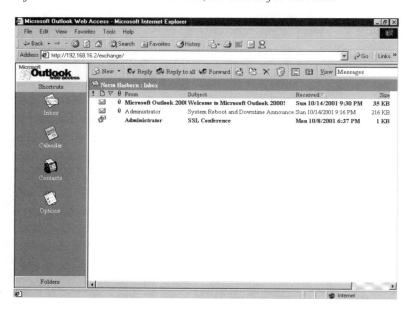

6. You will now send an e-mail to the SBS network administrator informing this individual that OWA is working. Click the **New** button on the OWA toolbar. Note that you may see the Windows Installer dialog box appear briefly as a few Outlook 2000 components are downloaded and installed on your client machine. No intervention is required by you at this time.

7. In the **To** field, type **Administrator**. In the **Subject** field, type **OWA is OK!**. In the body of the e-mail (the large text box beneath the e-mail header), type the following sentences: **I have tested OWA, and so far, so good. Please reply to this e-mail to confirm it is working for e-mail send and receive activity. Thanks! NormH.** Click the **Send** button.

BEST PRACTICE: Observe that the OWA-based e-mail message has much of the same functionality found in the regular Outlook 2000 client, such as the paperclip button for adding an attachment and the exclamation mark button for identifying the message as important.

You will also be pleased to know that this version of OWA is much faster and more stable than the version used in SBS 4.5 with Microsoft Exchange Server 5.5. In other words, it works very well this time!

8. Now go to your SBS server machine, log on as **Administrator** with the password **husky9999,** and launch **Outlook** (**Start**, **Programs**, **Microsoft Outlook**). You will recall that you configured Outlook for the Administrator on the server earlier today. Observe that the OWA-based e-mail sent by NormH appears in the Inbox. Double-click to open the e-mail, read and reply (click the **Reply** button) with a text message of your choice, such as **Thanks NormH! I got it!,** and then click **Send**.

9. Return to the workstation **PRESIDENT** where **NormH** should still be logged on to both the SBS network and OWA (otherwise log on at PRESIDENT as NormH and establish the OWA session again). Click the **Check for New Messages** in the center of the OWA toolbar for the Inbox to refresh with new e-mails. Note you must manually check for e-mail using this button, as OWA is not dynamically updated like the regular Outlook 2000 client (remember to tell your users to click the **Check for New Messages** button often!). The e-mail reply sent by the administrator in Step 8 appears in your Inbox. You have now sent and received e-mail in OWA!

The OWA client has several other features, many of which are poorly documented. I've already mentioned the Inbox, Calendar, and Contacts, but here are some others:

- **Address Book.** By clicking the **Address Book** button on the OWA toolbar, you can search for employee names on the Exchange-based e-mail system. After clicking the **Address Book** button, the **Find Names** dialog box appears as a browser window. Type **Linda** in the **Display name:** field and click **Find**. The name **Linda Briggs** will be returned in the lower part of the Find Names dialog box, assuming you entered all of the SSL users on the SBS network back in Chapter 4. Click **Close** to close the Find Name dialog box.

- **Options.** In the Shortcuts pane to the left, click **Options**. Several options appear including the **Out-of-Office Assistant,** which you can set to notify people you are absent (and you can include a short message explaining your absence). What's really cool is that you can set this from remote locations as needed. You will also observe settings for the **Date and Time Formats**, **Calendar Options,** and **Contact Options**.

- **Folders**. Click the **Folders** button at the bottom of the left pane and the entire mailbox structure for NormH will be displayed. This includes not only the **Inbox,** but **Deleted Items**, **Drafts**, **Journal**, **Notes**, **Sent Items,** and **Tasks** (in addition to **Calendar** and **Contacts,** which I've previously mentioned).

Needless to say, OWA has been very popular with my SBS clients, and I'm sure it will be with you and those you turn on to SBS!

Summary

With the end of Chapter 12 at hand, you now have the basic and advanced Outlook skills that you need to be successful with Outlook on your SBS network. I discussed several topics, including basic features, such as sending e-mail, creating a contact, and setting an appointment. Additionally, I presented advanced features using e-mail, calendars, and contacts. I also covered advanced configurations, security, use of third-party devices, and a couple of cool tools!

Chapter 13
Remote Connectivity

One of the drivers for implementing SBS 2000 is the remote connectivity function. Hyperactive business managers (known as Type-A) love this feature because, when they combine it with telecommunications technologies such as DSL, they can work from their home office after hours and on the weekend. Regular workers enjoy remote connectivity for checking e-mail early on bad traffic days. Remote connectivity not only justifies the implementation of SBS but catches on very quickly. In this chapter, using the SSL methodology, you will learn how to implement remote connectivity solutions in SBS. This includes running the Internet Security and Acceleration Server 2000 (ISA) virtual private networking wizard. I also cross-reference Terminal Services (presented in Chapter 8) and introduce NetMeeting as part of your possible remote connectivity solution. NetMeeting, a desktop control application, is one part of the remote connectivity solution employed by Springer Spaniels Limited (SSL), the sample company used across this book.

Understand that the world we live in today, with SBS 2000, is really about remote sites connecting to the SBS network. Much less frequent is the need for an internal user on the SBS network to dial out to a remote network. Why? Because outbound communication from an SBS network is mostly to the Internet. Other outside resources that one might "ring up," such as a bulletin board system (BBS) or a private business, have declined dramatically in popularity. Possible outbound communications include dialing the bank to conduct business, the credit bureau to obtain a credit report, or the drug testing laboratory to obtain a certain employee's urinalysis drug test reports (true story). But even many banks have migrated their transactional environments to the Web!

SBS Remote Connectivity Architecture

At its core, the remote connectivity solution is based on the first two components discussed below. Two other components are also presented.

Routing and Remote Access Service

The first component, Routing and Remote Access Service (RRAS), is what I'd call a core service. It is installed automatically as part of the SBS 2000 setup yet set to a disabled startup condition. RRAS needs to be configured in order to operate. That's because, while a core service, it is not preconfigured in SBS 2000. RRAS is managed from the **Routing and Remote Access** snap-in (accessed from **Start**, **Programs**, **Administrative Tools**, **Routing and Remote Access**).

Figure 13-1

Viewing RRAS from the Routing and Remote Access snap-in in its virgin state prior to any configuration activities.

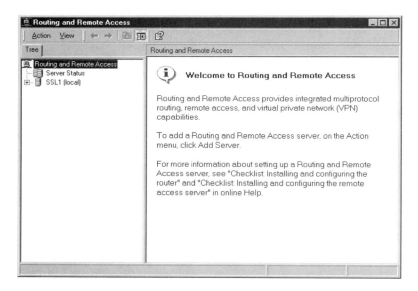

BEST PRACTICE: To learn more about remote access the official SBS way, click on the **Configure Remote Access** link on the SBS 2000 **To Do List** (accessed from the **To Do List** icon beneath **Small Business Server [BackOffice Manager]** on the SBS Administrator Console).

Note that in this chapter you will configure the ISA VPN Wizard that is discussed when the Configure Remote Access help screen appears. You will also activate remote access on SBS 2000 as part of the ISA VPN configuration process.

The role of RRAS is to handle inter-network routing and manage communications. I'll focus on the communications aspect in this chapter.

BEST PRACTICE: If you read the **Description** field on the **Routing and Remote Access Properties [Local Computer]** dialog box under **Services** (from **Start**, **Small Business Server Administrator Console**, **Computer Management [Local]**, **Services and Applications**, **Services**), you would see the following somewhat inaccurate description: "Offers routing services to businesses in local area and wide area network environments." This description really doesn't apply to SBS 2000 and its single network paradigm, does it?

A better and more accurate way to view RRAS in SBS 2000 is that it supports and manages the communication function. This includes supporting virtual private networks (VPN), providing underlying support for the ISA Server VPN wizard. Another area of support is providing modem management for inbound calls to the SBS network.

Shared Modem Service

Another communication mechanism is the Shared Modem Service, which is used for outbound modem-based communications. Search as you may in the SBS Administrator Console or the SBS Personal Console, you can't find a link or snap-in for the Shared Modem Service. But don't fret too long; it's only a Control Panel applet away (**Start**, **Settings**, **Control Panel**, **Shared Modem Service**). The Shared Modem Service property sheet is shown in Figure 13-2.

Notes:

Figure 13-2

Configuration tab sheet on the Shared Modem Service Admin on \\SSL1 property sheet.

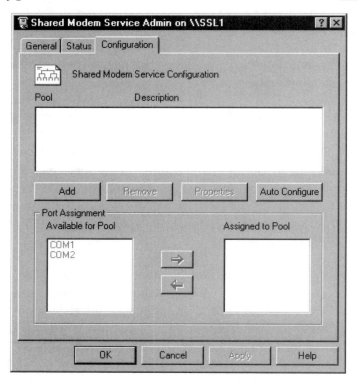

What's interesting about Figure 13-2 is that, while the Shared Modem Service is installed and started by default when SBS 2000 is set up, that's about it! You will note on the Configuration tab that no Shared Modem Service pool is configured by default.

> BEST PRACTICE: Use the **Auto Configure** button on the **Configure** tab seen in Figure 13-2 when you want to build your modem pool for outbound, modem-based communications. It really works, my friend! Existing modems installed on the SBS 2000 server will be detected and added to the modem pool that is created.

After the modem pool is built, because the Shared Modem Service starts when the SBS server boots, you are in business for outbound calls to be made from the Shared Modem Service. That's it! Okay, maybe one little thing to check. You

need to make sure your modems are connected via a telephone cord to a functioning telephone jack. While kinda silly to say, it's a step I've overlooked in the past.

So far, I've only shared with you the server-side of the Shared Modem Service.
But there is a client-side too. As you might recall from Chapter 4, the client-side
setup chapter, you could elect to install the client-side Microsoft Shared Modem
Service Client. In case you've forgotten this discussion area, please revisit
Figures 4-8 and 4-17. So then, you would expect the client-side application to be
something impressive, eh? See for yourself and click **Start**, **Programs**,
Microsoft Shared Modem Service Client and look at the program group.
Surprisingly, the only program item found is a Web page titled **Microsoft Shared
Modem Service Client Help**, as seen in Figure 13-3.

Figure 13-3

Viewing Microsoft Shared Modem Service Client Help.

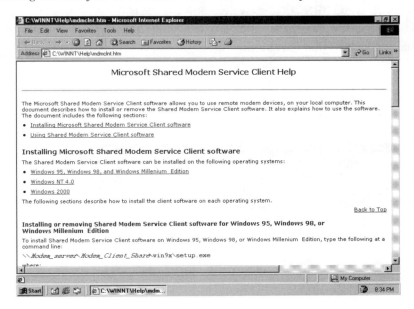

In a sense, there is nothing more on the client computer, at least as far as the eye
can see. The goal on the client computer is to redirect a physical communications
port (COM), such as COM2, to the server-side shared modem pool. In other
words, when a client computer communications application needs modem-based
communications, those communications will be directed through the SBS 2000
server machine. Whew! That was a mouthful.

BEST PRACTICE: I'll save a little timber here and direct your attention to the information displayed in Figure 13-3. I basically have nothing to add to this. But what's interesting to me is that it all comes down to a command line (yes—you've read correctly!). And just what is that command-line entry? You will type a command that starts with **netmodem**.

Fact of the matter is that the Shared Modem Service works well. I just don't use it very much in this era of Internet connectivity via broadband connections. However, when I delivered an SBS 2000 speech at a Direct Access event in Puerto Rico in the spring of 2001, I was educated that international markets still are very big users of modem-based communications with SBS 2000. This includes the Shared Modem Service.

Network and Dial-up Connections

Meanwhile, back at the SBS 2000 server machine, there is the Network and Dial-up Connections window. To display the **Network and Dial-up Connections** window (seen in Figure 13-4), right-click on **My Network Places** and select **Properties**.

Figure 13-4
Network and Dial-up Connection window.

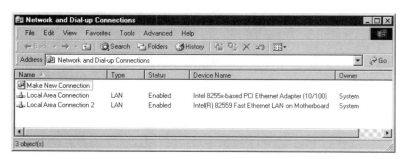

The Network and Dial-up Connections window is primarily used to configure the network adapter cards, as you may recall from prior chapters. But you can also configure dial-up communications, as the window name would suggest. If you double-click **Make New Connection** and click **Next** at the **Welcome to the Network Connection Wizard**, you will see the **Network Connection Type**

screen, as seen in Figure 13-5. This is the same screen that you see in Windows 2000 Professional and, as you can read below, a few of the options apply to Windows 2000 Professional rather than SBS 2000. The options are:

- **Dial-up to private network.** This really applies to a client computer running Windows 2000 Professional.

- **Dial-up to the Internet.** Here again, this is really something you'd use on a Windows 2000 Professional client computer.

- **Connect to a private network through the Internet.** DO NOT select this option with SBS 2000 as it's unlikely you would want to SBS 2000 server machine to connect to another remote network.

- **Accept incoming connections.** This is really oriented toward a Windows 2000 Professional client computer.

- **Connect directly to another computer.** Clearly, this is a Windows 2000 Professional capability.

Figure 13-5
The Network Connection Type screen.

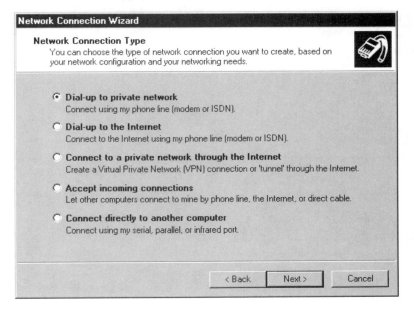

BEST PRACTICES: I want to emphasize two points about Figure 13-5.

First, you will use the ISA VPN Wizard to configure VPN connectivity in SBS 2000. Period. This will be demonstrated later in the chapter.

Second, the ability to accept incoming calls on the SBS server machine will be configured via the Routing and Remote Access snap-in.

Phone and Modem Options

A most pleasant surprise in SBS 2000 is that the underlying Windows 2000 Server operating system will, in most cases, detect and install modems. This is part of the Device Manager capability in Windows 2000. You may recall this occurred in the SBS setup in Chapter 3 in Step 20 of the SBS setup routine. Please revisit that now if you need a refresher.

To be honest, the good old Phone and Modem Options screen, shown in Figure 13-6, is about modem drivers, AT commands, and configuring TAPI providers. Yuck! But it is one place to confirm that your modem was correctly detected. Remember that it is these modems that can be added to the shared modem pools.

Notes:

Figure 13-6

The US Robotics modem setup in Chapter 3 is displayed in the Phone and Modem Options window.

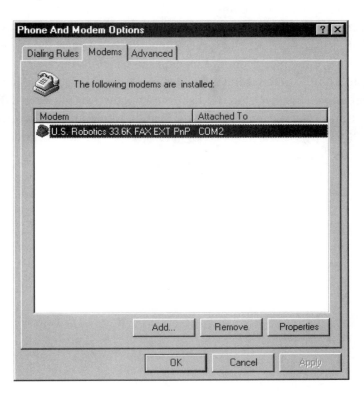

With that, I bring the remote connectivity technical architectural discussion to an end and move forward to discuss different types of remote connectivity in the next section.

Remote Control Versus Remote Node

Let's just cut to the chase. Everyone agrees remote connectivity is a good thing on an SBS network. What's much less clear—and the main point of this section—is the difference between remote control and remote node. By the end of this section, you might well join me in concluding that many people really want remote control as their remote connectivity solution. Why? Because a simple remote node connection has somewhat limited functionality and is often slower. Read on.

A Picture Is Worth a Thousand Words

I want to walk through a complex figure to aid in my discussion of this concept. Figure 13-7 is actually a drawing I've used with my clients to communicate a matter that is sometimes more maddening than mellow. I'll honor the SSL sample company framework in the drawing, but be advised that the only remote control solution proposed for SSL users is actually a combination of (A) and (D), which is a combination of VPN and NetMeeting. I include (B) which is Terminal Services in Remote Administration Mode to make my discussion inclusive and not lacking in alternatives. Likewise, in (C) I show a hypothetical Windows 2000 Server running Terminal Services in Application Sharing Mode to show you what the remote connectivity possibilities are. Note that I discuss Terminal Services in tremendous detail in Chapter 8.

Notes:

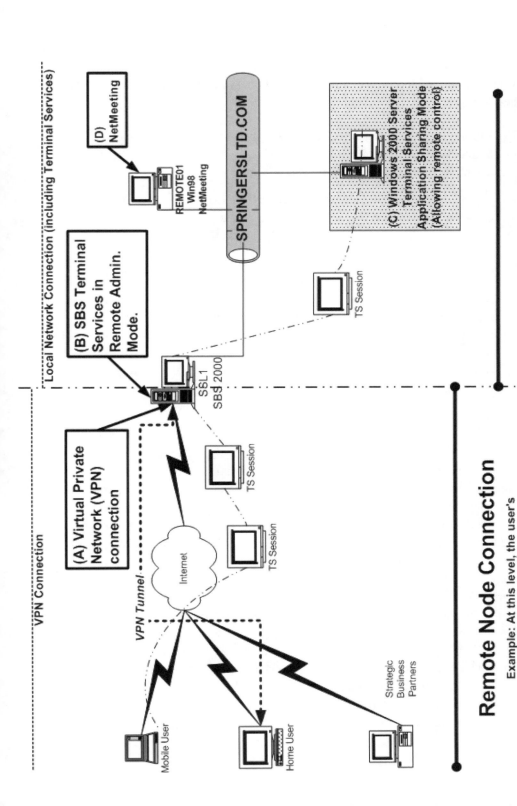

Figure 13-7

Framework for analyzing remote node and remote control.

So, exactly what is occurring in Figure 13-7? The short answer is "a lot." Seriously, starting on the left, you can clearly see three common remote connectivity needs:

- Mobile User. This would typically be a traveling business person trying to access the SBS network from the hotel. In the case of SSL, this is often Norm Jr. in his salesman role.

- Home User. This can be someone who is working from home during the day or a regular employee working from home after hours. Norm, the president of SSL, is known to remotely access the SSL SBS network from his home after hours.

- Strategic Business Partner. As an SBS consultant, I've seen many of my SBS clients (often going against my better judgment) allow their clients and vendors to have access to their SBS networks. Because the client is always right, it's not my role to quash their request, but rather to facilitate it. The facilitation means implementing a remote connectivity infrastructure that is secure and speedy! Note that in two cases the strategic business partner remote connectivity request came from accounting firms. Here, the idea was to allow accounting firm clients to access their financial information.

In the middle of it all is the SBS 2000 server machine through which all remote connectivity passes. In scenarios (A) and (B), the remote connectivity scenario ends there. Remote connectivity scenario (A) is explained in the next section and (B) is explained at length in Chapter 8. After establishing a remote connection, such as a VPN session over the Internet, you could connect to a non-DC Windows 2000 Server machine running Terminal Services in Application Sharing, as seen in scenario (C). And yes, even though it's deemphasized by Microsoft in this day and age, NetMeeting still has very much of a remote communications role. I discuss NetMeeting below in Remote Control and then again in a section near the end of the chapter on installing and configuring NetMeeting on a client computer.

BEST PRACTICE: Double-check yourself and confirm that you know what a VPN solution really is. Many of us do know what VPNs are, but you'd be surprised who doesn't and won't admit it in public. When I was involved with producing the Small Business Server 2000 Setup video prior to the release of SBS 2000, the script was specifically rewritten in one section to include a VPN primer, based on user feed-back. Note the Small Business Server 2000 Setup video is part of the Partner Guide referenced in Appendix A of this book.

Technically speaking, here's what a VPN is all about. You are effectively creating a secure tunnel across the Internet between the remote host (e.g., user) and the server (e.g., SBS 2000 server machine). This secure tunnel establishes a network connection between user and server. There are many fine texts that delve deeper into VPN technicalities, so after reading this book, feel free to avail yourself of those tomes.

Remote Node

I liken the remote node discussion to a college finance lecture on risk. Many of my clients will say that they want a VPN connection. End of discussion. Okay, once configured, they see it's really not all that exciting. Sure, you can map a drive to access data files. You can run an application. But typically my clients were expecting much more – that is, more bells and whistles, more system speed and responsiveness.

My point is this. In finance, there are many definitions of "risk." In remote connectivity, there are different definitions of "remote node." More often than not, my clients are confusing remote node with remote control, something I explore in the next section. So, the bottom line is that a remote node connection performs for you just as though you were sitting at your desk at work on the SBS network. An example of this is your e-mail account as managed through Outlook 2000 when you synchronize your mailbox to a local *.pst file. With a remote node connection, the Outlook session is much like an Outlook session at work. The user's Outlook mailbox contains the Inbox and other Outlook objects, such as Calendar. Upon closing, the mailbox synchronizes with the local *.pst file, allowing the user to work offline. This sounds good on the surface, but it can run very slowly.

BEST PRACTICE: I've found most people are disappointed with remote node connections alone because the speed and responsiveness are discouraging. Think about it. Even with a broadband connection, the remote node connection is still but a fraction of the connection speed found on a true LAN at work. Talk about an expectation management problem.

Don't forget the raw connection speed is also hampered by network overhead, such as broadcast activity, NetBIOS name resolution, and browsing. Go ahead and see for yourself with a basic VPN connection —it's not all it's cracked up to be.

Catch the headline on the bottom left side of Figure 13-7 that correctly depicts the remote node connection including the SBS 2000 server machine. Regardless of all the verbal babble I've laid on you the past couple of paragraphs, that's what you want to understand.

Remote Control

Even though your SBS network users or SBS clients might not exactly say it right, they are in all likelihood looking for a remote control solution. I've seen it many times. When you turn someone on to Terminal Services (C) or NetMeeting (D), as seen in Figure 13-7, they say, "Oh yeah…that's what I want." Properly implemented as discussed in Chapter 8, Terminal Services in Application Sharing Mode costs some bucks, which often causes small businesses to balk. A free remote control solution, NetMeeting, allows users to "remotely control" a workstation, just as if they were sitting at work.

Semi-technically speaking, what is occurring here is that "screen images" are passing to and from the remote user and the workstation is being controlled. These screen images are more efficient travelers than full network traffic. Note that includes mouse-clicks and keyboard activity traveling as part of the screen images.

Security

It helps to have friends in high places. When confronted with intense security discussions, I typically feign coughing, excuse myself from the situation, and call one of my security gurus on my cellular telephone from the parking lot. Hey – I'm an SBSer, not a security consultant. I only understand security matters to a certain level of depth, and I say that with a small smirk of pride. I've conferred with the security experts on the Microsoft SBS development team, a leading

MCSE security consultant, and even a hot-shot twenty-something hacker. All have signed off on SBS 2000's remote connectivity solutions as providing effective and sufficient security for the small business.

> BEST PRACTICE: As of the fall 2001, the Microsoft SBS team is releasing to its certified partners a ten-hour computer-based training (CBT) advanced course on SBS 2000. It is likely that this courseware will be made available to others for purchase, something you could determine by checking the SBS resources listed in Appendix A. If you have the opportunity to use this CBT, kindly turn your attention to **Module 1: Microsoft Small Business Server 2000 Administration** and then the **Small Business Server 2000 connectivity** learning event. The first learning object called **Using VPNs on Small Business Server**, a sample slide of which is shown in Figure 13-8, is truly an experience in being taken to school on VPN security. I found myself being soundly educated in an area where I can always afford to know more.

Figure 13-8
Microsoft's SBS advanced training for certified partners goes into great detail on security, both ISA firewall and VPN. Heck – it's even better than the Windows 2000 Server Resource Kit!

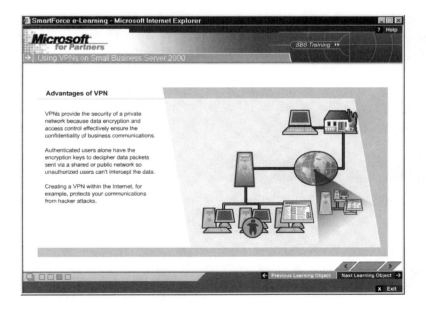

BEST PRACTICE: Just so you don't BBQ me for ducking and dodging the security issues surrounding remote connectivity, let's establish the facts. It's a fact that each of the VPN methods available under ISA Server 2000 are encrypted methods. It's a fact that the point-to-point tunneling protocol (PPTP) method that I'll use in the next section on configuring VPN connectivity via the ISA VPN Wizard is considered effective security. And it's a fact that the remote control methods I've suggested in the context of Figure 13-7 provide sufficient security (primarily because you establish a VPN connection first via the SBS 2000 server machine).

So enough theoretical hooey! Let's tickle the ivories and implement VPN capabilities in SBS 2000.

Server-side VPN Configuration

Time to get back to work and help SSL implement VPN connectivity. Here's the task before you.

1. At **SSL1**, log on as **Administrator** using the password **husky9999**.
2 Click **Start, Small Business Server Administrator Console**.
3. Expand **Internet Security and Acceleration Server 2000, Servers and Arrays, SSL1, Network Configuration**.
4. Click **View, Taskpad**.
5. Select **Configure a Local Virtual Private Network (VPN)**, as seen in Figure 13-9.

Notes:

Figure 13-9

The taskpad view displays a user friendly interface.

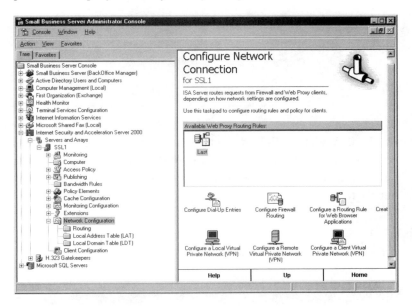

6. Click **Next** at **Welcome to the Local ISA Server VPN Configuration Wizard**.

7. Click **Yes** at **ISA Virtual Private Network (VPN) Wizard** dialog box that communicates the RRAS service must be started (see Figure 13-10).

Notes:

Figure 13-10

The RRAS service interacts with ISA in the context of VPN connectivity.

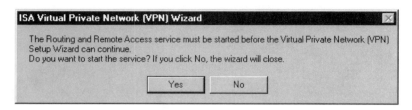

8. On the ISA **Virtual Private Network (VPN) Identification** screen, type **SSL-SBS** in the **Type a short name to describe the local network:** field. Type **Internet** in the **Type a short name to describe the remote network:** field. This is shown in Figure 13-11. Click **Next**.

Figure 13-11

Naming the VPN connection. This naming combination appears on other screens in ISA Server 2000.

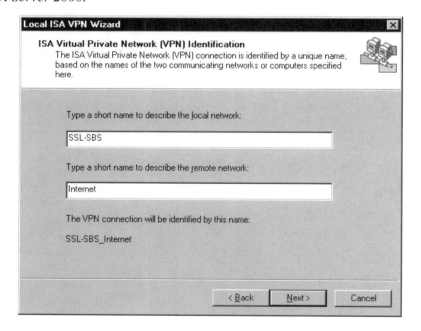

9. The **ISA Virtual Private Network (VPN) Protocol** screen is most important. You will select **PPTP**, as seen in Figure 13-12. Click **Next**.

Figure 13-12

Most small businesses are well served via PPTP in a VPN scenario.

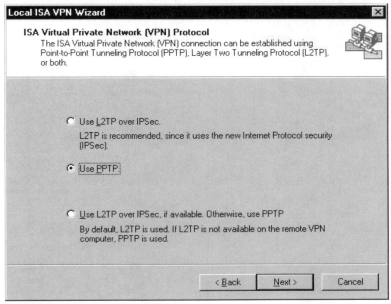

BEST PRACTICE: Oh, sorry to leave you hanging at that last step. The reason why it is incumbent upon you to select PPTP over the other options is for the following reason. The other options require you to set up a Certification Authority (CA) to issue the certificates. Let's not go there right now, although there are some great references to CA in the Windows 2000 Server Resource Kit.

10. To be honest, if you read really closely on Figure 13-13, the **Two-way Communication** screen doesn't apply to the single network paradigm of SBS. Make no selections and click **Next**.

Notes:

Figure 13-13

Leave the Two-way Communication screen alone and move on. This screen really applies to enterprise implementations.

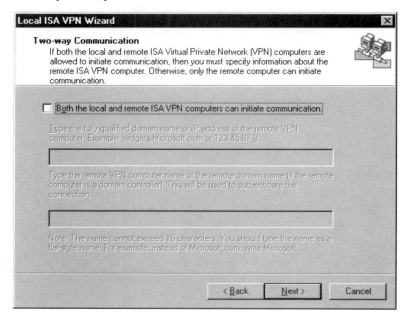

11. You arrive at the **Remote Virtual Private Network (VPN) Network** screen. Here again, if you look closely, it really speaks to enterprise implementations (not SBS). However, the problem is that you can't move on without performing some type of configuration. Why? Because the Next button is grayed out and inactive. Oh, what to do! Click **Add**.

12. A dialog box titled **ISA Virtual Private Network (VPN) Wizard** appears as seen in Figure 13-14. Enter the IP address range of **10.0.0.5** to **10.0.0.6** and click **OK**.

Figure 13-14

Enter a fictitious IP address range for a nonexistent remote network so you can continue to complete the ISA VPN Wizard. .

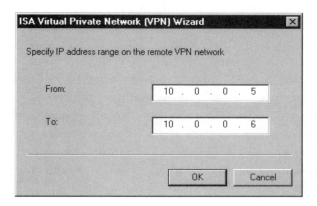

13. In Figure 13-15, observe that the **Next** button on the **Remote Virtual Private Network (VPN) Network** screen is now enabled. Click **Next** and move on.

Figure 13-15

You may now click the Next button and proceed.

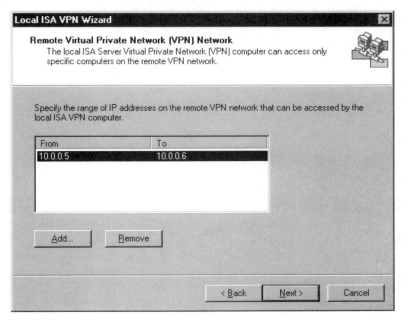

14. The next screen, titled **Local Virtual Private Network (VPN) Network**, is shown in Figure 13-16. For SSL, an adjustment is not required, so click **Next**.

BEST PRACTICE: Dismount the horse for a moment and pull up for a long-winded Harryb lecture. The screen in Figure 13-16 has two important roles. First, at the top part of the screen, you want to verify the external IP address for the SBS 2000 server machine and a two NIC scenario is displayed. This is the IP address that remote users will ring to establish a VPN session. Second, note the internal network address ranges displayed at the bottom of the screen. This is where you configure the ability for remote clients to access the entire network, not just the SBS 2000 server machine once a VPN session is established. By default, well-known private address ranges are listed, including the SBS default 192.168.16.x range.

Those SBSers who come from prior releases, that is SBS 4.x, will recall that under **Network** properties, **Services**, **Remote Access Service**, you made a VPN configuration that allowed a remote user to access the server machine or the entire network. You are effectively making that same setting in Figure 13-16.

Okay, time to mount the horse and ride again.

Notes:

Figure 13-16
Take an extra moment to read with interest this screen regarding wild-side IP addresses and internal network addresses.

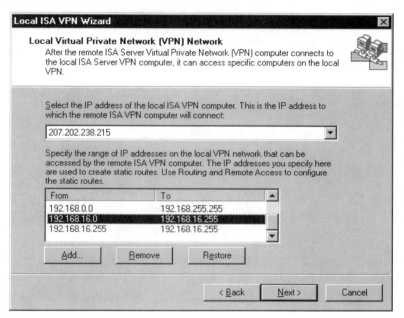

15. Well, the long journey to implement the ISA Server-based VPN solution is nearing the end. The **ISA VPN Computer Configuration File** screen, shown in Figure 13-17, allows you to save all this VPN stuff to a configuration file. In the SSL methodology, simply type **ssl** in the **File name:** field, leave the **Password:** and **Confirm password:** fields blank and click **Next**.

Notes:

Figure 13-17

The VPN configuration information is saved to a file for reference by ISA Server 2000.

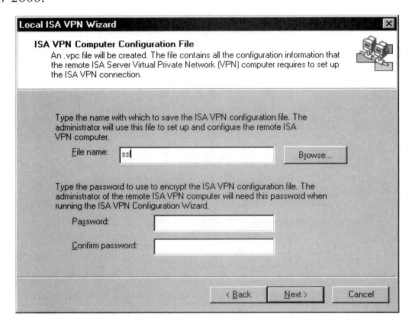

16. The **Completing the Local ISA Server VPN Configuration Wizard** screen appears. In a moment, you will click **Finish**. But first, click **Details** and observe the rich information on the **ISA Server Virtual Private Network (VPN) configuration summary** screen (shown in Figure 13-18). Click **Back** and **Finish**.

BEST PRACTICE: Highlight with your mouse this configuration text information and copy and paste it into your SBS network notebook. The SBS network notebook was discussed in Chapter 7 and other chapters.

Notes:

Figure 13-18

The VPN configuration information is saved to a file for reference by ISA Server 2000.

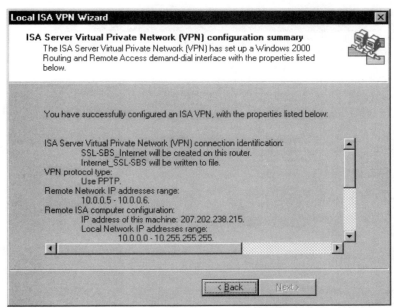

And that's it, my fine furry friend. You've implemented the suggested VPN solution in SBS 2000. But before moving on, let's do a tad of Missouri-state action. That is, "show me" where the configurations we just made are implemented. In the **Internet Security and Acceleration Server 2000** snap-in, you can see some PPTP packet filter entries under **IP Packet Filters** (beneath **Access Policy**). This is shown in Figure 13-19.

Notes:

Figure 13-19

The PPTP protocol settings are taken directly from the steps in the last section where you ran the ISA VPN Wizard.

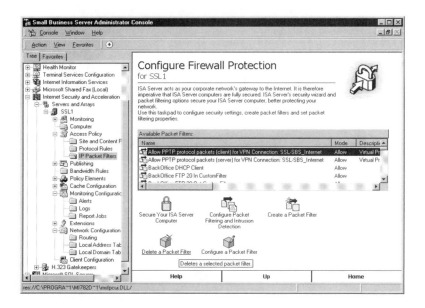

BEST PRACTICE: I'd encourage you to double-click and read with interest the two PPTP entries shown in Figure 13-19. You'll be taken to a property sheet that has a couple of tab sheets that better explains what in the heck is going on here!

And don't forget that RRAS was impacted by the ISA VPN Wizard activity. The place to see this is the **Routing and Remote Access** snap-in (**Start, Programs, Administrative Tools, Routing and Remote Access**). Expand **SSL1 (Local)** and click **Routing Interfaces**. On the right side you'll see the **SSL-SBS_Internet** demand-dial interface created by the ISA VPN Wizard. This is shown in Figure 13-20.

Figure 13-20

If you double-click the SSL-SBS_Internet entry, you'll see even more details than displayed here via a property sheet.

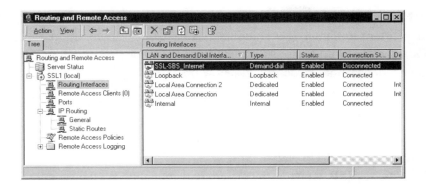

Client-side Remote Connectivity

With an eye cast toward pragmatism and an appreciation for the real world, I now present, in often painful detail, the complete client-side connectivity. There is a story behind this. After implementing VPN and Terminal Services capabilities on the SBS server-side for a client, I went home smiling. Another successful SBS surgery! Said client called back a few weeks later and communicated that, unfortunately, no one was using the mystical and magnificent solution. I was asked to return and create a remote user manual. I'm basically presenting that here for your benefit and that of your SBS users who will want to take advantage of some or all of the remote connection possibilities before them. Note that this could be considered a slight departure from SSL methodology because it is drawn from a real client.

> BEST PRACTICES: The examples below are based on Windows 98. And while many of the basic ideas hold true for Windows XP and Windows 2000, the actual keystrokes will vary. For example, in Windows 2000 Professional, you'll configure your VPN connection via the **My Network Places, Properties, Network and Dial-up Connections, Make New Connection** (as discussed earlier in this chapter under Network and Dial-up Connections in the SBS Remote Connectivity Architecture section).

End-User Remote Connectivity Guide

This guide will allow you to connection to the Internet and access the company SBS network. You will be shown how to establish a VPN connection.

Connect to the Internet

The first step, after turning on your computer, is to establish a connection to the Internet. Establishing a valid Internet connection is critical before either of the two communications solutions described below may be used.

To establish a valid Internet connection, you will to connect via the ISP.

1. In Windows 98, double-click **My Computer**.
2. Double-click **Dial-Up Networking**.
3. Double-click **ISP**, which is the dialer created by the SBS consultant. The **Connect To** dialog box will appear. Verify the **user account name**, **password**, and **telephone number,** and click **Connect**. Note that you may have a desktop icon titled "1. ISP Connection" allowing you to jump to step 3 immediately (avoiding steps 1 and 2 above).

> BEST PRACTICE: If you are in a hotel room or at a location with a PBX telephone system, you may need to modify the telephone number with a "9" and perhaps a short pause (a pause is denoted with a comma) to get an outside line. Note some hotel and PBX telephone systems require you to add an "8" to get an outside line.

Once an Internet connection is established, you will see a connection icon in the lower right-hand corner of your desktop. You may look at the status of your connection (to further verify the "fitness" of the connection) by right-clicking on the right-hand corner connection icon and selecting **Status**.

If you need to troubleshoot your Internet connection, consider the following:

- Verify ISP "Connect to" dialer settings.

- Verify ISP dialer property settings with the following steps.

1. Right-click the **ISP** dialer in **Dial-Up Networking**.
2. Select **Properties** from the secondary menu. The **General** tab sheet for ISP will appear.
3. Select the **Server Types** tab sheet. Verify that only the **Enable software compression** selection is made in the **Advanced** options section. Verify that only **TCP/IP** is selected in the **Allowed network protocols** section.
4. Click on the **TCP/IP Settings** button in the lower right-hand corner of the **Server Types** tab sheet. A **TCP/IP Settings** dialog box appears. Confirm that the **Server assigned IP address** radio button is selected. Confirm the **Server assigned name server addresses** radio button is selected.

At this point, you've completed the settings verification.

Perform Internet connection testing

Part of your troubleshooting effort should involve testing the connection. This will be accomplished by the Ping and Telnet commands, both of which will be typed at the command line. These are very simple, low-level tests that allow you to determine whether you have basic Internet connectivity. Granted, most of the time these tests need not be performed and you can proceed to using the Internet as described next. However, when you have connection problems, it is these tests that will indicate at what level the failure is occurring.

Let's start with the Ping test.

1. Click the **Start** button on the Windows 98 desktop.
2. Select **Programs**, **MS-DOS prompt**. The MS-DOS Prompt window will appear.
3. Type each of the Ping commands at the command line.

```
ping 209.20.130.41 (this is nwlink.com)
ping cnn.com (this is the CNN news network)
```

If the Ping command succeeds by responding with a positive result, proceed to troubleshooting via the Telnet command. If the Ping command is not successful (as denoted by a "host unreachable" response), see the next steps discussion later in the chapter.

Another way to test basic connectivity is to use the Telnet program.

1.   Click the **Start** button on the Windows 98 desktop.
2.   Select **Programs**, **MS-DOS prompt**. The MS-DOS Prompt window will appear.
3.   At the command line, type:

```
telnet nwlink.com
```

4.   If you see the Northwest Link logon prompt, your test was successful. Close the Telnet screen with the upper right-hand close box denoted by "**X**". If the test was unsuccessful, see the Next Steps discussion in a moment.

Connect Via VPN

After a successful Internet connection has been established, you may now attempt to create a VPN connection. The benefits of this type of connection are:

*   Use e-mail

*   Use the corporate database

*   Use Microsoft Office products

*   Manipulate files (read, save, delete) that are stored on network drives

*   Access other basic network functions

To create a Virtual Private Network connection, perform the following steps in Windows 98.

1.   Double-click **My Computer** on the Windows 98 desktop.
2.   Open **Dial-Up Networking**.
3.   Double-click the dialer connection titled **VPN**. (Note that this was created by the SBS consultant to dial the external IP address of the SBS server machine).
4.   The **Connect to** dialog box will appear. Enter your **user name** in the **User name** field ("Jon") and enter your **password** in the **Password** field. Verify the VPN Server address is a correct IP address as per the company technology policy book and click **Connect**.

5. The connection process may take up to several minutes depending on your location and the speed of your modem. If you are presented with a network logon dialog box (**Enter Network Password**), please enter your **user name**, **password** and make sure the **SBS domain name** (e.g., SPRINGERSLTD.COM) is listed.

You will note that you have a successful VPN connection when you notice a second connection icon on the lower right-hand portion of your desktop (similar to the original modem connection to the ISP). If for some reason a VPN connection can not be established, please reboot your laptop and try again. Note the reasons for VPN failures are varied, such as the telco (e.g., QWEST) providing erratic DSL service, an immediate disconnection notice on your screen after making a successful connection, and so on. If you are unable to establish a VPN connection after rebooting you machine, proceed to the next steps discussion below.

Next Steps

As promised, if you're high and dry and having connection problems, here's some last resorts. Consider these two alternatives for connecting to the SBS network to accomplish your work.

- Alternative Connection Method #1: Go to Kinko's and rent a PC by the hour. Kinko's stores are located in nearly every major city and college town. For approximately $10/hour or so, you can rent a powerful computer that has a high-speed connection to the Internet. From the Internet Explorer web browser, connect via Outlook Web Access to the e-mail system. This is an excellent method for reaching the SBS e-mail system.

- Alternative Connection Method #2: If your travels find you in another business office or at a friend's house, simply try to borrow a computer, log on to the Internet, and access the e-mail system via the Outlook Web Access.

Using NetMeeting

Granted, NetMeeting has become something of a second cousin to Terminal Services when it comes to managing the SBS server machine from afar. I'll give you that. However, NetMeeting is still one of the best darn remote control solutions (for free to boot) for the client computer. That said, it's the remote connection solution of choice for the SSL users in this book. You will recall from Chapter 2 that the old NetWare server was reformatted with the Windows 98 operating system to exclusively run NetMeeting (see Figure 2-6).

Amazingly, NetMeeting is already included on your client computers after you've run the SBS "magic disk." Follow these keystrokes to implement NetMeeting for SSL on the REMOTE01 client computer.

1. Log on to **REMOTE01** on the SSL network as **Administrator** with the password **husky9999**.
2. Double-click the **Internet Explorer** icon on the desktop.
3. Click **File**, **New**, **Internet Call**. The NetMeeting setup wizard launches.
4. Click **Next** at the first screen with the welcome notice.
5. On the next screen, complete the **First name:**, **Last name:**, **E-mail address:**, **Location:**, and **Comments:** fields similar to Figure 13-21. Click **Next**.

Figure 13-21
Completing a NetMeeting screen with user information.

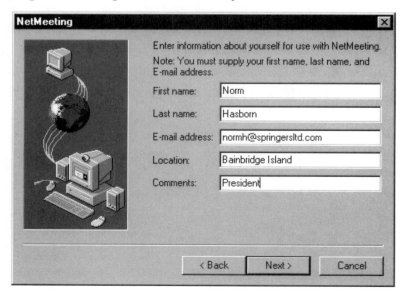

6. Complete the screen discussing directory services similar to Figure 13-22. The key point is that you don't want to have your name listed in a directory service. Click **Next**.

Figure 13-22
Make sure you actively shield your name from Internet-based directory services.

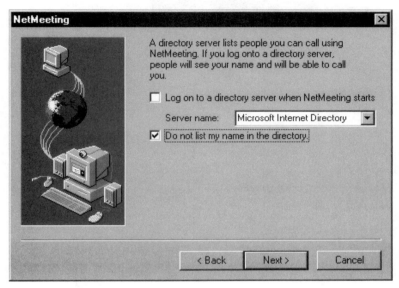

7. On the screen discussing connection speed, select the **Local Area Network** radio button and click **Next**.
8. Accept the default settings on the screen discussing shortcuts and click **Next**.
9. If you receive an error message regarding a missing sound card, click **Next**.
10. Click **Finish.**

And that's it! NetMeeting will automatically start and await the opportunity to answer a call and share the client computer desktop. NetMeeting is shown in Figure 13-23 and with the video camera attached to the client computer and functioning, you see yourself in the center screen.

Figure 13-23

Meet NetMeeting. Note the hand holding the box on the lower left is the desktop sharing button (that's where the remote control capability is invoked).

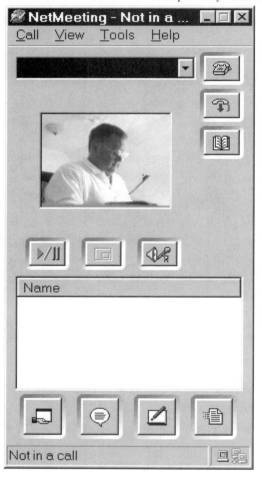

BEST PRACTICE: While I won't go into it completely here, you need to download and install the NetMeeting 3.x Resource Kit from www.microsoft.com/downloads. There is a setup configuration tool that allows you to richly configure how client computers will run NetMeeting. This includes configuring NetMeeting's desktop sharing capabilities so that it runs when the client computer boots. You can also configure the remote desktop sharing capability to request a user name and password before granting access. This last step insures that coworkers who access the SBS network remotely won't improperly access your client computer that has NetMeeting sitting and waiting to answer the call to duty. In other words, you can configure NetMeeting to only allow you to access and take remote control of your client computer desktop.

Other Approaches

Old habits are hard to break. So, instead of using Terminal Services on the one hand or the "free" NetMeeting on the other hand, some folks use the popular remote control solutions of PCAnywhere or VNC. PCAnywhere, shown at a real SBS site in Figure 3-24, doesn't need much of an introduction. Its reputation is legendary (and you can learn more at www.symantec.com as well).

Figure 13-24
PCAnywhere at work in the inner window.

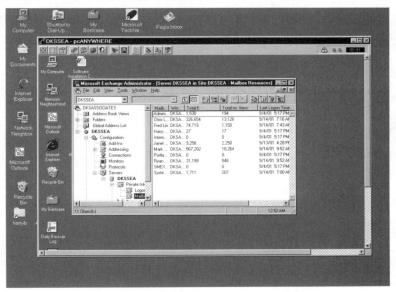

I discussed VNC in Chapter 8, so I kindly refer you back to that discussion at this time.

Advanced RRAS

Take a moment to explore the RRAS snap-in. Lurking under the hood are a few advanced settings that will separate the wheat from the chaff in SBS land. Follow these keystrokes to display the **SSL (local) Properties** property sheet.

1. Log on to **SSL1** as **Administrator** with the password **husky9999**.
2. Click **Start**, **Programs**, **Administrative Tools**, **Routing and Remote Access**.
3. Right-click on **SSL1 (local)** and select **Properties**.
4. Explore each of the tab sheets and click **OK**.

BEST PRACTICE: On the **IP** tab, you will notice that DHCP will assign the IP addresses to the remote hosts. On the **PPP** tab, notice that multilink connections are enabled by default. On the **Event Logging** tab, I suggest you select the **Enable Point-to-Point (PPP) logging** check box to assist in your VPN connectivity troubleshooting tab. This is shown in Figure 13-25. Note that when you select the last option mentioned, you will be asked to restart the RRAS service. Click **OK**.

Notes:

Figure 13-25

When working with VPN connectivity issues, it won't hurt a bit to turn on more aggressive logging features.

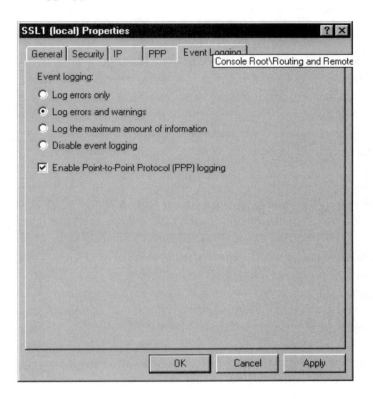

Guest Column

Your Mission—to create the ideal computer environment that allows you access to anything, anywhere, anytime and for it to cost nothing to maintain—well almost! Mission impossible or not the client wanted to reduce costs long term. This was the broad requirement one of our client set us. Basically they wanted to be able to bring their 9 remote stores into the 21st century and have them permanently online so that they could maintain a single accounting and stock control system. The client is in the fashion industry and sells name brand handbags, wallets, and fashion accessories. They have 9 stores, 4 in the Sydney area, and 5 in Melbourne (over 1000km away). A fully integrated accounting system was used for stock control, and normal accounting functions, with the stores providing manual reports on a daily basis via fax. They needed 2 full time staff to key these reports into the accounting system on a daily basis. In addition the client had buyers who often went overseas and needed to maintain full contact with the office during these trips. The existing network was a home built server running NT4 server with third party mail utilities giving selected staff email access via a central modem.

The Solution—this sounded like a job for SBS and Terminal Server. We felt that the store environment was ideal for a Terminal server solution and the existing accounting system had a Point of Sale module and this would provide direct input to the main central database. The only question was how to link them all together cost effectively. The terminal server had low bandwidth requirements which meant we could use modem connections from the stores to head office.

We looked at the location of the stores and found that two were in a local call zone—so these could be handled by SBS's RAS facility and dial directly into the head office LAN. The other two Sydney stores were outside the local call zone and this meant long distance - timed phone charges. The Melbourne stores were also outside the local call zone. We felt that a Virtual Private Network was the best answer to these problems. This allowed the remote stores to connect to the Internet and then create a virtual connection through to head office which had a permanent internet connection. They could then access the Terminal Server and run the POS application.

The Implementation—We did a site audit to determine the existing configuration of PC's and those at the stores. This revealed that key people in the organization were still running 486's—the financial controller being one of these. They could also benefit from the terminal server environment. We built an implemented the SBS server and migrated all of their head office applications over first. Whilst this was happening the ISDN connection to the Internet was being installed and configured. The router connected the SBS server to the Internet for all functions. The VPN was configured on the SBS server and user id's were setup for the remote stores. Because various sales staff at the stores used the system, we wanted to restrict access to email for internal use only—so this was configured in Exchange to allow the store user id's the appropriate level of access. The first store was setup and rolled out—we had a few hiccups which were easily resolved and the remaining stores were rolled out without too many drama's. We brought the stores online progressively over a two week period.

The client then needed to go on a buying trip to Europe—the VPN allowed him to connect to the office and see all the things he needed to see while he was away. Outlook Web Access also allowed him to shoot off a few quick emails whilst he was in the airport lounges waiting for the next flight.

The result—6 months after the implementation the client is happy with the solution provided. Recently they held a "warehouse" sale to sell off excess stock and it took a matter of hours to setup and additional "store" on a notebook PC and run the sale. A target was set to keep the store communications costs below $100 per store per month. A recent review of the costs found that we had achieved and average cost of no more than $30 per store per month—including phone charges. The client is very happy with the savings this represents and can now dedicate those two staff to other more profitable tasks. The client's not sure how he survived without all of these features like the VPN, OWA and Terminal Server. Overall I'd have to say Mission accomplished!

Wayne Small has worked in the IT Industry for over 15 years. He's an MCSE+I with a focus on Exchange Server. He currently runs Correct Solutions which is a Sydney based, dynamic IT Systems Integrator with a focus on Microsoft Small Business Server. They've been associated with Small Business Server since it's inception and focus on the small to medium business market. Wayne likes to spend as much time after-hours with his family and his hobbies include, astronomy, camping and reading.

Summary

Again, what a chapter. So many SBSers are justifying the implementation of SBS networks based on remote connectivity that you really need to master the ISA VPN Wizard approach. Before turning your users on to the VPN way, be sure to test the heck out of it first for stability purposes, etc.

Anyway, this chapter presented the theory behind VPN connectivity, introduced you to how SBS handles VPN connectivity, and showed you how to configure the SBS server machine via the ISA VPN Wizard. Client computer remote connectivity was presented next. And I'm sure that somewhere, somehow, I implored you to use the ISA VPN Wizard, not the RRAS VPN Wizard. Now on to the faxing chapter.

Chapter 14
Faxing

You're now well over two-thirds of the way through the book. The faxing topic is appropriately placed here, later rather than sooner, because it is usually one of the last aspects of the SBS network configuration that my SBS clients suddenly discover. Whereas e-mail and Web browsing are the main priorities out of the gate for most SBS sites, faxing is usually something I can demonstrate when things settle down and I have the client's undivided attention. After other SBS features, such as Outlook, are accepted and widely used, the time is ripe to introduce faxing.

To balance my introduction of the faxing topic, full disclosure is necessary. I have some clients who view faxing akin to religion. Implementing an electronic, network-based faxing solution, such as that found in SBS, was a key driver for that network implementation project. And not only do I know this firsthand from selected clients, but I also know it from the e-mails you (the readers) of my first SBS book sent me. Many of you commented at length how important faxing is in a small-business environment networked with SBS. In fact, the dialog between reader and writer (that's me) revealed a couple of interesting points:

- Faxing, when used, is considered very important.

- In general, SBSers where disappointed with the reliability and capability of the faxing application in previous SBS releases.

- SBSers in the past have opted to deploy third-party faxing solutions, such as GFI Fax, instead of using the native faxing capabilities inside SBS.

The good news is that Microsoft listened to the feedback in the SBS community on faxing. In SBS 2000, the fax application, officially called Microsoft Shared Fax, is one area that received some of the greatest attention. And the results show. It was actually a crack team of developers at Microsoft Israel who "rewrote" or reprogrammed the fax application from the ground up to take advantage of a more stable and robust Windows 2000 code base. The bottom line is this. If SBS previously lost your trust with respect to faxing, I think this is an application release will restore that trust.

In the first part of the chapter, basic SBS faxing is defined as well as configured. You will learn how to send and receive a fax as well. In the second half of the chapter, I discuss fax reporting and other advanced fax topics (such as the property sheet for the Microsoft Shared Fax).

SBS Faxing Defined!

One of the first hurdles to overcome when generating excitement for the faxing function is to educate both yourself and the SBS users as to what faxing really is. In this secular world of atoms, bricks, and mortar, people have long known faxing as the capability to feed a page into a desktop device and send the contents of the page to another fax machine at a distant location. The SBS faxing function, shown in detail in Figure 14-1, includes:

- Sending and receiving faxes via the fax modem attached to the SBS server machine

- SBS's capability to save faxes to the Shared Fax Inbox

- SBS's capability to print faxes automatically to a network printer (see the Fax Printer in Figure 14-1)

- SBS's capability to e-mail the faxes to a designated recipient (see the SBS User in Figure 14-1)

Figure 14-1
Basic SBS faxing function.

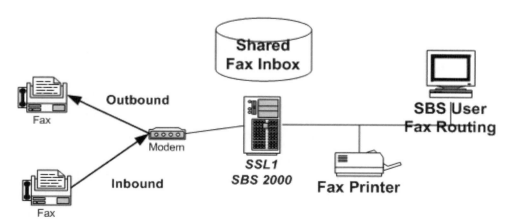

Outbound Faxes

One of the first questions SBS users ask regarding faxing is "How do you get the document into the computer?" This question, when unanswered, poses such a mental block that I've seen small businesses not embrace the powerful SBS fax capabilities. Here is the answer to this fear of faxing question. In reality, you will continue to use your existing fax machine for odd-sized outgoing documents, such as *Dilbert* comic strips that you're faxing to friends and family. You will likely continue to use the existing fax machine to transmit documents, such as letters, that need your signature (although later I'll show you how to scan your signature for your letters). And you'll probably use your fax machine to transmit handwritten notes. So there, I've now said it and clarified a major point of contention surrounding SBS faxing: You'll most likely continue to use your existing fax machine for very specific reasons.

But outbound faxing is in no way a total loser, either. Remember way back (in the first third of the book) when I discussed the landscaping company? The CEO of the landscaping company saw his greatest potential with outbound faxing, targeted to his landscaping customers. His idea was to send out spring planting notices. Here, the outbound faxing capability would be integrated with his Outlook Contacts, something that is easily done.

> BEST PRACTICE: Some progressive SBS sites are using low-cost scanners to scan in odd-shaped documents for use in outbound faxing scenarios. More firms will most likely use this approach in the near future as scanners become cheaper and enjoy greater acceptance (but heck, you can already buy a color scanner for $100, so what are you waiting for?). I'll offer one word of caution with this approach: The scanned images that result when you scan odd-shaped documents are larger than you think. Even moderate scanning activity can result in over 100MB of scanned images. As you can see, you'll quickly eat up hard disk space that you might need. (Even so, hard disks are much cheaper than just a few years ago).

A few key benefits to outbound faxing include:

- Marketing announcements and flyers
- Form letters with a scanned signature

- Standard forms your customers might request

- Other documents appropriate for broadcasting

BEST PRACTICE: Understand that the capability to fax the same document to multiple parties via SBS faxing isn't true broadcasting. Fax broadcasting, in its pure form, is a service provided by a telco with lots and lots of extra fax lines (that is, burst capacity) with the ability to get your document out to tens or hundreds of parties within a few minutes. The telco uses a pool of lines to do this and charges you accordingly for such a wonderful service.

SBS's outbound faxing capability is, shall I say, linear. Given a list of parties who are to receive the same document, the SBS server calls each party in succession and transmits the fax. Such a linear approach can indeed take hours to complete, as each fax call is made one at a time. But fear not, the good news is that this activity is automatic, meaning you do not have to attend to the process (allowing you to go home and slow-cook a great meal, go play golf, and so on).

Inbound Faxes

SBS faxing really shines where inbound faxes are concerned. Here the SBS server machine answers the fax line when a fax is arriving (the telephone line generates a ring like a normal telephone line). The fax is received by the SBS server and processed as an image file: printed, saved to the server's hard disk, or e-mailed to a single e-mail account (or alternatively, it can be sent to an e-mail distribution group).

SBS does not facilitate automatic routing or distribution of faxes to additional e-mail accounts like high-end stand-alone fax applications can do. Other third-party faxing solutions with more advanced features (and, I'll warn you, a much more advanced price tag) include GFI Fax, WinFax PRO (Symantec), Fax Sr., and RightFAX.

The benefits of having the SBS server machine receive a fax include:

- The capability to forward a fax image to others via e-mail.

- The capability to store fax images on the SBS server for future use or as a permanent record. You'd be surprised how important this is when your firm becomes involved in litigation (or better yet, if you're a law firm that provides legal services in the litigation area).

- The capability to refax a document to another party without any loss of fax quality (with real fax machines, when you refax a document to someone else, you suffer a significant resolution loss). I like to refer to this in techno-babble as "non-generational loss of image quality."

- The capability to use your computer network laser printer as a plain-paper fax printer, thus eliminating the curly or heat-transfer fax paper used by older fax machines (which a surprisingly high number of small businesses still use).

- The capability to view a fax on your computer display without printing it first. Under the SBS faxing model, when you receive junk faxes or faxes that simply aren't important, you can quickly glance at them with the SBS workstation fax viewer software (which I'll discuss in a moment) and then delete the fax, never sending it to a printer.

- The capability to read faxes remotely. When faxes received by the SBS server are either forwarded to me via e-mail or simply stored on the SBS server, I can dial in and read these faxes without having to cross the bridge and drive to the office just to retrieve my faxes. This feature alone has made a huge difference for me and my SBS clients, and we've all avoided a lot of unnecessary trips into the office to pick up faxes.

- The capability to scan graphics and signatures for use on your network. I'll show you how to do this later today.

- Using a third-party text-scanning application, such as GFI Fax, to convert the faxed text into text that you can manipulate in your word processing application (this is a technology called Optical Character Recognition or "OCR"). This is still an immature technology that doesn't always work correctly as yet. You still have to proofread text that was converted. One more comment on this area. Other SBSers and I have already offered our feedback to Microsoft's SBS development team that OCR would be a desirable feature in the faxing application in future SBS releases. The good news is that the SBS development team is very good about receiving sincere feedback, so I'd rate it at even or better odds that you'll see OCR in future SBS releases!

More Fax Features

A few other cool features are included with Microsoft Shared Fax, many of which I'll discuss in more detail later today:

- Fax Modem Pool Support. You can attach up to as many fax modems as are practical to the SBS server for faxing purposes. That is, the four fax modem limit from prior SBS releases has been removed in SBS 2000. Using the default modem pool actually supports limited group faxing on outbound faxing. That is, if everyone prints to the same fax printer from the desktop, the faxes can all be sent at the same time because each fax modem would use a separate fax line to initiate its call. This discussion is conceptually similar to printer pooling.

BEST PRACTICE: This fax modem pool capability also has a role for inbound faxing. When combined with a hunt-line capability from your telco, Microsoft Shared Fax allows you to offer never-a-busy-signal-level services for your customers trying to fax your firm. Essentially, all your customers send faxes to a single published fax line, say 206-123-1235 for SSL. If a customer attempts to send a fax, and the first fax modem is occupied, the telco's hunt capability provides the capability to have the second, third, or fourth modem receive the inbound fax call. Cool, eh?

Theoretically, all four fax modems, assuming you have that many, could receive faxes at the same time. And because a small business would almost never receive more than four faxes simultaneously, you could advertise your business as never having a busy fax line!

I should also note that a fax modem pool also facilitates simultaneous inbound and outbound faxing operations, something many small businesses can enjoy only if they have truly separate fax machines. It's a tip worth mentioning to the small-business owner seeking more information on how to use multiple telephone lines and a fax modem pool.

- Fax board support. At the SBS 2000 launch in Atlantic City in February 2001, there was a collective "halleluiah" when it was announced there is native SBS 2000 support for fax modem boards, such as the offerings from Brooktrout. In fact, a representative from Brooktrout was on hand to bask in his moment of glory and answer questions. This is a long-requested capability in SBS, and those who take faxing seriously greatly appreciate this capability.

- Cover Pages. The Microsoft Shared Fax also includes a set of fax cover pages for your use. You can also create your own fax cover pages via Microsoft Word or the Microsoft Fax Viewer software. Be advised that the use of a computerized faxing solution, such as the Microsoft Shared Fax, eliminates the ability to use the popular Post-it Fax Notes (the physical kind you paste onto manual faxes). These tiny scraps of paper, with a sticky backing, are typically attached to the header of the first fax page when using a real physical fax machine. Because you can't physically attach such as a Post-it Note, to a computer-generated fax, you need to be content with using Microsoft Shared Fax-based cover pages when transmitting.

- Control. Via the Manage User in the SBS Console, you can specify who may use the SBS faxing capabilities and who may not. Although not as critical a need as preventing Internet usage abuse, I do have SBS sites – granted, they tend to be old-fashioned companies – that want strict control over who can use the fax capability on the SBS network. And part of the reason for this control are those silly fax cover pages that people send out (like "Let's Seal The Deal" that has a cartoon of an Alaskan seal on an iceberg). You can limit people to a group or legitimate fax cover pages via the control capabilities of Microsoft Shared Fax.

SBS Fax Components

SBS's fax capabilities can be divided into server and client components. First I'll discuss the server side, where basic configuration issues are addressed. On the client side, I'll show what components are installed on an SBS user's workstation.

BEST PRACTICE: Before I go one sentence further, there is something you should know that was mentioned ever so briefly during the SBS setup discussion many days ago: YOU DON'T NEED TO HAVE A MODEM ATTACHED TO THE SBS SERVER MACHINE TO INSTALL AND CONFIGURE MICROSOFT SHARED FAX (I've used capitalization for emphasis – hope it worked). This is a huge improvement over prior releases of SBS and means you only need to physically attach a fax modem once you truly start to use the Microsoft Shared Fax services.

The Server Side: Microsoft Shared Fax

The actual faxing capability installed on the SBS server machine is known as Microsoft Shared Fax. This server-side capability is installed automatically when you install SBS using the complete installation feature (which I recommend). It is comprised of the following three server-side components: Shared Fax Service Server, Shared Fax Service Manager, and Shared Fax Service Console.

Shared Fax Service Server

This is the core server engine and is such a service it is (ov vay!). It is listed with other services (**Start, Small Business Server Administrator Console, Computer Management (Local), Services and Applications, Services, Microsoft Shared Fax**).

> BEST PRACTICE: Now is as good of time as any to impart the following faxing wisdom. If you look under the Printers folder (**Start, Settings, Printers**), you will see two fax printers listed. The **SharedFax printer** is the default fax pool created and used by Microsoft Shared Fax in SBS 2000. There is only the one fax pool used by Microsoft Shared Fax, a very important point to know. The other fax printer listed, Fax, is there for backward compatibility reasons and uses the NT fax driver (not the better Microsoft Shared Fax driver). You and your SBS users should only send faxes to the **SharedFax printer**, which is the default setting.

Shared Fax Service Manager

This is the "official" user interface to configure, manage, and monitor the Shared Fax Service. I show you this in Figure 14-2. Later in the chapter I discuss the Microsoft Shared Fax property sheet as the Swiss Army knife of faxing, where the real heavy lifting occurs. This is accessed by clicking **Start, Small Business Server Administrator Console, Microsoft Shared Fax (Local),** and selecting the **Normal** tab in the detail pane).

Notes:

Figure 14-2
The Shared Fax Services Manager as viewed in the SBS Administrator Console.

Shared Fax Service Console

This is more of a real-time user interface allowing you to view the sending and receiving of faxes as well as monitoring the fax queue and the all-important archiving function for sent and received faxes. This is useful for answering questions from business managers such as "Did we receive that fax from the Ferguson Companies yesterday afternoon?" Note that there are other forms of fax reporting, which I discuss later in the chapter. In the Shared Fax Service Console, accessed from **Start**, **Small Business Server Administrator Console**, **Microsoft Shared Fax (Local),** select the **Normal** tab in the detail pane and click **Manage Fax Jobs** is shown in Figure 14-3.

Notes:

Figure 14-3

Meet the Shared Fax Service Console, a snap-in that runs in an MMC.

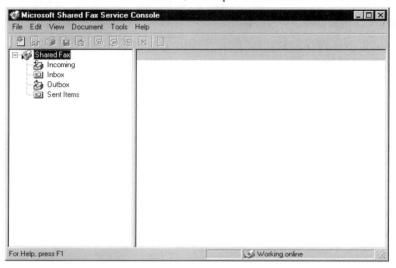

Fax Modem

Talk about a massive improvement in SBS 2000 (and an improvement that isn't obvious at first blush), the installation of a fax modem device in SBS 2000 is truly automatic. Yes, you heard right. When you add a fax modem to the SBS server machine, it is automatically added as a device in the default fax modem pool (SharedFax). This fax modem is automatically configured to send but not receive.

To see where the new fax modem was added as a device and to configure the Receive capability, perform the following:

1. Log on to **SSL1** as the **Administrator** with the password **husky9999**.
2. Click **Start, Small Business Server Administrator Console**, **Microsoft Shared Fax (Local)**, **Devices and Providers**, **Devices**.
3. The modem you added will be listed. Right-click the modem device and select **Properties**.
4. Click the **General** tab.
5. Under **Transmission settings**, select the **Receive Faxes** check box.
6. Select the number of rings before answers in the box next to **Rings** before answering.
7. Click **OK**.

You have now verified that a new fax modem has been added to the SharedFax pool and configured it to receive faxes.

> BEST PRACTICE: Be sure to use high-quality fax modems with your SBS network. A favorite of many SBSers on the Yahoo-based SBS newslist (sbs2k@yahoogroups.com) is the US Robotics V.Everything fax modem. The Yahoo-based newsgroup is discussed more in Appendix A.

Cover Page

You can select from several default cover pages that are sent along with the fax. The Cover Pages listing is shown in Figure 14-4 (**Start, Small Business Server Administrator Console, Microsoft Shared Fax (Local),** select the **Cover Pages**) and one of the fax cover sheet templates is shown in Figure 14-5.

> BEST PRACTICE: You can allow or prevent the use of personal cover pages (yes, the humorous ones) by selecting or deselecting the **Allow use of personal cover pages** on the **Outbox** tab of **Microsoft Shared Fax (Local) Properties** dialog box. See my discussion on the Swiss Army Knife later in the chapter for more on this topic.

Figure 14-4

Cover pages.

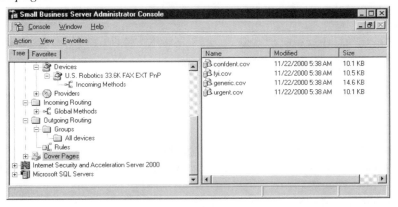

Figure 14-5

Cover page template (fyi).

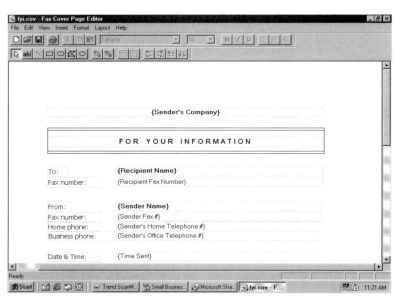

By default, a user is required to use one of the listed cover pages. These cover pages are stored at the following location:

```
%SystemRoot%Documents and Settings\AllUsers\Documents\
Microsoft\Shared Fax\CoverPages
```

> BEST PRACTICE: You can create a cover page for your company and have that cover page be the only fax cover page which can be used on the SBS network. To do this, right-click the **Cover Page** object beneath **Microsoft Shared Fax (Local)** and select **New**, **Cover Page** to launch the **Fax Cover Page Editor**. Create the cover page, with graphics if desired, and save the file with the *.COV extension. This new cover page you've created can now be used as a fax cover page on the SBS network. Be sure to delete the other cover pages so that your SBS users must use your new corporate fax cover sheet by default.

The Client Side: SBS Faxing

On the client side, you handle the main configuration and observation activity via the Microsoft Shared Fax Service Console (the same one as discussed above and displayed in Figure 14-3). This tool is installed when Microsoft Shared Fax is installed.

With the **Microsoft Shared Fax Service Console**, you can send a fax (**File, Send a New Fax**), complete a User Information page, select a personal cover page (if you're allowed to), and view the server status of the computer running the Microsoft Shared Fax server-side service.

User Information

Selecting **User Information** from the **Tools** menu allows you to complete the screen shown in Figure 14-6 so that basic user information is entered onto the fax cover pages. This, of course, would save the user time by not having to type basic identity information each time. This information is, unfortunately, not carried over from the same type of information you entered in Chapter 4 when you set up the user. Bummer.

Figure 14-6
Completing a meta-data user information screen that is used as part of the faxing process. This is for Bob Easter.

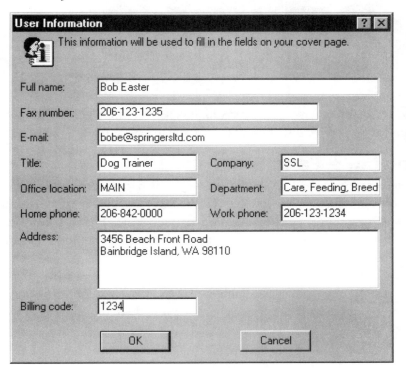

Cover Page

Select **Personal Cover Pages** from the **Tools** menu if you want to (and are allowed to) utilize personal cover pages. And just how do you create said personal cover pages at the workstation? On the **Personal Cover Pages** dialog box, click **New** and the **Fax Cover Page Editor** will launch. You can create the fax cover pages you so desire, even adding TIF photos such as the one of Brisker and Jaeger, the two patriarchs of SSL (see Figure 14-7).

Figure 14-7
Creating a personal cover page on a less-than-serious note for SSL.

After the personal fax cover page is saved, it is listed in the **Personal Cover Pages** dialog. You can and will use it later today to send a fax!

Receiving a Fax

A fax can be received any and all of three ways when the fax modem on your SBS server commences its reception: print the fax, store the fax in the Shared Fax Inbox folder, or e-mail the fax to an SBS user (who typically redistributes or forwards the fax to the receiving party). This was shown earlier in Figure 14-1.

Viewing a Fax

Viewing a fax is truly a point-and-double-click exercise, assuming you don't want to print it out to hard copy but rather keep it in digital form. Whether you receive the fax as an attachment over e-mail or use the Microsoft Shared Fax Service Console at the workstation (or heck, you can even view a fax this way from the SBS server machine but I wouldn't let your users work at the server machine), you simply double-click the *.TIF file that represents the fax. And like magic, the built-in Kodak image viewer (officially called Imaging for Windows Preview) displays the fax.

> BEST PRACTICE: Before jumping into the step-by-step on how to view a fax, I need to impart some wisdom that is essential for end-user success in using the Microsoft Shared Fax Service Console. Hear me out on this. By default, if a fax is received and stored on the SBS server. If a user dutifully launches the Microsoft Shared Fax Service Console application to view this fax, such viewing permissions are denied by default. Say what? You can't view the fax? Yes, it's true. Read on for the necessary permissions adjustments.

Back at the SBS server machine, the SSL administrator must perform the following steps.

1. Log on to **SSL1** as the **Administrator** with the password **husky9999**.
2. Click **Start, Small Business Server Administrator Console**.
3. **Right-click** on **Microsoft Shared Fax (Local)**.
4. Select **Properties**.
5. Click the **Security** tab.
6. Highlight **Everyone** in the **Name** field. Observe that, by default, Everyone is only given the Submit low-priority faxes and Submit normal-priority faxes permissions. This is a very low-level of fax permissions, so you'll want to consider adding fax-related permissions to Everyone to improve the functionality of the SBS faxing capability.
7. Select **View incoming messages archive** under **Permissions** for the purposes of viewing a fax from a workstation as part of the SSL methodology using the Microsoft Shared Fax Service Console.
8. I'm jumping the gun, but while we're here, please also select the **View outgoing messages archive** permission so that later on, when you send a fax, you can see how it is stored by SBS 2000 in the fax service outbox.
9. Click **OK**.

Now, look at Figure 14-8 and observe that the arriving fax on the SSL SBS 2000 server machine is now visible from NormH's machine using the Microsoft Shared Fax Service Console. This is a critical set of steps to perform for viewing received faxes.

Figure 14-8

Correct permissions for viewing incoming faxes, set at the SBS server level, allow NormH to view the fax Inbox.

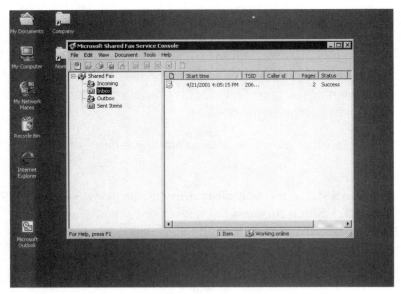

So, permissions properly set for the example to follow, let's get started with viewing a fax.

1. Log on as **NormH** at **PRESIDENT** with the password **Purple3300**.
2. Click **Start**, **Programs**, **Microsoft Shared Fax Client**, **Shared Fax Service Console**.
3. Click **Inbox**. Assuming you've faxed yourself a document to the SBS server machine (you could fax any document to yourself to complete this example), the Inbox will now display the fax that was received.
4. Double-click the fax in the details pane when Inbox is highlighted. Your results should look similar to Figure 14-9.

Figure 14-9

Viewing an important received fax with the Microsoft Shared Fax Service Console. This is the tax form that is displayed on NormH's workstation.

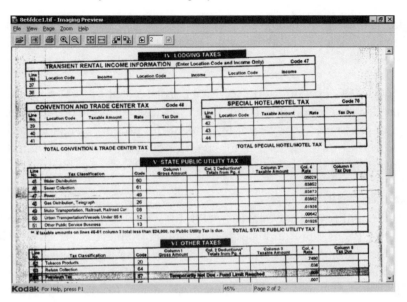

BEST PRACTICE: You can't navigate to a shared folder on the SBS server machine in SBS 2000 like you could in SBS 4.5. You might recall that, in SBS 4.5, you could navigate from a workstation via Network Neighborhood (or My Network Places in Windows ME or Windows 2000) to the FaxStore shared on the SBS server machine and simply double-click the *TIF file (representing the fax). There is no FaxStore share point on an SBS 2000 server by default. But if you wanted to create a shared folder called FaxStore to view you faxes like we could in the good old days, you would share the following folder on the SBS 2000 server machine:

```
%systemroot%Documents and Settings\AllUsers\
Application Data\Microsoft\Shared Fax\Inbox
```

By right-clicking on the above folder and selecting the Sharing command from the secondary menu, you could share this as SharedFax with allowing Everyone the Full Control permission. Then, when users run-and-shoot (make that point-and-click) their way through either Network Neighborhood or My Network Places, they can view their faxes in a shared folder called FaxStore.

When the fax is opened, you can rotate, shrink, resave, and otherwise manipulate the fax via the Kodak imaging application. Here you could print faxes on different paper sizes.

> BEST PRACTICE: I mentioned this once early on, but I'll do so again. Odd-sized faxes are modified to fit the default paper in the printer that prints received faxes. For example, a legal document on legal-sized paper would be printed as a letter-sized document if the designated laser printer used letter-sized paper (8.5 by 11 inches) by default.

Unusual Receive Uses

I've used the capability to receive faxes as .TIF files in two unusual ways. First, by having each SBS user proffer his or her signature on a piece of paper, which I fax to the SBS server machine, I effectively scan each SBS user's signature. These signature image files, which look similar to Norm Hasbro's signature in Figure 14-10, are then stored in a central location, such as Company Shared Folders on the SBS servers. In the future, when composing and faxing a letter from the desktop, all you do to add your signature to your letter is insert the signature image file. I discuss this approach in a moment under "Sending a Fax."

Notes:

Figure 14-10

Scanned signature via SBS faxing.

The second unusual use of fax reception is artwork. Similar to scanning a signature into a .TIF file as described earlier, you can also fax yourself maps, drawings, and photos. When received by the SBS fax server, the image is a .TIF image. The person receiving the fax can not only easily insert the image into word processing documents and Web pages but can also modify and manipulate it with popular drawing applications.

Guest Column

We all tend to do business with friends, whether we admit to it or not. When I was seeking a guest column for the faxing chapter, I turned to Burl Carr, a founding member of the West Sound Technology Professionals Association (WSTPA, see www.wstpa.org), a group that allows residents of Bainbridge Island, WA to join. Here's Burl's contribution:

When Harry asked me to share my experiences with you on how people are using computer-based faxing I quickly thought, 'they just do it'. And then, as I thought about it some more, it occurred to be that these folks in small business environments make use of a number of different methods to fax documents.

I recall a story told to me a number of years ago by a Personnel Manager friend of mine about the problem one of his young staffing assistants was having after the copy machine went on the fritz. As the story goes, the manager requested that the staffing assistant type up an urgently needed document from his hand written draft and make three other copies. The manager, noting her perplexed looks at his request, asked whether there was a problem. She explained that the copy machine was broken and that she did not think she would be able to type up all those copies in time. The manager suggested to her that she could use carbon paper, to which she replied, "What's that?"

Well, I believe that there will soon come a day when a similar "What's that?" reaction will be heard when someone suggests that one use a fax machine to send a document. Already the stand-alone fax machine is rapidly becoming a relic in the office environment. Sure, the fax machine is still heavily used in the professional services area like doctors, lawyers, and other businesses where digitized documents raise security concerns and multiple page documents are often sent. However, the operation and maintenance costs for the fax machine can be high and only one person at a time can send a fax.

Looking to keep overhead costs down and increase productivity, small businesses are using a range of faxing solutions including the popular fax/copier/printer machine combinations, fax software applications, and Internet faxing.

My experience with those businesses that have opted for the fax/copier/printer solution is that they soon discover that someone wants to fax at the same time as another wants to make a copy and another wants to print and they all have to take a backseat while an incoming fax is received. When that outgoing fax is a bid proposal that must be received by a deadline, sending the fax is critical. It can't wait. The business has probably outgrown the machine and needs to begin looking for a computer-based solution.

Most small businesses today are using fax software solutions that provide the tools to allow the delivery and receipt of documents through a fax-modem connected to a regular phone line. On the fax-sending side, documents are either acquired by the fax application from a scanner interface or produced by a word processor application and sent on for delivery, just like sending a document to the printer. On the receiving side, incoming fax documents are stored as a file on the system with the option to send the document directly to an attached printer.

These fax software applications offer some expanded functionality not found in a fax machine solution. Features like delayed delivery so that the fax can be sent at a time when the phone rates are at their lowest, sending a pager notification that a fax has been received, sharing the service within a workgroup or network, and the ability to create detailed reports of faxing activity.

Internet Faxing although not that new is certainly drawing more attention as the technology gains in maturity and computer systems rely more high-speed access for Internet connectivity. Several vendors offer Internet faxing solutions. The costs for an Internet Fax solution range anywhere from free to a few dollars per month for a subscription plus a nominal per-page cost. Of course the free solutions do come with some baggage. They generally include banner ads on the cover page an even some stick an ad on the faxed document itself. Not very professional in my mind so it may be worth a few dollars to subscribe. Some other shortcomings for the free versions may be that you will only get the ability to receive faxes and not be able to send them or the delivery may be delayed. Shop carefully here.

I have a client that desired faster access and, with the availability of affordable high-speed broadband access via DSL and cable modem technologies, chose the cable modem access, dropping the slower 56K dial-up service and in the process also dropped the extra phone line. They are what I would call a casual fax user and used a fax software application. At the time little thought was given to the impact their decision to disconnect the phone line would make on their faxing capabilities. Discovering that they had lost that ability, they asked if the fax cable modem could be used to send a fax. I looked at Internet faxing as a solution but as it turned out, the service lacked a local phone number in their particular area to be a viable solution. So, for the time being, they have returned to the fax software solution. From a cost standpoint they seem to have gained overall. The increase in productivity with the cable modem has over-shadowed the expense of the phone line for faxing.

Internet faxing can be 'cat's meow' for road warriors. There are Web-based faxing services where one logs on to a website, enters the fax number, attaches the document, and sends it on its way. Incoming faxes are sent to your 'fax number' provided by the service and forwarded to your email address as an attachment to the message.

A budding SBSer, Burl Carr works for ATECI in Kitsap County, Washington and can be reached at burl@ateci.com.

Sending a Fax

Sending a fax from an SBS workstation is very simple. At its most basic level, sending a fax from an SBS workstation is nothing more than printing (via the Print command on the File menu in the application of your choice) the document you seek to fax somewhere. In other words, you simply print to the fax printer. But here's a quick list of all ways to send a faxes from an SBS workstation:

- File, Print command from a Windows-based application.

- Send To command in a Microsoft Office application.

- Microsoft Outlook e-mail. There are two ways to do this. When composing an e-mail message, you can select an Outlook Contact, Exchange Global Address member (this is entered at the SBS server machine by creating a Contact via Active Directory Users and Computers found in the Small Business Server Administrator Console) or Personal Address Book listing with a fax telephone number. You can also fax directly by entering a fax number directly into the To: field using the following syntax: [fax:206-123-1235] (this is a sample telephone number, but you get the point).

- Microsoft Shared Fax Service Console by selecting Send a New Fax from the File menu.

BEST PRACTICE: Many of these options give you the opportunity to send to ad hoc fax recipients. These are fax names and numbers that are entered on the fly. This type of ad hoc information is typically in a To: and Fax # field as the following step-by-step example demonstrates.

Here is a step-by-step example of how you send a fax.

BEST PRACTICE: While attempting to associate prefixes with a long distance call, I've found it is better to handle this capability manually, instead of attempting to configure such activity via the Dialing tab. Here's why. Many local prefixes really aren't dialed as an 11-digit long distance call (1-area code-telephone number) but rather as a ten-digit local call (area code-telephone number). Such oddities are best handled by SBS end users when a fax is sent.

To send a fax from a word processing program (such as Microsoft Word) using the wonderful SSL methodology:

1. Logon as **NormH** at **PRESIDENT** with the password **Purple3300**.
2. While working on the document you want to fax using a word processor such as **Microsoft Word**, select the **Print** command from the **File** menu. The **Print** dialog box is displayed.
3. In the **Select Printer** field, select **SharedFax on SSL1** as the printer. Click **Print**.
4. The **Send Fax Wizard** starts. Click **Next** at the **Welcome to the Send Fax Wizard** page.
5. On the **Recipient Information** screen, complete the **To: Location:** and **Fax number:** field. You may also use an existing recipient name from the Exchange Global Address List by clicking the **Address Book** button (you will also have the chance to select **Personal Address Book** listings and **Outlook Contacts**). If you enter multiple names, these names will be listed in the **Recipient name** field. Your screen should look similar to Figure 14-11. Click **Next**.

Notes:

Figure 14-11

Entering names on the Recipient Information page. In this case, a fax will be George Sedoakes.

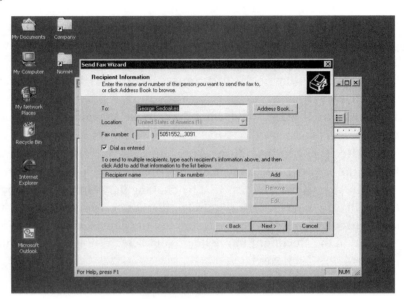

6. On the **Preparing the Cover Page** screen, click the **Select a cover page template with the following information** check box. Select the cover page of your choice, but select the "dawgs.cov" personal cover page that was created earlier today. Click **Next**.

7. On the **Scheduling Transmission** screen, confirm that **Now** is selected under **When do you want to send this fax?** and Click **Next**. Note that there are options for sending during a discount period (which is defined by an administrator at the server level and will be discussed later in the chapter in the Outbox section) or a specific time. You will also note that the user in this example, NormH, can only select the Normal or Low faxing priorities (by default, typically users such as NormH can not send a high-priority fax, so that option is grayed out, but the high-priority fax permission could be set on the Security tab discussed earlier today).

8. On the **Delivery Notification** screen, accept the default setting **Don't notify** under **How do you want to be notified of a successful or failed delivery?** and Click **Next**. And don't worry that you won't be able to

view that your fax was or was not sent (I'll show you an alternate way to view this in a moment).

9. Observe the summary information on the **Completing the Send Fax Wizard** and click **Finish**. The fax will be sent.

Assuming no problems are encountered, the party for which the fax is intended receives it. And because I promised that I'd show you how to view some "evidence" that your fax was sent, I now present you the **Sent Items** folder in the **Microsoft Shared Fax Service Console**, as viewed from NormH's workstation (click **Start**, **Programs**, **Microsoft Shared Fax Client**, **Shared Fax Service Console**). This is shown in Figure 14-12.

Figure 14-12
Proof positive that an end-user's fax was sent as seen in the Sent Items folder.

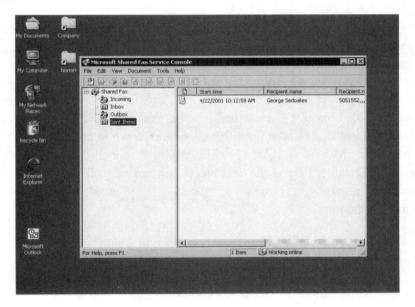

BEST PRACTICE: Back when "Windows" referred to glass panes set in the wall of a house or building, I had a client who used faxes like we used e-mail today – to send quick messages. This gentleman was a wealthy business owner who ran his business empire (he had several business entities in several states, including Alaska) in seclusion from his condo in Hawaii. He'd fax a one-line question on a fax cover page and have the recipient type out and fax the reply. There was rarely voice communication (much like business today with the use of e-mail). So, in memory of that client of long ago, I share with you a built-in tool on the client workstation side that does exactly what this gentleman did: fax a single cover page. At a workstation on an SBS network, click **Start, Programs, Microsoft Shared Fax Client, Send Fax Cover Page**. The **Send Fax Wizard** starts (which you will need to complete each screen; click **Next** six times and click **Finish**). However, this version of the Send Fax Wizard only allows you to send a message on a fax cover page (this is described to you on the Welcome to the Send Fax Wizard screen). So remember that when you're running your empire from a condo in Hawaii!

The Swiss Army Knife

Needless to say, I like the revamped and improved faxing capability in SBS 2000. But as I was learning it during the SBS 2000 beta cycle over the summer of 2000, I was bewildered at how all the pieces fit together. Fortunately, the program manager at Microsoft on the SBS 2000 team who had responsibility for faxing pulled me by the ear into his office, parked his telephone, and closed his door, giving me a whole hour of his undivided time to teach me about faxing, from A to Z. And when it was all said it done, it really came down to one thing: the property sheet for Microsoft Shared Fax (Local) on the Small Business Server Administrator Console. I'll use the next few pages to describe this property sheet; afterwards I'm hopeful you'll join me in believing it's your all-in-one Swiss Army knife for faxing.

First, perform the following steps at the SBS server machine while you are logged on as Administrator.

1. Click **Start, Small Business Server Administrator Console**.
2. Right-click on **Microsoft Shared Fax (Local)** and select **Properties**.
3. The **General** tab will be displayed by default.

General

As seen in Figure 14-13, the **General** tab displays general in-progress information under **Activity**. However, this is not its great strength. What's really valuable is the ability to disable specific fax activities via the three disable check boxes. And why would you ever do this? I can think of one reason I've already used in SBS 2000: to add a new fax modem to the server. By disabling the sending (**Disable transmission of outgoing faxes**) and receiving faxes (**Disable reception of new faxes**), you could replace a broken modem or add a new one (an external modem I'm assuming) without taking down the SBS server machine. More important, under this specific scenario, where the aforementioned two check boxes are selected, users could continue to submit faxes to the default fax queue for transmission at a later time (e.g., after you've added the new fax modem).

Figure 14-13
The General tab sheet is valuable for temporarily disabling faxing capabilities.

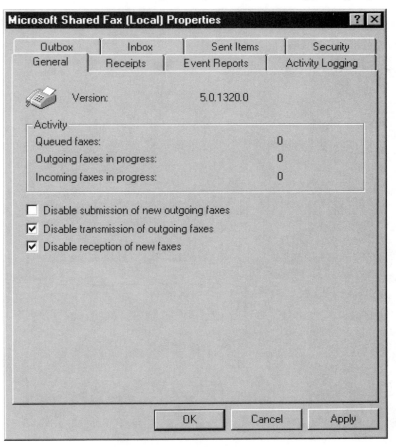

Receipts

Not surprisingly, the **Receipts** tab displays configuration selections for how delivery notification receipts should be handled. Under **Message Box**, the **Enable message boxes as receipts** checkbox is selected which allows users to elect how they would like to be notified when a receipt is sent.

More important, you can configure an SMTP e-mail box (either on the local SBS network or out on the wild side of the Internet) to receive delivery receipts. This occurs by configuring the SMTP e-mail section in a manner similar to Figure 14-14. You will note in the **From e-mail address:** field: that **MelindaO** will receive the receipts. You need to put **springersltd.com** (the Internet domain name) in the **Server address:** field, something that isn't entirely apparent at first blush. Leave the **Port:** field unchanged at **25**.

Figure 14-14

Spend a moment to understand and configure the Receipts tab.

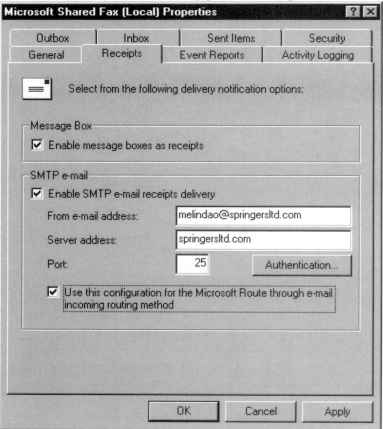

BEST PRACTICE: It's mission critical that you understand the importance of the **Use this configuration for the Microsoft Route through e-mail incoming routing method**. Why? A short story will explain. I set up SBS 2000 at one of my blue-chip client sites shortly after the product was released. This site, a property management company that I've mentioned throughout this book, is a big user of inbound faxes. Sure enough, early in the week after my weekend SBS 2000 installation, I received a call from Pat, the front desk receptionist. Turns out the faxes weren't getting routed to her desktop machine (that is, her Outlook 2000 Inbox) like they had with SBS 4.5. Hmmmmm. I logged on remotely via Terminal Services and poked around the Small Business Server Administrator Console, disbelieving I'd overlooked this important matter. Lo-and-behold, it turns out that the **Use this configuration for the Microsoft Route through e-mail incoming routing method** check box must be selected as a predecessor step to configuring e-mail routing of faxes in SBS 2000. See the Routing section later today for more discussion and steps to configure e-mail routing of faxes.

Event Reports

As they say in business, once you lose someone's trust, it is very hard to regain. Such is still the case with many SBSers who, twice burned by the faxing application in both SBS 4.x versions (4.0a, 4.5), are legitimately casting a wary eye towards the "new and improved" faxing capabilities of SBS 2000. Okay, fair enough. So on the **Event Reports** tab sheet, I recommend you set the levels for error tracking to **High** from the default position (which is one notch to the left of High) for each of the tracking areas (**General, Incoming, Outgoing, Initialization or shutdown**). That way, if you need to troubleshoot the Shared Fax capability of SBS 2000, you'll be capturing all of the information you need.

Notes:

Activity Logging

By default, the logging activity for incoming and outgoing fax activity is selected by default, as seen in Figure 14-15.

Figure 14-15
The Activity Logging tab is where incoming and outgoing logging is invoked.

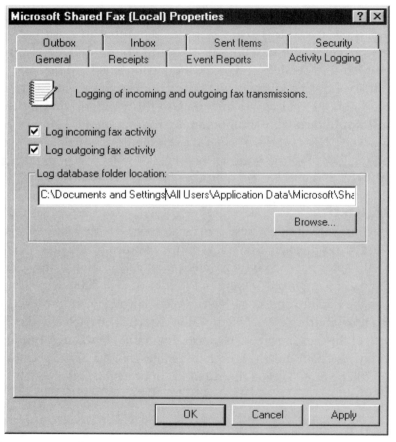

The logs are stored at:

```
%system root%\Documents and Settings\All Users\
Application Data\Microsoft\Shared Fax\ActivityLog
```

The location can be changed by clicking the **Browse** button. The actual logs look similar to the Figure 14-16.

Figure 14-16

The fax logs are text-based and somewhat difficult to interpret.

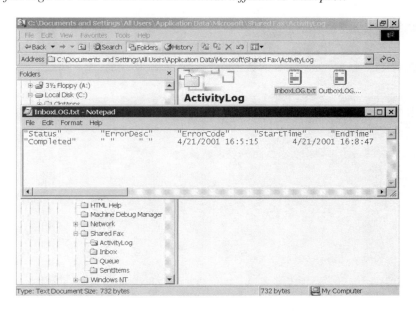

Obviously, the fax logs aren't meant to be artistic pieces of work like you had in SBS 4.5 (where the SBS Console presented a beautiful HTML-based Fax Report displayed in Internet Explorer as seen in Figure 14-17).

> BEST PRACTICE: Take this fax logging discussion seriously. I've billed good hours to SBS clients having to go back in time and prove or disprove that faxes were sent or received in matters involving litigation. When the pedals hit the metal in the courtroom, it is often necessary to resolve a "he said, she said" argument by showing SBS fax logs.

Notes:

Figure 14-17
The Fax Reports in SBS 4.5 were, in a single word, wonderful!

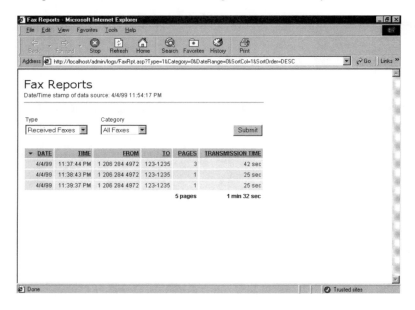

In SBS 2000, you're now left with looking at this fax log in Figure 14-16 (yucky) or the Sent Item folder in the Microsoft Shared Fax Service Console (this is better). There must be a better way to view fax activity?!?! Yes, one other way to view fax activity is to view Event Viewer in SBS 2000 with the following steps:

1. Assuming you are logged on to the SBS server machine as Administrator, click **Start**, **Small Business Server Administrator Console**.
2. Expand **Computer Management.**
3. Expand **System Tools.**
4. Select **System**.
5. To observe outgoing fax activity, look for an **Information** entry for Print that has an **Event ID** of **10**. This is shown in Figure 14-18 and reflects the outbound fax sent by NormH.

Notes:

Figure 14-18

Confirming the two page fax was sent from NormH to George Sedoakes.

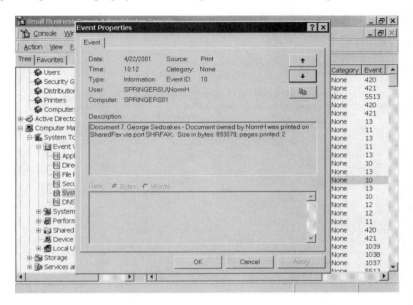

BEST PRACTICE: A Print entry #10 should be followed immediately by a Print entry #13 that confirms the document as deleted from the SharedFax queue after it was successfully sent.

Now, viewing incoming faxes via Event Viewer is a slightly different procedure. Here you would look for at the Application event log in Event Viewer, and for the Source equals Microsoft Shared Fax, look for Event ID# 32008. This confirms the fax was received.

BEST PRACTICE: The Application event log will record Event ID # 32092 if the received faxed is archived and Event ID # 32081 if the received faxed is routed to an e-mail address.

Outbox

By default, several check boxes are selected for you on the **Outbox** tab sheet (see Figure 14-19). One that stands out in particular is that, by default, users can use personal cover pages. This is because the **Allow use of personal cover pages** check box is selected, and if you or your clients find this to be unacceptable, you should deselect this check box. Remember that personal cover pages can be silly and offensive in many business climates.

Figure 14-19
The default view of the Outbox tab sheet.

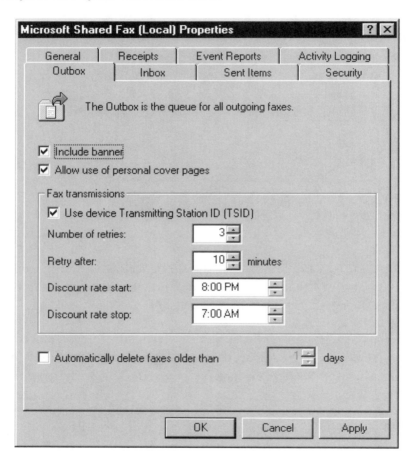

Note the Outbox tab sheet allows you to set some other important settings, such as number of times a fax call will be attempted (**Number of retries**), time between retries (**Retry after**), and setting the discount rate period (**Discount rate start**, **Discount rate stop**) that users can select when sending a fax.

Inbox

The **Inbox** allows you to make the selection that allows you to save incoming faxes (via the **Archive all incoming faxes to this folder check box**). This location was defined earlier in the chapter when I suggested you could create a shared folder on the SBS 2000 server called SharedFax for your users to browse. By default, the check box allowing Event log warning entries (**Generate warning in Event Log**) and deleting faxes over 90 days old (**Automatically delete faxes older than 90 days**) are selected. The Inbox is shown in Figure 14-20.

Figure 14-20
The Inbox in Microsoft Shared Fax (Local) Properties.

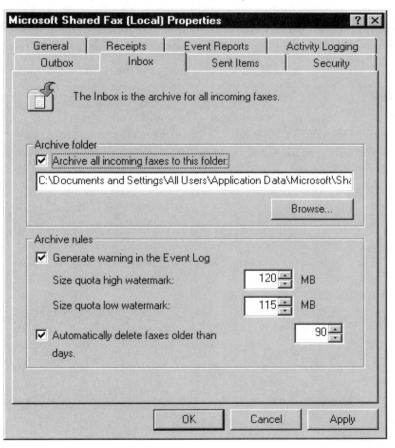

BEST PRACTICE: You might consider deselecting the **Automatically delete faxes older than 90 days** check box for one very important business reason. One of the key points to having inbound faxes stored in digital form is preservation. Have you ever lost a paper-based fax that you wanted again months later? Of course you have! By saving the inbound faxes in digital form forever, you can find the fax you're looking for one year later when you really need it! And law firms and government agencies are most excited about preserving these types of communications forever (for litigation, public records, etc.).

Sent Items

The **Sent Items** tab sheet looks very similar to the Inbox tab sheet. You can make **Archive folder** and **Archive rules** selections. And again, you, might deselect the **Automatically delete faxes older than 60 days** check box to preserve faxes indefinitely.

Security

Security is one of the more important tab sheets and is shown in Figure 14-21. It is with security that you'll define how a run-of-the-mill end user can interact with the faxing capabilities in SBS 2000 (Administrators are granted all faxing-related permissions by default and so are the members of the BackOffice Fax Operators security group).

Notes:

Figure 14-21

There are numerous fax security-related settings to select under Permissions.

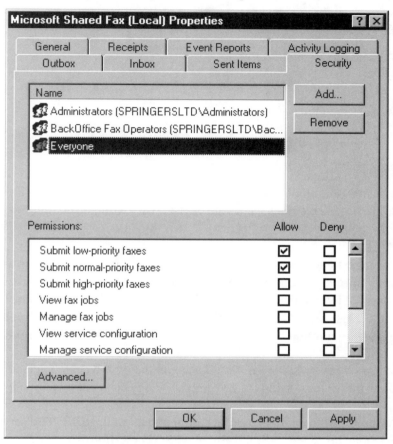

Here is a list of the permissions you can Allow or Deny under Permissions on the Security tab. I've placed an asterisk (*) next to the permissions I suggest you allow your end users (the Everyone security group) to have so they can the SBS 2000 fax service more effectively.

- Submit low-priority faxes*

- Submit normal-priority faxes*

- Submit high-priority faxes*

- View fax jobs*

- Manage fax jobs*

- View service configuration

- Manage service configuration

- View incoming messages archive*

- Manage incoming messages archive

- View outgoing messages archive*

- Manage outgoing messages archive

And that's it for walking through the in's and out's of Microsoft Shared Fax (Local) Properties. Remember – it's your Swiss Army Knife of faxing!

Routing

One of my longest journeys with the faxing application in SBS 2000 was the configuration of routing. There are three settings you must make. The first was to configure the SMTP e-mail section of the **Receipts** tab. This includes the all-important **Use this configuration for the Microsoft Route through e-mail incoming routing method** check box.

The second setting is to define the e-mail account that will receive the incoming faxes. Follow these steps, using the SSL methodology.

1. Assuming you are logged on as Administrator at the SBS 2000 server machine, click **Start, Small Business Server Administrator Console**.
2. Click **Microsoft Shared Fax (Local)**.
3. Expand **Devices and Providers**.
4. Expand **Devices**.
5. Expand the modem object named after your modem brand model.
6. Click **Incoming Methods**.
7. Right-click **Route through e-mail** and select **Properties**.
8. Select the **E-mail** tab.
9. In the **Mail to:**, enter the SMTP e-mail address of the person or distribution group to receive the incoming faxes. In this case, enter **MelindaO@springersltd.com**. Your **Route through e-mail Properties** dialog box should look similar to Figure 14-22.

BEST PRACTICE: So what happens if MelindaO is sick one day and is unable to forward the faxes via e-mail? You should either have the faxes printed automatically or sent to an e-mail distribution group instead of an individual (note my reference to a distribution group in Step #9 above). Such a distribution group might include other administrative staff members and be titled "FrontDesk" or something easily understood.

Also, I'd recommend you select all three reception methods: **Print, Save to archive**, and **E-mail** as an SBS site becomes familiar with the inbound fax capabilities of SBS Server. At a future date, you might elect to discontinue one or two of the fax reception methods to avoid massive duplication.

Notes:

Figure 14-22

*It's critical to correctly spell the e-mail name in the **Mail to:** field as there is no error-checking.*

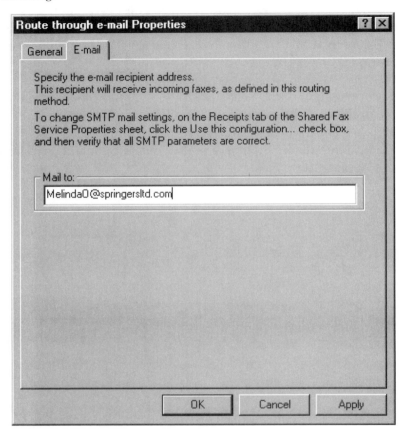

Now, a final act to complete the e-mail routing of faxes. On the **Route through e-mail** option under **Routing Methods**, perform a right-click and select **Enable** from the secondary menu.

You've now configured e-mail routing for the fax service in SBS 2000. MelindaO at the front desk of SSL will receive this e-mail. Note that if you in any way skip one of the first two steps outlined here, you would receive an error message when you try the third step (Enable). The error message dialog box reads somewhat unclearly: "You cannot enable a routing method before it has been configured. Configure the settings on the method-specific tab of the incoming method Properties sheet."

> BEST PRACTICE: In a similar routing vein, you actually need to perform a few steps for the automatic printing of faxes capability to work. Click **Start**, **Small Business Server Administrator Console**, expand **Microsoft Shared Fax (Local)**, expand **Devices and Providers**, expand **Devices**, expand the **modem object** (named after your modem brand model), click **Incoming Methods**, right-click **Print**, select **Properties**. Click the **Print** tab and put the Uniform Naming Convention (UNC) path to a shared printer in the **Printer Name** field. Whew! Then click **OK** and again right-click **Print** and select **Enable**. Then your incoming faxes will automatically print to the shared printer you elected. Got it?

> It is interesting to note that you don't have to perform such a convoluted series of keystrokes to save the incoming faxes to a folder on the SBS server machine. That election is made by configuring archiving on the Inbox tab sheet (discussed above).

On a final routing note, the **Incoming Routing** and **Outgoing Routing** folders directly beneath **Microsoft Shared Fax (Local)** are not used to configure these types of routing discussed in this section, so don't be fooled into thinking these folders hold your routing configuration answers. For example, if you drill deep enough into the **Incoming Routing** folder, clicking on **Global Methods** objects, you'll ultimately be looking at **property sheets** that simply display Dynamic Link Library (DLL) information for each of the three routing methods. Granted, the Global Methods folder is the place you can change the routing priority (one, two, three) of the three routing methods.

Faxing Alternatives

I want to quickly present a Internet faxing service that allows you to not use the faxing application in SBS 2000 but still have some of the benefits of computer-based faxing. This is a free service I use called OneBox at www.onebox.com. After completing a quick sign-up process, you will have free e-mail, voicemail (which is cool), and faxing tied to a regular telephone number in your area code and including a short telephone extension. So, when people want to fax to you, they enter the full telephone number followed by a few commas (pauses) and then your four-digit extension. The fax is received by OneBox and you're notified by e-mail that you have a fax waiting. It looks similar to Figure 14-23.

Figure 14-23
OneBox is a free Internet-based fax service that captures incoming faxes as a digital image. This is an advertisement for SBS 2000.

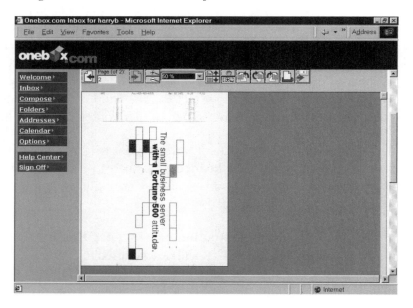

So, why in the world would you do this with the new faxing service so handy in SBS? I can think of two reasons.

- Carrot and stick. Set up a reluctant client on OneBox to turn them onto computer-based faxing and its benefits as a way to "hook" them. Then use that as leverage to implement the Shared Fax service in SBS 2000.

- The "heck with it crowd." Perhaps the reading you've done in this chapter has actually scared you about SBS's faxing capabilities. You might find a service such as OneBox easier to use. Whatever works, as they say in business.

Summary

So you've decided to become an SBS fax organization: You've decided to make the fax function part of your SBS network and everyday business world activity. You've possibly arrived at this decision, based on much of the discussion today and by considering the following about SBS network faxing:

- Reduced hardware costs - Not only have you eliminated the need to purchase an expensive, modern, fax machine, more important, you've eliminated the need to have each workstation equipped with its own fax modem and fax telephone line (I've seen it done). I've used the capability to eliminate multiple fax telephone lines in the past to help a firm justify the cost of an SBS conversion.

- Ease of use - Properly trained SBS users find sending certain types of documents and receiving any document to be easy with SBS network-based faxing. To read a typical fax, the user only needs to double-click to open the fax image. To send a fax, the user only needs to use the basic printing command.

- Monitoring and control - Again, depending on your unique situation, you might have an important need to control fax usage. That type of control is exceedingly difficult with a traditional fax machine, but with SBS, the network security model dictates who can use the fax service.

The next step to receiving and sending faxes is simple: Just do it!

Section 4

Extending SBS

Chapter 15
Extending SQL Server 2000

Talk about a career path. Not only can you find very good (and large) texts dedicated to the SQL Server 2000 database application (a database application helps you gather, organize, and report information), but more than one Microsoft Certified Professional (MCP) has made a good living doing the SQL thing. Studying SQL Server introduces you to one of the largest bodies of knowledge contained within SBS 2000. Given this overwhelming perspective, I've made the decision to keep the SQL Server discussion germane, practical, and relatively brief (and, as always, with an SSL point-of-view). If you so desire, I can recommend a great SQL Server book from my fellow Seattle-area author, Richard Waymire: *Sams' Teach Yourself Microsoft SQL Server 2000 in 21 Days*, ISBN: 0-672-31969-1.

If I were to delve into the depths of SQL Server at the level of the aforementioned book, you and I would not only be here late into the night, but we'd be together for many days and nights forward. I can appreciate your interest in learning more about SQL Server (more than I can reasonably deliver in one chapter), so bear with me and consider this a sampler.

On the one hand, you can say SQL Server 2000 is a very important part of SBS 2000. Call it the revenge of the good old "It's the data, stupid" crowd. When you really think about it, the whole reason any of us technology professionals are here is because the underlying data drives business computing. Get it? No? Then consider how I interact with my clients on any given day. The property management firm I serve calls when they can't run payroll, not because some SBS event log entry looks interesting. A true story: The payroll program at the property management firm needed Internet access to obtain updated tax tables and forms before it would cut the paychecks. The solution was to open a port in the firewall to allow the traffic through. But understand that the call I received from the client was much more about the "data" than asking me to come over and open up a firewall port. So it's truly "the data, stupid!"

On the other hand, I can't deny that, in its natural state, SQL Server is one of the least used components in SBS 2000. This is revealed in several ways.

- Microsoft reports that fewer than 10 percent of its installed SBS sites (that's you, the SBSers) have SQL Server installed.

- SQL Server is not installed by default when you set up SBS 2000. You must select SQL Server as an installation option, such as you did in Chapter 3.

- Rumors are circulating in Redmond that SQL Server may not be part of the SBS bundle in the future. But, fear not, for this only means you can still purchase it separately and run it on another server – which isn't a bad idea, you know, instead of loading up the poor old SBS server machine with everything it already has plus SQL Server and a business application. Personally I can see the merits of this thinking, especially if Microsoft lowers the price of SBS to reflect the absence of SQL Server.

So what am I really saying with these points? That SQL Server isn't emphasized in SBS 2000. One other interesting thought along these lines of de-emphasis (and don't worry, I get to the "emphasis" argument in the next paragraph) relates to being an actual SQL language programmer. It's highly unlikely that, as an SBSer, you'll program inside of SQL Server (using the SQL programming language) at an SBS site. With respect to building custom applications and other SQL goodies (such as stored procedures), SQL Server is much more at home in development and enterprise environments. It's not my world, but I sure like the business applications that SQL Server developers create!

Now for some good news about SQL Server, starting with the old saying about having nothing to fear but fear itself (with all due respect to United States President Franklin Roosevelt). SQL Server has a very important role that I haven't even discussed yet: supporting business applications. To understand this supporting role, you'll learn the basics of SQL Server in this chapter. Such an understanding will aid greatly in supporting applications that run on top of SQL Server.

To understand SQL Server at an appropriate level for an SBS site, you'll spend the first part of the chapter creating a simple table to manage some information for SSL via SQL Server (yes, that never-ending SSL methodology is utilized yet again). Later in the chapter, the focus shifts to advanced SQL Server tidbits (such as publishing data as a Web page) that you need to know about to better manage SQL Server. I do want to manage your expectations: This is not a chapter to master SQL Server; it is a chapter to meet and greet SQL Server.

> BEST PRACTICE: In all seriousness, I hope I've managed your expecta-
> tions to this point about what SQL Server is and isn't. More important,
> I want to emphasize that in no way, shape, or form is this chapter any-
> thing more than a SQL Server sampler. As stated previously, several
> thick books dedicated to SQL Server await your reading pleasure.

SQL Server Defined

The first of this chapter starts with defining SQL Server and ends with having you create a table to track Springer Spaniel registrations.

At its heart, SQL Server is a database, but you likely already knew that from the introductory discussion. Did you know, however, that it differs from other databases you might have worked with in the past in that SQL Server is a client/ server database? Perhaps you've worked with other databases, such as dBASE, which are relational databases (similar to SQL Server), but don't exploit the power of the network's server (the SBS server machine on an SBS network). Figure 15-1 shows how SQL Server works as a client/server database and how other databases (such as dBASE) work.

Notes:

Figure 15-1
SQL Server client/server versus other databases

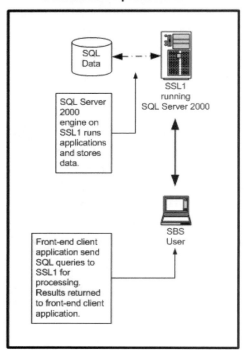

**Client/Server Model
SQL Server 2000
Database Implementation**

SQL
Data

SSL1
running
SQL Server 2000

SQL Server
2000
engine on
SSL1 runs
applications
and stores
data.

SBS
User

Front-end client
application send
SQL queries to
SSL1 for
processing.
Results returned
to front-end client
application.

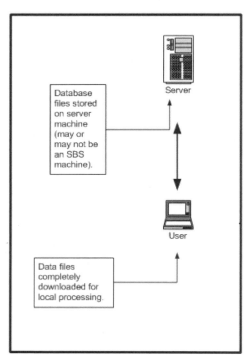

**Non-Client/Server Model
(other databases)**

Server

Database
files stored
on server
machine
(may or
may not be
an SBS
machine).

User

Data files
completely
downloaded for
local processing.

Notes:

The Server Side

On the SBS server machine, the data resides not only in tables but also is manipulated by the SQL Server engine. These SQL Server server-side capabilities include three functional areas: data warehousing, e-commerce, and line-of-business.

Data Warehousing

Microsoft has positioned SQL Server to act as a store of data for the organization. This is accomplished in several ways:

- **Comprehensive Analysis Services.** This speaks to SQL Server 2000's business analysis capabilities via online analytical processing (OLAP) and data mining.

- **Data Transformation Services.** These are the routines that automate the extraction and transformation of business data from multiple sources.

- **Web-enabled.** Not only can you publish your information to a Web page, but you can analyze data accessible from remote Web sites.

- **Meta-Data Services.** The idea here is that SQL Server supports the sharing of data between different tools and environments.

- **Indexed Views.** Microsoft is claiming that performance enhancements related to accessing your data can be gained by indexed views.

- **Office 2000 Integration.** In Microsoft Excel, you can use the pivot table capabilities to manipulate SQL Server-based data.

- **English Query.** Here's something many SBSers, who don't claim to be SQL gurus, will like. In SQL Server 2000, there is greater support for posing queries in English versus SQL speak (or as Microsoft calls it, "Multi-Dimensional Expressions"—MDX for short).

E-Commerce

- **XML Support.** One of the more promising developments in the database world is that of the Extensible Markup Language (known as XML). This is the capability to parse data into a meaningful format.

- **Web and Application Hosting.** SQL Server is clearly e-commerce-ready with its ability to interact in real time with Web pages, and by collecting and providing data.

- **Distributed Partition Views.** This is the ability to distribute the workload over several servers (call it another fancy term for load balancing). This would be very important for an organization that has much Web activity, such as a Web retail storefront.

- **Database Administration.** Not surprisingly, the database administration area has improved with this release of SQL Server including automatic tuning and maintenance features.

Line-of-Business

- **High Availability.** Short of getting the right data in the right hands, the other SBSer obligation to SQL Server is high availability. Consider the following. You're a king SBSer who knows infrastructure like no one else, and you've done a good job of advising your client or bosses on the use of a database. But without high availability, all of your credence might be shipped south. SQL Server 2000 is committed, as I can attest, to high-availability. One such way it demonstrates this is by its ability to make online SQL Server-based backups (say in the middle of the day) of critical databases.

- **Application support.** Ah, my favorite topic. Major line-of-business software application vendors are committing to SQL Server 2000 (granted, these software vendors may have committed to Oracle first, but that's a whole different story and book).

- **Application hosting.** Interestingly, with Microsoft's ascension to the altar of application service providers (ASPs) with its .NET (called "dot-net") initiative, Microsoft is promoting the ASP paradigm shift in SQL Server 2000. So perhaps you can act as a line-of-business server to other businesses. Hmmmmmm…shall we say the possibilities are truly endless?

- **Replication.** I suspect you join me on this one, but I truly believe that having your data stored in more than one place is a business technology success factor. I shared with you the importance of replication in Chapter 12 in the context of PDA replication. SQL Server essentially has the same capability with its transactional and snap-shot replication.

Primary server-side services

The main server-side services for SQL Server are:

- **MSSQLServer.** This is the SQL Server engine as you know it, the piece that processes the SQL statements (officially known as Transact-SQL). This service also allocates server resources (such as memory), manages the tables (for example, prevents collisions between users), and ensures the integrity of the data (via various tests). In SBS 2000, this service is set to automatically start, meaning that it will start when the SBS server machine starts.

- **Microsoft Distributed Transaction Coordinator.** This is a service which acts as a traffic cop, managing the sources of data that compose a transaction. In SBS 2000, this service is set to automatic start.

- **SQLServerAgent.** This is a service that manages scheduling activities and sends alerts. This service must be manually started in SQL Server 2000.

- **Microsoft Search.** This is an indexing-related service used by SQL Server 2000 and other SBS 2000 components (such as the Find command in Windows 2000 Server.

- **MSSQLServerOLAPService.** This service relates to the online analytical processing capabilities of SQL Server 2000. This service auto-starts when the underlying Windows 2000 Server operating system starts.

The SQL Server 2000 Services are displayed and managed via the SQL Server Service Manager displayed in Figure 15-2

Notes:

Figure 15-2

SQL Server 2000 services can be stopped, started, and configured via the SQL Server Service Manager tool.

The following SQL Server system databases are automatically constructed when SBS 2000 installs SQL Server 2000 (and watch my play on words here as these databases are automatically built but SQL Server 2000 is not automatically installed in SBS 2000!):

- **Master.** This is the mother of all tables in SQL Server. Lose it (with no back up) and you'll die. Simply stated, it controls SQL Server operations completely (including user databases, user accounts, environmental variables, system error message, and so on). It is critical that you back up this database on a regular basis.

- **Model.** A template provides basic information used when you create new databases for your own use. This is akin to the metainformation you entered when you installed SBS 2000 (company name, address, fax and telephone numbers) that reappears each time you add a user, via one of the SBS consoles, to your SBS network. You might recall that I defined *metainformation* early in this book in the middle of Chapter 3; it is information that is used globally by the computer system, not just in one place.

- **Msdb.** The SQLServerAgent uses this for scheduling and job history.

- **Tempdb.** This is another database that's very important to the operation of SQL Server. It's a temporary storage area used by SQL Server for working storage. This is akin to the paging file used by Windows 2000 Server (the underlying operating system in SBS).

- **Northwind.** Consider using this sample database as the prototype for developing your own company database. This was the sample database in Microsoft Access and is the "standard" sample company used in Microsoft's "Official Curriculum" training courses for MCSEs.

- **Pubs.** Yet another database used in most of Microsoft's SQL Server manuals, including the wonderful online books!

The built-in databases are shown in Figure 15-3 via the SQL Server Enterprise Manager (which I'll demonstrate later).

BEST PRACTICE: As part of the SSL methodology, you should have installed SQL Server 2000 as part of Step 35 located near Figure 3-14 in Chapter 3. You should have modified the SBS Administrator Console in Steps 1-10 near Figures 5-26 and 5-27 in Chapter 5. If for some reason you did not complete those steps, return to those respective chapters and do so at this time.

Notes:

Figure 15-3

Observing the built-in databases in SQL Server 2000. Note that the SQL Server Enterprise Manager incorrectly uses "NT" terminology next to the server name.

Server-side management

This is where you will spend your time with SQL Server: using the management tools. You've already seen two of the management tools: the SQL Server Enterprise Manager and the SQL Server Service Manager. But there are various other SQL Server administration tools and wizards, as well as the books online. To introduce yourself to the full array of SQL Server management tools (which are technically considered client applications even though they run on the server), simply display the contents of the Microsoft SQL Server program group (found via the Start button, Programs) as seen in Figure 15-4.

Notes:

Figure 15-4
Microsoft SQL Server program group.

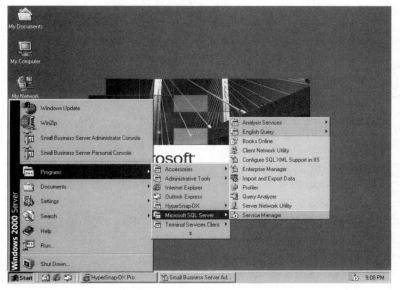

The Client Side

The client side speaks to the wide range of applications that use SQL Server, including:

- Third-party applications, such as Great Plains Dynamics accounting software.

- Microsoft Access running on the SBS user's workstations.

- Microsoft Excel spreadsheets that link to databases housed on an SBS server machine running SQL Server.

- Microsoft Visual Basic-created applications that use SQL Server. These are typically homegrown applications written by either an employee at an SBS site or a consultant to use data stored and managed by SQL Server.

- Other applications. I've seen a wide range of applications, including Microsoft Excel, Word, and PowerPoint, that access a SQL Server database to extract and place data. Rumor has it that the advanced pivot table feature in Microsoft Excel works very nicely with SQL Server-based data.

BEST PRACTICE: Client-side applications typically connect to SQL Server (running on the SBS server machine) via the following database application program interfaces (API):

• Open database connectivity (ODBC). ODBC is the connector by which many front ends running on the clients (a.k.a. client applications) connect to the SQL Server database. I'll show you ODBC in action shortly.

• Object linking and embedding (OLE). OLE, in English, is what I like to think of as copy-and-paste kept alive. When you paste data from one source to another and you change the data back at the source, it's automatically updated at the destination you created. With respect to SQL Server, imagine a Microsoft Excel spreadsheet containing financial information from a SQL Server-based table. The financial information changes in the table and the Microsoft Excel spreadsheet is updated automatically. Plain and simple!

• ActiveX Data Objects (ADO). This is a connector that, among other things, provides record-level access to VSAM, AS/400, and PDS data

• Remote Data Objects (RDO). RDO provides a framework for using code to create and manipulate components of a remote ODBC database system.

Common Uses of SQL Server on SBS Networks

First and foremost, the greatest need I've seen for SQL Server 2000 on SBS networks is support for third-party applications such as Great Plains Dynamics and other narrow, vertical-market applications in the legal, medical, and instrument-repair industries (to name just a few).

Secondary uses for SQL Server 2000 on an SBS network include creating your own databases and learning SQL Server 2000 for MCSE certification purposes. (I'm just calling it like I see it.)

BEST PRACTICE: For more information on SQL Server 2000 specifics, I can send you to two free resources! First, visit Microsoft's SQL Server Web site at www.microsoft.com/sql. Second, read the SQL Server Books Online (installed as part of the complete SQL Server installation process).

SQL Server and SSL

No chapter on SQL Server, in any book, would be complete without having you create a database and a table or two, enter some data, and then display the data you've entered. This book is no exception. But again, understand that this exercise is almost an exception to the rule on SBS networks; you're far more likely to work with third-party applications that sit on top of the SQL Server 2000 engine.

That said, revisit your friends at SSL. Assuming no third-party software exists that explicitly tracks dogs, you'll create a database to accomplish this business purpose.

> BEST PRACTICE: Whenever considering the creation of a database, be sure you understand the purpose for undertaking this project. Poorly considered database projects are like poorly written books: difficult to read and soon ignored.

Now get to work and create a database for SSL. Afterward, you will create a table and populate it with meaningful dog tracking information.

To create the database for SSL, perform the following steps:

1. Log on to **SSL1** as **Administrator** with the password **husky9999**.
2. Click **Start**, **Small Business Server Administrator Console**.
3. The SBS Administrator Console appears. Expand the following objects in the left pane: **Microsoft SQL Servers**, **SQL Server Group**, **SSL1 (Windows NT)**, as seen in Figure 15-5

Notes:

Figure 15-5

SQL Server Enterprise Manager.

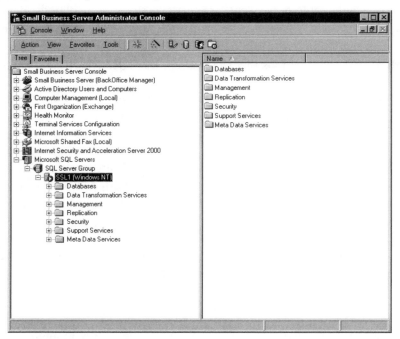

4. Highlight **SSL1 (Windows NT)** and select **View**, **Taskpad** to display the taskpad in the right pane with the **General** tab initially displayed, as seen in Figure 15-6.

Notes:

Figure 15-6

The General page on the taskpage. Note that the operating system is incorrectly reported as Microsoft Windows NT.

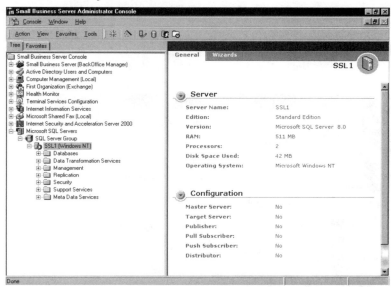

5.   Click the **Wizards** tab and the resulting screen should look like Figure 15-7.

Figure 15-7

The Wizards page on the taskpage offers a wizard link to accomplish nearly any task.

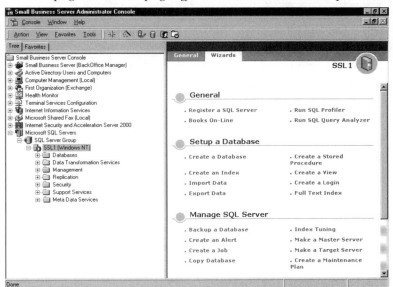

6. Select the **Create a Database** link under **Set up a Database on the Wizards** page of the taskpad. The **Create Database Wizard – SSL1** appears and the **Welcome to the Create Database Wizard** screen is displayed as seen in Figure 15-8. Click **Next**.

Figure 15-8
The Welcome screen lists the tasks to be accomplished including naming the database and creating files.

7. The **Name the Database and Specify its Location** screen appears. In the **Database name: field**, type **SSLDOG**. Accept the settings for the database location in **Database file location:**. Accept the settings in the **Transaction log file location:** field. Your screen should look similar to Figure 15-9. Click **Next**.

Notes:

Figure 15-9

Naming the database and accepting file locations on the Name the Database and Specify its Location screen.

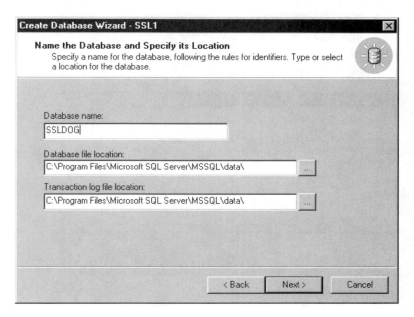

8. The **Name the Database Files** screen appears. Accept the default file name of **SSUDOG_Data** under **File Name** and type **10** under **Initial Size (MB)**. Your screen should look similar to Figure 15-10. Click **Next**.

Notes:

Figure 15-10

Changing the default database size on the Name the Database Files screen.

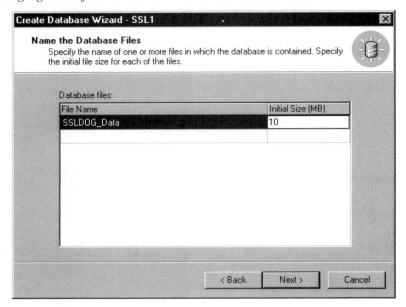

9. Accept the default settings, shown in Figure 15-11, on the **Define the Database File Growth** screen. Click **Next**.

Figure 15-11

Read and accept the settings on the Define Database File Growth screen.

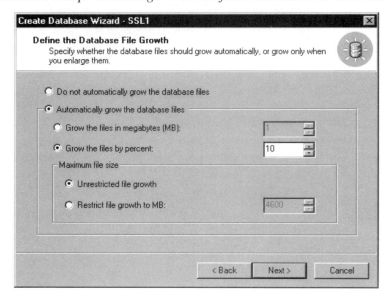

10. Accept the default settings on the **Name the Transaction Log Files** screen shown in Figure 15-12 and click **Next**. Note the initial size of the transaction log file will be 1 MB.

Figure 15-12
Read and accept the settings on the Name the Transaction Log Files screen.

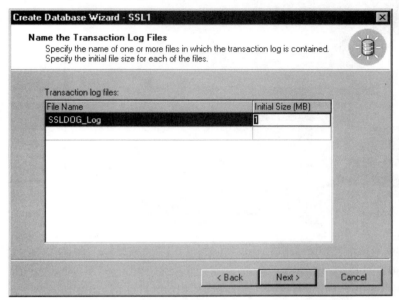

11. Accept the defaults on the **Define the Transaction Log File Growth** page and click **Next**. This page looks very similar to Figure 15-11 but speaks specifically to transaction log growth.
12. Click **Finish** on the **Completing the Create Database Wizard** page. This is shown in Figure 15-13.

Notes:

Figure 15-13

Finishing the database creation process.

BEST PRACTICE: Note that the configure information shown in the text field (in the center), as seen in Figure 15-13, can be selected via the mouse (hold down the right mouse button and drag across the text) and then copied by pressing CTRL-C. Open Notepad or some other text editor and paste this text. Then save the file as part of the network notebook discussed in Chapter 7. With these simple steps, you will have the whole database configuration at-a-glance!

13. Click **OK** when the **Create Database Wizard** dialog box notifies you that you have successfully created the database.

14. You are asked whether you want to create a maintenance plan for the database SSLDOG on another **Create Database Wizard** dialog box. Click **Yes**.

BEST PRACTICE: It is critical that you set up a daily maintenance plan for your key databases (the master database and any databases you create). On more than one occasion, I've had to rely on the SQL Server-based database backups when a traditional backup tape failed me. An SQL Server-based database backup places a bona fide copy of your database on another part of the SBS server machine's hard disk. It's unbelievably valuable!

15. The Database Maintenance Plan Wizard launches. Click **Next** after reading the **Welcome to the Database Maintenance Plan Wizard** screen. Note that the Welcome screen tells you which tasks the Database Maintenance Plan Wizard will run, including running database integrity checks, updating database statistics, and performing database backups (inside of SQL Server 2000).

16. Select **master** and **SSLDOG** under the **Database** column on the **Select Databases** screen, as seen in Figure 15-14. Click **Next**. Kindly note that Figure 15-14 displays the SSLDOG database as being selected in the Database column, but believe me that master is also selected. Given the constraints of the user interface for that dialog box, I can't get both selections to appear in a single figure (master is selected at the top of the databases list and has been scrolled out of the figure).

Figure 15-14
Select the master and SSLDOG databases on the Select Databases screen.

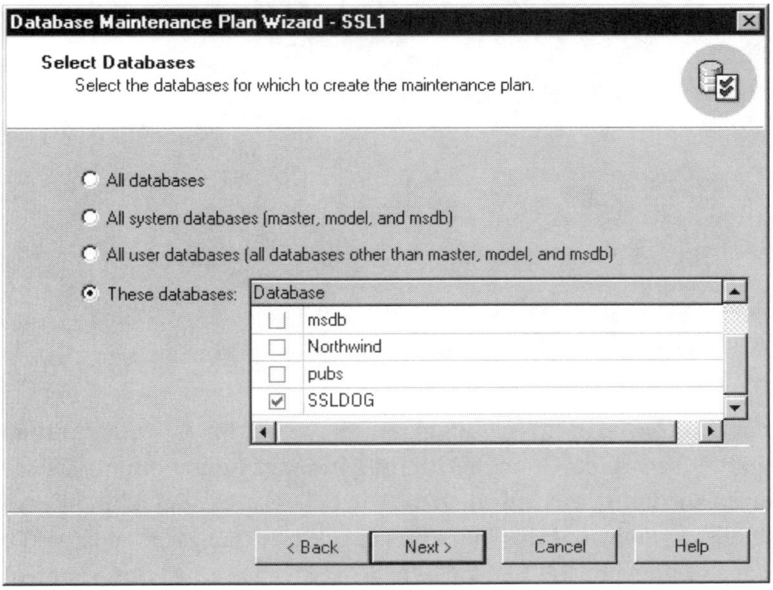

17. On the **Update Data Optimization Information** screen, select the
Reorganize data and index pages check box. Select the **Change free
space per page percentage to:** radio button and accept **10** in the numeric
value field immediately to the right. Select the **Remove unused space
from database files** checkbox and accept **50 MB** for the **When it grows
beyond field:**. Accept **10 % of data space** in the **Amount of free space
to remain after shrink:**. Accept the default schedule under **Schedule**: of
Occurs every 1 week(s) on Sunday, at 1:00:00AM and click **Next**.
Your screen should look similar to Figure 15-15. The selections you have
made relate to managing disk space from the SQL Server 2000 database
perspective. And managing disk space on a computer is considered an
important thing to do.

Figure 15-15
Your Update Data Optimization Information screen should look similar to this figure.

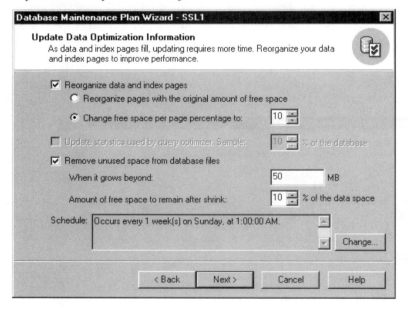

18. On the **Database Integrity Check** screen, select the **Check Database
Integrity** check box. Click the **Include indexes** radio button. Select the
Attempt to repair any minor problems check box. Select the **Perform
these checks before doing backups** check box. Your screen should look
similar to Figure 15-16. Click **Next**. What you have just done is invoke

the native SQL Server capability to maintain sound database integrity and to perform these actions before making an internal SQL Server backup. For your information, "integrity" is a commonly used word that basically has a favorable connotation.

Figure 15-16

The selections you make on the Database Integrity Check screen will allow you to keep your SSLDOG database healthy.

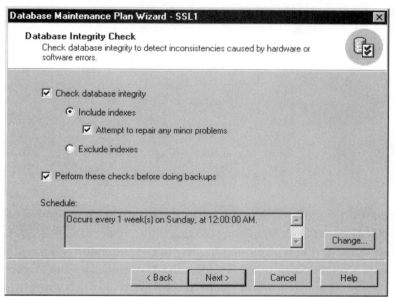

19. On the **Specify the Database Backup Plan** screen, select the **Back up the database as part of the maintenance plan** check box. Select the **Verify the integrity of the backup when complete** check box. Click the **Disk** radio button. Click the **Change** button and select **Daily** in the **Occurs** column when the **Edit Recurring Job Schedule** dialog box appears and click **OK**. You are returned to the **Specify the Database Backup Plan** screen, which should look similar to Figure 15-17. Click **Next**.

Notes:

Figure 15-17
Specify the Database Backup Plan to make your screen look similar to this figure.

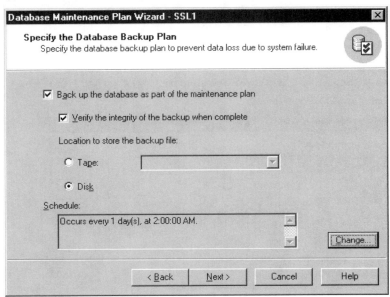

20. Accept the default selection of **Use the default backup directory** on the **Specify Backup Disk Directory** screen. Click **Next**.

21. Select **Back up the transaction log as part of the maintenance plan** check box on the **Specify the Transaction Log Backup Plan** screen. Accept the default settings of **Verify the integrity of the backup when complete**, **Disk**, and the **Schedule:** that backs up the transaction log every week on numerous evenings. Click **Next**.

22. Accept the default selection of **Use the default backup directory** on the **Specify Transaction Log Backup Disk Directory** screen. Click **Next**.

23. Select the **Write Report to a text file in directory** check box on the **Reports to Generate** screen. Accept the default report storage folder (c:\Program Files\Microsoft SQL Server\MSSQL\LOG\). Select **Delete text report older than** and accept the default time period of **4 Week(s)**. Your screen should look similar to Figure 15-18. Click **Next**.

Figure 15-18

You can configure the text-based reports you want to generate.

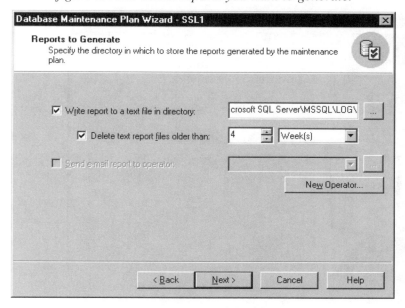

24. Accept the default settings of **Write history to the msdb.dbo.sysdbmaintplan history table on this server** and **Limit rows in the table to: 1000 rows for this plan** on under **Local Server** on the **Maintenance History** screen and click **Next**.

25. The **Completing the Database Maintenance Wizard** screen appears. Accept the default plan name of **DB Maintenance Plan1** under **Plan name:**. Note you could select all of the configuration information in the text box using your mouse (dragging) to copy it to the clipboard with the CTRL-C command and then paste it into a text editor such as Notepad for inclusion in your network notebook (which was introduced in Chapter 7). Your screen should look similar to Figure 15-19. Click **Finish**.

Notes:

Figure 15-19

Verify all of the configuration information on the completion screen, including the plan name.

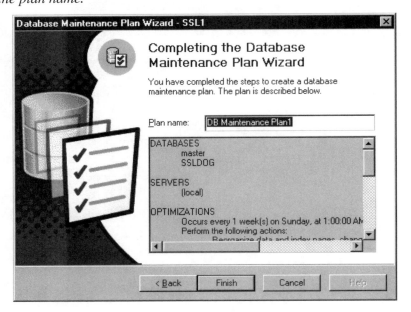

BEST PRACTICE: You might receive an error message via the SQL Server Enterprise Manager dialog box that informs you that the SQL Server Agent service is stopped and must be started to complete this processing. If you receive this message, simply click the **Start** button from your SBS server machine desktop (you might have to hold the **CTRL-ESC** keys to display the Start button). Click **Programs**, **Microsoft SQL Server**, **Service Manager**. When the **SQL Server Service Manager** appears, select **SQL Server Agent** in the **Services:** drop-down field. Click the **green arrow button** next to **Start/Continue**. Close the **SQL Server Service Manager**. Click **OK** on the SQL Server Enterprise Manager dialog box that appeared at the beginning of this note.

You have now successfully completed the creation of a database maintenance plan for SSL. You will receive no indication that this was successfully created (in SBS 4.5 with SQL Server 6.5, you received a notification dialog box that you had to click OK on). However, you can verify the database maintenance plan was successfully created by expanding the **Management** folder under the **SSL1 (Windows NT)** object in the **SQL Server Enterprise Manager**. Click the **Jobs** object in the left pane and the details for DB Maintenance Plan1 appear in the right pane as seen in Figure 15-20.

Figure 15-20

Observing that the database maintenance plan was successfully created.

Notes:

Creating the Tracking Table

You should always have a bona fide business purpose for creating a database and populating it with information. SSL is no exception. Here the underlying business purpose is clear: to use SQL Server to solve a problem. The problem is that, with the sheer volume of springer spaniels entering the world at SSL, you must have a method for tracking their whereabouts and exact origin. The simple table you'll create here, the Tracking table, achieves this important business goal.

Table 15-1 shows the data dictionary that you will use to create the database.

Table 15-1: SSL Data Dictionary

Item (Column Name)	Description
SSLDOG	Database name
Tracking	Table name for tracking Springer Spaniels
DogName	Name of dog (column name, Data Type = char, Length = 30)
ShowName	Long name of dog for show purposes (column name, Data Type = char, Length = 50)
FatherDN	Father dog's name (column name, Data Type = char, Length = 30)
MotherDN	Mother dog's name (column name, Data Type = char, Length = 30)
DDOB	Dog's date of birth (column name, Data Type = datetime, Length = 8)
AKCNum	American Kennel Club (AKC) registration number (column name, Data Type = char, Length = 15)

Now commence the task of creating your Tracking table:

1. Log on to the **SSL1** as **Administrator** with the password **husky9999**.
2. Click **Start**, **Programs**, **Small Business Server Administrator Console**.
3. The SBS Administrator Console appears. Expand the following objects in the left pane: **Microsoft SQL Servers**, **SQL Server Group**, **SSL1 (Windows NT)**.
4. Expand **Databases**, **SSLDOG** and then right-click the **Table** icon in the left pane. Select **New Table** from the secondary menu. This is shown in Figure 15-21.

Figure 15-21
Selecting New Table to create the table.

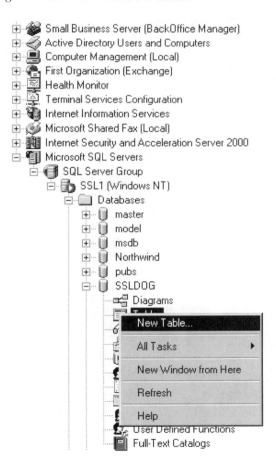

6. The **New Table in SSLDOG on SSL** screen appears. Create the tracking table based on the information contained in Table 15-1. For example, enter the column name under the **Column Name** column. Enter the data type under the **Data Type** column. Enter the field length in the **Length** column. You will not modify the **Allow Nulls** column. The result should look similar to Figure 15-22.

Figure 15-22
Tracking table setup.

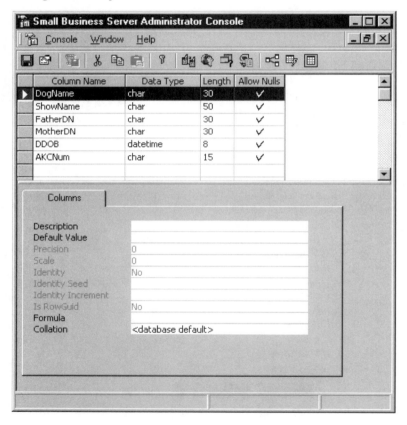

BEST PRACTICE: Move your cursor from field to field just like you would when using a spreadsheet. When your cursor is in the Data Type field, a down arrow appears. This is a drop-down menu containing the different types of data type fields you'll be working with (for example, datetime).

7. Click the **Save** icon on the left side of the toolbar (disk icon) on the **New Table in SSLDOG on SSL1** screen. Type **Tracking** in the **Enter a name for the table** field when the **Choose Name** dialog box appears. Click **OK**.
8. Close the Tracking Table window via the **X** in the upper-right corner of the screen.

If you look at the table listed for SSLDOG database in the SQL Server Enterprise Manager, you will see that the **Tracking** table is listed in alphabetical order right after the **sysusers** table.

Using Your SSL Database

You will now enter real business information into the Tracking table. Afterward, you will query the table to retrieve the data. Finally, I'll end the chapter with some advanced SQL Server topics.

Data Entry

It is now time to enter data into the Tracking table. In Table 15-2, I've provided the data needed for two Springer Spaniels. You will use this information to populate the database.

Table 15-2: SSLDOG Data

Item	Dog1	Dog2
DogName	Brisker	Jaeger
ShowName	Sir David Brisker	Sir Jaeger Matthew
FatherDN	Pepper	Pepper
MotherDN	Maria	Maria
DDOB	8-15-93	8-15-93
AKCNum	WA98119A	WA98119B

1. Log on to the **SSL1** as **Administrator** with the password **husky9999**.
2. Click **Start, Programs, Small Business Server Administrator Console**.
3. The SBS Administrator Console appears. Expand the following objects in the left pane: **Microsoft SQL Servers, SQL Server Group, SSL1 (Windows NT)**.
4. Expand **SSLDOG**.
5. Expand **Tables**. The list of tables will appear in the right pane.

6. Right-click on the **Tracking** table. From the secondary menu, select **Open Table**, **Return All Rows**.

7. The **Data in Table 'Tracking' in 'SSLDOG' on 'SSL1'** window appears. Enter the information from Table 15-2 into this window. For example, in the case of Dog1, enter **Brisker** under **DogName**, **Sir David Brisker** under **ShowName**, **Pepper** under **FatherDN**, **Maria** under **MotherDN**, **8-15-93** under **DDOBB** and WA98119A under **AKCNum**. After Dog1 and Dog2 have been entered, your screen should look similar to Figure 15-23. (You can move between fields with your **TAB** key.)

Figure 15-23
Completed Tracking table after Dog1 and Dog2 have been entered.

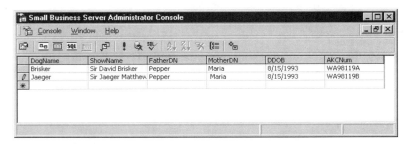

8. Close the **Data in Table 'Tracking' in 'SSLDOG' on 'SSL1'** window by clicking the **X** on the upper-left corner of the window. You have now entered the data for two dogs in the table of a SQL Server database that you have created. Congratulations.

Query the Data

You will now query the SSLDOG database, much like a client application does. Why? Because in and of itself, a table populated with data is relatively worthless. For your relationship with SQL Server to have true value, you must use the information. That's an action verb, as in *query*. Thus, after populating a table with information, you will query it to return the information in a synthesized or value-added form. And that's essentially the database food chain.

1. Log on to the **SSL1** as an **Administrator** with the password **husky9999**.

2. Click **Start**, **Programs**, **Small Business Server Administrator Console**.

3. The SBS Administrator Console appears. Expand the following objects in the left pane: **Microsoft SQL Servers**, **SQL Server Group**, **SPRINGERS01 (Windows NT)**.

4. Select and expand the **SSLDOG** database.

5. From the Tools menu, select **SQL Query Analyzer.** The SQL Query Analyzer program launches.

6. A **Query** window appears inside of the SQL Query Analyzer application. In the SQL Query Analyzer toolbar, confirm that **SSLDOG** appears in the database drop-down menu (upper right in Query window). If not, select SSLDOG from the database drop-down menu.

7. In the Query window, click the **blank space** in the upper-left part of the screen and type the following command: **select * from tracking**. This is shown in Figure 15-24.

Figure 15-24

Creating a select statement in SQL Server 2000 to query the SSLDOG database and, specifically, the Tracking table.

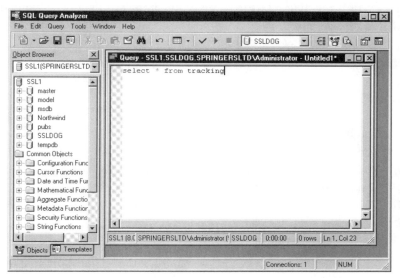

8. Select **Execute** from the **Query** menu (you can also press F5 or click the green right arrow on the Query window toolbar). The contents of the Tracking table are returned to you, as seen in Figure 15-25.

Figure 15-25

Successful query against Tracking with result returned to the display.

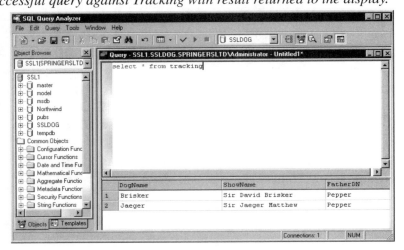

9. Close SQL Query by selecting **File**, **Exit**. Select **No** when the **SQL Query Analyzer** dialog box asks if you want to save the query (named **Untitled1** by default).

Success!

Enjoy your success. You've had a busy stretch of time so far performing the following SQL Server-related duties:

1. You learned SQL Server basics.
2. You created a SQL Server database title SSLDOG.
3. You created a table titled Tracking in the SSLDOG database.
4. You entered data for SSL in the Tracking table.
5. You queried (that is, used) the data in the Tracking table by executing a simple SQL query.

I want to emphasize one final point before you call it a day: This short chapter on SQL Server is only a start, and you have a lot to learn about SQL Server 2000 if you so desire. In other words, for those readers who complain in posted reader reviews at Amazon and other online book sellers that I don't cover specific SBS components at the Ph.D. level, I hope I've sufficiently managed your expectations about the depth which I can delve into individual BackOffice applications. No hard feelings, but there are many fine books (and large books at that) dedicated to individual applications, such as SQL Server 2000.

Advanced SQL: Publishing a Web Page

Now for some fun to wrap up this chapter on SQL Server 2000. Perhaps you didn't know, but you certainly will in just a few paragraphs, that your SQL-based data can easily be published as a Web page. This is actually one of the cooler features of SQL Server 2000 and very practical when you might want to publish information, such as real estate listings and product inventory sheets.

Publishing SSL data to a Web page

1. Log on to the **SSL1** as an **Administrator** with the password **husky9999**.
2. Click **Start**, **Programs**, **Small Business Server Administrator Console**.
3. The SBS Administrator Console appears. Expand the following objects in the left pane: **Microsoft SQL Servers, SQL Server Group, SSL1 (Windows NT)**.
4. Select and expand the **SSLDOG** database.
5. From the **Tools** menu, select **Wizards**. The **Select Wizard** dialog box appears.
6. Expand **Management** under **Please select the Wizard you wish to use:**.
7. Select **Web Assistant Wizard** and click **OK**.
8. The **Welcome to the Web Assistant Wizard** screen of the **Web Assistant Wizard** appears. After reading the welcome notice, click **Next**.
9. On the **Select Database** screen, select **SSLDOG** in the drop-down list of databases in the **Database name:** field. Click **Next**. This is shown in Figure 15-26.

Notes:

Figure 15-26

Selecting the SSLDOG database from the list of databases is an important step.

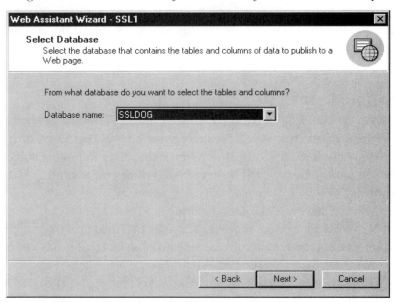

10. On the **Start a New Web Assistant Job** screen (see Figure 15-27), accept the default database name of **SSLDOG Web Page** in the **What do you want to name this Web Assistant job?** field. Accept the default selection under **What data do you want to publish to the table on the Web page?** of **Data from the tables and columns that I select** (this is a radio button). Click **Next**.

Notes:

Figure 15-27

Completing the Start a New Web Assistant Job.

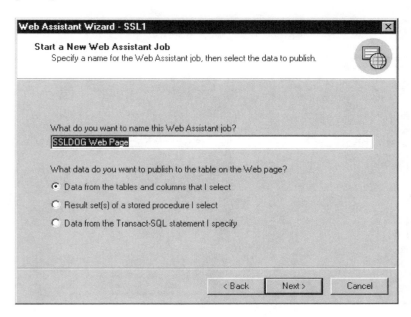

11. On the **Select a Table and Columns** screen, select the **Tracking** table
(which is the default selection) in **Available tables:**. Click the **Add All**
button so the columns initially listed under **Table columns** move over to
Selected columns. Your screen should look similar to Figure 15-28.
Click **Next**.

Notes:

Figure 15-28

Selecting the table and columns to use in the Web page.

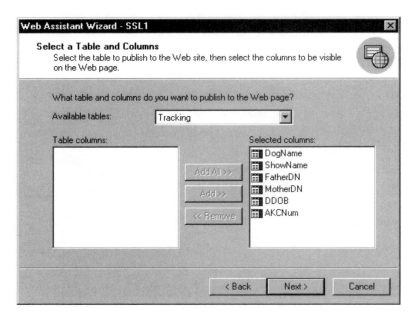

12. On the **Select Rows** screen, accept the default selection of **All of the rows** under **Which rows from the table do you want to publish to the Web page?**. Click **Next**.

13. On the **Schedule the Web Assistant Job** screen, accept the selection **Only one time when I complete this wizard** under **When should the Web Assistant update the Web page?** Note that this screen allows you to select the frequency the Web pages would be updated with data from SQL Server, as detailed in Figure 15-29. Click **Next**.

Notes:

Figure 15-29

You can specify how often the Web page is updated with database information.

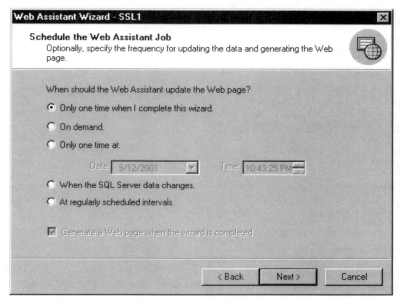

14. Accept the default file path and name of **C:\Program Files\Microsoft SQL Server\80\Tools\HTML\WebPage1.htm** in the **File name:** field of the **Publish the Web Page** screen. Click **Next**.
15. On the **Format the Web Page** screen, accept the default select of **Yes, help me format the Web page** and click **Next**.
16. The **Specify Titles** page appears. Under the **What do you want to title the Web page?** field, type **SSL Dog Registration Tracking Database**. Under the **What do you want to title the HTML table that contains the data?** field, type **AKC Registration Numbers**. Accept the default setting of **H3 - Large** in the **What size should the HTML table title font be?** field. Your screen should look similar to Figure 15-30. Click **Next**.

Notes:

Figure 15-30

Providing title information for the Web page you are creating to display the SQL data.

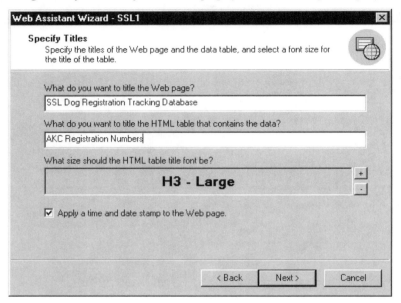

17. On the **Format a Table** screen, accept the default settings of **Yes** and display column names under **Do you want column names displayed in the HTML table?**. Accept the **Fixed** selection under **What font characteristics do you want to apply to the table data?** and keep the **Draw border lines around the HTML table** check box selected. Click **Next**.

18. On the **Add Hyperlinks to the Web Page** screen, accept the default selection of **No** under **Do you want to include hyperlinks on your Web page?**. Select **Next**.

19. The **Limit Rows** screen appears. Accept the default selection of **No, return all rows of data** under **Do you want to limit the total number of rows returned by SQL Server?**. Accept **No, put all data in one scrolling page** under **Do you want to limit the number of rows displayed on each Web page?**. Click **Next**.

20. Click **Finish** on the **Completing the Web Assistant Wizard** screen after reviewing the summary information.

21. Click **OK** when the **Web Assistant Wizard – SSL1** dialog box appears informing you that the **Web Assistant successfully completed the task.**

22. You will now view the Web page you just created. Launch Internet Explorer by clicking **Start**, **Programs**, **Internet Explorer**. Note you might have to hold down the **CTRL-ESC** keys to display the Start button.

23. When Internet Explorer appears, select **File**, **Open**. Navigate by clicking the **Browse** button to the file location specified in Step 14 above. This file in the **File Name** field of the **Microsoft Internet Explorer** dialog box (which appears when you click Browse) should be: **C:\Program Files\Microsoft SQL Server\80\Tools\HTML\WebPage1.htm**. Click **Open**.

24. Click **OK** when you return to the **Open** dialog box.

25. The Web page showing the AKC Registration Numbers for SSL appears, as seen in Figure 15-31. Close Internet Explorer after you've observed the Web page. Close the SQL Server Enterprise Manager.

Figure 15-31
Viewing SSL data in a Web browser.

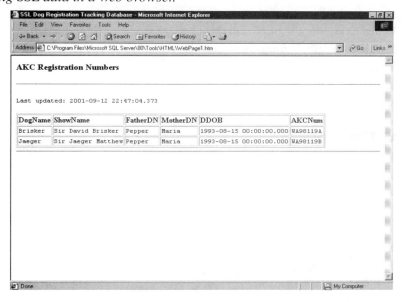

Next Steps - You've Only Just Begun

So you're still interested in learning more about SQL Server. That's great! It's a huge area where you can always grow; it has no upper knowledge limit. Aside from the advanced SQL Server books mentioned earlier today, there are several key areas to master as you continue in your quest to learn and use SQL servers.

These study topics are:

- Learn SQL basics including these SQL commands: <u>SELECT</u>, <u>UPDATE</u>, <u>INSERT</u>, and <u>DELETE</u>.

- Learn the rules: how to define primary keys, secondary keys, and indexes, and how to normalize a database.

- Learn the power of stored procedures. Create a stored procedure of your own.

- Learn, inside and out, the tools that ship with SQL Server 2000 including SQL Server Enterprise Manager, SQL Query Analyzer, and Books Online (to name my three favorite tools).

- Learn and master client-side connectivity, especially ODBC.

- Learn how third-party applications use SQL Server 2000. Such third-party applications include Great Plains Dynamics, an accounting application.

- Learn to connect sophisticated Web pages to SQL Server 2000 for online transactions (far more advanced than you learned in the last section). This is, of course, a very popular and in-demand skill set. It is the basis of many electronic commerce implementations.

Guest Column

Join me in welcoming Steve Bloom, an MCSE and MCDBA who servers as an IT professional at Versus Law in Redmond, Washington. Steve paints the picture of SQL Server for us.

An impressive feature of SBS is the fact that it comes bundled with SQL Server. I'm going to talk about the "What", "How", and "Why" of SQL Server; mention a potential drawback regarding licensing; and discuss best practices for making good use of SQL Server on your SBS network.

Originally, Microsoft and Sybase worked together to develop a database product. Parting ways in 1994, Microsoft proceeded to develop a database program that was tightly integrated with the operating system, which yielded higher performance and impressed industry experts such as the ones at Info World magazine.

In June of 1995, SQL Server 6.0 was released. Since then we've seen versions 6.5 and 7.0. Finally, in late 2000, SQL 2000 was made available and is literally ready for business.

SQL Server has become an industrial strength relational database product. It can be configured so that large numbers of users can query and insert data simultaneously. Routine maintenance tasks like running backups or checking the overall health of tables and indexes are very easy to configure. Entire databases can be quickly copied from one machine to another for redundancy. Or, one copy might be used for online transactions while the other copy is used for data analysis or decision support. There are also many wizards for performing more complex tasks like finding the worst performing queries or tuning indexes for optimal performance.

Developers can easily create web forms or Visual Basic programs for data entry. But the most important database decisions are made before any data goes into your tables.

Built into SQL Server is a diagramming tool for drawing tables, adding fields, and defining relationships between tables. The design decisions you make will affect the performance of your database for ever after, so take the time and or hire the expertise needed to set up your database correctly. There's a utility for generating sql scripts that you can use to save the structure of your database if you ever need to re-create it from scratch. It can be reassuring to know that you can rebuild your database from scratch if you need to!

If you plan to put your accounting system on SQL Server, there are several accounting packages that come with a database already designed and the necessary data entry and maintenance utilities already built for entering and maintaining your data. Within the last 30 days of this writing, Microsoft had just announced plans to purchase Great Plains Software, a well-known manufacturer of accounting software. If you plan to sell products or services on the web you might give some careful thought to how you will get your orders into your accounting system. Here's a hint: Eliminate manual entry and your staff can spend more time providing customer service and closing sales.

Access 2000 comes with the ability to upgrade Access databases to SQL Server with the use of some easy wizards. There is also the MSDE, the Microsoft Data

Engine, which allows a developer to work on his desktop and build a fully functional SQL Database which can be accessible from a limited number of users across a network. The MSDE provides a fine way to develop databases for easy deployment on your SQL Server. And maybe a necessary one.

Currently, licensing requirements for SQL and SBS require that the purchaser buy a separate version of SQL and use a Client Access License to have SQL server on a separate machine. Since best practices require a wise business owner to separate his mission critical database applications from his primary domain controller, SBS owners are a little bit constrained. If you must deploy your database on your SBS server, you have tight control over how much memory to allow SQL to use. Simply right click the server name in Enterprise Manager, click properties, and examine the Memory tab to adjust the memory settings for your server.

A workable compromise might be to have to pay a fee to "de-couple" SQL 2000 from the SBS server without having to pay full price for a second version when the first one can't effectively be rolled into production, but at this writing Microsoft has not commented on this possibility. Perhaps your best bet is to develop your database on Access 2000 using the MSDE, then deploy the tested database application to a separate server on your SBS network.

Summary

In this chapter you worked with SQL Server 2000, the powerful database included with SBS 2000. I hope that the exercise in creating a database for SSL went a long way toward debunking the myth that databases are hard to use. If you followed the steps in this chapter, you not only created a database, but used it as well. That said, I emphasize the following point again: On an SBS network, your interaction with SQL Sever 2000 will likely be limited to installed third-party applications that use SQL Server 2000 as a database engine. If for some reason you decide to program SQL Server directly, as you did in creating the SSLDOG database table for SSL, remember to keep your databases simple and friendly, very much like you did today. That's my $69.95 advice to you. Good day.

Chapter 16
Boosting and Monitoring Small Business Server Performance

This is a chapter many SBSers have been waiting for. Now that you have a fully functional SBS network up and running for SSL (the sample company used in this book), it's time to optimize it! I'll focus on three performance monitoring components: Server Status View, Server Status Report, and Health Monitor 2.1. But I also pay lip service to a few other performance monitoring techniques, such as listening to your end users, Task Manager, Performance Monitor, and Network Monitor.

All in Order Now

Bear, not bare, with me for a moment. Granted, in Chapters 6 and 7 I spoke of performance issues in the context of daily, weekly, monthly, and annual tasks. I'll weave that discussion in again here as I migrate you to some new SBS monitoring tools. This section is designed to list, in order, the different types of performance monitoring tools you should utilize in being a supreme SBSer! Let's start with end users.

End Users

First and foremost, your end users are always your best performance monitor in terms of immediacy. They are real-time squawkers that will alert you to nearly any problem. Once alerted to a problem, your task may be to determine exactly what is occurring on the network. Often you are armed with such helpful phrases uttered by the end user as "nothing works." It's an art and science to decipher the hidden meanings, but you become more skilled with experience. Better yet, once notified by an end user that nothing works, you can use the tools listed below to remedy various SBS network maladies.

Server Status View

This tool, first seen in Chapter 5 within the SBS management console discussion, is an at-a-glance current view of your system health. Three primary areas are monitored, including Health Monitor Alerts, Performance Counters, and Services. The Server Status View is explored in detail later in the chapter. The Server Status View in SBS 2000 is a huge improvement over the "Home" page in SBS 4.5 that showed basic disk space measurements and failed services.

Server Status Reports

Server Status Reports allow you to monitor the health of your SBS network on a daily basis. The mechanics are quite simple with a comprehensive report e-mailed to the system administrator or technology consultant with key system performance information and attached reports (such as event logs). This capability was first introduced in SBS 4.5, and has since been improved in a couple of ways. First, the basic performance monitor variables have been expanded. Second, you no longer need a special tool from the SBS Resource Kit to customize the Server Status Report to add reports of your liking. Third, the Server Status Report can be viewed from a special XML tool released by the SBS development team at Microsoft.

Health Monitor 2.1

Many SBSers equate themselves to a medical doctor when it comes to server surgery and patient (end user) care. In the spirit of preventive medicine, the SBS development team released Health Monitor 2.1. Note that a previous version of Health Monitor was available at the enterprise level with Microsoft System Management Server (SMS). You might think of Health Monitor, which is a true 7/24 'round-the-clock monitoring tool, that is sort of an x-ray of your system at a point in time. That is, it reports the here and now, but doesn't do a good job of giving your historical perspective (the historical views are better handled by Performance Monitor).

Task Manager

Task Manager is accessed by right-clicking the task bar at the bottom of the SBS desktop and selecting Task Manager. Not only will Task Manager tell you what applications and processes are running (or have stopped running), but the Performance tab is wonderful for viewing current processor activity and memory.

BEST PRACTICE: I really like the way that the Task Manager memory counter, displayed as both a histogram bar and a line chart, includes both physical RAM and paging memory space. That provides a more realistic view of how memory is managed as compared to three other memory reporting methods (one in Server Status View and two in Server Status Reports) in the SBS performance area. See the advanced topics discussion on memory near the end of this chapter.

Performance Monitor

This was highlighted in Chapter 7 with respect to periodically logging the performance of your system over a period of time. While the real-time charting feature in Performance Monitor is cool to look at, it is in its ability to log information and create long-term charts that this tool really shines, for this allows you to visually track long-term SBS system performance declines or improvements. Performance Monitor is installed by default in SBS 2000 and launched from the **Performance** program item in the **Administrative Tools** programs group (**Start**, **Programs**).

Network Monitor

This tool was the darling of the Windows NT 4.0 MCSE era with an entire two days of the five-day class – *Course 689: Using Windows NT Server in the Enterprise* – dedicated to its use and abuse. If you ever see a *Course 689* book sitting around an MCSE's unguarded desk, steal it and run. Seriously, the Network Monitor tool is a network sniffer that not only gives you wiretapping privileges to look at unencrypted communications from the bad guys, but allows you to troubleshoot intense network performance issues, such as a failed logon handshake or DHCP address issuance problems.

BEST PRACTICE: Go ahead and play around with Network Monitor and learn what you can from it. You might well enjoy viewing the network statistics, such as bandwidth utilization, in addition to snooping around the contents of packets. But be advised that there are very few good texts on network monitoring, and the real way you learn it is in the following way: paid Microsoft Product Support Service (PSS) incidents. I speak the truth: You will learn Network Monitor most thoroughly in a crisis condition while on the telephone with PSS.

Network Monitor is not installed by default in SBS 2000. Perform these steps to install Network Monitor on SSL1.

1. Log on to **SSL1** as **Administrator** with the password **husky9999**.
2. Click **Start**, **Settings**, **Control Panel**, **Add/Remove Programs**, **Add/Remove Windows Components**.
3. Select **Management and Monitoring Tools**. Click **Next**.
4. Accept the **Remote administration mode** selection on the **Terminal Services Setup** screen and click **Next**. DO NOT even select Application server mode.
5. If necessary, insert SBS Disc 1 when asked for the **Service Pack 1 CD**. Click **OK**.
6. Click **Finish** on the **Completing the Windows Components Wizard**.
7. Click **Close** on **Add/Remove Programs**.
8. Close **Control Panel** from **File**, **Close**.
9. Click **Start**, **Programs**, **Administrative Tools**, **Network Monitor**.
10. Click **OK** on the **Network Monitor—Select Default Network** dialog box.
11. When the **Select a network** dialog box appears, expand **Local Computer** in the right-pane. Select the **internal network adapter card** (e.g., ETHERNET, NDIS NPP, 00E018CB7FC2) that represents the 192.168.16.x subnet and click **OK**.

BEST PRACTICE: Granted, I just walked you into a box canyon. The visual element that described the network adapter card was via (MAC) value, not by network adapter card brand and model name or even LAN connection. So, just exactly how do you know which network adapter card relates to the internal 192.168.16.x network? Here's how. Click **Start**, **Programs**, **Accessories**, **Command Prompt**. At the command prompt, type **ipconfig /all** and look at which network adapter card (**Description**) is associated to the IP address **192.168.16.2**. Then look at the **Physical Address** field and write the MAC address value down. On the **Select a network** dialog box, pick the option with the same MAC address (00E018CB7FC2). Oh—and don't forget to close the **Command Prompt** box by clicking the close "**X**" in the upper right corner.

12. Click **Capture**, **Start**. Network Monitor will start to capture network packets and report network traffic activity similar to Figure 16-1. This is very interesting information, to say the least.

Figure 16-1
Network Monitor at work – capturing packets.

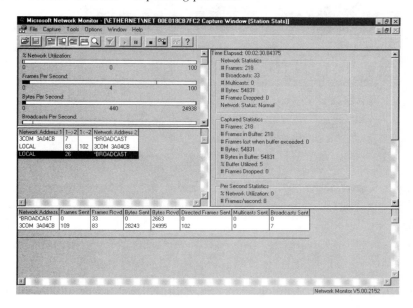

13. Click **Capture**, **Stop**.
14. Click **Capture**, **Displayed Capture Data**. Your screen should look similar to Figure 16-2. The lower pane is where you see the contents of the packet displayed.

Notes:

Figure 16-2

Viewing a packet capture in Network Monitor. Look at frames 320-322. Those three frames are the classic TCP/IP handshake between hosts (LOCAL and PRESIDENT).

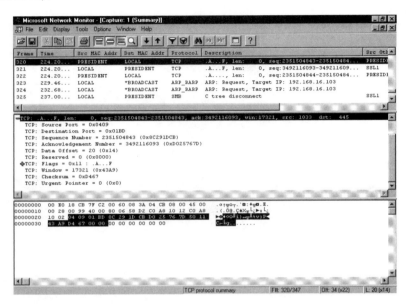

15. Close Network Monitor from **File, Exit**. Click **No** when the **Save File** dialog box appears. Click **No** when asked to save the names database on the **Save Address Database?** dialog box.

Meet Server Status View

When you open either the SBS Administrator Console or the SBS Personal Console, the Server Status View is displayed by default. First mentioned in Chapter 5, the Server Status View attempts to bring an "Executive Information System" (EIS) view to managing the SBS network. It does a good job of presenting three major categories in separate screen panes: Health Monitor Alerts, Performance Counters, and Services.

It is interesting to note that the middle pane of the Server Status View, shown in Figure 16-3, adheres to the fundamentals of network administration. Here is what I mean: In the Microsoft Network Essentials text – the entry point for many an MCSE – you learn the critical monitoring areas are disk, memory, processor, and network performance. The default counters listed in Performance Counters address three of the four: disk, memory, and process.

Figure 16-3
Meet and greet Server Status View.

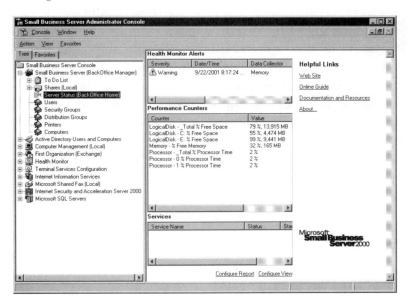

BEST PRACTICE: To monitor the fourth fundamental area of network administration, network performance, use Network Monitor's statistics screen, described in the preceding section.

Note the Services pane of the Server Status View only displays services that are stopped, start pending, or stop pending. You will not see services that are running. Basically we're talking exception reporting here, wherein only problems or potential problems are reported.

To customize the Server Status View, perform the following keystrokes.

1. Log on to **SSL1** as **Administrator** with the password **husky9999**.
2. Click **Start, Small Business Server Administrator Console**.
3. Click **Configure View** on the **Server Status View** page. The **Server Status View Configuration Properties** dialog box appears.

4. On the **SSL1** tab, select the **PhysicalDisk-Total Avg. Disk Queue Length** performance counter. This is shown in Figure 16-4.

BEST PRACTICE: Note that I won't have you add more services to display at this time for one simple reason. That reason is the services you can select from in Server Status View aren't especially meaningful to me. For example, I really need to select a couple of Exchange services that aren't present: Microsoft Exchange Information Store and Microsoft Exchange System Attendant. Hopefully the ability to select from any service listed under **Services** (found under **Computer Management (Local)**, **Services and Applications** in the SBS Administrator Console) will be available in the next rendition of Server Status View in a future SBS release.

Notes:

Figure 16-4
Selecting a counter to display in Server Status View.

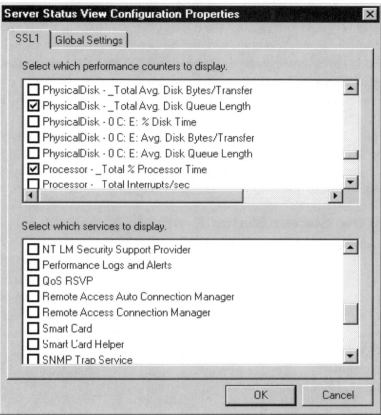

The counter you just added is now visible in the Server Status View even when these services are running just fine. That's all for that area, folks!

Meet Server Status Reports

I love the Server Status Reports. Not only do these reports allow me to monitor my client's SBS networks easily, but each day I can reply to my clients that everything is okay. So, in that context, the beauty of the Server Status Reports is half technical and half communications. And when you think about it, that's exactly what consulting is: half-and-half.

BEST PRACTICE: Not to play on the coffee analogy here, but I can't resist after that last sentence above (the half-and-half part). Understand that I set the Server Status Reports to be sent each morning just before the business opens, say 7 a.m. That's because I want the most current information, and the mere act of receiving the report means several things are going right, including the fact that the SBS server is functional, Exchange and other services are fat and happy and sassy, and the telco connection to the Internet is alive and kicking. The problem with having the reports sent any earlier is that the SBS network may well have been functional at 1 a.m. but somehow failed later in the morning, a fact you would be unaware of until your client called you in a fuss while you were gulping down your espresso. Not a fun experience, let me tell you (and one that I've had).

Creating the Server Status Reports

First, you'll configure the Server Status Report for SSL and have it sent to the Administrator. Part of this configuration includes adding custom reports for Backup Exec 8.x for Small Business Server 2000 and Trend's OfficeScan 5 for Small Business Server 2000. You'll recall that you downloaded and installed both of these products in Chapter 6. Next, you'll review the Server Status Reports, both in raw form and using the XML tool that you will download and install from Microsoft's SBS Web site. Finally, you will analyze the custom reports for Backup Exec and OfficeScan. Freshen up the cup of coffee, because that's a bunch of tasks in front of you!

1. Log on to SSL1 as **Administrator** with the password **husky9999**.
2. Click **Start, Small Business Server Administrator Console**.
3. Click **Configure Report** on the **Server Status View** page. The **Server Status Report Configuration** dialog box appears.
4. In addition to the default settings (**Performance counters**, **Services**, and **Health Monitor alerts**), select **Attach above data in XML format**.

BEST PRACTICE: Note that the XML format option relates only to the default three selections (Performance counters, Services, and Health Monitor alerts). It does not in any way, shape, or form relate to how data will be presented in an XML format from other sources, such as third-party reports.

5. Select all options under Application log files (**Application Event Log, Firewall Service Logs, IIS Logs, Security Event Log, System Event Log,** and **Web Proxy Log**).
6. Click **Add**. The **Add Report Log** dialog box will appear. Add the following custom reports based on the information in Table 16-1. Note you will need to click the **Browse** button and navigate to the specific files listed in **File Name:** field. After each entry, click **Add** to close the **Add Report Log** dialog box. (You'll repeat Step 6 once to add the second custom report in Table 16-1.)

BEST PRACTICE: Once you make an entry for a custom report, you might have noticed that there is no way to edit your custom report entry. If you've made a mistake or want to change the display name or description of a report, you will need to first remove it (**Remove**) and then add (**Add**) it again.

Table 16-1: Custom reports to add to SSL1 Server Status Reports

Display name:	Description:	File name:
Virus Detection Update Log	Reports virus definition file update activity	C:\Program files\Trend\ OfficeScan\PCCSRV\Log\update.log
Backup Report	Reports tape backup activity	C:\Program Files\VERITAS \Backup Exec\NT\BEX*.*

BEST PRACTICE: Did you notice that I was wild-carding in the second row under File name: in Table 16-1? Yep – the old start-dot-star. This is a very important point to understand. Basically what's occurring here is that you can use the *.* wild-card variable when adding a custom report to Server Status Report. This allows you to accommodate third-party applications that increment their file names each day, which is common and truly the case with Backup Exec and its tape backup log file names. You might be interested to know that this wild-card capability also exists with the Server Status Report customization tool from the SBS 4.5 Resource Kit in the last release.

After you have added the custom reports, the Report Options tab of Server Status Reports should look similar to Figure 16-5.

Figure 16-5
Note the custom report entry for virus detection file updates under the Application log files list.

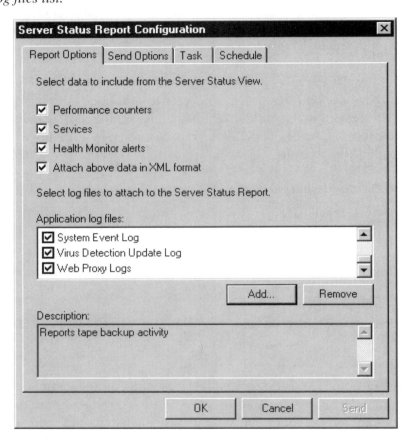

7. Meanwhile, back to the step-by-step nature of this example. Click on the **Send Options** tab and select **Send report via email**. In the field just below this selection ("**Type one or more email addresses...**"), type **administrator@springersltd.com**. This will send the reports to the administrator account for the SSL SBS network, as you might expect. This is shown in Figure 16-6.

BEST PRACTICE: You could also select the **Send report via fax** option. This would allow you to receive the core data listed on the **Report Options** tab (**Performance counters, Services, Health Monitor alerts**) but not the log file attachments.

I see the benefit of receiving the Server Status Report information via fax as a form of redundancy. Imagine this. You select both the e-mail and the fax options but you only receive the fax report one morning. You now know that the SBS server is alive and kicking and either the Exchange 2000 Server application isn't working correctly or the SBS client site is suffering from some type of Internet outage (say a down DSL line). Under this scenario, you could reverse engineer your solutions to a possible problem you've witnessed.

Closely related to that topic of e-mail and faxing the Server Status Reports is this: It's a crying shame that the selection boxes aren't organized in some type of "If…Then" construct. Here is what I mean. My preference is to receive one Server Status Report per client per day, first and foremost by e-mail. If for some reason the e-mail transmission of the Server Status Report fails, then I'd like to have it arrive via fax, so I can review the core SBS data and then determine why the e-mail report didn't arrive. And under that scenario, if I receive neither the e-mail or fax versions of the Server Status Report from a client, then I can conclude all hell has broken loose at the client site and either call, rush over immediately, or head for higher ground for personal protection!

Notes:

Figure 16-6

Configuring the Server Status Report to be e-mailed to the administrator account.

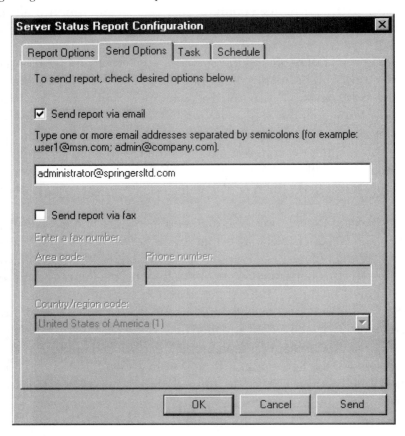

8. Click the **Task** tab. You will now create the job that can be scheduled for delivery. In the **Run as:** field, type **Administrator**.

9. Click the **Set password...** button. The **Set Password** dialog box appears. Type **husky9999** in both the **Password:** and **Confirm password:** fields. Click **OK**.

10. Click the **Schedule** tab and click the **New** button. Accept **Daily** in the **Schedule Task:** field. Type **7:00 AM** under **Start Time:** so this report is mailed just an hour before normal business hours commence. Accept all other settings such that your screen appears similar to Figure 16-7.

Figure 16-7
You have now configured the Server Status Report to go out every single day, including weekends and holidays at 7 a.m.

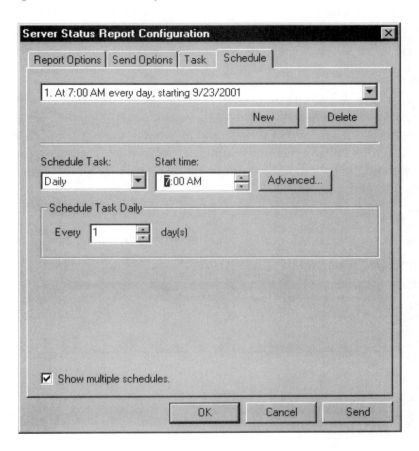

11. Click **Send** as part of this example to immediately send a Server Status Report (so you don't have to wait until 7 a.m. one day hence to view it!). Note that the Send command will close the **Server Status Report Configuration** dialog box and save your settings. This is the end of the configuration example.

Viewing the Server Status Reports

It's now time to view the server status reports. In this section, there are two ways to view this report: raw and XML Reporting Tool.

Raw

The first way is to simply open the Server Status Report e-mail in your Outlook 2000 Inbox. Double-click the e-mail titled **Server Status Report - <Springer Spaniels Limited/Bob Easter>** in the **Inbox**. The end result should appear similar to Figure 16-8 whereby the Performance Counters appear as "raw" text and the attachments are lined along the bottom. Leave this e-mail open for use in the XML Reporting Tool section below.

> BEST PRACTICE: Remember in the early chapters of this book when I spoke towards meta-data? Information you entered during the SBS setup process is often reused in strange and mysterious ways. One such way is the Subject line of the Server Status Report e-mail. The organization name and the user name are derived directly from an underlying SBS setup screen.

Figure 16-8
Meet the Server Status Report in its "raw" form. This is difficult to read and understand.

BEST PRACTICE: Don't reply to ServerStatusReport account listed as the From: (sender) of the Server Status Report e-mail. This is a nonexistent or null account that is simply a placeholder. Don't believe me? Well then, right-click on **ServerStatusReport** and select **Properties** from the secondary menu. You will note on the **E-mail Properties** dialog box that appears that the **Display name:** and **E-mail address:** are exactly the same. And the e-mail address of ServerStatusReport is not a valid SMTP address.

What's unfortunate about the use of a dummy e-mail address for the Server Status Report is the following. When I want to reply to my SBS client that everything is cool today, as reported in the Server Status Report I received, I have to remove the ServerStatusReport e-mail address from the To: field after clicking the Reply button on the message. Next, I type a valid SMTP e-mail address for someone (or a distribution group) at my client site. What a pain in the rear endski!

But have no fear. I've spoken directly with the program manager on the SBS development team about this reply-to-a-phony-e-mail-address malady and he has taken my observations under advisement. Hopefully, in a future release, this reply e-mail address will be configurable (and save me a few annoying keystrokes per client each day).

XML Reporting Tool

In order to view the reports via the whiz-bang XML Reporting Tool released by the SBS development team, you'll first need to download and install this tool. As of this writing, the XML Reporting Tool link is located on the main page at Microsoft's SBS Web site. Follow these commands.

1. Log on to **SSL1** as **Administrator** with the password **husky9999**.
2. Double-click the **Internet Explorer** icon on the desktop and surf to **www.microsoft.com/sbserver**.
3. Click on the link under **Top Downloads** (right-side) titled **XML Reporting Tool**.
4. On the **XML Reporting Tool** page, shown in Figure 16-9, first click on the **SBSXMLtool.doc** file link. When the **File Download** dialog box appears, click **OK** to accept the default selection of **Save this file to disk**. Double-

click **My Documents** in the **Save As** dialog box followed by a click on the **Save** button. Click **Close** on the **Download complete** dialog box.

Figure 16-9
Take a moment to read the XML Reporting Tool page.

Notes:

5. Now click on the **sbsxmltool.exe** link on the **XML Reporting Tool** page. When the **File Download** dialog box appears, click **OK** to accept the default selection of **Save this file to disk**. Double-click **My Documents** in the **Save As** dialog box followed by a click on the **Save** button. Click **Close** on the **Download complete** dialog box.

6. Double-click the **My Documents** shortcut on the SSL1 desktop.

7. Double-click **SBSXMLtool.doc** and carefully ready this document. Close WordPad from **File**, **Exit** when you've completed your reading assignment.

8. Double-click **sbsxmltool.exe**.

9. Select **I Agree** on the **License Agreement** screen. The InstallShield process will start.

10. Click **Finish** on the **InstallShield Wizard Completed** screen.

11. You are returned to **My Documents**. Right-click and select **New**, **Folder**. Name the folder **SSL1-XML**. Double-click on **SSL1-XML**.

12. If need be, launch **Outlook 2000** from the **Microsoft Outlook** shortcut on the SSL1 desktop and double-click the e-mail titled **Server Status Report - <Springer Spaniels Limited/Bob Easter>** in the Inbox.

13. Right-click on the attachment object titled **ServerStatusReport** at the lower far left of the screens (in the attachment section). Select **Save As** from the secondary menu. By default, the **Save As** dialog box will display **My Documents**. Double-click on **SSL1-XML** to open it. Click **Save**.

14. From the SSL1 desktop, click **Start**, **Programs**, **Microsoft Small Business Server 2000 XML Reporting Tool** (program group), **Microsoft Small Business Server 2000 XML Reporting Tool** (program item).

15. The Welcome screen for the XML Reporting Tool appears as seen in Figure 16-10. Carefully read the notice message regarding the need to download and install the Microsoft XML Parser (MSXML) 3.0. Follow the exact instructions on this Web page to download the parser from **msdn.microsoft.com/downloads/default**. When you complete the process, click **Refresh** as instructed.

Figure 16-10
This Web page regarding the parser used by the XML Reporting Tool is very important and should be followed exactly.

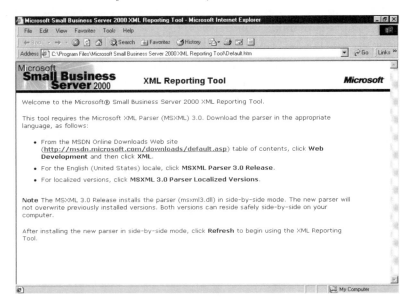

BEST PRACTICE: Note when you actually find the parser on the MSDN site as instructed by Figure 16-10, you will need to click **Download**, followed by **Yes** (on the Licensing page). When the **File Download** dialog box appears, click **OK** to accept the default selection of **Save this file to disk**. Double-click **My Documents** in the **Save As** dialog box followed by a click on the **Save** button. Click **Close** on the **Download complete** dialog box. Now you need to double-click the **My Documents** shortcut from the SSL1 desktop. Double-click **msxml3.exe**. Click **Next** when the **Welcome to the Microsoft XML Parser Setup Wizard** screen appears. Select **I accept the terms in this License Agreement** when the **End-User License Agreement** screen appears. Click **Next**. When the **Customer Information** screen appears, click **Next**. Click **Install** on the **Ready to Install** screen. Click **Finish** on the **Completing the Microsoft XML Parser Setup Wizard** screen.

16. Whew! Return to the **XML Reporting Tool** screen shown in Figure 16-10 and click the **Refresh** button. The **Welcome** screen takes on a new

appearance as shown in Figure 16-11. Carefully read that you need to create a folder structure for each client site. For the purposes of SSL, I had you create this folder in Step 11 above (the parent folder is **My Documents** and the child folder is **SSL1-XML**).

Figure 16-11

You will see this screen after you have successfully installed the XML Reporting Tool's XML parser and clicked Refresh. Congratulations!

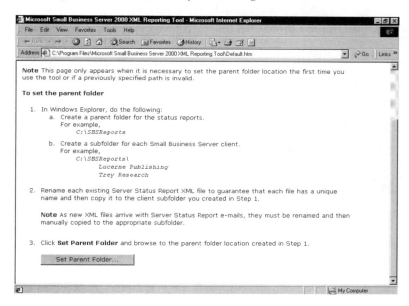

BEST PRACTICE: Did you catch the language in Step 2 in Figure 16-11? Do you know what the implications of this are? Simply stated, if you want to store any XML reporting history, say the XML reports from the start, middle, and end of month, you need to manually rename the XML file attachment titled "ServerStatusReport.000.xml" that is sent each time with the Server Status Report e-mail. This requires you to manually name the file something meaningful such as ServerStatusReport091501.xml for each client for the file you received on, say, September 15, 2001. If you simply save the daily XML report file over itself, you will not be able to generate any historical comparisons.

The funny thing is, the term "000" in the last part of the file name could be used for an incremental counter. And you guessed, I've asked the SBS development team to implement incremental XML report file naming in the next SBS release!

17. Click **Set Parent Folder** and select **My Documents** in the **Browse for Folder** dialog box. Click **OK**.
18. The **XML Reporting Tool** screen now displays the **TreeView Control** as seen in Figure 16-12. Expand **SSL1-XML** and select **ServerStatusReport.000.xml**.

Figure 16-12
You are so darn close to viewing your Server Status Report information via an XML report format.

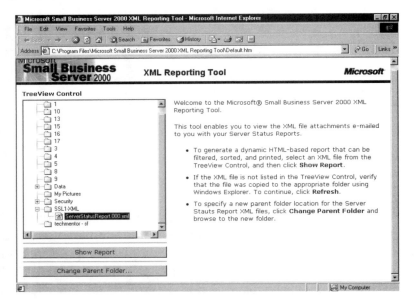

BEST PRACTICE: You'd expect that you could simply double-click the XML data file (ServerStatusReport.000.xml) and have it open up. The next step proves otherwise, as a double-click on the file will do nothing.

19. Click the **Show Report** button. The **Server Status Report** screen appears as seen in Figure 16-13. Note that I display the second part of this in Figure 16-14.

Figure 16-13

The top part of the XML-based Server Status Report.

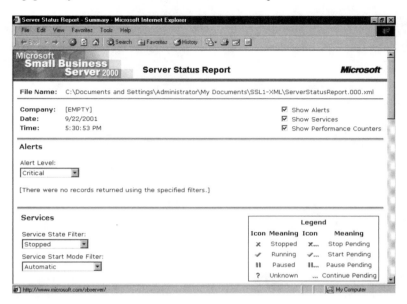

BEST PRACTICE: Take a moment to appreciate the thought that went into how the XML-based Server Status Report operates. For example, look at the Services section in Figure 16-13. You will see its exception reporting in action as the Service State Filter is set to Stopped and the Service Start Mode Filter is set to Automatic. This basically says "…show me all services that should have automatically started that are now stopped." An example of one such service that is to automatically started and must keep running is the Microsoft Exchange Information Store. When it comes to the Microsoft Exchange Information Store, I'd like to know if its not running.

Along those lines, play with each of the options in each of the drop down menus. The XML tool has powerful sorting capabilities.

Figure 16-14

The bottom part of the XML-based Server Status Report.

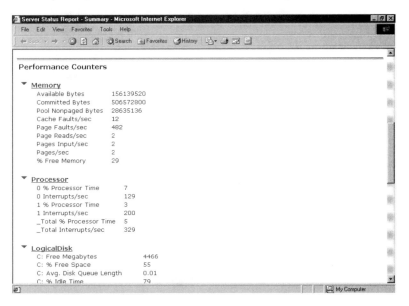

Guest Column

Here are some great words of wisdom by the SBS program manager in the performance monitoring area.

Monitoring Your Small Business Server 2000

by Eduardo Melo
Microsoft Corporation

Monitoring is one of the core features in Small Business Server. Monitoring tools allow VAPs to be more proactive, acting before problems occurs. For example, using our tools, you can notice that an SBS server is running out of disk space, giving you the chance to call your customer and discuss his buying a new, larger hard disk before he is actually out of space. And you know the magic formula well: You overcome your customer expectations, you get a happier customer, and you get more revenue!

Small Business Server 4.0 and 4.5 presented some monitoring tools. The most important was the Server Status Report (SSR) that allowed VAP to receive via e-mail or fax SBS health information. SBS 2000 goes one step beyond, introducing two new monitoring tools: Server Status View (SSV) and Health Monitor. SSV provides SBS administrators with a real-time snapshot of the server health. From the SBS management consoles, you can view information about the most important server services, performance counters, and alerts you have chosen to monitor. Small Business Server 2000 includes Health Monitor 2.1, a powerful real-time monitoring tool for system administrators. Health Monitor collects system data, such as performance counters and service status, and generates a detailed status view of the SBS server. You can also configure Health Monitor to automatically notify you, via e-mail or pager, when it detects a problem. Additionally, you can configure Health Monitor to perform automatic action whenever performance thresholds you configured are reached. You can, for example, configure Health Monitor to run a disk clean-up tool whenever the server disk space drops below 25 percent and to send you a notification whenever disk space is under 10 percent.

Finally, we added some cool new features to the Server Status Report. Now you can configure SSR to send you, via e-mail or fax, the same set of information you have from the Server Status View (alerts, services, and performance counters). You can also configure it to attach log files to the report. If you have configured a backup utility to run overnight, you can configure SSR to send you the backup logs, allowing you to keep an eye on whether the backup ran successfully or not. And all this information is sent according to the scheduling you defined.

The most important of the new SSR features is the ability to send the reports in XML format. XML is one of the current Internet buzzwords and stands for Extensible Markup Language. It allows developers to create their own customized tags, enabling the definition, transmission, validation, and interpretation of data between applications and between organizations. This means that VAPs, third-parties companies, and Microsoft, of course, are able to develop tools to create and, mainly, interpret data according to their particular needs.

This past spring, Microsoft released the Small Business Server 2000 XML Reporting Tool (XML Tool). It is available for free download from the SBS website (www.microsoft.com/smallbusinessserver). It's a great example of the XML power and the tools that we can build to manipulate data in XML format. Using the XML Tool, the XML files sent via the SSR can be viewed as dynamic

HTML-based reports, with options for sorting, filtering, and printing, Alerts, Services, and Performance Counters per predefined criteria. It is compatible with non-English Small Business Server 2000 installations and can display non-English XML file attachments. And since the tool is web-based, it doesn't require you to use a SBS2000 server to view the reports. All you need is a PC with Windows 2000 Professional (or higher) with Internet Explorer 5. With these requirements, you are able to view the reports even on the road, using your laptop.

The XML Tool was developed with the hottest web technologies, like XML, XSL and JavaScript. The tool uses these technologies to read the XML files sent via the SSR and generate good-looking and printing-friendly reports. If you are interested, you can find additional information about these technologies on the Microsoft MSDN website (http://msdn.microsoft.com).

But VAPs are not bounded to what the XML tool currently delivers. The decision to build the tool with technologies such as XML and XSLT allows VAPs to extend the tool, adding new features their customers require. For example, you would like to send an "executive report" every Friday to your customers, reporting any problems that happened during the week and also providing information about the backup job that runs on the SBS server every night. You can edit the HTML pages to display only Health Monitor alerts and add a section where you'll add the backup information. Since you can receive the backup logs via the Server Status Report, you can write some code to read the logs and add to the report the backup results (success or failure). Then it's just run the tool, generate the customized report, and send it back to your happy customer!

And we won't stop here. We're working hard to design and develop the next Small Business Server release. We'll expand the Server Status Report to allow you to receive even more information about server health and usage. Our team also wants to hear from you as to how you're using the XML tool and what we can add to the next release to make it more useful to you. Visit our website and give your opinion and feedback. It's very important to us.

Eduardo Melo graduated from Computer Science at the Federal University of Pernambuco, Brazil, and now works as a Program Manager on the Small Business Server team at Microsoft.

Meet Health Monitor 2.1

Moving even further into the depths of SBS performance monitoring, it's time to introduce you to Health Monitor. I'll present this huge area of study in the context of a discrete example related to SSL. Not that I'm trying to sell you short on Health Monitor, but more advanced Health Monitor issues will be explored in my monthly SBS newsletter, *Small Business Best Practices*, discussed in Appendix A.

Health Monitor, in a nutshell, is a 7/24 real-time SBS network monitor tool. It comes with hundreds of performance counters just waiting for your fine-tuning. To see these performance counters for yourself, simply expand all of the folders under **Health Monitor Sample Monitors** in **Health Monitor**.

I'll focus on one in the SSL methodology: the counter relating to free disk space. But first, a few more definitions. A key term in Health Monitor is "threshold alert." A threshold alert notifies you of potential performance problems. For example, you can set an alert to notify you when available disk space reaches a specified level. You can set three types of alerts to be generated under certain conditions (Informational, Warning, and Critical). You can also set multiple levels of alerts. For example, you can set an Informational alert when available disk space reaches 30 percent, a Warning alert when it reaches 20 percent, and a Critical alert when it reaches 10 percent.

You can specify how the system responds to problems by configuring the system to send notification by e-mail (which could include sending an e-mail to a paging service), write the problem to a text or log file, run a script, or configure a command-line action. For example, you might want the system to generate a log at all alert levels, but only call your pager during a critical alert. For some alerts, the system writes to the log and runs a script at one level, but writes to a text file and executes a command-line action at another alert level.

1. Log on to **SSL1** as **Administrator** with the password **husky9999**.
2. Click **Start, Small Business Server Administrator Console**.
3. Expand **Health Monitor, All Monitored Computers, SSL1, Health Monitor Sample Monitors, Windows 2000 Performance Monitors, Logical and Physical Disks, Logical Disk**.
4. Right-click **% Free Space < 10** in the **Thresholds** pane to the right. Select **Properties**.

5. On the **Expression** tab, change **Is less than** to **90** (from 10). Yes, this is a goofy value but it'll generate an alert for the purposes of the SSL methodology. Under **Duration**, select **Any time this occurs**. Your screen should look similar to Figure 16-15.

Figure 16-15
Completing the Expression tab with a goofy sample value.

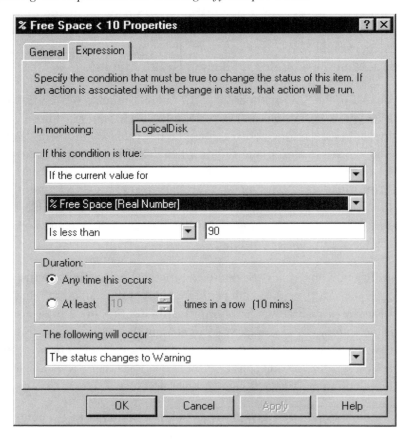

6. Click **OK**.
7. You will now configure the default e-mail action by expanding **Actions** beneath **SSL1** (**Health Monitor**, **All Monitored Computers**).
8. Right-click **Email <username>** and select **Properties**.
9. On the **Details** tab of the **Email <username> Properties** dialog box,

type **SPRINGERSLTD.COM** in the **SMTP server:** field. Type **Administrator** in the **To:** field. Your screen should look similar to Figure 16-16. Click **OK**.

Figure 16-16
Completing important e-mail addressing information in Health Monitor.

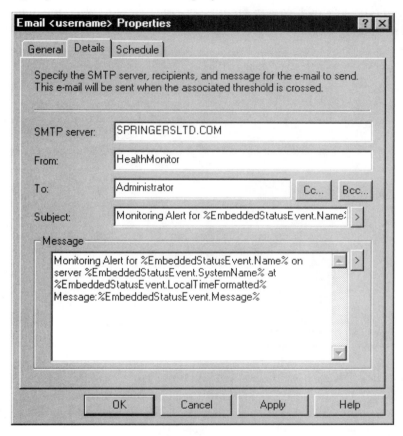

10. You now must link the performance monitor for disk space to the e-mail action you just configured. Right-click on the **Logical and Physical Disk** folder beneath Windows 2000 Performance Monitors and select **Properties.**
11. Click on the **Actions** tab.
12. Click on the "yellow" star icon, which is officially called **New Action Association**.

13. The **Execute Action Properties** dialog box appears. Verify that **Email Administrator** is selected beneath **Action** to execute. Select **Warning** under **Execution Condition**. This is shown in Figure 16-17. Set **Reminder** to **1 Minute(s)**. Click **OK**.

Figure 16-17
You're almost there with Health Monitor by completing the Execute Action Properties dialog box.

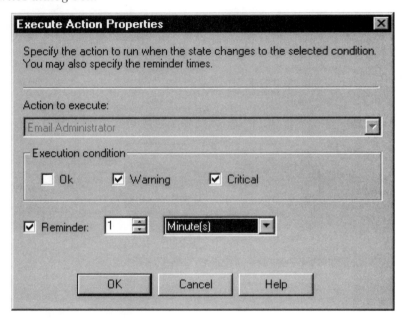

14. Click **OK** to close the **Execute Action Properties** dialog box.
15. Click **OK** to close **Logical and Physical Disks Properties**.
16. One last task! Please right-click **LogicalDisk** beneath **Logical and Physical Disks** and select **All Tasks, Enabled.**
17. Minimize the **SBS Administrator Console**.

BEST PRACTICE: By the way, the online help system for Health Monitor is absolutely wonderful. Print it out and read it if this is an area of interest for you.

Now, take a break and go get a cup of coffee. It takes a few minutes for Health Monitor to start rocking and rolling at this point for reasons I'm not completely sure about. When you return, launch **Microsoft Outlook** from the SSL1 desktop. Double-click the **Health Monitor alert e-mail** in the Inbox and read the message.

> BEST PRACTICE: Please work through the above steps again and re-turn the alert value to 10 percent free space in Step 5 above. Other-wise, you'll be bummed out with all the alerts you'll receive in the Outlook 2000 Inbox.

You can also customize Health Monitor to add a performance monitor for a specific component. For example, if you want to monitor a third-party applica-tion, you can add a performance monitor for that application. To do this, open the **SBS Administrator Console**. In the console tree, expand **Health Monitor**, and then expand **All Monitored Computers**. Right-click on **SSL1,** click **New**, and then click **Data Group**. Name the new data group **Testing1-2-3** and click **OK**. Right-click **Testing1-2-3,** click **New**, **Data Collector,** and then click the appropri-ate data collector. You may select from this list:

- Performance Monitor
- Service Monitor
- Process Monitor
- Windows Event Log Monitor
- COM+ Application
- HTTP Monitor
- TCP/IP Port Monitor
- Ping (ICMP) Monitor
- WMI Instance
- WMI Event Query
- WMI Query

Configure the necessary settings in the data group **Properties** dialog box for the data collector that you selected (e.g., **TCP/IP Port Monitor Properties**), and then click **OK**. The following list describes the settings that you can configure in the Properties dialog box.

- **General.** Enables you to specify the data group and add comments.

- **Details.** Enables you to specify the object that you want to monitor.

- **Actions.** Enables you to specify the action to occur, such as e-mail notification.

- **Schedule.** Enables you to specify the frequency and time that data will be collected.

- **Message.** Enables you to specify the text that is displayed in the Health Monitor console when the threshold is crossed or when the status is reset.

Advanced Topics

To wrap up the discussion herein on boosting SBS performance, I present a few random advanced topics, including a memory matter, two new performance monitoring tools in the small business realm, a war story, and a lesson on good communications.

Memory Reporting

One false—make that misleading—read on memory occurs with the Memory-% Free Memory counter in Server Status View because it reflects only the "physical" RAM memory on the SBS server machine. That is, paging space allocated to primary memory is ignored. This is also seen in the same counter in the Server Status Report (both raw and XML formats). So, on a SBS 2000 server machine with 256 MB RAM, you can get a free memory reading of 0% free. On an SBS 2000 server machine with 512 MB RAM, you may well see a free memory reading of 18 percent to 25 percent.

Fact of the matter is that if you look at the memory chart on the Performance tab in Task Manager, you'll see that the computer believes it has much more memory. That's because the paging space allocated to primary memory is correctly added back in. This is the memory reading, via Task Manager, that I suggest you use to assess the memory situation on an SBS server machine.

bCentral for Technology Consultants

Microsoft's bCentral service is a Web-based portal for small businesses and service providers. There is a technology consultant suite of services, expected to be made available in the U.S. early in 2002 that represents a budding courtship between SBS and bCentral. The Network Monitoring Service extends basic Health Monitor and Server Status Reporting in SBS 2000 by aggregating information from multiple customers on a single Web page. The value-add is that you don't have to look at server status reports one by one from each of your clients. A help-desk service allows you to accurately track your trouble tickets in ways that Outlook 2002 or Microsoft Project 2002 cannot. A customer lead generation service allows you to list your business in the "Find a Technology Consultant" service at www.bCentral.com where over 3.5 million customers visit each month. Finally, this service for technology consultants displays relevant news alerts on its home page for virus outbreaks, local event information, service packs, and security bulletins.

> BEST PRACTICE: To learn more about Microsoft bCentral for Technology Consultants, visit directory.bcentral.com/partner.

CA Unicenter for Small Businesses

Computer Associates, recognizing the size and momentum of the small business technology market, has launched a product similar to several SBS performance monitoring components. I quote directly from part of the press release announcing this product:

ISLANDIA, N.Y., July 30, 2001 – Computer Associates International, Inc. (CA), the world's leading provider of eBusiness management solutions, today announced the immediate availability of Unicenter Desktop Management Suite for Small Businesses – the simplest, most complete solution ever offered to help organizations, with little or no IT staffs, keep their businesses up and running smoothly.

The new solution, available on a subscription basis for only $30 per system, per year, provides all the elements required for desktop and laptop support in one easy-to-implement package. It enables small companies to significantly improve the reliability of their critical PC resources without requiring them to spend an inordinate amount of resources on management tools and IT staff. Free 30- and

60-day trials of the Unicenter Desktop Management Suite are available at http:// ca.com/unicenter/dm.

Enterprise Management Associates (EMA) Software Management and Outsourcing Trends for the SMB/SME and RBO Markets research report, scheduled to be released this week, identifies a strong demand for desktop management tools such as the Unicenter Desktop Management Suite for Small Businesses.

"The small-to-mid-sized market has been waiting a very long time for a PC management solution as comprehensive and easy-to-implement as Unicenter Desktop Management Suite for Small Businesses," said Martha Young, research director, EMA. "Using the subscription-based model that CA is offering is particularly easy for companies with limited IT budgets to swallow."

So the question I pose to you is – friend or foe of SBS?

War Story

Nothing like a Sunday a.m. e-mail from your largest client asking why their Web site is loading so slowly. Of course the client's version of the story is that the network is a "notwork" and running very slowly. This is an SBS 2000 site, and true to form, the external Web site is actually hosted at the ISP, not on the SBS server machine. I look, poke, and peek around, finding nothing out of the ordinary. Finally, in an act of desperation, I e-mail a Web-head buddy of mine and have him take a look. It turns out the Web visitor counter-linked back to a third-party site monitoring service that had gone broke. Each time the main Web page attempted to load, there was a delay until the little Web counter at the bottom timed out. We're talking tens of seconds here.

The point is that you never quite know where you're SBS network performance problems will crop up from. Perhaps left field, eh?

It's the Communication That Is Important

So what's the bottom line here in this chapter? Yeah – the technical tools are cool. But it's really all about communicating with your SBS stakeholders. The native SBS tools allow you to do this in a much more proactive manner than previously possible. And not only can you send a kindly reply e-mail each day saying everything is fine, but you know to man all battle stations if you don't receive your daily report!

Summary

So much to cover and so little space. Three performance monitoring areas in SBS (Server Status View, Server Status Report, Health Monitor 2.1) were covered via the SSL methodology. Downloading, installing, and using the new XML Reporting Tool was certainly a highlight of this chapter (in my humble opinion). A guest speaker from Microsoft fortified the topics presented in this Chapter, and his plea for feedback shouldn't be lost on you. A gaggle of advanced topics were presented to wrap things up.

Chapter 17
Internet Information Server and Index Server

In order to delve deeper into the SBS depths, it is mandatory to take a look at an integrated component in the underlying Windows 2000 Server operating system: Internet Information Server. And heck, while we're at it, I'll take a Sunday country drive and look at Index Server. Granted, neither of these components are implicitly a huge part of SBS 2000; nonetheless, some exposure to them is deemed necessary.

IIS is the Web-engine that has its paws into more things than you might imagine. I'll highlight a few of those features in a moment. Note that IIS is something that assumes a larger foreground role at the enterprise level where things like Web hosting (both for external Web sites and internal intranet sites) make much sense. However, such roles are deemphasized in SBS 2000. And you can't deny IIS has something of a publicity problem, being best known for its susceptibility to worm attacks such as CODE RED, CODE RED II, and NIMDA in mid-2001.

Index Server is something that was previously in the "foreground" in SBS 4.5 as its own program item in the Windows NT Option Pack program group. In SBS 2000, it's surprisingly hard to find Index Server, as it is hidden deep under the Computer Management snap-in in the SBS Administrator Console.

As always, the topics of this chapter will be presented in the context of Springer Spaniels Limited (SSL), the sample company used across the tome to teach you SBS 2000 in a safe, secure, and, most important, successful way!

IIS Architecture

As spoken by Microsoft itself, "...IIS is tightly integrated with the Microsoft Windows 2000 Server operating system to provide a powerful Web server for small business. This integration enables the small business to take advantage of the Internet and intranet use, while still maintaining the highest levels of security for applications and information."

So let's take a second to dissect Microsoft's IIS definition from an architectural viewpoint.

Integration

The United States Department of Justice can go pound sand on this one. Whereas the great barristers in the antitrust division at the Department of Justice may have to some degree proven their point that Internet Explorer (the Web browser) can be removed and/or replaced by a competing Web browser on the Windows platform, don't even try that argument with IIS. IIS is a bona fide integrated component of Windows 2000 Server and thus SBS 2000. Don't believe me? Just remove it, reboot, and try to return to your normal SBS operations. Just kidding – don't really do this. Just believe me on this one.

An example of this operating system-level integration is how the IIS Admin Objects (IISAO), which sets the following properties in Active Directory, uses the Active Directory Services Interface (ADSI).

- AccessFlags
- AccessSSLFlags
- AnonymousPasswordSync
- AnonymousUserName
- AnonymousUserPass
- AuthFlags
- IISCertMapper
- LogonMethod
- PasswordCacheTTL
- UNCAuthenticationPassThrough

BEST PRACTICE: As an SBSer, it is probably in your best interest not to modify the Active Directory schema. I present the above Active Directory schema objects only to make my point on IIS integration.

Another example of operating system-level integration is how Terminal Service's WebConsole, known in SBS as MyConsole, depends on IIS. Matter of factly speaking, Web-based Terminal Services session is managed, in part, by IIS. Also consider the IIS/SBS integration point at **Configure Internet Information Services** on the **To Do List** from the SBS Administrator Console. The SBS development team put this in to address security issues surrounding IIS and ISA Server running on the same machine. By binding IIS to the internal network adapter card, you secure it against some potential Internet maladies. These specific security measures are taken when you click this link and complete the **IIS Configuration Tool** that appears:

- The IIS socket pool feature will be disabled.
- IIS will be unbound from all IP addresses except your local (internal) network interface card.

BEST PRACTICE: When I've completed the IIS Configuration Tool in the past, I have found that it disabled the ability to use Outlook Web Access (OWA) to remotely check e-mail from a Web browser over the Internet. It may well be that I'm doing something wrong, as in my discussions with the SBS development team they asserted that OWA will still work. Other SBS users have e-mailed me that no such issue has existed for them. So whatever side you fall on this matter, just beware of this issue.

Back to the storyline at hand here now. Later, when I again ran the IIS Configuration Tool and selected **Restore Defaults** to reverse the IIS security setting I'd made, I couldn't get OWA to work again until I had run the Internet Connection Wizard (ICW) again. Note that the need to re-run the ICW under this scenario isn't communicated on the To Do List or the online help system.

I should mention that Instant Messaging in Exchange 2000 Server is integrated with IIS.

Enabling

Closely related to the integration assertion is the way that IIS enables so much of the functionality in SBS 2000. For example, Exchange 2000 Server is dependant on a happy, healthy, and wealthy IIS. You might recall the discussion from Chapter 6 where I outlined how, after installing Exchange 2000 Server Service Pack 1, you must reapply the cumulative IIS fix from August 2001 (or later) with the CODE RED fix. That's because the darn Exchange 2000 Server Service Pack 1 copied over the enhanced ISAPI.DLL file that the initial CODE RED fix implemented. And let me take another angle on this discrete discussion. If your SBS 2000 server machine was attacked by CODE RED, which played on IIS vulnerabilities, then Exchange 2000 Server wouldn't work properly.

Exchange's Web-based e-mail capability, known to you as the Outlook Web Access (OWA) capability, is largely managed by IIS under the Exchange Folder under the Default Web Site in IIS.

Another application that is dependant on IIS is ISA Server 2000. One interaction area between these two components that I'm aware of is Web Proxy Service and caching. Alternatively, you can configure ISA Server to pass HTTP requests through to Web pages hosted by IIS.

Security

Now we're talking IIS's claim to fame. As the front line in electronic commerce and the Internet solution set in the Microsoft Server's family, IIS is a very popular hacking target. Several of the most recent hacker attacks (CODE RED, CODE RED II, and NIMDA) have directed their fury at IIS. Not surprisingly, many Microsoft man-hours have been expended on creating IIS fixes, as the next BEST PRACTICES alludes to.

> BEST PRACTICE: A continual challenge for SBSers, as expressed in both Chapter 6 and Chapter 7, is to stay current with service packs, fixes, and whatnot. That was a fact of life for an SBSer yesterday, remains the same today, and will continue to be tomorrow. One Web site at Microsoft that I've found to be especially keen on IIS issues is at http://www.microsoft.com/technet/treeview/default.asp?url=/technet/security/current.asp which is the Security Bulletin Search page as part of Microsoft TechNet. Another hint is to consider using the Windows Update tool that is native in Windows 2000 Server.

In a nutshell, IIS has the following security mechanisms, which I'll present as is. (Please consult the *Microsoft Windows 2000 Server Resource Kit* [Microsoft Press] for much more detailed information on this matter).

- Certificate Storage (integrated with Microsoft CryptoAPI)
- Digest Authentication (various authentication methods)
- Fortezza (U.S. government security standard)
- Kerberos V5 Authentication
- Security Wizards (Web Server Certificate Wizard, Permissions Wizard, CTL Wizard)
- Server Gated Cryptography

Visualize IIS

IIS is managed from the **Internet Information Services** snap-in as seen in Figure 17-1 in the SBS Administrator Console. When you expand out the parts, it has the **Default Web Site** and the **Administration Web Site** by default.

Figure 17-1

Meet IIS.

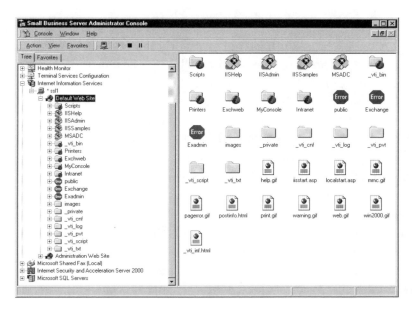

BEST PRACTICE: To be brutally honest and nothing less, it is possible that you'll never click the Internet Information Services snap-in. Seriously, you could operate just fine as an SBSer on an SBS network without ever interacting with IIS. That would assume that you're not going to implement the IIS functionality suggested in this chapter, including the SSL intranet page and FTP functionality.

SSL and IIS

So, let's break the mold and do a couple of things with IIS in the context of the SSL methodology. You'll lay down the infrastructure for the SSL intranet and install and configure FTP. Note that in the next chapter, Chapter 18, you will create the SSL intranet and then post it to the SSL intranet site you will now create. Let's get going, starting with creating a Web Site space for the SSL intranet.

Web Site

Follow me closely on this one. A Web page is placed in a Web site in the world of IIS. A Web page is created with FrontPage 2000 (the topic of Chapter 18). A Web site is created in IIS using the following keystrokes. Note you need to complete this next example in order to fully complete the examples in Chapter 18. You will first create a folder to physically hold the Web site and then create the Web site itself.

1. Log on to **SSL1** as **Administrator** with the password **husky9999**.
2. Click **Start, Programs, Accessories, Windows Explorer**.
3. Expand **My Computer, Local Disk (C:), Inetpub**.
4. Right-click in the details pane (right-side) and select **New, Folder**. Name the folder **SSLIntranet**. Also – please create another folder called **SSLFTP** in the same location that you'll need in the next section.
5. Close **Windows Explorer** from **File, Close**.
6. Click **Start, Small Business Server Administrator Console**.
7. Expand the **Internet Information Services** snap-in.
8. Right-click ***ssl** (the server object) and select **New, Web Site**.
9. The **Web Site Creation Wizard** launches. Click **Next** at the **Welcome to the Web Site Creation Wizard** screen.
10. Complete the **Description** field with **Springer Spaniels Limited Intranet** on the **Web Site Description** screen, as seen in Figure 17-2. Click **Next**.

Figure 17-2

Describing the SSL intranet.

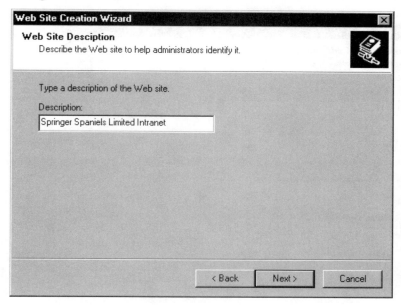

11. On the **IP Address and Port Settings** screen, select **192.168.16.2** under **Enter the IP address to use for this Web site:** and change the **TCP port this Web site should use (Default: 80)** to **8080**. Under the **Host Header for this site: (Default: None)** field, type **SSL Intranet**. This is shown in Figure 17-3. Click **Next**.

Notes:

Figure 17-3

Providing basic IP infrastructure information for the Web site.

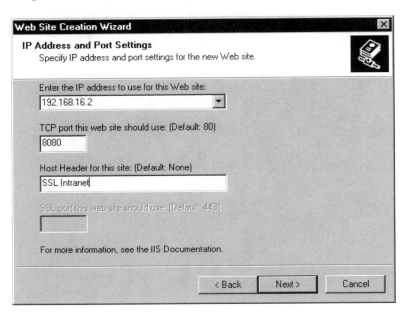

12. Click **Browse** on the **Web Site Home Directory** screen and navigate to
C:\inetpub\SSLIntranet. Once there, click **OK** to close the **Browse for
Folder** dialog box that magically appeared. Your screen should now look
similar to Figure 17-4.

Notes:

Figure 17-4

You have now selected the physical folder that will store the SSL intranet Web page you create in the next chapter.

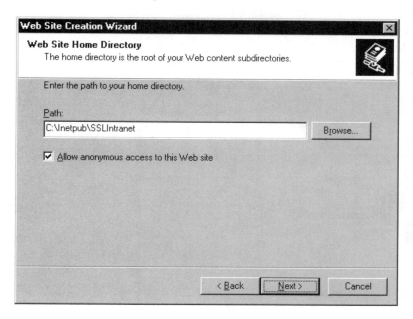

13. Select **Read, Write and Run** scripts (such as **ASP**) on the **Web Site Access Permissions** screen and click **Next**.
14. Click **Finish** on the **You have successfully completed the Web Site Creation Wizard** screen.

Notes:

Note the **Springer Spaniels Limited Intranet** should appear in the Internet Information Services snap-in similar to Figure 17-5. By default, the Web site is in a stop condition. And this is where you stop this portion of the example (you will resume with the Web site in Chapter 18).

Figure 17-5
Yo—you have laid down the Web infrastructure needed by SSL for its intranet site.

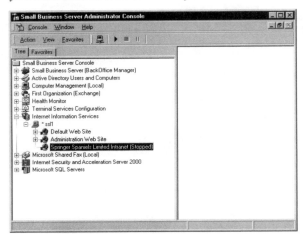

BEST PRACTICE: SBS 2000 IS NOT well suited to host your external Web pages. Better to host these with your ISP as per Microsoft's recommendation (for security, speed, and availability reasons).

You might be interested to know that a customer at the Microsoft/Gateway/Intel booths during the ITEC traveling road shows in the fall of 2001 had an interesting need. He ran a church that hosted Web pages for many churches. He wondered if SBS 2000 could host multiple Web pages by pointing multiple IP addresses to the external network adapter card (each IP address assigned to a different church's Web page). The answer was yes, this can be done. But this kind gentleman was discouraged from pursuing this strategy with SBS 2000 for all the reasons both I and Microsoft state about Web hosting and SBS.

FTP

Another way that SSL will interact with IIS is via FTP. There is a real-world need, more often than you think, to implement FTP. Why? Because many e-mail systems have 5 MB attachment limits. This is a true hindrance when working with large files. Just ask my client, a traffic engineering firm that is making big plans (and I mean big AutoCAD plans) for Seattle's new light rail system. When you're dealing with 60 MB CAD drawings, e-mail doesn't cut it. You typically need to look to FTP as a solution.

> BEST PRACTICE: FTP, officially known as File Transfer Protocol, is really about creating and managing a storage space to facilitate large file transfers. It's not very exciting, to be honest, except when you surface the words "security" and "FTP" in the same sentence.
>
> The security issue is this: FTP passes the user name and password, as well as the files being transferred, in clear text. So an evil gremlin with a network sniffer could view your information in an unkind and insincere way.
>
> But hang on to your hat. In the example that follows, I'll make it so that you can secure FTP by binding it to the internal network adapter card and thereby force external users to establish a secure and encrypted virtual private networking connection (VPN) prior to using their FTP client.

1. Log on to **SSL1** as **Administrator** with the password **husky9999**.
2. Click **Start, Small Business Server Administrator Console**.
3. Expand the **Internet Information Services** snap-in.
4. Right-click ***ssl** (the server object) and select **New, FTP Site**.
5. Ha! You got the error message **The service is not installed on this machine via the Internet Service Manager** dialog box shown in Figure 17-6, didn't ya! I get my jollies in strange ways, including walking readers headfirst into box canyons. Click **OK** and close the **Small Business Server Administrator Console**.

Figure 17-6

This message indicates that you need to install the FTP service on the SBS 2000 server machine. The FTP service is not installed by default on the SBS machine.

6. Click **Start, Settings, Control Panel, Add/Remove Programs, Add/ Remove Windows Components**.
7. Highlight **Internet Information Services (IIS)** on the **Windows Components** screen of the **Windows Components Wizard** that has appeared. Click the **Details** button.
8. Select **File Transfer Protocol (FTP) Server** as seen in Figure 17-7 and click **OK**.

Figure 17-7

Installing FTP on the server-side.

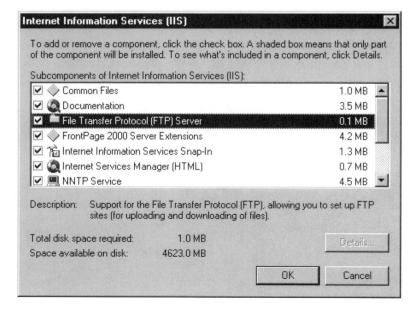

9. Click **Next** on the **Windows Component** screen.
10. Accept the **Remote administration mode** selection on the **Terminal Services Setup** screen and click **Next**. The configuration process will take several minutes.

BEST PRACTICE: Be extremely diligent not to select the Application sharing mode selection here, as major bad things will happen. Read the Terminal Services chapter (Chapter 8) for much more information on this topic.

11. If and when you are asked to insert the Compact Disc labeled **"Service Pack Files"**, simply insert **Disc 1** of the SBS 2000 setup discs and click **OK**. Remove your Disc when this step is complete.

BEST PRACTICE: You will need to also re-run Windows 2000 Server Service Pack 2 as detailed in Chapter 7 of this book to bring the service pack components into, shall we say, alignment. Please refer to Chapter 7 on the steps to perform this action.

12. Click **Finish** on the **Completing the Components Wizard** screen.
13. Whew! Click **Close** on the **Add/Remove Programs** window and then exit **Control Panel** window.
14. Return to the **Small Business Server Administrator Console** from **Start**. Right-click on *ssl under **Internet Information Services** and select **New, FTP Site**.
15. Click **Next** on the **Welcome to the FTP Site Creation Wizard** screen of the **FTP Site Creation Wizard**.
16. Under **Description** on the **FTP Site Description** screen, type **SSLFTP** and click **Next**.
17. On the **IP Address and Port Settings** screen, select **192.168.16.2** under **IP Address** and click **Next**. This screen is displayed in Figure 17-8.

Notes:

Figure 17-8

Assigning the internal IP address to the FTP site.

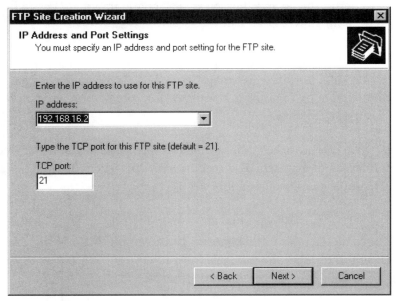

BEST PRACTICE: This step is very important. By binding the FTP site to the internal IP address, you've effectively made it more secure. An external party, seeking to use this FTP site, would need to first establish a VPN connection to participate on the internal SBS network.

18. The **FTP Site Home Directory** appears. Click **Browse. Browse to C:\Inetpub\SSLFTP** folder (that you created in the Web site section above). Click **OK**. Click **Next**.

19. On the **FTP Site Access Permissions** screen, select **Write** and verify that **Read** was selected. Your screen should look similar to Figure 17-9. Click **Next**.

Figure 17-9

Giving Read and Write permissions to the SSLFTP site.

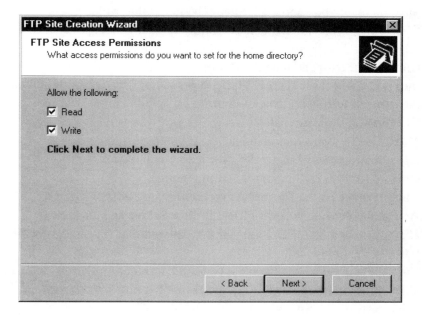

20. Click **Finish** on the **You have successfully completed the FTP Site Creation Wizard** screen.

Now, I betcha that you're just aching to use the FTP site you've just created, eh? Super! Let's do exactly that. In this example, you'll log on to PRESIDENT as NormH and download a free FTP client from a shareware site, install the client, transfer a photo file, and then FTP the file to the SSLFTP site. Refill your coffee, because here we go.

1. Log on to the client computer **PRESIDENT** as **NormH** with the password **Purple3300**.
2. Double-click **Internet Explorer** from the desktop and surf over to **www.shareware.com**.
3. In the **Search** field, type **CuteFTP** and click the **Search** button.
4. Click on the link **CuteFTP (32-bit)** that appears in the list of **CNET Downloads**.
5. Click **Download Now** on the **CuteFTP (32-bit)** page that appears.

6. When the **File Download** dialog box appears, select **Save this program to disk** and click **OK**. Save the file to **My Documents** when asked in the **Save As** dialog box and click **Save**. The file will download.

7. Click **Close** when the **Download complete** dialog box appears. Minimize your IE Web browser as you'll need it in a moment.

8. Click **Start, Run** and then the **Browse** button. Navigate to **My Documents** and select the **CuteFTP** file that was downloaded (it should have the name **cuteftp.exe**). Click **Open**.

9. Click **OK** at the **Run** dialog box.

10. The CuteFTP setup routine launches. If you receive an error message regarding Internet Explorer 5.5, just ignore it and click **Next**.

11. Click **Next** after reading the **Welcome!** notice.

12. Click **I Agree** on the **License Agreement** dialog box.

13. Accept the **default** setting on **Destination Folder** and click **Next**.

14. Click **Finished** on the **Installation Completed** dialog box. By default, **CuteFTP** will launch.

15. Click the **Start trial** button on the **CuteFTP Evaluation Period** dialog box.

16. Click **Close** to terminate the **Tip of Day** dialog box.

17. Click **New** on the **Site Manager** dialog box.

18. The **Site Settings for New Site** dialog box appears. Under **Label for site**, type **SSLFTP**. Under **FTP Host Address**, type **192.168.16.2**. Your screen should look similar to Figure 17-10.

Notes:

Figure 17-10

Creating a site to connect to, which in this case is the SSLFTP site.

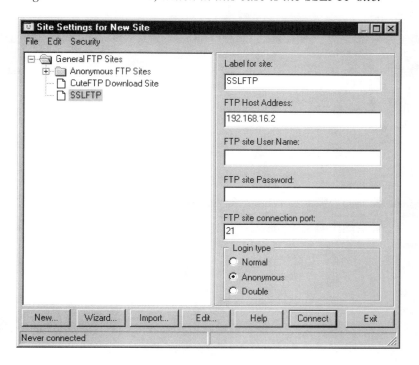

19. Click **Connect**.
20. Click **OK** at the **Logon Message** that indicates you've successfully logged on to the FTP site.
21. You are now viewing the CuteFTP client application. On the left pane, the default location is **My Documents**. Double-click **My Pictures**.
22. Select **Sample.jpg** with your mouse and drag this file to the right pane of CuteFTP. This right pane is **FTPSSL** on the SSL1 server (this is the FTP site you painstakingly created above).
23. Click **Yes** on the **Confirm** dialog box. The file will transfer quickly and your screen should now look similar to Figure 17-11.

Notes:

Figure 17-11

Another arrow in your SBS quiver! You've successfully transferred a photo file to the SSLFTP site.

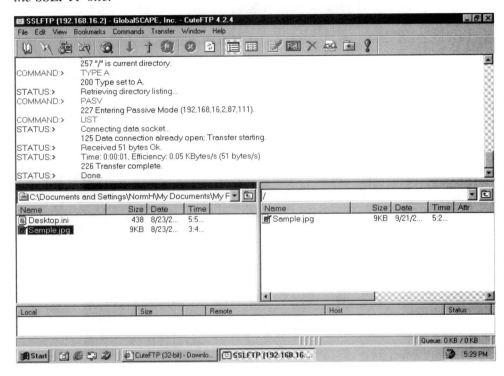

24. **Close** the **CuteFTP** application from **File, Exit**.

BEST PRACTICE: I've used CuteFTP as only an example herein. You could use the FTP client of your choice to complete the above example (but the keystrokes would be different). Heck—you can even use Internet Explorer as a rude and crude FTP client to complete this example. Ouch! Note that in the next section on Index Server, I actually have you use IE as the FTP client from the SSL1 server, just so you can see it in action!

Hey—a bit of SBS trivia for you. Microsoft doesn't have a robust FTP client application, so whenever you read Microsoft documentation and books about use of FTP, they'll typically use either the command line (the rudest FTP client of all, let me tell ya!) or the IE Web browser. It's this small fact that I enjoy about the writing a third-party book on SBS: I can show off third-party solutions.

And so it's now time to move on to the Index Server discussion. Let's do it.

Using Index Server

The reason that Index Server has a role in the SSL implementation methodology for SBS 2000 is that, once people see Index Server, the wheels start turning and they think of ways to use it in the real world. Index Server is basically a keyword search mechanism. True, you can fuss with the Find command and its mystical powers from the Start menu, but it's not quite the same no matter how you slice it.

In this example sitting at SSL1, you'll create a storage folder and download a set of important consulting documents from my company's Web site. You will then scan these documents for key words using Index Server and then perform a query against the "corpus" and afterwards you'll view the results.

1. Logon to **SSL1** as **Administrator** using the password **husky9999**.
2. Click **Start, Programs, Accessories, Windows Explorer**.
3. In **My Documents**, right-click and create a folder titled **Data** from **New, Folder**.
4. Close **Windows Explorer** from **File, Close**.
5. Double-click **Internet Explorer** from the desktop.
6. In **Address**, surf to **www.nethealthmon.com**. Select the **MCSE** button on the lower left. Note the IE has just become an FTP client.
7. Highlight all of the consulting documents with your mouse.
8. Right-click on the selected documents and select **Copy To Folder**. Select the **Data** folder under **My Documents** and click **OK**. The files will be transferred.
9. Close Internet Explorer from **File, Close**.
10. Launch **Small Business Server Administrator Console** from the **Start** button.
11. Expand **Computer Management**. Expand **Services and Applications**.
12. Right-click on **Indexing Service** and select **Start**. Answer **Yes** to the dialog box asking if you want to **Start the Indexing Service** each time the server machine starts.

13. Right-click on **Indexing Service** and select **New, Catalog**.

14. The **Add Catalog** dialog box appears. Type **SSL-DATA** in the **Name** field. Click the **Browse** button and navigate to the **Data** folder under **My Documents** in the **Browse for Folder** dialog box. Click **OK** followed by **OK** a second time.

15. Click **OK** when the **New Catalog Created** dialog box appears. Note this dialog box informs you that the Indexing Services needs to be stopped and started for the catalog to work. You will do this next.

16. Right-click on the **Indexing Service** and select **Stop**. Follow this with another right-click on **Indexing Service** and select **Start**.

17. Expand **SSL-DATA** and right-click on **Directories**. Select **New, Directory**. Click the **Browser** button and navigate to the **DATA** folder under **My Documents**. Click **OK** followed by **OK**. Your screen should look similar to Figure 17-12.

Figure 17-12
You've now created an Index Server corpus to be scanned and queried.

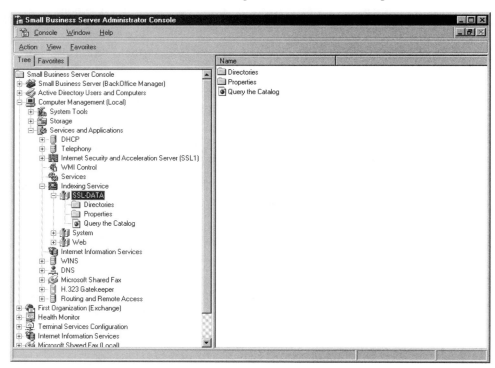

Hang in there! You're almost ready for action. But first go get a cup of coffee while the darn Indexing Service does its scan of the DATA folder. This can take a spell.

18. Welcome back from your coffee break. Expand **SSL-DATA** and double-click the **Query the Catalog** object.

19. In the **Enter your free text** query below: type **SBS**. Your screen should look similar to Figure 17-13. Click **Search**.

Figure 17-13

You will now query your consulting document corpus on the word "SBS."

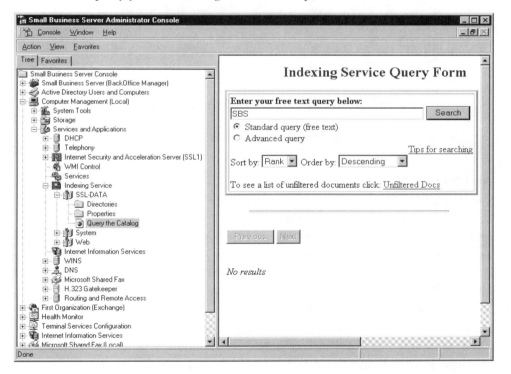

20. The results of the query are instantly displayed and can be opened by clicking on the document hyperlink in the **Title** field. Your screen should look similar to Figure 17-14.

Figure 17-14

Success! You've completed the example to create and search a data corpus with Index Server. Take a bow.

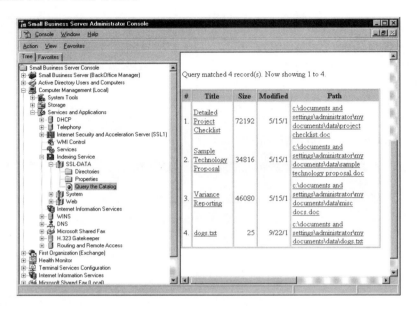

Summary

And that's all, folks, when it comes to working with IIS, including creating a Web site and FTP. Remember the Web site was created as part of the Web infrastructure needed to host the SSL intranet Web page (that you'll create in the next chapter). If you read closely, you would have caught my stern endorsement of Microsoft's best practice that external Internet Web pages should be hosted with your ISP, not on your SBS server. The FTP exercise was not only real world in nature, even to the point of using a third-party FTP client, but you learned one method for making FTP more secure (by requiring a VPN connection first). Finally, an often overlooked friend in the SBS community, Index Server, was presented in its full glory in an exercise that you can successful complete on your own.

Chapter 18
Publishing on the Internet/Intranet

So, now that you've laid down the small business networking infrastructure, what's the follow-up act? That is, up to this point, you've truly explored the workings of SBS 2000 from "A to Z" or start to finish. But your job doesn't end there, something the SBS 2000 development team thought of, believe me. This idea that you will now extend your use of SBS 2000 is best evidenced by the inclusion of Microsoft FrontPage 2000 in the product packaging. The belief is that you'll use the FrontPage to create intranet Web pages to enhance internal business communications. And, you guessed it, FrontPage can be used to create your external Web site. It's all part of the Internet "presence" thang!

In this chapter, you'll install FrontPage 2000 and create a very simple intranet Web page for Springer Spaniels Limited (SSL), the sample company used across this book. You'll use FrontPage 2000's FTP transfer approach to move your intranet Web page to SSL1's intranet Web site. You'll recall that in Chapter 17 you created the SSL1 intranet Web site in Internet Information Server (see the section "SSL and IIS" in Chapter 17). The good news is that this chapter isn't going to grow beyond the example that I've just laid out for you. There are plenty of wonderful books out on the market that address Web page creation and publishing. This chapter is just a quick-and-dirty sampler of that process.

Installing FrontPage 2000

Have you agreed to the enclosed license for FrontPage 2000 before proceeding another sentence? If so, read on. The reason I point this out is that the copy of FrontPage 2000 included with SBS 2000 is a single-user version. It may only be installed on one computer. And, as you might imagine, FrontPage 2000 shouldn't be on the SBS 2000 server machine (SSL1), as far as I'm concerned. Better to install FrontPage 2000 on a client computer, such as PRESIDENT, which is exactly what we'll do.

1. Log on to the client computer **PRESIDENT** as **NormH** with the password **Purple3300**.
2. Insert the **FrontPage 2000 Disc** into your CD-drive.
3. On the **Welcome** screen, enter your **customer information** and **FrontPage 2000 product key** (see the back of the disc gem case for this). Click **Next**.
4. Accept the license by selecting **I agree** on the **License** screen and click **Next** to continue.
5. On the installation page, click **Install Now**.
6. After FrontPage 2000 has completed its installation process, click **Finish** on the **Completing FrontPage 2000 Installation** screen.

BEST PRACTICE: To be honest, installing FrontPage 2000 is very similar to installing other Microsoft desktop products. No great mystery here.

Obtaining the Necessities

You'll need to quickly download the photo that will be used on the Web page. This is a picture of Jaeger and Brisker, the prize-winning Springer Spaniels of SSL! Perform the following steps.

1. Log on to the client computer **PRESIDENT** as **NormH** with the password **Purple3300**.
2. Double-click the **Internet Explorer** icon on the desktop.
3. Type the following in the Address field: **www.nethealthmon.com** and press **Enter**.
4. Select the **MCSE** button on the lower-left side.
5. Right-click on the file **dawgs.jpg** and select **Save Target As**. Click **Save** in the **Save File** dialog box to save the file to the default location of **My Documents**.
6. Close Internet Explorer from **File, Close**.

Notes:

Using FrontPage 2000

Let's cut to the chase and create an intranet Web page for SSL! Follow these keystrokes.

1. Log on to the client computer **PRESIDENT** as **NormH** with the password **Purple3300**.
2. Click **Start, Programs, Microsoft FrontPage.**
3. A blank Web page appears in the default view of Microsoft Front Page. Type and format the following text, shown in Table 18-1, such that it appears similar to Figure 18-1.

Table 18-1: Text input for SSL intranet Web page.

Text	Formatting
Springer Spaniels Limited	Bold, 18-point, Arial, left-alignment
Bainbridge Island, WA	Bold, 14-point, Arial, left-alignment
Intranet Web Site	Bold, 18-point, Arial, center-alignment
Jaeger and Brisker's Retirement Party – June 30th	Bold, Italic, 12-point, Times New Roman, left-alignment

Notes:

Figure 18-1

SSL Web page after entering Table 18-1 information.

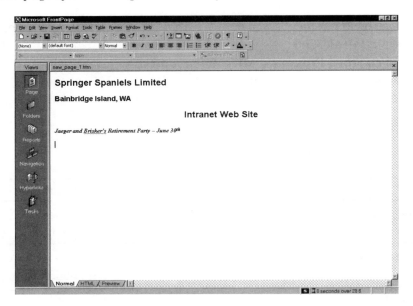

4. Just below the sentence **Intranet Web Site**, press **Enter** to create a blank line.
5. Click **Insert**, **Picture**, **From File**. When the **Select File** dialog box appears, navigate to **My Documents** and select **dawgs.jpg**.
6. Click **OK**. The picture of Jaeger and Brisker appears in the Web page.
7. Let's take a moment to save the file we're working on. Click **File**, **Save** and accept the default file name (**springer_spaniels_limited.htm**). Click the **Save** button.
8. Click **OK** when the **Save Embedded Files** dialog box appears, as seen in Figure 18-2.

Notes:

Figure 18-2
The step "embeds" the JPEG picture of the dogs (dawgs.jpg) in the Web page.

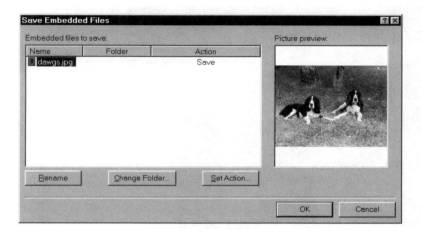

9. You might have noticed the JPEG photo of the dogs is very large. You will need to resize this down by clicking a corner of the photo and dragging it inward to make a small photo object. There's really no other way to explain this step.
10. Click on the **Preview** tab. Your SSL Web page should look similar to Figure 18-3. If this is the case, proceed to the next section. Otherwise, make sure that you've not overlooked a step above in the creation of this Web page.

Notes:

Figure 18-3
Your SSL Web site should now look similar to this.

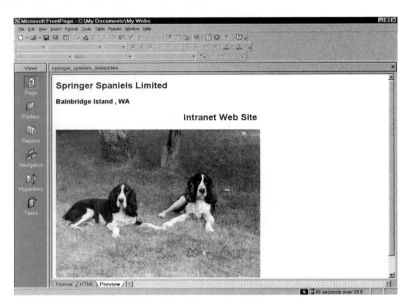

Transferring the Web page

Now that you've created the Web page, it needs to be transferred to the SSL1
server and start work as the intranet Web page. Assuming you haven't performed
other keystrokes since the last section (that is, FrontPage 2000 is open with
springer_spaniels_limited.htm in Preview mode, you're ready to proceed with
the following keystrokes.

1. In FrontPage 2000, click **File**, **Publish Web**.
2. The **Publish Web** dialog box appears. Complete the **Specify the location
    to publish your web to:** with **http://192.168.16.2/SSLIntranet**. This is
    shown in Figure 18-4.

Notes:

Figure 18-4

The "publish" process you are facilitating here is actually using an internal FrontPage 2000 FTP mechanism to transfer the Web page.

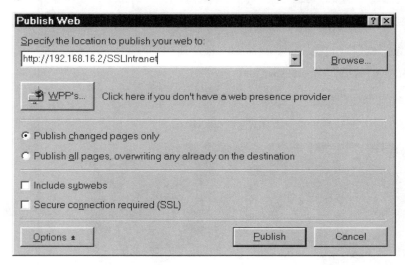

3. Click **Publish**. The SSL Intranet Web Site will be published pronto to the SSL1 server machine.
4. Close FrontPage 2000 from **File**, **Exit**.

Take a quick bow. There is really just one last step left – viewing the page!

Viewing the Web page

In this section, you'll simply launch Internet Explorer from the PRESIDENT desktop and surf on over to the SSL intranet Web page. Follow these steps.

1. Log on to the client computer **PRESIDENT** as **NormH** with the password **Purple3300**.
2. Double-click the **Internet Explorer** icon on the desktop.
3. Type the following in the Address field: **localhost/sslintranet** and press **Enter**.
4. The SSL intranet Web page should appear just as you see in Figure 18-5. Now take a huge bow. You've created and published a Web page in FrontPage 2000 as part of your SBS 2000 journey!

Figure 18-5

The finished look of the SSL intranet Web site. While not a "Picasso," it works!

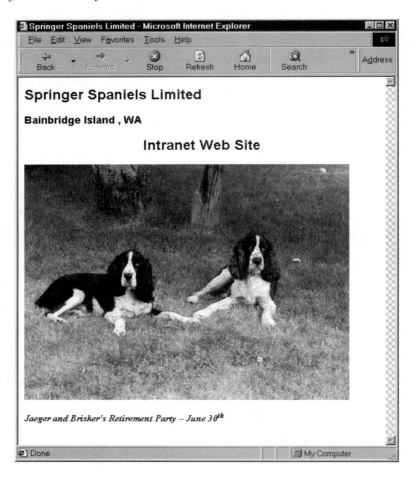

BEST PRACTICE: I'm sure you've followed that the example in this chapter relates to publishing an intranet Web site to SSL1, the SBS 2000 server machine for SSL. Remember that for external Web sites, you should use the Web hosting capabilities of your Internet Service Provider (ISP).

Alternatives

So what if you get serious about the Web thing and want to go beyond the simple example presented herein. There are three alternatives that I can think of (and I'm sure more!). These include using FrontPage 2000 for advanced Web sites, bCentral, handcrafted Web sites, and FrontPage 2002.

Advanced FrontPage 2000

Believe it or not, FrontPage 2000 can do much more than I've shared with you here. Might I suggest that you consider taking a course in FrontPage (see Figure 18-6) or hiring a Web-head to take your Web pages to a higher level?

Figure 18-6

Gateway Country Stores offer advanced FrontPage 2000 training.

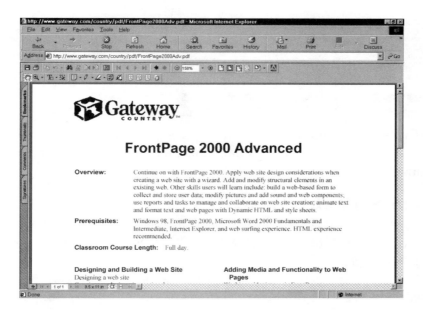

bCentral

Another alternative is to effectively outsource some of your Web site development, maintenance, and so on. This can be accomplished by using the Web building process offered from bCentral and seen in Figure 18-7.

Figure 18-7

Perhaps you'd prefer to do the bCentral thing when it comes to the Web.

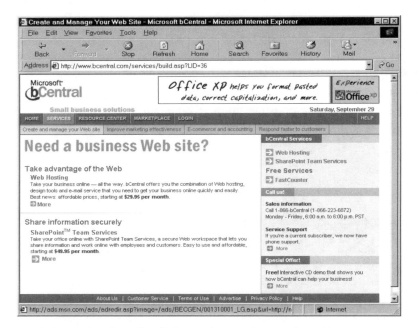

BEST PRACTICE: The bCentral portal even has SharePoint Team Services to support your internal communication needs, much like the intranet you created in this chapter.

Handcrafted Web pages

So, you want to be a Web-head from the coding perspective. Cool! I wish you well. Below you'll find some of the HTML code from the SSL intranet Web page created in this chapter.

```html
<html>

<head>
<meta http-equiv="Content-Language" content="en-us">
<meta http-equiv="Content-Type" content="text/html;
charset=windows-1252">
<meta name="GENERATOR" content="Microsoft FrontPage
4.0">
```

```
<meta name="ProgId"
content="FrontPage.Editor.Document">
<title>Springer Spaniels Limited</title>
</head>

<body>
<p><b><font face="Arial" size="5"><span style="mso-
fareast-font-family: Times New Roman; mso-ansi-lan-
guage: EN-US; mso-fareast-language: EN-US; mso-bidi-
language: AR-SA">Springer Spaniels Limited</span></
font></b></p>
<p><st1:place>
<st1:City>
<b><font size="4" face="Arial"><span style="mso-
fareast-font-family: Times New Roman; mso-ansi-lan-
guage: EN-US; mso-fareast-language: EN-US; mso-bidi-
language: AR-SA">Bainbridge Island</span></st1:City>
<span style="mso-fareast-font-family: Times New Roman;
mso-ansi-language: EN-US; mso-fareast-language: EN-US;
mso-bidi-language: AR-SA">, </span><st1:State>
<span style="mso-fareast-font-family: Times New Roman;
mso-ansi-language: EN-US; mso-fareast-language: EN-US;
mso-bidi-language:
```

In all seriousness, there are those in the Web community that still like to be close to the code so they can create the exact look and feel they want.

FrontPage 2002

While not included with SBS 2000, primarily because it was released after the SBS 2000 ship date, there is an upgrade to FrontPage you should consider. This release, called FrontPage 2002, is part of the Office XP genre. It's got more features, yadda yadda yadda. But you'll have to purchase this version, as there isn't a free upgrade available from the FrontPage 2000 included in SBS 2000.

Summary

Short, sweet, and to the point. I wouldn't have it any other way, as this Web discussion is really adjunct to the core SBS infrastructure mission presented in the previous 17 chapters. In this chapter, you installed FrontPage 2000 on the PRESIDENT client computer. Next, you downloaded a photo of Jaeger and Brisker for use on the SSL intranet Web page. You then proceeded to create this Web page. Afterwards, you transferred the Web page to the SSL server machine and viewed it with Internet Explorer.

This chapter represents the end of the tasks you can accomplish "natively" or out of the box with SBS 2000. In the next chapter, I explore more ways to extend SBS 2000, including downloading and installing more Microsoft software and running Office XP. See you there.

Chapter 19
More Microsoft Solutions for SBS

So what's an SBSer to do? You've planned, setup, managed, configured, communicated, published, and otherwise tweaked the SSL SBS 2000 network over several hundred pages. You have now reached the final chapter, which instead of mourning the end of the SSL journey, really celebrates the next steps you can take with SBS. In this chapter, you'll see what the SBS network has empowered you to do. You can sign up for services at bCentral. You can implement a Microsoft Digital Dashboard solution. You can use Outlook Team Folders. You can deploy and exploit Microsoft Office XP. Heck—you can even improve your financial management with Microsoft's new Great Plains small business accounting solution.

> BEST PRACTICE: If you're into tea leaf reading and lookin' between the lines, you might have guessed what I'm trying to accomplish here. SBS serves up the technology platform you need to do more good stuff! It may be that you simply use the suggested solutions in this chapter in your everyday use of SBS. Or if may be that you're an SBS consultant looking for a way to extend the engagement with your clients. Mastering one or two of the solutions presented here is a start. And I'd be negligent if I didn't underscore that last point. Honestly, SBS 2000 is in some ways too good. It installs seamlessly, runs like a Swiss watch and, quite frankly, needs a tad less care and feeding than prior SBS releases. This third-generation SBS release is the breakout version.

So, what's a poor SBS consultant to do if there is some evidence that SBS 2000 runs so well that there are fewer billable hours for maintenance? The answer is simple: Get smart about it! You may need to add a few arrows to your SBS consulting quiver. Read on, as the following solutions are some sharp arrows just waiting for you to grab and fire.

Microsoft bCentral

Truth be told, there are bona fide public rumors circulating that over the next several years, SBS and bCentral will get married and have babies. That is, these two Microsoft solutions will increasingly find synergistic ways to work closer and closer together. If you find that thesis to be credible, you should probably bookmark the bCentral Web page at www.bcentral.com and visit it regularly. You might even consider using some of bCentral's services, whether you are an SBS client or an SBS consultant.

The bCentral portal is focused on the small business community. Take a look at its Web site, shown in Figure 19-1.

Figure 19-1

Welcome to bCentral—a small business portal that effectively extends SBS 2000's reach and capabilities.

Digital Dashboard

Some SBSers have found Microsoft's Digital Dashboard to be an interesting avenue. It's a solution that's kinda hard to define. On the one hand, it's a data extraction tool that puts a pretty face on tables of data stored on backend servers.

On the other hand, it's the reemergence of the executive information system (EIS) concept from days of old. An EIS is a presentation tool that allows you to display complex information. One use of an EIS is to display the DuPont ratio model (this is a complex financial modeling system in business) to an executive using a red light, green light, yellow light metaphor. In this case, red light means holy hell is breaking loose in the company and bad things are happening. Yellow light suggests caution. Green light is groovy. Under the MBA belief of "management by exception," the executive would only manage the red lights.

So, how does that pocket MBA lecture relate to Digital Dashboard? Simply stated, the Digital Dashboard solution is how you can implement an EIS for a small business. And believe me, the legitimate billable hours that can accrue from a development engagement such as Digital Dashboard can simply be divine!

Digital Dashboard is shown in Figure 19-2. For more information, visit www.microsoft.com/business/dd.

Figure 19-2

Run, don't walk, and educate yourself on Microsoft Digital Dashboard.

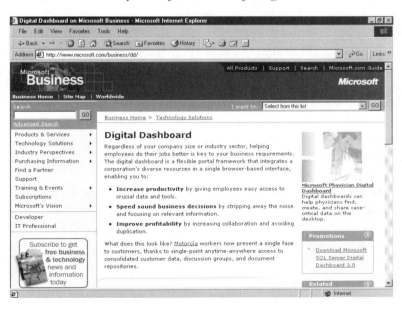

Guest Column

Join me in welcoming Jennifer Kern from Microsoft who will enhance my discussion on Digital Dashboard. You go, girl!

So, you've taken the first step and decided Microsoft Small Business Server is the right product for you. You've installed and deployed it and completely taken advantage of everything that SBS has to offer, right? There is so much more that you can do with SBS 2000!

Picture this—you are the owner of a business and, as you well know, it's important that you have your fingers on the pulse of crucial segments of your business. Right now, you can not view that type of information without constantly checking out multiple data sources which will eventually lead to your early retirement due to carpel tunnel syndrome. You dream of a customizable portal that integrates sales projections, customer data, and Internet news services in a single browser-based interface.

The vision that I have just described is a "Digital Dashboard." The dashboard is a customized solution that combines personal, team, corporate, and outside information with single-click access to collaborative and analytical tools. It is designed to help you and your employees make better decisions by allowing you to have instant access to key information.

Why is a Digital Dashboard a useful tool? Two words: Information overload. It enables you and your employees to handle it—finally! Today, information is sent to employees via a wide range of sources and it has become very difficult to manage and prioritize. The Dashboard can help you catch trends, avoid work duplication, and more.

- ***Gather information from a variety of sources.** The Digital Dashboard is capable of integrating with current business systems—legacy, Exchange Server, SQL Servers, or even Web servers—and combining that information in one central location and stored for either online or offline use.*

- ***Information integration.** The Digital Dashboard enhances the teaming capabilities of Outlook and Exchange 2000 by enabling employees to collaborate on shared documents, projects, and other team-oriented tasks. In addition, the dashboard can filter urgent customer or sales data and send important opportunity/problem updates to employees.*

- *Analyze and interact with information.* The Digital Dashboard allows employees to gain access to, analyze, and edit high-level sales data in reports that use Microsoft PivotTable Web components, Excel, or SQL Server online analytical processing integration. The dashboard can also include Microsoft NetMeeting and Windows Media Player, enabling intranet/Internet collaboration, streaming media content for online training, etc.

What can you do to get started with your own Digital Dashboard? Your first step is to download or order your Digital Dashboard Resource Kit, which includes all the tools and documentation you need to build SQL and Exchange digital dashboards—visit,

http://www.microsoft.com/business/DigitalDashboard/.

Next, take the time to determine what information is crucial to different areas of your company. You may want to review the Digital Dashboard Business Process Assessment Guide at www.microsoft.com/business/digitaldashboard/ddbpag.asp to help step you through this process.

Finally, check out an example of a Digital Dashboard at:

www.microsoft.com/business/digitaldashboard/ddoverview.asp. This example integrates the user's e-mail inbox, MSN Messenger Service, calendar, and important company information. This site also hosts an online tour of the dashboard to help you explore your options.

Start taking advantage of the possibilities that Small Business Server has to offer —and implementing a Digital Dashboard is the first step in that direction.

Jennifer Kern has worked at Microsoft for six years and is currently a Corporate Account and Channel Sales Representative in the Microsoft Pacific Northwest Sales office in Bellevue, Washington. She is a guest columnist for Computer Source Magazine.

Outlook Team Folders

If the future of the SBS realm involves some collaboration tools such as SharePoint Server, as early reports out of Redmond suggest, then today you need to learn about Outlook Team Folders. Outlook Team Folders are an add-in to Outlook that creates a bona fide, Lotus Notes-killing, collaboration-driven groupware environment. Specifically, Outlook Team Folders provide threaded discussion, a document repository, team calendar, team task list, and contacts list.

You can download and install Outlook Team Folders from <u>www.microsoft.com/outlook</u>. This is shown in Figure 19-3

Figure 19-3
Sharpen your SBS skill set by adding Outlook Team Folders to your arsenal.

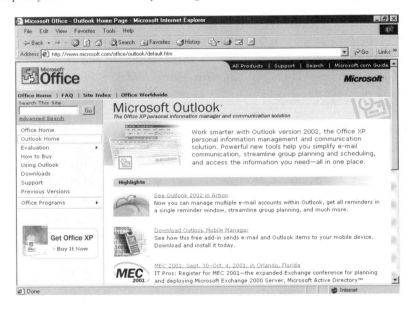

Office XP

All too often, the desktop productivity application suite spoken of in the context of SBS 2000 is Office 2000. While SBS 2000 was in development, that was the proper context. However, times change in technology very fast. As of this writing, the correct Microsoft Office version to install on client computers (including your own) is Office XP (shown in Figure 19-4).

Figure 19-4

Yee-haw—all you need to know about Office XP can be found at www.microsoft.com/office.

Personally, I like Office XP because I put Word 2002, the word processing component, to a true test as a work-a-day SBS beat writer. Seriously, you really appreciate the strength of your favorite application when you work with it all the time. And so far, Office XP won't let you down.

> BEST PRACTICE: I could well be imaging this, but I swear on books that the Office XP components are loading much faster than similar applications in the old Office 2000. It's almost as if the code overhead footprint has been reduced. Whatever it is, I sure enjoy how fast Word 2002 loads now!

Great Plains

Whew—something that barely made it in time for my press deadline was Microsoft's Great Plains new offering for small business. Released in the late fall 2001, the solutions is known as Small Business Manager. Basically, you're getting a capable Great Plains accounting solution at a fraction of the cost of "real" Great Plains Dynamics. This solution is shown in Figure 19-5 and can be accessed via www.greatplains.com.

Figure 19-5
Meet Great Plains Small Business Manager.

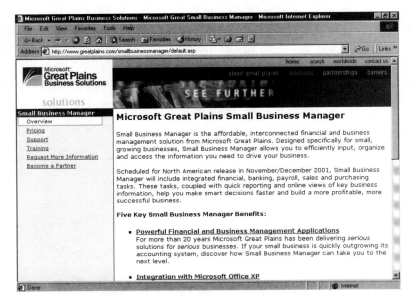

BEST PRACTICE: Many SBS consultants are adding the Great Plains capability to their list of services. It's a smart move, but know that planning for and deploying Great Plains requires an accounting skill set. You might partner with an accounting firm if you want to become a Great Plains partner with Microsoft.

Summary

This chapter presented several next steps for you to consider as an SBSer. With the SBS network infrastructure you have in place, you can consider supplemental paths including Microsoft bCentral, Digital Dashboard, Outlook Team Folders, deploying Office XP and Great Plains.

Huge hugs and congratulations are in order to you as you have reached the last paragraphs of this book. Assuming you've been a good student and followed the SSL-based examples in this book, may I be the first to bestow the SBSer title and designation upon you. Holding this title is an honor and a privilege, and it brings with it great responsibilities. You must now go forth, do good, and help your fellow SBSers along the way.

In this book, you've planned for, set up, managed, configured, and extended SBS 2000. That's no small feat, as SBS is a large product, pardon the pun.

So, it's time to go. You've been launched as an SBSer and I wish you the best. As for me, I'm headed to the pub mentioned in Figure 10-28 for a "black and tan." See you there, mate!

Section 5

Appendixes

Appendix A
SBS Resources

This appendix lists numerous SBS resources that not only allow you to get the most from your existing SBS network but also allow you to stay current with SBS developments. The resource categories are the Web, newsletters, newsgroups, E-mail distribution lists, and general resources.

Web

In this section, I list several important Web sites relating to SBS 2000.

www.sbsfaq.com

This Web site is dedicated to SBS frequently asked questions (FAQ) and is the strongest, non-Microsoft SBS site I've found to date. Not only are solutions posted to common SBS problems, but there are helpful links to other SBS-related resources. You should bookmark this as an SBS favorite. This Web site, run by Wayne Small from Australia, is shown in Figure A-1.

Figure A-1

Wayne Small's SBS site is current and informative.

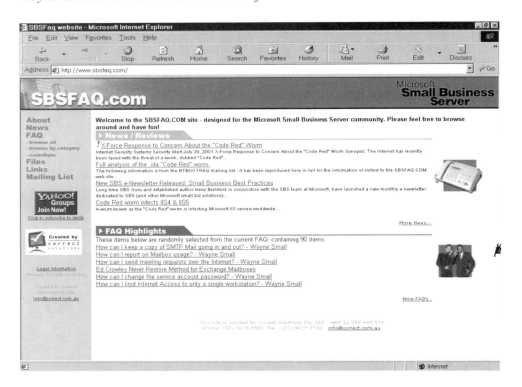

www.smallbizserver.com

This Web site is the grand daddy of them all. Founded and currently maintained by Grey Lancaster, there are surprisingly strong links and information about the SBS product. This Web site is shown in Figure A-2.

Figure A-2

Grey Lancaster's SBS Web site.

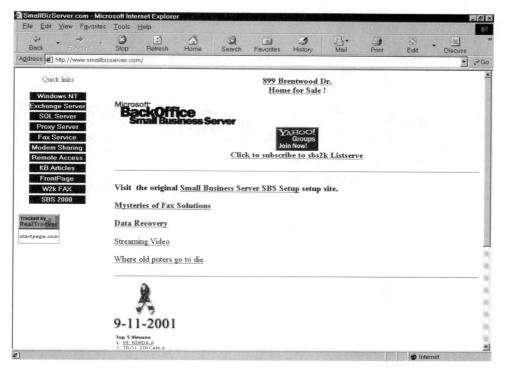

Microsoft Web Sites

Microsoft has several Web sites that are of interest to the SBSer.

- www.microsoft.com/smallbusinessserver. This Web site, shown in Figure A-3, is front and center for the official word on SBS. Use it!

- www.microsoft.com/partner. This Web site is for certified solution providers who sell, support and maintain SBS.

- www.bcentral.com. Here's the bCentral portal for both the small business and the SBS consultant.

- Individual products. Don't forget to visit the Web sites for individual SBS products such as Exchange 2000 Server (www.microsoft.com/exchange).

Figure A-3

Microsoft's SBS Web site.

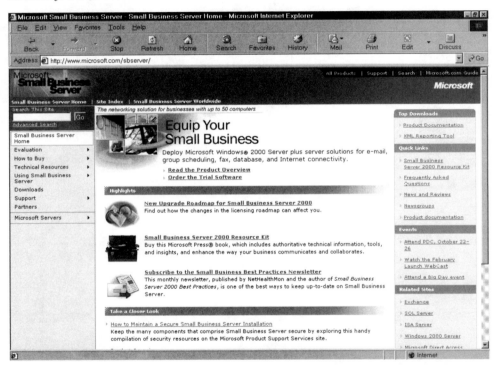

Microsoft Certified Professional Magazine

This magazine, dedicated to the MCP and MCSE certifications, has created a Web community for SBS. Check it out at www.mcpmag.com and look at the listed BackOffice/SBS link on the left-side.

www.windows2000advantage.com

This Web site, a joint venture between Compaq and ComputerWorld, has been very SBS friendly. Indeed an SBS article is front and center in Figure A-4.

Figure A-4

Bookmark this Web site for periodic SBS articles.

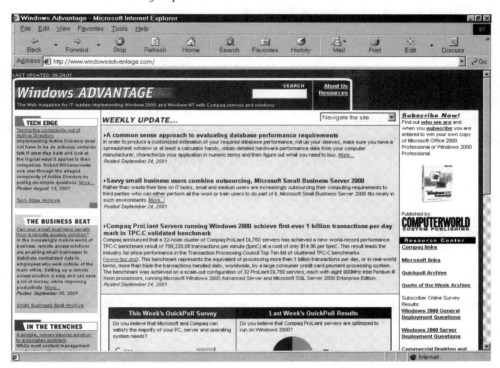

www.NetHealthMon.com

This Seattle-based company, run by yours truly, provides SBS network monitoring via SBS server status reports and Health Monitor 2.1 alerts. The site contains SBS educational materials and a monthly SBS newsletter (more on that in a moment). Network monitoring services start at $1/day.

Newsletters

Run, don't delay and subscribe to my monthly newsletter (Small Business Best Practices) dedicated to amongst other things, SBS 2000. My newsletter also discusses Windows XP peer-to-peer networking and Microsoft bCentral. Send e-mail to: subscribe@nethealthmon.com.

Newsgroups

Microsoft's own newsgroup is very active and monitored by Microsoft Most Valuable Players (MVPs) who are available to answer your questions. Simply point your newsgroup reader to microsoft.public.backoffice.smallbiz, and join in. See the Guest Column below for more information.

E-Mail Distribution Lists

The very best SBS e-mail distribution list is managed by Grey Lancaster and run on the Yahoo! newsgroup engine. To subscribe to the SBS list, point you Web browser to http://groups.yahoo.com/group/sbs2k/ and complete the signup process.

Guest Column
Microsoft Small Business Server Public Newsgroups —What, Where, Why

by
One of the Small Business Server Newsgroups MVPs

Somehow you have been given the task of supporting the company's new Microsoft Small Business Server (commonly referred to as "SBS"). After all, you've got a computer at home, and you're on the Internet all the time so you must know how to do this right?   And the company with just 10 employees certainly can't afford the big computer company downtown at $200 an hour.

Well, you read the book from front to back and some of it makes sense and some of it doesn't. You see a reference to the SBS Website (www.microsoft.com/ sbserver) and decide to look around. Here you will find lots of information about Small Business Server, including several "How To" White Papers. On the main page you see a link labeled Support. Now you're cooking! You click and see several topics and one of them say "Newsgroups - Join Small Business Server newsgroups to provide resellers and consultants peer-to-peer support on technical issues regarding Small Business Server."

What are these newsgroups really? Each newsgroup is devoted to a particular aspect of a particular Microsoft technology or software. For SBS there are two; one for Small Business Server 2000 (microsoft.public.backoffice.smallbiz2000) and one supporting the previous version (microsoft.public.backoffice.smallbiz).

Here folks from all around the world who use or support Small Business Server come to seek solutions or help others by offering free assistance based on their own experiences with this product.

Now that I know what they are, how can I get to these Newsgroups? You will need a newsreader program to access these newsgroups. Outlook Express is available as a free download as part of Internet Explorer. You will need to then configure the newsreader to connect to the server msnews.microsoft.com. This is a free server and does not require a username or password. For more information on connecting to the Small Business Server Newsgroups, go to http:// www.microsoft.com/sbserver/support/newsgroups/default.asp .

Finally, why use the Newsgroups? First, because it's FREE! Secondly, it is a community of people from all around the world helping each other with problems just like the ones you're having. Some of newsgroup participants are recognized by Microsoft and designated as MVPs for SBS. Microsoft MVPs (Most Valuable Professionals) volunteer technical answers and expertise in the newsgroups. The Microsoft MVPs come from a wide range of backgrounds and professions, with a willingness to give their time, expertise, and advice to enhance the technical skills of others within the newsgroups. In the SBS newsgroups we have MVPs from the US, Canada, Australia, United Kingdom.

Come join us in SBS newsgroups to get help with a problem, share a solution, or possibly even make some new friends.

General Resources

There are other SBS 2000 resources you should consider as well, including an online seminar site at Microsoft, a partner guide, the 2301a course and a Disc-based advanced SBS 2000 e-learning (similar to computer-based training) course.

Online Seminar

To attend an online seminar related to SBS, fist surf on the Internet to http:// www.microsoft.com/seminar/ and then expand the Server Products link on the left. Next, click on Small Business Server (left-side, under Server Products) and play the online seminar of your choice.

> BEST PRACTICE: As of this writing, there are only two seminars listed from the SB S 4.5 time frame. However, it's anticipated that more seminars, specific to SBS 2000, will be added.

Partner Guide

If you're a certified partner with Microsoft, you can obtain the Microsoft Small Business Server 2000 Partner Guide for free. This partner guide includes a 45-minute SBS 2000 setup video (featuring yours tulry), a copy of Course 2301a (discussed next) and a 120-day evaluation edition of SBS 2000. This 120-day edition is very interesting. It is the fully copy of SBS 2000, and once installed, it can be easily upgraded to the full version of SBS 2000 by simply running the retail product's Discs (this being the real copy of SBS that you have purchased post-hoc) through the SBS setup cycle. It's really quite simple. The idea here is that you can try before you by.

> BEST PRATICE: There are several ways to acquire the Microsoft Small Business Server 2000 Partner Guide including attending Course 2301a as a student, attending a local Microsoft SBS marketing event such as "Big Day" in your local area or simply signing up as a certified partner at www.microsoft.com/partner.

One-day Microsoft Official Curriculum Course

Titled *Course 2301a: Implementing Small Business Server 2000*, this is a one-day Microsoft Official Curriculum (MOC) course, is delivered at Microsoft Certified Technical Education Centers. Visit http://www.microsoft.com/trainingandservices.

Advanced SBS E-learning Course

Titled *Implementing & Supporting Microsoft Small Business Server 2000: Advanced Topics*, this course was released in the fall of 2001. With this 8.5 hour interactive course, you will learn to effectively manage many Microsoft Small Business Server 2000 components. This courseware commences where other Small Business Server 2000 training resources end. It includes the focus areas of networking planning, security, communications, and advanced topics.

In the network planning area, instruction on server and client computer setup is provided, followed by post-setup administrative tasks. The security topics offer an in-depth view of Small Business Server 2000 firewall protection, virtual private networking, and remote access best practices. Terminal Services is featured in the Remote Administration module. Communication topics include Exchange 2000 Server and Outlook 2000 configuration topics in addition to

Instant Messaging deployment. The details of Small Business Server 2000 fax management are unveiled in the faxing learning event, followed by how to configure Web components and a secure form of FTP. Advanced Small Business Server 2000 topics are: console customization, adding a non-domain controller Windows 2000 Server machine to a network, and data and system-state backup and restore procedures.

> BEST PRACTICE: So the SBS gurus out there are asking if this is truly an advanced course. And the answer is: Yes. The course includes advanced topics along with some background information for Small Business Server 2000 (for example, a few rollover pages are spent defining SBS2K). More important, this course does a good job of not repeating the content of Course 2301a. In that context, it meets the goals of becoming the "next step" in SBS education.

> Highlights of "advanced" course include discussions of the following:
>
> - Terminal Services
> - Instant Messaging
> - Exchange 2000 Server
> - ISA Server 2000

Here's how to obtain the advanced SBS course as of this writing:

- *MS Action Pack*: Course will be included in the October and January Microsoft Action Packs.

- *MS Partner Market:* Course will be sold on Microsoft Partner Market (access Partner Market by visiting www.microsoft.com\partner. Click on box titled, "The Microsoft Partner Market" in left-hand column.)

- *Website Promotions*: Course information will be available on Small Business Server 2000-related web pages including: www.microsoft.com/smallbusinessserver & www.microsoft.com/partner.

Appendix B
Upgrading to Small Business Server 2000

This Appendix addresses the SBS 2000 upgrade issue.

Editorial

Only when world events warrant will you see a publication issue a front page editorial. Such an event is the SBS 2000 upgrade issue. In writing this book, working in the glass tower hallways of Redmond, monitoring SBS news lists and working closely with real small businesses in dusty backrooms, I've drawn the following personal conclusion. The conclusion is that for me, there is no such thing as an upgrade to SBS 2000. That is, I'll only promote and undertake "freshies."

The term freshies has dual meanings. In the context of SBS 2000 upgrades, it means saving the data and e-mail (twice) to another computer or tape backup (verified!), then FDISKing (reformatting) the server machine and installing SBS 2000 fresh. In skiing, "freshies" means a kick-ass powder day (also called "pow-pow"). Granted, we're here to discuss SBS, not skiing, so read on.

What can I say? I started with the noblest of intentions when I commenced the creation of this book, but I learned a lot along the way. Some learning experiences were painful. The in-place upgrade from SBS 4.5 to SBS 2000 was one of these pain points. So in my usual Texan style, I've completely over-reacted and tossed the baby out with the bath water. Yes it's extreme to do a fresh SBS 2000 installation instead of considering an in-place SBS 4.5 to SBS 2000 upgrade. But you know what? In fresh SBS 2000 installation has an assured outcome in terms of task duration and quality control. Not only do I know the project will take some four hours or so, but that my demons and gremlins from the SBS 4.5 server machine will be exorcised along the way. Cool!

So you on your own at this juncture with respect to the SBS 2000 upgrade matter. Below are some resources to guide you through an in-place upgrade.

Resources

Microsoft has fulfilled its fiduciary obligations and posted some SBS 4.5 to SBS 2000 upgrade resources for you to read, digest and use.

WebCast

Perhaps the best of the best is the 35-min. Webcast created by a support engineer at Microsoft. This is not only cool but complete. It's a nice change from other technical resources too, this new fangled Webcasting approach! Find the Webcast at **http://support.microsoft.com/servicedesks/webcasts/wcd030101/ wcdblurb030101.asp** where you will see a screen similar to Figure B-1.

Figure B-1

The Microsoft Webcast on upgrading to SBS 2000.

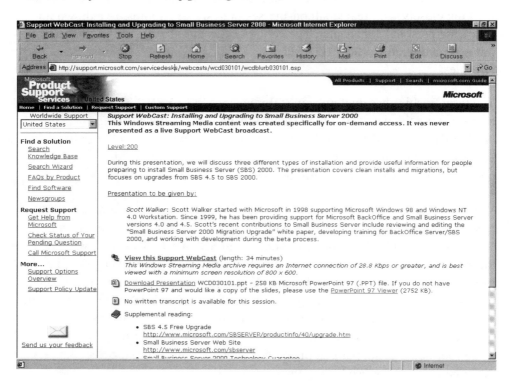

White Paper

As I write this, I'm holding in my hot hands the SBS 2000 upgrade paper released by the development team at Microsoft. You'll find this oil well of knowledge from the **Support** link of the Microsoft SBS Web site at **www.microsoft.com/sbserver**. This paper is also discussed in the Web cast mentioned above.

Licensing Road Map

Late in the writing of this book, Microsoft started to revise its licensing scheme. The resource found at http://www.microsoft.com/sbserver/howtobuy/roadmap.asp addresses both licensing and how to upgrade to larger environments from (or away from) SBS 2000. Hey—it's a nice problem to face: aggressive growth forces you to look at new and exciting Microsoft Servers solutions. The Web page related to this matter is shown in Figure B-2.

Figure B-2

Visit this page to learn more about the upgrade roadmap.

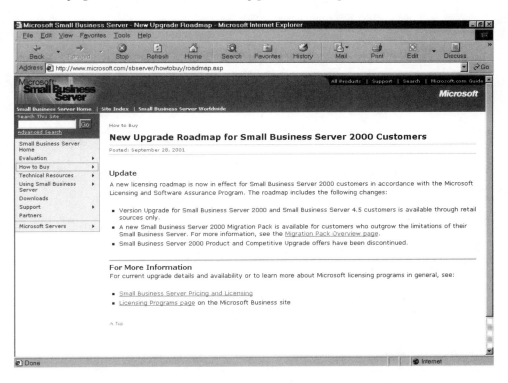

Appendix C
SSL Information

As promised, here's your source of Springer Spaniels Limited (SSL) information to enter as you setup and manage the SBS 2000 network in this book. This information is broken into common and unique information.

Common

This is information that is common to all users.

Phone	*206-123-1234*	Add User Wizard
Exchange Server	*SSL1 (default)*	Add User Wizard
Exchange store	*Mailbox Store (SSL1) (default)*	Add User Wizard
Description for User	*Founder and President*	Add User Wizard
Allowed to change password (Y/N)?	*No*	Add User Wizard
SBS Programs to Install:	*Complete:* *Internet Explorer (IE),* *Microsoft Shared Modem* * Service Client,* *Microsoft Shared Fax Client,* *Firewall Client,* *Outlook 2000 SR1*	Set Up Computer Wizard
Operating System:	*Windows 2000 Professional*	Set Up Computer Wizard
Verify available workstation hard disk space based on SBS Programs to install listed immediately above (for example, 300 MB required)	*Yes*	Misc.

Turn off programs at workstation such as anti-virus program.		Misc.
SBS server-based Shared Folders this user will access.	*User name (e.g. NORMH), USERS, COMPANY, ACCOUNTING, OLD, APPLICATIONS*	Misc.
Printers	*HP5MCOLOR*	Misc.
Network Protocols	*TCP/IP*	Misc.
IP Address (Static or Dynamic)	*Dynamic*	Misc.
Mapped Drives	*S: SSLI\%user name% T: SSLI\USERS U: SSLI\COMPANY X: SSLI\APPLICATIONS*	Misc.
Workstation Shares (shares on workstation)		Misc.
Additional Applications to install (for example, Great Plains Dynamics accounting):		Misc.
Special configuration issues		Misc.
Comments		Misc.
Tested Logon (Y/N)		Misc.
Repairs/Reconfiguration Needed		Misc.

Unique Information

This is information that is unique on a user-by-user basis.

First:	**Norm**
Last:	**Hasborn**
User Name (and e-mail alias):	NormH
Password:	Purple3300
Job Title:	President
Office:	Executive
User Template:	Power User
Computer Name:	PRESIDENT

First:	**Barry**
Last:	**McKechnie**
User Name (and e-mail alias):	BarryM
Password:	2Reedred
Job Title:	Accountant
Office:	Accounting
User Template:	User
Computer Name:	ACCT01

First:	**Melinda**
Last:	**Overlaking**
User Name (and e-mail alias):	MelindaO
Password:	Blue33
Job Title:	Front Desk Reception
Office:	Administration
User Template:	User
Computer Name:	FRONT01

First:	**Linda**
Last:	**Briggs**
User Name (and e-mail alias):	LindaB
Password:	Golden10
Job Title:	Manager, Registration
Office:	Registration and Scheduling
User Template:	User
Computer Name:	MANREG01

First:	**Bob**
Last:	**Bountiful**
User Name (and e-mail alias):	BobB
Password:	Bish4fish
Job Title:	Breeding Manager
Office:	Care, Feeding, Breeding
User Template:	User
Computer Name:	BREED01

First:	**Tom**
Last:	**Benkert**
User Name (and e-mail alias):	TomB
Password:	Whitesnow101
Job Title:	Scheduler
Office:	Registration and Scheduling
User Template:	User
Computer Name:	SCHEDULE01

First:	**Norm**
Last:	**Hasborn Jr.**
User Name (and e-mail alias):	NormJR
Password:	Yellowsnow55
Job Title:	Sales Manager
Office:	Sales and Marketing
User Template:	User
Computer Name:	SALES01

First:	**David**
Last:	**Halberson**
User Name (and e-mail alias):	DaveH
Password:	Grenadine2002
Job Title:	Marketing Manager
Office:	Marketing
User Template:	User
Computer Name:	MARKET01

First:	**Elvis**
Last:	**Haskins**
User Name (and e-mail alias):	Elvis
Password:	Platinium101
Job Title:	Researcher
Office:	Genealogy
User Template:	User
Computer Name:	GENE01

First:	**Bob**
Last:	**Easter**
User Name (and e-mail alias):	BobE
Password:	dogcatcher1
Job Title:	Dog Trainer
Office:	Care, Feeding, and Breeding
User Template:	Power User
Computer Name:	CAREFEED01

Index

Small Business Server 2000 Best Practices

Finally, the third-party Microsoft Small Business Server 2000 book that everyone has been waiting for. Based on shipping code and written by Microsoft SBS "insider" Harry Brelsford six months after the SBS 2000 release, this book is packed with real world, detailed SBS 2000 topics and lots of hard-fought SBS war stories.

The planning, setup, administration and management topics dominate the first half of the book and include references to KBase articles, hard learned workarounds and in-the-trenches best practices. This tome is also current for the operating system and application service packs (Windows 2000 SP2, Exchange 2000 Server SP1). And not only are the individual applications such as Exchange 2000 Server and ISA Server 2000 covered in-depth, but this discussion is put into context of how these applications are used in the SBS community (no enterprise sidetracking here). The book extends SBS 2000 with add-ons such as the new XML Reporting Tool, Exchange Conferencing Server, Digital Dashboard and Outlook Team Folders.

This book speaks to the entire SBS community ranging from the do-it-yourselfer newbie to the hardened SBS guru. A practicing SBS consultant, Brelsford deftly weaves introductory and advanced SBS 2000 discussion, as only he can do with his Texas accent, in a warm and collegial way into the pages of this book. And when that's not enough, the book includes guest columns from members of the Microsoft SBS development team and other leading SBSers!

Simply stated, this book picks up where the SBS 2000 Resource Kit, training videos and one-day MOC #2301 course leave off. By the end of the book, you will have correctly implemented a secure network for a sample company, Springer Spaniels Limited (SSL).

So buddy up with **Brelsford** and enjoy **Small Business Server 2000 Best Practices**. Not only will this book pay for itself immediately with an hour of your time saved, but it'll return its price back to you many times over by helping you avoid hidden hooks, pitfalls and box canyons along the SBS 2000 journey.

Order Form

QTY.		Price	Can. Price	Total
	Small Business Server 2000 Best Practices —Harry Brelsford	$69.95 US	$92.95 CN	
	Shipping and Handling Add $10 for orders in the US			
	Sales tax (WA state residents only, add 8.6%)			
	Total enclosed			

Telephone Orders:
Call 1-800-461-1931
Have your VISA or
MasterCard ready.

Fax Orders:
425-398-1380
Fill out this order form and fax.

Postal Orders:
Hara Publishing
P.O. Box 19732
Seattle, WA 98109

E-mail Orders:
harapub@foxinternet.net

Method of Payment:

☐   Check or Money Order

☐   *VISA*

☐   MasterCard

Expiration Date: _____

Card #: _____

Signature: _____

Name _____

Address _____

City _____ State ____ Zip _____

Phone (___) _____ Fax (___) _____

Quantity discounts are available.
Call 425-398-3679 for more information.
Thank you for your order!